Leslie Halliwell was born in Bolton. films and series screened by the ITV n to Hollywood in search of them; he h medium since childhood. He has mana tion and specialist cinemas and is a member of two National Film Archive committees.

Mr Halliwell spent several years as a film reviewer for *Picturegoer* and *Sight and Sound* and has contributed to other national publications. His published works include *Halliwell's Film Guide* and *Halliwell's Filmgoer's Companion* (both of which are available in Paladin), *The Filmgoer's Book of Quotes*, *The Clapperboard Book of the Cinema* (co-author), *Mountain of Dreams* and *Halliwell's Teleguide*.

LESLIE HALLIWELL

Halliwell's Hundred

A nostalgic choice of films
from the golden age

Granada Publishing

Paladin Books
Granada Publishing Ltd
8 Grafton Street, London W1X 3LA

Published by Paladin Books 1984

First published in Great Britain by
Granada Publishing 1982

ISBN 0-586-08490-8

Reproduced, printed and bound in Great Britain by
Hazell Watson & Viney Limited,
Aylesbury, Bucks

Set in Baskerville

Dedicated to the memory of
Mr Laurel and Mr Hardy

Contents

Foreword

I was born in 1929 into a family of cotton spinners, who enjoyed life as fully as they could in a grimy area of South Lancashire at a time when such domestic facilities as central heating, telephones, refrigerators and washing machines were only dimly heard of and barely comprehended. Church, the Co-op, and the Spinners' Hall were the centres of social activity, and by the time I began to notice the world around me, the slump was on. Work being scarce, the days could be hard, but people were still determined to laugh, at themselves if need be. Luckily Bolton and its environs boasted in the thirties no fewer than twenty-seven cinemas, including a new cathedral-like Odeon which offered to the masses an irresistible lure. Here, for the equivalent of two pence in modern money, the otherwise deprived might for three hours enjoy blissful comfort in a perfumed atmosphere, watching on a giant lustrous screen the activities of characters more fortunate than themselves, sharing the excitement of less restricted lives, and occasionally being stimulated by the touch of a superior intellect. Not that we despised humbler picture houses such as the Hippodrome, a converted music hall which naturally found its greatest success when playing the films of celebrated low comedians; here Will Hay, Sidney Howard, Gracie Fields, George Formby, Laurel and Hardy and the Crazy Gang came to seem like beloved uncles and aunts.

When one considers the contrasts involved, it is hardly surprising that my favourite films should come from this impressionable period of my life, or at least to belong to one of the genres which most attracted me then. Simple slapstick and violence always bored me. I looked for some cleverness in the presentation, some wit in the dialogue, some hint of the magician's wand. I could be serious-minded when the occasion required it, but I avoided the gutter and objected to having my nose rubbed in the mire. I kept a

11

sharp sense of humour, I loved a mystery; and I listened hard for messages.

As things turned out, watching films turned from a hobby into a profession. I was in turn journalist, cinema manager, publicity executive, television programme buyer and part-time author. One interest feeds the other, and my days are certainly well filled. People are always surprised however when I assure them quite truthfully that I see very few films apart from those which crop up on television. My memory retains those of the past which measured up to my standards; of today's crop I have soon had my fill. Most of them are obscurely told; they tell me things I don't wish to know, in language I find offensive; and they concern characters whom I would willingly cross the road to avoid. Cheap colour makes them unattractive to look at, and all the old studio crafts, so laboriously learned over a quarter of a century, appear to have been jettisoned in favour of obscenely large budgets which allow the film-maker to wander restlessly around the world crashing real aeroplanes and giving a distorted view of real locations instead of setting his own and the audience's imaginations to work. *The Maltese Falcon* was shot in five or six small sets, with scarcely an exterior scene. Does anyone suggest that it would be better if remade today on a multi-million-dollar budget, with the fashionable doom-laden photography and unintelligible sound track? How long in fact is it since a film of our time offered such wit, such performances, such sharp control?

Ah well, there is always the National Film Theatre, and the cassette revolution has finally begun. One way or another, all the films mentioned in this book can still be seen by those with plenty of patience and the determination to seek them out. I have myself, over the last eighteen months, seen all those which form the principal subjects of these affectionate revaluations; and if I have been disappointed with any aspect of them, I have said so. I could not catch up with all the secondary titles I have mentioned by way of bonus, but in these cases I am usually commending aspects rather than the whole.

I do not nominate these films as the greatest ever made. Few of them indeed are serious works of art, fewer still milestones of film history. But apart from one or two which earned a place for being so fascinatingly bad, they all measure up to some rather stringent private requirements. None is less than twenty-five years old. All are made with great craft and competence under the old studio system which was so abused and is now so much missed. All contain superb examples of scriptwriting, or narrative skill, or camera magic, or editing, or direction, or sheer imagination; all of them demonstrate a joyous ability to entertain, to repay most amply the time one spends with them. Taken together I hope they represent a consensus of the so-called golden age of film-making at its most likeable and efficient. Though I could scarcely resist the inclusion of such bobby-dazzlers as *Citizen Kane* and *The Grapes of Wrath*, I have generally tended to exclude what are likely to be the 'great' films of other collections, for this is intended to be an amusing book rather than a solemn one. However, the fact that Fassbinder and Kurosawa and Fellini and Eisenstein are not represented does not mean that I fail to recognize their virtues, only that they are not the chaps with whom I would choose to spend a holiday. They don't speak for me; they are not in my style; I admire and respect them without loving them.

My aim has been to give as much as possible of the original flavour by generous quotation, description and comparison as well as by stills carefully chosen to illustrate the angle of appeal. One way or another, I hope I have been able to convey the delight with which I am filled at each repeated viewing of this elegant bric-à-brac from a less grittily realistic age.

Leslie Halliwell
December 1981

Very Merry Men
The Adventures of Robin Hood

While King Richard the Lionheart fights his crusades against the Saracen, his brother Prince John plots to usurp the English throne but is foiled by the swashbuckling exploits of a Saxon knight and his followers who make their home in the depths of Sherwood Forest.

The image of the extrovert green-clad hero and his romping merry men is firmly fixed in the world's imagination. But who fixed it? Richard Greene in 143 television episodes? Certainly not the BBC's more realistic serial of the seventies. Nineteenth-century accounts are extremely vague, and probably for people middle-aged in 1980 it was the 1938 film with Errol Flynn which consolidated many centuries of scattered ballad references into one irrepressible and irresistible hundred-minute Hollywood adventure, cast with favourite actors and bathed in the glowing and glorious Technicolor of the period. I lean to the theory that great films are great not because they are planned that way but because of a happy combination of circumstances which strikes the public imagination and makes them both unique and beyond criticism. A study of the original script of this film shows that it might have been, and perhaps very nearly was, a relentless bore. But somebody touched it with a magic wand, and from its spirited beginning to its exhilarating end it now moves with the skill and grace of an Olympic athlete. More: Erich Wolfgang Korngold's superlative musical score gives it the overtones of a medieval light opera. This is a film which dates not at all: see it as often as you will, it comes up fresh and sparkling, brimming with more good humour than the story properly

15

demands, but delighting the audience with every hairbreadth escape and last-minute rescue, every threat and riposte, every knockabout fight and duel to the death. Give it a good print, and all the elements in this over-forty-year-old movie shine as though newly minted.

And yet, as with the superb *Casablanca* from the same studio, it seems to have been made up pretty much as it went along, with Michael Curtiz brought in midway to give some twang to the diligent but dull direction of his predecessor William Keighley. Curtiz was perhaps the magician in question, polishing, shortening, changing the emphasis here and there, enthusing the cast with the feeling of success. Or perhaps everyone realized that Errol Flynn, at that point in his career, could do no wrong. Test the film where you will, and it passes triumphantly. If we did not know that it was entirely shot around Thousand Oaks, California, we would swear that the locations were authentic English countryside, recorded during some unusually benevolent summer. Nor do any false accents disturb our ears. Claude Rains and Basil Rathbone make an admirably suave brace of villains. ('Any objections to the new tax, from our Saxon friends?' asks the former of the latter in an especially memorable interchange.) Olivia de Havilland is an entirely wide-eyed and wholesome Lady Marian Fitzwalter, wooed and won by Robin after she comes to understand his high ideals: 'It's injustice I hate, not the Normans,' he assures her. Melville Cooper, Ian Hunter, Una O'Connor and Alan Hale all present the proper British attitudes, and Eugene Pallette is such a perfect Friar Tuck, getting the better of Robin in their initial watery encounter, that he is promptly forgiven for being a transatlantic interloper. (Two years later he played an almost identical role in Mamoulian's dazzlingly pictorial *The Mark of Zorro*, which stayed so close to the *Robin Hood* format as to seem like a Spanish-oriented remake.) But of course it is the magnetic Errol Flynn – 'six foot four of British manhood', as Warners erroneously billed him – who seized the film bodily and carried it away over his shoulder like the deer he impudently brings into the palace banquet and slings on to the table in front of Prince John as his contribution to the feast. (It was a royal deer anyway.) No audience would need more than this short scene to realize that here was a star in the truest Hollywood sense, though one destined to be wasted on too many inferior

THE ADVENTURES OF ROBIN HOOD. Stalwart Errol Flynn gets the accolade from Ian Hunter's King Richard. Admiring spectators include Olivia de Havilland, Eugene Pallette (in hard hat), Alan Hale, Herbert Mundin and Patric Knowles

vehicles before he allowed his own vital spark to burn dry from self-indulgence.

The shape if not the style of this film was accurately copied by many cut-price epics during the twenty years which followed its première, and in 1956 *The Court Jester*, a pantomime which earns its own section in this book, burlesqued many of its situations. But the 1938 *Robin Hood* borrowed a surprising amount from Douglas Fairbanks' 1922 version of the subject, which also has a court jester in a significant role. It begins with a joust, which was also the start of the 1938 film according to the script, though the entire expensive scene was removed after being shot. Alan Hale plays Little John in both; other matching sequences include the king in disguise testing the

17

merry men's loyalty; the daring appearance of Robin in the castle and his escape via balcony and battlements; the steps around the inner tower (ideal for duelling down). It may well be that our modern concept of Robin was formulated by this astonishing 1922 film, its castle sets of a grandeur second only to Griffith's *Intolerance*, and its many splendours spread over a running time of just under three hours. I wouldn't care to sit through it very often, for it has a somewhat galumphing approach to narrative, but no one can deny that it is a revelatory experience. The only word for Wilfrid Buckland's sets is awe-inspiring, and there is a touch of genius too in the costumes of Mitchell Leisen, who also painted the huge tapestries (in burlap) and constructed the seventy-foot curtain down which Fairbanks slides (by means of an actual metal runway concealed within its folds). Cinematographer Arthur Edeson fills frame after frame, in what seems very like deep focus, with Brueghel-like groups of knights, peasants and followers, arranged as in a jigsaw puzzle to fill every available space and perspective; near the end of the film more than twenty merry men, sitting on a balcony wall, fall backwards from it in unanimous exhilaration at their own victory.

The critical eye of 1981 must appear to discern many faults in an epic nearly sixty years old made for the medium of silence; in fact however most of the obvious ones must have seemed no less so at the time. As an exciting yarn it is curiously disjointed and takes too long to come to the boil: one yearns to get through the first half, with its trusting king, off to the Crusades, failing to recognize John's perfidy even though it is as plain as the sneer on his lips. Fairbanks underuses himself, seems unattractively middle-aged, and for two-thirds of the film has to fail at everything he attempts, not to mention resisting the notion of romance. True, he starts by winning a joust, but when the king (played with amiable bluster by Wallace Beery) suggests that as the Earl of Huntingdon he might fittingly woo Lady Marian, his surprising plea is: 'Exempt me, sire, I am afeard of women.' So camp indeed is his Chaplinesque physical foolery with his peers that one would hardly be surprised to find his chief adversary renamed Sir *Gay* of Gisbourne. The king can only rub his chin: 'At such a time as this it were more befitting that he try his hand for a maid!' Only after his lands are stolen and Lady Marian is believed killed does this Robin dedicate his life to revenge

– which we are curiously told will be 'bitter but joyous'. Abruptly the film changes gear to give us the Fairbanks we all expected, lither and apparently younger, pirouetting like a ballet star and clearly immune to all physical dangers. The stunts in the film's climactic third are truly amazing: even the curtain descent is topped by a leap from a battlement straight across a void at an ivy-covered wall, and by his ascent via a moving drawbridge to Marian's boudoir window. True, Fairbanks goes too far at times by fighting eight men at once and by so protracting Robin's last-minute rescue from John's arrow squad that when a convenient shield finally deflects the executing arrows just as they have been fired, our only recourse is to laughter. He seems indeed to invite it, by drilling his merry men to hop, skip and jump all over the place when they might have saved their valuable strength on occasions by walking: these romping, beaming, demented dervishes must surely have produced an excessive reaction even in 1922, especially since the subtitles so frequently tell us how little they have to be cheerful about. (Danny Kaye in *The Court Jester* recruited a troupe of midgets as *his* merry men, and they were no funnier than this lot.) Nor are sniggers kept at bay by assiduously researched 'medieval' lines such as 'I'll knop your scop' or 'I'll lash them till they bleat'. All the same, a streamlined version of this quite amazing film would teach modern film-makers a trick or two; it makes one consider how many other silent wonders must be locked unjustly in neglected vaults.

The Adventures of Robin Hood. US 1938; Technicolor; 102 minutes. Produced by Henry Blanke for Warner/First National. Executive producer, Hal B. Wallis. Written by Norman Reilly Raine and Seton I. Miller. Directed by Michael Curtiz and William Keighley. Photographed by Sol Polito and Tony Gaudio. Music score by Erich Wolfgang Korngold. Technicolor consultant, W. Howard Greene. Art direction by Carl Jules Weyl. Costumes by Milo Anderson. Master archer, Howard Hill. Fencing instructor, Fred Cavens. With Errol Flynn as Sir Robin of Locksley; Olivia de Havilland as Lady Marian; Basil Rathbone as Sir Guy of Gisbourne; Claude Rains as Prince John; Alan Hale as Little John; Eugene Pallette as Friar Tuck; Melville Cooper as the Sheriff; Herbert Mundin as Much the Miller's son; Ian Hunter as King Richard; Patric Knowles as Will Scarlet; Una O'Connor as Bess; Montagu Love as the Bishop of Black Canons.

Robin Hood. US 1922; monochrome; silent; 175 minutes (at 16 frames per second). Written and produced by Douglas Fairbanks for United Artists. Directed by Allan Dwan. Photographed by Arthur Edeson. Art direction by Wilfrid Buckland; assistants Irvin J. Martin, Edward M. Langley, Mitchell Leisen. With Douglas Fairbanks as Robert, Earl of Huntingdon; Wallace Beery as King Richard; Enid Bennett as

Lady Marian; Sam de Grasse as Prince John; Paul Dickey as Sir Guy of Gisbourne; William Lowery as the Sheriff; Willard Louis as Friar Tuck; Alan Hale as Little John.

Life Upon the Wicked Stage
All About Eve

By devious means, a young Broadway actress fights her way to the top.

When in 1967 I first visited New York I never did get my jet lag right because on the second evening, when I should have been catching up on my sleep, I took a stayawake tablet in order to enjoy *All About Eve* on the TV late show. The temptation was simply too great. I had of course seen it before, perhaps half a dozen times, but to enjoy it here, within a stone's throw of Sardi's and Shubert Alley, surrounded by the theatre folk it treated so vividly, was a temptation I simply couldn't resist. Not that it was ever one of my private delights: with my critical hat on I found whole stretches of it flat and unsympathetic. But such considerations were always overcome by the fact that it breathed and smelled of theatre, which had been the overwhelming obsession of my younger life. As an amateur I had with modest success played the king in *Hamlet* and Grandpa Vanderhof in *You Can't Take It With You* and Sheridan Whiteside in *The Man Who Came to Dinner*, and a school friend, now a popular actor in Australia, had dreamed with me of someday opening our own theatre in the West End. Just to show that we defied superstition, we were going to call it the Macbeth. Well, my dreams of theatre ended, along with my acting, when I left university, having received for a performance in the wildly unsuitable role of the Stage Manager in *Our Town* the kind of notices I knew I could never better; since then I simply haven't found the time. But an in-show about actors still has me on tenterhooks, and the more bitchily they behave the better. Which might well have been the recipe for *All About Eve*.

It isn't a great piece of cinema, because Joseph L. Mankiewicz, who wrote and directed it, never did show much interest in camera angles or moody photography or cinematic story-telling, just in getting onto the screen as much briskly scintillating dialogue as possible. In this case he crafted it on to the bare bones of a creaky old Clyde Fitch-style melodrama about a middle-aged star slowly displaced by a scheming and insinuating young hussy. *All About Eve* is as close to a personal monument as he ever came, though it wouldn't be the slick entertainment it is without the gleaming studio production handed to Mankiewicz on a plate by Darryl F. Zanuck, who must have had misgivings about the script's box office potential. As fate would have it, it did very well indeed for several reasons. It collared several Academy Awards. It gave Bette Davis' career a massive shot in the arm: a larger-than-life role like Margo Channing was just what she needed when her show was slipping. It presented George Sanders as the smooth cynic everybody thought he was in real life. And in a bit part it featured Marilyn Monroe, who by the time the film was released had already become a name to conjure with. Oddly enough, nobody who enjoyed the movie remembers much about the lady of the title, and that isn't because she's such a nasty piece of goods, for Miss Davis made her name playing those. Nor is Anne Baxter a poor actress; but the fact is that Mankiewicz fails to make us believe in Eve or in the success of her rather obvious manipulations; we feel sure that in reality all those put upon would have booted her out into the cold cold snow before she could do so much damage. So the movie succeeds in spite of her, and in spite of the fact that she pretty well hogs the screen throughout the last twenty minutes, the dreaded Margo having been put in her place by then.

The entertainment begins hypnotically. Behind those simply but splendidly designed Fox credits of the post-war years, we see a stylish statuette, and presently backtrack from it to find ourselves invisible witnesses at a theatrical awards dinner. Addison de Witt, the savagely influential critic, begins his off-screen narration in the middle of a speech:

The distinguished-looking gentleman is an extremely old actor. Being an actor, he will go on speaking for some time. It is not important that you hear what he says . . . These hallowed walls, indeed many of these faces, have looked upon Modjeska, Ada Rehan and Minnie Fiske. Mansfield's voice filled this room. Booth breathed this air. It is unlikely that the windows have been opened since his death.

This is hardly the stuff for Halifax or Hoboken. And Mr de Witt will declare later: 'I have lived in the theatre as a Trappist monk lives in

ALL ABOUT EVE. Clearly no member of this edgy quartet is about to speak the unvarnished truth. Anne Baxter, Bette Davis, Marilyn Monroe, George Sanders

his faith' – another attitude unlikely to be understood in the sticks, which could absolutely be expected to abhor backstage dramas as firmly as they nixed hix pix. In a sense *All About Eve* is the last glorious gasp of the American high comedy tradition which brought forth such splendours as *Trouble in Paradise* and *The Philadelphia Story* (which Mankiewicz, wearing a different hat, produced); in another sense it foreshadows the Manhattan comedies of Woody Allen, for all the characters have feet of clay and are full of neuroses, though they don't yet recognize them as such and refrain from parading them round the less salubrious sections of the city. The presence of Broadway in this picture is almost entirely conveyed by suggestion, not by trailing round with a camera photographing marquees.

At bottom, the success of *All About Eve* at the box office was attributable not to the skill with which it dissects an aspect of the real American world, nor to its being recognized as the pinnacle of its author-director's career, nor even to the appeal of the stars previously mentioned, but to its generous allocation of insulting one-liners to almost every character in its cast. (Except Eve; but then, as we've agreed, she hardly counts.) Take Thelma Ritter as Birdie, Margo's dresser and part-time maid, who comments at the start of a party, as she returns from stacking the outer garments of rich widows: 'The bed looks like a dead animal act.' And when Eve spins her initial yarn of woe, Birdie is the only listener (except the audience) to remain unconvinced. 'What a story. Everythin' but the bloodhounds snappin' at her rear end.' And she is ever ready with a smart answer for her boss: when Margo says accusingly, 'You bought the new girdles a size smaller,' Birdie retorts, 'Maybe sumpn'else grew a size larger.'

Margo is not to be outdone. Struck by Eve's perfidy for the first time just before her own party, she has one drink too many before the jaded guests, and her producer, arrive. Lloyd remarks: 'The general atmosphere is very Macbethish. What has or is about to happen?' Margo tipsily mutters. 'Fasten your seat belts, we're in for a bumpy night.' She never fails to respond venomously to Addison's insinuations:

MARGO: I distinctly remember striking your name from the guest list.
ADDISON: Dear Margo. You were an unforgettable Peter Pan. You must play it again soon.
MARGO: I've been wanting you to meet Eve for the longest time.
ADDISON: It can only have been your natural timidity that prevented you from mentioning it . . .
EVE: I'm afraid Mr de Witt would find me boring before too long.
MISS CASWELL: You won't bore him, honey. You won't even get to talk.

Under all the invective Margo is the character most truthful to herself:

MARGO: Lloyd, I am not twentyish, I am not thirtyish. Three months ago I was forty years old. Forty. Four oh. *(She smiles.)* That slipped out. I hadn't quite made up my mind to admit it. Now I feel as though I'd suddenly taken all my clothes off.

Addison, when his protégée has failed an audition through stage fright, has waspish words for the theatre's younger sister.

ADDISON: Your next move, it seems to me, should be towards television.
MISS CASWELL: Tell me this. Do they have auditions for television?
ADDISON: That's all television is, dear, just auditions.

Addison also has glimmerings of divine truth. When by scheming he has made Eve his, the prize already seems tawdry:

ADDISON: That I should want you at all suddenly seems to me the height of improbability. But that in itself is probably the reason. You're an improbable person, Eve, and so am I. We have that in common. Also a contempt for humanity, an inability to love or be loved, insatiable emotion . . . and talent. We deserve each other.

If the above has conveyed a little of the bitter flavour of this attitudinizing 138-minute film, readers will not be surprised to hear that Mankiewicz's creative Hollywood career was a fairly compact one, at its best when he was under some head office control and skirting disaster when he was pulling rank after his big successes. Given rope, he hanged himself, for nothing kills most movies more surely than talk, even when the talk is erudite, witty and amusing. *A Letter to Three Wives*, his stepping stone to *Eve*, was a freshly observed three-decker romantic comedy which dutifully used up the studio's young talent. *People Will Talk*, which came after, is a witless aberration about a professor of anatomy and an unmarried mother: one critic retitled it *People Will Talk, and Talk, and Talk. The Barefoot Contessa* was even more lugubrious, a solemn in-joke about Hollywood folk who lost their marbles along with their inspiration. *The Quiet American* perversely changed the ending, and the point, of Graham Greene's book. *The Honey Pot*, massively cut by the distributors, took the sting out of *Volpone*. In between whiles he contrived with often elephantine competence to handle a few routine chores: *Five Fingers, Guys and Dolls, Suddenly Last Summer, Cleopatra, Sleuth*. They were all twenty minutes too long. At least.

For all that, Mankiewicz at his best was so talented a wordsmith that Hollywood did not dare to banish him. *All About Eve* may be a crumbled monument, its joints a little rusty and its speeches a little repetitive, but no one who has enjoyed disentangling its wheat from its chaff would deny it a preservation order.

All About Eve. US 1950; monochrome, 138 minutes. Produced by Darryl F. Zanuck for 20th Century-Fox. Written and directed by Joseph L. Mankiewicz from a story, 'The Wisdom of Eve', by Mary Orr. Photographed by Milton Krasner. Music score by

Alfred Newman. With Bette Davis as Margo Channing; Anne Baxter as Eve Harrington; George Sanders as Addison de Witt; Gary Merrill as Bill Sampson; Celeste Holm as Karen Richards; Hugh Marlowe as Lloyd Richards; Thelma Ritter as Birdie; Marilyn Monroe as Miss Caswell; Gregory Ratoff as Max Fabian; Barbara Bates as the girl.

The Devil to Pay
All That Money Can Buy

A nineteenth-century New England farmer sells his soul to the devil in return for seven years' good fortune.

It never seemed to belong to anybody. It was made in 1941, for RKO, but although I read about it in the odd American magazine, it didn't turn up in England until years later, when a small independent distributor, I think New Realm, offered it as a cheap component in a double bill. This was during my Cambridge cinema-managing days, and I snapped it up at once, partly out of curiosity and partly because it starred Walter Huston, who had alas just died. The title hadn't much box-office punch, so we second-featured it, but the print which turned up was a beauty, and I spent three winter afternoons gazing at it enraptured.

The film has a number of snags apart from the title. (The alternative, *Daniel and the Devil*, wouldn't have helped.) The cast lacks drawing power, and as for the director, who had now turned producer and was obviously the prime mover behind the entire effort – well, no one could even pronounce his surname. What's more, it dealt with characters from American history, and came from some highbrow poetic play by a fellow with three names. It wouldn't have helped, either, to say that it was a version of *Faust*. Commercially, in fact, the film was dead before it started production, and yet one can only be grateful to whoever financed it, for it has moments which rank with the best of Ford and Welles and even Hitchcock, and its final moments are guaranteed to send any audience home happy if once they can first be persuaded to part with the means of admission.

One would have guessed that the art direction was by William Cameron Menzies if the titles had not credited Van Nest Polglase.

Still, both are names to conjure with. It is the look of the film which first commands attention; the sheen and detail which combine a Matthew Brady photograph with a Currier and Ives print. It opens puzzlingly with Daniel Webster – never properly introduced for non-American audiences – trying to write a political speech while irritated by the whispered thoughts of the devil, whose shadow is cast on the wall, unmoved by the rapid strokes of Webster's pen: 'Why worry about the people and their problems? Start thinking about your own. You want to be president of this country, don't you? And you ought to be . . . Don't be a fool. Stop bothering with that speech and get busy promoting yourself instead of the people.' 'Be still!' roars Daniel, hurling an inkwell at the wall. The shadow vanishes. And so the scene is inevitably set for the final confrontation. We know the devil has wiles; but Webster has some of his own. As Eli remarks, 'They say, when he goes out to fish, the trout jump right out of the stream and into his pockets, because they know it's no use arguing.' And Jabez adds, 'Why, they say that when he speaks, stars and stripes come right out in the sky . . .'

But meanwhile it is to Jabez Stone and his problems that we are introduced. Jabez is a poor New Hampshire farmer of the 1840s, so badly off that we are instantly reminded of *The Grapes of Wrath*, especially as Jane Darwell is back to play Ma, whom nothing daunts. Everything goes wrong for Jabez. His wife has a fall, the bills and the mortgage are a-mounting, and the crops have failed. When he stumbles and spills a sack of corn into the mud, he finally loses his temper: 'That's enough to make a man sell his soul to the devil. And I would, too, for about two cents.' Slowly he realizes that two cents is just what he has in his hand. And there in the doorway stands a smiling, well-dressed figure, a little like a travelling salesman. 'Good evening, neighbour Stone,' says the newcomer smoothly. 'My name is Scratch – I often go by that name in New England.'

Needless to say, the honest farmer is no match for the smooth talk of the saturnine stranger. The promise of gold, and the magical stage management of its appearance, spilling up from under the floorboards, soon make him sign on the dotted line, though he balks a bit at the mention of losing his soul.

SCRATCH: Why should that worry you? A soul – a soul is nothing. Can you see it, touch it, smell it? No. Think of it, that soul, your soul, a nothing –

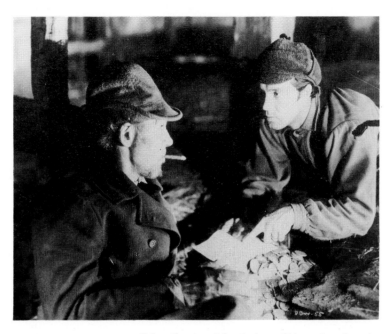

ALL THAT MONEY CAN BUY. Jabez Stone weighs the loss of his soul against the uses to which he can put a bag of gold. Walter Huston, James Craig

against seven whole years of good luck. You will have money and all that money can buy. Upon my word, neighbour Stone, if it weren't for my firm's reputation for generous dealing . . .

This may not seem a particularly persuasive speech, but all who have experienced Walter Huston's way with it will agree that it could make any victim turn into butter, melting in the devil's palm. Indeed the film could do with more of Mr Huston, though his occasional appearances are never less than effective, especially at the barn dance, when he is finally glimpsed as the fiddler up in the rafters, impelling all present to dance ever faster until they drop exhausted on the boards. But it is the farmer's fortunes that we follow, his sudden rise to riches and a great house, and his infatuation with the mysterious Belle, who comes 'from over the hill', and insists on staying to keep an eye on the family. We of course know from the backlit mist which accompanies her – for we have been to the pictures before – that she is the devil's emissary.

Stone's joy turns to distress when he throws a ball and nobody turns up except Miser Stevens, who confesses himself similarly in the devil's clutches. A little later he is found dead and a small moth fluttering around turns out to be the miser's soul – it speaks with his voice at least – but it's caught with practised ease by Mr Scratch, who uses a big bandanna handkerchief for the purpose, remarking, 'In the midst of life – one really hates to close these long-standing accounts. But business is business.'

When his seven years are up Jabez begs Daniel Webster to plead his case with Mr Scratch. The confrontation takes place one night in the barn, and Webster starts by citing the law that 'no American citizen may be forced into the service of a foreign prince'.

SCRATCH: Foreign? Who calls me a foreigner? When the first wrong was done to the first Indian, I was there. When the first slaver put out for the Congo, I stood on the deck. True, the North claims me for a Southerner, and the South for a Northerner, but I am neither. To tell the truth, Mr Webster, though I don't like to boast about it, my name is older in this country than yours.

Webster has no recourse but to insist on a jury trial and stresses only that the jurors be American. Scratch cheerfully agrees, and summons thirteen sinister phantoms from the barn cellar:

SCRATCH: Captain Kidd, who killed a man for gold . . . Simon Girty, the renegade . . . Governor Dale, who broke men upon the wheel . . . Asa the black monk . . . Floyd Ireson and Stede Bonnet, fiendish butchers . . . Walter Butler, king of the massacre . . . Big and Little Harp, robbers and murderers . . . Teach, the cut-throat . . . Morton, the vicious lawyer . . . and General Benedict Arnold. Dastard, liar, traitor, knave . . . Americans all . . .

To top it all, Scratch's selected judge is Hathorne, who persecuted the witches of Salem. But the trial which ensues does not go Scratch's way after all. Webster, by an impassioned patriotic speech, stirs the patriotic sentiment of even this hardened jury. 'Gentlemen of the jury: Don't let this country go to the devil! Free Jabez Stone! God save the United States and the men who have made her free!' The wraiths vanish with cockcrow, but Jabez has won the right to keep his soul, and Webster runs Scratch off the property before the family sits down to a celebratory breakfast. But when they lift the cover from Ma's peach-pie, the dish is empty.

'What the devil . . . ?' cries Ma. And, to the accompaniment of subdued poppity-pom music, we see Scratch, sitting on a stile, licking his fingers as he finishes off the pie, then getting out his notebook to select another client. He runs his finger down the pages, then catches sight of the audience through the camera. With a roguish grin he points his sharp little finger right at us, and the film irises out over it.

All That Money Can Buy is an immensely appealing movie in every respect, and it gains much from the lowering Teutonic direction which Dieterle brings to it: he was always at his best, as in *The Hunchback of Notre Dame* and *Portrait of Jennie*, with impressionistic studio settings which made no attempt to ape reality, and this kind of treatment is of course perfectly suited to a fairy tale for grown-ups. The adaptability of the Faustian subject matter was shown when in 1949 it was translated into modern politics for *Alias Nick Beal*, directed by John Farrow against lowering skies and darkened rooms. Here the victim is Thomas Mitchell, an honest politician beset by corruption; in desperation he falls for the promises of an apparently altruistic gangster without realizing the true identity of Mr Beal, who is played in a sinister snap brim by Ray Milland. It eventually takes all the power of bible-brandishing George Macready to corner Milland on a foggy jetty, from which, snarling 'You've jockeyed me into some kind of morality play,' he vanishes into the mist, and the sky brightens at once. This is a smart little movie which works out its fancies strictly according to Hollywood tradition; but there are more surprises in René Clair's *La Beauté du Diable*, in which Mephistopheles actually gives the aged Faust a young body for seven years, then wants it back. And last time I saw it there was much to be said for Murnau's 1926 silent version of *Faust* with Emil Jannings. Goethe would have been very surprised to find how many ways twentieth-century film-makers would find of beating his egg; but he didn't exactly invent the story either.

All That Money Can Buy. US 1941; monochrome; 106 minutes. Produced by Charles L. Glett and William Dieterle for RKO release. Written by Dan Totheroh, from 'The Devil and Daniel Webster' by Stephen Vincent Benet. Directed by William Dieterle. Photographed by Joseph August. Special effects by Vernon L. Walker. Music score by Bernard Herrmann. Art direction by Van Nest Polglase. Edited by Robert Wise. With Walter Huston as Mr Scratch; James Craig as Jabez Stone; Jane Darwell as Ma

Stone; Anne Shirley as Mary; Simone Simon as Belle; Edward Arnold as Daniel Webster; Gene Lockhart as Squire Slossum; John Qualen as Miser Stevens; H. B. Warner as Judge Hathorne.

Alias Nick Beal. US 1949; monochrome; 93 minutes. Produced by Endre Boehm for Paramount. Written by Jonathan Latimer, from a story by Mindret Lord. Directed by John Farrow. Photographed by Lionel Lindon. Music score by Franz Waxman. Art direction by Hans Dreier and Franz Bachelin. Edited by Eda Warren. With Ray Milland as Nick Beal; Thomas Mitchell as Joseph Foster; Audrey Totter as Donna Allen; George Macready as Rev Thomas Garfield; Fred Clark as Frankie Faulkner; Henry O'Neill as Judge Hobson.

The Leisen Touch
Arise, My Love

An American flyer condemned to death in the Spanish Civil War is rescued by an enterprising newspaper woman, and he romances her around Europe as the bombs begin to fall.

The name of Mitchell Leisen would not spring readily to the lips of most people asked to cast their minds back to Hollywood's golden age. Yet as much as any director he symbolizes the glamour, the light-hearted fluency and the box office success we came to expect of our packaged entertainment in the thirties and forties, and his inclinations straddle several peaks of Hollywood glory. Lubitsch, Sturges, La Cava, de Mille, Borzage, Von Sternberg – all influenced him or were influenced by him; and in between whiles he had a shot or two at the musical, the variety show, the aeroplane thriller, the suspenser, the historical pastiche, the psychological comedy and the *film noir*. Possibly his adeptness at so many styles accounts for his failure to be remembered for himself, yet he had a distinctive flair, and whatever he did, he did meticulously. His films were never less than elegant to look at, though he disclaimed any art of cinema; the camera never moves arbitrarily in my pictures, he said. This tended to mean that he told his stories in words and close-ups, with conversations that were sometimes too long and points that could have been better made by the unaided camera; but every shot was beautifully composed, and he demanded camerawork of the most lustrous kind.

Despite his talent and his understanding, none of Leisen's films is an outright masterpiece. Either he lacked a necessary touch of astringency, letting the sentimentality get out of hand, or he over-indulged his scriptwriters instead of compressing their verbiage into cinematic terms. *Arise, My Love* has all these faults, and it is also very dated by its propaganda content, but I choose it as a favourite because in it, if one mentally pares down its ten per cent of excess in all departments, the talents of all concerned can be seen to be working at full steam. Besides, it is an amazing instance of Hollywood's topicality in the days of fast studio production. Released in October 1940, it climaxes with the fall of France just four months previously, and was in fact written and made during July and August. As drama torn from the headlines, this must beat even *Confessions of a Nazi Spy* and *Five Graves to Cairo*. Incidentally, if Joel McCrea had been cast as originally intended, the resemblance to Hitchcock's *Foreign Correspondent* would have been underlined, for both films feature Americans cavorting around 1940 Europe and finally appealing to America not to stay isolationist.

Arise, My Love is said to be Claudette Colbert's favourite of her own films, and one can well believe it from her entirely deft and satisfactory performance as the modern woman of her time, doing a man's job and reluctant to find time for love. Amusingly we never see the right side of her face; Leisen gave in to her whim that the left side photographed better, which meant that poor Ray Milland, shouldering the role which was to make him a star, and proving only a trifle lightweight for it, was constantly obliged to show his right. The entire film can be viewed as one long romantic dialogue, alternating light banter with rather deadly seriousness and the odd touch of poetry. The title comes from the Song of Solomon, and Milland quotes it casually when he first falls for Colbert: 'Arise, my love, my fair one, come away.' It takes on a different meaning when they both decide to quit Europe for the safety of America, but at the end, after sinking with the *Athenia* and witnessing the fall of France, they take a firmer stand and elect to stay and warn the world. 'Say it to America,' says Colbert sternly. 'Arise, my love, and make yourself strong. Is it going to be their way of life, or ours?' It is an indication of the film's high style that the actress can get away with this line without evoking a horse laugh from the audience, which has already had to accept the scriptwriters' own poetic vision of the trees in the forest of Compiègne 'practising their curtsies in the breeze because they believe Louis XIV is still king'.

Most of the movie is set in Paris, and this cushions the sought-after whiff of reality because for Leisen, Paris can still be found on Paramount's backlot, just where Lubitsch left it. He re-creates it by an exterior café set, by a fairly lavish interior for Maxim's, and by the shape of some of the windows in the press office. In a romantic film like this, anyone impelled to pull the communication cord as the Berlin train steams through Compiègne will find a cosy isolated inn which Mrs Miniver would have loved, and a forest that is an art director's dream, with so much wild life bounding through it that one can understand the heroine's feeling that the seven dwarfs must be throwing a party. It is also the kind of film in which the climax of love is a chaste kiss, though more may be read into the scene which opens with the lovers having apparently spent all night on the forest floor without getting either pneumonia or their hair ruffled. The dialogue, as he lies with his head in her lap, fairly successfully suggests what may have happened during the preceding fade-out:

AUGUSTA: There's an ant crawling up your cheek.
TOM: I'd rather have a kiss. *(She kisses him.)* That's an awfully small kiss.
AUGUSTA: It was a small ant.
TOM: I wish it had been an elephant.

This kind of teetering on the brink reminds one that the script is by Charles Brackett and Billy Wilder, fresh from *Ninotchka*. This knowledge prepares one both for such playful gibes as the one about the Berlin correspondent who got fired because he went to a party at Von Ribbentrop's and kept yelling for gefilte fish; and for such running gags as Colbert's means of defending herself against men who get too fresh, which is to bite their noses. And, considering that the film was written while America was still defiantly neutral, they make their attitude to Hitler abundantly clear in the scene when Colbert settles down determinedly to read *Mein Kampf*. 'Wake me up,' says Milland, 'when you get to the part where he claims Milwaukee.'

If the film sells itself on its stars, it also has a memorable supporting performance by Walter Abel as Colbert's harassed editor, who goes around muttering: 'I'm not happy. I'm not happy at *all*.' He serves generally to deflate tension at the film's more

ARISE MY LOVE. The suave commandant of a Spanish prison is taken in by the wiles of an American lady reporter . . . or is he simply bemused by that hat? George Zucco, Ray Milland, Claudette Colbert

solemn moments. The Nazis invade Warsaw; the lovers gaze tearfully into each other's eyes; and in top hat and tuxedo Mr Abel flounces into the press office crying: 'I might have known. Every time I try to see *The Magic Flute*, something happens.' He also gets half-brained by a vase when he tries to invade Colbert's room and she thinks it's Milland. 'Just a slight skull fracture,' he assures her. 'I'll deduct it from your salary.'

This brings us to the vexed question: should *Arise, My Love* be classified as comedy or drama? The best description, probably, is to call it a comedy on a serious subject, a comedy which hopes that the world will appreciate the tension underlying its jokes. It begins solemnly enough to confuse, with credits against a rather unattractive grey symposium of clouds and sunbeams; then we track down into an impressively shadowed Spanish courtyard where a prisoner is being executed by firing squad as Milland in his cell wearily plays cards with a priest. 'He never heard that volley,' said Milland. 'Lead travels faster than sound.' The priest, unable to instil thoughts of repentance, mildly comments that the Spanish case against the Americans was not entirely without merit: 'after all, you have shot down seven of our planes.' 'Seven my foot,' replies Milland, 'it was twelve. One official communiqué said nineteen!' The mood suddenly changes as they are called to see commandant George Zucco, who has been persuaded by Milland's tearful 'wife', in fact a perfect stranger, to grant him a pardon. 'I hope heaven can wait, padre,' says Milland cheerfully as they leave. 'I think your chances of reaching heaven are very remote, my son,' replies the padre, who knows the truth but is bound by the confessional. Unfortunately Milland has left behind a regrettably frank and truthful will, so a car and plane chase ensues; and suddenly we are in Paris and everyone is getting drunk on champagne and crème de menthe (in the same glass). Milland lays siege to Colbert by sitting all night in the open-air café opposite her hotel room, but she resists the temptation to join him by having all her shoes locked up in the hotel safe. Within a few minutes we have moved from the world of Hemingway through Sturges to Lubitsch, and any director who can manage such switches must deserve the earnest consideration of posterity.

Of Leisen's other movies, *Kitty* commends itself as an elegant period rip-off of *Pygmalion*; *Lady in the Dark* is an expensive, witty, but ultimately charmless satire on psychiatry, much harmed by head office editing. *Hold Back the Dawn* and *To Each His Own* are women's pictures par excellence, and in the former Leisen makes a personal appearance as the recipient of Charles Boyer's story. *Easy Living* is a screwball farce which must have given its scenarist, Preston Sturges, a lot of pointers; *The Princess Comes Across* is one of the most polished comedy-mysteries of the mid-thirties. Perhaps the most perfect, the lightest, of Leisen's works, however, is a little bit of fluff called *Midnight*, also by Brackett and Wilder. Colbert is again in evidence in this elaboration of the Cinderella story (hence the title); the opening finds her in Paris, penniless in a gold lamé evening gown. After a series of chance meetings she is hired by rich John Barrymore to entice a gigolo away from his wife, but ends up marrying a taxi driver only to find that he is really a count. With a cast which also includes Mary Astor and Rex O'Malley, it's all great waspish fun, but as so often Leisen can't quite sustain the pace till the end title, and the final court scene goes on too long and lacks really funny lines. A Leisen near miss, however, is worth half a dozen of most other people's hits.

Arise, My Love. US 1940; monochrome; 113 minutes. Produced by Arthur Hornblow Jnr for Paramount. Written by Charles Brackett and Billy Wilder. Directed by Mitchell Leisen. Photographed by Charles Lang Jnr. Music score by Victor Young. Art direction by Hans Dreier and Robert Usher. With Claudette Colbert as Augusta Nash; Ray Milland as Tom Martin; Walter Abel as Phillips; Esther Dale as Susie; Dennis O'Keefe as Shep; Dick Purcell as Pink; George Zucco as Prison Governor.

Midnight. US 1939; monochrome; 94 minutes. Produced by Arthur Hornblow Jnr for Paramount. Written by Charles Brackett and Billy Wilder from a story by Edwin Justus Mayer and Franz Shulz. Directed by Mitchell Leisen. Photographed by Charles Lang. Music by Frederick Hollander. Edited by Doane Harrison. With Claudette Colbert as Eve Peabody; Don Ameche as Tibor Czerny; John Barrymore as George Flammion; Mary Astor as Helen Flammion; Francis Lederer as Jacques Picot; Hedda Hopper as Stephanie; Rex O'Malley as Marcel; Elaine Barrie as Simone.

A Show That Is Really a Show Sends You Out in a Kind of a Glow
The Band Wagon

A fading Hollywood dancer and an impresario of the legitimate stage team up to produce and star in a Broadway revue.

The Broadway revue of the Depression era, and the Hollywood putting-on-a-show musical which developed from it, had only one aim and that was to make people forget their troubles. Starting in 1943 with *Oklahoma!*, book shows with 'meaning' began to develop, until the sixties brought complex musical entertainments like *Cabaret* and *Fiddler on the Roof*, about the plight of the Jews, *Camelot*, about the impossibility of Utopia, and later *A Little Night Music*, about the self-delusion of middle age. The old musicals had no point to make; what was memorable about them was the stars and the numbers. Busby Berkeley was a name much associated with such endeavours, and in 1970 he was coaxed out of retirement to add his echo (and very little else) to a Broadway revival of *No No Nanette!*, one of the most inane of twenties musical comedies. It was propelled to new success partly by the addition of songs from other shows, but principally by the re-emergence after thirty years' obscurity of Ruby Keeler, the starry-eyed ingenue of many a Warner extravaganza of the early thirties, who had more or less retired after marrying Al Jolson. When she came strutting down the staircase and did her taps to 'I Want to Be Happy', arms akimbo and feet thudding on the stage in that old clumsy way of hers, the audience rose to its feet and caused reverberations which for once might really have been expected to raise the roof of the 46th Street Theatre. The real reason for the cheers was that the ageing watchers clearly perceived Miss Keeler to be still alive and on her feet, and felt therefore that there was still hope for themselves; accordingly, finding themselves also in the presence of such accomplished performers as Helen Gallagher and Bobby Van, they were prepared to sit back and be thoroughly entertained by beach ball girlie numbers and by the unlikely compromising of a bible publisher and by the straight-to-audience cynicism of a know-it-all Irish maid, just as their grandfathers and grandmothers had been entertained long before, in the age of innocence.

The last gasp of the light Hollywood musical, before such things became prohibitively expensive, was heard in the early fifties when the Arthur Freed unit at MGM was winding down; and among the best musicals of them all was *The Band Wagon*, built around Dietz-and-Schwarz songs that were first popular in the late twenties, like 'I Love Louisa' and 'Dancing in the Dark' and 'Louisiana Hayride'. Tongue-in-cheek from start to finish, it contrived to spoof not only the entire putting-on-a-show tradition but the slowly fading career of its imperishable star Fred Astaire, first seen travelling from Hollywood to Broadway in a silver train and finding fun in an amusement arcade before trying to pick up a stage career. The plot which follows is no plot at all, merely a link for the numbers, for some neat comedy performances, and for a touch of romance. Oscar Levant and Nanette Fabray more or less portray Adolph Green and Betty Comden, who wrote a lot of musicals including this one. Jack Buchanan, in a long-delayed return to Hollywood after mild success in the early thirties, plays a producer who wants to put on *Oedipus Rex*, and who after bombing in New Haven with a Freudian version

THE BAND WAGON. A quintet with no aim but to make you feel good. Oscar Levant, Cyd Charisse, Jack Buchanan, Fred Astaire, Nanette Fabray

of the musical entertainment we have seen rehearsed, is rapidly converted by the rest of the cast to the philosophy of making people happy instead of giving them sad shows like *Hamlet*.

> Where the ghost and the prince meet
> And everyone ends in mincemeat.

The lines are from *That's Entertainment*, the one new song in the movie and a rouser which quickly became a classic; even so it can't beat the magic of 'I Guess I'll Have to Change My Plan', sung and danced by Astaire and Buchanan as the most immaculate tail-coated duo on film against a clever set which is no more than horizontal bars in light pastel shades. The other highlights include 'Triplets', with Nanette Fabray joining Fred and Jack to form a terrible trio of screaming infants in cunningly devised baby clothes, and the elaborate 'Girl Hunt', an elegant take-off of all the private eye yarns that Mickey Spillane may have thought of but never bothered to write.

What chiefly distinguishes *The Band Wagon*, apart from the fact that it works so well and has no dull spots, is its light, sophisticated style. The artistic pretensions of its director have been held in check by the popular sense of its producer and the natural inclinations of its stars. Its design throughout is restrained but imaginative, from the wurlitzer which sparks into amazing life when Astaire kicks it, to the lamplit park for the romantic duet and the gleaming green alleyways and free-standing fire escapes of the ballet. Perhaps the best example of *The Band Wagon*'s rare stylishness is that it can convey a disastrous first night simply by the off-screen wailing of a Greek chorus and the single visual of a gigantic egg.

The Band Wagon has a night club ambience, and its chief motif might be that of a tail-coated man. Busby Berkeley's musicals concentrated on undressed women, and presented them in a honky tonk atmosphere that harked back to burlesque; perhaps his most typical image is that of the naughty little boy who cavorts gleefully through a couple of his numbers allowing us to peek through window shades at girls undressing; and one might also pause to consider the number of times Berkeley persuades his cameraman to track through a tunnel of girls' legs. Glamour-processed they may be, but the essential appeal of Berkeley's numbers is to the voyeur. They are millionaire versions of a schoolboy's erotic dream, filled to bursting point with multiple images of a kind that only dreams, movie magic, and the mind of a Berkeley can provide. The title number of *Dames* is typical, and its introduction confirms my thesis:

> What do you go for, to see a show for?
> It's to see those great big, gorgeous, wonderful dames . . .

Giant white alarm clocks rotate through a gleaming black floor, bringing into view fifty beds each containing a luscious girl stretching into wakefulness. The mini-sets revolve again into dressing tables, and the girls set about their toilettes. One of them recognizes the camera as a peeping tom, and thrusts a powder puff into it; the puff is withdrawn to reveal that the girls are now dressed and at the perfume stage. Presently an atomizer is sprayed into the camera, and when the mist is wiped away it is by a window cleaner gazing at an army of girls walking the city streets to work. Fully-dressed women, however, are not in Berkeley's scheme of things, so presently he contrives to have us gazing at sixty or so girls in black tights, spreading their legs in unison for the kaleidoscopic shots which turn them into pulsating geometrical patterns. Finally the group freezes subtly into a pulchritudinous still, through which Dick Powell symbolically thrusts his head to finish the song.

It sounds elementary in print, but while it's on the screen you can't take your eyes off it, for Berkeley knew exactly what the camera could achieve with a little coaxing, and at Warner he had the master art director Anton Grot to design the sets. 'By a Waterfall' and 'Remember My Forgotten Man' are more Grot than Berkeley, and the train which divides in 'Shuffle Off to Buffalo' is an eye-popping example of big studio expertise. If Spielberg or Scorsese did it today there would be cries about revelatory technique; in 1933 it was just another number in a movie called *42nd Street*. Again the lyrics are on the sexy side:

LEADING MAN: I'll go home and pack my panties,
You go home and get your scanties,
And away we'll go;
Then you'll see us shuffle, shuffle off to Buffalo.
GIRLS: Matrimony is baloney, they'll be wanting alimony
In a year or so;
Still you'll see 'em shuffle, shuffle off to Buffalo . . .

Sometimes the chorus girls, beaming overpoweringly into the camera, seem to be mocking the professed amorous intentions of the principals. The leaden dancing of Miss Keeler is anything but aphrodisiac, and the men are always strangulated tenors who look too impotent to rise to any of the occasions suggested by the lyrics:

I'm young and healthy, and so are you;
When the moon is in the sky,
Tell me what am I to do?
I'm young and healthy, and you've got charms;
It would really be a sin
Not to have you in my arms.

But most people barely notice the words in this fantasy land where a girl can step down from a taxi roof she wasn't even on a moment before, and a bare black floor can become an illuminated skyscraper in full perspective, with the principals waving from the top. It's a world trapped in Hollywood aspic, and at least we should be grateful for the proof that it did once happen.

The Band Wagon. US 1953; Technicolor; 112 minutes. Produced by Arthur Freed for MGM. Associate producer, Roger Edens. Written by Adolph Green and Betty Comden. Directed by Vincente Minnelli. Photographed by Harry Jackson. Songs by Howard Dietz and Arthur Schwarz. Art direction by Oliver Smith. Choreographed by Michael Kidd. Edited by Albert Akst. With Fred Astaire as Tony Hunter; Jack Buchanan as Jeffrey Cordova; Cyd Charisse as Gaby; Oscar Levant as Lester Marton; Nanette Fabray as Lily Marton; Robert Gist as Hal Benton; Thurston Hall as Colonel Tripp; James Mitchell as Paul Byrd.

Down These Dark Streets a Man Must Go
The Big Sleep

A Los Angeles private detective finds himself in some very complex trouble when he agrees to pay off a few gambling debts for General Sternwood's errant daughter.

It was about eleven o'clock in the morning, mid-October, with the sun not shining and a look of hard, wet rain in the clearness of the foothills. I was wearing my powder blue suit, with dark blue shirt, tie and display handkerchief, black brogues, black wool socks with blue clocks on them. I was neat, clean, shaved and sober, and I didn't care who knew it. I was everything the well-dressed private detective ought to be. I was calling on four million dollars.

That is the opening paragraph of Raymond Chandler's 1939 novel on which this cult film is based, and there is of course no way of conveying on celluloid such spare, laconic, character-building detail; all the actor can do is go up to the door and knock. But when the actor is Humphrey Bogart, we have most of the advantages we need, for Bogie was the natural personification of Philip Marlowe, on screen and off: tough, cynical, intelligent, honest, mildly intellectual, gallant when need be, and a sucker for a hard luck story. He also had a unique manner of half-lisping speech which enabled him to deal admirably with Chandler's clipped witticisms, without appearing to take a breath before each funny line as Dick Powell did in *Farewell My Lovely*, or playing for laughs as James Garner did in *Marlowe* and its tele-imitation *The Rockford Files*. Bogart was the star

Marlowe, for 1946 and all time, and Chandler himself was delighted by the performance, 'all he has to do to dominate a scene is to enter it,' he said. It seems a crying shame that Bogie played the part only once.

The Big Sleep is an insufferably murky film. It is murky to look at, because Warners always liked to hide their cheap sets behind lots of fog and quasi-artistic shadow, and in this case the longer the film goes on the darker it gets, becoming positively treacly by the last reel. As to plot, it is so deep, dense and maze-like that although we are given equal opportunity with Marlowe to understand the initial situation, there are many developments not made clear to him or to us, and confusion is compounded by the fact that a couple of important characters never appear, while those who do are bumped off at an alarming rate. When it came to tidying up the matter of who, out of the few left alive, killed whom, even Chandler had to admit himself baffled. The odd thing is that it doesn't much seem to matter: mood is all. The action never strays for more than a few seconds from the Warner backlot and sound stages, but interest skims along on the surface tension of threatened violence and incidental wit, buoyed by the splendidly insolent man-woman relationship of Bogart and Bacall, who prowl around each other like tigers in a cage. Their first meeting, as spoiled rich girl and perspiring private eye, he fresh from being interviewed by her father in a humid hothouse necessary for the old man's continued life, is not exactly auspicious for eventual romantic harmony:

VIVIAN: So you're a private detective. I didn't know they existed, except in books, or else they were little greedy men snooping around hotels. My, you're a mess, aren't you?
MARLOWE: Yeah, I'm not the orchid-bearing type.
VIVIAN: . . . I don't see what there is to be cagey about. And I don't like your manners.
MARLOWE: I'm not crazy about yours. I didn't ask to see you. And I don't mind your ritzing me, or drinking your lunch out of a bottle. I don't mind your showing me your legs. They're very swell legs and it's a pleasure to make their acquaintance. I don't mind if you don't mind my manners. They're pretty bad. I grieve over them on long winter evenings. But don't waste your time trying to cross-examine me.
VIVIAN: People don't talk like that to me. Do you always think you can handle people like trained seals?

As written, the role of Vivian's dying father seems almost perfect for Sydney Greenstreet, but an emaciated frame was required, and

Charles Waldron, an actor otherwise little known, does excellently with it:

BUTLER: How do you like your brandy, sir?
MARLOWE: Just with brandy.
GENERAL: I used to like mine with champagne. The champagne cold as Valley Forge and with about three ponies of brandy under it. You may take your coat off, sir. It's too hot in here for a man with blood in his veins. You may smoke, too. I can still enjoy the smell of it. That man is already dead who must enjoy his vices by proxy.

A little more of Mr Waldron would not have come amiss. There *is* more of him in the shooting script published by Appleton-Century-Crofts, two whole scenes in fact, but they have entirely disappeared from the finished film, along with a great deal of rather tiresome explanatory dialogue between other characters. All the film's climactic sequences, culminating in Bogart and Bacall smoking in the dark, waiting for the police to arrive, with a dead body on the doorstep, seem to have resulted from last-minute changes; that final image, so strong that it is also used under the credit titles, is not in the shooting script at all. There is no obvious merit in the missing scenes, just accusations and counter-accusations and recapitulations and snarls, but in throwing out so much, Hawks also jettisoned what sense there was in the plot development. He did however leave in all the violence, and critics of the time were quick to complain about it, even though most of the deaths discreetly take place offscreen. Some local authorities in Britain gave the movie an 'H' for horror, and counted up the number of corpses as fourteen. This seems absurd enough now, as there isn't a drop of even black-and-white blood to be seen, and no shock moments at all, while apart from the evil Canino the heavies are too roughly sketched to be menacing. In 1946, however, the suggested background of vice, gambling, perversion, pornography and nymphomania was strong enough in flavour to justify some of the disturbed comments. 'Often brutal and sometimes sinister,' said James Agee: 'it is a dream world, and doubtless it stimulates socially undesirable appetites.' 'Morbid and disturbing,' said Bosley Crowther, headlining his piece 'Violence Erupts Again'. Nowadays most Chandler fans recognize that his seamy Los Angeles and corrupt Bay City never really existed, forming merely a landscape of the mind through which violent and

THE BIG SLEEP. Bogie and Bacall wait for the final shoot-out

frustrated feelings could be dissipated in a pleasingly literary way; its creation was Chandler's way of staying sane in a drab but insufficiently dangerous world, and its guns were harmless fireworks serving merely to punctuate the story and eliminate characters who had outlived their interest.

When reading Chandler even now, it is impossible to prevent the mind's eye from seeing Bogart, especially in the first-person narrative of mental processes, and it is his personality above all which keeps *The Big Sleep* so fresh after thirty-five years. Howard Hawks used to say that it was the first film in which Bogie could be persuaded to laugh. Evidence shows that this is quite untrue, but it is certainly the first film in which he felt sufficiently assured of his star persona to play around with it in little ways, such as the lightly homosexual disguise he assumes while casing the pornographic bookshop:

MARLOWE: Would you happen to have a *Ben Hur* 1860?
ASSISTANT: A first edition?

MARLOWE: No, no, the third. The one with the erratum on page one-sixteen.
ASSISTANT: I'm afraid not – at the moment.
MARLOWE: How about a Chevalier Audubon – the full set, of course?
ASSISTANT: Not at the moment.
MARLOWE: You do sell books? Hm?
ASSISTANT: What do those look like, grapefruit?
MARLOWE: They look like books to me.

A delightful, memorable little scene, but one wouldn't instinctively cast Bogart in it. Yet he brought it off triumphantly, and who can forget the way he grinned to himself, turned up his hat and donned hornrims before going in? Of such tiny details is film history made; and from fun movies like *The Big Sleep* grew the *film noir* movement of the late forties and a goodly share of the Bogart cult of thirty years later.

The Big Sleep. US 1946; monochrome; 114 minutes. Produced and directed by Howard Hawks for Warners. Written by William Faulkner, Leigh Brackett and Jules Furthman, from the novel by Raymond Chandler. Photographed by Sid Hickox. Music score by Max Steiner. Edited by Christian Nyby. With Humphrey Bogart as Philip Marlowe; Lauren Bacall as Vivian; Martha Vickers as Carmen; John Ridgeley as Eddie Mars; Bob Steele as Canino; Charles Waldron as General Sternwood; Regis Toomey as Bernie Ohls; Charles D. Brown as Norris; Elisha Cook Jnr as Harry Jones; Dorothy Malone as Proprietress; Theodore Van Eltz as Geiger.

Medium Rare
Blithe Spirit

A best-selling novelist, staging a seance for research into his new book, unwittingly conjures up the mischievous spirit of his previous wife.

After the rather severe credits in careful handwritten italic comes a playful introduction in the form of a Victorian sampler:

> When we are young
> We read and believe
>   The most fantastic things.
> When we are older
> We learn with regret
>   That these things cannot be.

As this image fades, we hear the unmistakable tones of Noel Coward.

We are quite, quite, wrong!

Even if we had not recognized the voice or even read the credits, we would surely recognize this film as vintage Coward, for no other writer has such control over a dismissive line:

CHARLES: What do you suppose induced Agnes to leave us?
RUTH: The reason was becoming increasingly obvious, my dear.
CHARLES: Mm. We must keep Edith in the house more.

Or:

CHARLES: Anything interesting in *The Times*?
RUTH: Don't be silly, dear.

Or, as Charles describes the death of his first wife:

CHARLES: She was convalescing from pneumonia and one evening began to laugh helplessly at one of the BBC musical programmes and died of a heart attack.

Almost any one of these lines would to me make *Blithe Spirit* a film to treasure, but there is no accounting for the widely divergent standards set by critics of the different arts. In the West End theatre, though Coward himself dismissed it as a trifle cooked up during a four-day holiday at Portmeirion, *Blithe Spirit* was an instant success which ran almost throughout World War II and was promptly acknowledged as a modern light classic; its brittle lines making several acting reputations. The celluloid version, produced shortly after, was dismissed by almost all London's film critics as a stagey cocktail comedy of a kind long out of date, and did only moderately at the box office, although in fact it is in my view an improvement on the play, pruning much of the excess verbiage which Coward simply didn't have time to attend to before the West End première, which took place six weeks after delivery of his first and only draft. Now, I am the first to object to photographed plays if the play has no merit to start with and the camera is fixed in the sixth row of the stalls; but equally one does not wish to lose the chance of preserving in sharpened and highly cinematic form something which, although originally designed for the stage, is worthy of wider circulation. The film of *Blithe Spirit*, like that of *The Philadelphia Story*, makes an ideal compromise between the two art forms. It resists the temptation to open up the action, but ensures that the eye remains engaged by subtle movements of a camera which is always in the right place to catch an effective close-up. Every time I come back to it I sense that I am watching something not only well worth doing but done with rare discretion.

By including *Topper Returns* also among my hundred films, I may seem to be over-indulging myself in the direction of comedy ghosts, as both films depict spirits visible to certain characters and invisible to others. On analysis however we are considering two different genres. The *Topper* film is American pratfall farce in the noisiest tradition, with the ghost involved only for the boisterous fun to be obtained from it. *Blithe Spirit* is uppercrust English from first foot to last, seeming to emanate from the dead centre of Weybridge's St George's Hill. Its forte is malicious wit, the self-mockery if you like of a society which was already on its way out and probably knew it, and its method is to treat the abnormal as though it were the most normal thing in the world. 'Where is the little darling now?' asks Madame Arcati about the undead Elvira. 'My husband's driven her into Folkestone,' is the casual reply. And like an anxious weekend host, the novelist urges his unexpected ghostly guest: 'You must find out whether you're going to stay or not, and we'll make arrangements accordingly.' But poor Elvira's main concern seems to be what her husband has done to the garden while she has been wandering on her astral plane these last seven years: 'You've absolutely ruined that border by the sundial: it looks like a mixed salad. All those nasturtiums are so vulgar.'

This is a film which floats on a cloud of badinage, and the jokes have been so compressed that to see it with a full house is to lose half of them. Husband and wife fill in any empty spaces by taunting each other:

RUTH: You were hag-ridden by your mother until you were twenty-three. Then you fell into the clutches of that awful Mrs Winthrop whatever her name was . . . then there was Elvira, she ruled you with a rod of iron.
CHARLES: Elvira never ruled anyone, she was much too elusive, that was one of her greatest charms.
RUTH: Then there was Maud Charteris.
CHARLES: My affair with Maud Charteris lasted exactly seven and a half

BLITHE SPIRIT. Ectoplasmic Elvira plays a few tricks; Mrs Condomine only sees the chair. Kay Hammond, Rex Harrison, Constance Cummings

weeks, and she cried all the time . . . If you wish to make an inventory of my sex life I think it only fair to tell you that you've left out several episodes. I shall consult my diary and give you a complete list after lunch.

The cause of all the trouble has been the previous evening's dress-for-dinner party with Dr and Mrs Bradman, Madame Arcati the local medium, and 'Always' played on the gramophone. Unfortunately this happened to be the favourite tune of Charles Condomine's departed wife (one wonders why Coward didn't pick one of his own instead of Irving Berlin's), and this fact, together with the presence of a dim maid who later proves to be a natural medium, is enough to waft Elvira's spirit through the closed curtains while the port is still being passed. The enthusiastic efforts of Madame Arcati, despite her facility for smelling ectoplasm and the vigorous way she sends herself into a trance, appear to have been largely incidental, and she certainly sees no way of repairing the situation, but as she is played by the magnificently misshapen Margaret Rutherford she comes close to stealing the show. Her enthusiasms extend to bicycling:

MRS BRADMAN: I must say I find bicycling very exhausting. Those awful hills . . .
MADAME ARCATI: Just knack. Down with your head, up with your heart, and you're over the top like a flash and skimming down the other side like a dragonfly.

Elvira, grey-green all over apart from her lipstick and fingernails, is played by Kay Hammond with a pouty plum-in-mouth charm which makes us regret all the more that this unique actress's career was cut short by illness. The fact that only Charles can see or hear her leads to a fine conversational mix-up, Ruth being driven to the conclusion that he is merely drunk:

RUTH: Now, sit down, Charles. You can't relax standing up.
ELVIRA: African natives can. They can stand on one leg for hours and hours.
CHARLES: I don't happen to be an African native.
RUTH: You don't happen to be a what?
CHARLES: An African native. Oh, say no more about it.
RUTH: Would you like some more brandy?
CHARLES: Yes, please.
ELVIRA: Very unwise, you always had a weak head.
CHARLES: I could drink you under the table.
RUTH: There's no need to be aggressive. Here, drink this, then we'll go to bed.
ELVIRA: Get rid of her, Charles, then we can talk.
CHARLES: That's a thoroughly immoral suggestion, you ought to be ashamed of yourself.
RUTH: What is there immoral about that?
CHARLES: Oh, I wasn't speaking to you, I was speaking to Elvira. She's here, Ruth, a few yards away from you.
RUTH: Oh yes, dear, I can see her distinctly, under the piano with a zebra!

Soon after this Ruth quite naturally flounces off to bed alone, and Charles cuddles up on the sofa with his sexy ghost. At this point David Lean's normally tactful direction calls attention to itself with a tracking shot of real star quality, away from the couple, through a door which opens itself and into a mirror through which we can see the couple still reflected . . . but no camera. It has taken me more than thirty years to work out how it was done.

Blithe Spirit is by no means an important film in the history of the art, but it is a marvellous record of a comedy significant in its period, played by actors in touch with the author's intention; and it provided an important corrective at a time when the bulk of British cinema was resolutely lower class. It belongs in the Rank art gallery with *Caesar and Cleopatra, The Red Shoes, A Matter of Life and Death* and *Henry V*; such efforts in the gradual elevation of mass culture had however proved easier during the war itself, when queues formed at the pithead for Sybil Thorndike in *The Trojan Women*, and king and commoner alike crowded into the National Gallery to hear Myra Hess play at a lunchtime concert. Clearly this type of comedy could not be expected to last into the era of *Saturday Night and Sunday Morning*, but perhaps it may be thought ripe for revival next time the British film industry gathers its wits and elects to produce something at a higher cultural level than *Confessions of a Door to Door Salesman*. Meanwhile, let's hope someone looks after what's left of the negative of *Blithe Spirit*, which has already lost one of its primary colours and tends to look rather more unearthly than was originally intended.

Blithe Spirit. GB 1945; Technicolor; 96 minutes. Produced by Anthony Havelock-Allan for Cineguild/Two Cities and Rank release. Written by Noel Coward, from his play. Directed by David Lean. Photographed by Ronald Neame. Music score by Richard Addinsell. Art direction by John Bryan. With Rex Harrison as Charles Condomine; Constance Cummings as Ruth Condomine; Kay Hammond as Elvira; Margaret Rutherford as Madame Arcati; Hugh Wakefield as Dr Bradman; Joyce Carey as Mrs Bradman; Jacqueline Clark as Edith.

They Called Her Wicked Lola
The Blue Angel

An elderly professor, pursuing errant schoolboys to their tawdry nightclub haunt, falls for the leading singer and persuades her to marry him. She quickly tires; he becomes a buffoon in her act and, when they revisit his former home, he trudges through the snow to his classroom and dies there.

In 1951 I was a Cambridge undergraduate, writing for the weekly paper *Varsity*. As film critic, I discovered an obscure, badly situated, and chilly twelve-hundred-seater called the Rex, which had no booking power against the ABC circuit which held Cambridge in a stranglehold, and was now owned (I think he won it in a raffle) by a tough, bullying but somehow very likeable ex-haulage contractor who hadn't been inside a cinema for twenty years and would have seemed better suited to owning a few pubs. Sad to see so large a hall occupied by so few bodies, I asked him why he didn't try booking films to suit undergraduate tastes. It transpired that he hadn't seen a movie since *King Kong* in 1933, and fell asleep in that, so he eagerly asked for suggestions. Since the resulting programmes were naturally excellent, and I was saying so in my weekly column, George and I quickly became fast friends, and after two terms of success with the Marx Brothers and Hitchcock revivals I was growing rather experimental. 'Try *The Blue Angel*,' I said.

Oddly enough it was a film George remembered, and he put it in so quickly that I barely had time to regret my advice. I had seen it once, at the unsuitable age of five, in a Bolton fleapit called the Atlas, where it was said they loaned you a hammer along with your ticket. I think I expected to see a real angel bathed in ultramarine light, at any rate I was pretty disappointed with what I did get, but I had a vague memory of scratchy music and impressive visual compositions, and all the reference books called it a masterpiece, so I was eager to sample it again. A few days later I got a message to ring George: he said he had to decide whether he wanted the German or English version. Stifling an impulse to suggest calling the whole thing off, I plumped for the latter, remembering that the film had been shot in both languages and thinking that at least the songs would sound better if one could follow the words. As the booking date grew near I shivered a little in my shoes, and was glad that at least some of my other suggestions were turning up trumps and so would excuse the inevitable drastic failure of this primitive Teutonic talkie about dreary characters who could have no possible relevance to undergraduate tastes of the fifties.

The film was booked for four days beginning on a Sunday in May. Not only was the weather remarkably hot and sticky, but it was the main week of exams, which was at least an excuse. I rang George on the Monday and he said Sunday had taken sixty pounds, which was well below average but not disastrous. I deduced that he had seen the picture, so didn't ask him what he thought of it. I couldn't myself get up till the Wednesday, and having promised to have a late

THE BLUE ANGEL. 'Your boys should see you now,' murmurs Lola-Lola to the stuffy professor whom she has twisted round her finger with remarkable ease. Emil Jannings, Marlene Dietrich

Indian meal with George, I skipped the college offering of jugged hare and was up at the Rex by 6.30. George avoided my eyes, but his tone was recriminatory. Down to twelve pounds on Monday: disaster. Twenty-one on Tuesday. I coughed and mentioned the weather. George said he couldn't stand any more and was off to the pub. I nodded at the usherettes and climbed the stairs to the circle, which was totally empty. It was 6.50 and *The Blue Angel* had just ended. I looked into the stalls and saw three people. I wandered back onto the circle landing to watch the crowd arrive, madly bicycling up the hill after first Hall. The trickle was so intermittent that I could even hear the birds singing outside. Sensing the lights dimming behind me, I returned to my seat with a sigh, and tried to enjoy the second feature, another of my recommendations called *The Saxon Charm*. Why hadn't I at least given George a copperbottomed second feature, one I'd seen? This proved to be a heavy comedy drama about Broadway, and despite its pretensions quite terrible.

An hour of it had gone by when I looked up and noticed that at least half a dozen enterprising souls had joined me in the circle. There was a curious buzz from downstairs too: craning my neck, I was surprised to see torches flashing, and to discern that at least five rows of the mid-stalls were almost full, with gowned figures settling down like bats from every aisle. There seemed no possible explanation of this late influx except that everybody who had wanted to see *The Blue Angel* had been put off by the weather and the exams until the last night, and even then had decided to forgo the second feature in favour of an extra hour's swotting. I propelled myself through the swing doors of the circle and found below me a packed and noisy foyer, with an enthusiastic queue stretching not only down the street but, as I incredulously discovered, round the distant corner. Bicycles were stacked six deep against the cinema walls, and more approached in the gloaming; householders had come to their doors to see what on earth was the matter.

George had been sent for, and arrived at that moment in his Mercedes, his small eyes glinting in astonishment and greed. It was all rather like one of those 'putting on a show' musicals from Hollywood, in which disaster is averted by the magical last-minute appearance of a society audience including all the most influential backers and critics. Ours was an enthusiastic crowd indeed. Every one of the trailers was loudly cheered, and the interval was extended so that ice-cream sales could be completed before *The Blue Angel* began. When it finally did, every seat that wasn't broken was amply filled, and in absolute defiance of the fire regulations there were forty people standing at the back of the stalls. I stood in the circle gangway myself, deputizing for an usherette who was counting up the ice-cream money. And now came the test. *The Blue Angel* has a very slow start, and for a while I was anxious lest this crowded and critical house should vent its exasperation by mocking the heavily overstressed acting and the pretentious direction. But no, the wonderfully lustrous print supplied by long-forgotten Wardour Pictures Ltd seemed to hypnotize everyone present, and there was no more than a warm buzz of murmured comment, not even that when the situation took hold. Once the professor's predicament is established, the story tightens its grip like a tourniquet, and by the time Dietrich as the tawdry Lola has belted out 'Falling in Love Again' for the last time, lingering huskily on each syllable as the old man staggers back through the snow to die at his desk, you could have heard the proverbial pin drop. When the lights came on at the end it was five or ten seconds before anybody moved. Nobody spoke, either; for a chill second I thought they'd all been mysteriously frozen solid by rays from outer space. Gradually they began to reach for their belongings and move towards the exits, but whereas there was normally a mad scramble for bikes and a twenty-mile-an-hour dash down the slumbering streets, tonight the crowd filed out slowly and silently, like monks in a processional. They stood thoughtfully on the pavement until their bikes came to the top of the heap, then pedalled away so gently that their gowns didn't even flap in the breeze. The pedestrians melted away in almost equal silence, just a few of them obscuring the moonlit pavements by their earnest discussion. George came out and stood on the step with me until the last dark figure had disappeared round the furthest corner, then he said, 'That stunned 'em, boy, I told you it would,' and we went out for a celebratory chicken biryani at the Koh-i-noor.

The Blue Angel could no longer have that kind of effect. We are all too sophisticated now, and the prints available to us are several generations less gleaming than the one I saw on that famous Cambridge occasion, when we seemed almost to be able to smell the squalid nightclub and to feel the sweat on the professor's brow. A Hollywood remake in the late fifties was laughably mishandled, and somehow diminished the reputation of the original; by then, too, the Dietrich who was giving phenomenally successful cabaret turns around the world seemed to have no possible connection with the thick-limbed, sensual charmer of Sternberg's underworld. In a way *The Blue Angel* was her finest hour, and certainly she could never escape the image it created for her of a sex goddess, oblivious to her husband's final decline as she sits straddling a wooden chair, giving a relentless growling emphasis to each syllable of what for the emancipated women of the thirties came to be her most artfully stated defence of her sexual methods:

> Men cluster round me
> Like moths around a flame . . .
> And if their wings burn
> I know I'm not to blame;
> Falling in love again,
> Never wanted to;

What am I to do?
I can't help it.

Von Sternberg was in no doubt as to what he had created in the mythic figure of Dietrich: 'I am a teacher who took a beautiful woman, instructed her, presented her carefully, edited her charms, disguised her imperfections and led her to crystallize a pictorial aphrodisiac'. What seems to have jaundiced his outlook is that the creation became more famous than the creator, and her somewhat disappointing Hollywood career was later attributed to his Svengali-like influence. To him she was but a small and dispensable item in his scheme of things. He was after all the director, and:

a director's function . . . embraces all the arts. Every step and every moment is filled with imponderables. 'Trifles light as air' must be ready to become substantial. An audience of one, he controls the camera according to his vision, uses light, shadow and space as his mind dictates, dominates the tempo and content of sound, controls the sets, chooses and edits the actors, decides their appearance and make-up, arranges the scenes in rhythmic progression, eliminates and adds moments that have no meaning to those who stand in attendance, and is solely responsible for every frame of his film. He is chief of his crew of workmen . . . and in addition to that I wrote the manuscript on which the theme was based. My word was law, I was boss, my behaviour was known and that is why I had been called.

The Blue Angel is certainly a director's film, and a studio director's at that, for it never touches reality. Its first shot is of those packed and twisted roofs dear to German cinema, suggesting the Grimms' fairy tale which in a way this story resembles. In no scene is the dialogue memorable, which is hardly surprising as the English version is merely a flat transcription of the German original. One watches it for Dietrich; for Jannings, who despite the trouble he gave behind the scenes was on screen as powerful and sympathetic an actor as Charles Laughton, once one discounted his Teutonic tendency to play to the gallery; and for the story-telling technique of the director, handicapped here by the primitive techniques with which he was working (this was after all the first German film with sound), but nevertheless contriving to engage our eye and lead it from one shot to another according to the dictates of his ever darkening story, which he chose because it was like *Of Human Bondage*, but which, with its ever-more-humiliated hero, has in it the truer stuff of Shakespearian or Greek tragedy.

The Blue Angel. Germany 1930; monochrome; 98 minutes. Produced by Erich Pommer for UFA. Written by Robert Liebmann, Karl Zuckmayer and Karl Vollmoeller from the novel *Professor Unrath* by Heinrich Mann. Directed by Josef Von Sternberg. Photographed by Gunther Rittau, Hans Schneeberger and Fritz Thiery. Music score by Frederick Hollander. Art direction by Otto Hunte and Emul Hasler. With Emil Jannings as Professor Immanuel Rath; Marlene Dietrich as Lola-Lola; Kurt Gerron as Kiepert; Rosa Valetti as Guste; Hans Albers as Mazeppa.

My Only Weakness
The Bride of Frankenstein

Mary Wollstonecraft Shelley *explains to her husband and to* Lord Byron *that the monster did not die at the end of her* Frankenstein *novel, but persuaded his creator to fashion him a mate . . .*

Drenched in verbal and visual conceits of a sophistication not normally associated with Hollywood in the early thirties, this toothsome draught of nectar and vinegar might be imagined to have poured effortlessly from the minds of James Whale and his ex-Bloomsbury emigré friends during a long weekend in the California sun. It reads that way: a banquet of sensation, a comedy of horrors, a parade of perversities, a pinnacle of paradox, each scene giddier than the last, until finally the monster's mate, with her Nefertiti hair-do and her Hawaiian theme tune, is revealed to be in the image of Mary Shelley who is telling the story. The more sober truth is that the film was conceived as a straight horror sequel under the title *The Return of Frankenstein*, that the zaniness was injected piece by piece during production, and that simultaneously the cruder horror bits were eased away, to produce a final mix like a Monty Python prequel.

In fact the watchful student, while fully appreciating the overall exhilaration, will sense several jolts, mostly resulting from the excisions made after the first preview. (The length of the answer print is variously listed as 80 and 90 minutes, but the longest negative a year later ran 75.) Most of the *Castle of Otranto*-style prologue went for a start, including Mrs Shelley's explanation that she set her sequel a hundred years into the future: this of course accounts for Baron Frankenstein having Victorian lapels on his otherwise modern tweed jackets, and talking about a new invention called the telephone. (Some commentators declared that the mixture of periods and fashions was one of Whale's obscure surrealist jokes.) Again, central scenes were shot in which the monster killed several villagers including the burgomaster, actions which failed to mesh with Whale's conception of him as a sympathetic, even Christ-like creature, much more sinned against than sinning. So the entire sequence was eliminated, leaving the villagers with no real reason for their fury against the strange being, who after the mayhem of the first sequence only waves his arms and growls at them, not even unnerving an old gypsy woman whose dialogue has been restricted to 'Pass the pepper and salt'. Finally, in the version we now have, Frankenstein's wife Elizabeth is freed along with him at the end of the film, the monster uttering the immortal words: 'You go. We belong dead.' He then pulls the lever which appears to exist for the sole reason of blowing to smithereens everyone inside the laboratory; himself, his mate, and the cowering Dr Pretorius. The last shot of the film shows the potentially happy Frankensteins watching from a nearby hill; yet in the previous shot of the laboratory starting to explode, they are briefly but vividly visible behind the luckless monster. This curious *non sequitur* results from the vote for a happy ending having been taken after the alternative was already shot, an alternative which had the baron and his lady also perish in the holocaust. Indeed, an even more gruesome finale was discarded only during shooting; when Henry demands a fresh female brain, the hunchback was to have brought him that of his captive wife instead of the streetwalker whose end we now witness. This would have given real ironic meaning to the title, making the female creature both Henry's bride and the monster's; and the final cut still shows Henry's dawning suspicion that such is the case.

Forgetting the imperfect assimilation of the various facets (and one easily can, so finely honed and polished is the film's visual style), this is a simply marvellous piece of Grand Guignol which from the very beginning laces its horrors with wit and laughter. The villagers are dancing joyously round the dying embers of the great fire in which we saw the monster perish at the end of the first film. Or did we? Suddenly one of them falls through the pyre into some curious kind of underground river (on a hilltop?) where the monster naturally lurks. With fine timing he lunges into view, malevolently despatches the villager, and climbs a convenient ladder to be greeted by the villager's shortsighted wife, who gets thrown into the pit for her pains. Halfway down the hill he meets the incomparable Una O'Connor, who takes one look and runs boohooing all the way to Castle Frankenstein to raise the alarm. Here the stilted histrionics of Colin Clive and Valerie Hobson are surely intended to reduce any audience to fits of delight; but Whale's dizzy-making camera tracking, John Mescall's lustrous photography, and Charles D. Hall's gothic art direction give one insufficient time to argue the point. Promptly a visitor is announced in the shape of Dr Pretorius, Henry's evil genius from the university, now with a nameless past behind him; originally intended for Claude Rains, this key role is uniquely played, in the manner of an emaciated gargoyle with a nasty smell up its nose, by Ernest Thesiger, and if there were any justice in Hollywood it is his name which would be above the title. (Some commentators believe that, sharing many of Whale's proclivities, he contributed more roguish ideas to the script than anyone else.)

Pretorius has the secret of creating life, but his homunculi, though perfect in shape, lack size: 'I grew them, from seed,' he says glumly. He keeps them in glass jars from which an amorous Henry VIII constantly escapes under the eyes of an archbishop and pays court to Anne Boleyn, only to be flown back home in a pair of tweezers. This superbly effected scene, with its entirely invisible trickery, hardly meshes with the rest of the film; but I would not have it lost. We shortly proceed to the jolly episode of the blind hermit, who takes in the wandering monster as a lodger, teaches him to speak basic English ('Friend good. Fire bad.') and even to smoke, but gets his house burned down for his charity when an over-anxious huntsman recognizes his guest. Soon the monster is mad as hell, uncontainable by either chains or a form of crucifixion (to make sure we get the point, Whale lets the cross shape linger on the screen after all else has faded), so homing instinct (presumably) takes him to the cemetery. Here he descends into a crypt not far away from where Pretorius is paying off two grave robbers who have found him 'a nice fresh female corpse'. 'I think I shall stay here for a while,' the professor tells them in farewell; 'I find the atmosphere congenial.' Sitting on the nearest slab, surveying a pile of human bones, a

THE BRIDE OF FRANKENSTEIN. Not a barber shop quartet, though the monster may well be asking his mate where she had her hair cut. Colin Clive, Elsa Lanchester, Boris Karloff and Ernest Thesiger show Hollywood the British way of life

packed lunch and an interesting-looking bottle, he sets to with a will and is soon singing and carousing merrily, though we nervously prepare to take our leave of him as the shadow of the monster looms and the music wells ominously. Suddenly Thesiger glances round, with mild surprise but no fear. 'Oh,' he says to the monster, 'I thought I was alone. Won't you have a cigar? They're my only weakness.'

A film that goes on in this way must clearly become a cult, and *The Bride of Frankenstein* goes on in this way for its entire running time. Space permits no more than a reminder of the quite incredible creation sequence, with an electrical storm above, the monster raging below, and Elsa Lanchester in a white shroud being unwrapped and swaying from side to side, all edited in a profusion of fast unexpected shots and set to Franz Waxman's melodious and luxuriant Hawaiian score. These extraordinary six minutes would not have disgraced Eisenstein and have no parallel in Hollywood.

How can we have come so far without mentioning Karloff? Despite his own later misgivings, his performance here as the monster is a thing of sheer magnificence, the best by far he ever gave. For Whale himself, the London luminary who staged *Journey's End* and then went west, this was both the summit and the end of his horror career, so perfect that it left him nowhere to go. And after half a dozen more films of very diverse kinds, he plainly lost his touch altogether and faded from view. A great pity; for as Max Miller said in a different context, there'll never be another.

Were it not that *Bride* is so superb, Whale's original *Frankenstein* would certainly earn itself a section in this book. Made in 1931 before the talkies had learned their technique, it was necessarily a stark and primitive film, marred occasionally by backcloths and by one irreplaceable censor cut, and rather obviously lacking the final brush strokes of background music. But it didn't lack humour, or vigour, or cinematic ideas. Whale first lets us see the monster as it backs through a door and then slowly turns; then from long shot he jumps diagonally to medium shot, then diagonally again to close-up. (A few years later he imitated this nicely judged shock moment in *The Man in the Iron Mask* and in 1963 Hitchcock quietly borrowed it in *The Birds*.) Karloff's performance here is all hissing anger and violence, quite different from his later interpretation in *Bride*, but almost equally striking. He played the monster for the third and last time, rather coldly, in *Son of Frankenstein*. This rather ponderous 1939 film was given a big budget and is still very watchable, but it entirely lacks humour (unless one counts the unintentional kind in the performances of Basil Rathbone and Lionel Atwill). What it can boast is excellent art direction and Bela Lugosi's best performance. As Igor, who can commit what crimes he likes because he was hung once before and it didn't take, he gives a bravura display of malevolence and mischief, and physically is quite unrecognizable behind the whiskers. But the saga of the monster was about to enter its cheapjack phase, and from now on the creature, not played by Karloff, would become a stalking automaton with nothing in its heart but murder and not enough energy even for that until the electrical equipment began to crackle in the final reel.

The Bride of Frankenstein. US 1935; monochrome; 75 minutes (release version). Produced by Carl Laemmle Jnr for Universal. Written by William Hurlbut and John L. Balderston. Directed by James Whale. Photographed by John Mescall. Music score by Franz Waxman. Art direction by Charles D. Hall. Make-up by Jack Pierce. With Boris Karloff as the monster; Colin Clive as Frankenstein; Ernest Thesiger as Pretorius; Valerie Hobson as Elizabeth; Elsa Lanchester as Mary Shelley; Gavin Gordon as Byron; Douglas Walton as Shelley; Una O'Connor as Minnie; O. P. Heggie as the hermit; E. E. Clive as the burgomaster; Dwight Frye as Karl.

Frankenstein. US 1931; monochrome; 71 minutes (release version). Produced by Carl Laemmle Jnr for Universal. Written by Garrett Fort and Francis Edward Faragoh, from the novel by Mary Shelley (adapted by John L. Balderston from the play version by Peggy Webling). Directed by James Whale. Photographed by Arthur Edeson. Music score by David Brockman. Art direction by Charles D. Hall. Make-up by Jack Pierce. With Boris Karloff as the monster; Colin Clive as Frankenstein; Mae Clarke as Elizabeth; Edward Van Sloan as Dr Waldman; John Boles as Victor; Dwight Frye as Fritz; Frederick Kerr as the old baron.

Passion on Platform Four
Brief Encounter

During her weekly shopping visits to the nearest town, a middle-class housewife meets and falls in love with a married doctor.

When one reads the screenplay of *Brief Encounter*, the most surprising discovery is that it is set in 1939. All references to date were removed from the film as distributed in 1946, giving it a somewhat unreal flavour, as nobody in it makes the slightest reference to the recent war or to the present austerity; nor do they seem ever to have been shaken out of a certain smugness, an almost tangible lack of interest in anything outside their own rather parochial lives. The golf club, the picture house and the Kardomah Café seem to be the limits of their world. This does not reduce their interest as people, but if the film had made us appreciate the background which Coward intended, we would have known them that important bit better, and that especially goes for the comic relief. When the film was first shown, I remember the unkind sniggers which greeted Joyce Carey's barmaid with the cut-glass accent; but such pretenders were commoner before the war broke down class barriers.

A second way in which *Brief Encounter* seems puzzlingly at odds with itself is in its location. What we see is pure Weybridge, the milieu in which Coward himself was brought up; yet the trains run on steam, not suburban electricity. It was well publicized that the station which forms so vital a background was Carnforth, and the film is full of little indications, perhaps unintentional, that the setting is northern, not least a platform signpost to the train for Leeds and Hellifield. All very odd, and all the more remarkable that a film so schizophrenic in small ways should be so overpoweringly right in its intimate dissection of the two leading characters, who may have been picked out of a drawer marked English Types Mark A but down the years remain fresh, memorable and moving in one's memory, just as one's best friends remain so for their predominant characteristics rather than for their quirks and subtleties. On its first release *Brief Encounter* was likened by many to a French romance, in that the mood is downcast, the characters ordinary, the setting drab and the ending not exactly happy. Certainly it has its similarities to *Une Si Jolie Petite Plage*, but at the end the characters do not commit suicide but elect, in the English way, to make the best of their lot; and the sexual layer of it is English indeed, for no French couple who wanted to go to bed together would be put off by the priggishness of a character like Valentine Dyall, who by once interrupting them and looking disapproving seems entirely to kill their physical ardour and to bring them to a realization of what they henceforth see as a mistake if not a sin.

In 1975 *Brief Encounter* was remade for TV, with a good production and a cast headed by Richard Burton and Sophia Loren. It was a disaster, underlining the fact that the classic status of the original must be attributed to a happy coming together of rare talents rather than to any timelessness in the concept. Coward's script, though compelling enough as part of the whole, seems to me the least essential major element. Taken from an old one-actor called *Still Life*, it easily becomes risible in the wrong hands, though in context it has enormously moving moments, such as the heroine's unspoken narration to her cheerfully uncomprehending husband, who does not suspect that she has that day been on the brink of suicide:

I meant to do it, Fred, I really did. I stood there trembling right on the edge – but then, just in time, I stepped back. I couldn't. I wasn't brave enough. I should like to be able to say that it was the thought of you and the children that prevented me, but it wasn't. I had no thoughts at all, only an overwhelming desire not to be unhappy any more – not to feel anything ever

BRIEF ENCOUNTER. Apparent realism conceals a clever set

again. I turned and went back into the refreshment room: that's when I nearly fainted.

Rather oddly, the film then gives the docile Fred, who has hardly spoken during her reverie by the fire, the last word; and we find that after all he may have understood his wife better than she or we thought:

FRED: Whatever your dream was, it wasn't a very happy one, was it?
LAURA: No.
FRED: Is there anything I can do to help?
LAURA: Yes, my dear, you always help.
FRED: You've been a long way away.
LAURA: Yes, Fred.
FRED: Thank you for coming back to me.

This stuff is easy enough to satirize, but nary an audience sits through it without a sniffle or two; while the 'meeting cute' of Laura and Alec, when he removes a speck of coal dust from her eye, has its own niche in cinematic history. So irresistibly does the image sit in the memory that it sometimes seems that Celia Johnson built an entire career out of this one unexpected and unglamorous role: how commandingly she plays it, wide eyes, quavery voice, picture hat and all. Trevor Howard has the simpler task, that of limning out a middle-class professional gentleman, and accomplishes it with distinction and without embarrassment. We, like Laura, can easily imagine his return home after their first disturbing encounter, walking through the quiet streets, letting himself into the house with his latchkey and greeting his 'small, dark and delicate' wife (whom we never see): 'I wondered if he'd say I met such a nice woman in the Kardomah: we had lunch and went to the pictures. Then suddenly I knew that he wouldn't. I knew beyond a shadow of doubt that he wouldn't say a single word – and at that moment the first awful feeling of danger swept over me.'

Still, the major accolade must go to David Lean, whose first solo film this was. So brilliantly understated is the technique applied to the opening scenes, as the ill-starred pair say goodbye before we go into the flashback, that we are hooked despite our misgivings, and stay hooked even though the development of the plot may have somewhat less bite than we expect. We can scarcely believe that an entertainment film is starting in such drab documentary surroundings, the camera prowling round a railway refreshment room amid the stale sandwiches, watching a barmaid flirt with an elderly porter over the rock cakes. Over there in a dingy corner a man and woman toy with teaspoons, and as the camera approaches them we realize that they are to be our chief concern. Before we can even distinguish their conversation they are interrupted by a garrulous acquaintance of hers – Penelope Keith style, we would now say – who, we quickly realize from their pained expressions, is crashing in on a poignant moment. As soon as he has been introduced, and we have learned that he is off to Africa the following week, Alec quietly exits to catch his train; and the interloper goes on prattling, barely noticing the little squeeze he gave to Laura's shoulder as he passed. (We learn later, painfully, that this was their last goodbye, the end of their unconsummated romance.) A moment afterwards Laura dashes out uncharacteristically, to see the express go by; but she comes back, albeit rather white and shaky, and the two women shortly catch their own train. During the short journey the awful, non-stop-talking Dolly Messiter's mouth looms large in close-up; and Laura's unspoken thoughts, now and after dinner at home, begin to tell us the real story. When we get to the parting scene again, we are allowed to see, in vertiginous tilted shots of flashing lights, that Laura really did try to throw herself under the express; but by now we know too that the fever has passed, that she won't do it again, that for her the myriad unexciting rewards of family life will again come to take the place of the grand passion. And Mr Lean, with a little help from the actors and from Rachmaninov on the sound track, has made us care and wonder and remember.

Brief Encounter. GB 1945; monochrome; 86 minutes. Produced by Anthony Havelock-Allan and Ronald Neame for Cineguild and Rank release. Written by Noel Coward, from his play *Still Life*. Directed by David Lean. Photographed by Robert Krasker. Music from themes by Rachmaninov. Art direction by John Bryan. With Celia Johnson as Laura Jesson; Trevor Howard as Alec Harvey; Cyril Raymond as Fred; Stanley Holloway as the porter; Joyce Carey as the barmaid; Everley Gregg as Dolly Messiter.

He Just Went Gay
Bringing Up Baby

A mild-mannered archaeologist reluctantly assists a zany heiress to look after a pet leopard.

The later thirties were the heyday of, among other things, that brand of 'crazy comedy' by which Hollywood might have meant many styles but had in mind only one. The phrase did not signify the comedy thriller, as popularized by Bob Hope; not the anarchic farce of the Marx Brothers or Olsen and Johnson; nor the gentle fantasy of Laurel and Hardy with its Tom and Jerry violence which did damage to nobody; nor the debonair sleuthing of *The Thin Man*, nor the ghostly playfulness of *Topper*. The true crazy comedy of that era concerned the privileged classes, and the crazy part came in when they proved unwilling merely to enjoy their privileges, as they did in *The Philadelphia Story*, but insisted on adopting attitudes which the world saw as unfamiliar, unbecoming and undignified. There is always a hint of craziness in Capra, who liked to have everybody yelling at the top of his lungs, and spotlighted such characters as a millionaire giving all he has to the poor and an heiress running away from her wealth to marry a reporter, but Capra always had a social point to make. Crazy comedy preaches no gospel. It aims only to entertain, and does so by the constant pulling of a carpet from beneath the feet of dignity, by the contrast between how we expect the characters to behave and how they really do. (*Alice in Wonderland* should be kept well in mind.)

Across the years certain peaks are still evident. In *My Man Godfrey* the idle rich go on a scavenger hunt and vie to bring back a forgotten man. (Any hint of tastelessness in an era of high depression is removed by the fact that their choice turns out to be a rich man in disguise.) An extravaganza called *Twentieth Century* allowed John Barrymore to go engagingly berserk, backstage and on a train. *The Awful Truth*, which seemed to have been made up as it went along, started with divorce and gradually got its couple back together again. *Nothing Sacred*, in which Carole Lombard went on the razzle when she thought she was dying, had elements of satire and of black comedy; but nothing could be more in the crazy comedy tradition than the slogging match between her and Fredric March. In *Time Confession* an attorney's wife lies herself into a murder charge. All these themes crossed and divided and were imitated and developed: elements of them can be found in the forties work of Lubitsch and Leisen and Roach and above all of Preston Sturges, who found a crazy comedy style all of his own. But by 1938 the boundaries were well defined, and that year brought the most scatterbrained comedy, or high farce, of them all, in the shape of *Bringing Up Baby*.

This film satisfies all the requirements. Everything about it is a reversal. Even the infant of the title is a leopard, and the only way to keep it happy is by serenading it with 'I Can't Give You Anything But Love, Baby'. The collection of incidents which passes for a plot is exclusively concerned with the deflation of pretensions and the loss of dignity. The stars, both known for witty and sophisticated comedy-dramas, are required to fall on their faces, or behinds, with great regularity. The locale is allegedly Connecticut but seems closer to the land of Oz, being populated by such larger-than-life characters as an irascible old millionairess, a timid big game hunter, an incompetent sheriff, a pompous psychiatrist and a drunken Irish groom. And the director who so cunningly held these diverse elements together was renowned for he-man action drama.

Cary Grant is disguised as an absent-minded, bespectacled

professor of the Stuyvesant Museum of Natural History, who needs only an inter-costal clavicle to complete his reconstructed brontosaurus. His po-faced fiancée sees their forthcoming marriage as a dedication to their work, with the twenty-foot-high dinosaur as their child. And no sex, of course. Meanwhile, she expects him to coax some finance for the museum out of New York's philanthropists, starting with one million dollars from Mrs Carlton-Random, with whose lawyer, Mr Peabody, David is shortly due to play golf. The game is only the first of many plans to be disrupted by a carelessly attractive, non-stop-talking, rich female screwball named Susan Vance, who has an answer for everything, though not necessarily a sensible one. She starts by playing his golf ball and proceeds to smash up his car, under the impression that both are her own. David is naturally exasperated. 'The most important corporation lawyer in New York is waiting for me on the eighteenth green.' Her answer has its own logic: 'Then it's silly of you to be fooling around on the first fairway.' He doesn't realize it at once, but he is already trapped in her web. His shouted line across the golf course: 'I'll be with you in a minute, Mr Peabody', is all the funnier with each repetition because the audience knows that he won't.

That evening he is waiting in a snooty club to take Mr Peabody to dinner and plead his case all over again. But lo and behold, Susan is at the bar fooling around with an olive, which drops in his path. He skids on it, and not only falls heavily but sits on his hat in so doing. She leaves her purse with him, but she seems to have picked up one belonging to a psychiatrist's wife and David is nearly arrested as a thief. Susan explains to the monocled shrink that the foolish young man would steal anything of hers, as he's so madly in love with her. (The reply is: 'The love instinct in men frequently reveals itself in terms of conflict.') David's next remark to her however is something of a deterrent: 'Let's play a game. I will count to ten while closing my eyes, and when I open them, you will be *gone*.' But instead she accidentally splits his tail coat up the middle, and when he explodes she walks away without realizing that his foot was on the back panel of her dress, which has become detached and considerably altered the view of her rear end. She refuses to listen to his garbled explanation, which she takes for a belated apology, so he desperately clamps his crumpled hat on her derrière, a gesture which she naturally misunderstands. When light finally dawns, she panics,

BRINGING UP BABY. The unknown actor playing the cop looks as though he can't really believe what's going on. Nor could the audience, but they loved it anyway. Cary Grant, Katharine Hepburn, Walter Catlett, Fritz Feld

and they have to exit in close unison, music hall fashion, past the astonished lawyer who is just arriving. The exit line, of course, is: 'I'll be with you in a minute, Mr Peabody.'

Next day David is due to get married, but by a series of misadventures Susan virtually blackmails him into escorting her to her aunt's place in Connecticut with a pet leopard which her brother has sent to her, quite incredibly, from foreign parts. The journey is fraught with incident, such as buying 30 lb of steak from a bemused butcher ('It isn't for me, it's for Baby'), and they arrive somewhat dishevelled, so Susan has some excuse for sending off David's only clothes to be cleaned. When Aunt Elizabeth comes home he makes a rather bad impression in a lacy fur-trimmed white negligée which is the only wraparound he can find. 'Why are you wearing those clothes?' asks indomitable old May Robson. 'Because I just went *gay* all of a sudden,' he yells, springing in the air. (Question: Is it possible that the modern distortion of the word 'gay' has its origins in this moment of film history?)

It naturally transpires that David has blotted his copybook again, as Aunt Elizabeth is the wealthy Mrs Carlton-Random. Meanwhile his inter-costal clavicle, just delivered, has been stolen by her wire-haired terrier (the same canine who played Asta in *The Thin Man*). Much time and energy are now expended in following the dog round the 26-acre grounds, David having acquired an ill-fitting pair of jodhpurs for the purpose. Susan goes along rather reluctantly, not fully understanding the uniqueness of the missing clavicle. When David informs her that it took three experts five years to find that particular specimen, she replies cheerfully, 'Well, now that they know where to look, couldn't you send them back for another?'

By now Susan has explained away David's apparent eccentricity as the result of jungle fever allied to an incipient nervous breakdown. She has given him the name of Bone and allowed the leopard to escape, so that they have to search for that, too, with a butterfly net in which David's own head seems regularly to get caught. Between them they fall into poison ivy, slither down a small cliff, wade into a stream which turns out to be six feet deep, and get on the trail of a really vicious leopard which just happens to have escaped from a local circus. Through various complex misunderstandings the entire cast ends up in jail under the supervision of Walter Catlett, who plays the local Pooh Bah like an American Will Hay and has a whale of a time sniffing, staring and double taking.

SUSAN: Never mind, when they find out who we are, they'll let us out.
DAVID: When they find out who *you* are, they'll pad the cell!

Susan helps matters very little, if at all, by adopting a phoney Bronx accent and telling the sheriff she is really a gun moll, Swinging Door Susie. David blenches as she identifies him as Jerry the Nipper. 'Get me outa this joint, I'll unbutton ma puss and shoot the works.'

Since the movie is already overlong and must end somewhere, Mr Peabody arrives as *deus ex machina*, promptly followed by the more bad-tempered of the leopards. It remains only, in the coda, for David's fiancée to jilt him and for him to be left alone with his brontosaurus, on the top working platform. To him enters Susan, who in her enthusiasm mounts a rocky ladder to hand back the missing bone, grabs the brontosaurus for support, and is left swinging by one hand as the entire structure collapses.

Bringing Up Baby is not a particularly well made or handsome film – Hawks never seemed to care how his movies looked, provided the content was right – and time has been unkind to the sound track. However, to see it with a full house is to realize how many long, loud laughs it packs in. Alas and alack, in 1964 Hawks saw fit to remake it, more or less, as *Man's Favourite Sport*, and the result got no laughs at all, which proves that stars count for something after all. And as is well known, Bogdanovich's *What's Up Doc* was a reworking, if not a remake, with many of the sight gags intact (but no leopard). That wasn't too funny either, apart from the elaborate chase sequence tacked on at the end; but then, how could it be, with Streisand and O'Neal standing in for Hepburn and Grant? I mean, I've heard of second teams, but this is ridiculous.

Bringing Up Baby. US 1938; monochrome; 102 minutes. Produced and directed by Howard Hawks for RKO. Written by Dudley Nichols and Hagar Wilde. Photographed by Russell Metty. Music score by Roy Webb. Edited by George Hively. Art direction by Perry Ferguson. With Katharine Hepburn as Susan Vance; Cary Grant as David Huxley; May Robson as Aunt Elizabeth; Charles Ruggles as Major Horace Applegate; Walter Catlett as Constable Slocum; Barry Fitzgerald as Gogarty; Fritz Feld as Dr Fritz Lehmann; George Irving as Alexander Peabody.

Everybody Went to Rick's
Casablanca

In French North Africa in 1941, refugees from Nazi tyranny wait for exit visas, seldom granted by the Vichy French under German domination; but a cynical American casino owner is eventually stirred to sacrifice his own safety for a principle.

It's one of the paradoxes of Hollywood. A film written page by page, mostly after shooting had started; originally designed as a 'B' to star Ronald Reagan and Ann Sheridan; based on a play so mediocre that it appears never to have played anywhere; shot entirely on the studio backlot; falsely promoted as significant because the Big Three of World War II chose just before its release to hold a strategy conference in Casablanca. None of these conditions suggests the atmosphere in which an enduring classic is made, and yet, forty years after its première, *Casablanca* remains a movie which most filmgoers could happily see twice a year or more, for its witty characterizations, its romantic suspense, its carefully integrated situations, its technical expertise and its precisely timed comedy relief. Whatever the problems of its manufacture, all systems were clearly at go whenever they were most required to be so; and like most happy accidents it resisted imitation. Warners themselves tried a year later with *The Conspirators*, Republic soon after with *Storm Over Lisbon*; despite interesting casts, neither film is now remembered at all. And when in the mid-seventies Elia Kazan made a deliberate attempt to re-create the *Casablanca* set for his film within a film in *The Last Tycoon*, the result was ludicrous and horrible. You can't even spoof it – Neil Simon tried in *The Cheap Detective* – because the original already contained a strong element of self-mockery, and everyone knows you can't spoof a spoof.

I don't remember being exactly wild with enthusiasm when I first viewed it myself, at the Bolton Capitol one Saturday afternoon in 1943. I imagine I was disappointed that there wasn't any real action; indeed, apart from the explanatory opening scenes in a very unconvincing studio street, the film virtually takes place in the café set, with a few short sequences in a market, Renault's office, and a fogbound airstrip. (Does Casablanca really have fog and rain, or was Jack Warner cost-cutting again?) It wasn't until the fifties that the legend really began to grow, and it became clear that the magic of *Casablanca*, like that of *The Maltese Falcon*, lies in its classical restraint. From the very fact of there being no spectacle, and action only in the mind, one is forced back to watching the characters, and caring for them, and listening to their dialogue; and because there is such a gallery of good actors, and a director so capable of creating pace and mood, not to mention the wittiest and springiest of scripts, the piece comes off superbly as not only the acme of moody war romances but the very quintessence of Hollywood moonshine, suspense melodrama department.

The title can't have helped particularly. Bogart and Bergman in love in Casablanca, the ads screamed unpersuasively. Later, Istanbul and Timbuktu and Saigon, Tangier and Teheran and Calcutta had movies named after them, but all are now forgotten. Yet there may be something special about the word Casablanca, the satisfying sound it makes when one says it (and especially the way Bogie said it), that makes it a better box office bet than, say, *African Manhunt* or *They Met in the Casbah* or even the original *Everybody Comes to Rick's*.

It begins in ho-hum fashion. The writing credits are fascinating only in retrospect: at the time; Koch and the Epsteins, and Casey Robinson who isn't credited but says he had much to do with it, were only routine melodramatists. Here however they seem to have sparked something off in each other, like Mankiewicz and Welles in *Kane*, even though Robinson handled the project only intermittently and Koch mainly put together the Epsteins' bits and pieces after they had excused themselves from the assignment. Between them they somehow made a masterpiece of a film which starts with an incredibly clumsy and old-fashioned introduction, its stentorian commentator reading out a roller caption over a crudely-fashioned globe, followed by a rush of cameos from people not seen again to point up the corruption of Casablanca and of its Vichy head Captain Renault (Claude Rains in his most endearing piece of winning villainy, often stealing the movie from the presumptive stars). It is December 1941, and Rick Blaine, the mysterious American who sticks his head out for nobody, is running the Café Américain, which for reasons stated rather than shown is Casablanca's number one uppercrust gambling and gathering place. (We discover in a later flashback that Rick didn't leave Paris until June 1940), so he has done pretty well to establish his casino so indelibly in local folklore in the space of a mere eighteen months.) Ironically, the audience knows that America will very soon enter the war, but Rick is still an isolationist, out only for himself as a result of a broken romance, and not until the last reel, in the movie's most unconvincing speech, are his patriotic feelings even slightly stirred: 'I'm no good at being noble, but it doesn't take much to see that the problems of three little people don't amount to a hill of beans in this crazy world.' This very reluctant hero makes a characteristically late entrance, after everyone else has expressed a view of him; even then we see his hand scribbling OKs before we see him.

Casablanca is the penultimate stage in a trans-European trail for refugees able to finance and accredit themselves for escape to the new world: one plane hop to Lisbon and they're in neutral territory. Accidentally but quite fortuitously, Rick has in his possession two irrevocable letters of transit signed by General de Gaulle. These

CASABLANCA. Sam plays it with pleasure for Rick and prefers not to be transferred to Ferrari's Blue Parrot. Humphrey Bogart, Dooley Wilson, Sydney Greenstreet

unique documents are what Hitchcock would call the McGuffin of the plot, and the question set in the last reel is whether Rick will use them selfishly for himself and his lost love, who turns up married to an underground leader much in demand by the Nazis; or generously, as a belated wedding present for her and her husband; or even patriotically for himself and Laszlo, so that Rick can join the cause. The story goes that the production team didn't make up its own mind until the time came to shoot; oddly enough, it wouldn't much matter which of the alternatives had been chosen, except that the present one, with Rick staying behind to join the Free French at Brazzaville, spares us the cliché of a romantic clinch and offers instead a delightful moment as our hero walks into the darkness with Renault, who has also shown himself a prince among men by covering Rick's shooting of the Nazi general, and now wishes to join Rick in doing the right thing for France. 'Louis,' says Rick, 'I think this is the beginning of a beautiful friendship.' Not too surprisingly, scholars of the seventies have cast a little doubt on the respectability of this man-to-man relationship.

What makes *Casablanca* such a joy to watch is the incredibly fast pace given to it by Michael Curtiz: no scene opens without a flourish of camera movement, and none ends without a pointed gesture, even if it's only Sydney Greenstreet swatting a fly. Koch says that when he was worried about the logic of some scenes, Curtiz told him: 'Don't worry about logic, I make it go so fast nobody notices.' We are equally dazzled by the array of fine character players, each with his little share of the spotlight: Leonid Kinskey as Sacha the bartender, S. Z. Sakall as Carl the maitre d'; Greenstreet as a black-marketeering rival café owner; Peter Lorre as Ugarte, a small-time crook who has bitten off more than he can chew; Conrad Veidt as Nazi-in-chief, the famous vein in his forehead throbbing splendidly; Marcel Dalio, the croupier who apologizes to Rick when anyone wins; above all Dooley Wilson as the unforgettable pianist Sam, who sings 'As Time Goes By' more persuasively than its composers can have expected. After all this richness the nominal co-stars, Ingrid Bergman and Paul Henreid, might have been utter bores had they not been underplayed with such intensity; in any case they are never allowed to hog the screen for long unless someone wittier is sharing it with them.

Fragments of imperishable dialogue are scattered recklessly throughout the film. Take the thoughtful moment under the stars, when Renault tries to quiz Rick about his reason for being in Casablanca.

RICK: I came to Casablanca for the waters.
RENAULT: But we're in the desert.
RICK (*slightly shrugging*): I was misinformed.

Renault in particular is never at a loss for a good line, as when reproving Rick for helping a desperate young woman without taking advantage of her. 'How extravagant you are, Rick, throwing away women like that. Someday they may be scarce.' Or when finding an excuse, under Major Strasser's instruction, to close Rick down:

RENAULT: I am shocked, shocked, to find that gambling is going on in here!
CROUPIER: Your winnings, sir.
RENAULT: Oh, thank you very much.

The comedy is the more acceptable because every character in the movie is playing a game, showing one face to the world but eventually revealing another. Ethics are constantly stood on their head, even by the petty swindler Ugarte: 'You're a very cynical person, Rick, and just because you despise me you're the only one I trust.' And by Ferrari: 'As leader of all illegal activities in Casablanca, I'm a very influential and respected man.' And constantly by Renault: 'Realizing the importance of the case, my men are rounding up twice the usual number of suspects.'

If we haven't mentioned Max Steiner's music so far, we should, for it covers everything with rich nourishing soup and adds immeasurably to the film's distinctive style. But over and above all the other contributions stands the figure of Bogart, here at his apogee, self-effacing, unshowy but unable to give a bad reading to a line if he tried. Before 1940 he was thought too sinister to be a hero; after the war his sense of deep brooding introspection was out of fashion and his furrows, his toupée and his short stature were becoming ever more difficult to disguise (until in *The African Queen* he let it all hang out and became a character actor). But in the early forties he admirably portrayed a man who could take on the world at its own terms; a man whose ethics, and usually his morals, could be entirely trusted; a man who dealt fair and square with friends and enemies alike and in the end might sacrifice a woman or even his life for a cause. In his best films he allowed others to carry the guns, for he was tough in mind rather than behaviour: you seldom saw him in a fist fight. In the end, Bogart is *Casablanca*, but the film is perhaps the most perfect vehicle ever devised for a star.

Casablanca. US 1942; monochrome; 102 minutes. Produced by Hal B. Wallis for Warners. Written by Julius J. Epstein, Philip G. Epstein and Howard Koch, from a play by Murray Burnett and Joan Alison. Directed by Michael Curtiz. Photographed by Arthur Edeson. Music score by Max Steiner. Art direction by Carl Jules Weyl. With Humphrey Bogart as Rick Blaine; Ingrid Bergman as Ilsa Lund; Paul Henreid as Victor Laszlo; Claude Rains as Louis Renault; Conrad Veidt as Major Strasser; Sydney Greenstreet as Ferrari; Peter Lorre as Ugarte; Dooley Wilson as Sam; S. Z. Sakall as Carl; Leonid Kinskey as Sacha; Marcel Dalio as croupier.

The Body-in-the-Library Syndrome
The Cat and the Canary

Twenty years after the death of a wealthy eccentric, relatives gather in his swamp-bound house to hear the reading of his will, and the heiress is driven near to madness by the next heir, a dangerous lunatic who must be one of the stranded party.

The extraordinary thing about this entertaining little movie is not that it rocketed Bob Hope to stardom or that it started a new vein of horror comedy, but that its photography and art direction are so endurably stylish. The credits are superimposed on a shot of shutters flapping in the moonlight, perfectly encapsulating the gist of the entertainment; afterwards we barely venture outside the house, but we can smell the musty dampness of the unlived-in rooms, feel the spidery shadows of the secret passages which seem to run behind every wall . . . until in the climactic sequence we are led with the over-venturesome heroine into the narrow, dangerous darkness behind the library shelves. The panel closes at the touch of a claw-like hand on a lever, a knife flashes the end of an unneeded associate villain; and the dreaded cat creature, hardly glimpsed till now, chases his prey down sagging steps, round jagged brick corners, and up into an outhouse where in the nick of time, as the heroine cowers beneath a swinging lamp, he rips off his fright mask and gets his come-uppance from a vengeful housekeeper. This terrifying five-minute sequence, in shocking contrast to the preceding wisecracking, is so elegantly designed, so dramatically lit, and so nimbly directed, that for sheer cinematic bravura it ranks in my mind with the Odessa Steps sequence from *The Battleship Potemkin* and the charge through the palace from *The Scarlet Empress*.

When *The Cat and the Canary* first played at the Bolton Capitol in 1940, as a double bill with *Golden Boy*, the powers that were wouldn't let me in, as the local watch committee had disagreed with its national colleagues and raised its certificate from an 'A' to an 'H': 'H' for horror, that was, and forbidden to anybody under sixteen. When a couple of years later I joined a choir outing to Southport, the movie was playing on reissue under its original 'A', which meant that I could get in if accompanied by an adult. Luckily it began to rain very hard around 2 P.M. and I was able to persuade the vicar in charge of us that the surest way of keeping everybody happy would be to attend a matinée at a cost of sixpence per head, much less than we would otherwise spend on the funfair. Even at the age of thirteen I was clearly renowned for my researches into film, for he was convinced by my assurance that we would see a rare work of cinematic art. To this very day, I think he has not quite forgiven me; he enjoyed it himself, but on the way home some of my friends had assumed a delicate shade of green, and it may be that their mothers had a word to say to him next day. I had to admit that I was pretty scared myself in a couple of spots, though I knew that all would come right in the end: not until *Psycho* twenty years later did a damsel in distress actually fall victim to a lurking lunatic.

There isn't an ounce of fat on this film, not a single wasted moment. The original play, though a trifle hoary in terms of dialogue, is still a favourite with British repertory companies, and this sharpened version follows the plot closely, though it has extra icing in the form of Hope's one-liners and in the performances of such a team of endearing professionals as no local rep could hope to assemble. Take Nydia Westman, the perfect wide-eyed feed. 'Don't these big empty houses scare you?' she asks. 'Not me,' says Hope, 'I was in vaudeville.' A little later she does it again. 'Do you believe people come back from the dead?' Hope looks up in surprise. 'You mean like Republicans?'

She clearly can't be The Cat. Nor can her elderly companion Elizabeth Patterson, so angry at not being the heir that she is tickled pink at any sign that the heroine's mind is breaking under the strain of clutching hands and disappearing bodies. Gale Sondergaard, the archetypal sinister housekeeper, simply has to be a red herring who will turn sympathetic in the end. As for George Zucco, he of the receding hairline, thin lips and sepulchral tones, he is such a perfect Lawyer Crosby that we are sorry when he chooses the wrong place to stand by the library shelves and is abruptly carried off by a hirsute paw which emerges from the wainscoting. 1939 is too early for the kind of twist which would reveal the delightfully spunky and damned attractive Paulette Goddard as the mastermind, and besides, Hope has to pair up with somebody in the final clinch. We are fast running out of suspects, and to anyone requiring a hint we can only say look out for the most sympathetic, cheerful, altruistic and right-minded character. And never trust a man who smokes a pipe.

The mystery is worked out quickly, clearly and suspensefully. It doesn't play *entirely* fair, but near enough. I wrote a spoof of it once, called *A Night on the Island*, with parts for Sondergaard and Zucco: pity they never heard about it, though it did modestly well around the English provinces. I couldn't get much suspense into it because nobody was actually murdered, and my laugh lines didn't rival Hope's, though I was unnaturally delighted with one passage, as guest and housekeeper study the portrait of the old eccentric:

HOUSEKEEPER: It was painted from life, as he lay dying. I believe he saw his end approaching.
GUEST: How very uncomfortable for him.

As for *The Cat and the Canary*, I followed it everywhere. I saw it in Manchester, on a double bill with *The Miracle of Morgan's Creek*; in Cambridge, as a Sunday revival at the Central; in Klagenfurt, dubbed into Austrian; and at the National Film Theatre, where it evoked a spirited round of applause. Finally the BBC in the mid-sixties astonished me by considering it family entertainment suitable for showing at 6 P.M. on Boxing Day; it still scared me. And now it lies in limbo, its literary copyright having lapsed in favour of a remake so awful that it has barely been released. I can wait. And meanwhile the silent version of 1927 still has its moments.

The Ghost Breakers, which followed a twelve-month later, is a cruder affair with a looser plot, but works up to a scary-as-hell climax in a haunted Cuban castle with an eyeless zombie lurching through the fog. Goddard and Hope are again involved – 'Basil Rathbone must be throwing a party,' he remarks during a thunderstorm – but the honours are taken by Willie Best as the archetypal frightened black servant. (Jerry Lewis more or less took this role in the abysmal remake, *Scared Stiff*.) Best gets the lion's share of the lines, though Hope scores with his standard cowardly act, as when going upstairs to explore: 'If two men come down, let the first one go. That'll be me.' And Paul Lukas, from a suavely villainous entrance to being found dying in a glass coffin, is excellent value as red herrings go.

THE CAT AND THE CANARY. As choice a group of suspects as ever did a double take for the camera when nobody else was looking. George Zucco, Gale Sondergaard, Douglass Montgomery, Bob Hope, John Beal, Paulette Goddard, Elizabeth Patterson, Nydia Westman

Serious attempts in the spooky house genre are rare, but one which kept a straight face and worked was *The Spiral Staircase*, directed in 1946 by Robert Siodmak with all the trimmings. The period flavour helped the first sequence, as a silent film is being avidly watched at a matinée in a small town hotel while upstairs a crippled girl is strangled as she gets into her clothes. All we actually see is a lurking eye between the hanging clothes in the wardrobe; then as the girl's arms stretch upwards through the sleeves of her dress, the hands stiffen and cross in a physically unlikely but dramatically most effective manner. Among the audience at the movie show has been the deaf mute maid from the big house on the edge of town, and by the time we have followed her back home under an impending thunderstorm we have been made aware that there is on the loose a mad killer who can't stand imperfection, and therefore strikes at women with physical defects. We can be pretty sure that our heroine is going to be next on his list, and that the killer must be one of the rather uninspired bunch of men who live in the house: professor, handyman, stepson, doctor. Shortly indeed we see the livid eye again, and this time are treated to its viewpoint: the owner sees the maid with no mouth at all, just a blank from nose to chin. A close study of the billing will reveal to most film buffs who the murderer must be, not that it matters much; the look of the thing is what counts here, and the performances of Dorothy McGuire and of Ethel Barrymore. (The latter plays the bedridden old owner of the house who suspects madness in her family and therefore sleeps with a loaded rifle under her pillow.) The staircase of the title is somewhat irrelevant, simply the backstairs location for the final shootout; but the piece is so full of red herrings that the viewer will be too dizzy to count them. The superiority of style over material here may be judged by a glance at Peter Collinson's tawdry 1975 remake, which updates the same script, handles it flatly, and is unwatchable.

A who-done-it which manages without a thunderstorm but goes better than most by eliminating eight of its ten characters (the book had them *all* dead at the end) is *And Then There Were None*, which I first knew in less race-conscious days as *Ten Little Niggers*. In an effective reversal of cliché, all the murders here take place in a sunlit modern house on a seaside island, cut off from the mainland till the damage is done. When I first saw it in 1945 I was a great fan of the book and resented the movie's tampering with it; but later I came to appreciate the delicate performances, as well as the nervous tight-rope walked by director René Clair in deciding to make a black comedy from the material. He establishes his hand firmly with a neat who's-following-whom sequence near the beginning, ensures that his compositions are always elegantly framed, and gets poised performances from his superb cast of comedy actors before callously disposing of them one by one. Richard Haydn as the butler does his adenoidal drunk act before being chopped in half; Barry Fitzgerald and Walter Huston conspire like laughing hyenas the night before being shot and drowned respectively; Roland Young snaps his fingers and says 'I get it' just as a stone ornament falls and bashes his head in. There is also a splendid touch at the end, when the young innocents return to the house in realization that Mr U. N.

Owen must be someone previously thought dead: they find him playing billiards, but for a few seconds, to provoke an infallible laugh and send the audience home happy, his identity remains obscured by a hanging lampshade. It is actually possible to feel well disposed towards this murderer, for according to Agatha Christie, and to Dudley Nichols' very literate reworking, all the doomed ones richly deserve their fate.

The Cat and the Canary. US 1939; monochrome; 72 minutes. Produced by Arthur Hornblow Jnr for Paramount. Written by Walter de Leon and Lynn Starling, from the play by John Willard. Directed by Elliott Nugent. Photographed by Charles Lang Jnr. Music score by Ernst Toch. Art direction by Hans Dreier and Robert Usher. Edited by Archie Marshek. With Bob Hope as Wally Campbell; Paulette Goddard as Joyce Norman; John Beal as Fred Blythe; Douglass Montgomery as Charlie Wilder; Gale Sondergaard as Miss Lu; Elizabeth Patterson as Aunt Susan; Nydia Westman as Cicily; George Zucco as Lawyer Crosby; John Wray as Henricks.

The Spiral Staircase. US 1946; monochrome; 83 minutes. Produced by Dore Schary for David O. Selznick and RKO. Written by Mel Dinelli from the novel *Some Must Watch* by Ethel Lina White. Directed by Robert Siodmak. Photographed by Nicholas Musuraca. Music score by Roy Webb. Art direction by Albert S. D'Agostino, Jack Okey and Darrell Silvera. With Dorothy McGuire as Helen; George Brent as Professor Warren; Ethel Barrymore as Mrs Warren; Kent Smith as Dr Parry; Elsa Lanchester as Mrs Oates; Sara Allgood as Nurse Barker; Rhys Williams as Mr Oates; Rhonda Fleming as Blanche; Gordon Oliver as Steve; James Bell as officer.

I'll Bet You Five You're Not Alive if You Don't Know His Name
Citizen Kane

A lonely, rich old newspaper magnate dies, and we see his life through the eyes of his ex-wife and closest associates as they are interviewed by a newsreel journalist.

When *Kane* played Bolton, *Kane* lost. I turned up at the Lido at 4.15 P.M. on the Tuesday, only to find that owing to poor business it had been taken off on the Monday, and replaced by a reissue of *The Hunchback of Notre Dame*. I duly paid my fourpence to see the latter again, but my heart wasn't in it. I was particularly upset because the trailer for *Kane*, which I had witnessed the previous week, had been uniquely promising. Mr Orson Welles, then a tall, slim, impish and to me utterly unknown young man, showed us proudly around the RKO studio; I don't recall that he actually described it as 'the biggest toy train any boy ever had to play with', but he rather diffidently showed us a clip or two from his new film, mentioned his Mercury company of actors one by one, and introduced us to several of them sitting round a piano and singing with some chorus girls, rather scantily clad. 'Frankly,' murmured Mr Welles in our ear, 'the girls don't have too much to do with our picture. They're here for purposes of – ballyhoo?' It was the upward questioning inflection of the last word that won my heart.

I never caught up with *Citizen Kane* – didn't have a chance to – until ten years later when I had endured the army, and enjoyed the university, and was now booking movies for a Cambridge art house. Mammoth double features were the order of the day, run in continuous performances with the last complete show starting just after seven so that eager undergraduates had time to cycle up our hill after first hall. We usually had three changes a week, and one Thursday in November, early on in my tenure, I booked *Kane* along with *The Ox-Bow Incident*, a doom-laden combo hardly conducive to dancing in the streets. Because of the length of the programme, and especially of *Kane* (119 minutes), the projectors had to start turning at 1.15 p.m., which was much too early for our habitués; the lights went down on no more than a dozen of the faithful. I was prepared for this, and had long planned to join them. Seeing *Kane* after all those years of curiosity was a bit like opening Tutankhamun's tomb, the kind of encounter which should not be spoiled by noisy crowds. And so, surrounded by more than a thousand empty seats, on a cold afternoon, in a half-derelict cinema where heating rarely had any effect unless the seats were filled with bodies, I sat in my overcoat and came face to face with what, if there has to be one, is the best film of all.

Too much has been written about these 119 magical minutes for me to attempt a summing-up in this space, only a few quibbles, queries and tributes. It isn't a perfect film, certainly: one can point to the lack of real hard information about Kane's character, to the scant and unsatisfying mentions of his mother, to gaping lacunae in his biography. The script itself is a mystery. Who really wrote it? Neither Welles nor Mankiewicz ever demonstrated such style on his own account, so what sorcery made them so magical in double harness? Chemistry is one explanation, but you can't make water with neither oxygen nor hydrogen.

In my forties I went as a tourist to William Randolph Hearst's incredibly opulent California estate, San Simeon, given by his embarrassed heirs to the state as a number one attraction for travellers along the Pacific Coast Highway. I recognized Xanadu at once, and Welles' 1941 disclaimers must have sounded hollow indeed to anyone who had actually visited the magic castle, for a tour of the house and grounds is like reliving the movie. I didn't find Rosebud, though, and perhaps that's why this plot gimmick, the old man's dying word, seems so unsatisfactory when the truth is finally glimpsed as his schoolboy sled bearing the name is tossed into the furnace by his uncaring executors. A sled simply isn't the kind of boyhood memory a newspaper magnate would cling to; his own ambition, successes and failures would surely have given him more urgent matters to ponder in his old age. No, this was a strained Hollywood device to lock together the disparate strands of a movie which best succeeds scene by magnificent scene; Welles and Mankiewicz, who had both been guests at San Simeon, must have taken their best inspirations direct from the enchanted hill. No wonder they were struck from the guest list; but they had sealed its atmosphere in celluloid for all time.

Citizen Kane is an ingenious patchwork of conjuring tricks, patterns of sight and sound deftly blended and transformed by Hollywood expertise. It marks the coming together of every craft of studio film making in its most advanced form. In 1941, bewildered audiences found its impressionistic narrative impossible to follow with such effort as they had left after paying the price of admission. But for those with the courage to stick with it and work at it, a treasure trove was in store; while now, of course, its abrupt narrative devices seem almost too elementary. Some of its brightest stars were behind the camera: Gregg Toland's wondrous deep focus photography, Robert Wise's split-second editing, above all Bernard Herrmann's jaunty, insolent theme music which occasionally breaks into twangy song:

> There is a man –
> A certain man –
> And for the poor you may be sure

CITIZEN KANE. The dismantling of Xanadu. William Alland, Paul Stewart. (The bit-part player behind the girl with the picture is Alan Ladd.)

> That he'll do all he can . . .
> Who loves to smoke –
> Enjoys a joke –
> Who wouldn't get a bit upset
> If he were really broke;
> With wealth and fame
> He's still the same –
> I'll bet you five you're not alive
> If you don't know his name!
> What is his name?
> It's Mister Kane!
> He doesn't like that Mister, he likes
> Good old Charlie Kane!

The bursting in of this raucous melody to cover the end credits, after we have just seen Kane's possessions, and by implication Kane himself, go up in a billowing black cloud of smoke as we track back to reveal the same No Trespassing sign which opened the story, is one of my favourite moments from this or any film. Others include the capsule characterization of the second Mrs Kane's operatic career by a shot of a flickering and fading light bulb, backed by a rising shot into the theatre 'flies', where a stagehand sums up his impression of her tinny little voice by putting two fingers to his nose. The doubling up of parts reminds one of the old stage repertory tradition: Joseph Cotten and Gus Schilling, though they play a drama critic and a waiter respectively, are visible among the newsmen discussing Kane's life, and Alan Ladd has several bits before his clear appearance with a pipe in the final scene. The carefully faked old newsreel is a joy in itself, with scratched and blurred 'old' prints married into a perfect parody of the *March of Time* technique. And then there is Everett Sloane's marvellous moment as the aged executive ('Me, I'm chairman of the board, I got nothing but time') recalling lost opportunities, such as the beautiful girl he glimpsed on a ferry sixty years before and didn't dare speak to. 'She didn't see me at all, but I'll bet a month hasn't gone by since, that I didn't think of that girl.' And the screeching cockatoo superimposed over a particularly fraught moment near the end (but note that a hasty optical effect has robbed the bird of its eye). And the mischievous characterization of Walter Parks Thatcher's butch librarian. And the crude handwriting of the great man, giving a clue to his character. And the layers of meaning in casual lines, such as: 'He never gave anybody anything in his life; he just left you a tip.' Or: 'He was disappointed with the world, so he built one of his own – an absolute monarchy.' The clever obscuring of Kane's face, by tricks of shadow and make-up, in order not to show him physically so fully as to reveal that he is really a young man of twenty-four acting seventy. The use throughout of body outlines rather than faces to indicate character. The dovetailing of one scene into another by rapid panning shots and lively sounds on the track. The delightful montage of outrageous newspaper headlines, each making Kane's guardian more furious than the last. The endless jigsaw puzzles suggesting an unfinished life with a mystery at its centre. And of course the famous ceilings, not in fact a film first but here built lower and more decorative than usual so that they become part of the narrative.

Students of film grammar will note that *Kane* uses little camera movement (save in the famous breakfast scene, which by use of fast pans turns years into moments). The trick generally is to devise elaborate and interesting camera set-ups, and to allow the actors to move around within the frame. Whatever the method, the result is a film without a dull second, or a single shot composed less than cunningly. Perhaps, as some have said, it is all form and no meaning; but its form is wondrous to gaze upon, and it is a form which can never be seen again because it depends entirely on the technical resources of a giant studio; its impressionist effects simply can't be duplicated by today's aping of reality.

Welles' second film, *The Magnificent Ambersons*, is also a marvellous work until near the end, when the story lurches because Welles' last reels were ditched by the studio in his absence and replaced by a rapid and unconvincing coda. This time cinematographer Toland was replaced by Stanley Cortez, to a different but not a lesser effect, and Welles found a way of dispensing with titles altogether, instead holding the credits until the end and then speaking them over a static silhouette of camera equipment, ending: 'I wrote and directed the picture. My name is Orson Welles.' The sense of American small town life, of horses replaced by cars, of old manners giving way to new, is wondrously and most economically conveyed; and the famous backward tracking shot through a dozen doorways has been often imitated but never equalled. Agnes Moorehead's performance as the hysterical Fanny was much lauded, but Joseph Cotten and Ray Collins also give of their best, Richard Bennett has a touching moment, and Tim Holt as the arrogant youth who gets his come-uppance was coaxed into a performance which may have surprised even him. It was Welles' last major fling with a major studio, and that, along with his descent to the status of unreliable ham and TV food salesman, is much to be regretted.

Citizen Kane. US 1941; monochrome; 119 minutes. Produced and directed by Orson Welles for RKO. Written by Herman J. Mankiewicz and Orson Welles. Photographed by Gregg Toland. Music score by Bernard Herrmann. Edited by Robert Wise. Art direction by Perry Ferguson. Set decoration by Darrell Silvera. Special effects by Vernon L. Walker. With Orson Welles as Kane; Joseph Cotten as Jedediah Leland; Everett Sloane as Bernstein; Dorothy Comingore as Susan Alexander; George Coulouris as Walter Parks Thatcher; Ray Collins as Jim Gettys; Ruth Warrick as Emily Norton; Agnes Moorehead as Mrs Kane; Paul Stewart as Raymond; Fortunio Bonanova as Matiste; Erskine Sanford as Editor Carter; William Alland as Thompson.

The Magnificent Ambersons. US 1942; monochrome 88 minutes. Produced and directed by Orson Welles for RKO. Written by Orson Welles from the novel by Booth Tarkington. Photographed by Stanley Cortez. Music score by Bernard Herrmann. Art direction by Mark-Lee Kirk. Edited by Robert Wise. With Joseph Cotten as Eugene; Dolores Costello as Isabel; Anne Baxter as Lucy; Tim Holt as George; Agnes Moorehead as Fanny; Ray Collins as Jack; Richard Bennett as Major Anderson.

Is the Pellet with the Poison in the Flagon with the Dragon or the Chalice from the Palace?
The Court Jester

With help from hypnosis, the Fox's assistant routs a usurper and restores the rightful heir to the throne of Britain.

If this is my favourite star vehicle for an American comedian, that may be because it rather mysteriously plumbs the depths of English pantomime; one suspects also that its creators were old enough to remember Douglas Fairbanks' 1922 *Robin Hood*, so close does it come to being a spoof of that unique piece of swashbuckling. Its rather complicated but dramatically watertight plot contrives to upturn a fair number of basic Hollywood clichés while paralleling the development, and much of the spirit, of more serious historical adventures; it also recruits the dashing villain of many of them in the person of Basil Rathbone, still thoroughly able, at the age of sixty-three, to disport himself convincingly in a duel. Although by the time of the release of this film Danny Kaye's career was waning, it finds him as a performer at his multi-faceted zenith, and he is cunningly supported. Nevertheless, for me the chief attraction of the piece lies in its rich array of running jokes and elaborate puns such as delighted me in my infancy during provincial touring performances of *Aladdin* and *Jack and the Beanstalk*. True, nobody does the 'I can prove that you're not here' routine, but even more delightful, if such a thing is possible, is the impossible mnemonic given to the hero just before he drinks the loyal toasts and marches into mortal combat in the arena with the grim, grisly and gruesome Griswold. The sophisticated witch Griselda ('Gris-who'll-da?') whispers helpfully to him: 'The pellet with the poison's in the chalice from the palace. The vessel with the pestle has the brew that is true.' With some difficulty he masters this, just as she returns with the news:

'They've broken the vessel with the pestle. The brew that is true is in a flagon, with a picture of a dragon . . .' By this time Griswold has overheard most of the plot, so both armoured figures amble into battle trying in vain to get the couplet right. The whole sequence forms one of the great moments of Hollywood comedy: it is of course borrowed from *The Paleface*, made seven years earlier, in which Bob Hope, about to participate in a shootout with the fastest gun in the west, is advised: 'He shoots to the left, so lean to the right . . .' But the oldest known form of the gag occurs in a 1939 Hope comedy by Don Hartman, Frank Butler and (of all people) Preston Sturges; in *Never Say Die* the hero, a reluctant duellist, learns that 'There's a cross on the muzzle of the pistol with the bullet. There's a nick on the handle of the pistol with the blank.'

All films these days have to be judged by how they come up on TV. If *The Court Jester* fails in this respect it is on two counts only. Disappointingly fuzzy 16mm prints are all that can now be made from the brilliantly coloured VistaVision original; and the many pauses originally intended for audience laughter give one rather too much time to observe the slightly stilted direction, obvious glass shots and cardboard sets. To be truthful, there is also rather too much plot to be digested before the comedy can really start. Even so, within the first fifteen minutes Kaye has an opportunity for two songs (including the marvellously edited 'They'll never outfox the fox'), also a tedious love scene (which bolsters up Glynis Johns' part but might otherwise be sacrificed in favour of sharpness) and impersonations by the star of not only a deaf and aged rustic ('Who are you?' – 'Fine, thank you') but also the incomparable Giacomo, king of jesters and jester of kings. In the latter guise, which gets him inside the castle, he manages snatches of French, German and Italian, and later, for good measure, adds a touch of the Laurence Oliviers. ('And now, Ravenhurst, you rat catcher . . .') His first meeting with the said Basil Rathbone is a little masterpiece. Rathbone thinks Kaye is an assassin come to do away with the usurper so that Rathbone can succeed in his place: Kaye thinks Rathbone is an ally of his boss the Fox (Robin Hood to you) who will help Kaye find the key which unlocks the secret passage through which the rebels will storm the castle. The dialogue is admirably succinct:

The Musical Romantic Adventure Of This Or Any Year!

PARAMOUNT PRESENTS

DANNY KAYE in

THE COURT JESTER

Color by TECHNICOLOR

VISTAVISION

"Picture of the month!"
— THE AMERICAN MAGAZINE

"A very funny picture!"
— SATURDAY REVIEW

"...the funniest Kaye on movie record!"
— LIFE MAGAZINE

"...lot of fun... grand entertainment!"
— CUE MAGAZINE

"Good fun!"
— N.Y. TIMES

SONGS!
Where Walks My True Love
Baby Let Me Take You Dreaming
Life Could Not Better Be
The Maladjusted Jester
My Heart Knows A Lovely Song!
Outfox The Fox

co-starring
GLYNIS JOHNS · BASIL RATHBONE · ANGELA LANSBURY · CECIL PARKER

Words and Music by Sylvia Fine and Sammy Cahn · Written, Produced and Directed by NORMAN PANAMA and MELVIN FRANK

GIACOMO: All I want to do is get in, get on with it, get it over with and get out. Get it?
RAVENHURST: Got it.
GIACOMO: Good.

Special gags all the way through are devoted to Rathbone, burlesquing his roles in *The Adventures of Robin Hood* and *The Mark of Zorro*: there is even a neat spoof of Zorro's candle trick, as Rathbone slices through an illuminated candle without toppling it. Kaye, hypnotized at this point into believing himself 'a lover of beauty and a beauty of a lover', does the same trick with six at a time. Even as the credit titles unfurl, the Rathbone name keeps shivering, darting about, and zooming at Kaye, whose image heralds the long list of contributors while warbling 'Life Could Not Better Be': thus we are admirably entertained before the action even starts. The hypnotist in the plot is the princess's tame witch splendidly portrayed by that incomparable comedienne Mildred Natwick, and it is she who provokes the movie's biggest laughs, as her doggerel commands ('On your feet, be not afraid, you're the greatest with the blade') and finger snaps transform the increasingly dizzy hero from mouse to man and back again. In his swashbuckling persona he catches the lascivious eye of the petulant princess, whose father has given her a stern instruction: 'If it pleases me, you will marry Griswold,' to which her somewhat anachronistic answer is: 'If it pleases you so much, *you* marry Griswold.' The suave jester overcomes her resistance at once, with his rapid kissing from hand to neck, followed by the request: 'With your permission, ma'am, I'd like to go round again.' Or, more lyrically: 'I live for a look, I long for a kiss, I lust for a laugh, ha ha!' Irrepressible, he delights the usurper with tales of what the duchess did with her dirk to the duke and the doge; congratulated on his imagination and brilliance, he asks: 'Did you expect less?' Unlike Bob Hope, who played many similar roles of a coward in dangerous circumstances, Kaye can really manage the swashbuckling bit, and one almost believes it when one sees him apparently swing on a vine from one palace window to another. He also has the terpsichorean training which enables him to make the knighthood ritual hilarious, with Rockette-like lines of armoured men yelling 'Yea, verily, yea' as they revolve at top speed.

With its magnetized armour, its midgets to the rescue, and its true heir recognizable by a purple pimpernel on the royal backside, this is the kind of spoof of British traditions which could be made only in Hollywood – though with a mainly British cast. In a way it is the respect for the basic traditions which makes it so funny, plus the determination of all concerned to get the most out of the jokes without flattening them. Finesse may seem a curious word to apply to a romp of this kind, but it's what *The Court Jester* has.

Kaye's supremacy as a screen comic was short-lived, though he remained a big name on the live stage. Most of his later films were on the painful side, though his earlier Goldwyn ones all have their moments. *The Secret Life of Walter Mitty*, flabby and disappointing as a whole, is worth the price of admission for his heroic dreams ('It's nothing. Just a broken arm') and his song as a Parisian hat designer:

> I'm Anatole of Paris,
> I shriek with chic,
> My hat of the week
> Caused six divorces, three runaway horses . . .

Perhaps the best of them is *Wonder Man*, yet another man-and-mouse affair; this time a shy librarian has his body invaded by the ghost of his murdered brother, a nightclub comic bent on revenge. In all but name it's a *Topper* sequel, but there's nothing new under the sun, and among its more memorable scenes is his encounter with S. Z. Sakall as a delicatessen proprietor bemused and bewildered by his client, who is clearly not himself, ordering a pint of Prospect Park instead of potato salad. For good measure it's also the one in which Kaye impersonates a Russian baritone with hay fever . . .

The Court Jester. US 1956; Technicolor and VistaVision; 101 minutes. Produced, written and directed by Norman Panama and Melvin Frank for Paramount. Photographed by Ray June. Songs by Sylvia Fine and Sammy Cahn. Choreography by James Starbuck. Art direction by Hal Pereira and Roland Anderson. With Danny Kaye as Hawkins; Glynis Johns as Maid Jean; Angela Lansbury as Princess Gwendolyn; Basil Rathbone as Sir Ravenhurst; Cecil Parker as King Roderick; Mildred Natwick as Griselda; Robert Middleton as Sir Griswold; John Carradine as Giacomo; Edward Ashley as the Fox.

Unfamiliar Haunts
Dead of Night

Five ghost stories are linked by a sixth.

It wasn't until my third viewing of *Dead of Night* that I realized what I'd been missing. In Lancashire in the mid-forties, however palatial the picture house, many projectionists were ill-trained in the art of presentation. Breakdowns were frequent and sometimes quite prolonged, once we all had to be given free tickets for another performance because the projectionist had nipped off for a beer, the print had snapped, and the broken end reeled off all over the projection box. The chaps at the Theatre Royal in Bolton loved to make the credits unreadable by flooding them with coloured Brennergraph patterns, and I remember a ghastly moment when the organist at the Odeon rose colourfully from his depths to join in the entire finale of a Betty Grable musical. What was absolutely inevitable was that, once the music swelled to herald the end of the feature, on would flood the green footlights, swish would close the main tabs, and ice-cream would be on sale in all parts, with slides advertising bunion relief on the safety curtain.

The multi-story structure of *Dead of Night*, absolutely original at the time, has latterly become familiar via half-a-dozen Robert Bloch/Amicus horror compendiums, though they tended to replace its subtleties by great dollops of charnel-house gore. In this case the framing story was a little gem. A middle-aged architect awakes from a recurring nightmare, the details of which always flee away before he can recount them. The telephone rings: one Eliot Foley, recommended by a mutual friend, wants him to come down for the weekend to his country place, Pilgrim's Farm, and suggest some improvements. When he arrives, he finds everything, including host, guests, and the place to hang one's hat, frighteningly familiar, though common sense tells him that he has never been there, nor met any of them, before. It gradually dawns on him that Pilgrim's Farm has been the location of his dream, and that before the night ends something terrible will happen. The situation is seized on by members of the assembled company as an excuse to tell ghost stories from their own experience, and afterwards serious conversation dwindles into small talk; but eventually, left alone with the psychiatrist who has been explaining away every supernatural experience recounted, the architect impulsively murders him, is whirled into a nightmarish rigmarole of all the stories ... and awakes with no memory of the events he has so recently experienced. The telephone rings: a man called Eliot Foley wants him to go down to a place called Pilgrim's Farm for the weekend ...

At this point the end title was briefly glimpsed, and on my first two visits that was it: bright lights, bunion relief, and ice-cream. Luckily I liked the film well enough, despite its apparently abrupt finish, to seek it out for a third time, and so made my first contribution towards the upkeep of the Farnworth Palace, a tiny hall by the bus station. To my surprise it proved airy, comfortable and well-maintained, and at least the projectionist wasn't in a hurry to

DEAD OF NIGHT. Nobody seems to be believing Mervyn Johns at this point, though as it turns out they all have ghost stories of their own to tell. Frederick Valk, Roland Culver, Anthony Baird, Googie Withers

go home. For I found that after that deceptive end title there is a very slow roll-up of credits, and behind that at least another minute of essential action, underlining the fact that our hero does go down again to Pilgrim's Farm, in the same sequence of shots as at the beginning, and, wearing that same expression of blank bewilderment, is welcomed into the drawing-room by Eliot Foley and his friends . . . thus establishing beyond doubt that he is enmeshed in an endless series of recurring dreams from which he can never wake up. A suitably subtle and chilling end which was probably denied to four people out of five on the original release.

So much for the cherished intentions of film-makers. But *Dead of Night* had worse to suffer. Its master negative was destroyed in a fire, and the only prints now available are grainy dupes which obscure the original quality of the photography. In 1949 it was sent out on reissue with one of its stories missing, which not only upset the balance of grave and gay, but made Sally Ann Howes' part meaningless, as she was clearly about to tell a story but never did. At least the current television prints are complete, and despite some inevitable dating – Ealing did tend to approach the upper middle classes rather deferentially – it repays repeated viewing not only for the polish of its story-telling but for the urbanity of its performances. One final handicap suffered by the film was its original poster showing some kind of medieval demon, an image quite out of keeping with the contents and likely to alienate the audience which would have most enjoyed it.

Much of the weight of the film falls on Mervyn Johns as the little man to whom such curious and irreversible things happen; he is perfectly cast. Roland Culver is the perfect golf club host, and tells the kind of story you might expect; Sally Ann Howes is an absolutely smashing teenager, and Frederick Valk's bulk admirably sets off his heavy interpretation of the psychiatrist. On the whole the linking section could not be better done. Not that the interpolated yarns are poor, but somehow they seem to work against each other, as though fighting for top place; one feels that a better scheme would have been to reduce all except one to cameos, and have the one be something really substantial, like M. R. James' *O Whistle and I'll Come to You My Lad*. Well, that milk is spilt, and they all entertain in themselves. My favourite is in fact the slightest. A convalescent dreams of a hearse, with the driver saying, 'Just room for one inside, sir.' Recovering, he joins a bus queue, and when one pulls in, the conductor makes the same remark. Recognizing the face of the hearse driver, he steps back in alarm; the bus drives off and crashes over a bridge. (Be prepared for the most unconvincing of model shots.) The teenager's is a charming tale about meeting a sad little boy at a fancy dress party in a friend's baronial home; he is of course a ghost. Next comes the more formal tale of the haunted mirror; it belonged to a Victorian murderer, and when a modern young wife buys it for her husband, he begins to see himself in the role . . . This is the most stylishly acted and directed of the stories. Now as an entr'acte we are offered Radford and Wayne in the tale of the ghostly golfer who comes back petulantly after committing suicide for loss of his girl to his friend: he finds the friend had used a double-headed penny when they tossed for her. It's good fun in the *Topper* tradition but lacks finesse; this however is abundant in the stark finale about a mad ventriloquist whose dummy appears to take on a murderous life of its own. Michael Redgrave gives a masterly impression of schizophrenia, and Cavalcanti's impressionist techniques are dazzling. Thirty years later *Magic* told the same story, less dramatically, at four times the length.

Dead of Night encapsulates the world of upper-class Britain of the thirties rather than the forties: the war is not mentioned, and the world we see is that of Wodehouse and Sayers and Dodie Smith and Richmal Crompton. It might even have benefited from a period setting, for its gentle ghosts had no message for the age of austerity. It was however eminently exportable, proving a great favourite in America: and historically it inaugurated Ealing's great period, marking their dividing line between ancient and modern film-making. If only Alec Guinness had been discovered by then, he would have made a splendid architect . . .

Serious ghost stories are rare in the cinema. One which worked pretty well was *The Uninvited*, with Ray Milland saving a Cornish girl from the destructive spirit of her mad mother. The central setting for this film is a house on a clifftop, which I always wanted to own; but of course the scenery was created out of the thinnest Hollywood air, and the house never existed. Another curious feature of *The Uninvited* is that when it came out all the English critics congratulated the director for refraining from showing his ghosts. This must strike present-day researchers as odd, because on the prints now available the ghosts are certainly there, as wraith-like figures hovering on dark stairways, and very frightening they are too. The fact is that the British censor of the time cut them out so that the film could have an 'A' certificate; which the critics should have known if they'd done their homework properly.

As a teenager I was most impressed by the film of *Thunder Rock*, and tried very hard to have it produced as the school play. (I could have played Captain Joshua, but none of the other parts fitted, so we did *Saint Joan* instead.) Although I wasn't much interested in politics, I sensed the current urgency, in wartime, of this yarn about a famous journalist who, embittered when nobody heeds his warnings about Franco and Hitler, takes himself off to look after a lighthouse in the middle of Lake Michigan, finds the log of a ship called *Land o'Lakes* which foundered on its reefs a hundred years previously, and creates in his mind a gallery of ghostly passengers who, though finally shocked to hear that they are dead, persuade him that his destiny is to go back and fight for what he believes in, which is what they were doing when their ship capsized. I preferred to believe that Joshua and Melanie and Kurtz were real ghosts rather than figments of Charleston's imagination, and the author left this option open; but mostly I was impressed by the invention with which the Boulting brothers held my attention through a play which apart from a few flashbacks was set entirely within the great stones of a lighthouse. And I loved the moody performances: Mr Redgrave again, Mr Valk again, Finlay Currie, Lilli Palmer, Barbara Mullen. I wish I could feel that the cinema of the future held for me such a first-time thrill as *Thunder Rock* gave at the Princess Cinema, Blackpool, one night in 1943.

Dead of Night. GB 1945; monochrome; 104 minutes. Produced by Sidney Cole and John Croydon for Ealing. Written by John V. Baines, Angus MacPhail and T. E. B. Clarke. Directed by Basil Dearden, Charles Crichton, Robert Hamer, Alberto Cavalcanti. Photographed by Stan Pavey and Douglas Slocombe. Music score by Georges Auric. Edited by Charles Hasse. Art direction by Michael Relph. With Mervyn Johns as Walter Craig; Roland Culver as Eliot Foley; Frederick Valk as Dr Van Straaten; Mary Merrall as Mrs Foley; Anthony Baird as Hugh; Judy Kelly as Joyce; Miles Malleson as hearse driver; Sally Ann Howes as Sally; Googie Withers as Joan; Ralph Michael as Peter; Esmé Percy as antique dealer; Basil Radford as George; Naunton Wayne as Larry; Michael Redgrave as Maxwell Frere; Hartley Power as Sylvester Kee; Elizabeth Welch as singer.

Welcome to Bottleneck
Destry Rides Again

A no-gun deputy sheriff cleans up a western town.

It begins, exhilaratingly, with that famous stagecoach music by Frank Skinner, seeming to sum up fifty years of old-fashioned westerns with the elation of horses trotting at high speed, shaking and bumping their pioneering passengers into a new life in which danger was compensated for by the spirit of adventure. (The reality was no doubt a great deal more sordid, but it never does any harm to make the best of a bad job.) We find ourselves part of a brief pre-credits sequence (certainly one of Hollywood's first), with a sign saying 'Welcome to Bottleneck' being shot up. After panning across Boot Hill we come to some rowdy scenes of street life, these form a background for the credits, with energetic mayhem at every corner and doorway. And as the final credit fades the Last Chance Saloon stands before us, and in one of those exciting crane shots which seem to be a lost art we rise over the canopy to the shadowed room above, where little pools of light illuminate a card game which is clearly about to become crooked: we are not in the least surprised when Frenchy the sexy singer is recruited by town boss Kent (who is so villainous he ought to be called Jasper) to spill hot coffee into the victim's lap so that his cards can be changed. When earnest Sheriff Keogh takes up the case, a couple of shots signal his disappearance. As the shifty tobacco-chewing mayor, Hiram J. Slade, puts it to the assembled populace: 'The Sheriff's been suddenly called out of town on urgent business. He'll be gone permanent.'

Meanwhile the alluring Frenchy, not so much played as lived by Marlene Dietrich in the most popular role Hollywood ever gave her, goes into one of her rousing numbers, an elegy for a cowboy who pushed his luck:

> Little Joe, Little Joe,
> Oh, whatever became of him I don't know . . .
> Oh he sure did like his liquor
> And it would have got his ticker
> But the sheriff got him quicker . . .

An instance of the film's masterly control of narrative is that by the time the song ends we have been led along the crowded bar and introduced to several important subsidiary characters. There is Billy Gilbert as the explosive bartender who spends the whole film sliding foaming glasses of beer along the counter to the refrain: 'I put 'em up, you drink 'em down, I put 'em up, you drink 'em down. This is getting monotonous.' There is Mischa Auer as the emigré Russian whose wife keeps the boarding house and insists on calling him Callahan in memory of her first husband. There is Charles Winninger as Washington Dimsdale the town drunk, strumming on his banjolele and pulling up his shirt front whenever he gets mad. There is the aforesaid Mayor Slade, forever top-hatted like an undertaker, playing checkers with himself as he observes any building tension

DESTRY RIDES AGAIN. Jenkins, Hinds, Merkel, Winninger, Auer, Dietrich, Stewart, Donlevy, Hervey, Gilbert, Hymer: the cast lines up in the spirit of fun which pervades the whole movie. Mr Auer, it will be noted, is not wearing his pants

from the best vantage point in the saloon. Soon Frenchy sings another song, this time in a sensuous lather of close-ups and feather boas:

> You've got that look, that look that leaves me weak:
> You with your eyes-across-the-table technique . . .

Possibly no musical performer in film ever displayed such animal magnetism as does Dietrich in this number, especially as by now we are acquainted with her character: her cynicism ('The longer they wait, the better they like it'), her fatalism ('All or nothing, I always say') and her superstition ('Take my rabbit's foot and stay out of dark corners'). She is plainly destined to stop a bullet in the last reel, but her memory will go marching on.

The first movement ends with the unspeakable Kent arranging the election of the town drunk as sheriff to replace the nosey Keogh; but he doesn't reckon with Wash signing the pledge and sending for help in the shape of Thomas Jefferson Destry, son of the man who cleaned up Tombstone.

After the smoky night scenes and the villainy we have witnessed, a breath of wide open air acts as a tonic to our spirits, especially when accompanied by the vibrant music. Young Destry, twenty-five minutes in, is arriving in Bottleneck, and when the stagecoach grinds to a halt the assembled populace assumes it must be he who springs out to assault the driver for giving such an uncomfortable ride. But they're wrong; Destry is the one helping a lady down and carrying her yellow parasol. He also carves napkin rings (it soothes the nerves), and by the way he doesn't carry guns. Doesn't believe in them. ('You sure you're Destry?' – 'Folks is always asking me that.') What he does carry is a bottomless bag of moral stories about friends of his who've taken the wrong turning, and these yarns seem to be his only defence against villains who are better armed; but Hollywood naturally sees to it that he always wins. This is the archetypal James Stewart role, and as James Stewart is there to play it, things couldn't be better arranged. His first inspection of the saloon is perhaps the movie's centrepiece. Frenchy has been playing cards with Callahan, and bets him 'thirty bucks against your pants'. He is tempted, and of course she wins, so: 'Off with your pants,' 'But Frenchy,' he protests, 'it's undignified. I've met every king in Europe.' She is gleefully unrepentant. 'Now you met two aces in Bottleneck.' Destry walks in to find Callahan fleeing in his long johns; and Frenchy's taunting of the new lawman, handing him mop and pail to clean up the town, is interrupted by Mrs Callahan stalking in to retrieve her husband's only pair of pants. Her demands and insults provoke a spirited catfight, a hair-pulling and dress-tearing marathon, which comes to an end only when Destry tips the contents of the pail over the screaming, clawing harpies. Frenchy promptly turns on him with assorted bottles and small items of furniture and by the time he backs out discreetly we feel that we too have lived through this disgraceful but hilarious encounter between law and disorder.

Constantly throughout the film the mild-mannered but resourceful Destry is set against examples of the west at its wildest. 'Look at this post,' harangues Wash, 'soaked through and through with the blood of Saw-Tooth Magee.' When Destry is unimpressed, Wash suggests he takes the next stage before disaster befalls him. But Destry has at least inherited from his father a streak of stubbornness. 'I think I'll stick around. I had a friend once who collected postage stamps. Said the best thing about 'em was they stuck to one thing till they got there. I'm kinda like that too.' And he quickly shows his real worth by confiscating guns from a group of cowboys out to paint the town red. 'Aside from being nice ornaments a fellow can have a whole lot of harmless amusement with these toys . . .' He proceeds to shoot every knob off a distant street sign before sending the revellers out of town with a stern warning. And he is no less severe with the mocking Frenchy: 'I'll bet you have a lovely face under all that paint. Why don't you wipe it off some day and have a good look? And figure out how you can live up to it.'

This highly polished family entertainment is a gleaming example of how every talent in a Hollywood studio used to be bendable to a common aim, which was to give the audience a thoroughly good time in the most professional way possible. Direction, editing, music, script and casting are all honed to perfection. The story is not only deftly told, with innumerable undetachable hooks to secure the unwary viewer's interest, it contrives to include in its weave first-class roles for half a dozen popular supporting actors as well as the two leads. Nothing is left hanging high and dry, not even Callahan's pants. Mrs Callahan is accosted one morning by boarder Billy Gilbert, demurely wrapped in a curtain. In pained tones he enunciates: 'Prunes every day for breakfast I can tolerate. Torn sheets I get used to. But pants I cannot swallow.' At gunpoint Mrs Callahan gets the bartender's pants back from her fleeing husband, and Destry's are the next to go; but the plot then has Callahan allowed to keep the garment on condition he is sworn in as a deputy, a position in which he is finally able to prove his true worth to the community.

Destry Rides Again is an ample justification of the studio system, because, like *Casablanca*, it glows with the kind of expertise which simply can't be assembled from scratch for each new production. There are even little throwaway jokes for the villain, sidestepping as he leaves Frenchy's room in expectation that a vase will be thrown at him, which it is; and for Frenchy herself, in the middle of a song booting where it hurts a tart who is distracting the audience from the star. Behind it all is the expertise of producer Joe Pasternak, weighing the rich ingredients and apportioning them exactly, ready if interest should flag to bring in another shrewd comedy routine or a brilliant snatch of song for Dietrich, her final contribution being appropriately doomladen:

> And if I die, don't buy a casket
> Of silver with the candles all aflame:
> Just see what the boys in the back room will have
> And tell them I sighed
> And tell them I cried
> And tell them I died of the same!

Basically a comedy, this remarkable film even gets away with its tragic ending. After the climactic excitement, with the women of the town marching on the saloon, Kent shooting Frenchy in mistake for Destry and then being toppled himself, there is a neat coda to send us home happy. Bottleneck has been transformed into a haven of peace. Destry walks down the street whittling, and wincing just a little as a small girl sings 'Little Joe'. But the past is past, the new sheriff is engaged to a nice girl, and as the credits roll he is telling another story. 'I knew a feller once . . .'

Destry Rides Again. US 1938; monochrome; 94 minutes. Produced by Joe Pasternak for Universal. Written by Felix Jackson, Gertrude Purcell and Henry Myers, from a novel by Max Brand. Directed by George Marshall. Photographed by Hal Mohr. Music score by Frank Skinner. Songs by Frank Loesser and Frederick Hollander. Edited by Milton Carruth. With James Stewart as Tom Destry; Marlene Dietrich as Frenchy; Brian Donlevy as Kent; Charles Winninger as Washington Dimsdale; Mischa Auer as Callahan; Samuel S. Hinds as Hiram J. Slade; Una Merkel as Mrs Callahan; Allen Jenkins and Warren Hymer as Gyp and Bugs Watson; Irene Hervey as Janice Tyndall; Billy Gilbert as Loupgerou; Tom Fadden as Claggett; Jack Carson as Jack Tyndall; Lilian Yarbo as Clara.

Alter Ego
Dr Jekyll and Mr Hyde

A Victorian scientist discovers a formula which enables him to bring to the fore the depraved side of his character. Unfortunately it takes over his life and resists the antidote.

The Jekyll-Hyde myth seems so much a part of our heritage, its latest incarnation being *The Incredible Hulk*, that one is surprised to find it no older than 1885. It has certainly been well used since, with over a dozen film versions of the original story, to say nothing of scores of ever-zanier sequels and variations such as *Superman, Batman* and *The Wolf Man*. Even Bram Stoker, writing *Dracula* in 1897, must have been influenced by it. The original title still holds its fascination, perhaps because the names are so well chosen. One wonders why nobody ever thinks to film it in Stevenson's sequence of letters and documents, the development of which, with its slow unfolding of the truth, has its own peculiar power to generate suspense.

In seeking a favourite film version one is inexorably drawn towards the only real contender, though a nod for trying should not be withheld from the transexual Hammer variation *Dr Jekyll and Sister Hyde*, and respect is due to the high production values of the 1941 MGM treatment with Spencer Tracy, even if the resulting film was solemn, pretentious and very heavy going. I remember relishing with the wrong kind of delight the sub-Freudian dream sequence in which Hyde whips along Ingrid Bergman and Lana Turner, who have somehow turned into carriage horses. (One heard that Tracy would never afterwards speak to Somerset Maugham, who visited the set during shooting. Told that the actor differentiated the roles without any change in make-up, Maugham audibly enquired: 'Which is he playing now?')

No, it was in 1931 that the myth was most perfectly and elegantly filmed by Rouben Mamoulian, that master innovator who ran out of innovations. I first came across it as late as 1938, when it ran at the Bolton Lido as a reissue. It must have earned nothing stronger than an 'A' certificate, because Mother decided I might see it with her, though with curious logic she insisted that we sit further back than usual, in case I was frightened. It was clearly an excellent print, for I remember almost three-dimensionally my sense of the awesomely grand parlours contrasting with the dusty gloom of the doctor's laboratory and the raucous squalor of the East End slums. I remember too that a number of teenage urchins in the front rows fell to shrieks of laughter at the transformation scenes, the first example I can remember of hooliganism in a cinema; and when I enquired in a whisper why they were laughing my mother said it was because they were frightened and ashamed to admit it.

For more than a quarter of a century this 1931 film was unavailable, MGM having bought up the negative to preserve their later version, and it was not until the mid-seventies that I discovered, in my capacity as film buyer for ITV, that the negative was still in excellent condition and that prints were available from it. As it turned out, the rights went to the BBC, which suited me perfectly well as the ITV London companies, even if they had acquired it, might not have bothered to play it. And so, one summer Saturday at nearly midnight, it was chosen to herald a BBC2 horror season and I sat down to relive my childhood trauma. In fact I was enraptured, though with the passage of time the entertainment had lost several introductory scenes, which didn't seem to matter at all; indeed when they were imitated in the 1941 version they merely held up the plot. More crucial were the snips which had removed a moment when Jekyll sees Hyde's face grinning at him from the flames of his fire, and the famous sequence in which he involuntarily transforms after seeing a cat kill a bird in a tree. Rather meaninglessly he still says 'It is death, death', and runs off stimulated to kill Ivy Pierson, but we have lost the spur for this sudden change of mood.

Even those repelled by horror films must admit that technically Mamoulian has produced a masterpiece of cinematic flow and invention, and his ingenious devices are backed up by an unexpectedly literate script by Samuel Hoffenstein and Percy Heath, giving remarkably full display to the sexual element. The outwardly respectable Jekyll is an impatient lover, disquieting his dull friend Lanyon by asserting that liking to be kissed by a pretty girl is 'not a matter of conduct but of elementary instincts':

LANYON: Perhaps you have forgotten you are engaged to Muriel.
JEKYLL: Forgotten? Can a man dying of thirst forget water? And do you
know what would happen to that thirst if it were denied water?
LANYON: If I understand you correctly, you sound almost indecent.

Earlier the doctor has upset his fiancée's father by asking for a short engagement: 'If it is eccentric to be impatient in love, sir, I am.' That he is basically a good fellow is shown by his attention to poor patients:

LANYON: You know how insistent the duchess was on your coming. You
can't neglect her for a lot of charity cases.
JEKYLL: Can't I, Lanyon? It's the things one can't do that always tempt me.

In these snatches of dialogue the scene is cleverly and clearly set for Jekyll's eventual downfall, though the aim of his chemical experiments is above reproach: 'I want to be clean not only in my conduct but in my innermost thoughts and desires. There is one way to do it.' When Lanyon asks how, Jekyll replies. 'By separating the two natures in us.'

So much for the exposition, lucid and forthright. The development is equally swift. As Jekyll, a chance meeting with a sexy music hall singer; as Hyde, courtship, dominance, and murder of her. Then in savage fury he murders his fiancée's father; but he has been forced to reveal his secret to Lanyon, who leads the police to him. Now in his laboratory, he is Jekyll again and starts to bluff, but Hyde takes over before the horrified eyes of the constables, and the monster is shot dead, slowly reverting to Jekyll as the body lies on the experiment table. The camera tracks back through assembled retorts and test tubes until the grim scene fades out behind the flames of a brazier.

Outstanding among the elements which make this film a classic is Fredric March's performance; in the first place he is warm, vibrant and impulsive, then under the Hyde make-up an unrecognizable animal. Some have objected to the extent of the physical change, to the crooked teeth, the low simian hairline and the pointed head. The fact is that Mamoulian was aiming to show Hyde as a reversion to the ape stage in man, and there are very few shots in which the make-up, aided immeasurably by the actor's confident command of it, does not wholly work. What has seldom been commented on is its progressive concept, like Dorian Gray's picture: at the beginning

DR JEKYLL AND MR HYDE. A scene cut from the final print: the good doctor sees in the fire an image of his evil self

Hyde is an obscenely athletic young animal, at the end a weary, pouchy, hairy old pervert worn out by his own debaucheries. Nor can the other performers be faulted as in their various ways they contrast with the hero/villain. Miriam Hopkins in particular is a sensation as the deliciously sensual little trollop who gets more than her just deserts for flirting with Jekyll: there has seldom been a sexier scene in pictures than that in which the doctor examines her injured leg, tells her not to wear her garter so tight, then withdraws as she seductively swings her leg back and forth over the side of the bed, framed by the frilly bedclothes, like a metronome ticking as it fades very slowly indeed over the next scene of Jekyll walking home, unable to get it out of his mind any more than we can.

The most surprising trick of this very early talkie is its use of the subjective camera. It begins with what Jekyll sees as he arrives at the lecture hall to expound on his theme, and not until he actually begins to speak do we see his face. The technique recurs at intervals, most notably during the first transformation scene, when we gaze into the mirror at his reflection, then shake and stagger with him as the deadly potion takes hold, finally looking into the mirror again to get our first glimpse of the monster he has created from himself. This transformation is at least partially effected without the use of trick photography: layers of make-up were used, each successive one revealing itself under a different intensity of infra-red light. And the heartbeats which pound on the track were played backwards to give a weirder effect. Another favourite trick of Mamoulian's is to start a diagonal wipe, then hold it halfway so that we see two scenes at once, usually two women vying for Jekyll's favours, or his respectable friends waiting for him while he is off at an orgy. If technical dexterity and command of cinematic narrative do not impress you, then simply enjoy the *Dreigroschenoper*-like photography, or the audacious art direction which revels in such strokes as the vast hall of Jekyll's house with its single slender ten-foot-high candlestick on a central dais. This fifty-year-old film has excitement and ingenuity in every frame: there is no way at all in which it could be improved by the techniques of the eighties.

Dr Jekyll and Mr Hyde. US 1931; monochrome; 85 minutes (reissue version). Produced and directed by Rouben Mamoulian for Paramount. Written by Samuel Hoffenstein and Percy Heath, from the novel by Robert Louis Stevenson. Photographed by Karl Struss. Music from Schumann's *Aufschwung*. Art direction by Hans Dreier. With Fredric March as Dr Henry Jekyll; Miriam Hopkins as Ivy; Rose Hobart as Muriel; Holmes Herbert as Lanyon; Edgar Norton as Poole; Halliwell Hobbes as General Carew.

Just Wait Till He Gets Through with It
Duck Soup

The shyster president of Freedonia insults the ambassador of neighbouring Sylvania, and the countries go to war.

The Marx Brothers themselves always professed to prefer their MGM vehicles, with their high expensive gloss and contrasting romantic angles, to their earlier Paramount 'menagerie' romps (*Animal Crackers*, *Monkey Business*, *Horse Feathers*, *Duck Soup* – none of the titles having any relevance to the contents, even though behind the credits of the last-named four ducks are seen quacking in a simmering pot). Well, that just shows how much *they* knew. The MGMs certainly had magical moments and generously staged action climaxes, but the pure undiluted essence of these primitive zanies, for whom nothing is sacred, is to be found in the earlier movies with their abhorrence of love interest, their loathing of establishment ethics, and their generally unswerving endorsement of corruption, incompetence and greed. *Duck Soup* doesn't even pause for the accustomed musical interludes by Chico and Harpo, though sharp eyes may spot the point at which they appear to have been intended; but it does have excellent music and lyrics by Bert Kalmar and Harry Ruby. As these undervalued gentlemen also wrote the script, and performed similar services for the almost equally spell-binding *Horse Feathers*, they may well be considered the most formative source of Marxian onslaughts on the values of the early thirties.

The reason for the low esteem in which the brothers held *Duck Soup* is undoubtedly its poor performance at the box office, which almost cost them their Hollywood careers; luckily salvation came along in the form of Irving Thalberg, whom Chico met in a card game. It was at the Cambridge Film Society in 1950 that I first encountered *Duck Soup*. This august body, over a thousand strong, used to meet in the Central Cinema on Sunday mornings, and to enter the wide and sweet-smelling circle at 10.25 was to be deafened by the rustle of six hundred copies of the *Sunday Times* and blinded by the whiteness of newsprint held in undergraduate fists. I still have the programme for that memorable morning, but it gives little impression of the permanent and renewable joy the movie would bring. In answer to many requests Paramount had condescended to strike just one print of *Duck Soup*. It must have cost all of forty quid. It staggered round the art houses and film societies of Britain until it ran minutes short from splices, and it was an insult to ask money to see it: during my three-year tenancy of local cinemas, from 1953 to 1956, it must have had a score of bookings, first as feature and then as support, but although Paramount, knowing a good thing when they saw one, insisted on maximum percentages, they persistently refused to authorize another print. Luckily the negative, as may be seen from recent television transmissions, remained in first-class order.

DUCK SOUP. The new president of Freedonia shows his courtiers a thing or two

After that first screening I had to admit to a slight nagging feeling of depression, although my sides ached from laughing. The brothers' last film, the abysmal *Love Happy*, had just been released, and one knew that they were washed-up old men. To see them now so buoyant at the apogee of their careers was somewhat too sharp a contrast. But at second viewing – and the Film Society hurriedly arranged one – *Duck Soup* could be confirmed as a comic masterpiece of its own time, a time when dictators were raging in Europe (Harpo deliberately changed his real name from Adolph to Arthur), diplomats were failing to restrain the power-hungry or even to foresee the approaching cataclysm, and meanwhile the rich got richer and the unemployed stood in line. It isn't a sustained satire, more a satirical farce or even a war-themed *Hellzapoppin*, but it takes canny shots at all these elements and the Marxes themselves were not only at their most unfettered but had a director who shared their iconoclastic tendencies. Moreover their favourite foil, the stately

107

Margaret Dumont (Groucho claimed she never even understood their jokes, which was why she seemed able to rise above his insults with such dignity), had a central role as the millionairess who agrees to save the bankrupt country provided they appoint as president the celebrated Rufus T. Firefly. (We never do find out how he took her in, but he accepts with alacrity, and the cabinet is forced to concur.) At the posh function arranged to introduce him he is given an elaborate fanfare entrance, but after the third attempt we discover that he's still in bed. A fireman's pole gets him to the ceremony in double quick time, and he is shortly observed skulking behind the ballet girls who have been strewing flower petals in his expected path.

MRS TEESDALE: Oh, your excellency!
FIREFLY: You're not so bad yourself.
MRS TEESDALE: As chairwoman of the reception committee, I extend the good wishes of every man, woman and child in Freedonia.
FIREFLY: Never mind that stuff. Take a card. That's all right, you can keep it. I've got fifty-one left.

The badinage is incessant, though curiously for several shots in the middle of this scene Groucho sports a grey coat with black braid instead of the tails in which he entered, suggesting that the original script was telescoped after shooting.

MRS TEESDALE: Promise me you'll follow in the footsteps of my husband.
FIREFLY: Not that I care, but where is your husband?
MRS TEESDALE: Why, he's dead.
FIREFLY: I'll bet he's just using that as an excuse.
MRS TEESDALE: I was with him till the end.
FIREFLY: No wonder he passed away.
MRS TEESDALE: I held him in my arms and kissed him.
FIREFLY: So it was murder! Will you marry me? Did he leave you any money? Answer the second question first.
MRS TEESDALE: He left me his entire fortune.
FIREFLY: Is that so? Can't you see what I'm trying to tell you? I love you.

He rapidly adopts similar tactics with the Sylvanian ambassador, who accepts them less graciously.

TRENTINO: Your excellency, haven't I seen you somewhere before?
FIREFLY: I'm not sure I'm seeing you now. It must be something I ate.

And with the glamorous vamp: 'I could dance with you till the cows come home. On second thoughts, I'll dance with the cows and you come home.'

When Mrs Teesdale reproachfully tells him that the eyes of the world are upon him, he is playing hopscotch, and by the end of the scene all his new supporters have dashed off in a huff, whatever that is; but knowing that the script will have them back next morning, Firefly is not prevented from singing and dancing his unashamed manifesto:

> The last man nearly ruined this place
> He didn't know what to do with it;
> If you think this country's bad enough now,
> Just wait till I get through with it.

Pause for breath, and to meet Harpo and Chico, who for purposes of plot are spies for the other side: though Harpo's chief concern is to keep his scissors busy cutting off cigars, neckties and the tails of the ambassador's coat, and the plot is carelessly pushed aside while they both do a hilarious hat routine with a lemonade vendor played by Edgar Kennedy, he of the slow burn. The almost transparent Zeppo has already been introduced as Firefly's ineffective amanuensis, his finest moment being his entrance wearing half a hat after meeting Harpo in the corridor. Meanwhile Groucho is holding a cabinet meeting:

FIREFLY: Gentlemen, what we have to look for is a treasurer.
MINISTER: But you appointed one only last week.
FIREFLY: That's the one I'm looking for.

We shortly reach a high spot in which Groucho, in his nightshirt and nightcap but with cigar, is impersonated for reasons I can't entirely remember by both Chico and Harpo, both pretending to be his reflections in a broken mirror. This hallowed routine originated with Max Linder, and Harpo returned to it in the sixties in an episode of *I Love Lucy*, but it never worked so well as here.

The finale is a fast-moving sequence of war gags, the brothers in different costumes each time they appear. Told that 'General Smith reports a gas attack', Firefly's advice is 'Tell him to take a teaspoon of bicarbonate of soda in half a glass of water.' Chicolini as Secretary of War is not up to snuff:

FIREFLY: Don't you realize we're facing disastrous defeat? What are you going to do about it?
CHICOLINI: I've done it already. I've changed to the other side.

When Mrs Teesdale appears behind the lines to build their morale, Groucho sends off his men with a stirring speech: 'And remember, men, you're fighting for this woman's honour – which is probably more than she ever did!' And when she begins to sing the national anthem, they all throw rocks at her for a fadeout.

All this is merely scratching the surface of a hectic movie which tried not to let ten seconds pass by without a gag. As will have been noted, it is mainly Groucho's field day, for of all their films this is most clearly built round his irresponsible, irrepressible character with its penchant for verbal insult and near-the-knuckle innuendo. 'This shall be a gala day,' announces Mrs Teesdale. 'Well,' says Groucho, leering at the audience, 'a gal a day's all I can manage.' My other favourite line from this cavalcade of invective is: 'Excuse me while I brush the crumbs out of my bed, I'm expecting company.' I've been using it for years.

Harpo and Chico get a better share of the limelight in the other Paramount movies, Chico with some notable fractured English and illogical logic in *Animal Crackers*, and Harpo with some gargoyle-like facial contortions in *Monkey Business*. But it is always Groucho who can be relied on to steal a scene, even when merely hiding in a lady's wardrobe. 'Hey, what are you doing in there?' she calls, bemused. He opens the door and ogles her. 'Nothing. Come on in.' The later Marxian epics will be considered on another page, but it is worth noting here that when at the end of their careers Harpo got himself pride of place in *Love Happy*, and Groucho provided only a disenchanted narration, the balance was fatally wrong and nobody laughed, especially as Harpo had decided to take a leaf from Chaplin's book and become a lovable clown instead of a cheerful satyr. Marxism has a hard edge, and sympathy for the protagonists is not required: its essence, a kind of farcical nihilism, is expressed by Groucho in *Horse Feathers*, singing his way into the office of college president:

> For years before my son was born
> I used to yell from night till morn
> Whatever it is, I'm against it.

And I've been yelling since I first commenced it,
   I'm against it.

Duck Soup. US 1933; monochrome; 68 minutes. Produced for Paramount. Written by
Bert Kalmar and Harry Ruby, with additional dialogue by Arthur Sheekman and
Nat Perrin. Directed by Leo McCarey. Photographed by Henry Sharp. Music and
lyrics by Kalmar and Ruby. Edited by Leroy Stone. Art direction by Hans Dreier and
Wiard B. Ihnen. With the four Marx Brothers; Margaret Dumont as Mrs Teesdale;
Louis Calhern as Trentino; Edgar Kennedy as lemonade vendor; Raquel Torres as
Vera Marcal.

Hat, Cane and Baggy Pants
Easy Street and A Dog's Life

*A tramp becomes a policeman and cleans up a rough street. He
also fends off starvation with the help of a dog.*

I never really liked Charlie. I liked the tramp well enough, but even
from the first Chaplin film I saw – which was *Easy Street*, on 8mm in
a tent for a penny at a garden fete – I suspected that the amiable
character was assumed, that under the make-up was quite another
person, someone autocratic and boastful and rather mean, sentimental and preachy without the wisdom to temper his judgements,
brilliantly talented in a wholly natural way, proud of his success but
resentful of his low beginnings. All of these suspicions came to have
some foundation: Chaplin stage-managed his career well enough to
make each film an event until in the 1940s his faults began to
outweigh his virtues: then political exile and paternity suits and a
rather too self-revelatory autobiography brought about a whimpering climax to a famous career. He had lived too long, and in his later
films it became all too obvious that he had insisted too often on his
own way instead of welcoming advice from other talents. *A King in
New York* and *A Countess from Hong Kong* are among the most painful
experiences I have had in a cinema; and seeing them now, one
wonders what one ever saw in *Limelight* or *Monsieur Verdoux*.

Of his extreme liking for money, even against his own best
interests, I had one particular and personal experience. Around his
seventy-fifth birthday he arranged through United Artists a reissue
of three early shorts under the title *The Chaplin Revue*. At the time

111

I was devising a weekly television programme called *Cinema*, and would have liked to pay a birthday tribute, but the publicists announced that Chaplin was prohibiting any clips or trailers from being used, expecting his own name to be all the attraction that was needed. There was no way of mounting a half-hour programme without clips; but an influential friend of the great man encouraged me to approach him personally, and in those days I was game for anything. He was staying at the Savoy, and to my surprise the hotel switchboard put me through without demur. An unmistakable high-pitched voice said 'Hello' and took my breath away for a moment. I babbled my story about a tribute programme, and mentioned our mutual friend.

'Oh dear,' said Mr Chaplin, 'I hope you weren't expecting me to appear.'

'Well, of course we would love it, but I understand you don't care for being interviewed, so we would be very happy to settle for a few clips from *The Chaplin Revue*. We think it would help the release.'

'I see. How many scenes would you want?'

'Would three be too many? One from each film? Quite short ones, about three minutes each. Or less.'

'Mm. Well, I think it should be possible to help you. If you will be so kind as to ring my agent tomorrow – Mr Al Parker, that is – he will make the arrangements. I'll speak to him meanwhile.'

I rang off with profuse thanks. Puffed with pride, I dined out on the conversation that evening. Next day I rang Mr Parker and reported my conversation with his star.

'Oh yes,' said Mr Parker, 'he told me. You can have any three clips you like, and his fee will be twenty thousand pounds.'

The programme was not made.

Chaplin's technique of reissuing his films one at a time, at three-year intervals, with much drum beating, paid off handsomely throughout his middle age and concealed the fact that his last really satisfactory film was *Modern Times*, made in 1936. Before that, his only feature-length films were *The Kid*, *The Gold Rush*, *The Circus* and *City Lights*, and now that we can see them in a complete retrospective they seem considerably diminished. They all contain marvellous things, but none of them evokes the audience ecstasy of Keaton's *The General* or the warmth of Laurel and Hardy's *Sons of the Desert*. It became increasingly difficult for an acknowledged multi-millionaire to play a tramp, especially as he clearly revelled in all that the world could offer. Even as early as 1921, the poverty-stricken milieu he used for *The Kid* was bathed in a fake sentimental glow, and by the time he trotted it out again for *Modern Times* it was absurdly out of date.

It is to the early two-reelers that one must return for the essence of Chaplin's genius, for when he made them he could remember what it was like to be poor, and the mass audience knew it and could identify with him. Once they both grew affluent, they regarded each other with mutual suspicion and apathy. The tramp is essentially young and resilient: middle age would have found him either cynical or downtrodden. He resents being put upon, but his wants are few: a little cabin and a girl to look after it and grow old with him. He can be found in any milieu, but *Easy Street* is perhaps the most melodramatic. Here in this urban ghetto the squalor and the danger are real: families are oversized, hygiene is clearly unknown, and drug addicts are a common sight. The heavy is a real hulking menace whose head suffers not one whit from repeated truncheon blows and who has to be overcome, in typically ingenious tramp fashion, by being gassed with the lamp-post which he himself has bent as a demonstration of his strength. Charles is rewarded by being transformed from a cocky tramp into a cocky cop of the Keystone variety: we take our leave of a pillar of lower-class respectability, linking arms with the splendidly Victorian Edna Purviance on their way to the Salvation Army service. It is a marvellous short, full of acute observation and blinding fun; the social message is clear enough without Chaplin's having to break it over our heads as he later did in such misguided moments as the speech at the end of *The Great Dictator*.

If it had not been unfair to choose a Chaplin with no moral pretensions at all, I would have elected as my favourite either *The Adventurer*, which is pure farce, or *The Cure*, a comic ballet about a spa at which alcohol gets into the water. In the latter Chaplin has a way with a revolving door which seems almost like perpetual motion. I am even fond of the first two reels of *The Circus*, a muted film as a whole, far from strong enough for its own pretensions. (Chaplin's name appears six times on the credits, and one imagines he was furious at having to admit that Rollie Totheroh was responsible for the photography.) The first twenty minutes however

EASY STREET. Charlie is about to be reformed by the Salvationists

form a marvellously amusing episode in the old manner, with
Chaplin as the tramp on the run from the law. The pocket picking;
the mirror maze; the Noah's Ark with Chaplin as an animated
wooden figure; the circus roundabout; the conjuror's cabinet; the
cop chase; the rehearsal; the sleeping lion; the horse pill accidentally
swallowed; the ballet up a pole; the belligerent mule; all these are
perfectly timed for maximum effect, but alas, there follows a long
pause for sentiment, and the climactic slapstick with monkeys on
the high wire is simply unworthy of him.

Of the other features, *The Gold Rush* and *City Lights* have their
moments, but the sentiment, though here intermittent, again seems
too thickly laid on. As for *Modern Times*, after the magnificent
opening with Charlie going berserk in a factory, it dwindles into a
succession of half-thought-out routines which are not quite salvaged
by the walk-into-the sunrise fadeout.

My personal favourite of all Chaplin pictures is the little-known *A
Dog's Life*. It comes from the beginning of his middle period, so a

sufficient budget was available to make it slicker than his primitives, yet the half-hour running time allows no possibility of excess. The tramp is discovered at dawn, sleeping snugly in the open air behind a fence, with a loose board as draught protector. The stray dog, Scraps, a worldly and attractive black-eyed specimen, is asleep nearby in a paint pail; awake or asleep, his acting in this film is every bit as expressive as the star's. Charlie wakes up when a wad of paper keeps blowing out of its hole and causing a draught, and a passing cop decides to arrest him for vagrancy. There ensues a quick-fire ballet with every variation that can be worked on two men and a fence; the tramp runs round it, rolls under it, uses a hinged section to slap the cop's posterior or to hurtle himself to the other side, gooses the cop through it, unties his shoelaces under it. It is a sequence you can hardly fail to applaud; the dog merely waits his turn.

Charlie has another sequence to himself, trying to get in line at the labour exchange. He is always in the right place at the wrong time, or vice versa; every fleabitten tramp in the neighbourhood beats him to the available jobs. On emerging with a sigh, he is in time to save the dog from a fight, and poochie is grateful. He feeds it on milk by dipping its tail in a near-empty bottle and letting it lick off the drops. He tries to steal a cake for it from the nearest coffee stall: always the food is halfway delivered when the proprietor looks round, and Charlie has to cram it into his mouth and keep smiling, or pretend to be swatting a fly. Eventually the proprietor's suspicions bubble over into fury, but again it is the passing cop who gets slapped. Charlie escapes to a seedy dance hall – were they really like this in his childhood at the Elephant and Castle? – and in order to get the dog in, stuffs it down his trousers. Its wagging tail sticks out through a hole in the seat, and the helpless laughter which greets the ensuing sequence can be imagined. The room is filled with Chaplinesque types; bald pianist, bearded artist, middle-aged tart, a huge woman with a minute man, and a saintly singer with whom Charlie promptly falls in love. (Her song is so sad that the bartender promptly replaces, between tears, the money he has stolen from the till.) The plot now obtrudes with a lost wallet, which the dog is responsible for finding, recovering from thieves, and restoring to its rightful owner, and this includes a hilarious sequence of Charlie trying to get it back by coshing a cardplayer and then crouching so that his own arms emerge from the silent partner's armpits: the effect has to be seen to be believed. But let us leave the tramp, and his bride, one rosy dawn a year later, as they bend over a cot, smile benignly on the new arrivals, and listen to the patter of tiny paws.

Easy Street. US 1917; monochrome; silent; 22 minutes approx. Produced for Mutual. Written and directed by Charles Chaplin. Photographed by William C. Foster and Rollie Totheroh.

A Dog's Life. US 1918; monochrome; silent; 27 minutes. Produced for First National. Written and directed by Charles Chaplin. Photographed by Rollie Totheroh.

A Musical Education
Fantasia

Leopold Stokowski conducts the Philadelphia Orchestra in a concert of eight classical pieces, which are given cartoon interpretations.

It was my first visit to London, and my mother knew even less about the place than I did. It was 1941, and bombs were expected to fall. To me however our safety was somewhat less important than a visit to the New Gallery Cinema in Regent Street to see *Fantasia*, which was not scheduled for provincial release until the following year, if indeed such a 'highbrow' work ever made it to Bolton at all. The seats cost one and tenpence each – all of 9p in modern money – but we felt justified in our extravagance to see a film which was clearly so special. We went in during the Dance of the Sugar Plum Fairy, and sat entranced on the left-hand side of the centre aisle. It was a thin house, but scattered applause was heard as the item ended, with genteel laughter for the Chinese Dance as interpreted by mushrooms. We were enraptured by the whole of *The Nutcracker Suite*, a miracle of light and dancing patterns. Next came Mickey Mouse in *The Sorcerer's Apprentice*, the movie's closest concession to popular taste, but clearly superior in style and concept to the average Mickey adventure. It did nothing however to prepare us for the breathtaking power of *The Rite of Spring*, presented as an account of the rise and fall of prehistoric life. I had recently been reading H. C. F. Morant's *Whirlaway*, an admirable introduction to the age of

FANTASIA. The fight of the dinosaurs from *The Rite of Spring*

the dinosaur, so I was able to point out iguanadons and pterodactyls and *Tyrannosaurus rex*. The intermission brought a rather facetious interview with the sound track, which we felt let down the side a little; nor did we greatly care for the mythical gods and beasts of Beethoven's *Pastoral Symphony*, especially as they were presented in such a chocolate boxy style. Much more to our taste was the interpretation of the *Dance of the Hours* as a ballet for the world's most clumsy animals. Then, most marvellously, came Mussorgsky's *Night on a Bare Mountain*, with the Devil unfolding his wings from a giant rock and conducting a flaming sabbat performed by rubbery ghosts pulled out from shadowed graves. We disapproved of the way this tamely faded into a rather dim and formal *Ave Maria*, but at least the latter was brief and formed a suitable coda. We waited breathlessly through the newsreel for the magic to start again and were fascinated by the abstractions, something we had not previously experienced, which decorated Bach's *Toccata and Fugue in D Minor*. After watching the Dukas piece again, it was with great reluctance that we picked our way through the blackout to Waterloo; and when nearly a year later the film did reach Bolton, we were first in the queue.

Forty years later, I still don't know much about classical music, but all I do know germinated in this one visit to a cinema. When first released, *Fantasia* was caviare to the general because it told no story; now, I'm informed, it is hailed by young audiences as the ultimate trip. I saw it several times in the forties, then for years refused to visit it because it was turned into a SuperScope attraction by the simple expedient of cutting off the tops and bottoms of the images. At last, in the late seventies, it was restored to its proper ratio, and proceeded to break box office records at the Haymarket Odeon and points north, no doubt taking many times more cash than it did forty years earlier.

Is it still the wonder box of my youth? Well, it may be true that Disney's marvellous artists, of whom Otis Ferguson said that there isn't a snail or a puppy dog's tail that they can't give character or expression to, were most at home with more full-blooded concepts. The atmosphere of *Fantasia* is a little chill, a little rarefied, a little self-conscious; the immense skill is undeniable, but it is the music rather than the animation which evokes emotion and sympathy. It also seems now to be a misjudgement that the first two pieces are virtually abstract, unless one counts flowers and fairies as characters. Perhaps Mickey Mouse should have narrated in place of the disembodied Deems Taylor (of whom I know little else save that in 1943 he edited a Pictorial History of the Movies). On its own account however the Toccata and Fugue is still a most interesting illustration of what can be done with moving shapes and rolling sounds, its most interesting motifs being violin bows and bridges set against heavy waves, with one almost subliminal shot of what appears to be an upended coffin rocking its way into a cavern. The Nutcracker Suite now looks too much like more of the same, a succession of visual patterns woven by fairies, most notably in the form of frost, edging the landscape with white spikes, or gossamer webs being strewn with diamond dew in a world where the calyx of a flower can become a prima ballerina and leaping cossacks are finally recognizable as thistle stalks.

By this point in my 1981 reappraisal, I was aware that I could not be complimentary about the print on show. It was quite free of splices or scratches, and the music came through loud and clear, but

I had forgotten that Technicolor long ago abandoned its original three-strip process and with it any hope of reproducing the sharp and brilliant colours which were so essential to my enjoyment of *Fantasia* in 1941. Modern printing from a combined internegative can produce no more than a dingy facsimile of the original, with all the primary hues distorted and discoloured into an unattractive spectrum more suitable to a funeral than to a celebration. With many cartoons this would matter only marginally, but it knocks *Fantasia*'s subtleties for six: brightly lit scenes become hard and harsh, darker ones disappear into a grey-green mist and at several points we might have been watching a blank screen. Like so much in modern life, this is an example of progress backwards, the entertainment I received for £2.70 in 1981 was considerably less than I had had for 9p in 1941. For the young, the true brilliance of the pioneer work may now be not only unimaginable but unattainable.

At its best, the artistry of *Fantasia* is such as to make you disbelieve that you are watching a drawing. So swift and smooth are the imaginative transitions that, in these days of semi-animated yakkity-yak TV cartoonery one cannot imagine that animators once expended such time, energy and finesse to create an art form which has now been debased into a routine craft. In *The Sorcerer's Apprentice*, for instance, the choice of angle, expression and movement is so apt as to involve the spectator irresistibly in Mickey's plight. The magical animation of the hacked-up bits of broomstick sends a chill down the spine, and the wizard's final quelling of the flood is a masterfully moving image, with particularly apt timing in the last few seconds. Here as elsewhere in the film the bringing to apparent life of large amounts of flowing water is a major achievement in itself.

The Rite of Spring seems better than ever: in ten minutes we are given a complete scientific account of prehistory, and Disney's men allot to ungainly monsters a truly amazing grace. But the *Pastoral* is still uncomfortable when interpreted as Greek myth. The drawing seems now even thicker and cruder, the colours loud and shrill. The galumphing centaurs, the cute centaurettes (with breasts but no nipples) and the revolting Mickey Rooney-style cupids are redeemed only by a charming family of winged horses and by a brief but magnificent storm sequence, with Vulcan hurling down thunderbolts and Zeus finally tiring of the sport and pulling a chunk of black cloud over himself like an eiderdown.

By now one is conscious that one has sat through hundreds of single frames which, properly mounted, would in themselves be considerable works of art. The *Dance of the Hours* is an unqualified comic triumph, its irresistible music set to a farcical sequence of ostriches, hippos, elephants and magnificently saturnine crocodiles in ballet shoes, most of them at one point blown away like balloons. And the Walpurgisnacht of *Night on a Bare Mountain* remains Disney's most menacing melodramatic sequence, a fragment of Grimm's Fairy Tales for adults, enacted by assorted demons and a selection of local mittel-European dead. Its gleeful diabolism is scarcely countered by the *Ave Maria*, which now seems more anaemic than ever, giving the faded impression of old water colour rather than the richness of stained glass. It provides a regrettably anti-climactic end for so rich and varied a concert.

The place of Disney in cinema history has long been underrated, perhaps because his skills can't easily be compared with those of Welles or Lubitsch or Lean. In the thirties, though, the public certainly recognized his qualities; the short cartoons were often more popular than the features they nominally supported, and when the feature cartoons began with *Snow White and the Seven Dwarfs* they were treated as conversation pieces, almost as miraculous events. If I had to name his masterpiece it would be *Pinocchio*, for here music and sentiment and melodrama and characterization were perfectly blended in a timeless plot superbly backed by animation so evocative that you could almost smell the Bavarian forests. (Disney's own ancestry was German, and in whatever story he was telling the backgrounds and characters tended to look Teutonic.) Millions have grown up dreaming of the blue fairy and Old Gepetto the puppet maker, who was rescued from the belly of Monstro the whale, and especially of J. Worthington Foulfellow, the crafty fox who entices young Pinocchio away from home with dreams of simple glory:

> Hey, diddle de dee,
> An actor's life for me!
>> You tour the world in a private car,
>> You dine on chicken and caviare,
>> You smoke a pipe and a big cigar,
> An actor's life for me!

It is hard when an artist's audience expects of him nothing less than perfection. After the early forties Disney ceased to give it: themes were running thin and despite the sentimental triumph of *Bambi*, the story of a forest deer, he could no longer afford the meticulous creative processes involved in his best work. In order to keep solvent, the studio had to churn out entertainment at a rate which precluded the highest forms of inspiration. He became more commercial, which is not in itself a bad thing, but he was now *following* the public pulse rather than leading it. His instincts had not been commercial in the first place, and so he was less exact in his knowledge of the lowest common denominator of public taste than were, say, the creators of Bugs Bunny and Tom and Jerry. The family audience, always his mainstay, moved across to television; half of him moved with it, the other turned to animal documentaries and live action adventures, all fairly good of their kind but seldom the absolute classics expected of him. By the time he died in 1965, the truest expression of the Disney spirit was not on celluloid at all, but in the marvellous inventiveness and precision of Disneyland, a funfair unmatched anywhere in the world. Dopey and Dumbo and Jiminy Cricket would have loved it.

Fantasia. US 1940; Technicolor; 135 minutes (original version). Produced by and for Walt Disney. Supervisor, Ben Sharpsteen. Music direction by Edward H. Plumb.

A Rendezvous with La Duchesse de Guermantes
Father Brown

A parish priest retrieves a priceless artefact from a master thief.

Quirky, donnish and as literate as a *Times* crossword puzzle, *Father Brown* is undoubtedly the kind of movie they don't make any more, and you'd be darned lucky to find on television anything so quizzically acted, so lightly scholarly, so gleamingly polished in its comedy pace and timing. Not that it's a perfect film: there are *longueurs* when you long to stick pins into it, and certainly the narrative stops once or twice too often for irrelevant jokes. But this was true of such masters in a similar field as M. R. James, John

Collier and even Saki, and it is certainly true of the original stories of G. K. Chesterton from one of which, *The Blue Cross*, Thelma Schnee has fashioned this glowingly affectionate script, every foot of which has freshness and charm. For once the movies have produced a recognizable facsimile of a slightly recherché literary character, in this case a shortsighted little man of God who is fascinated by crime and detection but more concerned to save the criminal's soul than to hand him over to earthly justice; in his quest he is sustained by insatiable curiosity, by an amplitude of biblical quotations and by a sufficiency of Cadbury's Dairy Milk chocolate.

A later TV series about the character didn't come off, even with the wiles of Kenneth More to assist it, but in 1954 Alec Guinness was riding the crest of his particular wave of international popularity, and the 'angel with the flaming umbrella' was an amiable amalgam of his diffident inventor in *The Man in the White Suit*, his determined moneymaker in *The Card*, and his ancient cleric in *Kind Hearts and Coronets*, a sort of portmanteau Guinness performance. They might however have removed the script's references to his being fat; the original was, but Mr Guinness as filmed simply isn't.

The bemusing flavour of this somewhat unlikely entertainment comes up after nearly thirty years as freshly aromatic as new paint, which makes it a pity that problems of copyright have prevented the discerning public from seeing it for quite a while. Its similarity to an Ealing comedy is reinforced from the very credit titles by the tiptoe music of Georges Auric, which comes close to being a rip-off from his own score for *The Titfield Thunderbolt* the previous year; also by the subtle directorial presence of Robert Hamer and by our early glimpse of Sid James as a startled burglar making a getaway just as police cars roar down the street. Still at the open safe, however, is a strange little man dressed as a priest, and he is hurried down to the police station and accused of being on the premises for a burglarious purpose. He contradicts this politely: he was there for a *non*-burglarious purpose. He was putting the money back, having persuaded the thief to hand it over. Officialdom is unconvinced.

SERGEANT: Name?
F.B.: Brown.
SERGEANT: Sure it isn't Smith?
F.B.: No, no. Ignatius Brown, after Saint Ignatius Loyola, you know.

His belongings are counted out:

SERGEANT: One bible.
F.B. (*correcting*): One breviary.
SERGEANT (*firmly*): One book.

The little man asks permission to keep his glasses. 'I'm as blind as a bat without them. Though I often wonder whether all bats are blind, any more than all lords are drunk or all judges sober.'

Despairing of finding out the truth, the sergeant rings Scotland Yard: 'Get me "known to operate disguised as clergymen", will you?'

Freed eventually by the testimony of a sardonic monsignor, the priest is free to continue the process of converting the shamefaced Sid, who is hanging about outside the police station: 'I am disappointed in you. Not only did you do wrong, you did wrong in the wrong way. You are clearly incapable of earning a dishonest living: why not experiment with an honest one?'

By settling Sid down as chauffeur to a titled widow, Father Brown has again set his little corner of the world to rights. It is a calm and ordered corner close to London's river, suggesting the twenties rather than the fifties: everything is in its place and the whole cast goes to church on Sunday. The priest is the only paradox, eager to learn the skill of picking pockets and taking impromptu ju-jitsu lessons on the lawn outside his lych-gate. From this uncommon pursuit he is called to his bishop, who wishes to warn him that his revered blue cross, a relic of St Augustine, is likely to be stolen while on its way to Rome for an international church conference. The mysterious master criminal Flambeau is the suspected culprit-to-be. 'Flambeau?' asks Father Brown. 'Oh, I should so like to meet him.' 'The purpose of this visit is to frustrate such an encounter,' sighs the bishop.

Father Brown sees danger in the police plan for an ostentatious guard; surely it would be better if he carried the cross himself? ('Where do you hide a tree? In a forest. Where do you hide a priest? In a whole forest of priests.') The bishop demurs: Scotland Yard must be allowed to know best.

F.B.: But this is lunacy, my lord!
BISHOP: Father Brown, you will leave the matter in the lunatic hands of the

FATHER BROWN. Flambeau, in heavy disguise, is followed into the Paris catacombs by the intrepid parish priest. Alec Guinness, Peter Finch

inspector and myself. Scotland Yard will keep you informed of our further insane decisions. Good morning.

Needless to say, the priest determines to take the law into his own hands and sets off for Rome clutching at five brown paper parcels. Everybody on the train to Dover is a suspect, except a friendly bearded priest with whom he is able to exchange biblical aphorisms. Could Flambeau be the fellow who advises, as a guard against seasickness, two lightly boiled eggs and half a bottle of champagne? Probably not: he is as sick as the rest of them. By the time they are settled in the French train, the bearded priest has become Father Brown's aide in the search for Flambeau: 'any man may be he'. This journey is replete with highly suspicious characters, including a heavily veiled widow and an officer of the French Foreign Legion given to airing his views in a manner reminiscent of Mr Jingle in *The Pickwick Papers*: 'Widows make the best wives. If you are better than their first, they are grateful; if you are worse, they are not surprised.'

But they are all false alarms: in Paris, when his new friend orders a ham sandwich on a Friday, Father Brown realizes that *he* must be Flambeau, and that the mysterious pursuers they are doing their best to evade must be the police. Even so he allows Flambeau to lure him down into the catacombs, tie him up and steal the cross, all for the sake of saving his soul. The latter, unfortunately, is a commodity not recognized by the thief: 'When I was a child I was stuffed with religion as a Strasbourg goose with grain. I have no appetite left.' Father Brown is helpless to do other than congratulate Flambeau on the thoroughness of his deception. 'If I may say so, a "smoke" of an almost Mozartian elegance and simplicity.'

Now at a low point of his career, both as detective and as priest, Father Brown develops another ruse. Lady Warren must put up for auction her priceless Cellini chess set, which will surely lure Flambeau into the open. The delightful scene which follows introduces more amusing red herrings, including a maharaja who arrives just as the bidding begins and bows deeply to the lady:

MAHARAJA: My apologies. My aeroplane was late.
LADY WARREN: How many aeroplanes have you?
MAHARAJA: About as many as I have elephants.

Proceeding to acquire the set for fifty thousand guineas, the maharaja pauses before flying away to give it back to Lady Warren as a small token of his esteem. Recognizing an aged attendant as Flambeau (because his hands are much younger than his face), Father Brown allows him to steal the set rather than hand him over to the police. The suave crook however has an eye for Lady Warren and returns it to her, but begs to be excused from a battle of philosophy with Father Brown, who, shrugging, contrives to steal his crested cigarette case while assuring him that: 'Although I wear funny clothes and have taken certain vows, I live far more in the world than you do.'

Flambeau having absented himself again, Father Brown's only hope of getting his cross back, and salvaging his own status, is to follow the clue of his crest, which is a torch (or *flambeau*). The trail takes him to the French National Archive and a delightful encounter with its doddering custodian the Vicomte de Verdigris; involving themselves in a hilarious *pas de deux*, they manage to break each other's eyeglasses. The ancient curator regrets that it will not be possible to resume the search that evening. 'I have a rendezvous,' he says confidentially, 'with la Duchesse de Guermantes.' Luckily Father Brown finds an optician, followed in double quick time by a torch-bearing wine bottle label which sends him on a train to Burgundy during the wine harvest. Here Flambeau is revealed to be the melancholy squire of a fairy-tale château, hiding his priceless loot in a secret room which also contains the rocking horse of his childhood: 'the largest private museum in the world'. Father Brown is close to proving the error of his ways when the police again turn up, and Flambeau with a shrug makes a graceful exit, his tracks being covered by the priest. The result is a Louvre exhibition (which Flambeau attends incognito) of the gigantic haul of stolen goods, followed by a coda in Father Brown's church as he recounts to his congregation the parable of the prodigal son. During the last verses, Flambeau steals in, to sit by Lady Warren; and Father Brown's smile is positively beatific as he concludes his sermon: 'And they began to be merry.'

Reviewing *Father Brown* in 1954, Penelope Houston remarked that it had 'a detached, sophisticated, highly civilized tone the more welcome because it is, in the British cinema, so uncommon'. How much more true today!

Father Brown. GB 1954; monochrome; 91 minutes. Produced by Paul Finder Moss and Vivian A. Cox for Facet Films. Written by Thelma Schnee and Robert Hamer. Directed by Robert Hamer. Photographed by Harry Waxman. Music score by Georges Auric. Art direction by John Hawkesworth. Edited by Gordon Hales. With Alec Guinness as Father Brown; Peter Finch as Flambeau; Joan Greenwood as Lady Warren; Cecil Parker as the bishop; Sid James as Parkinson; Bernard Lee as Inspector Valentine; Gerard Oury as Inspector Dubois; Marne Maitland as the Maharaja; Ernest Thesiger as the Vicomte; Noel Howlett as the auctioneer; Ernest Clark as Monsignor.

Ze Roo-bees
Gaslight

In the 1860s, in a house in London's Pimlico Square, an old lady is brutally murdered. Twenty years later the detective who had been in charge of the unsolved case recognizes the new tenant of the house next door as the old lady's nephew, and guesses correctly that he is still seeking the jewels for which he murdered her, and is trying to drive his wife mad because she has innocently stumbled on his real name. In the end, it is he who is seen to be insane.

It was on a Saturday afternoon in 1940, towards the end of Battle of Britain summer, that this unique and unexpected British melodrama first grasped my attention. It caused a mild family panic.

Performances at the Bolton Odeon were continuous, and normally began around 2.30 with the main feature. After that, two complete programmes of about three hours each brought one to closing time. I had not long been allowed to make independent excursions to the cinema, but there I was on my own, trotting down Ashburner Street and smartly attired for the purpose. My bag of Maltesers lasted through the first performance of *Gaslight*, which I thoroughly enjoyed, and an ice-cream launched me into the second feature, a long-forgotten Joe Penner comedy called *Glamour Boy*. Soon came the temptation: *Gaslight* began again. I stayed for five minutes, then ten; shortly I realized that there was no possibility of tearing myself away before the end titles came up at 7 P.M. Subconsciously I knew that my tea would have been waiting for an hour, that my mother would be worried; all to no avail, for I was hypnotized. When the lights finally went up I recovered my wits as quickly as I could and headed for the exit; only to bump into my mother, who had come down in search of me. We stared at each other and smiled. 'Are you hungry?' she said.

'Not specially.'

'I've brought a cold meat pie. And some Maltesers. And I've paid to come in, so I might as well stop.'

GASLIGHT. The lady is being driven mad by her husband ... he hopes.
Diana Wynyard, Anton Walbrook

'I'll stop with you, then.'

So it was that I saw *Gaslight* three times in the same day. I enjoyed it, too; and my mother always counted it among her favourite films.

To tell the truth it was not a very suitable film for an 11-year-old boy, even a film-struck one. It treats of murder and madness, and other less specified evils. For hero-villain it presents a man whose dark Victorian garments and sombre mien conceal a spirit fascinated by sin and depravity; for heroine-victim we have the wife whom he sadistically goads into hysterical self-doubt so that she will not be believed if she innocently gives away his guilty secret. But my fascination, even then, was less with the subject than with the style. Of course I silently cheered for Diana Wynyard as she finally wrested herself from her husband's clutches and watched the police take him away, a gibbering lunatic himself; but it was the men who mainly captured my attention. That burly northerner Frank Pettingell was ex-Inspector Rough, a retired detective who was accidentally enabled to solve the mystery in ways closed to the official force; it was the best part this fine actor ever had. But above all it was Anton Walbrook who hypnotized me with his snake-like performance as the errant husband, slowly hissing his every remark so that his wife started at the very sound of his voice, yet capable of chucking the housemaid under the chin and making an assignation with her under her mistress' very eyes. 'Ze roo-bies, Bella . . . give me ze roo-bies.'

No one who heard Walbrook utter this simple line can possibly forget what he did with it, twisting and drawing out each syllable to three times its length while the whites of his eyes rolled in close-up and a lock of hair dropped dankly across his forehead.

In its original play form *Gaslight* was very popular in America under the title *Angel Street* (a most mysterious change since the action clearly takes place in Pimlico Square). It was therefore not surprising when MGM bought up the rights to remake the property in 1944 as a vehicle for Ingrid Bergman, then riding the crest of the wave. Alas, though she won an Oscar for it, she was way over the top in her performance, fluttery and simple-minded where Wynyard had been basically resilient and questioning. Charles Boyer, though quite adequate, was simply not as interesting as Walbrook, while Rough was turned into a romantic nonentity to suit Joseph Cotten. At 114 minutes the thing was half an hour too long, and all it really had going for it was opulent décor and a general tastefulness.

For years it was thought that the negative of the 1939 film had been destroyed by MGM in order to protect the remake, but in the sixties a supposedly pirated print was shown at the National Film Theatre and much appreciated. Not until 1978, however could the rights be cleared for television. On a summer evening, as the spearhead of a BBC2 season of British films of the forties, there appeared on the home screen the famous title, its letters outlined in the flame of a dancing gas jet, followed by credits in slightly shaky printing such as might have been found on a Victorian handbill. Immediately we were plunged into a flavourful reconstruction of a Victorian Sunday, all respectability and humbug. Pre-breakfast prayers with the servants, followed by the stately parade of well-dressed families to and from church, were presented for our inspection in a manner entirely cinematic, the camera constantly on the move yet always in the right place to pick up a significant detail, the lustrous monochrome photography exuding a more sinister atmosphere than colour ever could. The plot and dialogue of the original play were now carefully followed, though the narrative had been considerably reshaped. Rough is introduced at once, and his suspicions and investigations run parallel to the events in the Mallen house, affording useful relief from the strained atmosphere of mental torture. His apparently chance encounter in the street with Mrs Mallen is adroitly engineered: he asks her to assist him in distributing toys to a gang of urchins. 'But I don't know you,' she says. He shrugs: 'This is charity, ma'am, that blows convention out of the window.' It would have been interesting to see Sydney Greenstreet in the role.

All the time a deft music score is underlining the action, and the main set of the little square, round which the lamplighter pads his way at dusk, is cleverly constructed to allow a series of travelling camera shots and to display not only the august church at one end but the slums around the corner at the other. Felicitous little touches abound. When one dowager says to another after Diana Wynyard has passed, 'Charming, charming, quite a complexion,' the camera and the actress are allowed to show from her expression that she has heard and is pleased at the compliment. Her dressing for dinner is covered by a quick sequence of dissolves showing one flouncy petticoat dropping over another. The can-can sequence featuring the Darmora Ballet is no more than a series of brief impressions, yet clever editing makes us feel we have witnessed a rich entertainment without holding up the suspenseful action of the plot. The final shot tracks back from the house all the way across the square until a gas lamp settles into close-up; the perfect image on which to fade away. This is in fact a perfect film in almost every sense: a one-set play has been subtly transformed into a superior example of the film as narrative art.

Although this is Thorold Dickinson's masterwork, and a fine transcription of a now classic play, it is the acting to which memory brings one back time and time again. The painful scenes in the first half, of a man coldly and deliberately driving his wife mad, culminate in Walbrook's suavity being ripped away as he fiercely seizes a chance to tell his wife: 'You will die, raving, in an asylum.' At this point the actor's eyes and lips seem as out of control as the character. But help is at hand. As she is left alone, murmuring to herself that her suspicions must have been a dream, the shadow of

Rough falls across the doorway and his voice booms out. 'Was I a part of this curious dream?' The audience cheers to itself at this point, for it knows that the villain's gig is up: from here on it is simply a matter of confronting and exposing him.

The triumph of *Gaslight* is all the more satisfactory because it is a masterpiece from a period when British studios were supposed not even to know the grammar of their trade. Even more remarkable, it is the work of a studio which never again reached the same creative standard, despite a fairly interesting output which included *Love on the Dole* and *Pimpernel Smith*. The final surprise is that it was produced during the frantic period which followed the outbreak of World War II, a time when the thoughts of the people might be expected to be on anything but Victorian melodrama.

In 1948 Thorold Dickinson had Walbrook mad again in period costume, this time trying to wrest from the devil the secret of winning at cards. Even the credit titles again used broken handbill-style type. But *The Queen of Spades*, though ravishing to look at, was dramatically insecure and took too long to get to its climax which, when it came, with Edith Evans' dead eye popping open to menace the marauder, was an undeniable masterstroke. The real trouble was that the audience never cared about the outcome.

Gaslight. GB 1940; monochrome; 88 minutes. Produced by John Corfield for British National. Written by A. R. Rawlinson and Bridget Boland, from the play by Patrick Hamilton. Directed by Thorold Dickinson. Photographed by Bernard Knowles. Music score by Richard Addinsell. Art direction by Duncan Sutherland. With Anton Walbrook as Paul Mallen; Diana Wynyard as Bella Mallen; Frank Pettingell as Inspector Rough; Cathleen Cordell as Nancy; Jimmy Hanley as Cobb; Robert Newton as Vincent Ullswater.

A Fine Romance
The Gay Divorcee and Top Hat

***At a holiday resort, mistaken identity causes an innocent
dancer to be labelled a Lothario, but true love prevails.***

In the first film the resort is 'Brightbourne' on the English south
coast, and in the other it is Venice; but otherwise the same
synopsis, and largely the same supporting players, will serve. But
no audience ever complained about being offered warmed-over
goods – the plot was not what they had come for. Their hope was
that for the price of admission they might gain temporary entrance
to a charmed world.

All the Astaire-Rogers musical comedies of the thirties had
pleasing segments, and *The Story of Vernon and Irene Castle* was a
uniformly effective piece of dramatic nostalgia in a more subdued
vein, but in the case of the two films mentioned above the very
titles bring a rosy glow to the cheeks of habitués. For here the
entire soufflé rose perfectly to provide unfaltering after-dinner
entertainment, and that at a length generally undreamed of in the
early thirties. To view them now is like opening a time capsule: the
nostalgic fragrance is almost unbearable. Based on a stage original,
The Gay Divorcee, with certain adjustments (including the title,
which gained an extra 'e' in deference to the Hays Office's feeling
that divorces should never be gay), worked so well on the screen
that *Top Hat* was immediately planned as a follow-up which would
shine with even more self-confidence but would otherwise stick as
closely as possible to the original mixture of light sophistication,
wisecracks and style against a nimble musical backing. As to which
is the best, that's an unanswerable question. *Top Hat* may have
most polish, and a few more good gags, but *The Gay Divorcee* has
'The Continental', which may be the most overwhelming musical
number ever filmed, and at seventeen minutes is certainly the
longest. Its mindless beat and rhythmic cadences are so infectious
that most people will be surprised to read among the credits below
that it isn't by Kern or Porter or Berlin but by two fellows called

THE GAY DIVORCEE. The chorus prepares to dance 'The Continental'

Con Conrad and Herb Magidson, who might charitably be called unknown. They got an Academy Award all the same.

Is it only to those who grew up in the thirties that the tunes in the Astaire-Rogers musicals seem so instantly whistleable, so freshly sophisticated, so achingly sweet? Could it be the plangent saxophones, with which orchestras of that decade were so overloaded, which gave every song a throatily suggestive, edgy appeal, like a happily purring cat? Or is it the understatement which seems so desirable when remembered from the age of punk rock? The lyrics were unassuming, the melodies simplicity itself, yet no more was needed to set the world dancing. Listen carefully to any one of these tunes and the odds are that you won't get it out of your head for days, for what is most irresistible about it is its clarity of structure. 'The Continental', for instance, consists basically of seven notes, once repeated and then slightly varied, all in soft shoe tempo, punctuated by an occasional yawning trombone phrase such as 'beautiful music' or 'kiss while you're dancing'. The dance is also an engagingly simple exercise for about a hundred performers, half in black and half in white, who come tapping on to an exterior ballroom floor in the approved Busby Berkeley tradition and give a pretty convincing demonstration of perpetual motion. What they actually do may lack imagination, but they do it repeatedly and hypnotically, with brief cutaways for breath and to keep the plot on the boil, for song and dance duets by the stars, and for comic verses by Erik Rhodes and Eric Blore. And the night is still, and the moon, though we don't glimpse it, has to be beautiful.

At RKO the numbers were always worked into the plot, not separated from it by footlights as was the rule at Warners and Fox. The plot usually needed the support; but such as they were, all the expected elements were firmly established in *The Gay Divorcee*. Meeting cute, initial rapport, misunderstandings, double entendres, and a repertory of friendly show-offs in comic support. Eric Blore repeats his stage bit as a baleful waiter, rolling monosyllables round his quivering lips. Erik Rhodes plays the professional co-respondent, whose motto is: 'Your wife is safe with Tonetti, he prefers spaghetti . . .' There is also Edward Everett Horton, improbably cast as a philanderer but providing his own incomparable form of comic dithering, and Alice Brady as the friend of the heroine whose advice is as unreliable as her memory. They are all fantasy figures from stage musical comedy – Horton and Betty Grable even have a beach number called 'Let's Knock Knees' – and indeed the best moments of the series took place in a never-never land which correspond even momentarily with the realities of the thirties. The stars' numbers are also *de rigueur*. A dance solo for him, a comedy routine for the pair of them, a major spectacle, and a dramatic/romantic duet, in this case 'Night and Day', which could scarcely be bettered even if the treatment is a bit glum.

Top Hat mostly takes place in a Venice which could never exist outside a sound stage: they might as well have called it Oz. Every structure in sight seems to be composed of white marble. The canals are sanitized, the gondoliers seem to have escaped from a fancy dress ball, the bridges have been borrowed from an Ivor Novello musical. Reality has been banished, even colour would be an intrusion, for this is a gleaming monochrome world with the occasional touch of stainless steel. Even the lyrics of Berlin's big number, 'The Piccolino', point up the fantasy:

It was written by a Latin –
A gondolier who sat in
His home out in Brooklyn
And gazed at the stars . . .

The number takes place in an enormous white set which one supposes must be a mad designer's interpretation of St Mark's Square; in its sublime idiocy it is matched only by the ship's engine room in *Shall We Dance*. But while Fred and Ginger are dancing around it, we care not: and we willingly make similar allowances for the script, which an uncharitable critic might fairly analyse as a collection of blithering inanities mouthed by people who should be smart enough to know better. The fact is that these people, and this production team, not only get away with it but would be grounded by wittier or more substantial lines. The mixture jells. While the picture lasts, and they all cavort around these elegant surroundings in their optimistic way, looking innocent and decorative, we welcome them as friendly relics from an age that never was. It is as though the bright young things of the twenties had been revived and purified, for these characters never have time for any actual sinning (they're too busy talking about it) and their heaviest alcohol consumption is of champagne cocktails well spaced by horse's necks. It is also like a charade played at an annual family party, for here is Blore again, as a valet who is always being sacked but proves his worth in the end; and here is Horton again, in what seems to be the same part; and here is Erik Rhodes again with a new motto: 'For the man the sword, for the woman the kiss.' Brady must have been busy, for Helen Broderick steps in as Horton's suspicious wife/Rogers' friend, and gives it all she's got.

For sheer comedy the pre-Venetian sequences of *Top Hat* are perhaps the best. We start in a sleepy London club which Astaire can't resist rousing on his way out by a few staccato taps on the parquet. His first number is 'No Strings', danced in the privacy of his hotel bedroom; when Ginger, below, complains that he's disturbing her sleep, he scatters sand and turns the dance into a soft shoe. Then there's the park, the rain, and 'Isn't It a Lovely Day', a joyous duet in a deserted bandstand. And so to Fred's most memorable solo, presented for once as a number from his show:

I'm putting on my top hat,
Tying on my white tie,
Dusting off my tails . . .

This is the image that made Fred a star and stuck with him all through his career, that of the cheerful, elegant man about town, lighting up the city with his optimism, delighting with the precision of his movement, setting an example for the world. No number on film is more exhilarating – unless it be Fred's own 'Putting on the Ritz' from *Blue Skies*.

Like MacDonald and Eddy, Astaire and Rogers paid the price of their own enormous popularity. The very best they could do seemed merely the same all over again, and no writer who came their way could rise above the required plot contrivances. *Follow the Fleet*, in the name of desperate novelty, miscasts Astaire as an able seaman; its plot is a suet pudding enlivened by such marvellous numbers as 'We Saw the Sea', 'Let's Face the Music and Dance' and 'I'm Putting All my Eggs in One Basket'. *Swing Time* returns to luxury but can't shake off a rusty, creaking plot about rival nightclubs and the pretence that Ginger is about to marry some Latin. (How could she?) The songs are choice if sparse: 'A Fine Romance', 'The Way You Look Tonight', and Fred's spectacular if somewhat dislikeable 'Bojangles of Harlem'. *Shall We Dance* looks expensive as all get out, but again the storyline hovers leadenly and even the numbers show signs of novelty for its own sake: roller skates for 'Let's Call the Whole Thing Off', masks for the title number. After disappointing returns the stars took a breather from each other, and when their return gambit was the brief and modest *Carefree* in which Fred's opening number with golf balls is about the best of a meagre ration: the big novelty number, 'The Yam', just didn't catch on. A recommended change of direction brought the Castle film with its re-creation of period dances, and then suddenly the glorious teaming was over: the war brought brasher and cruder musicals than these stars could handle. Besides, Ginger had acting ambitions, which so startled Hollywood that they gave her an Academy Award for *Kitty Foyle*. When in 1949 they got together again for *The Barkleys of Broadway* it was a dismal mistake, for though Fred was as nimble as ever she had become stately and entirely lacked the old mischief;

Oscar Levant walked off with what honours there were. Oddly enough, the nightclub act she perfected in her late sixties revealed a Ginger who, though plumper and less sprightly, more closely resembled the Ginger of the great days than anything she did on film after 1939; and despite her frequent disclaimers she was careful to choose a dancing partner who in a dim light could pass for Fred.

The Gay Divorcee. US 1934; monochrome; 107 minutes. Produced by Pandro S. Berman for RKO. Written by George Marion Jnr, Dorothy Yost and Edward Kaufman, from a musical play by Dwight Taylor. Directed by Mark Sandrich. Photographed by David Abel. Special effects by Vernon L. Walker. Music direction by Max Steiner. Songs: various. Art direction by Van Nest Polglase and Carroll Clark. Choreography by Dave Gould. With Fred Astaire as Guy Holden; Ginger Rogers as Mimi Glossop; Edward Everett Horton as Egbert Fitzgerald; Alice Brady as Hortense Ditherwell; Erik Rhodes as Tonetti; Eric Blore as waiter.

Top Hat. US 1935; monochrome; 100 minutes. Produced by Pandro S. Berman for RKO. Written by Dwight Taylor and Allan Scott. Directed by Mark Sandrich. Photographed by David Abel. Special effects by Vernon L. Walker. Songs by Irving Berlin. Art direction by Van Nest Polglase and Caroll Clark. Choreography by Hermes Pan. With Fred Astaire as Jerry Travers; Ginger Rogers as Dale Tremont; Edward Everett Horton as Horace Hardwick; Helen Broderick as Madge Hardwick; Erik Rhodes as Beddini; Eric Blore as Bates.

Golden Silence
The General

During the American Civil War a Southern train driver foils a Yankee plot to steal a locomotive.

It is perhaps remarkable, or perhaps not in the present joyless age, that a silent film more than fifty years old can still delight one by one's own fireside and positively convulse audiences at the National Film Theatre. But *The General* is a remarkable film, not merely a brilliantly designed star vehicle, but a comedy wholly imaginative in concept and innovative in detail, with more sight gags to the reel than Chaplin or even Stan Laurel ever dreamed of. It also happens to provide the most accurate movie reconstruction, not excluding *Gone with the Wind*, of the famous war of the 1860s; and its story is based on a true incident, later recounted more solemnly but less excitingly by Walt Disney in *The Great Locomotive Chase*.

The unsmiling Buster Keaton is now regarded as among the greatest performers in cinema history. His original audiences saw him simply as a funny man with a 'great stone face', who despite his unathletic build and his tendency to be accident-prone always proved sufficiently tenacious and indomitable to right the prevailing wrongs and win the girl. He seemed to be at his funniest when battling against immense mechanical or constructed objects, such as the ocean liner in *The Navigator* and the house in *One Week*: here his nemesis is also his pride and joy, the faithful steam locomotive called *The General*. By the end of the adventure we seem to know its foibles as well as we know Keaton's: trains have been used for physical comedy by every screen funny man you might name, but Keaton is the first and only practitioner to make the train a character with a personality all its own. He also milks it for more laughs than are to be found in the combined running time of *The Titfield Thunderbolt*, *Silver Streak* and *The Marx Brothers Go West*.

The film begins slowly with the outbreak of war in a small, sunlit Southern town: Marietta, Georgia. Fort Sumter has been fired upon, says a title, and the streets come alive as men queue to enlist. Buster's girlfriend wants him to fight, and he tries hard enough for a uniform, but the recruiting officer tells him that he is of more value as driver of the Western and Atlantic Flyer. 'If you lose the war, don't blame me,' he tells them. Unfortunately his betrothed, pudding-faced Marion Mack, doesn't believe that he has been rejected, and refuses to speak to him again until he's in uniform. So the first movement draws to a close, as Buster sits despondent on the cross bar of his locomotive and, uncaring, is slowly propelled by it, by an eccentric motion, into a tunnel. A year later the girl has picked up with another fellow, and Buster's expression is more hangdog than ever as he goes about his daily tasks. Suddenly, with the omniscience of film audiences, we are made aware of a Yankee plan for spies to enter the South as civilians, steal the train, take it north and burn all the bridges behind them. The daring raid takes place at Big Shanty during the twenty-minute dinner stop, and as luck would have it Buster's fiancée is aboard, though not of course speaking to him. The tale shifts into action as our hero sees his beloved train disappearing up the line. He valiantly gives chase on foot, waving the other inhabitants of Big Shanty to follow; but eventually he realizes that he is alone – the only one with that kind of courage (or foolhardiness). He manages to catch up by means of a trolley, leaping up and down at each stroke because his weight is insufficient to control the vehicle in any other way. Disaster strikes when the clumsy vehicle is derailed, but he is able to commandeer a penny farthing bicycle.

At Kingston he manages to recruit army assistance, but a faulty coupling results in his steaming away without the soldiers. Discovering his plight, he has recourse to a cannon on a small trolley which he tows behind his locomotive. Unfortunately he just can't get the charge right. The first cannon ball merely burps out of the muzzle and lands on his footplate, nearly braining him, so on the second occasion he gives treble the dose. Unfortunately he gets his foot stuck at the back of the loco, and the cannon, running over a few bumps, shudders itself down to point straight at him. Petulantly he throws a stick of wood at it, to little effect. At the critical moment the train reaches a bend; the ball is fired exactly where it was first intended, straight at the train ahead, and scores a direct hit. All this is most cinematically told, with an economy of style which would not disgrace any modern master who could be persuaded to attempt something so modestly effective. The angle of vision is always exactly what is required to set off the joke, and the side-on shots of the train in motion are an excitement in themselves.

A reel or so later, Buster is so intent on chopping wood that he fails to notice the retreating Southern army, followed by the victorious Northern army, passing him in the opposite direction. He is now behind the enemy lines, and when spotted has to jump for it into an uncomfortably wet forest of whose biggest danger, a marauding bear, he is happily unmindful. Hopelessly lost, helplessly cold, and horribly hungry (as a subtitle puts it) he takes refuge in the nearest house, which just happens to be where the Northern generals are meeting to discuss their strategy. Under the table and managing not to sneeze, he is amazed to see through a cigar hole in the cloth none other but his fiancée, who has been captured and held hostage. Of course he must rescue her, and promptly does, against all odds; but she proves to be more of a hindrance than a help. Remarkably full of bright ideas after another wet wait in the forest, and having observed his beloved *General* being loaded up with supplies, he climbs on with the girl in a sack over his shoulder, and steams away with the Northerners in full pursuit. With the train's

THE GENERAL. Keaton always battled objects of intimidating size, but in the end proved more than match for them

help he drags a telegraph pole across the tracks, and is then torn between tossing packing cases on to the track behind him and finding fuel for the boiler. At the latter task he is not conspicuously successful, and watches in dismay when the girl first throws away a log because it has a knot in it, then offers him a twig about six inches long. His face a picture, he offers her a chip two inches long, and she helpfully places it on the fire. Half-playfully, he half-strangles her, but kisses her instead. He also falls for the waste of time involved in her demonstrating her idea to stop the pursuing train by tying a rope across the track between two saplings: silent exasperation is all he can muster this time. Just before a steep downward slope involving a U-turn, he leaves her in charge while he checks something and is dismayed to see the train steam on, out of her control. He scrambles down the slope to meet it; but by now she has found reverse and is shunting backwards.

And so, on the last lap, they reach and cross Rock River Bridge, a remarkably ramshackle structure at best. Near it, Northern and

Southern forces are massing for battle, and the Yankees are anxious to take their train across. There's just one snag: Buster has set the beams afire with oil from his headlamp. The Yankee general considers matters. 'That bridge is not burned enough to stop you.' But it is: the train chugs across and the whole structure collapses into the river, in a scene more spectacular than the climax of *The Bridge on the River Kwai*. And it isn't a model.

We leave Buster not merely enlisted but promoted to Lieutenant. Sitting as we first encountered him, spooning with his girl on the cross bar of the locomotive, he is distracted by dozens of other ranks saluting on their way to the messhouse. By a simple adjustment of his posture Buster still manages to salute regularly enough without distracting himself from the more important business of kissing.

Watching *The General* is like glancing through a book of splendid historical photographs, except that it tickles the funny bone as no actuality could or should. A true work of comic genius, it is also immensely likeable from first frame to last, the most universally accessible of classics. Yet when it first appeared, it was a box-office flop which harmed the star's career.

The General. US 1926; monochrome; silent; 79 minutes (at 24 frames per second). A Buster Keaton production for United Artists. Written by Al Boasberg. Charles Smith, Buster Keaton. Directed by Buster Keaton and Clyde Bruckman. Photographed by J. Devereux Jennings and Bert Haines. Edited by Fred Gabourie and Sherman Kell. With Buster Keaton, Marian Mack, Glen Cavander, Jim Farley.

Vintage Run
Genevieve

Two young couples compete in the London-to-Brighton vintage car race.

In the early fifties, apart from the university-controlled Arts Cinema, Cambridge had five ABCs, giving that circuit a stranglehold on all commercial bookings, and two specialized independents. For three years I managed and booked the latter, my main hope being to snap up items before the ABC booker got to hear about their usefulness, for he didn't have much notion of what films had university appeal. Naturally, if he found out that I was angling for a

GENEVIEVE. 'We'll have that,'says traffic cop Geoffrey Keen as the old crock rushes past at forty miles an hour. His partner is Harold Siddons; John Gregson and Dinah Sheridan are the worried contestants

particular film, he would use his weight to stop me from getting it; and I wasn't allowed even a nibble at the really big attractions, for he would book them for a week into the massive Regal, followed by three or six days at the Central and later, a run of some kind at the outlying Tivoli and Playhouse (which like most Cambridge cinemas were places to avoid in the winter unless they were likely to be full, as their gas radiators were mainly for show and they could be warmed only by bodies in seats).

Sitting one summer day in the overcrowded and seldom-cleaned cubbyhole which passed for the Rex's managerial suite, I was trying to book the autumn term and had my eye on a revival of *The Lavender Hill Mob*, then two years old. The question was what to put with it, as all the other Ealing comedies had recently been run to death. 'Try *Genevieve*,' said Johnny Knell, the Rank salesman. 'It'll have had its ABC runs by then. Not tearing up trees, but your lot'll like it. Quite sexy in spots.'

'How many ABC runs?'

'Well, it's in for four as usual, but the whisper is they'll take it out after two.'

There Johnny was wrong, for although I allowed myself to pencil in the double bill, I had to wait for it until January: for ABC let *Genevieve* run its course. British quota was in short supply that summer, and I glumly watched it play at all four cinemas. The odd thing was that it did better at the Central than the Regal, and during the autumn its national reputation started to build. ABC didn't have the gumption to bring its third run forward, so it played for only one day in term, after which all the undergraduates went home. That day broke a couple of records, though, and the following week Johnny came back and had the nerve to request a cancellation of our booking because ABC wanted another week at the Central. 'Not on your life,' I said, with the smell of war in my nostrils. 'What's more, I'll extend my bookings to a guarantee of two full weeks before the summer.'

The point of the story is that the growing popularity of *Genevieve* became the nationwide sensation of the Christmas season, and over the next three years we brought it back to the Rex fourteen times in all. Its first week broke our house record with ease, and its third would have exceeded that but for a December ice storm on the Friday. We varied the co-feature every time, but *Genevieve* was what people were coming to see, over and over again, people we hadn't seen before and who looked as though they hadn't been inside a cinema since *The Birth of a Nation*. Even my senior tutor, who often boasted that the pictures weren't for him, turned up on his bicycle and had it stolen from the racks outside; he still went home chuckling.

Even today, nearly thirty years later, one can understand why this modest movie tickled the nation's funny bone, for it had charm and freshness which are absolutely unique. The mystery is why it took so long to be discovered: even the Sunday critics, who usually know better, were pretty ho-hum about it. Obviously Larry Adler's catchy harmonica score helped, as Anton Karas and his zither helped *The Third Man*, but people could buy the record of that (and did, in their millions). Another attraction must have been the pastel colour photography of English countryside and suburb, even though the locations cheat more than a little: the Brighton road on which the action is supposed to take place often turns into little more than an unmarked country lane.

But above all *Genevieve*'s triumph was to present a quartet of thirtyish characters in whom one instantly believed and who could not be forgotten. They bounded complete into the public imagination and stayed there. Readers of the *Sunday Times*; conscious of the necessary pursuit of sex and money; filled with the best and worst of the public school spirit; the men obsessed by their hobby and capable not only of spending their last pennies on it but of squabbling like schoolboys – or as the wife of one of them says in a moment of temper, hawling like brooligans – over the respective merits of their venerable vehicles. The comedy of the first half derives largely from the characterization of sexual tension and frustration, that of the second from the innumerable variations performed on a single theme, i.e. which team can get back to London first? In the many delays and detours, parts are played by expectant fathers, traffic cops, publicans, and children who drop their ice-cream on a zebra crossing and insist on scooping it all up again. In between is the overnight interlude in Brighton, with its special brand of hilarious tension. Ambrose's hopes of 'combining the London to Brighton run with a really beautiful emotional experience' are shattered when his date passes out after drinking too much champagne and playing the trumpet; while the less extrovert pair are forced by their own tardiness to spend the night in a hotel of horrors presided over by Joyce Grenfell at her toothiest, enunciating firmly that 'hot water is provided every day between the hours of two-thirty and six; when you take a bath, please sign the book behind the bedroom door'. When after eight hours on the road the lady guest explodes at this news and stalks upstairs, dear old Eddie Martin totters on to commiserate with the proprietress and enquire: 'Are they Americans?' The bedroom which locates itself within inches of Brighton's version of Big Ben, its innards whirring, clanging and reverberating on the stroke of each hour throughout the night, is a masterstroke of outright farce. When our heroine expresses her mind loudly on the subject, and the next-door neighbours bang on the wall in protest, it is a pleasant touch to have her respond by blowing up and bursting a paper bag. One scream from next door, then silence. Nice.

Some of the best jokes in this timeless comedy are about sex, and even though they might be made franker today, they couldn't be funnier. At the end of the prologue, when after a chapter of disasters Gregson and Sheridan fall into bed and begin to look interested in each other, the scene fades out very slowly as a commentator's voice intones: 'What you see happening here is by now a very old story, but strange to say it was illegal before 1896 . . .' We fade in to find that Leslie Mitchell is talking about the vintage cars lined up next morning for inspection in Hyde Park. Much later, the abandoned girls commiserate with each other, Rosalind complaining that 'Ambrose only seems to think about two things. That silly old car – and the other thing.' And Wendy replying, 'What other thing? Oh. My husband only thinks about the car.'

Although Gregson has the fewest funny lines, he is by far the most sympathetic character. Impecunious (though as he's a junior barrister we don't have to worry overmuch about his future), loyal, careful but impulsive, he shows his true worth when, five minutes from the end of the race and with his rival rolling ahead, he allows himself to be detained by a distinguished old gentleman who wants to rhapsodize about the car. Arthur Wontner, in his day one of the screen's better imitators of Sherlock Holmes, has this cameo and milks it to the full. 'A Darracq! By Jove, a Darracq! My dear sir, it was in a car like that that I asked my wife to marry me. Pangbourne, 1904. She said yes: but it was the car, I'm sure of that, it was the car!'

Genevieve is not the film of a major stylist, but it is the film of a quiet wit, and one deeply regrets that Henry Cornelius was not spared to make more like it. Come to that, why were William Rose's later scripts so variable after he had cut his teeth on this little masterpiece? Consider the scene where Wendy has to stop to powder her nose, and dashes to the pub across the road. She runs back, and her husband starts the engine, but she has only come to say that she needs a penny. All this is beautifully handled in long shot, with an accompaniment of train whistles to underline the joke. Consider Geoffrey Keen's sardonic traffic cop, who when the antique Genevieve rattles blithely past him at forty miles an hour in a built-up area, smiles grimly to his partner and says: 'We'll have that!' Perhaps most of the wit is in the handling of the Rosalind character, who brings a large shaggy dog on a dirty weekend and is appalled at the things she has to do, not in bed but as co-driver. (Kay Kendall and Kenneth More match each other splendidly.) Before the race starts, Ambrose tries to cheer her up: 'Never mind, when that car gets started, you'll be intoxicated by the exuberance of your own velocity. Get that?' To which Rosalind glassily replies, 'I said I'm not drinking anything today. Nothing at all.' He tries again. 'I say, old girl, if we win, we'll fly over to Le Touquet next weekend, what?' She is properly scornful: 'Ambrose, that Le Touquet routine went out with high button boots.'

Nowadays the powers that be would call this scampi belt comedy. Under whatever label it is still rare enough to be welcome whenever it appears. Probably it has never appeared to better advantage than in this cheerful anecdote of two couples braving the British weather and the British character on the roads of Surrey and Sussex.

Genevieve. GB 1953; Technicolor; 86 minutes. Produced and directed by Henry Cornelius for Rank. Written by William Rose. Photographed by Christopher Challis. Music composed and played by Larry Adler, and directed by Muir Mathieson. Edited by Clive Donner. Art direction by Michael Stringer. With John Gregson as Alan; Dinah Sheridan as Wendy; Kenneth More as Ambrose; Kay Kendall as Rosalind; Joyce Grenfell as hotel proprietress; Edie Martin as hotel guest; Geoffrey Keen and Harold Siddons as speed cops; Arthur Wontner as elderly gentleman; Reginald Beckwith as fussy motorist.

Hate Is an Exciting Emotion
Gilda

A down-and-out gambler in Buenos Aires resumes a love-hate relationship with his former flame . . . after she has married his dangerous new employer.

In the mid-fifties there was a perfectly awful Joan Crawford vehicle in which the invincible star remarked to Jeff Chandler after a quarrel: 'I wouldn't take you if you were covered in diamonds . . . upside down!' One had to imagine that she or her scriptwriter had ten years previously seen and learned from *Gilda*, which started the love-hate business in a big way, having its tight-lipped characters toss at each other such endearments as 'I hate you so much that I would destroy myself to take you down with me' and 'Statistics show that there are more women in the world than anything else – except insects'. Statistics don't, of course, but a producer-writer team sporting such names as Virginia Van Upp and Marion Parsonnet, whose greatest monument this is, would be unlikely to take much notice of scientific fact.

Historically *Gilda* can now be seen as the first of Hollywood's post-war *films noirs* in the pre-war French manner: in it Columbia uncharacteristically came up with a steaming brew of sexual and other aberrations which, despite the fact that nobody in it is seen to go to bed with anybody, seemed at the time to set a new standard of sophistication comparable to that of Vivian Connell's notorious novel *The Chinese Room*. The reason for its box office success however was that in it Miss Rita Hayworth, then at the very height of her fame and beauty, mouthed a very torrid number (Anita Ellis actually sang it) and peeled off some long black gloves. On later inspection this very mild form of simulated striptease proves to cover only a couple of verses of 'Put the Blame on Mame, Boys' before the drunken performer is hustled off the floor and slapped around by her icicle-cold protector. With duel-scarred George Macready among the players this sounds like type-casting, but at the time Macready is temporarily absent from the plot and the ill-treatment is meted out by his partner, whose behaviour causes Gilda to comment bitterly: 'You wouldn't think a woman could marry two insane men in one lifetime.' Since hubby number two is played by Glenn Ford, one may confidently assume that he reforms in time for the final fadeout, but all three corner-pieces of this dingy triangle are sufficiently perverse and unsympathetic to have caused a few raised eyebrows in 1946.

It's a schizophrenic movie in more ways than a few. By closing in frequently on Miss Hayworth's coiffures it gives an impression of great gloss and luxury, but even a casual study of the sets, with their familiar Columbia economies, might make one guess that they were on short lease from *Crime Doctor* or *Boston Blackie*. Vidor's direction is sporadically inventive, but for long stretches falls as flat and lifeless as the lighting, which insists on illuminating every corner equally and permitting no interesting shadows. There is an almost total lack of background music unless an orchestra is supposed to be playing in the casino. Yet despite these deficiencies, the disparate elements of this long and claustrophobic film are held together by some torrid overacting and that weird but highly influential script. I'd like to have met Miss Parsonnet.

The movie begins with a shot which reminds one of going up in an elevator: we *rise* to floor level in time to have Mr Ford, looking almost too young for long pants, throw giant dice at us. 'To me a dollar is a dollar in any language,' says his off-screen voice. 'It was my first night in the Argentine . . .' And it's nearly his last, for the Argentinians don't take to his form of cheating, and he has to be saved by a suave passer-by with a swordstick. 'It is a faithful and obedient friend,' says the glacial Ballin Mundson; 'it is silent when I wish it to be silent and it talks when I wish it to talk.' Only a little more plot is required to turn Johnny into a walking semblance of the stick, for Mundson owns a casino and needs a front man. Grateful, Johnny asks only that there be no questions asked. 'I was born last night when you met me in the alley; that way I'm all future and no past.' There would seem to be an inkling of decadence in the way they then toast 'the three of us', i.e. the two chaps and the swordstick; but their eccentric idyll is presently shattered. One night Johnny hurries to Ballin's home to welcome him back from a trip. 'You didn't think I'd have a woman in the house, eh, Johnny?' asks the older man, calling into the womb-like bedroom: 'Are you decent?' 'Me? Sure I'm decent' is the answer, and, thirty minutes in, Miss Hayworth swings her tresses provocatively up into the frame. From Johnny's expression (for this is not the first movie we have seen) we guess that Gilda is Johnny's old flame from back home, and indeed she later confirms that she met and married Mundson on what must have been the slowest of rebounds. Uncharacteristically, Mundson is bubbling with boyish pride: 'Imagine, Johnny, she told me she was born the night she met me. Just think of that, the three of us with no pasts, only futures.' But as he leaves the house Johnny's thoughts are heavy with the bitterness of impending melodrama: 'I wanted to go back in that room and hit her. I wanted to watch them. I wanted to know.' And in his ears rings Gilda's taunting voice: 'Johnny. Such a hard name to remember and such an easy one to forget.'

Uncle Pio, the imperturbable casino lavatory attendant whom threats can't prevent from calling Johnny a peasant, observes the growing tension and tells Johnny so as he sits on the floor to shine his shoes. ('I find this a convenient vantage point. From here I can see people as they really are.') But Johnny sullenly subsides into loyalty to Mundson, and obediently carries out such errands as getting Gilda back from dancing with another man. ('Pardon me, your husband is showing.') 'Doesn't it bother you that you're married?' he asks her. She is incorrigible: 'What I want to know is, does it bother you?' For a while Mundson remains captivated by her spoilt behaviour: 'You're a child, Gilda, a beautiful greedy child. It amuses me to give you things because you eat with such a good appetite.' But to Johnny he is soon changing his tune and fingering his swordstick: 'Hate can be a very exciting emotion.' Meanwhile Johnny is telling us: 'I hated her so, I couldn't get her out of my mind for a minute.' And Gilda is flaunting herself at him in the most alluring gowns Harry Cohn could buy, but occasionally hinting to Johnny that she might be a shade ashamed of herself: 'Here's the laundry waiting to be picked up.' She knows that retribution will come: 'The Argentinians say, three days of sowing wild oats, and then the harvest.' The Argentinians probably say nothing so picturesque, but the movie isn't designed to improve the good neighbour policy.

Everything comes to a head on carnival night, with lots of streamers and grotesque head-masks. Mundson has been operating a tungsten cartel. ('Is it worth being shot at for the pleasure of monopolizing it?' asks Johnny after the Nazi element has shown its displeasure at his business methods.) Mundson is driven to commit murder and apparently dies while escaping in a private plane. Johnny inherits his empire and becomes like him, to the point of marrying the widow only to ignore her and hold her a virtual captive, paying her back not only on his own behalf but on Mundson's, not only for marrying him but for betraying him. 'What she heard was the door closing on her own cage. She hadn't been faithful to him when he was alive; she was going to be faithful to him now he was dead.' But of course Mundson isn't dead, and just as the lovers finally get together ('Nobody has to apologize because we were both such stinkers') he turns up bent on his own jealous revenge, only to be speared by Uncle Pio with his old friend the swordstick. And the lovers would have walked out into a rosy dawn if Harry Cohn could have afforded one; instead the scene fades out peremptorily as they leave the bar.

How this sexual hothouse got past the Hays Office is hard to imagine. It even has shots in which Miss Hayworth appears to be nibbling at Mr Ford's most vital parts, though the script says she's

GILDA. It's all over for Ballin Mundson. Joseph Calleia, Steve Geray, Glenn Ford and Rita Hayworth compete for the last close-up

only lighting a cigarette from a match he's holding very low. But it did get past, and proved to be catnip at the box office, the one Hayworth film everybody remembers (perhaps because she's the only female in it with a speaking part). And despite the deficiencies mentioned, as entertainment it has an irresistible electric charge, especially when Hayworth sails into her big number:

> One night she started to shimmy and shake,
> And that's what started the Frisco quake.

We believe it, we believe it. Hayworth in *Gilda*, even if she can't quite make sense of the role (and not even Bette Davis could have done that), is as pulchritudinous as the other characters so frequently say she is; but her career success brought personal setbacks. As she is reported to have said later: 'Every man I've known has fallen in love with Gilda – and wakened with me.'

Gilda. US 1946; monochrome; 110 minutes. Produced by Virginia Van Upp for Columbia. Written by Marion Parsonnet, from a story by E. A. Ellington adapted by Jo Eisinger. Directed by Charles Vidor. Photographed by Rudolph Maté. Music score by Marlin Skiles. Art direction by Van Nest Polglase and Stephen Gooson. Edited by Charles Nelson. With Rita Hayworth as Gilda; Glenn Ford as Johnny; George Macready as Ballin Mundson; Steve Geray as Uncle Pio; Joseph Calleia as Obregon; Joe Sawyer as Casey.

Ashley and Melanie and Scarlett and Rhett
Gone with the Wind

A well-to-do Southern family is overwhelmed by civil war, and its surviving daughter ruins her own life in her determination to keep the family mansion going.

It was one of the *causes célèbres* on the home front during World War II. 'Mrs So-and-so has seen it: how did she get in?' 'Queued for eight hours, she says.' Certainly it ran at the London Ritz for more than four years, and was booked for an unprecedented three weeks at my local Capitol, at advanced prices, displacing Field-Marshal Rommel as the centrepiece of conversation. I was disinclined to queue so long – I'd done it for *Mrs Miniver* and been sadly disappointed – so I didn't deign to go at all, suspecting that it really wasn't my type of picture: too much misery, and people dying in childbirth, by all accounts. However, when three months later it came to the Queens for an indefinite run, I considered it my duty to attend as soon as the crowds began to thin. I was overwhelmed.

At three hours and forty minutes it was of course the longest film we in Bolton had ever experienced. A few of us had heard about *Greed*, but no one had actually seen it, not in the original version, and as it was silent anyway it hardly counted. All my sisters, aunts, uncles and cousins who had seen *Gone with the Wind* before me agreed on one thing apart from its sheer blissfulness, and that was that the time passed without one's noticing the length at all. I had to concur, but it took me almost another forty years to realize why. The eye is never permitted to get jaundiced because the entire production has been storyboarded. Conversations which might have seemed flat and vistas which might have been merely depressing were composed, shot by shot before production started, by that master designer William Cameron Menzies, who performed a similar function on such films as *Foreign Correspondent* and *King's Row* and *Ivy*, all most notable for their visual sense. Menzies is the real director of *Gone with the Wind*: Fleming, who is credited, and Cukor and Wood, who aren't, merely got performances out of the actors. It is Menzies who made the film so entrancing to the eye; to experience it is like walking through an art gallery. One of Selznick's own memos confirms that 'Menzies prepared a complete script of the film in sketch form, showing actual camera set-ups, lighting, etc.' The effectiveness of this technique, which was used also by Hitchcock in every film subsequent to the idea being put forward to him, can be seen in the way one remembers the angle of an actor's head or the placing of him in relation to the surrounding furniture or scenery. Think of the breathtaking receding shot of Scarlett under the tree as she swears that she will always look after Tara. Think of the first sight of Rhett Butler at the foot of the stair, his face alight with impudence. Think of the burning of Atlanta and its aftermath, lit and angled like a gothic fairy story. First the escape from the house by night, with candles throwing flickering circles of light onto the wallpaper and landings. Then through the eerie streets by carriage, with danger from looters, and horses and humans silhouetted against the orange flames which begin to light up the sky, including a marvellous shot of a four-storey building which suddenly crumples in flames as the little procession passes it. Each scene is like a painting by a new stylist come to challenge the great masters with his montages of simple forms, a stylist who has studied Grimm and Disney and *The Wizard of Oz*. Roofs, fences, trees, bridges, all acquire menace and meaning in his hands: the scene in which Scarlett and Melanie, in a rainstorm, have to hide waist-deep in water under a bridge is breathtaking in its visual melodrama. And then the mood is suddenly, craftily broken when the unpredictable Rhett announces that he is off to war and Scarlett will have to find the rest of the way home alone. 'You're no gentleman,' she tells him. He smiles against the lowering sky. 'A minor point at such a moment,' he replies, galloping away as he tosses over his shoulder his restated conviction that she will make out as well as usual.

She does, of course, for the main attraction of this saga is not its Civil War background, however magnificently and extravagantly depicted; it is the progress of its temperamental, unscrupulous but

GONE WITH THE WIND. Rhett and Scarlett escape from Atlanta

curiously sympathetic heroine who decides, whenever she falls into sin or life seems especially hard, to think about her problems tomorrow. She marries three times without getting the man she wants; her adult life is filled with tragedy and hardship; yet when at the very end she is left alone again, we thrill to hear her telling herself that tomorrow is another day. Vivien Leigh never had a better role; and yet Selznick must have had another actress in mind, for shooting had already begun when Miss Leigh was first introduced to him. Paulette Goddard and Evelyn Keyes were known to be leading contenders, and the testing took so long that Warners conceived and completed a rival tale of the old South and one of its richest bitches, *Jezebel*, before Selznick's cameras even turned. (Bette Davis had wanted to play Scarlett, but Warner refused to loan her.) Another sustaining influence of the film is the amusing badinage between Scarlett and the slightly rascally Rhett, who is no great respecter of women or believer in patriotism but has his own code of ethics. The part might have been written for

153

Gable, though astonishingly Gary Cooper, Errol Flynn and even Ronald Colman were also seriously considered for it, and Gable was only obtained from MGM at the high cost of allowing them to distribute the movie and keep most of the residual rights. From his first appearance you know why Gable came to be called the King of Hollywood; as Scarlett says, 'He looks as though he knows what I look like without my petticoats on.' To help her flee from Atlanta he has to be roused from a session at Belle Watling's whorehouse, which he leaves as casually as he leaves anywhere, calling: 'Any of you ladies know where I can steal a horse for a good cause?' And Selznick very properly fought the Hays Office for the right to keep his famous last line: 'Frankly, my dear, I don't *give* a damn.'

It is these two characters, almost standing up from the pages of Margaret Mitchell's novel, so vivid is their combination of good instincts and bad, who turn what might have been an interminable soap opera into a memorable adult version of the way things might have been a hundred and more years ago. For the supporting cast, though long, is not studded with memorable performances. Ashley Wilkes is safe in the hands of Leslie Howard, but he is too old for real conviction; Olivia de Havilland can make little of Melanie but an intolerable goody-goody. These are mere foils for the principals. Thomas Mitchell has a few moments as Scarlett's father, as do Harry Davenport as Dr Meade, Hattie McDaniel as Mammy, and Barbara O'Neil as Scarlett's mother, but one doesn't think back on them afterwards with rekindled affection, for this is a two-character marathon.

Nowadays this kind of story is filmed only badly, as a TV serial or mini-series, for costs have risen and the family audience has dwindled, and the theory is that no one who watches TV notices detail. It should be a signal for the grinding of teeth throughout Hollywood that, forty years after *Gone with the Wind*, standards have sunk so low. Those with any sense of critical standards can't bear to watch the modern equivalent of this spectacular saga, for invariably the narrative is jumbled, the diction poor, the spectacle mere child's play; while the actors seem to have been introduced only recently to their costumes. *Gone with the Wind* is a magnificent monument to the Hollywood which, like the old South, has been swept away; and only the ballyhoo necessary for its commercial survival prevented it from getting its critical due at the time. As so often, the public knew a good thing when they saw it, and transmitted enough enthusiasm to their descendants for this to become by far the oldest film in constant commercial circulation. It even survived an attempt to stretch it to CinemaScope proportions, thus robbing it of most of the virtues detailed above. It now commands massive fees for television exposure, despite the regrettable fact that of its leading actors, executives and technicians only one, Olivia de Havilland, still lives.

Gone with the Wind. US 1939; Technicolor; 220 minutes. Produced by David O. Selznick for his own Company and MGM release. Written by Sidney Howard (and David O. Selznick), from the novel by Margaret Mitchell. Directed by Victor Fleming (and Sam Wood, George Cukor). Production design by William Cameron Menzies. Photographed by Ernest Haller and Ray Rennahan. Music score by Max Steiner. Edited by Hal C. Kern and James E. Newcom. Art direction by Lyle Wheeler. Costumes by Walter Plunkett. With Vivien Leigh as Scarlett O'Hara; Clark Gable as Rhett Butler; Leslie Howard as Ashley Wilkes; Olivia de Havilland as Melanie Hamilton; Hattie McDaniel as Mammy; Thomas Mitchell as Gerald O'Hara; Barbara O'Neil as Ellen O'Hara; Harry Davenport as Dr Meade; Victor Jory as Wilkerson; Evelyn Keyes as Suellen; Ann Rutherford as Careen; Butterfly McQueen as Prissy; George Reeves as Stuart Tarleton; Rand Brooks as Charles Hamilton.

Californy Er Bust
The Grapes of Wrath

In the mid-thirties, refugee farmers from the Oklahoma dust bowl set off for a new life as fruit-pickers in California

Americans have always been surprisingly willing to wash their own dirty linen in public. *Our Daily Bread, One Third of a Nation, I am a Fugitive from a Chain Gang, They Won't Forget, Storm Warning, Pinky, Gentleman's Agreement, Angels with Dirty Faces, Mr Smith Goes to Washington* and hordes of imitators in the thirties and forties pointed dramatically to skeletons in the national cupboard. Although the pill was in every case sugar-coated in the hope that it could provide entertainment as well as instruction, the combination was usually successful in both respects, and these films may have had a more far-reaching effect on national conscience than would be thought possible by those who regard movies as a mere placebo for the masses; but only one of them, perhaps, can stand out in retrospect as an example of the highest form of filmic art. That one is *The Grapes of Wrath*.

It is also the one which failed most signally at the box office. The trials and tribulations of the Joad family were just too depressing for an escapist audience to accept, especially when a world war was beginning and there were more desperate things to fight about. Soon the injustice meted out to the Joads and their like by corrupt officials and con men would give place to hypocritical patriotic pleas which would put them in well paid jobs making aeroplanes and machine guns. But in the late thirties their plight was real enough, and the film, while streamlining their story somewhat, made no concessions towards those bankers and corrupt middlemen who traded on the plight of the Oklahomans to make a fast buck. Their land would no longer produce crops, so it was confiscated by its mortgagors. The farmers were lured by promises of work in California, but so many of them answered the call that wages could be dropped to starvation level in the knowledge that families would fight for the chance to pick peaches at five cents a crate, living in insanitary conditions and making barely enough to keep body and soul together because the shops skyrocketed the prices of essential foods. The Okies, good and decent people for the most part, were quickly labelled as unattractive parasites and shunned by whatever community they asked to join. The film climaxes with their finding a clean, cheerful, government-run camp; the book by John Steinbeck was much less hopeful and more angry.

It is customary to denigrate the half-dozen moguls who ran Hollywood through the pre-CinemaScope age: Mayer, Goldwyn, Cohn, Laemmle, Warner, Zanuck. The fact remains that *The Grapes of Wrath* was filmed only because Zanuck thought it would be a good thing; what's more, he made it a personal production, selecting the low-key accordion score, adding dramatic touches here and there, and above all writing the final scene, which is not in the book, when Tom Joad has run away from the law and his Ma and Pa are again at the wheel of their truck, on a journey to who knows where:

PA: You the one that keeps us goin', Ma. I ain't no good any more, an' I know it. Seems like I spen' all my time these days a-thinkin' how it use'ta be – thinkin' of home – an' I ain't never gonna see it no more.

MA: Woman can change better'n a man. Man lives in jerks – baby born, or somebody dies, that's a jerk – gets a farm, or loses one, an' that's a jerk. With a woman it's all one flow, like a stream, little eddies, little waterfalls, but the river it goes right on. Woman looks at it like that.

PA: Maybe, but we're shore takin' a beatin'.

MA: I know. Maybe that makes us tough. Rich fellas come up, an' they die, an' their kids ain't no good, an' they die out. But we keep a-comin'. We're the people that live. Can't nobody wipe us out. Can't nobody lick us. We'll go on forever, Pa. We're the people.

Nobody who has watched Jane Darwell perform this small scene can doubt the justice of her Academy Award. Large, double-chinned and ungainly, Miss Darwell was a solid presence in Hollywood films from the early talkies until *Mary Poppins* in 1964. She played society matrons, prison wardresses, cooks, maids, hotel keepers. But Ma Joad was her finest hour, and she put everything she had into it. She rather than Henry Fonda is the sustaining presence of the movie, her other notable scene being a silent one as she prepares for the great journey by sitting in semi-darkness by an open stove and emptying a shoe box of her souvenirs. A picture postcard of greetings from New York City; a newspaper clipping of Tom's conviction; a china relic of the 1904 Louisiana Purchase Exposition; some earrings which she holds against her face as she looks into a broken piece of mirror. Most of them she puts into the fire, but her optimism will not let her cry for what might have been.

John Ford also won an Oscar, for his controlled yet poetic direction; and there were nominations for Henry Fonda, Nunnally Johnson and for best picture. How Gregg Toland's luminous photography came to be omitted is a mystery. The critics went even wilder than the Academicians. 'A genuinely great motion picture which makes one proud to have had even a small share in the affairs of the medium,' wrote Howard Barnes. 'The most mature motion picture that has ever been made, in feeling, in purpose, and in the use of the medium,' wrote Otis Ferguson. Frank Nugent, for his review, got a lifetime's job as a Fox scenarist: 'In the vast library where the celluloid literature of the screen is stored, there is one small uncrowded shelf devoted to the cinema's masterpieces. To that shelf of screen classics 20th Century-Fox yesterday added *The Grapes of Wrath*.'

Zanuck himself received no honours for the picture, but his biographer Mel Gussow knew the score:

In 1939 it took considerable daring and courage for Zanuck to film *The Grapes of Wrath* while it was hot, and to do it so faithfully and movingly . . . Viewed again today, it is not so dense or so harsh as Steinbeck's book, but as a movie it is surprisingly successful, full of evocative moments that speak much longer than their duration on screen, full of character detail that is as true as it is sensitive . . . Zanuck took an urgent problem and dramatized it, making it palatable to a wide public not by softening it but by humanizing it.

The picture is filled with unforgettable moments and images, not least its first shot of a sun-baked crossroad towards which Tom Joad doggedly walks in his ill-matched grey cap and dark serge suit, the gifts of a caring government after his prison term. Soon, on his way home to his family of sharecroppers, he meets the defrocked preacher Casy, one of John Carradine's most memorably eccentric performances.

CASY: I lost the call. But boy, I sure used to have it. I'd get an irrigation ditch so squirmin' full of repented sinners I pretty near drowned half of 'em! But not no more. I lost the spirit. At my meetin's I used to get the girls glory-shoutin' till they about passed out. Then I'd go to comfort 'em . . . and end up by lovin' 'em. I'd feel bad, an' pray, an' pray, but it didn't do no good. Next time, do it again. I figgered there just wasn't no hope for me.

It may seem cynical to compare this story with that of the forty-niners, but the resemblances are obvious: an arduous journey westwards to the land of supposed plenty, with a dilapidated truck instead of a covered wagon, rascally ranch-owners instead of Indians, and Highway 66 instead of a scouted trail. The simplicity of the characters reinforces the comparison, as when Grampa dies en route and Tom leaves a note on the body before they bury it: 'This here is William James Joad, dyed of a stroke, old, old man. His fokes bured him becaws they got no money to pay for funerls. Nobody kilt him. Just a stroke and he dyed.'

Checotah, Oklahoma City, Gas, Dr Pepper, Bar-B-Q, Joe's Eats, Bethany, This Highway is Patrolled, Amarillo, End of 25 Mile Zone, Vega, Drive-Inn, Lucky Strikes, Nutburger, Glenrio, Free Water, We Fox Flats, Used Cars, Flagstaff, Water 5c Gallon, Water 10c Gallon, Water 15c Gallon, California. The roadside legends almost tell the story, except that the land of milk and honey proves to have

THE GRAPES OF WRATH. The Joads take a stand against authority. Eddie Quillan, Dorris Bowdon, Henry Fonda, Jane Darwell, Russell Simpson, Frank Darien, O. Z. Whitehead, John Carradine

dangers of its own, like the rancher who brands the surplus itinerants as communists and rouses mobs to set fire to their camps. A quiet fruit-picker has the story: 'There was a young fella jes' come out an' he was listenin' one day. He kinda scratched his head an' he says: "Mr King, what *is* these reds you all a time talkin' about?" Well sir, Mr King says: "Young man, a red is any fella that wants thirty cents an hour when I'm payin' twenty-five."'

The Grapes of Wrath is not faultless. Some backcloths are evident, and the way the paid troublemakers are evicted from the state camp is more Hollywoodian than realistic. But many pages could be filled with descriptions of its felicities, and its praises are often sung most loudly by people who have to be forcibly persuaded to endure a story so apparently full of human misery and degradation. Perhaps above all it is the look of it which takes the curse off the depressing material: the bleached dusty earth, the flat horizons, the long shadows, the gnarled and stunted trees, the stillness. And the name of the man who caught all this so memorably in black and white – as it could never be caught in colour – is Gregg Toland.

The Grapes of Wrath. US 1940; monochrome; 128 minutes. Produced by Nunnally Johnson for 20th Century-Fox. Written by Nunnally Johnson, from the novel by John Steinbeck. Directed by John Ford. Photographed by Gregg Toland. Music score by Alfred Newman. Edited by Robert Simpson. Art direction by Richard Day and Mark-Lee Kirk. With Henry Fonda as Tom Joad; Jane Darwell as Ma Joad; Russell Simpson as Pa Joad; John Carradine as Casy; Charley Grapewin as Grampa; Zeffie Tilbury as Granma; Dorris Bowdon as Rosasharn; O. Z. Whitehead as Al; John Qualen as Muley; Eddie Quillan as Connie; Frank Darien as Uncle John; Frank Sully as Noah; Grant Mitchell as superintendent.

The Least Unlikely Person
Green For Danger

During the doodlebug raids of 1944, Inspector Cockrill investigates a double murder at a country hospital.

Little was thought of it by the critics of the time, and less by the Rank Organization who distributed it. It might be nearer the mark to say that they allowed it to escape, for nothing was done to bring it to public attention as more than a programmer, and it was left for the paying customers to discover its quality, as they did with *Genevieve* seven years later. Since the stars were not exactly attention-grabbing I nearly missed it myself. Cockrill is now remembered as Alastair Sim's best part, and it's a crying shame he wasn't signed up for a series, but in the credits he's fourth billed, and few newspapers at the time could afford more than two stars in their single-column billing. Sally Gray and Trevor Howard in *Green for Danger* sounded almost humdrum, and it was only by passing the Bolton Lido that I came to realize via poster and stills that Sim, with homburg and umbrella, seemed to dominate the goings-on, and that this was a film by Launder and Gilliat, who had written *The Lady Vanishes* for Hitchcock and themselves cooked up *The Rake's Progress* in the previous year. Well, apart from a few scenes, *The Rake's Progress* seems very faded these days, but *Green for Danger* still gives off the unmistakable aroma of a modest audience-pleaser in which every detail is brought off as well as possible.

It introduces a set of interesting people, one of whom is a murderer. It isn't too difficult to guess who, for why else in a who-done-it would an actor be billed above the title and not be either the detective or part of the romantic team? But *why* is as interesting as *who*, and the intricate plot, with its attendant wartime topicalities (a mere memory by the time the movie was released), is worked out with the very minimum of complication and the maximum of jocularity, so that the audience which really listens has a fair chance of solving the puzzle before the witty but on this occasion not exactly successful detective.

It is Cockrill who narrates, though for the first forty minutes we see no more of him than his fingers pounding away on a typewriter. 'The amazing events which I am reporting may be said to have begun on the evening of August 17th, 1944 . . .' Over the operating table we meet one by one a team of doctors and nurses, and also a postman injured during a raid, and the sonorous voice continues: 'By August 22nd two of these people would be dead, and one of them a murderer.' Suddenly the flickering eyes behind the masks become more compelling: we are in Agatha Christie land, and on the alert for clues. Relationships, we find, are distinctly edgy. Mr Eden, a proficient surgeon, is the hospital Lothario who leaves a trail of broken hearts in his wake. Sister Bates is one of them. Nurse Linley has just broken off her engagement to short-fused anaesthetist Dr Barnes. Nurse Sanson is on the verge of a nervous breakdown following her mother's death in an air raid. Plump Nurse Woods is everybody's auntie but from the shadow which occasionally crosses her face we know she has something to hide. And why does Joe Higgins, the postman who dies on the operating table, say he knows her voice?

The death is taken as accident, and the staff dance goes on. But Sister Bates drinks too much, and in the middle of a well-staged Paul Jones she foolishly announces that Higgins' death was murder, and that she has evidence showing the who, when and why. Even more foolishly she dashes off to retrieve it from the operating theatre, in a fine chase through the gardens by night, with witches' sabbath music making us expect a villain behind every bush. But it isn't until she crouches over her evidence that she finds herself locked in the operating theatre with a chilling white-gowned figure who murders her with a scalpel. This moment, with its high wind outside, its

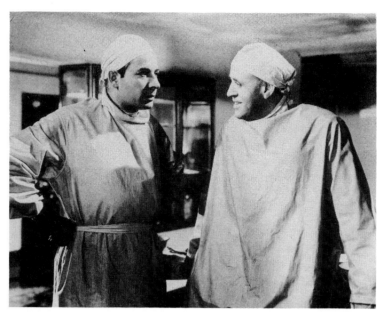

GREEN FOR DANGER. Even during a reconstructed operation, Inspector Cockrill can't resist taunting Mr Eden. Leo Genn, Alastair Sim

banging shutters and swinging doors letting in slices of light to illuminate the dreadful scene, is a classic highpoint of mystery film fiction; and when Nurse Linley discovers the dark deed we are treated to an equally memorable reprise, peeping in this time through the porthole-like window of the swinging door and seeing the body stretched out on the floor, alternately visible and invisible as the shutters continue to blow in and out.

Abruptly the mood changes to one of 'softly softly catchee monkey'. 'It was early the following morning that I myself, in person, arrived on the scene.' Armed with nothing more protective than an umbrella, Mr Sim is first seen making an ignominious escape from a distant buzz bomb. Recovering his aplomb, he introduces himself with amiable diffidence. 'Scotland Yard, I'm afraid. Sickening, isn't it?' But he is deaf to the hospital director's entreaties:

DIRECTOR: I do hope everything can be arranged discreetly.

COCKRILL: Shouldn't think so for a minute. Press, you know.
DIRECTOR: Do we have to have them in?
COCKRILL: They don't bother me. Anyway, they always give me a good write-up.

He promptly assembles the suspects and is brutally frank:

BARNES: Are you implying that one of us did it?
COCKRILL: Well, it seems very likely, don't you think?
BARNES: Did you get us here just to insult us?
COCKRILL: No, I merely like to strike an informal note.

The inspector is stung when Dr Barnes accuses him of being 'as insensitive as any flatfoot on the beat'. 'The police force has not a monopoly of fallen arches, Dr Barnes. Ask any chiropodist.' Dr Barnes simmers down and explains the mysteries of laughing gas: 'Actually it's the impurities that cause the laughs.' Cockrill nods sympathetically: 'Just the same as in our music halls.'

After the banter we turn our attention back to the puzzle, for the inspector can be direct and purposeful when he chooses, and indeed his ripostes have had a serious purpose, to unnerve. He is unable to prevent the murderer from attempting Nurse Linley's life by turning the gas on while she sleeps, but he does uncover Nurse Woods' secret: her twin sister is Lady Haw Haw on Nazi radio. And he undermines Mr Eden's romantic prowess by being present behind a bush to continue the Shakespearian quotations with which the surgeon beguiles pretty nurses in the garden by night. 'The next morning,' he boasts, 'my presence lay over the hospital like a pall . . . I found it all tremendously enjoyable.' When the nurses return to their quarters after night duty, they find him emerging: 'Good morning, ladies. Aha. No need to be alarmed, we were only searching your rooms.' He fences successfully with smooth Mr Eden:

EDEN: Are you trying to make me lose my temper?
COCKRILL: That was only a secondary object.
EDEN: The inspector has a charming aptitude for travelling in ever-decreasing circles, which I fear can have only one end.

Pride goes before a fall, and Cockrill's ingenious scheme of restaging the fatal operation goes wrong when the murderer, seeing that the game is up, takes poison before his very eyes and he shortsightedly prevents the antidote from being administered. There is only one way for him to conclude his report. 'In view of my failure – correction, comparative failure – I feel that I have no alternative but to offer you, sir, my resignation, in the sincere hope that you will *not* accept it. Full stop.'

An unimportant picture, yes, but perfectly done; which is what gives it, especially in America, the status of a minor classic. It delivers no message, states no social case; it simply entertains as efficiently as it knows how, without pandering to the groundlings. It is there to be enjoyed by those with wit enough to appreciate its humours, and enjoyed it has been for over thirty-five years, a period which does not appear to have dated it in the least. Only the blindness of some programmers prevents it being seen more frequently on television and at the National Film Theatre. Apart from providing Alastair Sim with one of his finest hours, it allows all the other actors to give excellent accounts of themselves, while Sidney Gilliat as co-writer and director probably reached his peak here. (The idea almost certainly stemmed from his involvement in three *Inspector Hornleigh* mysteries of the early forties, in which Sim played Sergeant Bingham.)

The uniquely delightful thing about *Green for Danger* (the title by the way refers to the murderer's ingenious plan of repainting a green carbon dioxide cylinder so that it is thought to be oxygen) is its unmistakable middle-class Englishness, a tradition which in the forties produced such classics as *The Way to the Stars*, *Brief Encounter* and *Blithe Spirit*, but in our modern world, where the few British films which get produced concern characters who drop their trousers more frequently than they raise their hats, seems to have disappeared for ever.

Green for Danger. GB 1946; monochrome; 91 minutes. A Frank Launder-Sidney Gilliat production for Rank. Written by Sidney Gilliat and Claud Gurney from the novel by Christianna Brand. Directed by Sidney Gilliat. Photographed by Wilkie Cooper. Music score by William Alwyn. Production designed by Peter Proud. Edited by Thelma Myers. With Alastair Sim as Inspector Cockrill; Sally Gray as Nurse Freddi Linley; Trevor Howard as Dr Barnes; Rosamund John as Nurse Sanson; Leo Genn as Dr Eden; Megs Jenkins as Nurse Woods; Judy Campbell as Sister Bates; Henry Edwards as Mr Purdy; Ronald Adam as Dr White; Moore Marriott as Higgins; George Woodbridge as Det. Sgt. Hendricks.

The Trail of the White Rabbit
Harvey

A gentle dipsomaniac whose constant friend is an invisible six-foot white rabbit embarrasses his elder sister, who tries to have him certified.

To tell the truth, *Harvey* is not very satisfactorily filmed; but then, I have never seen a stage production which quite harnesses the irresistible lunacy it can conjure up on the printed page. At least the film's sets are substantially satisfactory – and satisfactorily substantial – and it is held together, if not by style itself, then by a heavy absence of style. It never pretends to be taking place anywhere but on a studio sound stage. Two of the sets, including the imposing forecourt of the Chumley Rest Home, turned up in other Universal features of the time (one of them, *You Never Can Tell*, was double-billed with *Harvey* in some quarters), and when James Stewart walks happily towards the sunset at the end, we know that the end title will have to hurry along if he is not to step straight into the backcloth.

It did seem at the time a curiously cheeseparing way to treat a major enterprise with a major star, in a property which had cost a great deal of money but wasn't an obvious box office attraction. Certainly it alienated a few of the Stewart fans, and it didn't even satisfy him, as he felt he was far too young to play the worn-out lush. The role really requires a red-nosed comic of the vaudeville persuasion: Sid Field at London's Prince of Wales Theatre in 1948, though forced to play in sets that looked more like corridors, was the best Elwood P. Dowd I ever saw, though when Stewart returned to the role in the same theatre in the seventies, he was pretty marvellous himself. This is not to say that his 1950 stab at the part was an abject failure: he may not have been altogether convincing as the man, but he had a wonderful way with whole sections of Mary Chase's inimitable dialogue. There is for instance a sublime moment in the bar, when the rather boring young people have given in to the concept of Harvey, and ask Elwood exactly what he and the furry

HARVEY. Talk of a six-foot white rabbit alarms Mrs Chauvenet. Josephine
Hull, James Stewart, Grace Mills, Victoria Horne

quadruped find to do all the time. Stewart holds up his hands
expressively and replies as follows:

Well, we sit in the bars – have a drink or two – and play the juke box. Soon
the faces of other people turn towards me and they smile. They're saying
'We don't know your name, mister, but you're all right, all right.' Harvey
and I warm ourselves in these golden moments. We came as strangers –soon
we have friends. They come over. They sit with us. They drink with us.
They talk to us. They tell us about the great big terrible things they've done,
and the great big wonderful things they're going to do. Their hopes – their
regrets. Their loves – their hates. All very large, because nobody ever brings
anything small into a bar. Then I introduce them to Harvey and he's bigger
and grander than anything they can offer me. When they leave, they leave
impressed. The same people seldom come back.

A little later he explains how he first met his long-eared friend:

I'd just helped Ed Hickey into a taxi. Ed had been mixing his drinks, and I
felt he needed conveying. I started to walk down the street, when I heard a

voice saying: 'Good evening, Mr Dowd.' I turned, and there was this great big white rabbit leaning against a lamp-post. Well, I thought nothing of that! Because, when you've lived in a town as long as I've lived in this one, you get used to the fact that everybody knows your name . . .

I have always felt that in some inexplicable way *Harvey* is a great play. In the matter of theatrical technique impeccably finished, in the realm of the heart it offers us a world to retreat into when the one we normally inhabit is too uncomfortable; a place of comfort, an Erewhon, a new wonderland for Alice. Of course, as with Alice, you have to expect that its characters and situations won't always make precise sense. The dialogue certainly throws one a googly now and then without bothering to explain it, as when Wilson the male nurse, eminently sane but none too bright, hears that Harvey is a pooka, decides to look the word up in the dictionary, and finds the book talking back at him:

WILSON: P-O-O-K-A. Pooka. From old Celtic mythology. A fairy spirit in animal form. Always very large. The pooka appears here and there, now and then, to this one and that one, at his own caprice. A wise but mis-chie-vi-ous creature. Very fond of rum-pots, crackpots, and how are you, Mr Wilson?
(*He starts, then looks more closely at the book.*)
How are you, Mr Wilson?
(*He looks up fearfully, drops the book on the table, and runs off with a cry.*)

The film version should certainly be cherished if for no other reason than its preservation of the indescribable performance of Josephine Hull as Elwood's sister Veta Louise. This late lamented actress can never have been a beauty, and in 1950 her dumpy figure resembled several misshapen rubber tyres heaped loosely one on top of the other. But she gives a star performance if I ever saw one. To watch her nervously hosting a ladies' afternoon tea, with Mrs Ethel Chauvenet singing 'Pale Hands I Love', while anticipating the imminent return home of her disreputable brother and his pooka, to follow the startled, manic expressions which flit involuntarily across her twitching face, is an experience which alone repays the price of admission; and her fury with herself when she finally comes to believe in Harvey's existence is an accomplishment few actresses could muster. The Academy Award was for once well deserved.

Forget the rather unsympathetic photography and the unhelpful *mise en scène* which never allows one to see the outside of the bar, the town, or even the street in which the Dowds live. Think of the film as a reading by professionals of a simply marvellous play, and you will find it all joy. Forget the young people: it's the ones over fifty who matter in this piece, including the cabby who won't wait while Elwood has his voluntary treatment. Nice people go into the rest home, he says, and nasties come out.

CABBY: They got no faith in me or my cab – and we're going back over the very same road! It's no fun – and no tips!

VETA: Oh, but my brother would have tipped you. He's very generous. Always has been.

CABBY:Not after this he won't be. After this he'll be a perfectly normal human being – and you know what bastards they are!

Yes, like *You Can't Take It With You*, Harvey is a plea for escapism, for rose-coloured glasses, for heads in the sand. It wouldn't do for all of us to follow such a philosophy. But a few of us can; and the rest can share the vicarious pleasure of allowing them to.

A chilly matinée at the Bolton Odeon marked my first acquaintance with *Harvey* the film, and I may have been a little disappointed that, as in the play, we weren't given even a fleeting glance of the rabbit except in the portrait which Elwood proudly stands on the mantelpiece. Next day, as a kind of surrogate teacher, I joined a party of boys from my old school on an Italian trip. We spent one night on a coach heading for London, and the next sitting up in a train between Paris and Milan. When at the end of the third day we all poured ourselves out in Rome, the first thing I saw was a poster for *Harvey*; and on the next evening we all went to see it, with Italian sub-titles.

Another film in which a confused hero plays with white rabbits is *The October Man*, directed by Roy Baker in 1948; but here his fingers nervously make them out of handkerchiefs as his brain remembers that he was making one for a little girl when their bus crashed and she was killed. A year later, suicidal, guilty and nervous, he is the obvious suspect when a girl staying in the same private hotel is murdered; but since he is John Mills, we know he'll prove his innocence in the end.

This little film, which hardly anybody remembers, has haunted me down the years for its almost tangible sense of place. I knew when I first saw it that the Rank Organization didn't think much of its chances, for it played fifty-fifty on a double bill with a reissue of *Margie*. This was at the Salisbury Picture House, now a community centre; then it was a superb modernistic cinema with a large limpid screen which would have made even the Bowery Boys seem classical. It made *The October Man* seem like an amalgam of the greatest virtues of the British cinema of the forties: understatement, quiet wit, careful characterization, enjoyable and thoroughly reliable acting, and above all the sense of being in a recognizable milieu. The Victorian boarding house with its failed and frustrated inhabitants, on the edge of a common which might well be Barnes or Clapham though the film calls it Brockhurst, is an authentic recreation of a type which can still be found. Much of the film takes place at night, and I can still hear the clip clop of heels on rainy pavements along paths illuminated by infrequent blobs of light. Most vivid of all are the railway station scenes with their deserted, other-worldly air, and the iron-trellised footbridge where Mills hovers so frequently, undecided whether to throw himself under a train; there is a moment when one passes screaming below, and until the steam has cleared we are not sure whether after all our little entertainment is going to have an unhappy ending in the Gabin style. The film is full of good cameo performances, all subordinated to the star as though they may turn out to be mere effusions of his disordered brain. When one of them casually reveals himself as the murderer, you can almost hear the snap of the audience's changed mood, for the film has changed from a despondent nightmare into a mystery for which the author clearly intends to provide a satisfactory and suspenseful ending. The author incidentally is Eric Ambler, harking away from his habitual stamping ground of the international spy thriller but still presenting his favourite hero, a mature professional man backing away from a danger he doesn't wholly comprehend.

Harvey. US 1950; monochrome; 104 minutes. Produced by John Beck for Universal. Written by Mary Chase and Oscar Brodney, from the play by Mary Chase. Directed by Henry Koster. Photographed by William Daniels. Music score by Frank Skinner. Art direction by Bernard Herzbrun and Nathan Juran. Edited by Ralph Dawson. With James Stewart as Elwood P. Dowd; Josephine Hull as Veta Louise Simmons; Victoria Horne as Myrtle Mae; Peggy Dow as Miss Kelly; Charles Drake as Sanderson; Cecil Kellaway as Dr Chumley; Jesse White as Wilson; Nana Bryant as Mrs Chumley; Wallace Ford as taxi driver.

The October Man. GB 1947; monochrome; 105 minutes. Produced and written by Eric Ambler for Two Cities and Rank release. Directed by Roy Baker. Photographed by Erwin Hillier. Music score by William Alwyn. Art direction by Vetchinsky. Edited by Alan L. Jaggs. With John Mills as Jim Ackland; Joan Greenwood as Jenny; Edward Chapman as Mr Peachey; Kay Walsh as Molly; Joyce Carey as Mrs Vinton; Catherine Lacey as Miss Selby; Frederick Piper as Godby.

Anything Can Happen and It Probably Will
Hellzapoppin

No synopsis is given because none is possible. Or if it were, it wouldn't matter.

In May 1979 I saw in San Francisco the first tryout of a show called *Sugar Babies*, which subsequently went on to a surprising Broadway success. It was a plotless revue attempting to echo the great and formerly despised days of American burlesque, with its dubious jokes, its elaborate gag routines, its blackout sketches, its vulgar songs and its easy relationship with the audience. *Hellzapoppin* represents the truest flavour of burlesque that the Hays Office would ever allow the cinema audience to savour before the whole style became old-fashioned; and thanks to Hollywood craft, it is a good deal slicker than the original.

Themselves relics of burlesque, Olsen and Johnson refrain from hogging the limelight. Previously flops in movies, it was they who had nursed and nurtured an ancient collection of gags and girls to Broadway success in the late thirties, and it was on the crest of this wave that they were invited back to Hollywood, where they proceeded to turn Universal Studios into a disaster area. (See the first reel of their second picture, *Crazy House.*) Theirs was a firework that quickly fizzled out, but *Hellzapoppin* works not only because they lavished upon it the cream of the old gag crop, but because its editing and photography (including some nifty tricks) are right out of the top drawer, and the idea of putting the zany proceedings under the megaphone of a high comedy director like H. C. Potter was an inspiration: he ensured that every gag is played to the limit without ever outstaying its welcome. The culprit responsible for imposing a routine love story onto the proceedings never owned up, but for the most part it is sent up something rotten and only momentarily impedes the flow of gags.

Hellzapoppin is no easy film to describe. It opens in a projection box, with crumple-faced Shemp Howard muttering to himself as he laces up the reels: 'A fine thing I'm doin'. Fifteen years I've been runnin' these pictures and now all of a sudden I have to be an actor.' He finally gets the picture on (oddly enough in modern wide screen format) and we see a bevy of underdressed girls singing 'I Had a Vision of Heaven' as they descend an ornate staircase. Suddenly the steps flatten out into a slide and they all disappear amid screams and explosions to – well, where else? They fall right through the titles, and by the time the last card fades ('Any similarity between *Hellzapoppin* and a motion picture is purely coincidental') we are in Hell itself, or at least a streamlined Universal version of it, where all the demons sing the title song in close harmony. The girls are being roasted on spits, and new arrivals are sealed in tubs labelled 'Canned Gal' or 'Canned Guy'. A taxi arrives and disgorges assorted animals including Olsen and Johnson. The latter remarks: 'That's the first time a taxi driver ever went straight where I told him.'

Another arrival, dismayed at his fate, leaps from a high ledge, falls through the floor and causes an oil gusher. The stars step forward and ask the projectionist to run the last section again: he does. The hell scene turns out to be part of a movie Olsen and Johnson are making. They sit down in a corner with the director, who insists they have a story in it. They point out that they managed pretty good without one on Broadway. Johnson is interrupted for a phone conversation of which his end is: 'That's good. That's bad. That's good. *That*'s good. That's bad.' 'What are you doing?' cries the director. Johnson looks amazed that anyone should have to ask: 'Sorting strawberries.'

The discourse is interrupted by a burly woman braying for someone called Oscar; she reappears throughout the picture. So does the mild little man calling for Mrs Jones: he carries a potted plant which grows in size until it has to be brought in on a truck. The three conversationalists stroll through various studio sets, changing instantaneously into the appropriate costume for each, from French Revolution to Eskimo. While posing as the latter Johnson comes across a replica of the sled from *Citizen Kane*. 'I thought they burned that,' he says.

HELLZAPOPPIN. Olsen and Johnson make a spectacular arrival in their natural habitat

Elisha Cook Jnr is the assistant director whose good advice is never taken and who when asked 'How much do you charge to haunt a house?' replies 'How many rooms?' The director thinks the picture should finish with a big Broadway tryout. 'Not another picture with a show in it, per-lease,' says Johnson, no doubt echoing the feelings of the audience. (But wait till they see this one.) The director sits them down to watch some of the footage already shot, and suddenly there they are in the movies, mingling with rich girl and poor boy:

OLSEN: He isn't going to give her his love until he can support her on his own.
JOHNSON: That's crazy.
OLSEN: That's movies.
JOHNSON: That's crazy.

Mingling too are assorted supporting comics, a nap hand including

172

Mischa Auer as a fake Russian prince who doesn't want to be found out because the smart folks won't find him amusing any more, and if they don't find him amusing they won't invite him down for the weekend. And Hugh Herbert as a bumbling private eye with such a penchant for disguise that he can present five faces in rapid succession simply by looking out from different sides of a tree. ('Don't ask me how I do it, folks.') And Martha Raye as a sex-mad ingenue who sets her sights on Auer and inflicts on him various kinds of mayhem while singing 'What Kind of Love Is This?' (Her 'Watch the Birdie' is also something of a classic.) Her role is to suffer indignities and insults. 'Did anyone ever tell you you look like Deanna Durbin?' asks Olsen. 'Why, no.' 'No wonder!' yell our hosts in unison.

There has to be a pause for breath, and we reluctantly accept that Robert Paige is going to sing a love song to Jane Frazee. But this is quickly interrupted by a slide reading: *If Stinky Miller is in the audience, will he please go home?* At the third similar interruption the singers stop to join in the plea, and the dejected shadow of a small boy rises up into the screen and wends its way sadly to the exit.

The next interruption is a problem in the projection booth. Shemp has got to wooing his fat girlfriend, and the film is all over the floor. When he gets it back into the machine the picture is first in reverse, then upside down; then the stars who find themselves in this predicament utter harsh words which have to be censored. Nor are they greatly pleased to find themselves with the wrong background, being shot at by Indians; and even when they are restored to their moonlit terrace an Indian chief gallops through and asks: 'Which way did they go?' ('Thataway!')

Our resident gremlins enlist the services of Hugh Herbert. 'Would you know anything about love?' 'Who, me?' he burbles; 'I'm a married man!' (Mr Herbert also pauses at this point to address the audience: 'Hello, Mom, I'll be home to tea. Have meat.') We are arriving at the first night of our pre-Broadway revue, with an important backer in the audience, and the plot rapidly provides an excuse for our heroes to wreck every act. (Don't ask why, it doesn't matter.) The performance begins with an usher who gives tips instead of receiving them. There's a man who only wants to read a dime novel, and follows the ballerina and her spotlight in order to do so. The seekers after Oscar and Mrs Jones are well in evidence. The

Frankenstein monster is on hand to toss back on to the stage any performer who chances to fall into the orchestra pit. The ballet is ruined by sneezing powder, fly paper, and a bear on a scooter. There are exploding firecrackers, tintacks on the floor, a squirting accordion, sharp currents of air to play havoc with the girls' skirts, and (shame on them) a Cuban finale. ('It's the Cuban conga with the Yankee twist.') Two gags I especially care for. Johnson tries to scare two dignified gentlemen by putting on a fright mask and saying boogie boogie boogie. In vain. When he takes the mask off and sinks back into his seat, the lady next to him faints. Then there's the special announcement: 'Will Mr Robert T. McChesney please go home, as he has become the father of twins?' A perspiring and embarrassed gentleman rushes for the exit amid general applause, but suddenly stops to ask himself: 'What am I running for? My name's Miller.'

It all winds up with somebody trying to shoot the bear, who responds: 'You missed me. You need glasses.' Which causes one dog to remark to another: 'Can you imagine that? A talking bear.' Then there's a trick effect enabling Olsen to make his bottom half invisible and Johnson his top; the two halves join up for a military march. Finally, back in the studio, the stars quit and the director shoots his assistant, who calmly remarks: 'You can't hurt me that way. I always wear a bulletproof vest around the studio.' So saying, he drinks a glass of water, which squirts from his body in all directions.

This kind of cinematic slapstick may bore you to tears. It would bore me if it were badly done, but *Hellzapoppin* is honed to perfection, technically superlative and with each gag perfectly timed and weighted. I am grateful however to have seen the more ribald stage show, or at least the British touring version of it, which visited Portsmouth when I was in the army there in 1948. There was a man who kept coming on, loudly offering rubber balloons for sale. Then some of us were induced up on stage to dance with chorus girls whose pale green bras had black hands on each cup. Suddenly my partner fainted on the floor, and the cast began to offer helpful advice. 'Rub her forehead.' 'Rub her cheeks.' 'Rub her neck.' And then: yes, on he strode. 'Rubber balloons!' It is comforting to find that times don't change. Broadway audiences flocking to *Sugar Babies* are still laughing at the same joke.

174

Hellzapoppin. US 1941; monochrome; 84 minutes. Produced by Jules Levy for Mayfair Productions, released by Universal. Written by Nat Perrin and Warren Wilson. Directed by H. C. Potter. Photographed by Woody Bredell. Music direction by Charles Previn. Special effects by John Fulton. With Ole Olsen and Chic Johnson as themselves; Martha Raye as Baby Betty; Hugh Herbert as Quimby; Mischa Auer as Prince Pepi; Jane Frazee as Kitty; Robert Paige as Jeff; Shemp Howard as Louie; Clarence Kolb as Mr Rand; Nella Walker as Mrs Rand; Lewis Howard as Woody; Richard Lane as director; Elisha Cook Jnr as assistant director; Andrew Tombes as the backer.

Cry God for Larry
Henry the Fifth

In 1415 England declares war on France, and peace comes about after a great English victory at Agincourt.

Even at fifteen I must have had some precocious reputation as a film buff, for one day over school lunch the headmaster said to me: 'Well, young Halliwell, will *Henry the Fifth* ever be shown in Bolton?' Slightly startled at being consulted, I expressed my certainty that in view of the money J. Arthur Rank had poured into the production, he would be bound to ensure that it was played at his local flagship Odeon. 'And do you think it will draw the crowds?' I said I thought it might surprise everyone, Shakespeare or no Shakespeare.

Well, it did eventually arrive at the Odeon, but so late that I imagine district office must have been in great doubt about it; and in case he hadn't noticed I duly notified my headmaster. Normally I would have dropped in to see it on my way home from school on Monday afternoon, but I decided that since this was something of an occasion, the connections of Bolton with the bard of Avon being extremely tenuous, I would go home first for a scrub and attend the evening performance. I didn't expect a great queue, but was dismayed to observe as I crossed Ashburner Street towards the familiar marble façade that not a soul was to be seen. I managed my familiar seat with ease: twelve rows from the front, as far back as one could go for sixpence, the centre aisle seat on the right hand block. The Odeon that evening had a cathedral-like air, and smelled sweeter than I could remember; with a sinking feeling I realized that this was because the air was polluted by next to no cigarette smoke

HENRY THE FIFTH. All's well that ends well: Laurence Olivier, Felix Aylmer, Renée Asherson

and very few bodies. The giant red curtains finally parted before the most scattered and paltry house I remembered seeing in that vast auditorium, and I suspected that everyone present had distinct grammar school connections.

The dedication, screened in silence before the film started, made the atmosphere even stranger, not at all like the beginning of an entertainment:

To the Commandos and Airborne Troops of Great Britain – the spirit of whose actions it has humbly attempted to recapture in some ensuing scenes – this film is dedicated.

Misguided, irrelevant, pretentious and ungrammatical, I thought. But the magic swiftly began, with that first inspiriting shot of a playbill fluttering about in a blue sky, coming to rest before the camera as trumpets sounded:

The Chronicle History of
KING HENRY THE FIFT
with his Battel fought at Agincourt in France
by
Will Shakespeare
will be played by
The Lord Chamberlain's Men
at the
Globe Playhouse
this day the first of May 1600

Suddenly we were floating over medieval London, by courtesy of that celebrated, impeccably detailed scale model which has done duty as stock footage in so many subsequent and inferior films. We passed the Bear Playhouse and tracked inexorably towards the open cockpit of the Globe, where a flag was being hoisted. A cut to a close-up of the flag enabled us to enter the life-size theatre interior, a masterpiece of research and reconstruction with its thatched roof, its oak galleries, its apron stage with rear balcony, its groundlings buying apples in the seatless pit, and its noblemen taking their joint stools on to the very stage itself. A chronicle history, with a battle, to be enacted in these surroundings? A formidable problem, but of course Shakespeare had a way of solving it. After the boy had crossed the stage with the title board, on strode Leslie Banks, that mesmeric actor, as Chorus, to ask our indulgence and our assistance:

> O for a muse of fire, that would ascend
> The highest heaven of invention!
> A kingdom for a stage, princes to act,
> And Monarchs to behold the swelling scene! . . .
>   Can this cockpit hold
> The vasty fields of France? or may we cram
> Within this wooden O the very casques
> That did affright the air at Agincourt?
> On your imaginary forces work!
> . . . Piece out our imperfections with your thoughts;
> Think when we talk of horses that you see them,
> Printing their proud hooves i'the receiving earth;
> For 'tis your thoughts that now must deck our kings,
> Carry them here and there, jumping o'er times;
> Turning the accomplishment of many years
> Into an hour-glass . . .

177

And so we watch a few scenes in the 'wooden O', stagily contrived, with obvious make-up and frequent stumbling, the long-winded reading of the Salic law turned into farce; until gradually, in the celebrated technique devised by Olivier for this film, we suppose that the exhortations of Chorus are beginning to work on us as well as on that long-ago audience, and we begin to see scenery, rudely painted at first, then increasingly stylized and artistic, until at last, an hour later, Agincourt bursts upon us in full panoply, with the French charging on real horses, racing on real green grass into the terrifying hiss of the English arrows. And at the end of the film the process is reversed, with a stylized wooing scene between Henry and Katherine followed by Burgundy's speech, during which the French countryside recedes into a tapestry, then for a final curtain call we return to the Globe Theatre itself, on the stage of which the mighty and triumphant king is again recognizable as a nervous boy playing his first leading role.

This then was no mere play on celluloid, no dull Shakespeare transcript, but a fully creative movie shot in Technicolor much fresher, firmer and more varied than we had come to expect. The text of course had been cut, and why not? Shakespeare himself was no sluggard at borrowing other people's work and adapting it to his purpose, and none of his plays is innocent of padding which fascinates only the scholar. Every scene in the film is long enough to justify its presence on the screen, and no longer; but it is packed with detail to entrance the eye and performances to surprise the student who finds this play on the printed page so much dead wood apart from a few stirring speeches. The low comedy of Pistol, Nym and Bardolph is safe in the hands of Robert Newton (an overwhelming strutting braggart), Frederick Cooper and long-nosed Roy Emerton, with George Robey as a dying Falstaff smuggled in from *Henry IV*. Harcourt Williams is the doddery king of France, with Max Adrian delicious as the dauphin and Leo Genn, a new find, stealing most of the notices as the sardonic Constable. Each of the smaller parts was filled by a theatrical star, and the costumes by Roger Furse could scarcely have been more fetching than they seemed against Paul Sheriff's sets. As for Olivier, whose entire concept this was, his adaptation of film techniques to essentially theatrical purposes was audacious and successful, his direction firm and confident, his performance suitably diffident and his verse-speaking as mellifluous as one would expect.

One's only reservation at the time was that as a piece of political propaganda, showing England taking up arms against a European foe (and of course winning) it might have been more useful a couple of years earlier. But that matters not a jot when one looks at it now, and how satisfying it is that the negative has been so well preserved that prints from it can come up as fresh and sparkling as the first ones did on the day they were minted.

Compared with the airy delicacy of *Henry the Fifth*, Olivier's *Richard III*, made eleven years later, is more of a comic strip in stained glass. All else is subjugated to the star's famous presentation of the king as villain, a grotesque creature deep dyed in evil and addicted to macabre jokes. Those who insist that Shakespeare's view of Richard was to say the least jaundiced should stay away, and even the poetry seldom takes wing, for blank verse is used only to decorate a black comedy. Apart from the hunchback hero only Ralph Richardson gets a share of the limelight as the 'deep-revolving witty Buckingham', and even he is quickly slapped down when he requests a reward for his corruption and is savagely told: 'I'm not in the giving vein today.' Sets and performances in this case are stylized throughout until we come to the climactic battle scene, which comes as rather too much of a bloodthirsty shock; it certainly seems roughly assembled and dull to look at after the careful positioning of all that has gone before. Nevertheless it's a rich and immensely entertaining film, and it grieves me to report that when in 1956, on a Rank trainee course, I was assistant manager at the Radcliffe Odeon and played it for three days, we never took more than seven pounds a night with it.

Olivier's other Shakespearian films are less remarkable. Its Oscar notwithstanding, *Hamlet* suffers from a text too drastically pruned to make way for a lot of aimless camera tracking over draughty battlements and corridors, and from unengaging performances including Olivier's own: Stanley Holloway steals the show as the first gravedigger. *Othello* is boringly shot from the front stalls, and in CinemaScope to boot, with no cinematic magic to obscure the mechanics of performance and make-up. However, the mature spirits who remember his performance in the 1936 *As You Like It* have words of commendation for it, though from the standpoint of the eighties it is hard to imagine Olivier young and blithe enough to get away with lines like:

> Run, run, Orlando! Carve on every tree
> The chaste, the fair, and inexpressive she.

Henry the Fifth. GB 1944; Technicolor; 137 minutes. Produced and directed by Laurence Olivier for Two Cities and Rank release. Adapted by Laurence Olivier, Reginald Beck and Alan Dent from the play by William Shakespeare. Photographed by Robert Krasker. Music score by William Walton. Art direction by Paul Sheriff, with Carmen Dillon. Costumes by Roger Furse. Associate producer, Dallas Bower. With Laurence Olivier as Henry; Leslie Banks as Chorus; Robert Newton as Pistol; Renée Asherson as Katherine; Leo Genn as Constable; Felix Aylmer as Archbishop of Canterbury; Robert Helpmann as Bishop of Ely; Harcourt Williams as King Charles VI; Max Adrian as the dauphin; Esmond Knight as Fluellen; Niall MacGinnis as MacMorris; John Laurie as Jamy; Michael Shepley as Gower; Ivy St Helier as Alice; Valentine Dyall as Duke of Burgundy; Freda Jackson as Mistress Quickly; Frederick Cooper as Nym; Roy Emerton as Bardolph; George Robey as Sir John Falstaff.

Sons of Bitches
His Girl Friday

A Reporter jeopardizes her impending marriage for one last scoop about a condemned murderer who escapes on the eve of his execution.

The Front Page is the blackest of black comedies, and when the first film version appeared in 1930 it must have boasted the least prepossessing cast of characters ever exposed to small-town America. For sheer callousness in the face of someone else's imminent death, Edward G. Robinson as Little Caesar has nothing on the reporters and corrupt officials who assemble in the forlorn press room of Chicago's jail on the night before the execution of mild little Earl Williams, who has inadvertently shot a policeman. The authors, Ben Hecht and Charles MacArthur, have been reporters themselves and must therefore be presumed to know of what they spoke. The grubby room, filled with stale air and littered by cigarette stubs and packs of greasy cards, is populated by the kind of people one might normally avoid like the plague, hacks who would readily sell their own grandmothers into white slavery for a byline. (For contrast there is one fairy who writes doggerel verse in the

worst possible taste.) Even Hildy Johnson, the reluctant hero, leaves his fiancée waiting at the church when he finds he has the escaped murderer tucked away in a rolltop desk; and then all is forgiven between him and his hardboiled editor as they figure out how they can smuggle the fugitive out of the building and back to their editorial offices so that they can hold the local politicians to ransom.

Lewis Milestone's 1930 version, even if prints were generally available, would be found these days to move at somewhat too stately a pace for comfort; the dialogue is sedately spaced out in order to accommodate the primitive sound equipment, and Milestone fills in with tricky panning shots remembered from his own *All Quiet on the Western Front*. It gives a fair rendering of the play, and communicates the right sense of claustrophobia, but in the circumstances it isn't surprising that a few years later, when movies were slicker, the idea of a remake occurred to Howard Hawks, who loved comedy melodramas about tough guys linked in some common aim. By 1940 however censorship had closed in on Hollywood, the war was imminent, and the project needed a lighter touch. Taking it at one hell of a clip was one solution which would recommend itself automatically to Hawks; he had skated over similarly thin ice in *Twentieth Century* by persuading his actors to imagine themselves in some kind of verbal steeplechase. Exactly who had the idea of changing Hildy Johnson into a woman and offering the role to Rosalind Russell is open to doubt; there are many versions of the truth. But the more Hawks thought about the idea, the more he liked it. Russell was popular in smart comedy and had a ready wit; what's more, if Hildy were divorced from her editor, and if he wanted her back, extra piquancy would be added to the central situation. The overbearing Walter Burns had to be softened too; how better than to have him acted by that elegant smoothie Cary Grant, whose Machiavellian manoeuvrings would now suggest mischief rather than malevolence? The finally jilted fiancée would now have to be a man, and a weak man, which meant he had to be funny. After *The Awful Truth* Ralph Bellamy was such obvious casting, as to invite an in-joke in the script. (Planning Bellamy's second – or is it third? – arrest in one afternoon, Cary Grant explains on the phone to a fellow conniver: 'He looks like that fellow in the movies – what's his name, Ralph Bellamy.') The in-joke syndrome proved infectious, for a little later Grant tells his boss: 'The last man who said that to me was Archie Leach a week before he cut his throat.' Mr Grant's real name is Archibald Leach.

The resulting romantic comedy melodrama, seen with a lively audience, is one of the most enjoyably exhausting experiences on celluloid. It doesn't let up for a minute: never in the field of screen comedy have so many talked so much at one time without ever confusing their listeners. There is no movement for its own sake, and the low set costs must have delighted Harry Cohn, but neither actors nor director are ever caught with egg on their faces: you can't take your eyes off the screen for ninety minutes, and in that time the entire essence is caught of a play which on stage takes nearly three hours to unfurl.

The first half hour in fact is mostly new, a knock-down, drag-out fight between the principals in the newspaper office and, with Bellamy intervening, over lunch in a nearby restaurant. Walter is all out to stop Hildy from remarrying: 'Hildy, don't be hasty, remember my dimple.' She replies, 'You wrote that on a wall outside the courtroom. Delayed my divorce twenty minutes, while the judge went out to look.' There are interruptions for the latest bulletin from the jail; Walter tells an aide to tell the governor they'll support him for senator if he'll reprieve Earl Williams. When the aide protests, 'You can't do that, this paper's been democratic for twenty years,' Walter replies, 'We'll be democratic again after we get that reprieve.' But Hildy is mostly on Walter's mind: 'Come back on the paper,' he tells her. 'If we find we can't get along in a friendly fashion, we'll get married again.'

Bruce Baldwin (Mr Bellamy) is no match for this kind of repartee. He can only tell Hildy, with moon eyes to match, that: 'Even ten minutes is a long time to be away from you.' With Walter he has a man-to-man talk about the insurance business: 'We don't help you much when you're alive, but when you're dead, that's what counts.' Hildy finds him too eager to consider her ex 'a charming fellow': 'Oh, Walter's got lots of charm. He comes by it naturally. His grandfather was a snake.'

Walter soothes Hildy's suspicions by signing a fat cheque in Bruce's favour to cover an insurance policy, in return for Hildy's doing one last story from the jail. Naturally, being a careful fellow, Walter sends Diamond Louie after Bruce to steal the cheque back and to get Bruce himself arrested as a thief. From here in, everyone converges on the jail and the plot thickens so impenetrably that you could stand up a spoon in it. Bruce is perpetually arrested to keep him out of the way, Hildy hasn't time to bail him out, Earl Williams shoots a psychiatrist 'right in the classified ads' and hides in the desk, the sheriff and the mayor try to suppress a reprieve because hanging will better suit their political book, Diamond Louie gives Bruce's mother the fireman's lift and carries her off to an asylum for dipsomaniacs, and Walter is furious because with such a great story he can't get his city editor on the phone because the man is injecting himself with insulin. 'Diabetes. I ought to know better than to hire anybody with a disease.'

There are seldom fewer than two people talking at once, but Hawks still finds time for throwaway jokes, as Walter's reply when Hildy asks him the first name of the mayor's wife: 'You mean the one with the wart on her – ? Fanny.' And Hildy's reminiscence: 'Remember the time we stole old Ada Haggerty's stomach from the coroner's physician?'

It all comes out more or less right in the end with Bruce sent packing (of course) and Earl Williams getting his reprieve, while Hildy and Walter are clearly made to double-cross each other for ever and ever. My only regret is that the last line of the original play could not, for censorship reasons, be accommodated. Here Walter had behaved like a gentleman and let the male Hildy hurry away to meet his intended at the station, first giving him a sentimental address and the gift of an inscribed gold watch. Walter is still smiling as Hildy leaves, but one minute later he is on the phone to the office: 'Duffy! Listen, I want you to send a wire to the chief of police of La Porte, Indiana. Tell him to meet the twelve-forty out of Chicago, and arrest Hildy Johnson and bring him back here . . . The son of a bitch stole my watch!'

His Girl Friday begins with a disclaimer: 'It all happened in the "dark ages" of the newspaper game – when to a reporter "getting that story" justified anything short of murder.' If this were true, Hollywood was living in the dark ages right through World War II, for the image of the reporter which it sent round the world was a far cry from the Lou Grant we all know and love. I must mention one other Ben Hecht brainchild, *Nothing Sacred*, in which a newspaper turns a backwoods girl into a national heroine because she is thought to be dying of an obscure disease. If anything more biting even than *His Girl Friday*, this savage comedy also begins with a cynical preface: 'New York, skyscraper champion of the world, where the slickers and know-it-alls peddle gold bricks to each other and truth, crushed to earth, rises more phoney than a glass eye . . .'

In this environment one newspaper man can describe the ethics of another as follows: 'The hand of God, reaching down into the mire, could not elevate you to the depths of degradation.' I think I like best the moment when the reporter first goes to the backwoods town and finds the populace actively hostile when not merely monosyllabic. After several examples of this he is walking down a quiet street when through a picket gate dashes a small boy to bite him in the leg . . .

His Girl Friday. US 1940; monochrome; 92 minutes. Produced and directed by Howard Hawks for Columbia. Written by Charles Lederer, from the play *The Front Page* by Ben Hecht and Charles MacArthur. Photographed by Joseph Walker. Music score by Sydney Cutner. Edited by Gene Havlick. With Cary Grant as Walter Burns; Rosalind Russell as Hildy Johnson; Ralph Bellamy as Bruce Baldwin; Gene Lockhart as Sheriff Hartwell; Clarence Kolb as the mayor; Ernest Truex as Roy Bensinger; John Qualen as Earl Williams; Helen Mack as Mollie Malloy; Roscoe Karns as McCue; Cliff Edwards as Endicott; Porter Hall as Murphy; Frank Jenks as Wilson; Regis Toomey as Sanders; Abner Biberman as Diamond Louie; Frank Orth as Duffy; Billy Gilbert as Joe Pettibone; Alma Kruger as Mrs Baldwin.

Quick, Watson, the Rathbone
The Hound of the Baskervilles

Sherlock Holmes sends Watson to Dartmoor to protect a young nobleman threatened by a family legend.

'1889. In all England there is no district more dismal than that vast expanse of primitive wasteland, the moors of Dartmoor in Devonshire.' Thus the gothic-styled introduction to Hollywood's 1939 version of Sherlock Holmes' most famous adventure. There have been half-a-dozen English-speaking film versions of it, even an abysmal 1978 parody with Peter Cook and Dudley Moore. (This unbelievable piece of celluloid drek is memorable only for one of the most strained puns ever conceived, when a medium is blown up by a volcanic explosion, and Holmes' spiritualist mother (!) remarks: 'I've lost a medium rare in a world where the stakes are high.') This is clearly the worst, and the 1939 version is generally regarded as the best, partly because it tries hardest to match the atmosphere of its original and partly because it was here that the excellent Basil Rathbone first donned the deerstalker and played the familiar violin. It even manages, in the midst of the Hays Office's most protective period, to end with the line: 'Quick, Watson, the needle.' Perhaps the censor felt that he needn't meddle with a classic.

The most remarkable lack of this production should be mentioned at once. It has next to no background music, and in a suspense thriller this is a most curious omission, robbing the audience of quite a few frissons. Think of Hitchcock's *Psycho* without the music, or turn the knob down next time you watch the shower scene, and see the difference it makes. No horror, no suspense. That the Rathbone film succeeds so well in the circumstances is surely evidence that with the right score it could have been a minor masterpiece. It would certainly have persuaded us to forgive the fog-shrouded studio rocks which pass for Dartmoor's tors.

185

And there is an end to my cavilling. In all other respects, this is a highly satisfactory picture, equivalent almost to reading the original. Elements of the story have suffered alteration, but only members of the Sherlock Holmes Society are likely to notice. Most of the familiar dialogue is there, albeit in simplified form. We even begin with Watson's deductions based on the stick so conveniently left behind by Dr Mortimer: 'Has anything escaped me?' he asks Holmes, who replies, 'Almost everything, my dear fellow.'

The sets are solid and pleasant to the eye, their outlines amplified by Peverell Marley's limpid lighting, which as in all Fox films of the period achieves interesting compositions and deep shadows without sacrificing clarity of detail. Typically he contrives to have daylight through windows reflect itself up to the ceiling, which doesn't happen in any house I've visited.

The prologue has a fine brisk style. An elderly man is running for his life and collapses on the path outside his home. A fearsome bearded fellow steps from the shrubbery and tries to rob the corpse, but runs away when a housekeeper steps through the front doorway of Baskerville Hall, holds the lantern high, and screams. Then the inquest, with veiled suggestions of murder and at least one witness clearly telling less than he knows. And so to the overstuffed parlour in Baker Street, and to a pair of actors who are immediately recognizable as the best Holmes and Watson the screen is ever likely to give us. Rathbone has a rather severe hairstyle reminiscent of his Mr Murdstone, much more in character than the fancy coiffure he was to adopt later at Universal: his eyes are commanding, his gestures economical, his speech firm, clear and precise. When the scene is set for Holmes by Lionel Atwill as Dr Mortimer, the perfect red herring with eyes glinting suspiciously through pebble glasses, we are reminded of another occasion in 1939 when these two met and over-acted outrageously, i.e. the darts scene in *Son of Frankenstein*; here they are in perfect control of themselves and their effects.

The heir soon arrives, and we go through all Conan Doyle's effective business of the warning letter (its words cut from that morning's *Times* and pasted on to a sheet of paper); the stolen boots; and the threat from a hansom cab whose occupant has the supreme nerve, after eluding the great detective, to tell the cabby that he has been driving Mr Sherlock Holmes of Baker Street. And so Watson is sent to guard the heir on his return to Devonshire, and for the next

THE HOUND OF THE BASKERVILLES. Investigators must always be on the alert. Basil Rathbone, Nigel Bruce (as if you didn't know)

half hour Nigel Bruce holds sway with a Watson courageous but by no means foolhardy, liable to leap to the wrong conclusions but not the open-mouthed buffoon he later became. But of course Holmes makes a dramatic return, in outlandish disguise, to point out the villain, even giving a satisfactory account of his deductions, which is something rare in Hollywood mystery stories. Despite its minor lapses, this is a film to please Sherlockians, who have proved willing to forgive such curious aberrations of detail as the front door to 221B, which has leaded lights when Holmes opens it to leave, but solid wood panels when viewed a moment later from the outside.

This *Hound* has a mild-spoken but acceptable villain in the person of Morton Lowry, an English actor who after a few more years in small Hollywood roles (you can spot him in *The Picture of Dorian Gray*) caused a minor mystery of his own by disappearing from the scene. Holmes' definitive antagonist however is not Stapleton but Moriarty, who turned up in the next Fox chapter, smiling and smiling and being an absolute bounder. *The Adventures of Sherlock Holmes* is even more satisfying in its period re-creation than its predecessor, despite a May fog which causes one to wonder; but the plot is a poor thing, consisting largely of an elaborately unconvincing red herring to keep Holmes busy while Moriarty steals the crown jewels. We are also slightly distracted by Rathbone's assumption of the disguise as a music hall comedian, in which he sings two verses of 'I Do Like To Be Beside the Seaside'; but there is no gainsaying the absolute rightness of George Zucco as his malignant adversary, glinting and gloating from under his elegant top hat, and on the whole quite stealing the picture.

After this, the series of twelve second features made by Rathbone and Bruce between 1942 and 1946 are admittedly a letdown, though lovable for their parts rather than their wholes: and there is always the fun of deciding on what Conan Doyle original, if any, they are supposed to be based. *Spider Woman*, for instance, has a touch of *The Final Problem*, a soupçon of *The Empty House*, and the dwarf from *The Sign of Four*. *House of Fear* actually claims to be derived from *The Five Orange Pips*, but isn't. The straightest pair are *Sherlock Holmes Faces Death* (a sober amplification of *The Musgrave Ritual*) and *The Pearl of Death*, which is reasonably faithful to *The Six Napoleons* but adds a Hollywood horror figure in the shape of Rondo Hatton, a real-life victim of acromegaly, as the Hoxton Creeper. And *The Scarlet Claw*, allegedly an original, is as near as dammit *The Hound of the Baskervilles* again.

In most of these latter day adventures Holmes' deductions are correct, but he signally fails to reduce an average of one murder per reel. He is always ready however with a moral or patriotic summing-up for the coda: in *Voice of Terror* it was borrowed from *His Last Bow*: 'There's an east wind blowing, Watson. It will be cold and bitter, and a good many of us will wither beneath its blast. But it's God's own wind none the less, and a cleaner, better, stronger land will lie in the sunshine when the storm has cleared.'

I almost forgot to mention that for economy's sake the later films had been updated to World War II, which was raging at the time of their production. To begin with they were heralded by a somewhat ingenuous disclaimer: 'Sherlock Holmes, the immortal character of fiction created by Sir Arthur Conan Doyle, is ageless, invincible and unchanging. In solving significant problems of the present day he remains – as ever – the supreme master of deductive reasoning.'

I once arrived in New York on a Sunday night and found myself in the Warwick Hotel with instructions to fasten all three bolts on my door. Outside on the corner there was actually a knife fight in progress, and lines of yellow taxis were honking furiously to no apparent purpose. Room service had ended, and I felt suddenly lost and miserable in an alien land. I switched on TV and, lo and behold, I found Rathbone and Bruce in *Dressed to Kill*, just beginning. This final episode of the series is generally reckoned to be the weakest, but that evening, even though divided by commercials every five minutes, it shone with a most kindly light. I lapped it up like cream, and afterwards slept soundly for twelve hours. This is one of the best recommendations I can think of for a series whose merits must clearly outnumber its defects, for statistics show that throughout the world it is the most popular series of films ever televised, and the prediction is that it will go on running until the negatives wear out. For though it may sometimes have misread the letter of Holmes, it perfectly preserved the spirit of a warm and enquiring male friendship which no one ever accused of being gay, and of a time when for villains and heroes alike the excitement of the problem, its solution and the chase were all that really mattered.

More recent Holmes films have signally failed to hit the mark, and only one TV series, in the sixties, showed the proper characterization and spirit. But even though a second Rathbone seems hard to find, the power of the stories is undiminished, and critical assessments and pastiches pour from the press in ever-increasing numbers. Conan Doyle, who wrote the originals so hastily that they are packed with contradictions and *non sequiturs*, who indeed used the same plot three times under different titles, never really understood that he had accidentally fashioned a national and international hero for all ages. Luckily, as with Laurel and Hardy, the public proved to be the best and most important judge.

The Hound of the Baskervilles. US 1939; monochrome; 80 minutes. Produced by Gene Markey for 20th Century-Fox. Written by Ernest Pascal, from the novel by Sir Arthur Conan Doyle. Directed by Sidney Lanfield. Photographed by Peverell Marley. Music score by Cyril Mockridge. Edited by Robert Simpson. Art direction by Thomas Little. With Basil Rathbone as Sherlock Holmes; Nigel Bruce as Dr Watson; Richard Greene as Sir Henry; Morton Lowry as Stapleton; Wendy Barrie as Beryl Stapleton; Lionel Atwill as Dr Mortimer; Beryl Mercer as Mrs Mortimer; Barlowe Borland as Frankland; John Carradine as Berryman; Eily Malyon as Mrs Berryman; E. E. Clive as cabby; Mary Gordon as Mrs Hudson; Nigel de Brulier as Selden.

Films I Love to Hate
House Of Dracula

Dr Edelman, a research scientist living in Frankenstein's old castle, is visited by Dracula and the Wolf Man, both of whom want to be cured.

Even among bad films one is allowed a few favourites, but the term needs qualifying. Some films are so clearly doomed from the outset, and leave such pathetic images on an already overtaxed retina, that one wonders why the attempt was ever made. Michael Redgrave in *Mourning Becomes Electra* murmuring 'I must go and clean my pistol.' Mickey Rooney weeping buckets in *The Human Comedy* and being comforted by a ghost. Spencer Tracy as a benevolent spirit in *A Guy Named Joe*. Leslie Howard and Norma Shearer as a near-geriatric *Romeo and Juliet*. Bob Hope with too many kids and no script in *Eight on the Lam*. Ingrid Bergman as a shiny-armoured, angelic-visaged and totally uninspiring *Joan of Arc*. James Mason high on cortisone in *Bigger than Life*, an inflated Reader's Digest article. Cary Grant as a gloomy cockney in *None but the Lonely Heart*. Chaplin in *A King in New York* and, even more so, *A Countess from Hong Kong*. Ronald Colman in *A Double Life* (though he got the Academy Award for it from sheer gratitude for a long and distinguished career). *Adventure* ('Gable's back and Garson's got him'; whoever thought they had chemistry?). Hitchcock's intolerable *Marnie*. Anything with Jerry Lewis or Laurence Harvey.

These are projects with a long and expensive way to fall. They are of course outnumbered by the thousands of inept programme fillers which most of us with a glimmering of critical sense manage to avoid seeing. I personally shudder at the thought of ever again encountering such abominations as *I was a Dancer*, with Diana Napier; *He Found a Star*, with Vic Oliver; *Look Before You Love*, with Margaret Lockwood; *Zis Boom Bah*, with Ginny Simms; *Hi Buddy*, with Dick Foran; or almost anything from Republic or PRC; for these must have been known even to their producers as beyond redemption.

But a favourite bad film is something else. Clearly it must be the *kind* of film one normally likes, with an interesting cast and theme. Equally clearly something must have gone sadly wrong with it, and this must have produced some perverse kind of entertainment value, along with a regret for the film that might have been. Some of the films I have celebrated in this book will be thought by certain readers to have no merit whatsoever, but I hope I have proved that for me at least they work. My favourite bad films are of similar mould, except that their mixture has failed to rise. It seems to me useful to recapitulate them because it is always fun to spot someone else's mistakes; because they serve as awful warnings; and because one simply can't believe that professionals could embark on such calm and familiar seas and end up shipwrecked.

Pride of place in this category must be given to *House of Dracula*, the last of Universal's 'serious' monster films before Abbott and Costello took over. Although the series in my Lancashire experience always drew full houses, this one was never released in Britain at all until it was more than ten years old, when I caught up with it at London's Praed Street Classic on a double bill with the original *Frankenstein*. It is a gem of ineptitude. Its badness lies in its extremely flat handling and in the fact that the writers were not allowed to transfer to the screen the fun they must have had in cooking up its absurd plot. As it is, the laughter it evokes is clearly unintentional, yet to me it is a better horror spoof than Mel Brooks' much vaunted *Young Frankenstein*. Consider the following.

The mad doctor, Edelman (played by Onslow Stevens in view of Boris Karloff's having suddenly remembered an appointment elsewhere), starts off as an amiable enough chap living with his hunchback nurse in their all-mod-cons castle on the edge of a beetling Bavarian cliff but within screaming distance of the village. He has discovered a plant mould which softens calcium, thus permitting operations without surgery. As soon as he has enough mould he proposes to straighten up his nurse, but it's slow-growing stuff, and one evening he is distracted by a bewildering variety of patients. First Count Dracula turns up, coffin and all, pleading to be released from his centuries-old bondage. The doctor puts his trouble down to over-active glands affecting his metabolism and gets him on a course of blood transfusions via a unique apparatus which draws off the doctor's good blood and pumps it directly into the count. Next Larry Talbot the Wolf Man comes knocking on a similar errand. The doctor this time diagnoses runaway hormones stimulated by mental obsession, and recommends a little cranial adjustment – when he's saved up enough mould, that is. Petulant at having to wait, Talbot jumps off the cliff and is washed into a cave. The valiant doctor goes down to rescue him, narrowly escapes being savaged (lots of full moons in this part of the world), and on the way back they see something very odd indeed in a muddy underground corner. 'Oh look,' says Talbot in mild surprise, 'it's the Frankenstein monster.' It is indeed, and the dormant lump has obviously been slurped down here from the swamp where we left him in *House of Frankenstein*; to prove it, Dr Niemann's skeleton lies across his chest. Naturally the new find becomes another trophy for the doctor's lab, reached from the cave by a convenient secret staircase.

The next development is unfortunate – for Edelman. Dracula decides that he rather likes batting it around after all, and switches the transfusion tap so that his nasty blood is pumped into the doctor. The count shows his hand once too often and is disposed of, but the good doctor develops a set of nasty twinges and after an elaborate montage by courtesy of shots from older and better movies, turns from Dr Edelman into Mr Hyde and goes on the nocturnal prowl, murdering village folk with many a menacing he-he. Luckily he has restored the slightly puzzled Talbot to full health before the village folk turn out with their flaming torches, the monster is reactivated, and the castle goes up in smoke along with most of its inhabitants. Talbot is left to gaze into the sunset with the doctor's charming receptionist, and thus becomes the only monster ever to have a happy ending (temporary, as fans will know).

This cornucopia of comic-strip corn has a certain whimsical charm for addicts, who will be left wishing that James Whale had directed it instead of Erle C. Kenton. But what can be said of the same studio's *Night Monster*, an irredeemable cheapjack effort made in 1942? This gem of incompetence was written by one Clarence Upson Young, whom I strongly suspect to have been a pimply schoolboy whose derivative and pusillanimous farrago was accepted by Universal on a desperate afternoon when they had several actors sitting around waiting for a script. *Any* script. After a main title badly supered over an irrelevant still of the forest glade from *The Wolf Man*, it postulates a spooky house owned by a desperate but very rich cripple (the budget prevents our seeing more of it than the

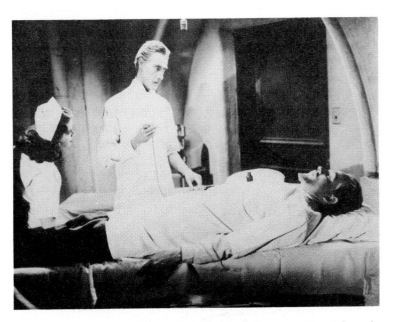

HOUSE OF DRACULA. Dr Edelman's kind intention is to cure Count Dracula by transfusing some of his own blood, but the evil Count is about to turn the tap the wrong way

front door and the lodge gates). A doctor, we're told, has been murdered in nearby Pollard's Slue. The sinister housekeeper is forever cleaning up spots of blood on the carpet. The cripple's sinister swami tells the twisted gateman that he has been communicating with the frogs – which always stop croaking when danger threatens. The owner's sister thinks she is mad and has sent for a psychiatrist. Giant bare footprints are observed in the mud. Man-eating dogs are spoken of. The chauffeur is a lecher.

These are mere preliminaries to the actual start of the plot. A tarty maid is murdered offscreen, in Pollard's Slue, to the accompaniment of wisps of studio fog and the cessation of the froggy chorus. The rich cripple welcomes for the weekend three surgeons, who it appears by their operations have made him even worse than he was before. He wants to say no hard feelings: 'You've never been properly rewarded – but you will be, you will be.' He reveals that he now has neither arms nor legs, though a local 'mechanic' has fixed him up an artificial arm by means of 'a few steel bars, electric wires and dry cells'. The swami does after-dinner tricks such as materializing on the carpet a kneeling skeleton which, apart from dripping blood, offers a box containing a ruby and a warning. ('This manuscript is in ancient Greek: it is the curse of death.') The three doctors and the chauffeur are then murdered one by one, the half-mad sister sets fire to the house, *Rebecca*-style, and the lady psychiatrist is chased through the bog (why doesn't she keep to the paths?) by the slow-moving monster who turns out to be the rich cripple (he had to be the villain as he's played by Ralph Morgan). It seems he has absorbed sufficient of the swami's teaching to grow himself limbs for occasional use, 'as a lobster grows a new claw'. Sure enough, after he has been shot in the nick of time they melt away, and the spots of blood all over the place are vaguely attributed to his imperfect mastery of the theory.

The greatest mystery about *Night Monster*, apart from the matter of why it was made at all, is the billing. Bela Lugosi, who gets half a screen to himself, plays the butler, who as my synopsis will show not only didn't do it but has no part in the plot. Co-featured with him is Lionel Atwill, who as the first of the doctors to be murdered has at most ten lines. Why didn't they keep him till last? Did he in the middle of production receive a call to another, better, film?

Another strong contender for the Halliwell lemon is *The Story of Mankind*, assembled in 1957 by Irwin Allen with a credit to the published 'work' of Henrik Van Loon, who must have been revolving in his grave after the movie came out. It all takes place on one of these draughty astral planes, with the devil and the Spirit of Man attending a heavenly tribunal to decide whether mankind should be destroyed by the super H bomb. The visual evidence then adduced by Vincent Price (with suitably arched eyebrows) and Ronald Colman (wearing a weary expression and Bogart's old trench coat) prove nothing to anybody, being largely culled from the stock shot library or laboriously acted out by the so-called cast of thousands, which actually consists mainly of character actors doing their best with undernourished cameos. Edward Everett Horton is billed as Sir Walter Raleigh, but one has barely time to recognize the figure who enters, smoking, before a courtier throws water over him under the impression that he is on fire. (Yes, that's the level.) As for the Marx Brothers, who but Mr Allen could have the idea of hiring them only to separate them? Groucho has a few moderate moments as Peter Minuit, buying Manhattan Island from the Indians, but Chico is merely a feed to Christopher Columbus, while Harpo as Sir Isaac Newton does the silent apple-on-head bit. The central ecstasy to be obtained from this gloriously bad movie derives from the scene between Agnes Moorehead as Queen Elizabeth and Reginald Gardiner as Shakespeare; the only explanation of the grotesque performances given by these normally reliable actors is that they knew themselves to be sunk by the script and thought they might as well have fun. The resultant exchange of grimaces, gestures and exclamations is I believe without peer since the days of Sarah Bernhardt and Tod Slaughter.

House of Dracula. US 1945; monochrome; 67 minutes. Produced by Paul Malvern for Universal. Written by Edward T. Lowe. Directed by Erle C. Kenton. Photographed by George Robinson. Music score by Edgar Fairchild. Make-up by Jack Pierce. With Onslow Stevens as Dr Edelman; Lon Chaney Jnr as Lawrence Talbot; John Carradine as Count Dracula; Lionel Atwill as Inspector Holtz; Martha O'Driscoll as Miliza; Jane Adams as Nina; Glenn Strange as the monster.

Night Monster. US 1942; monochrome; 73 minutes. Produced and directed by Ford Beebe for Universal. Written by Clarence Upson Young. Photographed by Charles Van Enger. With Bela Lugosi as Rolf; Lionel Atwill as Dr King; Irene Hervey as Dr Harper; Don Porter as Dick Baldwin; Ralph Morgan as Kurt Ingston; Nils Asther as Agor Singh; Fay Helm as Margaret Ingston; Leif Erickson as Laurie; Doris Lloyd as Miss Judd; Francis Pierlot as Dr Phipps; Frank Reicher as Dr Timmons; Robert Homans as Captain Beggs.

California French
I Married a Witch

A witch and her sorcerer father are burned at the stake in 1690. Released as puffs of smoke when lightning strikes the tree which pins down their remains, they take on human form to harass the modern descendant of the Puritan who had them executed.

The style of this cracklesome comedy is as delightfully mixed as its contributors, who include the author of *Green Pastures* and the elegant refugee Frenchman whose light touch distinguished *Le*

I MARRIED A WITCH. Smoke is the only covering Jennifer has for her new body, until kind unsuspecting Wallace finds her a fur coat

Million and half a dozen other durable classics of European wit. Dry and elusive of flavour, it mildly tickles the tongue in the best champagne manner, and is like no other Hollywood comedy, natural or supernatural. Some admirers attribute this to the fact that it was produced by Paramount, has Paramount background music, a Paramount supporting cast and a Paramount end title, yet the word Paramount is nowhere to be found among its credits, it having been made by that studio to the orders of United Artists. This was due to the wartime fact that Paramount had more production facilities than its distribution outlets could cope with, and UA found studio space at a premium. The resulting company, Cinema Guild, made only two or three films before other means were found of regulating the economic situation.

I Married a Witch was said during production to have a hex on it, probably because the stars hated each other and said so loud and clear. March looked down on Lake because she was not professionally trained; she thought him supercilious and played as many pranks on him as she could devise. (Her remarks about him in her autobiography are surprisingly vicious.) I knew nothing of this when I caught up with the film at the Kingston Odeon, on a release double bill with *Seven Miles from Alcatraz*. The latter was a forgettable RKO cheapie, but I had to sit through part of it twice in order to get a second look at the first half of *I Married a Witch*. (I couldn't stay for all of it because of catching the last bus to Weybridge, where my sister lived.) I remember waiting afterwards at the bus stop by the Saxon king's stone after which the town is named, and wondering whether the stone had any magical properties by deft use of which a warlock or two might be summoned. In the time at my disposal however I couldn't get it to work.

One can see now that *I Married a Witch* was economically made, hypnotizing us by means of very few sets and minimal special effects. It isn't particularly witty or wise, and even for those days it's very short indeed. (An 82-minute version is said to have existed, but no cuts are visible in the 76-minute form.) Yet one recognizes it within a minute or two as a warm and cuddly movie, from its puppy-like playfulness and from the mischievous smile which seldom leaves the lips of its spell-casting heroine. We are taken initially back to 1690 and an outdoor Puritan festivity presided over by portly Robert Greig, who as town crier announces: 'And now, while we prepare for the extinction of the sorcerer father of this witch, there will be a short intermission . . .' and a man comes on selling popmaize. It is clear even by this time that although the same original author wrote *Topper*, which leaned in its film version towards farce and invisibility tricks, the farce here will be limited to such moments as the hero stubbing his toe, while the tricks will be pleasantly handled but incidental to the main drift. Comic characterization is the thing, and the fact that Robert Benchley heads the supporting cast should be sufficient indication of the way things are expected to go.

So witch and warlock are put to death, but not before their persecutor, Jonathan Wooley, has had flung at him a curse that he and all his descendants will be unhappy in love. A few brief cameos then demonstrate the curse in progress, the Civil War scene being especially amusing. As the Wooley of that generation backs nervously away from his spouse towards the front door, the negro servant hurries in with the news that there's a war on. 'Where is the nearest recruiting office?' asks Wooley, to have his wife exclaim, 'Oh, running off to war like a coward!'

The 1942 Wooley is called Wallace, and like all the others is played by Fredric March in his nimblest straight comedy style. We can see at once that the curse is still in effect, for his fiancée as played by Susan Hayward is the most fearsome rich bitch in films. Even her father, a newspaper proprietor (Robert Warwick) who is busily getting Wooley elected governor, tells her at her eve-of-nuptials party: 'Will you try to be a little more pleasant, at least until after the wedding?'

Presently two puffs of smoke, released from their bondage by a lightning flash, are approaching the house, and the male puff is sampling the inside of a whisky bottle. The witch can't understand how the house is so brightly lit. 'Is it on fire?' she asks. 'Not yet,' replies her father with gurgling craftiness. It seems in fact that his magic works best by fire, for he sets off a blaze whenever either of them wants to materialize; her turn first. 'Goodbye, Jennifer, be a bad girl,' he calls, leaving her in a blazing hotel to be rescued by Mr Wooley on his way home, by which time the sexy-voiced puff of smoke has become the girl with the careless curl. Wooley takes the imperturbable and rather naked lady to hospital, but she promptly and mysteriously embarrasses him by turning up in his home as soon as he gets there. There is a small miracle of timing and film narrative at this point. Wooley is just entering his bedroom as his friend calls goodnight from the front door. Under his arm we see the girl sit up in his bed, and then Wooley sees her, and we hear the front door close as a cry rises to his lips.

So he is seduced into spending the night with her – quite innocently, for this is 1942 – and spends his wedding breakfast feeding her waffles, to the distress of his housekeeper. By now she thinks she has used enough charm to make him marry her, so that she can follow the curse and make him even more miserable than Susan Hayward would. But duty eventually calls him, so she has recourse to a love philtre. Unfortunately he feeds it to her as water while she is temporarily knocked out by a falling picture of his disapproving ancestor, so now she has an even more pressing reason for stopping his society wedding. Father has by this time material-ized into Cecil Kellaway, giving an Oscar-deserving performance of roguish malevolence, and he starts the chaos by sending a whirlwind ripping through the wedding parlour just as the bride to be is putting on her fiercest smile and a stately dame is giving out with 'I Love You Truly'. After this the groom remembers several pressing engagements upstairs, where the witch is threatening to reveal herself and her wicked old dad wants Wooley to shoot him so that he will fry in the electric chair. When Wooley demurs, he arranges things by remote control:

> Pistol, pistol, let there be
> Murder in the first degree

he murmurs, assuming a beatific smile as a shot rings out and he slumps in the armchair. By now Wooley is in no state at all to get married, and eventually his intended storms out in a fury of white lace despite his weak plea in mitigation: 'Did you ever have one of those days when just nothing seems to go right?'

Meanwhile witch blackmails father into putting new life into his old body, but while smoky he has been in the whisky bottle again, and falls out of the window. Taken to jail as drunk and disorderly, he finds that he can't remember any of his spells, thus giving witch and Wooley time to get married. The lady now uses her powers to get her new spouse elected: any X against his opponent's name on the ballot paper has a curious way of preferring to slide down against his. It is a landslide victory; as Wooley notes in bewilderment, his opponent didn't even vote for himself. He is even more incredulous when his wife tells him how she did it. ('Ever hear of the decline and fall of the Roman Empire? That was our crowd.') But the warlock has now worked up another diabolical revenge against his telltale daughter and her too successful spouse. It involves a flying taxicab and a fatal crash. 'Back to the tree,' he screams gleefully, and indeed the concussion seems to have killed the lady, who has become mortal through love. But love also has a power to heal, and as Wooley mourns over her she recovers her life and her wits, dashing across the room to stopper up the whisky bottle in which Dad is again hiding. He is given pride of place on the mantelpiece, from which in years to come he is able to witness, no doubt gleefully, that the Wooley's infant daughter is showing worrying signs of loving her broomstick more than her lessons.

This is indeed a film to keep by one on cassette, for it would repeatedly soothe away a wakeful night. Almost carelessly it uses the most professional means to entrance eye and ear throughout its running time. It is not the kind of film which requires roars of approving laughter: the occasional quiet chuckle is much more in its line, as it dispenses what the New York *Morning Telegraph* called 'a delightful sense of oddity and enchantment'. Enthusiasts for Clair's earlier *The Ghost Goes West* will certainly recognize the mood, though that comedy was more primitive and less piquant than this mischievous piece of Hollywood glitter. And perhaps in the end, what one relishes most, whether they got on or not, is the curious contrasting rapport between the stars: a slip of a girl with a sultry look but no acting experience, cosseted by a great director into appearing the equal of a serious actor who throughout his twenty-two years of increasing eminence has been prepared to take on the occasional light comic role. The film's only sin is that it more or less wastes Mr Benchley, though he has one delightfully confused exit line after light has dawned on him that his friend's wife really is a witch: 'Oh well, it's late, I've got to be getting into my strait jacket. I'll call a broom.'

I Married a Witch. US 1941; monochrome; 82 or 76 minutes. Produced and directed by René Clair for Cinema Guild. Written by Robert Pirosh and Marc Connelly from *The Passionate Witch* by Thorne Smith. Photographed by Ted Tetzlaff. Music score by Roy Webb. With Fredric March as Wallace Wooley; Veronica Lake as Jennifer; Robert Benchley as Dr Dudley White; Cecil Kellaway as Daniel; Susan Hayward as Estelle Masterson; Robert Warwick as J. B. Masterson; Elizabeth Patterson as Margaret.

Encounters of Too Close a Kind
Invasion of the Body Snatchers

In the small Californian town of Santa Mira, a doctor discovers that extra-terrestrial spores have taken root nearby and produced pods capable of taking over human beings by growing into their absolute likeness. He is finally able to escape and warn the authorities.

For a few months in 1956 I worked on the staff of a fan magazine called *Picturegoer*, later *Picturegoer and Date*, later *Date and Picturegoer*, later defunct. In between interviewing Michael Balcon, Melina Mercouri and Peter Finch I actually reviewed a few films. I came back one morning in a lather of excitement from a Studio One press show and knocked at the editor's door. 'Sir,' I said (one did in those days), 'I wish to propose a candidate for the *Picturegoer* Seal of Merit.'

Picturegoer had a one- to four-star rating system, with an open star for a real lemon; recently instituted at the other end of the scale was a rosette for outstanding merit, the *Picturegoer* Seal. Recipients included such as *Richard III* and *The King and I*, but we were not above honouring the odd unsung piece of new and unexpected talent. However, eyebrows were not merely raised but arched at my enthusiasm for what sounded from title and synopsis like a tuppenny horror flick from Hollywood's Poverty Row. Two colleagues were accordingly despatched to check whether I had been imbibing too freely before the screening; they returned as glowing as I was. It all took on the feeling of an H. M. Bateman cartoon; anyway, *Invasion of the Body Snatchers* got its seal, its director became a cult hero, and small towns have seemed sinister to me ever since.

The title suggests horror augmented by violent action, and the film has very little of either, unless one counts the destruction by garden fork of some slimy, slithery seed pods found growing, with many a plop and hiss, in King Donovan's garden greenhouse. This is a film in which the horror is all in the mind: the horror of being taken over during sleep and being replaced by an exact double from outer space; worse still, perhaps, the horror of finding that all one's friends are aliens. (Irritatingly, neither film nor book ever does explain what happens to one's original body.) The hook of the movie, in its later stages, is that the four friends fighting the invasion are taken over one by one, and the most terrifying moment comes when the exhausted heroine, who has been all night on the run, falls asleep for a moment: the hero kisses her to wake her up, but starts back in horror. It is too late: she has instantaneously changed into a screaming cloned harpy who yells their position to the aliens in hot pursuit. The last sequences, featuring a chase over the hillside which separates the little community of Santa Mira from the main highway, have a wonderful sense of familiarity giving way to strangeness. Sounds float up from both sides to the scrubby heights where it appears for a moment that pollution may have been avoided . . . and what seems at first to be a celestial choir turns out to be a commercial programme on a truck radio in the valley.

INVASION OF THE BODY SNATCHERS. It's a little unnerving when your own double grows before your very eyes on your own billiard table. King Donovan (twice), Kevin McCarthy, Dana Wynter

However much or little secondary meaning Jack Finney may have intended in his unique novel, there is no doubt that the film version had something to say for its generation, which had survived the implacable facelessness of the Cold War and the incredible era of supposed UnAmerican Activities when free thinkers were accused of nameless sinister objectives and robbed by plaster saints like Joe McCarthy of all they had believed in and worked for. It came as a plea for individuality and emotion at a time when people were being coerced into taking sides in a battle with no heroes. Santa Mira was a symbol of Shangri-La, unthreatened by either Sodom or Gomorrah until an even more inhuman enemy drifted in remorselessly from space. Reality, in the twenty-five years since the film was made, has proved that the small town was no match for man in the shape of urban planners and ecology destroyers: the corner shop was razed beneath the tractors of the conglomerates, and chemical fertilizers combined with man's own poisonous waste to pose a new threat to the healthy future of mankind. For this reason the expensive but unpersuasive 1979 remake of *Invasion of the Body Snatchers* was set not in a small town but in San Francisco, for big cities are now at risk and small towns already a lost cause; but the story simply as a story doesn't convince in this context, despite such nice in-touches as giving Kevin McCarthy, our hero in the original, a brief moment as the running man, still shrieking his warning to humanity before being run down by a passing car.

It has to be admitted that, cinematically, the original *Invasion of the Body Snatchers* works rather less well than it did. To begin with, one hadn't remembered it in SuperScope, which not only makes the black-and-white photography pale and lacklustre but is far too wide and action-orientated a ratio for a story which depends on whispered suggestions and the constant expectation of the unexpected. It also shows up the parsimony of the budget, by leaving too many empty corners where the eye can't rest. Being used to low budgets, Siegel covers up the cracks as best he can, but it's a struggle. It is fashionable to sneer at the front office's last-minute addition of a flashback prologue which sets up McCarthy's incredible story, but it is smartly done, with a splendid shock moment of the hero's first wild appearance as a door is opened, and it conjures up an air of brooding menace without which the first two reels might seem too plodding and dull as they set up the nuances of change which are worrying one or two people in Santa Mira. McCarthy, the local doctor, is called back from a conference to deal with a curious outbreak of mass hysteria among his patients: they all claim that their relations aren't really their relations at all. When they later recant (having been 'podded' themselves), he is more rather than less concerned. As Miles, McCarthy gives an amiable if slightly actorish performance, his rock-hewn features expressing alarm a shade too easily, though he certainly wins our vote as the best leader around. The real action begins when his friends the Bellicecs find an almost lifelike pod on their billiard table, just about ready for the final wrinkles which will turn it into the head of the house; and from then on the movie is a steadily-developing nightmare, its only hiatus coming when the doctor and his girl manage to snatch a few hours in the most unexpected place in town, his own office. Even here, next morning, they are confronted by a remodelled Bellicec and by the friendly neighbourhood psychiatrist, who puts over the film's anti-message. 'Love . . . faith. Without them life's so simple.' The pods are placed which will shortly absorb the personalities of the hero and heroine. 'Relax. There's no pain. While you're asleep they'll be taking you over, cell by cell. You'll walk into an untroubled world.' Miles speaks for us: 'Where everyone's the same?'

While maintaining the increasing pace and urgency, Siegel finds time for plenty of neat little touches. When Miles and Becky mount a hundred steps up a hillside, the reverse tracking shot showing their pursuers is worth the trouble it obviously took. When the blank on the billiard table suddenly opens an eye in semi-close-up, it's the kind of shock moment you chuckle over and remember. The daily distribution of truckloads of fresh pods is very properly watched only from the viewpoint of Miles in his office, where the distant, silent action seems far more unsettling than close-ups would have been. The fast-rolling clouds and softened drums under the credits have precisely the right air of menace. And the sense of place throughout the movie is excellent. You can almost smell the dusty sunlit office, sense the chill of the dark stairway leading up to it, touch the tacky plastic of the seats in the uneasily empty restaurant. The pods themselves, when closed, look a bit rubbery, but the scene of their accelerated development is truly horrendous.

From the viewpoint of the 1980s this little film may seem less exceptional, because it was only one of several science-fiction thrillers using similar themes and locations. *It Came from Outer Space*, made three years earlier in 3-D, has almost the same plot, except that in this case the aliens touch down by accident and want to leave again as soon as their craft is mended: the essential difference here is its exploitation of the eeriness of the Arizona desert, with its straight roads, heat haze, and spiky joshua trees. Slightly stiffly handled by Jack Arnold, it maintains a good sense of the strangeness of familiar things, and he and Siegel both use the trick of a hand coming suddenly into frame and grasping the hero's shoulder while his back is turned. In fact, Arnold uses it twice; but neither of them invented it. He also borrows Hitchcock's old trick of a girl screaming mixing quickly into another noise, in this case a telephone ringing. And Harry Essex's script (from Ray Bradbury's story) has some decent lines, as when the sheriff comments, 'Did you know that more

murders are committed at 92 degrees than at any other temperature? At lower temperatures people are easy-going; higher it's too
hot to move. But just at 92, people get irritable.'

If this sounds like a western in disguise, then maybe it is, with
jeeps instead of horses. But no western ever had a villain like *Them*,
made in 1954, also set in the desert, and again with a disturbing
music score to set the mood. The first half hour of this movie is
simply marvellous; but once the mysterious menace is revealed to be
giant ants, the entertainment dwindles to a matter of stop-frame
animation, plus a nice performance by 84-year-old Edmund Gwenn
as the enterprising professor. In England at this time, the challenge
of fighting the unknown was left to Professor Quatermass, who in
three intelligent thrillers, all condensed from TV serials, implanted
in thousands of young minds the need to keep an open mind on the
possibility of strangers from other planets finding ways to impinge
on our quiet, self-satisfied but intellectually disturbed post-war lives.

Invasion of the Body Snatchers. US 1956; monochrome; SuperScope; 80 minutes.
Produced by Walter Wanger. Written by Daniel Mainwaring, from the novel by Jack
Finney. Directed by Don Siegel. Photographed by Ellsworth Fredericks. Music score
by Carmen Dragon. Art direction by Edward Haworth. With Kevin McCarthy as Dr
Miles Bennell; Dana Wynter as Becky Driscoll; Larry Gates as Danny; King
Donovan as Jack Bellicec; Carolyn Jones as Theodora.

It Came From Outer Space. US 1953; monochrome; 3-D; 80 minutes. Produced by
William Alland for Universal-International. Written by Harry Essex, from a story by
Ray Bradbury. Directed by Jack Arnold. Photographed by Clifford Stine. Music
score by Herman Stein. With Richard Carlson as John Putnam; Barbara Rush as
Ellen Fields; Charles Drake as Matt Warren; Russell Johnson as George; Joe Sawyer
as Frank.

Give That Boy a Spotlight
The Jolson Story

*A fictionalized account of the road to success of the first
singing star of the talkies.*

It shouldn't have worked, even in 1946. Seven years later *The Eddie
Cantor Story*, a carbon copy, didn't work at all. Two years earlier, Al
Jolson couldn't get a job in Hollywood. He had paid the penalty of

too much fame in the late twenties, when in *The Jazz Singer* he broke three decades of movie silence by telling audiences 'You ain't heard nothing yet' and launching into 'Toot Toot Tootsie Goodbye'. (Every man and boy in the world became a Jolson imitator; some of them still are, and thirty years after his death he has one of the healthiest fan clubs in show business.) Five years after *The Jazz Singer* his vein was played out, and though he later tried experiment (*Hallelujah I'm a Bum*), nostalgia (*Swanee River*) and a recapitulation of his old hits while playing second fiddle to Faye and Power in *Rose of Washington Square*, his career in Hollywood was all washed up.

Jolson's urge to show off, to stand before an audience and belt out his schmaltzy, jazzy, Negro-Jewish numbers, was undiminished by this taste of adversity, and he didn't need money, despite the large amounts he lost on the horses. So in World War II he was one of the first stars to volunteer for overseas duty entertaining the troops, and his vibrant warm tones became known to a whole new generation of young people. Still Hollywood was slow to respond; in 1945 his cameo in *Rhapsody in Blue* was cut to one chorus of 'Swanee'. But there was one feared and hated minor mogul, a song plugger from way back, who knew Jolson's worth. Harry Cohn's studio, Columbia, was then on the brink of Poverty Row, grinding out cheap programme fillers featuring such charismatic characters as the Crime Doctor, the Whistler, and Blondie. True, he made an occasional biggie with Astaire or Hayworth, but it was big only by his standards, and he couldn't afford to have it flop. When a Hollywood journalist named Sidney Skolsky brought in the Jolson idea, Cohn intuitively knew it would go, but to his board it was an insane risk. On the train from New York to discuss it, Jolson met Jack Warner, who had already turned down the idea; when he heard that Cohn wanted it, he offered the *Yankee Doodle Dandy* team, and Cagney to play Jolson. Jolson was in demand again; he finally signed with Cohn, who he felt would spotlight the production whereas at Warner it might get lost in the shuffle; but he got 50 per cent of the profits, which made it, as things turned out, a multi-million-dollar deal.

There was one remaining snag. Who could play Jolson? Jolie thought he could do it himself, but Cohn shook his head: the mammy singer had never been good-looking, and he had long passed sixty. Danny Thomas was offered the part if he would have

THE JOLSON STORY. Larry Parks as the new star achieves his ambition: to sing to an audience with the house lights up

his nose shortened, but refused. Richard Conte and Jose Ferrer were considered, but lacked the pizazz. Finally, almost by accident, a minor Columbia contract player named Larry Parks was trained and tested, and afterwards no one had any doubt that he was the man for the job. The rolling eyes, the mischievous lips, the gravelly voice, the grand manner, were all there; with Jolson singing the songs to Parks' miming, the effect was uncanny, probably more mesmeric than Jolson had been himself when young. Jolson did insist on making one personal appearance: when at the height of his success the star moves up and down the runway singing 'Swanee', that's the real Jolson in longshot. As for Parks, the movie made him a major star, but he never really hit the top because he couldn't escape the Jolson image. Perhaps he didn't have a real personality of his own: at any rate in *Down to Earth* three years later he was still playing Jolson, and when he appeared as a seventeenth-century Scot in *The Swordsman* you expected him to get down on one knee among the heather and sing 'The Spaniard Who Blighted My Life'.

The script of *The Jolson Story* is fictionalized and sentimentalized beyond belief. Some of Jolson's youthful actions would not have been sympathetic on screen, and his ex-wife Ruby Keeler, round whom a good part of the story must plainly revolve, refused to allow her name to be used. Scenarist Sidney Buchman, after much hair-tearing, came up with a typically Hollywood compromise; the theme of the movie would be Jolson's need to perform, to see upturned faces appreciating his performance, and it was this that would wreck his personal life. The star wholeheartedly approved, and it is the wife, rechristened Julie Benson and attractively played by Evelyn Keyes, who in the film seems the less sympathetic, walking out on the great man just because he is recognized in a nightclub and persuaded to sing.

What made the film a hit is the ease and sympathy with which it moves, punctuated by no fewer than thirty-one songs. There are no big production numbers, but the Jolson manner makes up for that. Even the stereotyped introduction, with the young Jolson tearing himself away from his cuddly Jewish parents to embark on a life in show business, is accomplished with slick pace and movements of asperity among the schmaltz. These latter are mainly provided by William Demarest as the vaudeville pratfaller who becomes Jolson's mentor and later his manager, but much of the film's warmth comes from the outrageously but enjoyably tenderized performance of Ludwig Donath and Tamara Shayne as the elder Jolsons who get so confused when trying to follow their son's career in *Variety*. ('Poppa, what is sockaroo?')

Other attributes of the picture are its unassuming air, probably traceable to its unassuming budget; its lack of any villain except occasional glimpses of the Mr Hyde in Jolson; and its ability to suggest that 'Mammy', and the 'Kol Nidre' are part of the same emotional outpouring. The big 'new' musical hit it produced was 'The Anniversary Waltz', a song for old people; and perhaps the movie finally stands as the last of the big family successes so beloved of Louis B. Mayer. (He didn't make it, but he must have mightily approved of it.) Since director Alfred E. Green did not otherwise enjoy a notable career, we must assume that this was a composite effort and that he merely did what he was told; certainly Joseph H. Lewis was brought in to handle the musical numbers. Throughout the movie one somehow senses Harry Cohn calling the shots.

Although it runs 129 minutes it never slows down and never seems too big for its boots. A rolling roller title quickly gets it off the mark, with Jolson singing 'Let Me Sing a Happy Song' offscreen, and by the time Scotty Beckett merges imperceptibly into Larry Parks during a harmonica montage, we are as putty in its hands.

It all seems a long time ago, but I shall never recapture the excitement I felt one Friday night in Bolton in 1946. Unprecedentedly, the movie was booked at both the Queens and Rialto for two whole weeks, and I had to wait till the second week for the queues to abate, for Jolson songs were already flooding the radio airwaves and the fans had promptly rediscovered their old favourite.

I chose the Rialto and took my seat as a top-hatted Jolson was romancing his lady love with song:

> The stars are going to twinkle and shine
> This evening around a quarter to nine.

Two and a half hours later I emerged into what seemed a much better world. And a month after that I gathered up my family to luxuriate in the evident affection bestowed upon *The Jolson Story* by a packed audience at the Tivoli, a cinema which smelled of cottonseed oil transferred from the clothes of the spinners who were its principal patrons. After that I caught it on several revivals, and then its popularity waned and it went to television, which in this country at least has given it insufficient attention. In the late sixties, in the middle of the expansive 70mm years when fortunes were being made by *The Sound of Music*, some Columbia bright boy had the idea of cutting off the top and bottom of the image of *The Jolson Story* to give a 70mm ratio, and adding stereophonic sound. I shuddered at the thought, but went to the première, prepared to avert my eyes, for the sake of hearing the sound track in stereo. Despite much loss of colour and definition, the dastardly trick worked rather better than I expected, and there were so many among that stuffed-shirt West End audience who actually cried at 'Mammy' and burst into enthusiastic applause at the end. The only comparable feeling I've had in a place of entertainment was in New York in 1970, when *No No Nanette* was revived live on stage and Ruby Keeler came tap-tap-tapping her way downstairs to centre stage, flung her arms akimbo in that clumsy way she always had, and thudded her feet alternately against the boards as though Dick Powell were still waiting in the wings. I thought the roof was really going to be raised that night, because all the rich sixty-year-olds in the audience were reliving their own moments of glory along with Ruby and thinking: if she can still do it, so can I. Similarly *The Jolson Story* on its first release appealed mainly to the vast number of happily marrieds who had been youngsters when Jolson first hit the airwaves. There is a religious fervour to Jolson's performing, but the only religious object is himself. The deep brown, nasal tones belting out the assurance to his mammy that 'I'd walk a million miles for one of your smiles' . . . that's show business. And even in his sixties, after losing a lung, he could still make new converts and sell records by the million. The thrill is one that can never be entirely recaptured by another generation; but alas, what is there for the middle-aged fans of 1980 to recall with such affection? What film has enough bouncing optimism to do so many people so much good as *The Jolson Story* did?

Although a hundred musicals must have been made about the Jolson era or burlesque or vaudeville or minstrel shows or that final big night at the Palace, only a handful stand out vividly in the memory. We have mentioned *Rose of Washington Square*, which Jolson more or less takes away from the principals, acquiring in the process a curious comedy sidekick in the form of Hobart Cavanaugh. We have mentioned *Yankee Doodle Dandy*, which is basically a one-man patriotic extravaganza on the life of George M. Cohan; when the man is Jimmy Cagney, no more is required. *Alexander's Ragtime Band* had most of the required brassiness, some of it provided by Ethel Merman: if only she'd been allowed to play in *Gypsy* instead of Rosalind Russell! Donald O'Connor and Jack Oakie were *The Merry Monahans*. MGM made several efforts, but their touch was always too genteel. *There's No Business Like Show Business* had the songs but didn't seem to take place in a real world at all. For me the movie most evocative of that tawdry backstage milieu, where nervous amateurs got the hook on Friday nights and the star was likely to have his career blighted by the demon rum, was *Show Business*, made by RKO in 1944. Almost forgotten now, it gathered together a splendid quartet in Eddie Cantor, Constance Moore, Joan Davis and George Murphy. The last-named sang 'They're Wearing 'Em Higher in Hawaii' (pronounced how-a-yuh), the first-named reprised 'Whoopee', and they all seemed to sing 'It Had To Be You' at least half a dozen times. There's glory for you.

The Jolson Story. US 1946; Technicolor; 129 minutes. Produced by Sidney Skolsky for Columbia. Written by Stephen Longstreet. Directed by Alfred E. Green (dance numbers, Joseph E. Lewis). Photographed by Joseph Walker. Musical direction by Morris Stoloff. Songs, many and various. Art direction by Stephen Goosson and Walter Hoscher. Edited by William Lyon. With Larry Parks as Al Jolson; Scotty Beckett as young Jolson; William Demarest as Steve Martin; Evelyn Keyes as Julie Benson; Ludwig Donath as Cantor Yoelson; Tamara Shayne as Mrs Yoelson; Bill Goodwin as Tom Baron; John Alexander as Lew Dockstader.

Never Trust Elderly Men on Ships
Journey into Fear and Across the Pacific

Just before World War II, an American engineer on loan to the Turkish government is pursued by Nazi assassins. In 1941, a US army officer trails Japanese spies to Panama.

You know the kind of friend one hangs on to through thick and thin rather because one knows him intimately than because of any sterling qualities he may possess. So it is with me and *Journey into Fear*. I have researched it and understand its history; it was made by people who did incomparably better things; but I know it warts and all. A Mercury Production by Orson Welles, it came two years after *Citizen Kane* and a year after *The Magnificent Ambersons*. By then RKO was trying to wriggle out of its contract with Welles, for his nuisance value was far higher than his box office returns: with *Kane* they narrowly avoided a major lawsuit, and *Ambersons* was in their view so uncommercial that they had to lop off the last half hour and send it out as a second feature. The budget for his third film was therefore minimal: something that could be shot quickly on a few sets, with moody photography and lots of mist to obscure the lack of dollars. Welles himself was restless, anxious to work on a semi-documentary about South America; but it was the first of many projects he was not to complete. His fine repertory of actors was breaking up, there being lucrative offers from other employers; but Joseph Cotten was faithful, and it was probably he who suggested an adaptation by himself of Eric Ambler's thriller. Somehow production got going, though Cotten's writing was more replete with literary allusions than with film sense, and Welles at the last minute found himself too busy to direct, though he did purloin the small but meaty role of the head of the Turkish secret police.

The result had mood, all right, and years later *The Third Man*, with Cotten in an almost identical role, borrowed and improved upon its atmosphere and style. But there is scarcely enough plot to pad out the meagre running time, and too many scenes either start with menace and build up to nothing, or begin and end in the middle of conversations, as though not enough was shot and the final film had to be pieced together as extracts from the framing letter which the hero writes to his wife but never sends. The ladies in particular have a raw deal: del Rio's role is elusive at best, and she doesn't even serve the familiar purpose of stopping a bullet meant for Cotten, while Warrick and Moorehead are reduced to a couple of sentences each. The plot makes little sense, for the Turks could find a hundred better ways of protecting their charge, just as the Nazis could find a hundred easier ways of disposing of him. And the boat gives no sense of being at sea, only at the far end of one of RKO's lesser sound stages.

What remains on the credit side? A number of delightful fragments, an indication of the kind of movie it might have been with a little more care and attention. The biggest impression is made by a character who says nothing. In the very first shot we zoom up to the window of a sleazy room in Istanbul, where an obese and perspiring man vaguely attends to his lank hair and wipes the comb on his already dirty coat, while listening to a gramophone the needle of which repeatedly sticks. He dons a pre-Columbo mackintosh, caresses and pockets a revolver, adds pebble glasses and an oddly pointed black hat, and emerges into the night as the most nightmarish villain in filmdom. He is Banat, and his mission is to kill our hero as inconspicuously as he can; his real name is Jack Moss, he was Welles' agent, and he never acted again.

After Banat murders the wrong man in a dingy cabaret, all the suspects are rounded up and taken to Colonel Haki, who is Welles in a false nose and astrakhan hat, making a barnstorming entrance which belies the modesty of his credit. He rolls a few sinister lines round his tongue and tells our hero: 'Do not worry about your wife. I will take care of her personally.' This is not at all reassuring.

Most of the movie is set on the boat, which boasts the expected motley collection of passengers, one of whom must be Muller the

Nazi. Is it the Sydney-Greenstreet-style archaeologist who has been 'investigating the pre-Islamic cultures'? Or the Peter-Lorre-style tobacco salesman? ('I am neutral, you understand, I know nothing. I sell tobacco.') How about the mild Frenchman who scares his wife by pretending to be a commie? ('War is the last refuge of the capitalists.') Or one of the dancers from the nightclub? Conceivably Muller is a member of the crew? At the first stop, noises from a newly occupied cabin tell Cotten only that there is a new passenger; but we recognize a gramophone with a needle that repeatedly sticks. And soon the archaeologist produces a gun, and lines like: 'Please do not move. When one gets to my age one grows to resent any movement except that of the respiratory organs which keep one alive. For movement means change, and change means death.'

Somehow the protagonists get off the boat, and suddenly the film lurches into action, exploding into a firework display of vertiginous shots, including a famous low one as Cotten leaves the boat and a little later, during a chase in the rain round a hotel balcony, a high one in which the raindrops spike down like icicles. At this point Haki makes a reappearance, only to be shot so that he can collapse spectacularly through a window; but our hero's dander is up, and seconds later both Muller and Banat lie in the gutter with rain splashing around them. 'I got *mad*,' he tells Haki later. And yes, perhaps the movie after all is just another allegory for America's entrance into the war.

Another shipful of spies is the focus of *Across the Pacific*, which gets second place here because it was made as a hasty follow-up to *Maltese Falcon*, boasts the same star team and director, and isn't so good. But what could be? Judged on its own merits this is an amusing, suspenseful and well-written entertainment built around several rock-hard talents, and we can now forgive it the propaganda content which caused it to be promoted as a 'Jap-slapping sensation'.

Presumably the significance of the title is to remind America where the danger lies; the boat however only winds its way down the east coast from Nova Scotia, and gets no further than Panama. Bogart is on it, as Richard Lomas Leland, a cashiered army officer now sporting a trench coat and a chip on his shoulder. Sydney Greenstreet is on it, as Dr Konrad Lorenz, a professor of sociology

JOURNEY INTO FEAR. Joseph Cotten battles it out on a hotel ledge with Jack Moss. Guess who slips

from the Philippines, a connoisseur of Dimple Haig and an ardent Japophile: 'A much misunderstood people, sir. To know them is to feel the greatest affection for them.' Mary Astor is on it as Alberta Marlow from Medicine Hat: she makes a lot of jokes about seasickness and worries about Bogie going to Yokohama. She needn't, for during the New York stopover we are shown that Bogie after all is a right guy (we know it all along) on the trail of master spy Greenstreet, who shortly thereafter makes his disarming move: 'I never discuss being a traitor with a man. You'll find it easier if you don't think about that part of it.'

It seems that Leland has vital information to impart about the Panama defences, and accepts 2,000 dollars for it. Lorenz, being a cad, has him beaten up and takes back the money before a newspaper date – 6 December 1941 – gives us a clue what he's up to. And Miss Marlow, it transpires, is really the daughter of D. Morton, a dipsomaniac so much in Lorenz's power that he is allowing his plantation to be used as a Jap air strip. Lorenz's manservant, T.

214

Oki, turns out to be a Japanese crown prince who as pilot will have the honour of 'knocking over the canal'. And wincingly all-American Joe Totsuiko (Sen Yung) is what the script naïvely calls a 'Japanese gunsel'. All that remains is for Leland to save the day, which he does rather splendidly by escaping from a squalid cinema with a sinister Jap at every exit (how? round the screen of course) and barging in where angels might understandably have feared to tread. 'I am surprised,' chuckles the imperturbable doctor; 'but that is the way with you, you are always furnishing surprises.' There is then a short pause for propaganda

RICK: You guys have been looking for a war, haven't you?
JOE: That's right, Rick, that's why we're starting it.
RICK: You may start it, but we'll finish it.

So saying, he leaps into action, bounds into the jungle, takes over a handy machine gun post, and brings down T. Oki just as his wheels leave the tarmac; whereupon the good doctor tries to commit hara kiri, but finds that his Japophilia doesn't stretch that far.

Put together with Warners' usual cunning at concealing a paucity of sets, and with their usual heavy photographic gloss, *Across the Pacific* is ideal for a Saturday night out, even forty years after the events about which it took such pains to be topical.

Journey into Fear. US 1942; monochrome; 72 minutes. Produced by Orson Welles, for RKO. Written by Joseph Cotten and Orson Welles from the novel by Eric Ambler. Directed by Norman Foster (after preparation by Orson Welles). Photographed by Karl Struss. Art direction by Albert S. D'Agostino and Mark-Lee Kirk. Music score by Roy Webb. With Joseph Cotten as Graham; Dolores del Rio as Josette; Orson Welles as Colonel Haki; Ruth Warrick as Stephanie; Agnes Moorehead as Mrs Mathis; Jack Moss as Banat; Everett Sloane as Kopeikin; Eustace Wyatt as Dr Haller; Edgar Barrier as Kuvetli; Frank Readick as Mathis; Jack Durant as Gobo.

Across the Pacific. US 1942; monochrome; 97 minutes. Produced by Jerry Wald and Jack Saper for Warners. Written by Richard Macauley from a serial, *Aloha Means Goodbye*, by Robert Carson. Directed by John Huston. Photographed by Arthur Edeson. Music score by Adolph Deutsch. Art direction by Robert Haas and Hugh Reticker. With Humphrey Bogart as Rick Leland; Mary Astor as Alberta Marlow; Sydney Greenstreet as Dr Lorenz; Sen Yung as Joe Totsuiko; Charles Halton as A. V. Smith; Monte Blue as Dan Morton; Chester Gan as Captain Higoto; Richard Loo as First Officer.

Eighth Wonder of the World
King Kong

Made curious by traveller's tales, a film producer takes his crew to Skull Island, the mystery of which turns out to be a fifty-foot ape which carries off his leading lady. She is rescued, and the ape transported to New York, where it wreaks havoc and is shot down by airplanes from the top of the Empire State Building.

This extremely tall story is a seminal film in so many respects that it is hard to know where to begin. (Like so many seminal films it was ignored in its own day by everybody except the paying public: no Academy Awards, no critical commendation.) To 1933 audiences it was so slick and so modern that they couldn't believe the ape wasn't real, but its essential theme is that of an age-old legend, as the last line of dialogue makes clear: 'It wasn't the airplanes, it was beauty killed the beast.' Promised 'the tallest, darkest leading man in Hollywood', actress Fay Wray had to admit that she had not been deceived, for *Kong* is indeed a love story.

It is also the grand-daddy of all the monster animal pictures which proliferated so boringly in the fifties and sixties, when for no very good reason they were labelled 'science fiction'; *Kong* thought of itself as an adventure thriller, which is both a more exciting and a more dignified term. It is the last work of Edgar Wallace, though according to producer Merian C. Cooper he wrote 'not one damned word' of it before dying of pneumonia in February 1932; his screen credit is contractual but also appears because his famous name was expected to add something to the box office receipts, which it certainly did. Undoubtedly Cooper had been dreaming up *Kong* since 1929, when his partner in globe-trotting documentary drama, Ernest Schoedsack, had temporarily left him in Hollywood for a solo voyage to Sumatra. Cooper, reluctant to allow an eventful career to dwindle into that of a mere business executive, and spurred by the reported discovery of the Komodo dragon, devised a fictional story in which an island cut off from the evolutionary progress is found

KING KONG. Master of all he surveys – for one magnificent night of rampage

still to harbour forms of prehistoric life. He seems even to have named his giant gorilla Kong. When asked later what made him devise such a yarn, Cooper replied: 'To thrill myself. And to please the audience, of course. I wanted to produce something that I could view with pride and say, "There is the ultimate in adventure."' One thing Cooper certainly invented was the 'old Arabian proverb' which opens the picture: 'And the prophet said: Lo! the beast looked upon the face of beauty. And it stayed its hand from killing. And from that day it was as one dead.'

But several coincidences had to happen before *Kong* could be put before the cameras. First, David O. Selznick was appointed head of RKO Studios. He found on his books a stop-frame animation project called *Creation*, the brain child of Willis O'Brien who had activated the monsters for the 1924 version of *The Lost World*. It lacked plot values, and Selznick was about to cancel it when Cooper answered his summons to become head of production. Cooper saw a way of diverting the technical talent amassed for *Creation* to fit his own yarn, which Selznick conceded was more likely to be box office, and O'Brien agreed cautiously that a fifty-foot gorilla could be animated in such a way as to appear to share the screen with normal-sized people. Schoedsack was back and eager to work, and his wife Ruth Rose, an expert geographer, set about the screenplay as though she were writing another documentary, taking the more sensational bits from sailors' yarns overheard on her trips, and deliberately avoiding any explanation of how Kong could possibly have been transported in secret from Skull Island to the stage of a Broadway theatre. The project was then known as *The Eighth Wonder*.

Before long the budget, even while production was still in the preparatory stage, began to cause concern in the front office, and an ingenious method was adopted to pare it down. The studio was about to start shooting *The Most Dangerous Game*, another tropic island story about a mad hunter who deliberately wrecks travellers and then hunts them down for sport with his pack of fierce and hungry hounds. Cooper had the forest set for this comparatively cheap film made bigger than necessary, and the *Kong* crew moved in between takes to use it for their own purposes saving a fortune in tests of photographic and animation techniques. By the time *Game* wrapped, *Kong* was ready to go, and while watching the dailies Cooper had even cast his monster movie. Robert Armstrong, who played one of Count Zaroff's victims, was given the key role of the film producer, and became a life-long friend of Cooper. (Oddly enough, they died on the same day, forty-five years later.) Fay Wray, whose quivering lips perfectly registered terror, was an obvious choice. Joel McCrea was also offered the crossover, but his agent wanted too many of his stunts doubled, so the lead in *Kong* went to the athletic Bruce Cabot. Max Steiner's throbbing, pounding music in the two films is very similar, as is Schoedsack's direction of the chase scenes, and the 'exterior' night photography has the identical chiaroscuro effect.

Kong premièred in February 1933 and became one of the greatest successes in talking picture history: the paying customers were astounded. It is perhaps Willis O'Brien's movie more than anybody's because it was he and his team who animated the monsters one frame at a time into a semblance of live movement and blended them into the studio background; in most of his appearances Kong is no more than eighteen inches high, only the head and an arm having ever been built to scale. One misjudgement on O'Brien's part and the thing would have become a farce instead of a heart-stopping suspense thriller. (In fact Kong's first appearance is his least convincing, because his rabbit fur skin has rippled differently as each frame is shot, giving the impression of an electric current playing through it.) The processes used were kept fairly secret at the time, though I remember reading in a magazine that the roars of fifty lions and tigers were blended to make Kong's voice.

I was fated not to see *Kong* until I was in the army, when a 16mm print shown in the private cinema of a military mental hospital in Dorset gave me a nervous walk home along dark country lanes. On its first release it had been denied a general certificate by the British Board of Film Censors, and the local bodies had variously labelled it Adult or Horrific. Bolton plumped for 'A', which should have allowed me in if accompanied, but added a firm *Adults Only*. This was a contradiction in terms, but being scarcely of an age to write and complain, I could only skulk past the cinema and absorb the stills, which were all drawn anyway, as frame blow-ups would not have looked impressive and there was no other way to combine all the delicate trick work onto a photographic plate. But having eventually caught up with *Kong*, I saw it again and again with undiminishing delight, at the Bolton Capitol, the Bournemouth Savoy, and London's Studio One; while in the early fifties I played it during my tenure as manager of the Cambridge Rex, even donning a tatty ape skin for the occasion and galumphing about behind bars at the rear of an advertising truck. I believe my performance did several passing ladies no good at all, but it livened up the box office no end.

Kong now turns up regularly on television and is still simply marvellous. There has never been so persuasive a monster movie. Even the opening reels are deliciously of their period, with the faded flower being picked up on a foggy waterfront and made to rehearse meeting something very frightening and very tall. The scenes in the native village are rousingly staged, with crescendos of unnerving music and a war dance rivalling anything Busby Berkeley was doing over at Warner. And once Kong has carried off his delectable morsel and made a pet of her, the chase scenes are breathtakingly paced and stunted, with authentically reconstructed prehistoric monsters popping one after another out of shady undergrowth, and on one occasion rising silently from a deep dark lagoon. Kong's attractively designed split-level lair brings further splendours, including the fight between Kong and a passing pterodactyl, which ends as usual with the giant ape testing for signs of life in his opponent's broken and bloody jaw. Cabot and Wray finally escape down what must be the longest reed in the world (if it's a rope, what *is* it doing there?) and every audience, fearful that we are nearing a happy ending too soon, bursts into applause when Kong begins to haul them up again. But they fall with a splash into the muddy waters below, and when he pursues them he is overcome with tear gas. The New York scenes, leading to his inevitable demise, please me less, but there is one glorious moment among the mayhem when he sticks his head up through the rails of the elevated railway and we hear the hum of the distant train approaching disaster, its packed contingent of commuters just seconds from a spectacular fate.

Few people now recall that a sequel was completed and rushed out only eight months after the original. The result is regretfully what one would expect. *Son of Kong* takes Armstrong and Wray back to the island, but most of it is poor talk; the animation when it comes is mainly unconvincing and the situations more hilarious than suspenseful, so that RKO was obliged to release it with the slogan: 'He's just as funny as his old man was fierce.' Interesting to archaeologists of the cinema, it is justly forgotten by the public, as indeed is the much ballyhooed 1976 remake with the emphasis on sex; Kong was played by a man in a skin when the forty-foot robot failed to work. But the great original goes marching on in undiminished grandeur; and *The Most Dangerous Game* wears pretty well too.

King Kong. US 1933; monochrome; 100 minutes. Produced and directed by Merian C. Cooper and Ernest Schoedsack for RKO. Executive producer, David O. Selznick. Written by James Creelman, Ruth Rose and Merian C. Cooper from an idea by Merian C. Cooper and Edgar Wallace. Photographed by Edward Linden, Verne Walker and J. O. Taylor. Chief technician, Willis H. O'Brien. Music score by Max Steiner. Edited by Ted Cheeseman. Sound by E. A. Wolcott. Art direction by Carroll Clark and Al Herman. With Robert Armstrong as Carl Denham; Fay Wray as Ann Redman: Bruce Cabot as John Driscoll; Frank Reicher as Captain Englehorn.

Through Lace Curtains, Darkly
King's Row

In a small American town at the turn of the century, a young medical student finds that one of his mentors is a sadist who unnecessarily amputates the legs of his best friend; another murders his own daughter and commits suicide from fear of insanity.

Some movies haunt the mind because of direction, or performance, or a shock scene. *King's Row* has two rather unusual reasons for being unforgettable. One of them is its music. Erich Wolfgang Korngold, a European infant prodigy, composed only a handful of Hollywood scores, and that for *The Sea Hawk* is perhaps the best known; but I think this one surpasses it. A masterpiece of melodic simplicity, it seems almost to have been written for the alphorn. Three low sonorous notes. Pause. The same three notes again. Pause. Six more, taking the movement to an alighting point; then a slightly faster, sharper exposition, and a satisfying conclusion. No doubt Korngold could have written it on the back of a cigarette packet, but it floods this entire movie with its subdued light. Its effect is minatory, ominous; it makes one think of cheerless times of history, like England after the Romans left, or America recovering from the Civil War. It is the kind of sound that summoned the malevolent spirit in M. R. James' *O Whistle and I'll Come to You My Lad*. It can't be ignored.

The other great distinction of *King's Row* is its production design by William Cameron Menzies, whom I also credited, quite accurately I think, with being the creative driving force behind *Gone with the Wind*. Here he performs a similar task for one of the directors of that epic, Sam Wood, a man whose films are not normally thought of as having great pictorial merit. Menzies matches the music by filling his studio skies with lowering dark clouds, by putting black evil mansions behind white picket fences, by letting us see just as much of the town as the story makes necessary, and no more. This last trick, the withholding of shops, churches and other meeting places, makes the characters turn in on themselves and appear greater than lifesize, fragments of a mighty melodrama; without it, and Korngold's score, *King's Row* might seem no more than *Peyton Place* in fancy dress.

Basically, of course, that is what it is. One doesn't really believe that such a collection of nasties could congregate in one otherwise pleasant and sweet-smelling place, and in Bellamann's original novel they are really too much to take, especially in the sequel when one of them thinks he's a werewolf. (It was never filmed.) But the film transmutes them into figures of grand opera, chilling us not with a picture of people like ourselves, but with symbols of evil incarnate. The evil is not necessarily deliberate or sinful. It includes Madame Von Eln's cancer and Drake McHugh's pride and Parris Mitchell's weakness. And at the end it is triumphantly cleared away by poetry and optimism and true love. Yes, it's that kind of picture, but scorn it not until you have experienced its final justification of a hoary old cliché: a dazzlingly framed shot of the lovers running across a field to meet each other as the music soars into grandeur, the end titles fade in, and the audience puts its handkerchiefs away and goes home transfixed by a dream of life lived at a more exalted and passionate level than is possible for most of us.

One should perhaps add a third distinction: the lambent camerawork of James Wong Howe, who did many fine things in his career but none finer than this. Television slightly diminishes his great talent; but see a good 35mm print of this film on a big screen, and you will feel you have lived in these great gothic-arched rooms, hidden in the shadow of the decorated staircases, pushed aside the velvet curtains, ridden through Main Street in a brand new buggy, gasped for summer breath in the tiny cottage on the wrong side of the tracks, tumbled in the straw of the stables and met a train in the winter snowdrifts of the station approach.

I first heard of *King's Row* through *Picturegoer*, a weekly paper which was my bible in the forties, and for which I later briefly worked. Paper being scarce during the war, there were never enough copies to go round, so every Thursday I was in town by eight to queue for my copy at the only likely newsagent. One week there was a special picture section on *King's Row*, which was described as 'an adult film with no concessions to nitwits'; sitting on the back seat of the 'N' tram bearing me to school, I shivered pleasurably at the

KING'S ROW. Robert Cummings is inspiring the legless Ronald Reagan by spouting poetry at him. Ann Sheridan seems to be saying: 'Don't worry, dear, he'll soon go away'

thought of the forbidden thrills this might imply, and when the film itself turned up at the Capitol I decided I had better not invite my mother to accompany me, in case she disapproved. I certainly found it riveting, but discerned no element which should debar a sensible thirteen-year-old from seeing it; so when it went on its second runs I took both mother and sister to see it at the Farnworth Ritz, a cinema with a dreary stalls but an extremely cosy circle, from which we enjoyed the high-flown melodramatic shenanigans most thoroughly.

The oddest thing about the success of this picture – and it *was* a commercial success all over the world, despite a publicity campaign which made it look like the story of a modern good time girl – was that it was cast by Warners with what appeared decidedly to be a second team. Ann Sheridan was perhaps due for a dramatic lead, but it was daring to make her the box office draw, especially as she does not play the central character. Ronald Reagan never looked like making a star of the first rank, though this film certainly marked the peak of his acting career, and many years later he called his autobiography *Where's The Rest of Me?*, which is the line he utters after waking up to find that he has no legs. Robert Cummings, though curiously satisfactory as Parris because the character is so weak, was not much of an actor at all, more of a light comedian, and even in 1942 audiences must have been led by his name to expect a comedy. But the casting director made up for these aberrations by the solid power of his supporting cast. Charles Coburn as the sadistic surgeon, Claude Rains as the mad one, Judith Anderson as an icy wife, Harry Davenport as the town's one amiable senior citizen, were never more memorable, while Nancy Coleman and Betty Field, two young and untried actresses, were remarkably successful in suggesting different degrees of psychopathology. As for Maria Ouspenskaya, this may be the role for which her wonderfully ugly face is best remembered, dying behind the shutters of the white house on the hill while her young grandson learns about life in the streets below.

From the very beginning, as children pass a sign reading 'King's Row, a good town to live in', the mood is one of irony amounting sometimes to savagery and of dramatic contrast which on occasion almost tumbles over the fine line of discretion into the world of a Charles Addams cartoon. You never laugh, however, even though Parris Mitchell is such an insufferably nice wide-eyed boy that a rude awakening just has to be round the corner. Unknown to him his beloved grandmother ('I'm crazy about you, lady') is dying. The birthday party he attends is marred by suggestions that the girl's father deliberately performs operations without chloroform, and on the way home Parris hears the screams for himself. His tutor Dr Tower allows *his* daughter to be seen by nobody, and when he finds that she plans to run away with Parris, he poisons her. Mentally however Parris is stronger than he looks. His reaction to these shocks is a long trip to Vienna (where else?) to study psychiatry; he returns years later to cure his legless friend of despondency (rather absurdly, by shouting poetry at him) and for himself finds romance with the new young tenant of his grandmother's house.

It may not seem the stuff of which classics are made, but few who have been exposed to it can resist its spell, for it combines the effects of a number of magnificent behind-the-scenes talents which firmly pick you up in reel one and don't let you go until they're good and ready. No concessions to nitwits, indeed, and not a masterpiece of the intellect either, but a supreme example of the challenging, thought-provoking and memorable melodrama which the Hollywood studio system could provide in its heyday but which now comes to us only in television's economy versions, with no attempt to emulate the great talents of Howe, Korngold, Menzies and their peers. The talkies were only ten years old when Hollywood got into its first giant stride; how long before it takes another?

King's Row. US 1941; monochrome; 127 minutes. Produced by David Lewis for Warner. Executive producer, Hal B. Wallis. Written by Casey Robinson, from the novel by Henry Bellamann. Directed by Sam Wood. Photographed by James Wong Howe. Music score by Erich Wolfgang Korngold. Production designed by William Cameron Menzies. Art direction by Carl Jules Weyl. With Robert Cummings as Parris Mitchell; Ronald Reagan as Drake McHugh; Ann Sheridan as Randy Monaghan; Betty Field as Cassandra Tower; Claude Rains as Dr Alexander Tower: Maria Ouspenskaya as Madame Von Eln; Charles Coburn as Dr Henry Gordon; Judith Anderson as Mrs Harriet Gordon; Nancy Coleman as Louise Gordon; Harry Davenport as Colonel Skeffington; Karen Verne as Elise Sandor; Ernest Cossart as Tom Monaghan.

Days of Steam and Spying
The Lady Vanishes

During the build-up to World War II, on a train bringing holidaymakers back through Europe, an elderly lady spy is abducted by mysterious enemies, and the young girl who has befriended her is almost persuaded that she never existed.

I always thought it was an MGM film. I remember in 1939 sitting on a tram, rounding the corner by the Queen's Cinema in Bolton and being confronted by a vast red 48-sheet with a train excitingly steaming out at me surrounded by pictures of the stars, among which was the MGM lion. (In fact *The Lady Vanishes* could scarcely be more in the Gaumont-British tradition, but the mystery was later solved when I discovered that for a short time that company did distribute through MGM.) Four years later I booked the movie for the school film society and we had to turn people away. In 1952 it made a splendid evening's entertainment at the South Bank Telekinema, now the National Film Theatre, and since then I must have

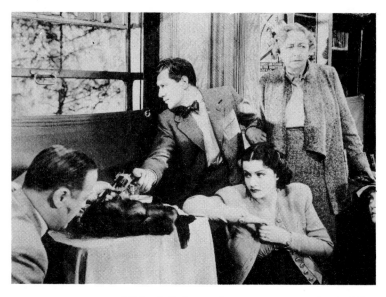

THE LADY VANISHES. Michael Redgrave keeps an eye on the baddies, Margaret Lockwood watches Basil Radford, and Dame May Whitty sees a way of escape

seen it at least once every couple of years. I was even able to assure the Rank Organization, when they press-showed it for a recent reissue, that they had the reels on in the wrong order. None of the national critics, incidentally, had noticed.

For a movie which is regarded throughout the world as one of Hitchcock's lighter masterpieces, the oddest thing about it is that it was conceived for, and set up by, another director altogether. Roy William Neill, who later made most of the Basil Rathbone/Sherlock Holmes thrillers, even did a week of shooting before being mysteriously replaced. Having been called in, Hitch clearly did a fast and skilful job, and probably injected a few humorous moments of his own, though the script by Launder and Gilliat is a classic in its own right and virtually director-proof: even the awful 1979 remake couldn't ruin *all* the jokes. This is by no means to diminish Hitch's marvellous ability to get exactly the right weight out of each actor's speech and gesture, or to linger with excruciating suspense over some detail which a lesser director would let go. The fact remains however that this has to be one of his least personal films in the sense that he never worked with his accustomed care on the storyboard; while Neill, perhaps, not sharing Hitch's contempt for realism, might have spared us the truly appalling model shots, including a car with no driver, which jerk about and get unintentional laughs right after the main credits. Come to that, while we are apportioning credit where credit is due, even Launder and Gilliat took their plot development and much of their characterization straight from Ethel Lina White's original novel, an early edition of which I was able to buy in 1977 for ten francs on the left bank near Notre Dame.

The first half hour of the adventure is not an adventure at all, but a rather jolly comedy about Charters and Caldicott, the perennial Britishers abroad, being forced to share the maid's room in a mittel-European railway hotel and then finding, when they have dressed for dinner, that there is nothing left to eat; and of Margaret Lockwood as a spoilt heiress being forced to share *her* room with Michael Redgrave after she has had him ejected for making too much noise with his peasant clog-dancing. Wonderfully in period, this section of the entertainment is full of lines like: 'Ze train she is a little bit uphold.' This presumably explains the fragments of German we hear, though the manager does seem to be Italian, and Dame May Whitty clearly states: 'Badrika is one of Europe's undiscovered corners.' (Later on, someone supplies the information that it is a train connection from Basle which is expected, so I suppose one is free to make up one's own geography.) Other stranded guests include the British politician (obviously a Tory) who has been on an illicit vacation with his light of love. (Cecil Parker and Linden Travers had an equally amusing undercover relationship ten years on in *Quartet*.) Their ardour has clearly cooled. 'My dear,' he expostulates at the hotel counter, 'a room at the back in a place like this!' 'You weren't nearly so particular in Paris last autumn,' she says sulkily. 'But that was quite a different matter,' he responds stiffly. 'Then the exhibition was at its height.' The film could well be considered worth seeing for this line alone, especially with an audience sufficiently quick to ring the rafters with it, and Miss Travers' raised eyebrows wring the joke dry.

Basil Radford and Naunton Wayne, who later made a whole career out of Charters and Caldicott, are tucked up in a double bed, with more than a suggestion of Laurel and Hardy, before the first sinister scene. Tweedy old Miss Froy has been listening carefully from her balcony to a street serenader, and she has just tossed a few coins and closed her window when hands reach out from the shadows and the singer is quietly strangled as the scene fades out. Why the British Foreign Office should require an elderly lady to travel across Europe's more dangerous zones remembering a coded tune when the same information could have been conveyed more quickly and efficiently by morse tapper, telephone or pigeon post is a question with no possible answer; but the film is so much fun that one does not begrudge it its lunatic McGuffin, 'the vital clause in a pact between two European countries'.

Next morning on the station platform, the young heroine, a debutante returning to London to marry an aristocratic oaf, receives on her head a flower pot clearly meant for Miss Froy. Comforting her with the promise of a cup of Harriman's Herbal Tea ('a million Mexicans drink it', if that's a recommendation), Miss Froy steers her into the restaurant car, then into a comfortable first-class seat where she quickly nods off; but half an hour later when she awakes, though the train has not stopped the old lady has disappeared; and the others aboard, for their own various if hardly convincing reasons, conspire to convince our Margaret that she never existed. The politician fears scandal, Charters and Caldicott don't want to miss the test match; but the lying waiters and the sinister baroness may have another motive. A brief glimpse inside a smoky third-class carriage brings Mr Redgrave back into the plot, but he also puts down Miss Froy as a figment of the girl's imagination, attributable to that bump on the head. Credibility is strained when they go back into the restaurant car and sit at the same table where Miss Froy so recently held sway, and Miss Lockwood sees the name Froy written in the condensation on the windows, as we the audience saw it written by the old lady herself. The cheat is that the letters are now quite different in style and position, and they disappear completely at a critical moment before Redgrave sees them, as the train goes through a tunnel, even though they are traced on the *inside* of the glass. There follows a frivolous scene in the baggage car when Redgrave pretends to be Will Hay with the help of a stray pair of pince-nez which Lockwood recognizes as Miss Froy's; he is then abruptly attacked by a manic conjurer, and the plot can start again in earnest, even the train appearing to pick up speed at this point.

'What was your friend dressed in? Scotch tweed, wasn't it?' 'Oat-meal tweed.' 'I knew it was something to do with porridge.' Lines like this one feel that Launder and Gilliat's natural successors are Frank Muir and Denis Norden.

Now the urbane foreign-accented doctor, played with sympathy and style by Paul Lukas, appears at last to believe our heroine's story; the audience of course knows that as he is so prominently billed he must be the chief heavy, especially as the nun attending his totally bandage-swathed patient wears high heels. Can the patient be Miss Froy? Of course she can. Will the doctor successfully dispose of Redgrave and Lockwood with a drugged drink? Of course not. As for the nun, she's really a likeable cockney who turns up trumps: if these heathens mean murder she isn't going to help them even for ready money. Charters and Caldicott nudge each other when they observe the unravelled Miss Froy's return to the restaurant car: 'Bolt must've jammed, old man.' But they turn out to be dab hands in a crisis, which comes when the nasties shunt the restaurant car into a siding and take pot shots at it. The only passenger who comes to harm is the politician, who discovers too late that these bounders don't even respect a white flag; when the rest by their own devices restart the train and escape into Switzer-land, even the heavy doffs his hat and says 'Jolly good luck to them.' But by now the lumpy and likeable Miss Froy has decided that she had better be going, through an offside window and across a stream, where she may or may not have been hit by a stray bullet; but first she bequeaths the tune to Redgrave and Lockwood, who spend the next two days whistling it.

In the hurried coda in London, several things happen in rapid succession. Hitch makes his fleeting personal appearance in Victoria Station. Charters and Caldicott find that the test match has been abandoned because of rain. Lockwood jilts her oaf, preferring after all not to be 'a slightly sunburned offering on an altar in Hanover Square', and accompanies Redgrave to the Foreign Office, where, surprise surprise, Miss Froy has arrived well before them; by what possible means is hard to imagine but the reunion causes a pleasant swell in the music, a delightful fade-out image, and a happy walk home for all concerned.

The Lady Vanishes is pure, harmless entertainment of a kind which is no longer considered commercial. One supposes kindly that the

1979 remake tried hard, but it totally lacked the charm and expertise which turned the 1938 version into an unexpected light classic. It preaches no message, unless one counts the passage near the end which reminds one that it came out in the year of Munich. 'I don't believe in fighting,' says the politician, getting out his white handkerchief. 'Won't do, old boy,' says Charters: 'Christians tried it and got thrown to the lions.' It offers no spectacle, except the nostalgic one of a train which looks comfortable, has polite attendants, and travels efficiently from place to place. It offers the merest whiff of sex and only the occasional suggestion of violence. But with superb control it pleases and satisfies, and years after seeing it one remembers its characters with the affection usually reserved for the oldest and dearest of friends.

The Lady Vanishes. GB 1938; monochrome; 97 minutes. Produced by Edward Black for Gainsborough Pictures. Written by Frank Launder and Sidney Gilliat, from the novel *The Wheel Spins* by Ethel Lina White. Directed by Alfred Hitchcock. Photographed by Jack Cox. Music direction by Louis Levy. Edited by Alfred Roome and R. E. Dearing. Art direction by Alec Vetchinsky, Maurice Cater and Albert Juillon. With Margaret Lockwood as Iris Henderson; Michael Redgrave as Gilbert; Paul Lukas as Dr Hartz; Dame May Whitty as Miss Froy; Cecil Parker as Todhunter; Linden Travers as Mrs Todhunter; Basil Radford as Charters: Naunton Wayne as Caldicott; Mary Clare as the Baroness; Googie Withers as Blanche; Catherine Lacy as the nurse; Philip Leaver as the magician.

London Suburban
The Lavender Hill Mob and Passport to Pimlico

A timid bank clerk conceives and executes a million-pound bullion robbery; residents of Pimlico discover that they are on Burgundian soil and declare an independent state.

When people speak of Ealing comedy, it is these two films they really mean; for Ealing is a suburb of London, and the films concern downtrodden Londoners getting their own back on society, by foul means and fair. The theme can be extended into the idyllic British countryside (*The Titfield Thunderbolt*) and a dour Scottish island (*Whisky Galore*), but it is the London worm turning which was

230

dearest to the little studio on the green, as though one of those thousands trudging to work over Waterloo Bridge suddenly elected to turn and go the other way, against the crowd. Notably these are two original scripts by T. E. B. Clarke, who also devised the 1946 comedy, *Hue and Cry*, which hesitantly introduced the genre, though itself plainly derived from the German *Emil and the Detectives*. Here teenage boys discovered that their favourite 'tuppenny blood' was being used to carry a crooks' code, and in the spirited finale hundreds of boys converged on the villains in and around a massive bomb site. Curiously stiff and dated apart from a couple of typically eccentric scenes with Alastair Sim as the author of the serial, *Hue and Cry* is now more historical than entertaining, its city skies seeming more constantly overcast than the plot warrants. But a few years later the same settings were given a fresh lease of life by the same director in *The Lavender Hill Mob*, one of the most perfect character comedies ever devised, and one which fully justified its Academy Award. Excepting the regrettable necessity to have the criminals caught at the end, this is a film so sure of itself as to delight for that reason alone: there is in it hardly a cut or a dissolve of an angle which does not serve the purpose of making you laugh. Or, rather, smile: until the final impeccably choreographed chase, with police cars colliding with other vehicles and radioing to headquarters a spirited rendering of 'Old Macdonald's Farm' (don't ask why, see the film), the mood has been the mood on Alec Guinness' face as he wryly contemplates the easy method by which he can make himself a fortune. Passed over for promotion at the bank, he has an answer which we appreciate the more because we know what has been in his mind:

MANAGER: The trouble with you, Holland, is that you haven't enough ambition. When a good opportunity comes along, grab it with both hands. It may not occur again.
HOLLAND: Very well, sir, I'll follow your advice.

Only Guinness, perhaps, could have squeezed so much juice – the raising of an eyelid, the emphasis on the word 'follow' – out of this simple reply.

We next see our hero in his Lavender Hill boarding house, holding knitting wool for one inhabitant and discussing mystery stories with another. But as he sips his soup he is making his plans, and arriving at the same stumbling block. The theft is comparatively easy – but how to get the bullion out of the country? The solution arrives in the shape of Stanley Holloway as a new lodger who makes base-metal Eiffel Towers and exports them to Paris. One evening Holland carefully explains his hypothesis, as pure fantasy of course, and we know by the other's wide-eyed expression that he is hooked, even before his famous close-up reaction: 'By Jove, Holland, it's a good thing we're both honest men!'

T. E. B. Clarke recalls in his autobiography that Michael Balcon had originally set him to work on a serious crime drama, which eventually became *Pool of London*. When he saw a promising comedy idea in the bank robbery, he was told to follow his head, and went to the Bank of England to ask the best way they could think of to steal gold bullion. Much to his surprise, his naïve request was given serious consideration. In fact, he writes: 'I sat in contented silence while they worked out the most essential part of my plot for me.' But even after seeing what a marvellous job Charles Crichton and the actors had made of his script, he still believed that the result was inferior to *Passport to Pimlico*, and left the Venice Festival the day before it was awarded the Golden Lion.

Passport to Pimlico, though it now seems over-contrived, was certainly the film which first established the Ealing vein in the public imagination. Anyone could recognize in this pleasantly tall tale innumerable spoofing references to the age of austerity and strained foreign relations through which Britons were then living. The story takes place in dilapidated London streets, transformed by a heat wave which gives the atmosphere a kind of magic. The opening shots, music and all, suggest a West Indian location, with white suits, venetian blinds and sunshades, but the camera pans down to include the sign 'Frying Tonight' and a radio voice announcing that we have been listening to Les Norman and his Bethnal Green Bambinos. (In-joke: Leslie Norman was then a studio executive.) A jogger in shorts sets the story going as he passes a group of boys rolling a big wheel into a crater containing an unexploded bomb, which blows up and reveals a cavern full of treasure, including documents which prove that the locals are not English at all, but Burgundians. Slowly they realize that this gives them certain privileges, such as not needing ration books providing they can

THE LAVENDER HILL MOB. Master criminals Stanley Holloway and Alec Guinness see their scheme at the point of fruition

persuade manufacturers to regard their requirements as export orders, and a few disadvantages, such as being invaded by black marketeers. Whitehall, in the predictable persons of Basil Radford (Home Office) and Naunton Wayne (Foreign Office), is in a tizzy over its cups of tea:

F.O.: I thought that since the treasure is the spoils of war I'd pass it over to the War Office.
H.O.: They wouldn't touch it. These people are aliens. It's your pigeon.
F.O.: But they're undesirable aliens. It's your pigeon.

The ingenious development of this situation, displayed mainly in newspaper headlines and illustrative montages, formed an irresistible fantasia for austerity Britain, especially when interpreted by a cast of comedy favourites. The laws of Burgundy, for instance, are declaimed by Professor Margaret Rutherford, who urges the new

Burgundians to form a parliament with the approval of the descendant of the duke. He turns up conveniently from Dijon, having thought it might be amusing to claim his inheritance, and Miss Rutherford is ecstatic:

PROFESSOR: Nothing could prevent me from instant communication with the living heir of Charolais. Forgive me – are you a bleeder? When you cut yourself, do you bleed excessively?
DUKE: I don't think so.
PROFESSOR: Pity. It's in the family.

A cod newsreel subsequently shows the grocer (Stanley Holloway) as prime minister, the bank manager (Raymond Huntley) as chancellor, and a customs post set up at the end of the street. The British government asks to negotiate, but the Burgundians can't agree terms. (Headline: BURGUNDIANS USE VETO.) When water runs short, they cut through Whitehall's barbed wire to turn on the hydrant, but in doing so unwittingly flood their own food supply. When they come near to surrender, however, the world accuses the government of starvation methods, and food parcels are thrown in from buses and trains, with an air lift including milk from a helicopter and a pig in a parachute. It's all a matter of the English behaving as the English are popularly supposed to do, but nobody had thought of making a comedy about it before, wartime morale boosters such as *This Happy Breed* seeming extremely artificial by comparison. Anyway, 1949's audiences lapped it up, especially the compromise ending which has the Burgundians giving Britain a loan in return for protection. This means that they have to have their ration books back, and all concerned, including the gentlemen from Whitehall, are invited to a gala al fresco lunch.

F.O.: Do you think we shall get more than two main dishes?
H.O.: Oh I hope so. I haven't had a good meal since that last deadlock in Moscow.

But a shade too obviously, the minute the prime minister announces 'We're back in Britain', the long-awaited thunderstorm starts, and the picture ends as it began with the jogger running through the scene, as the temperature falls rapidly to zero.

The Man in the White Suit and *The Titfield Thunderbolt* (with *Whisky Galore*) are treated separately in this volume. Other Ealing comedies are fewer on the ground than the novice film buff, bemused by the phrase, might think. Though not a comedy at all, *The Blue Lamp*, Ealing's tribute to the London police, is most in the familiar vein, with Jack Warner as P. C. Dixon being killed off but later resurrected for a twenty-year television run. Full of well-observed cameos in the sentimental manner, it stands comparison with Hollywood's *The Naked City*. *A Run for Your Money* is an enjoyable but very mild comedy about Welsh rugby supporters up for the cup and distracted by London's pleasures; it has its moments, but criminally wastes Alec Guinness. *The Ladykillers* I never liked at all: its gang of crooks, concerned to murder their elderly landlady because she knows too much, but coming to grief themselves one by one, falls hopelessly between black comedy and British music hall farce, while since there is no reality there can be none of Ealing's apt observations on it. *Kind Hearts and Coronets* is quite another kettle of fish, not only unique among Ealing comedies but the only British film ever made in this lightly macabre vein. Not by any means a warm or likeable film, it is remembered with affection because of Alec Guinness' playing of eight roles as the noble victim of Dennis Price's plot to get himself nearer to a dukedom; and for Price's marvellous touch as the elegant murderer, the best (and perhaps the only) performance he ever gave. But the script by Robert Hamer and John Dighton has many felicities of its own, notably Price's remark after seeing his first victim, plus light of love, over the waterfall in a canoe: 'I was sorry about the girl, but found some relief in the reflection that she had already presumably suffered a fate worse than death over the weekend.' My own favourite scene has Guinness as the aged parson unwittingly showing his murderer-to-be round his church: 'I always say that my west window has all the exuberance of Chaucer, without, happily, any of the concomitant crudities of his period.' *Kind Hearts and Coronets* is a film for connoisseurs willing to overlook its stiffness for the sake of such incidental delights along the way.

The Lavender Hill Mob. GB 1951; monochrome; 78 minutes. Produced by Michael Truman for Ealing Studios. Written by T. E. B. Clarke. Directed by Charles Crichton. Photographed by Douglas Slocombe. Music score by Georges Auric. Art direction by William Kellner. With Alec Guinness as Holland; Stanley Holloway as Pendlebury; Sidney James as Lackery; Alfie Bass as Shorty; Marjorie Fielding as Mrs Chalk; Edie Martin as Miss Evesham; John Gregson as Farrow.

Passport to Pimlico. GB 1949; monochrome; 84 minutes. Produced by E. V. H. Emmett for Ealing Studios. Written by T. E. B. Clarke. Directed by Henry Cornelius. Photographed by Lionel Banes. Music score by Georges Auric. Art direction by Roy Oxley. With Stanley Holloway as Arthur Pemberton; Barbara Murray as Shirley Pemberton; John Slater as Frank Huggins; Margaret Rutherford as Professor Hatton-Jones; Basil Radford as Gregg; Naunton Wayne as Straker; Raymond Huntley as Wix; Paul Dupuis as Duke of Burgundy; Betty Warren as Connie Pemberton; Jane Hylton as Molly; Sidney Tafler as Fred; Hermione Baddeley as Edie; Charles Hawtrey as Bert Fitch.

Moon over Malaya
The Letter

The wife of a successful rubber plantation owner is tried for the murder of another.

Behind the titles, a lambent moon passes behind banks of cloud. Trees strain their shadows diagonally across the frame, as though waiting for something to happen. The camera pans slowly down a rubber tree to watch the precious liquid dripping into a cup; then crosses the night-shaded lawn to a native compound where amateur musicians strum desultorily in the sultry air. Further to the right, the veranda of the big house eases into view. As unexpectedly as a thunderclap, a shot rings out; a white cockatoo flutters across the screen. More shots, and dogs start from their sleep. Through the screen doors staggers a well-dressed man, falling down the steps into a heap. A woman with an expressionless face follows, holding a gun before her and pumping bullets into his body even after he has slumped and lies still. The camera is still tracking forward into a close-up of her face, but learns nothing. The Malayans edge towards her in astonishment, looking up to watch the moon again pass behind a cloud. The woman stares up too as she is left in sudden darkness.

It is one of the most famous openings in cinema, and the years do not dull its impact: for this sequence alone, cinematographer Tony Gaudio joins the ranks of Toland and Garmes. As a studio, Warners always had a great facility for making much out of little: shadows and low-key lighting served the purposes of economy in addition to atmospheric effect. *The Letter* is an entire justification of this policy:

all the expensive location shooting in the world could not have improved on this backlot re-creation of plantation life and of the by-ways of Singapore.

By the time the audience gets its breath back, officialdom has arrived in the shape of a nervous young colonial servant. The woman locks herself in her room until her husband and his lawyer friend arrive, then emerges hesitantly to tell her story. The man was an old acquaintance who called unexpectedly, rather drunk, and suddenly tried to rape her. No one questions what she tells them. As whites, they believe her automatically, as someone who has survived one of the less common dangers of an alien land. 'Take your time, Mrs Crosbie,' urges the young official; 'remember, we're all friends here.' Though the tension is so acute that we don't even smile to ourselves, the dialogue in cold print does sometimes border on the laughable:

MRS CROSBIE: He looked me straight in the face and said, don't you know I'm awfully in love with you?
CROSBIE: Swine!
OFFICIAL: It's quite obvious the man only got what he deserved.

These days Mrs Crosbie might have been expected to fend off unwanted attentions with a sharp word or even a joke, but with this story we are back in the thirties or earlier, and we listen with bated breath while she tells her story as only Bette Davis can. Now we have time to realize we are in the presence of a master director. For a minute or more we look solidly at four backs, beautifully composed within the frame. A little later there is a flirtation with subjective camera as the men follow her description across the carpet, through the doorway and down the steps. All the time the family lawyer is watching and listening. His expression is not quite one of disbelief, though if we bear it in mind we shall not be too surprised at the subsequent turn of events. 'Would I have to be arrested?' Mrs Crosbie asks him during a lull in the discussion. He purses his lips slightly: 'I think you're by way of being arrested now.' Still, the only suspicion aroused in the audience at this point, and then only because frequent filmgoing will have made it clear that sudden remarks are seldom made in movies without a point, is by the breakfast table comment: 'Funny the head boy running off in the night.' We are shortly allowed to discover that the head boy has run

THE LETTER. Crosbie (Herbert Marshall) is congratulated on his wife's acquittal. But Bette Davis will find that the worst is yet to come

off to fetch the dead man's Eurasian widow, a stately tigress who, as the white party drives off to meet the requirements of law, emerges from the shadows to view the body and utter a barely audible cry.

Mrs Crosbie has had the first act to herself, but the lawyer now takes centre stage, first reassuring his client and then being confronted by his confidential clerk, a wily young oriental played to perfection by the underrated Sen Yung. This soul of discretion whispers in the lawyer's ear that in relation to the Crosbie case a friend of his is in possession of a letter written by Mrs Crosbie to the deceased on the day of the shooting, which appears to contradict her evidence that they had not corresponded for several months. The lawyer's face is a mask as he is allowed to read a copy of what turns out to be a note of suppressed passion, and his light dismissal of it is a cunning piece of acting, intended to convince the clerk but not the audience. Here it must be said that James Stephenson, an English stock actor in Hollywood who sadly died shortly after *The Letter* was released, gives in this film one of the most consummate star performances on record, even stealing the show from Miss Davis. Bosley Crowther called him 'superb, as the honest lawyer who jeopardizes his reputation to save a friend – a shrewd, dignified, reflective citizen who assumed a sordid business with distaste. He is the strongest character in the film, the one person who really matters.' One feels that even Miss Davis would agree.

Even after forcing Mrs Crosbie into a confession that the letter is genuine, and agreeing to defend her – 'I don't want you to tell me anything but what is needed to save your neck' – the lawyer continues the long conversation with his clerk, which is the heart and centre of Maugham's original story. He is assured that the highly incriminating letter, though in possession of the widow, need not go to the public prosecutor: it can be obtained for a mere ten thousand dollars.

MR JOYCE: Ong Chi Seng, what are you getting out of this?
ONG: Two thousand dollars, sir, and the greatest satisfaction of being of service to you and to our client.

Mrs Crosbie's voice echoes in the lawyer's ears: 'Are you going to let them hang me?' He persuades the husband to bankrupt himself by producing the money; the wife gets off, and the husband's reward is to hear from his ungrateful spouse: 'With all my heart, I still love the man I killed.' The tight little story has developed to Maugham's conclusion, with all three having to live with their guilt. Sadly this was not enough for the Hollywood censors of 1940, who insisted that a murderess must pay for her crime, and so the film is rounded off on another still and moonlit night as the vengeful widow stalks and stabs Mrs Crosbie . . . and herself is immediately whisked off by police as the credits roll. Even this false addition is handled by the director with immense style, a matter of billowing curtains, silent movement and deep shadows.

The Letter is a simple enough film, more a fully fashioned anecdote than a story, but will never, to any audience of the future which can see an unblemished 35mm print, be less than beautiful to watch. It is the work of a lapidary craftsman, relying on the superb techniques of a studio which can summon up at the drop of a hat the mood of Malaya, Manchester or Massachusetts. William Wyler was never much at home with realism, but immensely so with the kind of theatrical mood that camera, editor and actor could create. Most of his best films were in fact from plays, though they never stayed rooted in the stalls; even *The Letter* is shaped from the stage version rather from the original story, in which the shooting is only reported. In this area Wyler's reputation enabled him by the late thirties to go his own way with a series of up-market adaptations of semi-classical material which stand among Hollywood's major monuments.

Wuthering Heights, for instance, may have been adapted for the screen by two cheerful hacks who didn't even bother to read the original novel, preferring to work from a summary; its heather may have been painted tumbleweed; but even for the unromantically inclined it is a non-stop pleasure to watch, respecting the melodrama but never going over the top, even in the death scene with Cathy held in Heathcliff's arms at the open window so that she can see her beloved moors again. Wyler also manages the ghosts with discretion, both the distant ones at the end and the unseen one at the beginning, frightening Lockwood with its tapping at the window until Heathcliff bundles him out and bursts open the shutter, throwing out his arms to the raging night: 'Oh, my heart's darling! Hear me this time, at last! Cathy, I love you. Come in to me: come to me, Cathy, my own . . .' Shouted above the storm, it is one of Laurence Olivier's finer moments and also an unforgettable fragment of cinema, something to set the spine tingling in memory for the rest of one's life.

The Little Foxes is something else again, fashioned not from emotions but from spring steel. Its deceptively romantic opening images of the old South quickly give way to the deadly cat and mouse gamble between members of a callous and grasping family, of whom the most horrifying is the female of the species who finally lets her husband die for want of medicine because he intends to change his will rather than give in to her grand designs. Wyler's motif for this claustrophobic film is a staircase, a grandiloquent curve which renders the main set more interesting to look at by allowing action on several levels at the same time and from a variety of angles. He is a man devoted to the fullest utilization of his sets: think of *Dead End*, of *The Heiress*, of *Jezebel*, of *Detective Story*, and remark on your recall not only of the stories but of the buildings in which they took place. Better still, go and luxuriate in these remarkable movies again.

The Letter. US 1940; monochrome; 95 minutes. Produced by Robert Lord for Warner (Hal B. Wallis unit). Written by Howard Koch, from the story and play by W. Somerset Maugham. Directed by William Wyler. Photographed by Tony Gaudio. Music score by Max Steiner. Art direction by Carl Jules Weyl. With Bette Davis as Mrs Crosbie; Herbert Marshall as Mr Crosbie; James Stephenson as Howard Joyce; Sen Yung as Ong Chi Seng; Bruce Lester as John Withers; Gale Sondergaard as Mrs Hammond; Tetsu Komai as head boy.

The Other Side of the Mountain
Lost Horizon

Escaping by plane from an Eastern revolution, a British diplomat and four others are kidnapped and taken to a remote Himalayan lamasery which enjoys perfect weather and encourages extreme longevity. Though entranced by its philosophy and offered the position of high lama, Conway eventually makes the arduous journey back to white civilization at the urging of his brother, but after a period of amnesia returns to Shangri-La.

I have to make it very clear that the following remarks apply strictly and solely to the 1937 version of this haunting piece of Hollywood moonshine, and to the film as originally released rather than to the truncated reissue of the war years. Cinephiles should of course be grateful that President Roosevelt, when asked where the planes came from that bombed Tokyo, said Shangri-La, for the film was hastily dusted off and reissued. But in order better to fit a double bill, twelve vital minutes were edited out by the simple process of stopping some scenes just when they were getting interesting and by eliminating altogether Chang's account, as essential as it is delightful, of the Shangri-La way of life. I quote from the original script:

CHANG: To put it simply, I would say that our general belief is in moderation. We preach the virtue of avoiding excess of all kinds, even including, if you will pardon the paradox, excess of virtue itself.
CONWAY: That's intelligent.
CHANG: We find in the valley it makes for considerable happiness. We rule with moderate strictness, and in return we are satisfied with moderate obedience. As a result, our people are moderately sober, moderately chaste and moderately honest.

241

CONWAY: Aren't there any disputes about women?

CHANG: Only very rarely. You see, it would not be considered good manners to take a woman that another man wanted.

CONWAY: Supposing somebody wanted her so badly that he didn't give a hang whether it was good manners or not?

CHANG: In that event, it would be good manners on the part of the other man to let him have her.

CONWAY: Most convenient. I like that.

CHANG: You would be surprised, Conway, how a little courtesy all round helps to smooth out the most complicated problems.

One would have thought that this urbane conversation might have been retained rather than some of the slabs of bland romantic interest; but at least we were still allowed to hear the dying high lama's vision of the future, when man has battled himself to destruction and Shangri-La's ultimate purpose is to be fulfilled. Imagine a man so old that his eyes are mere pinpoints and his voice a scarcely audible whisper, his white hair backlit by candlelight so as to look like a halo, summoning all his visionary fervour to deliver himself of the following:

Time will come, my friend, when the orgy must spend itself – when brutality and the lust for power must perish by its own sword. When that day comes, it is our hope that the doctrines of Shangri-La will spread throughout the world. Here we shall stay with our books and our music and our meditations . . . Here will be found such wisdom as men will need when their passions are spent. Yes, my son, when the strong have devoured each other, the Christian ethic may at last be fulfilled, and the meek shall inherit the earth.

Not too many Hollywood films of the thirties can be found to encompass thoughts of this kind, though one might have preferred to retain James Hilton's original language rather than Robert Riskin's rather verbose variations. The project in fact seems to have over-awed both him and director Frank Capra, and the polish which remains is principally supplied by the actors, the little scenes between Ronald Colman and H. B. Warner being particular masterpieces of mutual appreciation.

The fact that *Lost Horizon* came to be filmed at all was, as so often, a matter of several success stories coming to a simultaneous head. Ronald Colman was born to play the self-effacing visionary Conway, but in the normal way of Hollywood he might never have been given the chance. James Hilton's dreamlike novel came out in 1933 and won the Hawthornden Prize as well as leaping into the bestseller lists, where it has remained, in various paperback incarnations, more or less ever since. The name Shangri-La passed into the language, and even today is borne by private houses and Chinese restaurants the world over. In 1936 Frank Capra reached the top of the Hollywood tree as a result of his easy-to-like comedies. *It Happened One Night* and *Mr Deeds Goes to Town*, both of which implied that the common man, Mr Honest Joe American, shall inherit the earth: in Capra's philosophy the underdog was king and always got the better of conniving millionaires and industrialists. It is easy to see why *Lost Horizon* appealed to Capra now that the world was his oyster, for in it a heaven on earth, in which wealth means nothing, is provided for those with the intelligence to appreciate it. The enterprise however was nearly Capra's disaster, perhaps because a self-made Italian-American is not the likeliest person to interpret matters of Eastern philosophy to the world at large, even with the practised help of Riskin, a writer well versed in American myths but uncomfortable with larger issues. The project seems to have driven them both, out of awed respect for its implications, into a substandard appreciation of both character and drama. Among Capra's obvious slips was the approval of a main lamasery set which was fatally thirties modern despite the script's allegation that it was devised and constructed in the eighteenth century, and a prologue and epilogue in a London club which further demonstrated his tendency to reduce characters and situations outside his own experience to hilarious cliché. ('Shangri-La may be a fact, or it may be a state of mind, but one thing will always remain with me – its magnificent conception.')

Despite these initial blemishes, *Lost Horizon* still manages for middle-class audiences to be a thoroughly entertaining film and a thrilling adventure of the mind. The script in fact made a number of basic changes from the book which may have been typical of Hollywood but are said to have won the approval of James Hilton, who allegedly wished he had thought of them first. His aged missionary, Miss Roberta Brinklow, became an American tart with TB (cured in a couple of days by the air of Shangri-La). The intolerable Mallinson became Conway's younger brother, the better for the audience to understand why Conway should drag himself away from his idyll to escort the whining George back to 'civilization'. Instead of four people being kidnapped at random to replenish

243

LOST HORIZON. Chang (H. B. Warner) explains to Conway (Ronald Colman) the principle of moderation

Shangri-La's dwindling population, the film makes it a deliberate mission to secure Conway, Britain's 'man of the East', diplomat, scholar, adventurer, next foreign secretary and general Anthony Eden lookalike. (The script rather than the movie as cut makes it clear that this was the idea of the new character Sondra Bizet, who is thirty years old, laughs a lot, and seems to have the ear of the High Lama; it does not prevent Conway from falling in love with her.) Most curiously, the film transplants the book's setting-off point, Baskul, from Afghanistan ('over the hills from Peshawur') to China; in fact Baskul never seems to have existed anywhere, though the book and two films have probably persuaded millions that it did. There may have been political reasons at the time for not placing Afghanistan's real capital, Kabul, as the site of a bandit revolution.

Capra premièred his 130-minute colossus in Santa Barbara early in 1937. It went badly; people laughed in the wrong places and a man he met at the lobby drinking fountain said: 'Did you ever see such a goddamn Fu Manchu thing in your life? People who made it should be shot.' In a cold sweat at the thought of having given birth to a two-million-dollar disaster, Capra spent a sleepless night and arose next day with an inspiration: junk the first two reels. (He claims he did, but in fact the script shows that most of the missing scenes were cut into later stages of the movie.) The result is a somewhat lame start, with three screens full of pretentious titles preparing one for a romantic fantasy about 'what lies over the hill'. However, the airfield evacuation scenes are so exciting and self-explanatory that we are plunged into the story and easily pick up the character backgrounds en route, absorbed by the predicament of these ill-assorted people who shortly find themselves crash-landed in a snowy wilderness with no food and a dead pilot. The emergence through the snowy mist of Chang and his rescue party is one of the magical moments of cinema, and after that we don't even mind that the golden valley itself is no more than an unconvincing matte shot, for the talk is now the thing.

The American Film Institute has spent many years reconstructing the 118-minute 1937 release version, and one looks forward to seeing again some of the comic banter between Edward Everett Horton and Thomas Mitchell as well as the famous climax when Margo, who has insisted on escaping with the brothers, suddenly ages and dies on the glacier. The reissue version denies us not only most of this but her admission that she lied about being only twenty years old, and although we can deduce it for ourselves we are momentarily puzzled and distracted by what seems a flaw in the film's drift. One remains grateful basically for the fact that the film was made at all, allowing the tale to become a popular classic, which as Capra's prologue might have said, will stay in men's hearts forever. For Colman, too, his remarkably expressive eyes shown repeatedly in close-ups which are more revealing than his dialogue; for H. B. Warner, impeccable as the discreetly cosmopolitan Chang; and for Sam Jaffe, superbly grotesque and looking every one of his two-hundred-odd years. Joe Walker's photography and Dmitri Tiomkin's music add lustre to a unique production which is to be enjoyed, warts and all.

Ross Hunter's reviled 1972 remake is in fact a fair stab at an update until the travellers arrive in Shangri-La, after which they do little but sit around and chant Burt Bacharach's tedious songs. Even Peter Finch, theoretically the perfect Conway casting for the seventies, lacks the means to cope with a sung soliloquy; Charles Boyer's lama is surprisingly dull; John Gielgud as Chang wears an absurd headdress that looks like a tea cosy; and Shangri-La itself is all too clearly a hurried revamp of the *Camelot* castle. No, the 1937 version is the one for posterity.

Lost Horizon. US 1937; monochrome; 118 minutes. Produced and directed by Frank Capra for Columbia. Written by Robert Riskin, from the novel by James Hilton. Photographed by Joseph Walker. Music score by Dmitri Tiomkin. Art direction by Stephen Goosson. Costumes by Ernst Dryden. With Ronald Colman as Conway; H. B. Warner as Chang; Edward Everett Horton as Lovett; Thomas Mitchell as Chalmers Bryant; John Howard as George; Sam Jaffe as the High Lama; Jane Wyatt as Sondra; Isabel Jewell as Gloria; Margo as Maria.

The Son of a Gun Is Nothing But a Tailor
Love Me Tonight

A Parisian tailor, owed money by a nobleman, is passed off as a count and falls in love with an heiress.

It is of course *Cinderella* in reverse. Charlie Ruggles as the impecunious Vicomte de Vareze is the fairy godmother who whisks our poor hero into the ball, where he is fêted by all; his own skill with a needle proves to have the same effect as the stroke of midnight, for it reveals the truth about him and he is banished; but true love naturally finds a way. It is also a Rodgers and Hart musical with a marvellous score including 'Mimi', 'Lover' and 'Isn't It Romantic?'. It is a comedy with a script by three Hollywood professionals, based on a serviceable European original. It is a Rouben Mamoulian film, which means delicate experiments in sound and vision performed with unerring theatrical sense, and in this case the satisfaction of seeing Lubitsch outwitted at his very own game. It is certainly Maurice Chevalier's most entertaining star vehicle. And it features C. Aubrey Smith singing. That should be enough points of interest to be going on with.

Some *aficionados* deny that it is dated. But of course it is, having been made in 1932, delightfully encased in a period when wit and precision and subtlety counted for something. One may admit that its sense of overall pace is a little languid but that is all the criticism

I for one will allow. Whenever it is shown before the audiences at the National Film Theatre, who are not exactly easy to please, the end title always produces an ovation, following affectionate chuckles and scattered applause as it unspools.

Let us enumerate some of its felicities. It begins in the kind of Paris street set so dear to Paramount (who borrowed the blueprints from René Clair) except that in this case every detail looks absolutely right, from chimney to gutter. It is morning, and all is silent. The first sound is made by a wheelbarrow, then we hear the picks of roadmenders. From inside a bedroom comes a snore; an old lady brushes leaves off the pavement; puffs of smoke billow from chimneys; a baby cries; an alarm clock rings; the knife grinder starts work, as do two cobblers at their lasts; a shutter goes up; a housewife beats her carpets. Music unnoticed at first, has picked up all these sounds and woven them into a delicate rhythm to make a musical number that only Mamoulian could have conceived. As a finale we glide into an open bedroom where a familiar silhouette with a jutting lip is drawn on the wall, with a straw hat hanging from a nail, just where it should be to complete an already recognizable picture.

Maurice – and that's his character name as well as his own – opens his tailor's shop just as one of a team of runners peels off and proves to be the Vicomte in his underwear, having escaped from an embarrassing situation. Maurice loans him the wherewithal to get home, but the nobleman has been recognized by various creditors who make Maurice worry about ever getting back the cost of sixteen suits, not to mention sundry loans. We realize by now that the scheme of the entertainment is to make dialogue flow into recitative, and recitative to turn into song, and for every character around to play his part in it. The song of the moment being 'Isn't It Romantic?', it is taken up from Maurice by a creditor, a taxi driver, an artist, soldiers on a train and on the march, a gypsy violinist and our heroine Miss Jeanette MacDonald; meanwhile we have been transported across country to the château where she lives with her guardian C. Aubrey Smith, his son the Vicomte, and three dotty aunts who contribute their comments from time to time like an eccentric Greek chorus or the witches from *Macbeth*. Also on hand is Charles Butterworth as Miss MacDonald's diffident suitor; her song from her balcony is ended by the thump of his ladder at her waist, for it is his intention to woo her.

PRINCESS: I'm going to bed.
SAVIGNAC: I've just come out to join you. I've brought along my flute hoping
to entertain you.
(She pushes him away and we hear him crash.)
Oh, I'll never be able to use it again!
PRINCESS: Did you break your leg?
SAVIGNAC: No, I fell flat on my flute.

The château is filled with guests who seem so bored with their lot
that they seldom have the strength to rise from the bridge tables,
where they yawn and snooze all day long. C. Aubrey Smith, not
noticing, summons his butler after breakfast to plan the day: 'Bridge
at three . . . dinner at eight. And after dinner, bridge. Rather an
amusing day, eh, Flamand?'

We have not yet mentioned the princess's man-mad cousin
Valentine, played by Myrna Loy. When the princess feels faint after
her first romantic brush with Maurice on the way home, the would-
be suitor asks her to get help: 'Can you go for a doctor?' 'Certainly,
bring him right in.' (She is later asked: 'Don't you think of anything
but men?' Her answer is: 'Oh yes, dear: schoolboys.') The doctor
does come, and his interview with the clearly frustrated princess
turns into another recitative number:

PRINCESS: Why do I wake up in bed, and why does blood rush to my head?
DOCTOR: At night?
PRINCESS: Quite right. At night.

Maurice arrives, is persuaded to pass himself off as a count, and
sings 'Mimi', which is reprised next day by Mr Smith (waking up),
Mr Ruggles (shaving), the aunts (working on their tapestry) and Mr
Butterworth (during his dumb-bell exercises). The programme for
the day includes hunting, and Miss MacDonald arranges for
Maurice to have a horse called Solitude, because it always comes
home alone. He not only calms the horse but saves the stag, and
from then on the princess is putty in his arms. But the jealous
Savignac has a report to make to the Duke: 'There's no such person
as the Baron Courtelin: I've even been through the better-class
illegitimates.' The duke is in any case getting pretty fed up with his
new guest, who is always the centre of attention: Valentine has even
bored a hole in his door so that she can watch him dress.

DUKE: That door has come down to us through generations.
VALENTINE: So have my instincts.

Maurice causes his own undoing by criticizing the talents of the princess' dressmaker:

DUKE: Madame de Beauvoir has been insulted.
SAVIGNAC: At her age? Remarkable.

By triumphing with the princess' riding habit, Maurice shows himself up for what he is. 'The Son of a Gun Is Nothing But a Tailor' is the next song, and everybody in the picture seems to get a verse, including the scullery maids and the kitchen staff. (By now the three aunts are barking like dogs in their excitement.) Maurice leaves by train, but the princess races it on horseback, sings to him, and calls to the driver: 'Stop the train: I love him!' ('That's not a railroad problem,' he replies.)

I have clearly failed to give an impression on the printed page of effects which can be produced only on celluloid, where image and sound track are perfectly blended. I have certainly been unable to give any indication of the magnificent sets by Hans Dreier and A. E. Freudeman, including a double door fifteen feet high. The whole delicious confection was of course caviare to the general, and Mamoulian's heyday at Paramount was over; but the critics gave it qualified praise. Philip K. Scheuer in the *Los Angeles Times* called it 'a picture I would like to take home with me, so that on dull evenings I could bring it out and display it to my friends, and make them happy too'. Over the years its fame magnified among cinéastes, as did that of the Marx Brothers; but there was only one *Love Me Tonight*, and it belonged to no school, so between the occasional retrospective screenings it languished in limbo. By the end of the sixties, however, John Baxter could confidently write: 'If there is a better musical of the thirties, one wonders what it can be.'

As for Mamoulian, he chiefly recalls that the enterprise started off with discord between himself and his star:

Lubitsch, Chevalier said, always had him present at all pre-production meetings. I said that was all very well; that was the way Lubitsch worked; but Lubitsch wasn't doing *Love Me Tonight* – I was, and I worked my way, and I especially didn't want him on hand at story conferences. He was hurt and said he would complain to the front office. I told him to please do so,

LOVE ME TONIGHT. Chevalier flirts with the chorus of aunts. Elizabeth Patterson, Blanche Frederici, Ethel Griffies

that I hadn't wanted to do this picture and was only doing it as a great favour to Mr Zukor, and would consider it a very special favour if he could get me taken off it. Maurice, of course, didn't go to the front office at all. He loved the script when it was shown to him, and was enchanted by all the Rodgers and Hart songs. *Love Me Tonight* turned out to be one of my happiest film productions.

Love Me Tonight. US 1932; monochrome; 92 minutes approx. Produced and directed by Rouben Mamoulian for Paramount. Written by Samuel Hoffenstein, Waldemar Young and George Marion Jnr, from a play by Leopold Marchand and Paul Armont. Photographed by Victor Milner. Songs by Richard Rodgers and Lorenz Hart. Art direction by Hans Dreier. Sets by A. E. Freudeman. Costumes by Travis Banton. Edited by Billy Shea. With Maurice Chevalier as Maurice; Jeanette MacDonald as Princess Jeanette; Charles Ruggles as Gilbert; Charles Butterworth as Count de Savignac; C. Aubrey Smith as the Duc D'Artelines; Myrna Loy as Valentine; Elizabeth Patterson as first aunt; Blanche Frederici as second aunt; Ethel Griffies as third aunt.

The Stuff That Dreams Are Made Of
The Maltese Falcon

Villains congregate in San Francisco on the trail of a priceless statuette, and after his partner has been killed a private detective finds himself in control of the situation.

There is sometimes no telling why a western or a mystery or a romance works better than others of its kind. It just does, the elements falling together in an entirely desirable way. However, one can usually predict that the first major film of a director with talent will be worth watching and rewatching, simply because he will be doing his damnedest to please, probably after a long apprenticeship. On this occasion only he will be thinking of his future rather than his immediate bank balance, and operating as economically as possible within a system which will reward him for doing so. So, certainly, with John Huston, whose later movies have been a wildly variable bag in unpredictable veins. *The Maltese Falcon* was his first chance to direct after years as a writer, and he wanted to get it right, for himself, for the audience, for the front office, and for Dashiell Hammett.

He did get it right. Even during the commendably brisk credit titles the sense of power and thrust and confidence is unmistakable, and in the first elliptical scene, set in the office of Spade and Archer, there is already a distinct sense of everything clicking into place as intended. Throughout the picture, despite the apparent excess of talk, there is never a boring shot: actors move in and out of exciting groups, and the camera tracks and pans just enough to underline what the actors are saying: the backgrounds of apartments and hotel rooms and studio streets are never dwelt upon, but what we see of them is sufficiently convincing as a background for the increasingly tense conversations. Unassuming though it was, the result was immediately labelled a classic and has remained as clear and fresh an entertainment forty years later as it was at the first rough-cut. Nobody concerned was ever quite able to repeat its success.

What had Huston done that was so clever? His choice of subject seemed absurd: a studio property which had already been filmed twice in the previous nine years, and which in 1940 belonged to an out-of-date genre. Staying as close to the original novel as possible, and thus risking the suspicion that he had no original ideas of his own, he kept most of the dialogue and eliminated only one character. For actors, he made a careful choice from the studio roster, striking lucky when George Raft refused the lead and Humphrey Bogart accepted it; for balance and freshness he did add a couple of outsiders, including a stage actor who at sixty-one had never been in a film before. Here again fate stepped in, for the preview cards said that the performance most enjoyed was that of 'the fat man', and Sydney Greenstreet promptly became one of the most popular and recognizable stars of the forties. However enjoyable his performance in his three longish scenes, Huston does not allow him to overbalance the picture: we equally relish the acting of Bogart, Astor and Lorre, and we sense that they are enjoying themselves too. As for Elisha Cook Jnr as the homicidal Wilmer, he made so indelible an impression that he was associated with the role throughout his career. (Bogart, and Hammett before him, describe Wilmer as a 'gunsel', which most people would take to indicate a small-time hood. In fact it is a slang term for a homosexual, and a 'gay' relationship between Wilmer and Gutman is clearly present for those with eyes to see it, especially in the last scene when Gutman very reluctantly agrees that the police shall have Wilmer for their 'fall guy'.)

Its 101 minutes made *The Maltese Falcon* a long film for its time, though it never seems to outstay its welcome: so fascinating are these characters that we are reluctant to let them out of our sight when the end title is finally superimposed on that marvellously gloomy shot of Bogie shrugging his way down the stairs as Mary Astor, in custody, descends by elevator. We certainly come to know our way around Bogart's apartment, with its worn furniture, untidy bedroom and cheap three-pronged chandelier (which Huston always tried to keep in shot, though television scanning usually eliminates it). Adolph Deutsch's music adequately pastes the scenes together, but essentially this is a movie carried by the words, by the actors, and by the direction, and at least equally by Arthur Edeson's gleaming black-and-light-grey photography, which creates its own world of shadows and half-truths.

THE MALTESE FALCON. The opening scene: Cowan and Bogart are ready to receive customers

The script plays remarkably fair by the audience, who are given just as much information as Spade, though they may be less adept at putting it together. Unlike *The Big Sleep*, which hinges on violence and relies on an atmosphere of sulphurous evil to obscure the gaping holes in its plot, *The Maltese Falcon* is a battle of wits, and intelligence is required not only to follow it but to act in it. Bogart's performance is so satisfactory because he seems to take his detection seriously, and not only because 'when a man's partner's killed, he's supposed to do something about it'. You can sense his brain cells multiplying at each new piece of information, and you warm to his appreciation of his secretary (a perfect supporting performance by Lee Patrick) as the indispensable girl Friday ('You're a good man, sister'). You can also sense the actor putting everything he has into the part which will consolidate his stardom, flexing his acting muscles to make the most of all those enjoyable reaction shots which Huston confidently places on his shoulders. Mary Astor, in something like a comeback role, has a less happy time, though her Brigid O'Shaughnessy, alias

Miss Leblanc, alias Miss Wonderly, did lead to other Warner roles including one in *The Great Lie* which would deservedly win her an Oscar. Here she can barely avoid an exterior performance, and the occasional unmeant laugh, as a congenital liar who turns out to be the real murderer of Spade's partner.

It has lately become fashionable, in such unworthy films as *The Black Bird* and *The Cheap Detective*, to parody *The Maltese Falcon*, while its plot has been unofficially borrowed for programmers from *Hell's Island* to *Mara Maru*. Predictably it is the parodies and imitations which are quickly forgotten, while the original goes from strength to strength. For one instance of the perfection which makes this so, in an age when most new movies seem to be not so much assembled as thrown together, one need look no farther than Joel Cairo's first entrance, after sending in a visiting card soaked in gardenia. ('Quick, darling, in with him,' grins Spade to Effie.) The appearance of Peter Lorre would provoke a rustle of appreciation from any audience in 1940, and they would relish his dapper appearance, his new curly hair-style, and his way with his first line: 'May a stranger offer condolences for your partner's unfortunate death?' Only Lorre could so caress and elide the syllables while still making his meaning abundantly clear. He continues:

CAIRO: I am trying to recover an ornament that has, shall we say, been mislaid. I thought and hoped you could assist me . . . I am prepared to promise that, er, what is the phrase, no questions will be asked . . .
SPADE: You're not hiring me to do any murders or burglaries, but simply to get it back, if possible, in an honest, lawful way?
CAIRO: Er, if possible. But in any event with discretion.

This six-minute scene, in which Cairo points a gun at Spade; is disarmed; proves to be travelling with French, Greek and British passports; gets his gun back and points it again, was long ago extracted by Britain's National Film Archive as a model for students of economy in acting and filmcraft.

The later meeting with Greenstreet is more expansive in mood. Why a man with the name Kaspar Gutman should speak such thespian English, and so relish the sound of his own voice speaking it, is probably impossible for anybody to explain, but the performance is all. Greenstreet, in cutaway morning coat, white collar and watch chain (pretty formal wear for midday when he doesn't seem to be going anywhere) is photographed as much as possible from below so that his stomach looms largely before him. Grasping Bogart's arm after he has shaken his hand, he leads him to a chair and begins pouring whisky.

GUTMAN: You begin well, sir. I distrust a man who says 'when'. He's got to be careful not to drink too much, because he's not to be trusted when he does. Well, sir, here's to plain speaking and clear understanding. You're a close-mouthed man?

SPADE: No, I like to talk.

GUTMAN: Better and better. I distrust a close-mouthed man. He generally picks the wrong time to talk, and says the wrong things. Talking's something you can't do judiciously, unless you keep in practice. Now, sir, we'll talk if you like. I tell you right out, I'm a man who likes talking to a man who likes to talk.

This is richness indeed, especially for the audiences of the 1980s, used to heroes who shoot from the hip and seldom utter words of more than one syllable (and fail to enunciate even those). If television should ever fail to dust off the print of *The Maltese Falcon* for its annual exposure, the script was published a few years ago with 1,400 sequential frame blow-ups from the movie. It's certainly the next best thing.

The Maltese Falcon. US 1941; monochrome; 101 minutes. Produced by Henry Blanke for Warner. Executive producer, Hal B. Wallis. Written by John Huston, from the novel by Dashiell Hammett. Directed by John Huston. Photographed by Arthur Edeson. Music score by Adolph Deutsch. Edited by Thomas Richards. Art direction by Robert Haas. With Humphrey Bogart as Sam Spade; Mary Astor as Brigid; Sydney Greenstreet as Kaspar Gutman; Peter Lorre as Joel Cairo; Gladys George as Iva Archer; Jerome Cowan as Miles Archer; Lee Patrick as Effie Perine; Elisha Cook Jnr as Wilmer; Barton MacLane as Dundy; Ward Bond as Polhaus.

What Closes Saturday Night
The Man in the White Suit

A single-minded young inventor makes a fabric which never gets dirty and never wears out: the consequences alarm both capital and labour.

It was released at the height of Ealing's greatest comedy period, just three months after *The Lavender Hill Mob,* and its comparative commercial failure came as a sad disappointment, for Balcon's men thought that in it they had achieved their finest hour. Posterity may say so too, but at the time even the popular critics were hard put to find a good word for it. Luckily the posh papers redressed the balance, and *Sight and Sound* hailed it as consolidating Sandy Mackendrick's pre-eminence among British comedy directors. The reasons for the general discontent are easy to find, for *The Man in the White Suit* is not the usual warm Ealing character comedy of a section of familiar English society resisting the invasions of bureaucracy. It is satire, erupting on occasions into farce, and every schoolboy knows that satire is what closes Saturday night, while farce is something which only the lower classes enjoy: the mix appeals only to a rather rarefied audience which was seldom found in the Odeons of 1951.

The Man in the White Suit hardly goes in for character at all. It is peopled with symbols, types, cameos and buffoons, and its general tone is even, subdued, calculated and slightly bloodless. It was too far from the common run to be recognized for what it was, a perfectly poised fantasy in the tradition of Clair, a witty and stimulating production which can be enjoyed for its sheer technical skill, for its crisp acting, for its deft balancing of age-old class antagonisms, or for being what the BBC recently called it, a satire on the age of obsolescence.

It has to be admitted that Alec Guinness, the bright new star of the time, is unable to wring much juice out of the leading role of Sidney Stratton, a mere two-dimensional outline who is put up only to be knocked down. He gets few laughs and induces little pathos, for once the plot is under way he is no more than the hub around

THE MAN IN THE WHITE SUIT. Sir John Kierlaw (Ernest Thesiger) takes charge. Crawford, Gough, Guinness and Parker take orders

which various Anglo-Saxon attitudes revolve. He is also handicapped by being too old for the part: his toupée lacks conviction and in an effort to look young he falls back on a single headscratching Stan Laurel expression of wounded or expectant innocence which works well enough while the film is on but leaves one with no pleasant memories to take home afterwards. At the very end he switches to a Chaplinesque shrug at his problems and a walk away from camera, down the mean streets towards a brighter sunlight; but he does not walk into our hearts. There is more fun to be found in the extensive supporting gallery, notably in Ernest Thesiger as Sir John Kierlaw, ancient godfather of textile manufacturers. He enters late, but proceeds to steal most of the scenes thereafter. He is most cunningly introduced as a skeletal hand in the dark recesses of a Rolls-Royce, then as a pair of shuffling feet and a deep fur-collared coat, finally as a wheezing asthmatic to whom the only enjoyment left is the ruthless use of power. The most alarming moment of Thesiger's performance comes when he laughs: the sound is that of a rusty cistern distantly heard. But his first speech, as he flops down exhausted into a wing armchair and arduously recovers his breath, shows what kind of business he means: 'Now. Some fool has invented an indestructible cloth. Where is he? How much does he want?' Altogether this Sir John is a grotesque worthy to set beside Thesiger's Horace Femm in *The Old Dark House* or his Dr Pretorius in *Bride of Frankenstein*, both of them highlights of cinema caricature.

Of the rest, one might mention any one of a dozen first-rate supporting actors, but for me two tiny roles stand out. George Benson is perfectly cast as the lugubrious and timid lodger disturbed in the final chase through Guinness' digs. 'Will you please kindly leave the room?' he hopelessly asks of several manic pursuers who almost force him through the wall with each opening of the door. 'I'll fetch Mrs Watson,' he adds as an afterthought; and the relish of this jest is that Mrs Watson is played by dear frail Edie Martin, seventy-odd at the time, who a little later has her own moment of glory when she confronts the fleeing white-suited Guinness in the dark cobbled street of the Lancashire mill town where the action takes place: 'Why can't you scientists leave things alone? What about my bit of washing when there's no washing to do?'

Though the final varnish of the production seems less shiny than it did, either because the negative has been poorly looked after or because one originally overlooked imperfections in the happy glow of audience reaction, this is technically a highly refined piece of work in which photography, writing and direction come together in perfect accord. Mackendrick in particular directs with a controlled bravado rare in the British cinema, achieving small throwaway miracles of timing, underlining nuances of comedy acting, and carefully building climactic scenes in the Eisenstein-approved manner. When Guinness furiously attempts to gain entry to Cecil Parker's house one rainy night, despite the adverse reaction of a Japanese butler who ends up falling all over the vase he is trying to protect, the comings, goings, dodgings and slammings are reminiscent in their orchestration of Laurel and Hardy at their peak.

The unfurling of the narrative is a joy in itself. Oblique at first, it presents millowner Michael Gough showing round the rival (Cecil Parker) with whom he hopes to join forces. To the discomfiture of both they stumble on a complex apparatus for which no one on the staff can account but which is later found to have cost the company more than four thousand pounds. (The rushing hither and thither of officials in search of this information is like an animated H. M. Bateman cartoon, with characters amply delineated by a single well-chosen shot.) The culprit is not found, though Parker's daughter (the sultry Joan Greenwood) clearly suspects the wide-eyed janitor who is forever edging away from the centre of attention. Deciding that discretion is the better part of valour, Guinness quits and takes on a menial job at Parker's mill, where by an amusing accident he is taken to be the custodian of a new electro-microscope. Later Miss Greenwood comes across a familiar gurgling, plopping mass of glass tubing and retorts which this time turns out to have cost her own father more than double the Michael Gough version. She is only prevented from giving the game away by Guinness' desperate explanation, hardly calculated to sweep a girl off her feet: 'You know the problem of polymerizing amino-acid resolutes?' She doesn't, but that night her father is surprised to see her carrying upstairs as bedside reading two volumes of the *Encyclopaedia Britannica*.

Success comes to the inventor after several more misunderstandings and an even greater number of mild explosions which increase the cost manifold and turn the head of research into a nervous wreck. Meanwhile he has aroused the maternal instincts of a lady shop steward (Vida Hope) who sees him as 'flotsam floating on the floodtide of profit'. Her comment on his achievement, 'The whole world's going to bless you', is obviously the end of part one; but the audience knows how quickly she is to be proved wrong, not least by her own socialist principles. A thread which never breaks or wears out, though it later helps its inventor to escape from a building, will obviously reduce labour and capital at one fell swoop. Both sides finally agree that it must be suppressed, and that the angry inventor must be prevented from telling his story to the press. Luckily for them, the moment they lay hands on his luminous suit, which was so strong that the pattern had to be cut from templates, it proves to be unstable and comes apart like cotton wool, making a fittingly neat ending apart from that final gleam of hope for better luck next time.

Interestingly enough, only a few years later *I'm All Right Jack* did achieve commercial success with a parody of the problems of management and labour, but this was less a sustained satire than a matter of allowing a number of well-established comic actors to do their thing. One remembers with affection Peter Sellers' communist shop steward, forever dreaming of life in Russia – 'all them cornfields, and ballet in the evening' – but the theme falls apart long before the end, and it is to the slighter, more diffident Ealing film that one must now turn for the classic elaboration of this theme.

The Man in the White Suit. GB 1951; monochrome; 85 minutes. Produced by Sidney Cole for Ealing Studios. Written by Roger MacDougall, Sandy Mackendrick and John Dighton, from the play by Roger MacDougall. Directed by Sandy Mackendrick. Photographed by Douglas Slocombe. Music score by Benjamin Frankel. Art direction by Jim Morahan. Edited by Bernard Gribble. With Alec Guinness as Sidney Stratton; Joan Greenwood as Daphne; Cecil Parker as Birnley; Michael Gough as Corland; Ernest Thesiger as Sir John Kierlaw; Howard Marion Crawford as Cranford; Henry Mollison as Hoskins; Vida Hope as Bertha; Miles Malleson as tailor; George Benson as lodger; Edie Martin as washerwoman.

Old Parties
The Man Who Came to Dinner

A celebrated but waspish radio personality breaks his hip on a lecture tour and makes life a misery for his unwilling midwestern hosts.

In a sense this famous piece of theatre by Kaufman and Hart wasn't so much a play as a farce for the Broadway in-crowd, who could be expected to appreciate that Sheridan Whiteside was a mischievous portrait of Alexander Woollcott, that Banjo is Harpo Marx and Beverly Carlton Noel Coward. (Opinions are divided as to the real identity of the man-eating Lorraine Sheldon.) And the film isn't so much a film as a slightly diluted photographed version of the stage original, mostly in one set and with some pretty choppy editing where the front office decided it was getting too esoteric. Nevertheless it still has me in stitches whenever I see it with an audience, though the plot holds very little water (why doesn't he go to a nursing home?) and it seems a little too much to discover that Lizzie Borden was a relative of the much-abused Stanleys and can be used as blackmail to force them not to interfere with the lives of their grown-up children. Still, there must be quite a bit of rarity value in any Hollywood film which in the course of 112 minutes contrives to mention Ethel Barrymore, Winston Churchill, Jude the Obscure, the Hound of the Baskervilles, Eleanor Roosevelt, the Duke of Windsor, Jascha Heifitz, Alexis Carrel, Haile Selassie, Schiaparelli, the Lunts, William Alan White, Betsy Ross, Katherine Cornell, Zasu Pitts, Winnie the Pooh, Deanna Durbin, Gypsy Rose Lee, Somerset Maugham, Admiral Byrd, Horace Greeley, Walter Winchell, Jock Whitney, Cary Grant, Barbara Hutton, Elsa Maxwell, Lana Turner, Mrs Vanderbilt, J. Edgar Hoover, the Khedive of Egypt, Mr Moto, Dr Dafoe, H. G. Wells, Toscanini, Ethel Waters and the Mount Wilson Observatory. There are also convicts, some penguins, and an octopus. And Bette Davis.

In another sense the show is an extended cabaret turn for the actor playing Whiteside, an elderly boor who is centre stage in a wheelchair for almost every minute and has to coo, berate, whinny, cajole, sentimentalize, moan, shout, plead and bellow, not to mention his occasional bursting into some such recherché ditty as:

> I'se jes' a little wabbit in the sunshine,
> I'se jes a little wabbit in the wain.

(At least he doesn't, as Woollcott did, recite *Goodbye Mr Chips* at the slightest provocation.) He maintains in his skull a ragbag of the choicest insults ever penned, though his stage opening line, on being wheeled from his private room to meet his assembled beaming hosts, was cut from the movie. For those who feel deprived, it was: 'I may vomit.' (The film substituted: 'Please stand back, I have several contagious diseases.') Similarly, his remark to his nurse, 'You have the touch of a sex-starved cobra', became 'You have the touch of a love-starved cobra': one hadn't realized that cobras were so romantic. The local physician is referred to as 'the greatest living argument for mercy killing', and his book of memoirs, *Forty Years an Ohio Doctor*, as *Forty Years Below the Navel*. Miss Davis is called Minnie the Moocher or 'cow-eyed Sappho'; but his nurse, played by the imperishable Mary Wickes, gets the brunt. When she tells him that in his condition he ought not to eat chocolates, he smiles sweetly upon her and enunciates through his snowy-white beard: 'My Great Aunt Jennifer ate a box of chocolates every day of her life. She lived to be a hundred and two, and when she had been dead three days she looked healthier than you do *now*.' (The last word is so relished that it almost turns into three syllables.) But the nurse finally gets her own back by quitting:

I am not only walking out on this case, Mr Whiteside, I am leaving the nursing profession. I became a nurse because all my life, ever since I was a little girl, I was filled with the idea of serving a suffering humanity. After one month with you, Mr Whiteside, I am going to work in a munitions factory. From now on anything I can do to exterminate the human race will fill me with the greatest of pleasure. If Florence Nightingale had ever nursed you, Mr Whiteside, she would have married Jack the Ripper instead of founding the Red Cross!

Even his reluctant host has a parting shot: 'I am now going upstairs to disconnect my radio, so that not even accidentally will I ever hear your voice again!'

What passes for plot complication in this movie is simplicity itself. Whiteside's faithful amanuensis falls for a local reporter, Mr Average Joe Small Town American. Deciding that this is not in her best interests (he means his own), Whiteside arranges for Joe to be smitten by a long-fanged Broadway actress. Finally repenting (most improbably), he gets rid of the actress by locking her in a convenient mummy case and consigning her to Nova Scotia in Howard Hughes' private plane. Just how this will break up Joe's infatuation is not clear, but it's been a long film, and Jimmy Durante has done his manic stuff as Banjo, and we are all waiting for the predictable sting in the tale, which is that on his way out Mr Whiteside again slips on the ice and is again carried in pain back to the Stanley's sitting-room. When last seen, Mrs Stanley has fainted on the rug and Mr Stanley is beating his head rather savagely against a pillar.

For any audience which can remember the period, and any company which can afford the right cast, this is still a richly enjoyable theatre experience, and one wishes that the film had been directed with a little more panache, for only the lines and performances now keep it nimble. Warners didn't build any sets for it: the railroad station is left over from *King's Row*, and apart from a skating scene everything else is played against two chairs, a fireplace and a staircase. Even the credits are a bit old hat, inscribed on visiting cards being placed on a silver salver. But of course it is the lines and the actors that matter, and here the film is richly endowed. Monty Woolley, Yale professor turned actor, and close friend of Cole Porter, delivers the most insulting epithets in tones as sweet as

THE MAN WHO CAME TO DINNER. The plot thickens: Monty Woolley, Reginald Gardiner, Bette Davis

succotash. It was an unexpected elevation to stardom after years of bit parts as judges and doctors in comedies from *Nothing Sacred* to *Midnight*, and his subsequent trouble was to find star roles to suit his Whiteside image. (After *The Pied Piper* and *Holy Matrimony* they were few and not too choice.) Bette Davis was thought by many to be misguided in accepting the decidedly secondary role of Maggie Cutler, but in fact she gives one of her most attractive and unselfish performances, wry and witty, without demeaning herself in the rather stodgy romantic interludes. The rest are turns: Reginald Gardiner brilliant as Coward, Ann Sheridan decorative as whoever (Gertrude Lawrence?), Ruth Vivian eerie as the formerly axe-wielding Aunt Harriet, George Barbier a bundle of bluster as the doctor, Grant Mitchell and Billie Burke the perfect flabbergasted hosts, and Durante kept for top of the bill, popping in to cause assorted mayhem and sing at the piano:

Did you ever get the feeling that you wanted to go?
And still get the feeling that you wanted to stay?

It may not make sense, but it's fun.

As a newcomer Monty Woolley got third billing in *The Man Who Came to Dinner*. Josephine Hull and Jean Adair, who had starred on Broadway for years as the sweetly murderous aunts in *Arsenic and Old Lace*, got eighth and ninth spots respectively when that was filmed by Warners, without even an 'and introducing' credit. There's no justice in Hollywood, especially if you're past sixty, but at least the ladies must have had the satisfaction of knowing that they remained the centrepiece of the entertainment even though Cary Grant tried to upstage everybody with nineteen double takes to the minute, and John Alexander as mad brother Teddy, burying supposed yellow fever victims in the basement, stole the notices. (In case anyone still doesn't know, the sweet old ladies in this more than eccentric family take it upon themselves to polish off lonely old men with elderberry wine laced with arsenic; they are rather pleased that one of their victims found time to say 'How delicious' before he died.) This is another one-set piece, but Frank Capra directs it with such whizz-bang pyrotechnics that you scarcely have time to notice: it isn't what you'd call one of his major films, but it certainly uses all his skill in handling crowds of people all yelling at once. When the people include, in addition to the above, Peter Lorre, James Gleason, Jack Carson and Edward Everett Horton, you just know you're in for a good time. The odd unsatisfactory thing is the casting of the role of evil brother Jonathan, who has been the victim of a plastic surgeon with a film star obsession, and subsequently knocks off people who say he looks like Boris Karloff. Mr Karloff played the part himself on the stage, which made the notion hilariously funny; Warners preferred to cast Raymond Massey, who does a good job but inevitably strikes an unpleasant and irrelevant note.

How pleasant to remember other comedies in which senior citizens have walked away with the honours. Charles Coburn enjoyed a twenty-year star career after winning an Oscar at the age of sixty-six for his performance as the elderly Cupid in *The More the Merrier*; he certainly made more of the part than did Cary Grant in the remake,

Walk Don't Run. Edmund Gwenn, still a star at the age of eighty-four in *Them!*, had perhaps his finest hour when he was seventy-two, winning his Oscar as the reputed Santa Claus in *Miracle on 34th Street.* Clifton Webb was only fifty-four when he played the elderly babysitter in *Sitting Pretty*, a modest comedy which did much to enliven the austerity year of 1947, but those who remember the splendid scene in which he quiets a fractious baby by dumping porridge over its head will agree that he counts all right: the generation gap was never so marked.

The Man Who Came to Dinner. US 1941; monochrome; 112 minutes. Produced by Jack Saper and Jerry Wald for Warner. Executive producer, Hal B. Wallis. Written by Julius J. and Philip G. Epstein from the play by George S. Kaufman and Moss Hart. Directed by William Keighley. Photographed by Tony Gaudio. Music score by Frederick Hollander. Art direction by Robert Haas. Edited by Jack Killifer. With Monty Woolley as Sheridan Whiteside; Bette Davis as Maggie Cutler; Ann Sheridan as Lorraine Sheldon; Reginald Gardiner as Beverly Carlton; Jimmy Durante as Banjo; Richard Travis as Bert Jefferson; Billie Burke as Mrs Stanley; Grant Mitchell as Mr Stanley; Ruth Vivian as Harriet Stanley; George Barbier as Dr Bradley; Mary Wickes as Miss Preen.

Arsenic and Old Lace. US 1941 (released 1944); monochrome; 118 minutes. Produced and directed by Frank Capra for Warner. Written by Julius J. and Philip G. Epstein, from the play by Joseph Kesselring. Directed by Frank Capra. Photographed by Sol Polito. Music score by Max Steiner. Art direction by Max Parker. Edited by Daniel Mandell. With Cary Grant as Mortimer Brewster; Josephine Hull as Abby Brewster; Jean Adair as Martha Brewster; John Alexander as Teddy Brewster; Priscilla Lane as Elaine Harper; Raymond Massey as Jonathan Brewster; Peter Lorre as Dr Einstein; Jack Carson as O'Hara; Edward Everett Horton as Mr Witherspoon; James Gleason as Rooney; Grant Mitchell as Dr Harper.

A Distinct Smell of Fried Onions
A Matter of Life and Death

A pilot bales out of a blazing bomber without a parachute, and lands in the sea. Surprised to find himself still alive, he has hallucinations of being summoned to the hereafter. The heavenly court gives him leave to appeal and select a defence counsel from the ranks of the dead; he appoints his doctor friend who has been killed in an accident. Meanwhile in the real world he undergoes a brain operation and is 'cured' of his fancies, just as, in heaven, he wins his case.

I knew it was partly in colour and partly in what the ads called 'dye-monochrome', and I quite imagined that the heavenly scenes would have the colour. Much to my surprise it was the other way round: they were a very pale green. So was I, and very sleepy, during that first encounter at the Bolton Lido, for I had spent the previous night rather wakefully in a prison cell. Two of us had been on a hike across Brontë country and decided to walk back over the moor at midnight. Startled at one point by my own shadow magnified on a fog bank, like the spectre of the brocken, I had fallen into a ditch, sprained my ankle, and limped at two into Todmorden, where the police station was the only building open and a friendly sergeant had offered me the only hospitality he could. It was a disorienting experience, so I was in the right mood for *A Matter of Life and Death*, which apart from its plot made my mind dance with its imaginative asides; but with Morpheus overcoming my resistance I had to go back on the following night to fix the movie firmly in my mind while I was alert.

Any film by Powell and Pressburger (the Archers, they chose to call themselves, though they didn't always hit the bullseye) was bound to be out of the common run, for they were a mischievous, witty, literary, technically very competent pair; and now that a rich uncle in the shape of J. Arthur Rank was guaranteeing them as the latest addition to his expensive 'art gallery', they were no longer restricted by the taint of mere commercialism. This eye-popping and

266

A MATTER OF LIFE AND DEATH. The heavenly court descends to chat to a prospective new recruit. Massey, Hunter, Niven, Livesey

supremely self-confident fantasy was an obvious choice as the first Royal Performance film, though far from everybody applauded it: it was too offbeat to be anything but caviare to the general.

Michael Powell, whose share of the work was mainly production and direction, is of course British; but Emeric Pressburger, like Korda from whom his ideas sometimes seemed to derive, is Hungarian, and in the early forties, though he could write English, he certainly couldn't speak it. Yet the image he clearly painted in this film is that of an imperishable England with all the traditional middle-class trimmings: an idyllic village, viewed by the doctor through his *camera obscura*; a country house with amateurs rehearsing *A Midsummer Night's Dream* under instruction from the vicar; quotations from the more popular poets; an infinite beach so unfrequented that the goatherd can sunbathe in the nude and play his pipes while tending a docile flock. This beach scene, by the way, is beautifully handled. Niven, washed ashore, has to feel that he is in heaven. Blue

267

skies help, and we observe his initial acquiescence as he divests himself while walking of items of his flying kit, leaving them in a trail behind him; we notice his surprise that he still has a shadow; we witness his displeasure that even Heaven has Keep Out signs; then with a shock he is brought back to reality when a four-engined bomber from the nearby aerodrome whizzes straight over his head from the other side of the sand dunes.

Clearly a highbrow by normal movie standards, Pressburger even contrived to get into his script not only initial mentions of Plato, Aristotle and Jesus Christ but a later consideration of the various qualities of Plato, Richelieu and Lincoln as defence counsel. Then there are quotations from Andrew Marvell and Sir Walter Raleigh. ('I'd rather have written that than flown through Hitler's legs,' says the supposedly doomed pilot in between dictating a letter to his mother and falling in love with the American radio operator who has caught what appear likely to be his last moments.) There is also a light but spirited discussion of the works of Spinoza (cut from the final print) and quite a bit about chess gambits. Where he and Powell often seemed just a little confused was which side of the war they were on, for throughout their joint career they tended to cast in heroic roles Germans (Veidt, Walbrook) or German characters (*Ill Met By Moonlight, The Battle of the River Plate*), while displaying Britons (*Colonel Blimp, The Red Shoes*, even to an extent David Niven here) as likeable nincompoops. Certainly the prosecuting counsel (Abraham Farlan, in 1777 the first American to be killed by a British bullet) is given a tirade against the British which may seem to contain rather too many home truths.

So this was a film on which no expense had been spared and in which anything could happen. The trick photography in particular was beyond criticism, and the moving stairway to heaven an unprecedented prop never bettered by Hollywood and especially convincing when accompanied by Allan Gray's memorably simple score, which seemed to consist of six piano notes repeated again and again. Indeed it was argued in some quarters that the real stars of the picture were Jack Cardiff for his controlled colour and marvellous effects (note particularly his careful flooding of monochrome images with colour, as when the heavenly messenger comes to earth, notes with satisfaction that his *boutonnière* grows properly rose-coloured, and jokes disarmingly with the audience: 'One is so starved for Technicolor up there.'); and Alfred Junge for his apparently limitless heaven sets, especially the gleaming trial arena and the tracking down shot from Airman Trubshawe as he gazes through one of several circular holes in the high ceiling of the celestial record office. But the overall style is of course that of Powell and Pressburger: the careful juxtaposition of one sequence against another, the insistence that the audience's mind shall be put to work, the sensuous lingering over attractive irrelevances like the rhododendrons and the *camera obscura*, the semi-circular tracking round the doctor's book-piled sitting-room to warn us that something eerie will soon happen. The subjective sequences shot from the patient's viewpoint as he is wheeled along hospital corridors work beautifully, but the Archers' regulation lapse of taste comes with the 'going under' shot of a screenful of closing flesh-coloured eyelids, especially as the lashes seem to be pointing in instead of out (though the enthusiastic creators redeem themselves with the very next shot of blotchy inkwash colours, which perfectly represents the sensation of undergoing an anaesthetic).

The preface of the movie disclaims any supernatural element:

This is the story of two worlds, the one we know and another which exists only in the mind of a young airman whose life and imagination have been violently shaped by war. Any resemblance to any other world, known or unknown, is purely coincidental.

But by the end, despite the cunning revelation that God and the surgeon conducting the operation are played by the same actor (superb Abraham Sofaer), the heavenly characters have taken on a distinct life of their own, and the ambivalence is underlined by the mysterious return of a borrowed chess book from heaven to earth, a clear case of a scriptwriter wanting to eat his cake and have it, as with the scarf in *Portrait of Jennie* and the coin in *Miracle in the Rain*.

Despite the unsatisfactoriness of fantasies for the mass audience, we have here a romantic extravaganza which plays with time and death and love and yet within its own terms contrives to dot every i and cross every t. It is a true work of the intellectual imagination, and the European imagination at that: the Brothers Grimm, for instance, would have loved it, and Korda almost certainly wished he had made it himself. One can imagine the effect its exuberant richness of colour and wit must have had on the audience for that first royal film of 1946, soon after post-war austerity had set in. When clips from it were shown at the 1979 royal performance, they were received with astonishment and applause by watchers who had forgotten that films could be so breathtaking in their creative splendour, and many were heard to whisper afterwards that they would have preferred to see it in full rather than sit through the beggarly contrivances of *California Suite*, a flimsy star vehicle which contrasted strikingly with a genuinely creative old movie whose stars had been content to subjugate their own talents to a unique whole of greater significance than any collection of individual performances. As *Time Out* remarked when it was shown on TV later in 1979, 'There are few true masterpieces in British cinema, and most of them are Powell/Pressburger pictures . . . nobody who truly loves cinema can fail to be both moved and astounded by this extraordinary film.'

Pressburger must surely have borrowed his heavenly messenger theme from *Here Comes Mr Jordan*, made five years earlier in Hollywood, though adapting it entirely to European requirements. The American comedy, recently remade as *Heaven Can Wait*, was a hard-boiled whimsy of indeterminate style, at its best perhaps when viewed as a series of gags for such accomplished scene-stealers as Claude Rains, Edward Everett Horton, Donald McBride and James Gleason, with a meaty leading role for personable Robert Montgomery. Its plot, which seemed so weird at the time, gave a myriad of later films plenty to chew on, and Harry Segall (original play) and Sidney Buchman (script) deserve their share of kudos. A boxer, just before his plane crashes, is mercifully whisked off to heaven by a benevolent messenger. Once there, he finds he was to have survived, and must return to earth; but by the time the heavenly red tape has been sorted out his body has been cremated and he must find another. In doing so he brings a couple of murderers to book and resumes his pugilistic career. This curious rigmarole may well be seen as a predictable outcrop of a generally unspiritual and mammon-worshipping nation in the midst of total war; the supernatural was also enjoying considerable resurgence in the form of horror films, for a people aghast at the death of loved ones naturally balked at accepting death as the end. In England after the war ended, *A Matter of Life and Death* could hardly fail to seem a little tasteless, with its queues of dead airmen waiting for their heavenly wings. Thirty-five years later however it is *Here Comes Mr Jordan* which seems brash and unsympathetic, while *A Matter of Life and Death* stands fresh and vivid as an undated work of cinematic imagination and a rich feast of tragi-comical-romantic entertainment.

A Matter of Life and Death. GB 1946; Technicolor and monochrome; 104 minutes. Written, produced and directed by Michael Powell and Emeric Pressburger for the Archers; Rank release. Photographed by Jack Cardiff. Music score by Allan Gray. Art direction by Hein Heckroth. Edited by Reginald Mills. With David Niven as Peter Carter; Roger Livesey as Dr Frank Reeves; Kim Hunter as June; Raymond Massey as Abraham Farlan; Abraham Sofaer as the judge; Marius Goring as Conductor 71; Robert Coote as Bob Trubshawe.

Here Comes Mr Jordan. US 1941; monochrome; 93 minutes. Produced by Everett Riskin for Columbia. Written by Seton I. Miller and Sidney Buchman, from the play *Heaven Can Wait* by Harry Segall. Directed by Alexander Hall. Photographed by Joseph Walker. Music score by Morris Stoloff. Edited by Viola Lawrence. Art direction by Lionel Banks. With Robert Montgomery as Joe Pendleton; Claude Rains as Mr Jordan; Edward Everett Horton as Messenger 7013; Evelyn Keyes as Bette Logan; Rita Johnson as Julia Farnsworth; James Gleason as Max Corkle; Donald McBride as Inspector Williams; John Emery as Tony Abbott; Halliwell Hobbes as Sisk.

Et Voilà!
Le Million

Tradesmen, crooks and opera singers are drawn into the search for a winning lottery ticket which has been lost.

It defies criticism, as perfect things do. To analyse it is almost like breaking a butterfly upon the wheel. But the attempt must be made, if only to convince a modern audience that a film made in 1931, when less than half the world's cinemas were wired for sound, can have employed such delicacy and charm in its conquest of the new medium. When I first saw it in 1949, its merit was no less than I had come to expect from René Clair, but by then the golden age of light cinema had come and gone, and in the joy of my discovery I failed to appreciate the breakthrough it had represented at the time of its release. Now that charm, fun and romance are dirty words to film-makers, the achievement of *Le Million* can at last be properly understood.

Clair has been unfashionable for a few years now, and so must be ripe for revaluation. Many self-styled cinéastes must be totally unfamiliar with his work, so I may be forgiven for reminding them that his métier was to enrapture us with fantasies of the sunny side of life, especially of life in suburban Paris in his own time and the generations before, a milieu filled with concierges and creditors and taxi drivers and baker's men, all presented with sly exaggeration but also with affection for their foibles and for their warmly comic appearance. He had a trick of setting his characters against light grey backgrounds, so that the outlines of their portly, emaciated or otherwise eccentric figures might be fully taken in by the eye; graduates from an English childhood may be reminded of the illustrations in books by Enid Blyton. And in case familiarity were to breed contempt, he would toss in from time to time a minor character whose sole purpose was to make one blink, such as the bald and moustachioed gentleman in *Le Million* who is glimpsed in the police station wearing only a bowler hat and undershorts. No explanation is given, or required.

When towards the end of his career Clair made a colour film, it disappointed everybody, for he seemed to bring none of his old flair to it. The truth was that he had always created his own colour. Even though his settings were the less salubrious quarters of Paris, and his palette the old 'square' black and white screen, he was able to send us home with the feeling of having enjoyed all the colour and gaiety we could possibly need. His characters sing and dance and mime as to the manner born, with none of the strain so often evidenced in the works of Chaplin or Tati or Pierre Etaix. *Le Million* opens with a breathtaking panning shot over the crooked roofs of his milieu, with their smoking chimneys and sloping tiles. Presently Clair closes in on a skylight through which two inquisitive onlookers are peering down at a party in the studio below, where characters of all kinds are careering around the room in a perpetual daisy chain, singing triumphantly. Why the commotion, they are asked. A spokesman looks up and cries that he will willingly tell their story. As they dance on, the figures disappear, leaving an empty room in which the recapitulation of the day's events can begin. François, an artist, young and poor, is assailed by creditors whom he can't pay. Suddenly, reading the lottery results, he finds that the winner is either himself or his friend Prosper. Prosper tends to sulk when he finds that the winner isn't him, and to smile when François can't find the old coat in which reposes the essential piece of paper. Alas, we have seen that his well-meaning girl friend has given it to an elderly gent on the run from the law; and we now find that said gent is actually Père La Tulipe, an amiable Moriarty of the French underworld, who operates from palatial premises behind what we would now call a boutique. By the time François catches up with him he has sold the coat to a passing opera singer who thinks it would be just the thing for his leading role in *Les Bohemiens*. At the urgent request of the girl friend, La Tulipe agrees to get it back, and gives suitable instructions to his minions. Meanwhile François is mistaken for a thief and arrested; and Prosper refuses to bail him out, having extracted a promise that if he finds the ticket he shall have half the prize.

Already most agreeably stimulated by characters who refuse to talk when they can dance and sing instead, whether in garret corridors or police station waiting rooms, we now shift our attention expectantly to that night at the opera. I use the phrase advisedly, for if I were told that the Marx Brothers a few years later drew several bright ideas from M. Clair's extravaganza, I wouldn't be at all surprised. By now a number of comic crooks and four leading characters, including the escaped François who has the police on his tail, are in desperate search for the coat, and their paths frequently collide. There is a delicious moment in Signor Toscarelli's dressing room when hands reach for it from different hiding places and recoil as they touch. Presently there is a pause for breath, in delicate romantic mood, as the young lovers are trapped on stage behind a bush and have to listen to the duet, every line of which seems to apply especially to them; then the chase begins again. François and Prosper find themselves on stage amid the chorus, ready to grab for the coat when Toscarelli tosses it aside on cue. They get a cuff each, and won't let go, holding the garment up like a banner. But the singer who has to play victim of the duel falls heavily on the coat, leaving our heroes each with a detached sleeve. In the ensuing backstage mêlée, presented with the addition of a sound track borrowed from a rugby match, the coat is thrown out of the window onto a passing car. François leaves the opera in despair and goes home in the taxi which has been circling all evening waiting for him. Naturally, it turns out to be the very vehicle on which the coat fell,

LE MILLION. A toast to the happy ending which we all suspected was coming

and still reposes; but the prize is snatched away by La Tulipe's men. We wait for the happy ending, and it comes just as the despondent artist begins to explain the situation to his impatient creditors: La Tulipe turns up with the coat and the ticket intact, as promised. It is indeed he who has been telling the story, which he rounds off with an expressive gesture before returning to the dance, in which the entire cast now joins. *'Et voilà!'*

In such a film one obviously misses a great deal by not possessing a fluent command of French, like the little unsubtitled joke of the concierge who calls a fleeing tenant by increasingly rude names: *'Cochon! Assassin! Artiste!'* Some gags must be lost while chasing the words, but one does not however fail to appreciate the superb control with which we are passed from one shot to the next in a succession of perfectly framed pictures, for *Le Million* is never less than pleasing to the eye. Something I had not noticed until my most recent viewing, which was probably my tenth at least, is a rather curious but undeniably effective trick employed by Lazare Meerson in his set design. Towards the rear of each 'room' the atmosphere seems pleasantly misty, and I suddenly realized that this is because the rear wall is not three-dimensional but a photograph projected from a slide. (On one occasion, in the police station, a seated gendarme is even frozen in the still.) The intention is clearly to give a subtly fantasticated air, a delicacy of visual texture, to all the sets, and by gum it works.

The characters of *Le Million* may be caricatured, but never cruelly. One never doubts the real people under the exaggeration, and one appreciates especially that the hero is not some anonymous manly stalwart but an unathletic, crumple-faced failure; also that La Tulipe, who seems such a benevolent old crook when moustachioed, shows a thin businesslike mouth when his hirsute disguise is removed. There are here men and women of all shapes and sizes, including a truly massive prima donna and a little wisp of a crook, and much of the fun is in seeing them collide with or narrowly miss each other, to tumble down corridors and skip down stairs as though life were nothing but fun and games. To René Clair in Paris in 1930, it probably was.

Le Million is told almost entirely in recitative and song, a method infrequently copied. Mamoulian in *Love Me Tonight*, which is treated separately, had some good stabs at it, and Lubitsch in *One Hour With You* applied it rather daringly to high comedy, adding some speeches aimed directly at the audience by his star Maurice Chevalier. Milestone in *Hallelujah I'm a Bum* flopped rather desperately and more or less killed the career of Al Jolson; so by 1933 the brief fashion had waned. One might claim that it was revived in the sixties by Demy's *Les Parapluies de Cherbourg*, but that film was almost entirely sung and this invites comparison with light opera rather than with Clair's fluffy combination of styles.

Le Million. France 1931; monochrome; 80 minutes. Produced and directed by René Clair for Tobis. Written by René Clair, from the musical comedy by Georges Berr and Guillemaud. Photographed by Georges Périnal. Music score by Georges Van Parys, Armand Bernard and Philippe Parès. Art direction by Lazare Meerson. With René Lefèvre as the painter; Louis Allibert as friend; Annabella as his girl friend; Paul Olivier as the master crook; and Wanda Gréville, Raymond Cordy, Odette Talazac, Allibert Prosper.

On a Clear Day You Can See the Catskills
Mr Blandings Builds His Dream House

Exasperated by city living, a New York advertising executive determines to move his family to the Connecticut countryside, but fails to anticipate the difficulties.

I love this civilized comedy both for its own sake and for the fact that it sends me back so frequently to the book on which it was based, a book which in my opinion is one of the great achievements of light literature in this century or the last, fit to be classed alongside *The Diary of a Nobody* and *Alice in Wonderland* and the *Sherlock Holmes* stories, and to be turned to time and time again on winter evenings when the world needs brightening up. The film is perfectly cast, and when I read and re-read the book it is of Grant and Loy and Douglas and Denny that I think; but no film can match the immense satisfaction given by Eric Hodgins' feel for the English language. Try, for instance, putting the following onto celluloid:

Another winter came to Bald Mountain, and Mr and Mrs Blandings saw their growing house only at irregular intervals. As he viewed it now, on a warm mid-January weekend, it made Mr Blandings think of what a flayed elephant must look like. The brick veneer which was to form the lower exterior ended at different courses in different places; above it, the diagonal sheathing of yellow pine, crusty with resin and punctured with knotholes, rose to the eaves. The roof was a wavy expanse of tar paper, dotted with the big shiny discs that acted as washers to keep the holding nails from tearing its feeble substance. The house's appearance was the nakedness of muscle, minus skin and fat.

Or this:

There was nothing so, well, so aphrodisiac as a set of building plans, Mr Blandings said to himself. Even in the days when the Blandings' idea of a new home was merely a different apartment out of which someone had just moved, the plans, with their thick black lines and their crisp lettering, had roused in them an instinct that obviously was something deeper and finer than mere cupidity. It was the nest-building instinct, damn it, thought Mr Blandings, and let anybody go ahead and laugh who wants to. His head buried in Mr Simms' exquisite draughtsmanship, Mr Blandings was

MR BLANDINGS BUILDS HIS DREAM HOUSE. Cary Grant and Myrna Loy are impulse buyers, Melvyn Douglas the voice of restraint

dreaming again; dreaming happily. The vexations and frustrations and checks and naggings of mischance were all in the proper perspective of the far and insignificant background; something for a hearty laugh in the days when the Blandings' house would be a mellowed, weathered shrine; ivy-shrouded, garlanded with lilac, the shade trees casting their waving silhouettes upon the pure green suede of an English lawn.

One marvellous sequence that does get through more or less intact concerns the instructions given by Mrs Blandings, once the builders have left, to Mr PeDelford, the boss interior painter, who interrupts her monologue only with different inflections of the affirmative:

The living-room is to be a soft green, not as bluish as a robin's egg, but not as yellow as daffodil buds. This sample is a little too yellow, but don't let whoever mixes it go to the other extreme and get it too blue. It should just be a sort of grayish apple green. The dining room is to be yellow, and a very gay yellow. Just ask one of your workmen to get a pound of the A & P's best butter and match it *exactly* . . . For our bedroom here is a small sample of chintz. As you will see, it is flowered, but I don't want you to match any of the flower colours. There are some blue dots in the background, and it is these dots I want you to match exactly . . . The kitchen is to be white. Not a cold, antiseptic, hospital white, however. It should have a warm effect, but it should not suggest any other colour except just pure white . . .

The expression on Mr PeDelford's face during all this would match that of Uriah Heep, but as soon as Mrs Blandings is out of earshot he seems to straighten up considerably. 'Green, yellow, blue, white,' he murmurs to his assistant. 'Check?'

The film concerns only the nicest people, and is warmly funny from beginning to end, but one does have regrets about its omissions, especially as the bumping into each other in the New York apartment goes on rather too long; one would gladly have passed up a little of this in return for a scene with the estate agent conning his city slickers into paying three times the going rate for the old Hackett place. 'You've gotta be able to visualize', is the phrase that sells them. Also, a little more of Mr Blandings' problems at the office and his skilled solutions to them would have provided a welcome contrast to the difficulties in which he finds himself when dealing with well-drillers, cement contractors and the like. As his lawyer friend tells him at one especially fraught moment, when a supposed fifty-acre property has proved to survey at thirty-five, 'more or less': 'Every time you get a little tight, you weep on my shoulder about what a terrible thing the advertising agency business is for a sensitive soul like yourself because you make your living out of bamboozling the American public. I would say that a small part of this victimized group has now redressed the balance.'

It is this friend, Bill Cole, who narrates the story: the part has been pleasantly built up to accommodate Melvyn Douglas and to provide the merest wisp of a comedy triangle, with Mr Blandings indulging in quite unjustified jealousy of his old friend. Blandings is one of Cary Grant's most apparently effortless portrayals; after 94 minutes we feel we know exactly what his reaction will be to any given situation. He comes equipped with wall-to-wall women, including two daughters and an unseen schoolteacher, Miss Stellwagon, who reportedly regards him as 'very American, very grass roots, very blueberry pie'. His wife, charmingly portrayed by Myrna Loy, switches his alarm back on when he switches it off in the hope of more sleep, squeezes his toothpaste from the middle of the tube, and steams up the bathroom mirror when he's trying to shave. And his coloured cook takes no notice at all of what he wants for breakfast, insisting on serving up Wham, the stuff he has to advertise. ('Wham, the whale of a ham.')

He is thus easy prey to the lure of the countryside, where a man can breathe in the grounds of his own dream castle, and with insufficient research finds himself the owner of a tumbledown relic of the revolutionary war. 'Just to see it is to love it,' he assures Bill Cole, whose reply after inspection is: 'Good thing there are two of you, one to love it and one to hold it up.' The day comes when Mr Apollonio the construction engineer has to give him some unwelcome advice: 'If your chimney was shot and your sills were OK I'd say go ahead, fix her up. If your sills were shot and your chimney was OK, again I'd say go ahead, fix her up. But your sills are shot *and* your chimney is shot, so I say OK, you better tear her down.' So the old house has to be torn down (the film omits the wrath of the local residents at what their newspaper calls DESTRUCTION OF FAMED BALD MOUNTAIN EDIFICE) and another put up; thus the second half of this engaging movie concerns itself with lally columns, lintels (rabbeted or unrabbeted), ledges, artesian wells, two-by-fives, and Zuz-Zuz water softeners. It is a field seldom, if ever, previously explored by Hollywood, and its uniqueness is indeed refreshing, the Blandings family being absolutely recognizable as the equals of the average audience watching them. Thirty years on, indeed, Mrs Blandings' laughable cry of defiance as the costs escalate does not seem wholly unreasonable: 'I refuse to endanger the health of my children in a house with less than three bathrooms.'

Every film needs a conclusion, and plainly it would not be enough for Hollywood for the family simply to settle snugly in its new house. Mr Blandings has to have trouble finding a slogan for Wham, and to be on the point of resignation because his domestic problems have prevented him from coming up with anything better than the following:

> Compare the slice –
> Compare the price –
> Take our advice –
> Buy Wham!

Or even:

This little piggy went to market
As meek and as mild as a lamb.
 He smiled in his tracks
 As they slipped him the axe:
He knew he was going to be Wham!

Luckily his own coloured cook comes to the rescue as she calls the family to breakfast with:

If you ain't eatin' Wham
You ain't eatin' ham!

Would that all happy endings were so simply achieved.

Mr Blandings Builds His Dream House. US 1948; monochrome; 94 minutes. Produced and written by Norman Panama and Melvin Frank, from the book *Mr Blandings Builds His Dream House* by Eric Hodgins. Directed by H. C. Potter. Photographed by James Wong Howe. Music score by Constantin Bakaleinikoff. Art direction by Albert S. D'Agostino and Carroll Clark. Edited by Harry Marker. With Cary Grant as James Blandings; Myrna Loy as Muriel Blandings; Melvyn Douglas as Bill Cole; Reginald Denny as Mr Simms; Louise Beavers as Gussie; Sharyn Moffett and Connie Marshall as the Blandings girls; Jason Robards as Mr Retch; Nestor Paiva as Mr Apollonio; Harry Shannon as Mr Tesander; Emory Parnell as Mr PeDelford.

The Best of All Possible Worlds
Mr Smith Goes to Washington

Conniving politicians arrange the appointment of a young scoutmaster to fill an unexpired senatorial turn, but he soon begins to sniff out their corruption.

It is a film to have delighted the heart of Gary Cooper, who was obsessed by the idea of playing 'Mr Average Joe American' and indeed had already done so for Capra, most successfully, in *Mr Deeds Goes to Town*. The Smith version merely restates the identical theme: an earnest hick comes to the big city, survives a lot of laughter behind his back, and teaches the smart urban types a thing or two about life and love and morality. The city here is Washington, which momentarily blinds him with its shining visions of Lincoln and his glorious predecessors; the crooked little apple cart to be upset is the purchase by his fellow senator and the local political boss, under false names, of a strip of barren land which will then be sold at a huge profit when it is found to fit in with a new development. Our young hero may be imbued with the naïvest political ideals, but his virtues include diligence and tenacity. Surprising the conspirators by reading everything he is required to sign, he stumbles on enough evidence to expose the whole plot; whereupon the purchases are shifted to him, via forged signatures, and he is himself accused of the crime. By the kind of fortuitous timing known only to Hollywood he is able to halt the juggernaut of public vengeance, and restore his good name, by staging a twenty-four senatorial filibuster which prevents the passage of the law enabling the scheme to go through, and causes the senior conspirator to break down and attempt suicide.

This fairy tale might clearly have been intolerable: it was so in the seventies when remade as *Billy Jack Goes to Washington*, and versions of it came and went without much comment during the forties and fifties. As a television series it seemed merely bland. But apart from striking just the note of sentimental optimism which was required by 'New Deal' Americans at the time of its release, and providing a tonic too for the rest of the free world, it is lit by a brand of cinematic ingenuity and directorial panache which has all but disappeared from our screens and is (alas) contemptuously dismissed by the new breed of film-maker when it does surface. Capra and his writer Sidney Buchman can be seen here to be working with that assurance which comes only from being at the very top of the professional tree, and the resultant film is an intricate jigsaw of brilliant set-pieces blending perfectly into a satisfying stew under the supervision of a gourmet chef. As Graham Greene wrote in his days as a film critic:

A week later one remembers the big body of Pallette stuck in a telephone box, the family dinner of the weak crooked governor whom even his children pester over the nomination, the whole authentic atmosphere of big bland crookery between boss and politician – the Joes and the Jims, the Christian names and comradeship, the wide unspoken references, and one remembers too the faces chosen and shot with Capra care – worried political faces, Grub Street faces, acquisitive social faces and faces that won't give themselves away.

In other words, it's the Capra touch that means so much. James Stewart may have deserved an Academy Award for his performance (he got one the following year) and in the hoarse idealism of his final speech he wonderfully toes the line between pathos and bathos.

('You think I'm licked. You all think I'm licked. Well, I'm not licked and I'm going to stay right here and fight for this lost cause even if this room gets filled with lies like these . . .') It's marvellous stuff, but we wouldn't root for him as we do if Capra were not constantly cutting from one reaction shot to another, from long shot to close up, from angle view to frantic pan. Thus mundane elements are whipped up by sheer professionalism into what passes very adequately for a high plane of wit, emotion and dramatic invention. The result on the screen looks deceptively direct and simple, but the professional eye singles out this dexterity as the single most rare and valuable item in the film-maker's portfolio, whether in terms of time, patience, stamina or overall vision. Capra's political morality could hardly have been simpler: for him the underdog must always triumph. His film technique however was the most complicated in Hollywood, except perhaps for that of Orson Welles and the team who made *Citizen Kane* the experience it still is. *Mr Smith* entertains by refusing to allow the eye to rest for a single second, by creating a constant hubbub. Not until the second or third viewing is one able to see through the surface and admire the superb control of fundamentals, down to the finest detail. A score of people may be shouting and jostling on that little old-fashioned screen, but you still see what Capra wants you to see, no more and no less, and you remember down the years a descriptive angle or a laugh line which may seem thrown away but which Capra knows is audible because he shot it a dozen times until it came out exactly the way he wanted.

In this kind of production the technical team may be foremost but the venture will fail without the right actors to interpret Capra's simplistic stereotypes. With the exception of Claude Rains, who strives valiantly if not quite successfully to make a man out of Senator Paine, the half-corrupted 'silver knight' of the senate, all the leading actors had worked for Capra before or would do so again: they admirably suited his purpose, and so were recruited to his repertory. Jean Arthur, the smart city girl who despite herself comes to love a bumpkin; Edward Arnold, the very quintessence of crooked capitalism; Thomas Mitchell, the epitome of drunken Irish reporters. Harry Carey, Eugene Pallette, Guy Kibbee, H. B. Warner, Charles Lane have their moments too. Singly or in unison, they flesh out the living tapestry of Capra's America, to a grateful Italian immigrant a land of wondrous opportunity, where the right guy will

MR SMITH GOES TO WASHINGTON. A splendid array of villains: Kibbee, Pallette, Arnold, Rains

always triumph even if he *is* a little pixilated. It's a theme he returned to again and again. In *It Happened One Night* a reporter wins an heiress after a peripatetic courtship in buses and motels. In *Lady for a Day* soft-hearted gangsters enable an old apple-seller to persuade her long-lost daughter that she's a queen of society. In *You Can't Take It With You* Grandpa Vanderhof, who retired at thirty-five and doesn't pay income tax, persuades his large family to concentrate on doing their own thing despite what society expects. In *Mr Deeds Goes to Town* an unexpected millionaire proves that he isn't mad just because he wants to give his fortune away to poor farmers. In *Meet John Doe* a tramp is turned by a newspaper into a public hero. Even in *Arsenic and Old Lace* the two sweetly murderous old ladies are presented to us as the salt of the earth.

Capra himself seems to favour as his masterpiece the post-war *It's a Wonderful Life*, which he personally produced for his own company, Liberty films. The consensus of critical opinion, however, has it that, vastly enjoyable and Capraesque though the film is to an audience in the right mood, the director steered it a shade too far in the direction of hysteria to produce the American *Christmas Carol* he intended. In it, bankrupted by local villainy, an entirely honest small-town business man contemplates suicide. After ninety minutes of his life in flashback a bumbling white-haired old angel – yes, an angel, delightfully played by Henry Travers – is sent down to show him how much worse off the town would have been had he never lived, and just as this magical lesson strikes home, his many friends rally round to bail him out of his financial doldrums. This almost unbearably emotional finale, with outside a snowstorm raging and inside a roomful of joyous beaming people all talking at once and throwing cash into the kitty as the Christmas bells ring, has to be experienced to be believed. Without doubt it stands as one of the great climactic moments of American cinema, but alas, Capra has taken too long to get to it, and the overall mood of the movie is closer to sentimentality than to sentiment. But to test its quality, one has only to compare his version of the story with the languid three-hour television remake which appeared in the seventies under the title *It Happened One Christmas*: neither colour nor real snow nor Orson Welles playing Lionel Barrymore could replace the cinematic sorcery of the Capra team at its height.

Perhaps because of his disappointment at the lukewarm reception of *It's a Wonderful Life*, which at the age of eighty he was still showing every Christmas Eve in his home, Capra's career now started on the downgrade: he never did anything else but warmed-over variations on his thirties successes and a couple of mild originals in similar vein, and as the years progressed his work became more obviously out of key with the increasingly cynical times. There was one exception in a more astringent vein, a rare case of his directing work by people outside his own charmed circle. In 1948 he made a thoroughly enjoyable movie from the stage comedy *State of The Union*, about a presidential nominee trying to maintain his integrity in face of political pressures. It is now remembered less as a Capra movie than as a brilliant vehicle for the team of Spencer Tracy and Katharine Hepburn, she as what his agent called 'the most beautiful plank in your husband's platform'. No one could blush like Hepburn as she replied: 'That's a *heck* of a thing to call a woman!'

Mr Smith Goes to Washington. US 1939; monochrome; 130 minutes. Produced and directed by Frank Capra for Columbia. Written by Sidney Buchman, from a story by Lewis R. Foster. Photographed by Joseph Walker. Music score by Dmitri Tiomkin. Art direction by Lionel Banks. Montages by Slavko Vorkapich. Edited by Gene Havlik and Al Clark. With James Stewart as Jefferson Smith; Jean Arthur as Saunders; Claude Rains as Senator Joseph Paine; Edward Arnold as Jim Taylor; Guy Kibbee as Governor Hopper; Thomas Mitchell as Diz Moore; Eugene Pallette as Chick McCann; H. B. Warner as Senator Fuller; Beulah Bondi as Ma Smith; Harry Carey as President of the Senate; Astrid Allwyn as Susan Paine; Ruth Donnelly as Emma Hopper; Porter Hall as Senator Muroe.

Things That Go Arggggggh
The Mummy's Hand

Members of an archaeological expedition are threatened by a marauding mummy.

Although I am repeatedly hypnotized by the 1932 phantasy entitled *The Mummy*, it does take itself very seriously indeed, and is more an eccentric romance than a horror film. Boris Karloff's famous appearance in matted bandages is limited to a couple of seconds, and all he really does by way of acting is open one eye; we don't see him walk unless you count the trail of his loose ends across the floor. (This brief performance does however drive a young archaeologist mad, causing him to babble the famous line 'He went for a little walk', which the director, as an in-joke, arranged to have repeated in his next film, *Mad Love*.) For the rest of the movie Karloff has been magically restored to something resembling normal human appearance, assuming you know a few very wrinkled humans; mentally rejuvenated, however, he spends the remainder of his existence mooning over a young woman who resembles his lost love of 3,000 years ago. Then Isis (or Osiris, or one of those gods) reduces him to dust, and we can all go home happy.

The Mummy's Hand is a sequel in very different mood, clearly made as a second feature and utilizing almost intact its predecessor's flashback to ancient Egypt. (Look carefully and you'll even see Boris Karloff in the long shots.) It touches my life rather closely because of all the horror movies I've seen, this is the one that came closest to scaring me to death, perhaps because I came upon it by accident. I was twelve, and my history master thought that as a relief from sitting in smelly shelters during air raids his class might enjoy an educational afternoon at the pictures, threepence to be contributed by Mother. His choice was a yawnworthy piece of cardboard propaganda called *This England*, with John Clements and Emlyn Williams gracing a series of studiobound charades about the White Cliffs resisting invasion. I was all for having an afternoon off, and missing games, so a dozen of us met at 2 P.M. by the tram terminus and settled into the Lido's mid-stalls just as the big picture was starting. The history master almost broke his seat laughing at its ineptitudes, and as soon as it was over said we might stop for the cartoon if we liked. What he'd failed to notice was that it wasn't a cartoon but *The Mummy's Hand*, which by some fluke had got through with nothing more restrictive than an 'A' certificate. The green footlights increased in brightness as the houselights dimmed; and some of the green had rubbed off on us when we emerged sixty-five minutes later into the bright afternoon sunlight, giving all corners and alleyways a wide berth on our way home in case a malevolent mummy might be lurking.

I suppose this is a back-handed tribute to a pretty efficient little movie of its kind, and to the team of dedicated thespians who made it seem so real. Closely examined, it doesn't make much sense at all, even if initially one suspends sufficient disbelief to accept that a love-struck loon buried alive 3,000 years ago can be revived through imbibing the juice of tana leaves and used by a sinister secret society – via instructions in English – as an instrument of revenge against trespassers in his girl friend's tomb. (Surely shooting them would have been simpler?) Conveniently, each of the victims is too petrified with terror to get out of the way of this nauseous but slow-moving and one-armed collection of old flesh in dirty wrappings; and it's the kind of movie in which the heroine, after three violent deaths in one evening, retires unafraid in her silken shimmy to a lonely tent. It isn't long before the music wells up, the mummy's shadow falls on the canvas, and after a few helpless screams she ends up on the sacrificial block, just like Fay Wray in *The Mystery of the Wax Museum*, to be saved in the very nick of time by dashing Dick Foran. When I caught up with the movie for the second time I found that forty minutes of it is innocuous banter and the horrific cavortings round the pyramid take only twenty minutes to unspool. It seemed much

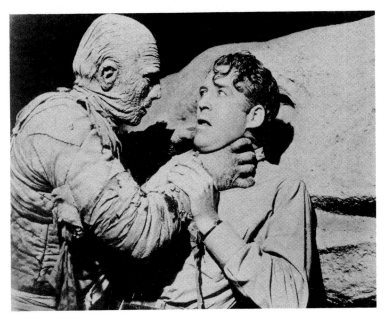

THE MUMMY'S HAND. Tom Tyler has a strong right arm for so desiccated a 3,000-year-old. Dick Foran feels the pinch

longer on that first afternoon; and I have to admit that when in 1979 I saw it for the umpteenth time on television, I made my way rather gingerly to bed through the darkened house.

One of the aspects worth commending about this little monster marathon is the wholeheartedness of its script. The rhetoric is penned with real vigour, especially in the opening reels when thin-lipped George Zucco, wearing a smart fez as the new high priest of Karnak (and who could be better suited for the job?) gets his instructions from his predecessor, who in a scene clearly pinched from *Lost Horizon* dies in mid-sentence as a candle blows out. Eduardo Ciannelli in this modest role displays the best set of shakes I have ever seen on film, but ensures that his words of wisdom come across with deadly clarity: 'Who shall defile the temples of the ancient gods, a cruel and violent death shall be his fate,' he whispers as his head quivers dangerously on his shoulders; 'I fear I shall not see the sun rise again over the valley of the jackals.' His frailty does

not prevent him from recounting the interminable history of Kharis'
disgrace, which surely Mr Zucco, as a senior member of the cult,
might have been expected to know:

Daring the anger of the ancient gods, he stole the forbidden tana leaves . . .
now he waits, asleep, to bring death to those who defile Ananka's tomb . . .
three of the leaves will make enough fluid to keep Kharis' heart beating . . .
once every night during the cycle of the full moon . . . nine leaves to bring
life and movement . . . but never for any reason must you brew more than
nine . . . he would become an uncontrollable monster, a soulless demon with
the desire to kill, and kill, and kill . . .

The exposition of the modern plot is then given at a fast clip, with
pauses for comedy concerning Cecil Kellaway, as an inebriated Irish
conjuror who finances the expedition and always gets his tricks
mixed up. (It is delightful that Mr Kellaway, who has been savaged
by the mummy, turns up hale and hearty in the final scene.) When
the full moon finally rises, the jackals howl, and the mummy walks,
the pace quickens even more, and no scene is allowed to go on too
long: the mummy's appearances tend to last only two or three
seconds each, probably to reduce the arduous post-production work
on his eyes, which have clearly been inked out frame by frame to
give the appearance of a rather nasty jelly. (The sharp-eyed in the
audience will spot a few scenes in which someone forgot to bother.)
Tom Tyler does valiant work in the title role, with a lurching walk
which is absolutely definitive, yet he is billed seventh; when Lon
Chaney Jnr donned the glad rags for three unpersuasive sequels, he
got star billing even though most of the role was performed by a
stunt man. There ain't no justice.

Incidentally, those who wonder how a second feature could afford
such splendid sets as the ruined temple steps and the massive
altarpiece should take a look at *Green Hell*, released by the same
studio a few months earlier. Well, there was absolutely no point in
wasting them.

The trick with the mummy's eyes reminds me of another pacy
Universal horror film of the same year, *Man Made Monster*, released
in the UK as *The Electric Man*. Karloff was to have starred as an
unfortunate who could absorb almost unlimited amounts of electricity, with Lugosi as the mad scientist who gradually increases the

dose and turns him into a murderous robot; but at the last minute the roles were given to young Chaney and Lionel Atwill. When it was finished, the studio judged the serial-like goings-on to be insufficiently startling, so John Fulton was brought in to handpaint an eerie glow round Chaney's head and hands in every scene of rampage, and it is this effective trick which gives the film its mild distinction.

Universal had casting trouble too on *Black Friday*, made in the same year. Here Lugosi was to play a saintly professor who, after an accident, has part of his brain replaced by mad doctor Karloff with that of a dead hoodlum. When he recovers, the plot becomes a replay of *Dr Jekyll and Mr Hyde*, with the transformed gangster stalking off periodically to seek revenge on the pals who took him for a ride. Lugosi, with his pidgin English, was quite incapable of sustaining such a role, though he could have managed the mad doctor and Karloff, one imagines, would have done well by the dual personality. (Instead he was allowed to stay where he was and give one of his stiffest performances.) Lugosi kept his star billing but was allotted an insignificant role as one of the gangsters, even his death scene being fumbled; and Stanley Ridges was brought in to play the professor, giving such a startlingly vivid account of himself that one wonders why so little was heard of this sensitive and professional actor.

Whether or not because he failed to sustain it, the studio ruined another of Lugosi's potentially most interesting performances, when he finally played a role for which he was originally cast in 1930, that of the monster in *Frankenstein Meets the Wolf Man*. This was Universal's first attempt to revive flagging returns by offering more than one ghoul in the same adventure. Chaney had recently played both the monster and the Wolf Man, and there was no way he could have the final fight with himself; so he opted for the lycanthrope and Lugosi was summoned to oppose him. The old Hungarian had little physical power, and his voice was weak, but that might have suited the part as written, for the monster was supposed to be blind until the final sequence, which is why in countless imitations the monster is visualized as stalking about with outstretched arms. So the film was shot; and then, for reasons lost to history, the studio cut out all the references to blindness along with some potentially interesting monster dialogue, and left poor Lugosi lumbering around to no purpose in another much truncated role. The movie is still worth a look for its genuinely frightening opening sequence in a Welsh crypt, for the curious air of doom and pessimism which pervades it, and for Maria Ouspenskaya's indomitable performance as Maleva the wise gypsy, ever ready with her doggerel warning:

> Even the man who is pure in heart
> And says his prayers by night
> May become a wolf when the wolfbane blooms
> And the autumn moon is bright.

Especially if he has seen a few Universal monster pictures.

The Mummy's Hand. US 1940; monochrome; 67 minutes. Produced by Maxwell Shane for Universal. Written by Griffin Jay and Maxwell Shane. Directed by Christy Cabanne. Photographed by Elwood Bredell. Music score by George Robinson. With Dick Foran as Steve Banning; Cecil Kellaway as Solvani; Peggy Moran as Marta; Wallace Ford as Babe Jenson; Tom Tyler as the Mummy; George Zucco as Adoneb; Eduardo Ciannelli as the High Priest; Charles Trowbridge as Dr Petrie.

For Your Added Entertainment
Mysterious Mr Moto and Charlie Chan at the Opera
The Japanese detective exposes a murder-for-hire syndicate, and the Chinese one foils a backstage murder plot.

Two men escape from Devil's Island by night, one a Japanese murderer. Lurching through a swamp infested by leopards as well as crocodiles they survive a hail of bullets from their pursuers. As an old-fashioned Hollywood montage, this sequence takes all of a minute and a half, and very exciting it is. We, of course, have recognized the 'Japanese murderer' as our old friend Mr Moto, and have surmised correctly that he had infiltrated the dreaded island prison for the sole purpose of escaping with his friend, who will doubtless lead him to the head of an international gang. (That was the fun of movies in the thirties: regular attenders knew all the plots.)

Before the ship sails for Europe Mr Moto has improbably taken on a job as the other's London houseboy. ('Cleaning immense,

CHARLIE CHAN AT THE OPERA. The star red herring, Boris Karloff, is visited on the set by Mr Moto-to-be, Peter Lorre

cooking pretentious, cocktails supreme. Suiting you?') Big Ben strikes, and before long the plot is unfolding itself at a Limehouse tavern. It is all very like Hollywood's concept of Sherlock Holmes; and if Mr Moto has a fault, it is not in the ingratiating performance of Peter Lorre, but in the lack of a Watson to be the viewer's eyes and ears. In fact the British come off rather badly in this adventure: the lower classes are ruffians and the officials, be they customs agents or policemen, are rude to foreigners. As for the amiable character called David Scott-Frensham, he turns out to be the head of the League of Assassins, out to murder Czech industrialist Anton Darvak because he proposed to give his steel secrets to the wrong side. By one of the occasional perversities of Fox's casting department, Darvak is played by Henry Wilcoxon, who couldn't be more English; while Scott-Frensham, whose dialogue is peppered with such remarks as 'I say, how does a chap get some attention around here?' and 'My dear girl, one can't go around town killing people, it simply isn't done', is played by the elegant Erik Rhodes, who used to play the amorous Italian in Astaire/Rogers musicals ('Your wife is safe with Tonetti, he prefers spaghetti') and is about as English as taramasalata.

Now Moto, or Ito, is secure in the kitchen of a Half Moon Street flat, serving to the extremely incompetent master criminals cocktails called 'memories of St Joseph', which graduates of Devil's Island will best appreciate. On his day off however he calls on the head of Scotland Yard (who keeps round his wall death masks of executed murderers) and tells him enough of his mission to get him interested, but not so much as to allow him to interfere. 'It seems so incredible,' says Sir Charles, 'an organization that offers murder for sale!' They were so naïve in 1938. It never becomes quite clear why Moto, who already knows everything about the plot, has to go so frequently for information to the Blue Peter pub in Limehouse, but he does, and on one occasion provokes the most splendid brawl ever seen outside an 'A' feature, with enough sinister characters lurking in the shadows outside to fill the Rogues' Gallery twice over. As the story builds to its climax Mr Lorre, or his double, gets plenty of opportunity to demonstrate ju-jitsu; there is also the obligatory scene in which he returns to his kitchen not realizing that his elaborate cover is blown. And so to the finale in an art gallery. Darvak, a connoisseur with clearly abysmal taste, is known to wish to see a particular picture, so arranged by the villains that in order to get the right light he will have to stand in the very spot where a chandelier can come crashing down on him. According to the plot, the villains who know what he looks like can't be present, so the big boss will come in and address him by name, at which signal the band will strike up a particular tune and the accomplice in the roof void will send the chandelier crashing down. As Mr Moto has overheard these elaborate and extremely silly plans, all he has to do is disguise himself as a bristly German professor and at the appropriate time address the evil Scott-Frensham as Darvak. Crash. He then pauses over the broken body long enough to explain his deductions, before leaping upstairs – the police can't find the way to follow him – to polish off the lurking murderer. 'Catchee monkey,' he smiles through a hole in the ceiling at the fade-out, 'but not very softly!'

I hope it is clear from the above not only that this is enjoyable

Boy's Own Paper stuff, but that its lapses are at least as endearing as its merits. This is the world of the 'B' picture, but the Bs from a major studio like Fox, with its plethora of standing sets and attendant technicians, were often more enjoyable than someone else's As. The Motos, whose appeal not so mysteriously waned with Pearl Harbor, were the paciest of all the action series of the thirties; they played top of the bill at secondary halls but might well be found in support at the local Odeon. First-rate familiar actors were available on contract to play assorted suspects, and the star after a while began to seem like one of the family. Today the place of these entertainments has been taken by TV series such as *Kojak* and *Charlie's Angels*; but alas they are so force-fed, so restricted in length, that the likeable details go by the board and we are stuck with the boring plot. In what TV series, for instance, would one be likely to find the following exchange?

'Didn't someone say that the best way to avoid death is not to have too much aversion to it?'
'Sounds like Schopenhauer.'

Yes, it really happens in *Mysterious Mr Moto*.

The most famous oriental detective of all was of course, Charlie Chan, whose adventures throughout the thirties were coming out at the rate of two a year from the same studio as the Motos. They are at least equally well produced, and the solutions play reasonably fair, but most of them tend to have dated rather badly, largely because of a surfeit of talk. The sprightliest of them is probably *Charlie Chan on Treasure Island*, which delves into the world of fake spiritualists; but the most unusual is certainly *Charlie Chan at the Opera*, for which Oscar Levant, no less, was commissioned to write sizeable scenes of an original opera, and Boris Karloff was recruited to play the heavy. The credits bill the stars as Warner Oland *versus* Boris Karloff, which isn't quite fair, as Mr Karloff plays an amnesiac opera singer who turns out not to have done it at all, even though he may think he has. After seven years in a sanatorium he remembers that his wife and her lover tried to burn him to death, and skulks around the theatre seeking revenge; but someone else gets in before him. The plot clearly derives from *Phantom of the Opera*, but misses quite a few possible frissons of that theme, spending too much time over the pratfalls of a dumb cop (William Demarest) and over Charlie's own aphorisms. 'Politeness golden key that open many doors,' he says approvingly to himself, informing the police chief in the same breath that he is going home to his family, 'like murderer always return to scene of crime'. When the cop thinks he has his murderer in Karloff, 'Correction please,' says Charlie, 'case still wide open, like swinging gate.' And at the final fadeout, when his son rushes up with fresh evidence, Charlie sighs. 'Excellent clue, but like last rose of summer, bloom too late.' Not a mention of Schopenhauer anywhere, and one feels the lack.

The suspects are a dull lot, and there aren't enough of them once we've decided that Karloff must be innocent, which we do early on; but Karloff himself is excellent value, his style of acting being so operatic that one isn't surprised when people think him mad. In 1937 audiences must have been bemused by memories of *A Night at the Opera*, for Karloff's character name, Gravelle, sounds like Chico, and his bushy black eyebrows made him look like Groucho. Still, he does marvellous things with his eyes and his lower register, and seems unable to avoid lurching forward like the Frankenstein monster.

Most of the other series of the thirties would be dull to sit through now, especially *The Saint*, which I've tried. But Philo Vance was often in safe hands, and *The Kennel Murder Case*, made in 1933, is still a splendid sealed-room murder mystery with a most intricate explanation and a charmingly casual performance by William Powell. *Arsène Lupin* and *The Lone Wolf* were basically one and the same, and always seemed long on elegance but short on the vital spark which leaves one craning for more when the end title rolls up: but the first film under the former title at least united John and Lionel Barrymore and built to an exciting climax in the Louvre as an attempt was made to steal the Mona Lisa. *Dr Kildare* had his criminal cases, and was always good for a weep and a laugh as well as a thrill; and away from crime altogether there was *Blondie*, the effervescent suburban housewife with her dumb but lovable husband Dagwood Bumstead, their son Baby Dumpling, their long-eared mutt Daisy, and that unfortunate postman of whom the most we saw was a cloud of letters cascading through the air after Dagwood made his sudden sprint for the 8:10. Simple, happy days.

Mysterious Mr Moto. US 1938; monochrome; 62 minutes. Produced by Sol Wurtzel for 20th Century-Fox. Written by Norman Foster and Philip MacDonald from the character created by John P. Marquand. Directed by Norman Foster. Art direction by Lewis Creber. With Peter Lorre as Mr Moto; Henry Wilcoxon as Anton Darvak; Erik Rhodes as David Scott-Frensham; Mary Maguire as Ann Richman; Harold Huber as Ernst Litmar; Leon Ames as Paul Brissac; Lester Matthews as Sir Charles Murchison.

Charlie Chan at the Opera. US 1937; monochrome; 67 minutes. Produced by John Stone for 20th Century-Fox. Written by W. Scott Darling and Charles S. Belden. Directed by H. Bruce Humberstone. Photographed by Lucien Andriot. Music score by Oscar Levant. With Warner Oland as Charlie Chan; Boris Karloff as Gravelle; Keye Luke as No. 1 son; Margaret Irving as Lilli Rochelle; Gregory Gaye as Barelli; Charlotte Henry as Mlle Kitty; William Demarest as Sgt Kelly; Frank Conroy as Whitely; Nedda Harrigan as Lucretia Barelli.

Shaggy Face Story
The Mystery of the Wax Museum

A wax sculptor is disfigured when fire sweeps through his museum, but some years later starts up business again in New York and seeks a model for his Marie Antoinette.

Significant strands of American cinema criss-cross in this wax museum, which on its first release was thought to be no more than a sixpenny shocker. The fact that for twenty-five years it was believed lost may have a little to do with its new attractiveness, but qualities of many kinds seep unmistakably from any screening. On a purely technical level it is one of the few remaining relics of the Two-colour Technicolor period which was swept away by *Becky Sharp* in 1935, and primary hues of orange and turquoise lend an unfamiliar soft outline to its horror. Colour is in fact one reason for its long disappearance. Dupes being expensive, only one master negative was kept. When the story was remade, more or less, in 1953 as *House of Wax*, an enterprising British publicist requested a copy of the original for a comparison showing to the press. He was sent the original; never used it; and instead of sending it back, had it destroyed to avoid storage and shipping costs. Rumour has it that he wasn't even fired, for the loss of the original seemed commercially unimportant when the remake was doing so well.

Twenty-odd years passed and Jack L. Warner, retiring from the business, asked a minion to dispose of the stock of prints he held for personal use in his garage. They were sent to United Artists, which had meanwhile acquired all rights to the pre-1948 Warner films. And yes, one of the salvaged copies was an unused, slightly watermarked, but otherwise whole print of *The Mystery of the Wax Museum*. As buyer for ITV, I heard the trade gossip and taxed UA with it; for money they produced two prints for the quality of which they apologized. To me they were sensational. They took me back to a night at the Bolton Hippodrome in, I suppose, 1934, when I had witnessed a trailer for this charismatic film. Now, the Bolton Hippodrome was economy-minded and normally advertised its forthcoming attractions on crudely coloured slides; for the management to spend four and sixpence on a talking trailer, albeit in black-and-white, must surely presage an event of monumental importance. This was just before the introduction of the 'H' certificate, so nothing got higher than 'A' and I was able to persuade my mother to take me on the following Monday. I distinctly remember that we settled into our seats some five minutes from the end, while the heroine was strapped beneath the bubbling wax and help arrived at the very last minute at the top of the Gothic steel staircase: I can see that upward-looking shot now, followed by a short but desperate struggle and the villain falling spectacularly into his own multi-coloured apparatus. I also remember vividly my mother on the way home declaring 'That's the last time I take you to a film like that,' so I must have emerged rather green about the gills.

The plot turned out to be extremely complex. The gimmick of course is that although the sculptor in his New York incarnation moves around in a wheelchair, with withered hands which force him to entrust the model-making to apprentices, he is in fact the ghastly loping nocturnal figure which we have been occasionally allowed to see frightening young girls and snatching bodies from the morgue to be encased in molten wax – a form of do-it-yourself Madame Tussaud's kit. Moreover his bearded face, which seems perfect enough, is a wax mask which at the story's climax the heroine batters away to reveal something extremely nasty below. Paralleling this main theme are the official investigation of several disappearances which are eventually laid at Igor's door; the problems of one of his assistants who is a drug addict; the love affair of Fay Wray (fresh from the arms of Kong) who nearly becomes Igor's new Marie

Antoinette; Igor's revenge on his former partner; and the arguments between a news editor and his brash girl reporter who finally solves the case. All in 77 minutes. And sharp eyes will catch Queen Victoria blinking.

The newsroom scenes are the best record we have, after *The Front Page*, of that hazy early talkie era when newsmen always wore pale hats and were better at crime-solving than the police; the wisecracks don't reproduce well, but in context they are perfectly in period. 'I'm going to make you eat dirt, you soap bubble,' says lady reporter to tough Irish news editor; and when he finally asks her to marry him her reply is: 'I'm going to get even with you, you dirty stiff – I'll do it!' The art direction shows Anton Grot near his best, with an unerring sense of the sinister in every design and a breathtaking, girdered, subterranean set for the last reel, approached by crooked stairs and unexpected upward-sliding doors. Director Michael Curtiz does not pace the film very well, and his famous infatuation with shadows is seen to better effect elsewhere, but scene for scene he never loses his grip on our tender parts. The acting is perfectly in period. Glenda Farrell and Frank McHugh, as the newsroom archetypes, come off best; Lionel Atwill's acting is full of foreboding but necessarily inhibited, as half the time he is an extremely unpleasant monster ('he makes Frankenstein look like a lily') and the other half is supposed to be wearing a wax mask. (How *did* he get the mouth to open and close?)

To sum up giddily – and you too will be giddy after sitting through this hectic ride on a funfair ghost train – *The Mystery of the Wax Museum* is a no-holds-barred exploitation thriller of its day, decorated with every kind of interesting detail, and I am delighted to have played some small part in preserving for posterity such virtues as McHugh's retort to a raspberry: 'A cow does that and gives milk besides.'

As for the remake, *House of Wax*, it seemed pleasantly ghoulish when first released, but then it was shot in 3D, and the best part of the entertainment, if you can believe it, was to have chairs, knives, guillotine blades and even less savoury objects apparently propelled towards one at high speed. Seen 'flat' it reveals itself as a quickie which cannot be said to improve on the original in any way, except perhaps for the catchy theme tune played while the barker is bouncing elasticated ping-pong balls into the camera. (The British

THE MYSTERY OF THE WAX MUSEUM. Arthur Edmund Carew lurks around an Anton Grot set, with shadows by Michael Curtiz, as Glenda Farrell investigates

censor excised the shot of chorus girls wiggling their behinds into the orchestra stalls.) It does however merit a small footnote in film history as the movie which introduced Vincent Price to the horror field in which he subsequently made himself so very much at home.

A year before opening their wax museum, Warners had set much the same team to work on another piece of Grand Guignol, *Doctor X*, which wears much less well but like its successor is fascinating to analyse and would be even more so if prints were still available in the original colour. The real trouble here is a script so ludicrous as wholly to suspend belief, which seems to have persuaded the producer to allow Lee Tracy, as the unprincipled reporter hero who keeps his hat on indoors, to give the impression of making up his lines as he goes along, with many a wink and nudge to the audience even amid the climactic horror. The yarn has police baffled by a string of moon murders in which the victims have been cannibalized. The scalpel used is one supplied only to Dr Xavier's academy of surgical research; even more conveniently it is vacation time, so that only the good doctor and four resident professors can be suspected. With remarkable indulgence the police allow Dr X forty-eight hours to check the physical reactions of his four shackled colleagues while he stages disturbing scenes of murder before their eyes. Needless to say, the monster turns out to be the one who can't possibly be guilty because he has only one hand; the secret is that he has stirred up a quantity of synthetic flesh which he daubs onto his stump rather like a man making an ice-cream cone, bringing it to useful life by immersing it in a crackling electric current. (For no very good reason except to look horrific he also spreads the goo on his face.)

The whole rigmarole is merely an excuse for a few thrills and as many gags, and its main interest is historical, in the chance it gives us to watch several major talents at work on what was clearly a hurried aping of another studio's success with *Frankenstein*. Warners' usual cut-price New York sets are in evidence, with comic strip dialogue to match them. Michael Curtiz directs without overall style, the editing being especially lumpy; his best shadow shot here is when the examining doctor is silhouetted on a cloth held over a corpse, and there is one effect which will be repeated in *Wax Museum*, namely the sudden sitting up of a corpse in the morgue, though this time it is the hero in hiding rather than the side effects of formaldehyde. Anton Grot gets a big credit for his sets, which are impracticable enough to be remarkable. Bookshelves at least twenty-five feet high are included in his Gothic manor, which contrasts low beams and baroque carving with ultra-modern offices and labs full of giant glass chemical fixtures kept merrily bubbling at all times ('My hundred milli-ampere high frequency coil with magnetic rotators,' says Dr X proudly). Actors who progressed to the later film include Fay Wray and Lionel Atwill; the latter has a sympathetic part for once, but you wouldn't know it from the sinister relish with which, abetted by highly shadowed lighting, he delivers each innocent line.

No care at all is taken to make this tall tale plausible. The main setting is given as Cliff Manor, Blackstone Shoals, Long Island, where scenes of nocturnal fog and raging wind are followed by Tracy and Wray lolling on a sunlit beach in bathing suits; the same night, inside the house, Tracy wears his overcoat with the collar turned up. Then Wray is finally saved by Tracy, who has taken the place of one of the supposed wax figures on display; but he waits until the monster has explained himself and half-strangled her before leaping into action. There are however some delightful if irrelevant echoes of the period. Tracy phones in his story from a brothel, for this was pre-Legion of Decency; and there is much play with a joy buzzer, which he holds in his palm to administer a mild electric shock to those with whom he shakes hands. (He is justly repaid by the gift of an exploding cigar.) For some reason too he arrives at the manor in a horse-drawn hansom, which must have been so unlikely in 1932 that one assumes a gag reminiscence of *Dracula*. He is the archetypal nosey reporter of the period, forever climbing drainpipes and peering through windows, and one really can't think what the heroine sees in him, or why the monster retires so gracefully on two early occasions when it almost has its claws in his neck. Preston Foster has little to do before going mad in a white overall and transforming himself, in a bravura sequence of lap dissolves, dry ice and burping apparatus into Hollywood's least convincing gargoyle; but his final fight with Tracy in a low arched corridor, before making a fiery descent through a window and out onto the rocks below, is sufficiently well staged.

They don't make absolute nonsense like this any more, not at any rate with the same gusto. It's the equivalent of the penny dreadful, without the nastiness which disfigures its modern equivalent, and the hardened film buff ought to find a place for it on his fun shelf.

The Mystery of the Wax Museum. US 1933; Technicolor; 77 minutes. Produced by Henry Blanke for Warners. Written by Don Mullaly and Carl Erikson from the play by Charles S. Belden. Directed by Michael Curtiz. Photographed by Ray Rennahan. Art direction by Anton Grot. With Lionel Atwill, Glenda Farrell, Frank McHugh, Fay Wray, Arthur Edmund Carew, Edwin Maxwell, Allen Vincent, Gavin Gordon, Holmes Herbert.

Dr X. US 1932; Technicolor; 70 minutes. Produced by Hal Wallis for Warners. Written by Robert Tasker and Earl Baldwin from a play by Howard W. Comstock and Allen C. Miller. Directed by Michael Curtiz. Photographed by Ray Rennahan and Richard Towers. Art direction by Anton Grot. With Lionel Atwill, Fay Wray, Lee Tracy, Preston Foster, John Wray, Harry Beresford, Arthur Edmund Carew, Robert Warwick, Thomas Jackson, Mae Busch.

Lady, Ever See a Man Looks Like This?
The Naked City

New York police catch the murderer of a society girl, and
expose a crime ring.

'There are eight million stories in the naked city . . . this has been
one of them.' It became a cliché in the sixties, when a slick television
series ran several years and made the name of a writer called
Sterling Silliphant, who delighted in odd-ball episode titles like
Ooftus Goofus and *King Stanislaus and the Knights of the Round Stable*, but
always remembered to end with a chase. Being in black and white,
the series is all but forgotten, except by cranks like me, so there
shouldn't be much hope for the equally monochromatic movie on
which it was originally based. But in fact it still entertains; some
historians would call it a classic; and commercially it's a seminal
piece indeed. From it were spawned not only the TV series in its
own namesake, but other features by the hundred and TV shows all
the way from *Highway Patrol* and *The Felony Squad* to *The Streets of San
Francisco*. Always there's a young cop who wants to learn, and an old
cop who wants to teach him, and it ends in sirens screaming against
the real streets of some real American city, usually photographed on
a Sunday morning when there are fewer real people to get in the
way. In 1979, for instance, the same processes were being instigated
by a black guy named *Paris* and a white guy named *Eischied*: a little
grittier, a little rawer, a little franker, but the essential recipe was
first tasted and approved in the summer of 1948, when *The Naked
City* startled an audience used to having its cops and robbers shoot
each other up on the Warner backlot under California skies rather
than in Lexington Avenue.

The Naked City was the brainchild of a New Yorker named Mark
Hellinger, a journalist who died before his Hollywood career really
got started. He knew the real New York, he did his own narration,
and his simple but fresh approach really worked. Barry Fitzgerald
and Don Taylor caught the imagination of 1948's paying audiences
just as surely as Karl Malden and Michael Douglas captured the

stay-at-homes a generation later, despite Taylor's curiously floppy trousers and the fact that Fitzgerald at his dwarfish height could never have been recruited into the police force in the first place. It hardly seemed to matter while the sniffy little Irishman was able to make the most of such dialogue as:

TAYLOR: Every high class jeweller in town? Oh, my poor feet!
FITZGERALD: Be glad you're not a horseback cop.

There is no denying that the basic tone of *The Naked City* was a little pretentious. 'This is the city as it is,' Hellinger intones, 'the children at play, the buildings in their naked stone.' He thought he was doing something important, whereas I, enjoying a night off from the army in the sweetened atmosphere of the Salisbury Picture House, saw only a gleaming entertainment with a few unusual trimmings. The critics complained that for all the brouhaha it was a mere murder mystery; I found myself delighted that it was, especially as I guessed the *modus operandi* before the police did. (The smart society doctor is blackmailed into tipping off a gang of burglars: 'A lamb led to slaughter, an idiot robbed of self-respect,' he calls himself.)

Another twenty years were to pass before I experienced New York in the flesh, or rather in the concrete. When I did, it looked exactly as *The Naked City* had suggested it would, apart from the smell, which the movie was naturally unable to convey. On a humid summer day, and especially before air-conditioning, it must have been the most intolerable atmosphere north of the equator, and Hellinger's film does let you sense the sticky discomfort as well as the frustration and the restlessness: 'It's one o'clock on a hot summer night and this is the face of New York when it's asleep, or as near asleep as it ever is . . . Every murder turns on a bright hot light, and a lot of people, innocent or not, have to walk out of the shadow to stand investigation.' They would do it less pseudo-poetically today. Even in 1948 it must have been difficult to accept crooks who hovered on the waterfront after committing a murder and spoke like this: 'I don't know what I'm going to say to God when my turn comes,' 'How can a man like me trust a man like you?'

The scene which, at that first post-adolescent encounter of 1948, etched itself most vividly on my memory as the real stuff of drama comes off equally falsely today. The victim has to be identified at the

THE NAKED CITY. The cameras turn in the baking summer heat of New York. The fugitive has just shot the blind man's dog, but don't worry, he'll pay for his misdeeds

morgue by her parents from the midwest. He is a desiccated old man who says very little, but his wife is an aggressively ugly woman in black, who before she goes in keeps telling the police how she despised her own daughter: 'I told her – I knew she'd turn out no good – I hate her. So clever she was – even had to change her name.' But as soon as the corpse is revealed her grim mouth opens in dismay and she runs forward with a cry of 'My baby!' A tactful fade-out here might not have been so bad, but Momma is allowed to give us a further dose of Acting before she returns to the midwest by the night bus: 'Dear God – why wasn't she born ugly? What a heartache. You raise a child, you nurse it, you pet it, you love it, and it ends like this.' I now prefer Hellinger's concentrated version of the same thought: 'This time yesterday she was just another pretty girl. Today she's the marmalade on ten thousand pieces of toast.'

Despite some choppy editing, nine-tenths of The Naked City has stayed crisp. Superbly photographed city scenes (remember the elevated railway?), cameos of the eccentric and worse who get themselves involved in the investigation, fascinating details of police procedure, the heavy routine of detective work ('Lady, ever see a man looks like this?'). Linking the elements is the pawky humour of Barry Fitzgerald, obsessive in his search for his J. P. McGillicuddy, the unknown man, but never too tired for a joke, as in his thoughtful aside to a legman when a girl witness has just left the office:

'Lovely young girl, isn't she?'
'Yeah.'
'Lovely long legs,'
'Yeah.'
'Keep looking at 'em.'

But he can disarm a suspect by his quiet fierceness, as when he rounds on Howard Duff, playing a man whose every alibi crumbles into thin air. 'I have been thirty-eight years on the force, but in a lifetime of investigation you are probably the biggest and most willing liar I have ever met.' Frank Niles may be the best role Howard Duff ever got, a character who should confuse nobody if they remember Mary Astor in *The Maltese Falcon*: no matter how guilty he *seems*, he really *is* guilty. But the actual murderer is Ted de Corsia, whom we barely glimpse until Don Taylor tracks him down over a root beer and inadvisedly confronts him in a Bronx tenement; the scene is then set for a chase across the rail/foot bridge (including the famous moment when the fleeing criminal disengages any lingering sympathy by shooting a blind man's dog, thereby alerting the police to his whereabouts). The villain is then beset by a peculiarly Hollywoodian form of insanity, starting to climb up an edifice from which there can be no possible escape.

The only serious message of *The Naked City* is that the swarming humanity of a metropolis can produce more absorbing interest than a casual passer-by might suspect. Also that when it comes to crime investigation, persistence is more useful than brilliance. The format was borrowed a few years later by Britain's Ealing Studios, who applied all the devices to London and came up with *The Blue Lamp*, which for the pretentiousness of Malvin Wald substituted the sentimentality of Ted Willis. His chief stroke of originality was to have his elder cop killed off after we had basked for half an hour in his warmth, his omniscience, and his determination to retire and grow cabbages. (Shortly thereafter, PC George Dixon was miraculously revived for a TV series which ran twenty years.) *The Blue Lamp*, running a spare 84 minutes, is a smart example of intelligent plagiarism, its format and development almost identical with those of its progenitor except for the removal of the unseen commentator, which takes with it the sense of the gods watching little victims at play. The investigative routines, the locations and the final cornering of the criminal run along precisely parallel lines and in their turn led to the British brand of TV cop show in which Covent Garden and the Old Kent Road stand in for the more photogenic aspects of the Big Apple.

The filmed-where-it-happened syndrome was of course not new to the film business when *The Naked City* picked it up and polished it off; it had merely fallen into disuse. As early as 1912 D. W. Griffith had filmed *Musketeers of Pig Alley* in the streets of Gotham and it was only in the thirties that backcloths and models were found to be easier than locations. *The Naked City* wasn't even a trail blazer. In 1945 Louis de Rochement had filmed a drama documentary in his best *March of Time* manner and called it *The House on 92nd Street*. Basically the story of the FBI's routing of atom spies, this was less concerned with the face of New York than with revealing the inner workings of a vast law enforcement organization, and it finally settled for melodrama in its revelation that the elusive Mr Christopher was a transvestite. It's a fascinating film to watch for its incisive development of a fragmentary story, for the performance of Leo G. Carroll as a bored but edgy master spy, and for its revelation of such tricks of the trade as two-way mirrors: the FBI never had a more glowing tribute, not even from Jimmy Cagney in *G-Men*. That organization too of course had many glorious hours to come on television, with Efrem Zimbalist standing in for J. Edgar Hoover; who incidentally had made crime pay as early as 1939 by spinning out his book *Persons in Hiding* into the basis of no fewer than four Paramount programmers offering heavily disguised accounts of the short but gory careers of Ma Barker, Bonnie and Clyde, and Pretty Boy Floyd.

The Naked City. US 1948; monochrome; 96 minutes. Produced by Mark Hellinger for Universal. Written by Malvin Wald and Albert Maltz. Directed by Jules Dassin. Photographed by William Daniels. Music score by Frank Skinner and Miklos Rozsa. Music direction by Milton Schwarzwald. Art direction by John F. de Cuir. With

Barry Fitzgerald as Muldoon; Don Taylor as Halloran; Howard Duff as Frank Niles; Dorothy Hart as Ruth; Ted de Corsia as Garzah; House Jameson as Dr Stoneman; Tom Pedi as Detective Perelli; Adelaide Klein as Mrs Batory.

The Old Man in the Bright Nightgown
Never Give a Sucker an Even Break
W. C. Fields tries to sell a script to Esoteric Pictures.

'If at first you don't succeed, try again. Then give up. No use being a damned fool about it.'

The image of W. C. Fields, who hated dogs and children, suffered from a variety of incapacitating ailments, drank to excess, developed in consequence a fine red nose which shone like a traffic beacon, once was a juggler, distrusted banks, used modified forms of impermissible expletives, and invariably found himself behind the eight ball, is so strong thirty-five years after his death that he has become the symbol of the American anti-hero: a whole nation still roots for him to win despite his unattractive personal habits, his anti-social attitudes and his mean-spirited cunning. His slightly bewildered biographer Robert Lewis Taylor said: 'His main purpose seemed to be to break as many rules as possible and cause the maximum amount of trouble for everybody.' He appeared in so many films during the twenties and thirties, and in one was such an unexpectedly imperishable Mr Micawber, that it would be unthinkable not to celebrate him in a retrospective such as this. The truth about Bill Fields however is that he is much funnier to think about than his films are to sit through. One starts them off with a ready smile on one's face, but in most of them the pacing is so irregular, the padding so intrusive and the handling of the gags so desultory that after twenty minutes one tends to be already thinking of other things if indeed one has not entirely succumbed to the temptations of Morpheus. (The Fieldsian phraseology is catching.)

Fields was a monster, even more in real life than on the screen because his misanthropy at home was not tempered by sentiment. Few who savour his celluloid image could have tolerated the reality for an hour, though it is impossible not to be amused by his putdowns of other people. The story goes that a polite young lady journalist invited him to lunch at Chasen's in hope of a story. Lunch in his case was a liquid affair, and left him uncommunicative. Noticing the passion with which he shooed away the hovering waiter with the ice water jug, she seized an opening. 'Mr Fields, could you tell me the reason for your well-known aversion to water?' 'Delighted, my dear,' he replied with suddenly increased bonhomie. 'Never touch the stuff – very unhealthy. Fish fuck in it.'

In similar vein he once announced himself as president of the FEBF, which on request he was happy to translate as Fuck Everybody but Fields. One also heard that he was seen outside his Beverly Hills house shooting birds in the tree branches which overhung his closely mown lawn. A lady neighbour hurried out in horrified protest, but he was unrepentant. 'Go on shooting the bastards,' he muttered, 'till they learn to shit green.' And I heard from a Universal publicist of the embarrassing evening when, in order to promote *My Little Chickadee*, he and Mae West were supposed to cook dinner at her home for selected press dignitaries. It was made clear to him that the continuance of his contract depended on his performing this charade, so he agreed . . . but proceeded to get rapidly and deliberately drunk and fall prostrate on the carpet, a form of comment which came easily to him. He and John Barrymore must have been the most unwelcome guests in Hollywood in the late thirties.

If I perversely include a Fields film among my hundred, it is mainly because his image must be cherished, if only as a harmless outlet for our own misanthropy. (It also enables me to choose another film (cf *House of Dracula*) so bad that one is surprised to find a professional studio perpetrating it on a paying public; the badness of both is so overwhelming that they become perversely and memorably entertaining.)

The choice should surely be made from his last four films for Universal which his fans feel were least fettered by commercial considerations. *You Can't Cheat an Honest Man*, however, is straight-forward and rather dull, its best gag being Fields' character name as the circus owner, Larson E. Whipsnade. In *My Little Chickadee* the stars are so busy upstaging each other that the comedy never gets going, apart from a ribald scene when Mae West substitutes a goat for herself in the nuptial bed and he is so unable to tell the difference as to compliment her on her perfume. *The Bank Dick* was written by

Fields under the pseudonym of Mahatma Kane Jeeves, but despite characters called Og Oggilby, J. Pinkerton Snoopington and Filthy McNasty one is desperately conscious of a falling-off towards the end. This is not so with *Never Give a Sucker an Even Break*, because it never achieves a level to fall off from. Its entirely irrelevant title aptly sums up not only its star's philosophy of life but his attitude to the film's producers, who paid him 25,000 dollars for a story line which he delivered on the back of a postcard but which could have been got on to the stamp.

In fact his credit, as Otis Criblecoblis, is very small, and it is the two studio writers sharing better billing who should be thoroughly ashamed of themselves. One almost suspects that they were instructed by the studio to allow the visibly collapsing comic, who in some scenes seems unable to stand unaided, to stew in his own juice so that the result would demonstrate his future unemployability. Certainly this is one of the most inept pieces of film-making ever to emerge from Universal or anywhere else. Its extremely loose format has Fields offering a story line to an incredulous and increasingly hysterical producer who throws him out of the studio after hearing it. One sympathizes, for the yarn involves its hero diving off a moving airplane in pursuit of a whisky bottle, landing on a trampoline atop a mountain where dwells a maiden who has never seen a man and therefore falls in love with him, and finally setting his sights on her rich but ugly mother. A good deal of time is wasted on kissing games, and wandering in and out to no purpose are a sabre-toothed Great Dane, an amorous gorilla, Leon Errol (in a miserably truncated part, his introductory scenes having been cut before release) and Gloria Jean, who plays the great man's twelve-year-old niece and has to keep gazing into the camera, Oliver Hardy style, and saying 'I still love him'. (She also holds up the story, such as it is, by singing two quite dreadful songs.) When this apology for a script has been wrung dry, the producers tack on a quite irrelevant but well-staged chase finale, with Fields driving a woman to the maternity hospital at top speed under the mistaken impression that she is about to deliver. Universal thought so highly of the stunt shots that five years later they reused them intact as the finale of Abbott and Costello's *Buck Privates Come Home*.

What can one salvage from this cut-price cornucopia of half-jokes and discarded fragments, incompetently translated from a drunk-

NEVER GIVE A SUCKER AN EVEN BREAK. The ape is as fake as the scenery, but the bottle no doubt contains the real stuff

ard's dream? Mainly a few glances and remarks from the half-addled star, even though many of his better lines he doesn't quite bother to finish, as though he lost interest half-way through. The same with whole scenes. He enters a café at one point and orders a milk shake, taking care to notify the camera: 'This scene was supposed to be set in a saloon, but the censor cut it out. It'll play just as well.' In fact it doesn't play at all, as it does not develop the plot, contains no jokes, and is utterly pointless. There are frequent references to the star's well-known partiality for the grape and the grain. 'Do you think he drinks?' asks Oulietta Hemoglobin. Her mother scornfully replies: 'He didn't get that nose from playing ping pong.' And his first reaction on meeting the gorilla is: 'Suffering sciatica! Last time it was pink elephants . . .'

It seems almost incredible that less than twelve months later the studio which so roughly assembled this haphazard rigmarole of apparent off-cuts could have produced the highly professional, zippy, gag-filled and still very funny *Hellzapoppin*, which used precisely the same story premise. Perhaps the difficulty lay in persuading Fields even to turn up on the set; certainly there isn't much in the movie of him actually doing anything. No billiard act, no golf game, just a kind of half-hearted drunken doodling and one bright moment with a candle flame which burns more fiercely when he breathes on it. To his fans that seems to be enough. After all, occasional jokes do get through whole:

WAITRESS: And another thing, you're always squawking about something. If it isn't the steak it's something else.
FIELDS: I didn't squawk about the steak, dear. I merely said I didn't see that old horse that used to be tethered outside here.

One should also commend a number of trick falls, mainly off mountainsides, as when Fields and niece are plummeting earthwards in a pulley basket with no one at the pulley:

GLORIA: We're falling two thousand feet!
FIELDS: Don't worry, dear. Don't start worrying till we get down to one thousand, nine hundred and ninety-nine. It's the last foot that's dangerous.

Luckily, before any solution to this predicament is required, the producer chooses this moment to tire of Fields' script altogether. The producer's wife was to have starred in it, but Fields has cast her as a bearded lady. The splendidly glaring, twitching Franklin Pangborn plays the producer, and could doubtless have extracted some laughs from the role had he been given any jokes. As it is, he is stuck with the likes of: 'Impossible, inconceivable, incomprehensible, and besides that it's no good.' This line was undoubtedly written in by the head of the studio when he discovered what he'd got for his 25,000 dollars. But Fields wouldn't care: he still had five more years to refrain from giving even breaks to suckers before the old man in the bright nightgown, his curious metaphor for death, came for him. Incidentally his longtime companion Carlotta Monti appears briefly in the film as a switchboard operator who is reproving her boy friend on the phone when Fields, quite reasonably, thinks she is talking to him:

OPERATOR: Someday you'll drown in a vat of whisky.
FIELDS: Drown in a vat of whisky. Death, where is thy sting?

Never Give a Sucker an Even Break. US 1941; monochrome; 70 minutes. Produced by Anon for Universal. Written by John T. Neville and Prescott Chaplin, from a story by Otis Criblecoblis (W. C. Fields). Directed by Edward Cline and Ralph Ceder. Photographed by Charles Van Enger. Music score by Frank Skinner. Edited by Arthur Hilton. Art direction by Jack Otterson and Richard H. Riedel. With W. C. Fields as The Great Man; Gloria Jean as His Niece; Franklin Pangborn as The Producer; Leon Errol as The Rival; Margaret Dumont as Mrs Hemoglobin; Susan Miller as Oulietta Hemoglobin.

And Two Hard-Boiled Eggs
A Night at the Opera, A Day at the Races and A Night In Casablanca

The Three Marx Brothers prevent two opera singers from being fired, a sanitarium from becoming a casino, and a renegade Nazi from escaping.

Though Marxists may agree that the true essence of the higher lunacy is to be found in *Duck Soup* (qv) and the other Paramount menageries of the early thirties, a small tribute must be paid here to Irving Thalberg, MGM's frail grand vizier who took over the Marxist cause during a card game, at a time when the brothers seemed to be commercially washed up, and singlehandedly extended their Hollywood careers over four more years at the top and a further seven of gradual decline. In fact the first two MGM films are eminently satisfactory in their way. It is the MGM way and the brothers had to fit in with it, but, given a big budget and plenty of time to hone the sketches to their sharpest (the company went out on tour to time and perfect the laughs), it works. Thalberg's theory was that the laughs would be twice as big if there were fewer of them, that they would appeal more generally if separated by chunks of more varied entertainment such as light romance and elegant musical numbers. This was tenable providing that these subsidiary attractions were as good in their way as the comedy, but after two sterling efforts carelessness set in. One winces at the memory of Kenny Baker in *At the Circus* singing about 'Two Blind Loves', and of Florence Rice telling her horse to 'Stand Up and Take a Bow'; critical faculties reel at the thought of Tony Martin in *The Big Store* singing 'The Tenement Symphony'; while whatever John Carroll sang to Diana Lewis in *Go West* was so utterly dispensable that the comedy segments might just as well have been separated by blank spacing.

It is reasonable also to complain that the Marxes themselves suffered a sea change enroute to Culver City. They are less anarchic, less intent on the main chance, prone even to play Cupid on occasion. They come on as recognizable human beings (well, almost) instead of walking cartoons from the pages of the *New Yorker*. Chico is less larcenous, Harpo less lecherous; Zeppo has vanished altogether; Groucho rather shamefacedly displays a sentimental streak amid the insults, which now have very little basis in social comment. Still, we would not willingly part with the memory of these extravaganzas, and *A Night at the Opera* at least is packed with classical inventions. A preliminary musical sequence having been lopped off at the last minute, it begins with famous abruptness in a fashionable restaurant where the magnificent Margaret Dumont as stately Mrs Claypool has waited for her host, Otis B. Driftwood, only to find that he has been entertaining a blonde at the table behind her. Mrs Claypool expects this con man (whose painted moustache wouldn't con anybody) to get her into society, and it turns out that his very best idea is that she should invest two hundred thousand dollars in the New York Opera: 'Don't you see? You'll be a patron of the opera. You'll get into society. Then you can marry me and they'll kick you out of society. And all you've lost is two hundred thousand dollars.'

He introduces her to Gottlieb the opera director, played apoplectically by the great Sig Rumann, who kisses Mrs Claypool's hand. Driftwood inspects the hand to see that the rings are still there, and adds *sotto voce*: 'Now listen here, Gottlieb, making love to Mrs Claypool is my racket. What you're after is two hundred thousand dollars . . . and don't forget, I saw her first. Of course, her mother really saw her first, but there's no point bringing the Civil War into this.' After this unpersuasive line in polite conversation it isn't too surprising when Driftwood finds that Gottlieb on the boat to New York has assigned him the smallest cabin ever devised by a maritime architect. There isn't really enough room for him and the bed, but promptly the script forces a score of people into the tiny cube of space, including a young woman who wants to know 'Is my Aunt Minnie in there?' ('No,' says Driftwood, 'but come on in.') When he hears what opera singers get paid he decides to become an agent and ignore the insult: 'You're willing to pay a thousand dollars a night just for singing? Why, you can get a phonograph record of "Minnie the Moocher" for seventy-five cents. For a buck and a quarter you can get Minnie.'

In quoting from a Marxian epic one inevitably gives the impression that Groucho is the be-all and end-all of the entertainment. He certainly sets off most of the verbal fireworks, but Chico has his moments too, notably in the contract scene where he and Groucho throw out every item, including the sanity clause. ('Ha ha, you can't-a fool me. There ain't-a no Sanity Claus.') And Harpo comes into his own in the *Hellzapoppin*-style finale, when the opera must for purposes of plot be sabotaged. Grotesquely impersonating a gypsy hag in the chorus, swinging through the flies à la Tarzan, ripping the skirt off a leading dancer, he is a child's hilarious idea of perpetual motion.

A Day at the Races has a less classy background, veering between a sanitarium and a nearby race track, both means of relieving the idle rich of their idle riches. For diversion this time, alas, we have a boring water ballet, a negro pied piper ensemble and a couple of tiresome ballads, but the comedy set-pieces are if anything more rousingly conceived and executed than before. Dumont and Rumann are again along for an uncomfortable ride, suffering variations on the familiar insults from Groucho, here disguised as Dr Hugo Z. Hackenbush. (To her: 'Marry me and I'll never look at any other horse.' To him: 'Don't point that beard at me, it might go off.') He is unflappable at interviews:

WHITMORE: Running a sanitarium calls for a doctor with peculiar talents.
HACKENBUSH: Look no further. I've got the most peculiar talents of any doctor you ever met.

He is ungallant in a clinch:

FLO: Hold me. Hold me closer, closer.
HACKENBUSH: If I hold you any closer I'll be in back of you.

He has a novel way of taking a temperature: 'Either he's dead or my watch has stopped.' His brothers as usual get their share of his venom. On Harpo he comments: 'Last time I saw a head like that was in a bottle of formaldehyde.' And he is quick to suspect the offer made by Chico as a racetrack tout:

TONY: One dollar and you remember me all your life.
HACKENBUSH: That's the most nauseating proposition I ever heard.

If *Races* has a fault it is that it too slavishly follows the structure of *Opera*. Again there is a Groucho-Chico bargaining dialogue, a Harpo-Chico mime, a centrepiece of outright slapstick, a piano sequence, a harp sequence, and a finale in which a public occasion is meticulously wrecked. This time it's a racetrack opening, and I shall never forget the elation with which it was received one Saturday in 1947 in Edinburgh, when I saw it through twice in an angular and uncomfortable cinema called Poole's Synod Hall. I thought the building would disintegrate around me, so loud were those Scottish laughs.

Passing over the decreasingly impressive MGM follow-ups (though *At the Circus* has some convincing fun on the high trapeze and Groucho singing 'Lydia the Tattooed Lady') the best of the later Marx is found in their independent venture *A Night in Casablanca*, made in 1945. It's cheaply made, takes a while to get going, and hardly involves the boys at all in its runaway plane climax, but it does contain Harpo's holding-up-the-wall joke and gives Groucho his last fling as Ronald Kornblow, manager of a hotel in which all his predecessors have been mysteriously murdered. His treatment of the guests is as cavalier as one might expect, especially of a dignified gent who comes in with his lady and addresses him as 'clerk':

KORNBLOW: Any baggage?
GUEST: It's on its way from the airfield.
KORNBLOW: In all my years in the hotel business that's the phoniest story I ever heard. I suppose your name is Smith.
GUEST: No, sir, it's Smythe, with a 'Y'.
KORNBLOW: I see, the English version. Mr and Mrs Smythe and no baggage. Let me see your marriage licence.
GUEST: What? How dare you?
KORNBLOW: Puts a 'Y' in Smith and expects me to let him in the hotel with a strange woman.
GUEST: Strange woman?
KORNBLOW: She is to me, I never saw her before.
GUEST: Sir, I am president of the Casablanca Laundry Company.

A NIGHT AT THE OPERA. Groucho watches to see that Margaret Dumont's rings are still in place when Sig Rumann has finished kissing her hand

KORNBLOW: (*removing shirt*): You are? Then take this and have it back Friday – and no starch. Meanwhile this is a family hotel and I suggest you take your business elsewhere.
GUEST: Sir, this lady is my wife. You should be ashamed.
KORNBLOW: If this lady is your wife, you should be ashamed.
GUEST: You'll hear from me, sir.
KORNBLOW: Do that, even if it's only a postcard.

The Marxes are gone. No wonder our world today seems grey, dishevelled, and empty.

A Night at the Opera. US 1935; monochrome; 94 minutes. Produced by Irving Thalberg for MGM. Written by George S. Kaufman and Morrie Ryskind, from a story by James Kevin McGuinness. Directed by Sam Wood. Photographed by Merrit B. Gerstad. Music direction by Herbert Stothart. Art direction by Cedric Gibbons, Ben Carre and Edwin S. Willis. Edited by William Levanway. With Groucho Marx as Otis B. Driftwood; Chico Marx as Fiorello; Harpo Marx as Tomasso; Margaret Dumont as Mrs Claypool; Sig Rumann as Herman Gottlieb; Allan Jones as Ricardo Baroni; Kitty Carlisle as Rosa Castaldi; Walter Woolf King as Rudolfo Lassparri.

Alfred Hitchcock Re-Presents
North By Northwest

A New York advertising man is mistaken by enemy agents for a CIA man who doesn't even exist, having been invented as a decoy.

If one professes to be a Hitchcock fan one simply has to like *North by Northwest* because it is a compilation of all his favourite effects in the field of the chase, presented in his most accomplished and expensive Hollywood style. It is scattered with variations on his favourite jokes: Hitch is glimpsed as a man missing a bus, and the hero sums up the plot in terms of his own initials, R. O. T. All the clichés of the genre, mostly established by Hitch himself, are present. Count them:

1. The McGuffin, i.e. what the spies are after, is left extremely vague, and Hitch even drowns out an explanation of it by aircraft noise.
2. The villain is urbane, witty, and an art collector.
3. The hero is abducted to a country house and threatened by hoodlums; but when he takes the police back there, it is occupied by demonstrably respectable people.
4. Wanting the hero dead, the villains take an extremely indirect route to this end, i.e. by making him drunk and *hoping* he will drive off a cliff.
5. When he goes for help to an eminent person, that person is stabbed, and our hero is not merely seen but actually photographed with his hand on the knife.
6. With both police and villains on his trail, he feels obliged to solve the mystery before giving himself up.
7. The girl who befriends him on the train turns out to be not merely a spy but a double agent.
8. Caught in a public place (in this case an art auction) with baddies at every door, he escapes by making a spectacle of himself.
9. The finale takes place against a well-known natural location, in

this case the presidents' heads on Mount Rushmore. (As usual with Hitch, the trick work does not shine.)

10. A number of schoolboyish sex jokes are worked in.

Most of these elements date from, and are present in, the 1935 version of *The 39 Steps*; other directors have successfully copied them in films as diverse as *The Prize* and *Three Days of the Condor*. Hitch was of course capable of ringing further changes on all of them, but by 1959 he had begun to get a little stiff in the directorial joints, and the pace overall is slightly laboured unless one allows for the response of a packed house at each viewing: one would have liked to see a pyrotechnic director like Preston Sturges have a go at this kind of entertainment. Where Hitch could still score was in playing with the set-pieces, and here he undoubtedly distinguishes himself in dealing with that other cliché, the scene where the hero is alone, defenceless and in fear of his life from the thugs. As Hitch has frequently explained, it usually takes place in a city by night, with wet streets and a black cat prowling around; so he deliberately turned it inside out by setting his hero in the blazing sun on a flat turnpike road west of Chicago, with no building in sight. He has been told to get off the bus here and wait for a contact, but had no idea that the site would be so isolated. High shots emphasize his apprehension of possible danger. Occasional traffic passes, but doesn't stop. Eventually a farm truck deposits a man across the road, but he turns out to be waiting for a bus which promptly picks him up, leaving our hero to savour his parting remark: 'That's funny. That plane's dusting crops where there ain't no crops.' By the time he has glanced again at the distant low-flying crop-duster, and taken in its implications, the horizon is empty and it is too late. Letting off loose trails of white powder, the plane turns menacingly towards him and slowly swoops, its intention perhaps being a decapitation by propeller, with a second threat from machine-gun bullets. Luckily there is a nearby field of tall corn in which our hero can hide, but he has forgotten Alfred Hitchcock's dictum: always use the props to the full. A crop-duster must dust crops; so let it. Half blinded and choking, he dashes back into the road in the path of a diesel truck which looks as though it can't stop. But it does, in the nick of time, and the plane, unable to vary its dive, crashes straight into it.

Even for the fortieth time, this famous sequence is a dilly to sit through. Although one can feel that a few of the shots are held just half a second too long, as a piece of storyboard construction it is impeccable. Logically, of course, it doesn't hold water for a second: shooting from a passing car would be a much more reliable means of murder than this clumsy method. But Hitchcock never did much care for logic, priding himself on being able so to involve his audience in the fate of his hero that they will gladly leave their brains under the seat until they are ready to go home. He is immensely helped, of course, by having a hero with the stature and resource of Cary Grant, who can produce a merry quip in even the most dangerous circumstance and hold the audience with him throughout by virtue of his familiarity, his dependability, his impeccable appearance, his way with a line, and his apparent willingness at the age of fifty-five to go through the most trying action scenes and emerge not even breathless.

One wonders why Hitch chose to make *North by Northwest* so long. It's all good stuff, but one gets the feeling that some of the dialogue is there only to paste the highlights together. Even so, insufficient screen time is allotted to James Mason's silky villain: he comes across as a cardboard threat, propped up only to be knocked over. Nor is any particular use made of the colour, and one imagines that the movie might have seemed tighter and more suspenseful if Hitch had been able to indulge his penchant for melodramatic framing in black-and-white, as he did in his next film, *Psycho*. Critics have also complained that the title is never alluded to, let alone explained. There is no such compass direction, and even though the chase takes the characters in a vaguely northwesterly direction, the fact seems irrelevant. It must have been in Hitch's mind, though, for at one time he planned to include a sequence in a Detroit car factory: we were to watch a car being assembled by robot machinery, and on completion find a body in it. This is typical of his concern for the momentary effect over the plot; but luckily or unluckily, he couldn't find a way to crack the problem of incorporating it. It has also been recalled that Hamlet, when thought mad, replied: 'I am but mad north-northwest; when the wind is southerly, I know a hawk from a handsaw.' But this merely confuses the issue, as Thornhill is thought to be not mad, but a murderer.

As usual, Hitch is never in too much of a hurry to stop for a joke.

NORTH BY NORTHWEST. Only Cary Grant could get out of this

Thornhill warns his mother (played by Jessie Royce Landis, exactly Grant's age) that the men following them are out to get him. She doesn't believe him, and as the elevator doors close on them all, says brightly: 'You gentlemen aren't really trying to murder my son, are you?' Then there is the scene where Thornhill escapes through the hotel room of a lady of uncertain years, who when she first sees him cries: 'Stop!' Then, having taken in his qualities, she adds in a very different voice, almost a plea: 'Stop . . . ?' The final joke, a visual one, does not even appear in the script and was obviously one of Hitch's impromptu ruderies: the phallic image of train disappearing into tunnel just as hero and heroine finally get together on an upper berth. In fact it was vital to the film's success, for it sent critics and audience away happy after the somewhat routine skirmishes atop Mount Rushmore, with microfilm concealed within an *objet d'art* and the CIA appearing quite mysteriously in the nick of time to save the day.

Probability is thrown to the winds with equal recklessness in the 1934 version of *The Man Who Knew Too Much*, two-thirds the length of Hitch's 1956 remake and twice as effective. After a slightly hesitant beginning it settles down into a series of tight corners, which might be thought of as gassing the dentist, infiltrating the tabernacle, and foiling an assassination attempt at the Albert Hall, with a finale clearly influenced by memories of the siege of Sidney Street. Linking these set-pieces is the story of a kidnap, and if Leslie Banks sometimes seems a little cheerful considering that his little girl's fate hangs in the balance, that may be because the script was originally conceived as a Bulldog Drummond story. Despite the occasional light relief there is a sense of doom about this picture: it all takes place after dark, mostly in a depression-struck East End; it features a number of callous shootings; and as chief villain, curiously named Abbott, it has Peter Lorre at his giggliest, with a scar over one eye and a streak of white through his hair. If it all seems more than a little distant as a whole, especially at the beginning with its appalling back projection of snowscapes, over every set-up there hovers Hitch's cinematic intelligence, especially in the scene in which knitting wool gets entwined between *après*-ski dancers, and Pierre Fresnay gets shot at the moment when it snaps. Again however one wonders at the inefficiency of Hitch's spies. With telephones to hand, why in heaven's name does Pierre Fresnay go to the trouble of concealing in his shaving brush a message which reads, under a drawing of a symbolic sun, WAPPING G. BARBOUR EIGHT PM A. HALL. This cryptic clue takes Leslie Banks the rest of the film to solve, but the complete message might have been instantaneously transmitted to his superiors in Whitehall. Why indeed is such an elaborate international cover necessary for one man with one gun to shoot one diplomat? Because, dear children, inessentials and *non sequiturs* are the stuff of which Hitchcock's thrillers are made, and surely no one would wish to hand back the pleasure they have given us for the sake of a little reality and truth?

North By Northwest. US 1959; Technicolor; VistaVision; 136 minutes. Produced and directed by Alfred Hitchcock for MGM. Associate producer, Herbert Coleman. Written by Ernest Lehman. Photographed by Robert Burks. Music score by Bernard Herrmann. Art direction by William A. Horning and Merrill Pye. Edited by George Tomasini. With Cary Grant as Roger Thornhill; Eva Marie Saint as Eve Kendall; James Mason as Philip Vandamm; Leo G. Carroll as Professor; Jessie Royce Landis as Mrs Thornhill; Martin Landau as Leonard.

The Man Who Knew Too Much. GB 1934; monochrome; 84 minutes. Produced by Michael Balcon and Ivor Montagu for Gaumont British. Written by A. R. Rawlinson, Charles Bennett, D. B. Wyndham Lewis, Edwin Greenwood and Emlyn Williams. Directed by Alfred Hitchcock. Photographed by Curt Courant. Music score by Arthur Benjamin. Art direction by Alfred Junge and Peter Proud. Edited by Hugh Stewart. With Leslie Banks as Bob Lawrence; Edna Best as Jill Lawrence; Peter Lorre as Abbott; Frank Vosper as Levine; Hugh Wakefield as Clive; Nova Pilbeam as Betty; Pierre Fresnay as Louis Bernard.

Faster! Faster!
Occupe-Toi D'Amélie

A lady's maid turns cocotte and is persuaded to feign marriage to a playboy so that he can inherit a fortune from his visiting uncle; but her boy friend's jealousy is a problem, especially as a foreign prince also wishes to bed her.

I well remember the impatience with which in 1950 I sat almost alone in the upper circle of the Cameo-Poly in Upper Regent Street and watched the interminable parade of credit titles pass slowly in barely decipherable white manuscript over a rather uninteresting street scene. As with most French films of the time, there seemed to be about four producers and innumerable hangers-on; nearly every actor had a screen to himself, prefaced with '*et*' or '*avec*' and on one occasion '*avec le participation de*'. Then I realized with some pleasure that the action had already begun, for behind the lettering a rotund, moustachioed personage was running towards the camera, which was tracking back along grey cobbled streets. At no time did the film which followed adopt a pace slower than that of the running man, who, perspiring profusely as the last credit finally faded, turned into the stage door of the Théâtre du Palais, where it transpired that he was the actor playing the rich uncle in the farce to be presented that night, namely *Occupe-Toi d'Amélie*. My spirits picked up at once, for it was clear that I was in for a stimulating afternoon of what Brecht might have called alienation effects, that is an alternation between telling the story as though it were to be believed and frequently pointing out that it was in fact only a tale told by actors. *Henry V* had performed this trick most successfully, but it was even more interesting to find it applied to French farce. Distancing it in this way, the director clearly hoped to avoid any criticism that the Feydeau original was too artificial, by first sustaining and then shattering the audience's suspension of disbelief.

Autant-Lara's success in this intention was almost total, especially when compared with Anthony Asquith's failure three years later to decorate *The Importance of Being Earnest* with more than the occasional drop of a curtain, or to offer more than a flatly photographed view from the sixth row of the stalls. *Occupe-Toi D'Amélie* is cinema from first shot to last. Indeed, the camera is seldom still for more than five seconds: delving into crowds, careering down corridors forwards and backwards, following its characters up and down stairs, swinging round occasionally to reveal the theatre audience, pirouetting round cluttered rooms in semi-circular pans, cutting from one actor to another, and then to a third, in a diligent attempt to keep up with the rapid-fire dialogue. Sub-titles, alas, are set an almost impossible task, and unless one is able to appreciate this film in the original French one is bound to miss quite a bit of either the sense or the performances. Which is a pity, for although most of the fun is in the handling, quite a bit derives from the accomplished face-pulling of a thoroughly professional cast, each member of which clearly enjoys fooling to the top of his bent. As to the rat-tat-tat of the repartee, one can judge only by the English translation:

I was taking a bath.
In your boots?
They're waterproof.

Or perhaps you prefer: 'To deceive your friend with a prince is no deception. Besides, he need not know.'

However, when particular tribute has been paid to the nimble, exhilarating exhibition of predatory innocence which is given by Danielle Darrieux in the title role, and to the fluent script of Jean Aurenche and Pierre Bost, it is to Autant-Lara that one must return, for in this film the real star is the director. It must be so, for when later on the master himself, Noel Coward, adapted the same farce as a Vivien Leigh vehicle for the West End stage, it seemed not nearly so irresistible. Surely no other film-maker, with the possible exception of Billy Wilder in *One Two Three*, has required so many actors to deliver so much dialogue on the run, yet ensured that so many nuances are given their full weight.

322

OCCUPE TOI D'AMELIE. Jean Desailly and Danielle Darrieux pretend to get married. Except that they really are married

To revert to our running actor, he finds waiting in his dressing room a group of rather puritan-looking friends. Donning his overcoat and moustaches for the role of rich Uncle Putzeboom, he persuades them to take a stage box despite their misgivings about the play.

'Not too spicy? No drawers?'
'No, no, only a couple. Excuse me, I've just arrived on the Antwerp Express.'

And so as the curtains part he hurries into the action, keeping up behind a cardboard train which wouldn't deceive an infant for an instant. Then he beams and burbles his way like Nigel Bruce across a few backcloths to announce to his nephew that he proposes to give him a fat cheque on the day of his marriage. But nephew doesn't want to get married, and arranges for an elaborate charade to be played by his friends, so that when uncle calls he is greeted by a demure fiancée and some acceptable if over-effusive in-laws. Luckily the real fiancé of Amélie is off to the army for a spell; but when he is forced by mumps to return, he finds that nephew and Amélie have spent the night together and rather enjoyed it, though they are too drunk to remember whether they accomplished anything before-hand. Fuming, he bides his time. Meanwhile the lecherous prince of Palestria, a full-blooded performance by Grégoire Aslan, has sent a blimpish general ahead to arrange with Amélie a cosy misalliance. In the middle of these sundry plots and humours we and the theatre audience have enjoyed an interval, complete with advertising slides and a final patriotic picture of President Poincaré.

Returning to the play, having watched the scene shifters at work, we find the style so developed that the curtain can now rise, as in those old Busby Berkeley musicals, on an impossibly vast street scene complete with moving cars. Indeed, at the end of a second act of alarms and excursions, we follow a car off into the wings and watch Amélie hurry from it to change into her wedding gown for the hilarious third act. Rich uncle has insisted on staying for the ceremony; fiancé has promised to replace the mayor by an actor friend, Toto Béjard. But of course he does no such thing, considering it a fine revenge to have the two lovers hooked for ever. So all through the ceremony the plotters are chuckling hysterically at what a fine actor Toto Béjard is, while the mayor, played by an actor with a distinct touch of James Finlayson, grimaces uncomprehendingly at them, especially when they whisper to him how convincing they think the large wart on his head. Immediately after the wedding, the bride has to leave for an assignation; the prince is already waiting for her, without his trousers, 'to save time'. But meanwhile, nephew has discovered the truth. His first instinct is to tear out the page from the wedding register, but Putzeboom's puritan friends swarm onto the stage from their box to prevent this; so he decides that after all he rather likes being married, and dashes off to save Amélie from a fate to which in truth she is plainly quite accustomed. Behaving like a gentleman, the prince grandly waves nephew to the bed he was keeping warm for himself, but causes consternation in the street when he walks to his car without remembering his trousers. The scene shifts to the railway station where the lovers are due to leave for Venice. The truth comes out, but they get their cheque anyway, and Uncle Putzeboom is left to remove his moustaches as he strolls off the set, musing that he wouldn't have minded keeping an eye on Amélie himself . . .

If all this sounds rather confusing, that's because it is; but it's also the stuff of which prize farces are made, and no other film I know has ever kept up style and pace with such magnificent self-assurance.

The English style of farce does allow its characters occasionally to move at walking pace instead of the regulation French trot. If I favour Ben Travers'*Rookery Nook*, made in 1929, it is not because of any quality in the film itself, which is as undisciplined and primitive as only a British film of that era can be; but because the stage original is perhaps the best British farce of all, and deserves to become a classic of our theatre. The film is a necessary point of reference because it uses the original cast, though none of them is at ease under the camera's unblinking eye; the pity is that they never remade it when their film technique was better. All that happens is that a young married man (dithering, monocled Ralph Lynn) precedes his wife to their holiday home at a seaside resort, and reluctantly spends the night furtively but innocently with the girl next door, who has escaped in pyjamas from her rather melodramatic stepfather Putz, who is nuts and won't let her eat wurst. The farcical situations result from the snooping of his housekeeper (Mary Brough) and from the often unhelpful assistance of his playboy brother-in-law (Tom Walls), but they are quickly resolved: the fun is all in the telling. Fragments of dialogue float melodiously down the years. 'The other rooms is elsewhere.' 'Earlier than that I cannot be.' 'There is also a cat. It lives in the kitchen. It has been trod on once tonight already.' 'You swine of a Twine.' 'Poppy Dickey, flags for the lifeboat.' And even in this creaky version Ralph Lynn's first sight of the fugitive, who has slipped in while he was getting the luggage from the car, is a joy to behold. He drops his baggage. Drops his monocle from his eye. Puts it in again. Does a double take. Goes to the door to make sure he's in the right house. Tries to cough but can't. Extends a finger but can't bring himself to touch her. Ditto with a loofah. And so on, and so on: a masterpiece of milking.

A later farce with the same Aldwych team, *A Cuckoo in the Nest*, has an extremely similar plot, with Lynn this time forced by circumstance to share a bedroom with a lady not his wife. It is memorable for one splendid line which Ben Travers gallantly admitted was written not by himself but by Mr Lynn, who has very nervously signed a false name in the hotel register. It is scrutinized by the landlady, who comments: 'You don't write very clear.' 'Er, no,' admits Mr Lynn: 'I've just had some very thick soup.'

No film containing this line can be entirely worthless.

Occupe-toi d'Amélie. France 1949; monochrome; 98 minutes. A Lux Production. Written by Jean Aurenche and Pierre Bost from the stage farce by Georges Feydeau. Directed by Claude Autant-Lara. Photographed by André Bac. Music score by Rene Cloërc. Art direction by Max Douy. Edited by Madeleine Gug. With Danielle Darrieux as Amélie; Jean Desailly, Carette, Coco Aslan, Bourvil.

Joe the Cockeyed Miller
Oh Mr Porter

A disaster-prone railway wheeltapper is sent to be stationmaster of a derelict halt in Northern Ireland, and inadvertently exposes a gang of gun-runners posing as ghosts.

They say that imitation is the sincerest form of flattery, and one can only hope that Arnold Ridley thought so when he saw the plot of his thriller *The Ghost Train* being borrowed for this marvellous all-comedy variation. (It later served not only for the same team's *Ask a Policeman*, with a police station haunted by a headless horseman, but for an Arthur Askey comedy called *Back Room Boy*, about a lighthouse beset by Nazi spies; and you can trace it through to a score of other movies including Abbott and Costello in *Hold That Ghost* and Peter Sellers in *Up the Creek*.) There isn't much doubt that this Will Hay version represents its most glorious screen incarnation, or that it is the best thing Hay ever did. To see a full house rise to it at London's National Film Theatre is an experience to be savoured, and the house is always full whenever it is announced.

I first came across it at the Bolton Hippodrome, a converted music hall which in my infancy was the local home of British comedy. Very little of the output however had the cinematic style of *Oh Mr Porter*, which gives the impression, probably erroneous, of having been lovingly polished and rehearsed and edited until every expression or inflection gets a laugh as surely as the repartee, the visual gags, and the thrill comedy sequences. I remember that after queueing we got in (as usual) about ten minutes from the end of the first house; the train was whizzing along at eighty miles an hour or more, with the crooks taking pot shots from their carriage at the highly inexperienced drivers, and being whacked from the roof by Graham Moffatt's shovel. Until the lights went up we had to sit in the front row, and although I was glued to the screen I can still smell the paper grass which covered the disused orchestra pit and lay so close to the dim red footlights that I feared conflagration. The supporting programme included a Floyd Gibson two-reeler called *Attic of Terror*. Mr Gibson was a patch-eyed New York reporter of sensational true stories, and whatever he had to report on that occasion, my attention was chiefly struck by his resemblance to the similarly afflicted 'ghostly' villain of the Hay film, One-Eyed Joe the Miller. Ecstatic in my enjoyment of the comedy when it came on again, I visited the Hippodrome at least once more that week, and also contrived to catch up with *Oh Mr Porter* on a wet afternoon in Blackpool. I even went so far as to look up some critical reviews of it in the public library, and was downcast to read the supercilious remarks of the *Punch* reviewer: I consoled myself with the thought that he couldn't know what delights he was missing by being so toffee-nosed.

Oh Mr Porter works beautifully from beginning to end. From the moment the sniffing, bespectacled, blustering and totally inefficient ex-wheeltapper drops off the Buggleskelly bus on a rainy night, with a two-mile walk to his dilapidated halt at which nothing halts any more, all is sheer delight. Mr Hay's ill-balanced *pince-nez* and his air of seedy incompetence and sly roguery (despite which one always rooted for him because of his irrepressible crooked grin) were the assumptions of a master comedian, but without his famous foils, of whose success he proved rather foolishly jealous, he seemed to lack something in richness. Luckily they were both fully present, and hopelessly incorrect, in this case. Graham Moffatt was Albert, the cheeky fat boy; Moore Marriott the toothless, whippety old Harbottle. Between them they run the station for no wages by dint of sidetracking any merchandise which may be unlucky enough to pass through their hands. When a local farmer calls for his pigs, for instance, the new stationmaster suddenly loses his appetite for the bacon he is eating. He is also disconcerted to find that his predecessors have had such remarkably short tenures of office. 'Got your clock?' asks Harbottle, adding the hideous presentation timepiece to a dust-collecting group of marble lookalikes on the mantelpiece. But like all new brooms he is determined to sweep clean, and next morning they make a start on the platform, removing the line of washing which might get in the way of an express, should one chance to pass by, and painting every stationary object in sight, including the chocolate machine which coughs up its prizes more readily to a well-aimed kick than to the insertion of a coin. 'You're wasting your time, wasting your time,' the leprechaun-like local postman assures him in an annoying piping voice, but by the end of the day Mr Porter has more or less restored to health a wheezing old locomotive called Gladstone, though most of the rolling stock has been accidentally shunted down a quarry, or turned into firewood by a passing train which deals it a glancing blow when it is left overhanging the main track. All this is marvellous stuff for grown-up boys who have always enjoyed playing with trains, but now the main plot must start. Mr Porter orders from head office an excursion train, and sells tickets (or rather exchanges them for produce) in the local pub. During the inevitable Irish brawl, while taking refuge from the flying furniture in a back room lit by flickering firelight, he meets the one-eyed manager of the local football team, who expresses a desire that next morning the excursion train should take him and his chaps to Connemara. They turn up in good time, but the train disappears before reaching the first signal box, and his minions don't even believe that it started at all, hangovers having prevented them from getting up early enough to see for themselves.

By now Mr Porter has been made aware of the local ghost story about One-Eyed Joe the Miller:

> Every night when the moon is bright
> The Miller's ghost is seen:
> He haunts the station, he haunts the hill,
> And the land that lies between.

It is this same phantom which has discouraged the locals from using the station; and of course he begins to realize that the 'football team manager' bore a striking resemblance to it. After a good deal of

OH MR PORTER. Will Hay arrives at Buggleskelly, to be greeted with derision by Graham Moffatt and Moore Marriott

argument the trio, with Gladstone's help, discovers the missing train in a disused siding in a tunnel below the old windmill, which it now becomes clear is a haven for gun-runners. The resulting chase around the mill, or rather up its rickety stairs, is fast-moving slapstick, and the escape down its sails a rousing and expertly edited sequence of thrill comedy in which our heroes find themselves each at the extremity of a sail just as a strong wind blows up. They recover in time to link Gladstone to the robbers' train and steam away at full speed for Belfast, burning everything in sight and by various means preventing the robbers from jumping out. Nothing from Hollywood, not even Buster Keaton in *The General*, has bettered this elaborate action sequence; but then, the British have always had a soft spot for trains.

The only way to appreciate a gusty comedy like this is to see it once for the laughs, then see it again in order to take in its myriad subtleties of invention and timing. Hay was never properly acclaimed in America, perhaps because he is so firmly in the alien

British music hall tradition; but a land which cherishes Lloyd, Keaton, and Laurel and Hardy should surely find a small corner of affection in its heart for this irrepressible colleague from across the sea.

A year later the same team turned up in *Ask a Policeman*. Here they constitute the entire police force of Turnbottom Round, a village with a long record of no arrests. They decide to do something about this by knocking out a few motorists, sousing them with whisky, and arresting them for drunken driving; unfortunately their first victim turns out to be the chief constable. The local ghost this time is the headless horseman of a phantom coach, and when Albert's girl friend sees it she staggers in and faints on the rug. 'Feel 'er 'eart, feel 'er 'eart,' squeaks old Harbottle. 'Nark it,' says Albert, 'she's my bird.' The ghost this time is meant to deflect attention from the local pastime of brandy smuggling, and Harbottle has an even more ancient old Dad who remembers a rhyme about it:

When the tide runs low in the smugglers' cove
And the 'eadless 'orseman rides above,
He drives along with his wild hallo,
And that's the time when the smugglers go in their little boats to the schooner and bring back the kegs of brandy and rum and put them all in the Devil's Cove below.

The One-Eyed Joe figure in this version is the lighthouse keeper, the splendidly dour Herbert Lomas, who raises no suspicion among our heroes when he so frequently asks permission to place a light on the roof of the police station and so warn his distant family that his little girl is sinking fast. But eventually the horseman makes a spirited and slightly alarming appearance, and the resulting chase somehow lands Hay and company in a driverless bus whizzing round Brooklands motor track in the middle of a race.

The Ghost Train itself, which was a silent in 1927 with Guy Newall and a talkie with Jack Hulbert in 1931, turned up again in 1941 as an Arthur Askey vehicle, and lo and behold the station master, with his lugubrious tale to tell ('If it be a natural thing, whar do it come from? Whar do it go?') was played by Herbert Lomas, still sporting his black oilskin from *Ask a Policeman*. And the plot still worked.

Oh Mr Porter. GB 1938; monochrome; 84 minutes. Produced by Edward Black for Gainsborough. Written by Marriott Edgar, Val Guest and J. O. C. Orton from a story by Frank Launder. Directed by Marcel Varnel. Photographed by Arthur Crabtree. Musical direction by Louis Levy. With Will Hay as William Porter; Moore Marriott as Harbottle; Graham Moffatt as Albert; Dave O'Toole as postman.

Bats in the Belfry
The Old Dark House

During a nocturnal thunderstorm in the Welsh mountains, stranded motorists take refuge at the decidedly odd house of the Femms, some of whom are merely eccentric, one extremely old, and another a homicidal lunatic.

My first chance to see this delectable chapter of grotesquerie came in 1937, and I muffed it. Reissued, it was showing on a double bill at the Bolton Lido with *The Invisible Man*, and neither bore anything more prohibitive than an 'A' certificate. The stills displays having proved especially enticing, I persuaded my mother to take me along. Alas, it transpired that the management, ignoring the official categories, thought they would drum up more custom by advertising 'strictly adults only'; so after a friendly but frustrating conversation with our pet commissionaire (the one with flat feet), we disappointedly took his advice and wandered round the corner to the Theatre Royal, where we made our first acquaintance with Old Mother Riley.

Ten years later I was in the army, at Bury, a place famous only for the invention of black puddings. *The Old Dark House* had been reissued once again, even reviewed in the *Monthly Film Bulletin* ('an unpleasant thriller which might well have been left in the vaults from which it was resurrected') and was on view at the Palace from Monday until Wednesday. I hastened along and was enthralled, not only by the movie itself but by the incredibly glossy print, the like of which I have never seen since. Granted, the few interpolated bits of romantic stodge were stodgy indeed, and it was my first encounter with a Universal film so old as to bear the monoplane-round-the-world logo (not to mention the valedictory legend, 'A Good Cast is worth Repeating'). But for sixty minutes out of seventy-two I sat back in ecstasy, realizing myself to be in the presence of a curious offbeat directorial talent who had contrived to bring a minor piece of English literature to Hollywood as a horror story and yet preserve its subtleties unimpaired for those inclined to seek them out. Priestley in his introduction to the novel explains that his intention was an allegory of post-war Britain, a gallery of grotesque types with unnecessary but ineradicable fears and inhibitions. Benn Levy was careful to preserve this flavour in his script, together with most of the original dialogue, but it is James Whale who, putting the anecdote together before the cameras, did the most dazzling job by keeping the balance of the material without upsetting the commercially minded front office.

Faded prints harm this movie. You need all the lustre of 35 millimetre to bring out the smells of the rain, the musty rooms, the log fire, the undercooked potatoes. The landslide is unconvincing in the Hitchcock manner, but once the huge door scrapes open to reveal a single glowering eye, prepare to be disconcerted. Karloff as the lumpish butler is more ominous than comical, but when prissy Ernest Thesiger as Horace Femm descends the stair and pauses by a gargoyle bearing an uncanny resemblance to himself, the intention to amuse is obvious. He is a desiccated cowardly cynic who scuttles away like a rabbit at the first sign of danger; his sister Rebecca, a squashed toad of a woman played to the hilt by Eva Moore, is a riveting example of religious bigotry, and deaf to boot. 'No beds,' she screams in the faces of her unexpected guests, 'they can't have beds!'; and later, while watching one of the ladies change, 'That's fine stuff,' she cries, pointing to a silken dress. The next moment her grubby hand touches the girl's throat, and she hisses: 'That's fine stuff too, but it'll rot, it'll rot!' Morgan the manservant is a dangerous oaf who drinks himself stupid on stormy nights, a simile for people who don't want to know; upstairs lies ancient Sir Roderick, symbolizing those who no longer care. (It seems somehow typical of Whale that he would cast a woman to play old Roderick, thus enhancing the tremor in the voice; the actress is Elspeth Dudgeon, disguised in the credits as John.) And as for Saul . . . he crouches behind the locked door on the second storey, and woe betide the household if anybody lets him out, for despite his meek demeanour he has a rolling white eyeball which indicates manic frenzy. Somebody does let him out, of course.

THE OLD DARK HOUSE. Lost souls in Charles D Hall's sepulchral set include Eva Moore, Ernest Thesiger, Gloria Stuart, Raymond Massey, Charles Laughton and Lillian Bond

These animated wax figures reveal themselves one by one to the weary travellers, who gaze at them in disbelief from the comparative safety of the hearth in the vast hall which seems to take up a large proportion of this unconventionally designed house. The front door opens straight into it, and at the far end under the great oak stairway there is a dining dais, with a corridor of kitchens and bedrooms off to the left. The daunting stairs lead straight to the double doors of Sir Roderick's haven, and side landings to a secondary stairway. Lit by candles and a flickering fire, this hall is an awesome setting for adventure, though probably very draughty in winter.

Into this Stygian inferno, this domain of the half-dead, stagger the heroes and heroines whose conventional lives are to be changed by this night of adventure; the stalwart young Wavertons; their cynical friend Penderel, shell-shocked in the war; businessman Sir William Porterhouse and his weekend fling. ('My goodness, what a night,' he

333

announces in Charles Laughton's thickest Yorkshire, dripping rain onto the slab floor.) The cast is now complete, with Karloff as a mute and dangerous master of ceremonies. By normal Hollywood standards not much happens, though by the time the sun peeps through the rainclouds next morning one man is dead and all the rest have had a most uncomfortable time. But Morgan is civil again, handing out bags like the doorman at the Dorchester, and Horace has an almost beatific smile for his departing guests. Oh, and Penderel has found romance with the chorus girl, and won't be cynical any more; pity.

It's a small enough film, but one which bears any number of reshowings because writing and performances are alike clearcut and the whole bears such an unmistakable stamp of personality. Perhaps Whale and his cast thought of themselves, all exiles, as the travellers, and Hollywood as the old dark house breathing various forms of menace down their necks. Certainly the story would never have come across so vividly if filmed in England: it would have been conventionalized out of all character. Incidentally the so-called remake by Hammer in the sixties retains only the title and is not worth a second glance; the original remains fresh as rain and wind and thunder, and every time I drive through the Welsh mountains I hope wistfully and in vain to turn a corner and find before me the house of the Femms.

During the very same year, back in the old country, the Aldwych farce team was on view in *Thark*, which on casual glance might appear to be taking place on the same set as *The Old Dark House*. For Thark is a haunted house, or at least so says its tenant Mary Brough; and the rest of the familiar farceurs play the owning family, who come down to prove that it isn't. Naturally, Ralph Lynn and Tom Walls end up sharing a bed in the haunted room. *Thark* is a rudimentary film, partly because British films of 1932 usually were, and partly because it is directed by Tom Walls, who never saw much more to the art than lining up the actors and telling the camera to roll. (In this case he also seems to like the actors' heads as close as he can get them to the top of the frame, which leads to some odd compositions.) It has to be admitted too that Ben Travers' original play was never much more than a protracted sketch, ending quite arbitrarily as the bed collapses; its theatrical popularity must be attributed almost entirely to the 'business' arranged nightly by these popular actors. What the film has to offer is a slightly stiffened version of one of those twenties nights at the Aldwych, and it often seems enough, as the dialogue is full of small jewels, as when Sir Hector Benbow growls to his butler: 'The mistress is coming home.' 'Very good, sir.' 'Very good be damned, it's very bad.'

Then there are the haunted room gags:

'Somebody moaned.'
'It was the wind.'
'I don't know the cause of his suffering, but somebody moaned.'

Or perhaps you prefer:

'She walked right into his bedroom. He must have been tight.'
'Why, what did he do?'
'Nothing, he thought she was a ghost.'

There are also some amiably garrulous lines for the indignant old battleaxe: 'It isn't easy to say what you've seen when all you know is you've seen something and you don't know what it is.'

The best recurring gag in the movie is Mr Walls' soda siphon, which he carries with him on all occasions and which, on each of its frequent uses, sounds like a startled soul in torment. But the scene-stealing performance, oddly enough, is that of Gordon James (actually Sidney Lynn, Ralph's brother) who plays a cadaverous and doomladen butler addressed by Miss Brough as Jones because she doesn't like his real name, Death. Clearly from the same stock as Boris Karloff in the Whale film, home address probably Cold Comfort Farm, he twitches and quirks and hisses his way to a lot of laughs, with sepulchrally-delivered lines like 'What time would you like your call?' and 'You go up and I'll bring the sheets.' When asked what he has in his hand, there can be only one answer: 'The last post, sir.'

Unexpectedly, the Aldwych team had another unmistakable fling at *The Old Dark House* four years later, in a minor film called *Pot Luck*, in which the crooks' hide-out was yet another eerie mansion, with Mr James again doing his creepy butler act. This time however the ominous hand which hovers uncertainly at the top of the oak staircase, just like that of Mr Brember Wills, turns out to be attached to Robertson Hare.

The Old Dark House. US 1932; monochrome; 71 minutes. Produced by Carl Laemmle Jnr for Universal. Written by Benn W. Levy, from the novel *Benighted* by J. B. Priestley. Directed by James Whale. Photographed by Arthur Edeson. Make-up by Jack Pierce. Art direction by Charles D. Hall. Edited by Clarence Kolster. With Melvyn Douglas as Penderel; Boris Karloff as Morgan; Ernest Thesiger as Horace Femm; Eva Moore as Rebecca Femm; Charles Laughton as Sir William Porterhouse; Raymond Massey as Philip Waverton; Gloria Stuart as Margaret Waverton; Lillian Bond as Gladys; Elspeth Dudgeon as Sir Roderick Femm; Brember Wills as Saul.

The Very Dickens
Oliver Twist and Great Expectations

A poor boy falls into the hands of thieves but is rescued by his true relations; another is given an expensive education by a secret well-wisher.

David Lean reached the pinnacle of his profession with only fourteen films to his credit as solo director. He is such an accomplished and subtle technician that one wishes there had been more, that *The Bridge on the River Kwai* had not driven him into the epic class, for he was thereafter plagued by the kind of elephantiasis requiring four years or more to be spent on the planning of multi-million-dollar spectacles which prove so unwieldy that for general release they have to be trimmed down to more manageable but sometimes incoherent proportions. *Doctor Zhivago* was allegedly still being cut on the afternoon of its world première, and despite its many pleasing qualities and some impressive scenes, the result looks it; Lean had for so long been so close to the project that he did not realize he was cutting some of the essential links which would have explained characters whose aberrations in the released film seem baffling. Similarly, after four hours of *Laurence of Arabia* we were no closer to knowing what made the hero tick, and the question of his homosexuality had been skated over so lightly as to have been better left unposed. *Ryan's Daughter* is a simple Irish love story, somewhat eccentrically cast. At 206 minutes it is also so absurdly prolonged that it prompted Alexander Walker to remark: 'Instead of looking like the money it cost to make, the film feels like the time it took to shoot.'

Despite these reservations about his later achievements, no one with a love for the art of film would turn down a chance to see a Lean movie. He may not be a master story-teller, but scene for scene he can make magic by effortlessly producing the right angle, the right movement, the right expression and inflection. He is the subtlest of our craftsmen, and his smaller canvases remain for me the most satisfactory. *Brief Encounter* and *Blithe Spirit* have sections of this book to themselves, and I have also a yearning regard for *Summer Madness*, which not only gives Katharine Hepburn the opportunity for one of her most sensitive portrayals but also so captures the feel of Venice that you may come out deciding, if you haven't been there, that you no longer need to go. *Madeleine* is equally beautifully made, but has the obvious drawback that since one never knows whether the heroine poisoned her lover or not, one doesn't really care. *The Passionate Friends* confused the paying public by its liberal use of flashbacks within flashbacks, and was dismissed at the time as a rich man's *Brief Encounter*, but for anyone anxious to learn about filmcraft, here is a complete manual. *The Sound Barrier* and *Hobson's Choice* seem unlikely to have been subjects that Lean passionately wanted to make, but no one watching them is likely to take his eyes off the screen for more than a moment. About *This Happy Breed* there is even more doubt, as both Lean and Coward seemed out of their depths in this affectionate but rather patronizing study of the British proletariat between the wars; but it was welcomed as superior propaganda, despite the extreme unlikeliness of Robert Newton as a mild-mannered suburbanite.

There remain the two Dickens adaptations, and here for me is the essence of Lean, letting a better man tell the story and himself decorating it in cinematic terms as well as he possibly can. The result is like watching the novels come to life. Both have been filmed again since, *Great Expectations* as a television musical which then had the music removed; the blandness of the result can be imagined. *Oliver!* however had such enormous commercial success that it almost totally eclipsed Lean's *Oliver Twist*; yet in almost every aspect I have to prefer the latter. Lionel Bart's songs are marvellously in keeping, but I like my Dickens straight, and most of Carol Reed's decoration was borrowed from Lean anyway. Since the later film doesn't fit too well onto television, and since television is the only real future for any movie, perhaps good sense will prevail and the Lean version will eventually come back into its own.

For a year or two it seemed that its claim to fame might be its banning in America because of the so-called anti-Semitic portrayal of Fagin (copied from the original illustrations). Eventually that particular piece of nonsense was forgotten, and for several years the film made frequent appearances in all-time top twenty lists. I first encountered it on a Saturday afternoon in the Portsmouth Odeon and found it a breathtaking piece of cinema, comforting despite its horrific passages because one knew there had to be a happy ending for Oliver after his passage through the hands of so many evil grotesques. To look at, it was truly magnificent, a gleaming feast for the eyes. *Sight and Sound* even reproduced its opening sequence in storyboard form, as a lesson in film-making. The bare windswept heath under heavy raincloud; an angle-shot of the forbidding workhouse gates; the poor mother staggering towards them in the last stages of pregnancy, the trees bending and straining in the wind to suggest her agony. We meet young Oliver, perhaps a mite toffee-nosed as presented by John Howard Davies, but then so is Dickens' character; the sufferings of a tough little creature would have provoked no interest. In the 'Please sir I want some more' scene the angles are especially cunningly chosen to ensure freshness, and in Francis L. Sullivan, an unjustly forgotten actor, we have the finest Bumble it is possible to conceive, the very quintessence of callous but comic greed. When Oliver is sent as apprentice to Mr Sowerberry the undertaker, the emaciated Gibb McLaughlin comes into his own; and when he falls into the more loving hands of old Mr Brownlow, we seem to know that Henry Stephenson, a Hollywood exile for so many years, was waiting to be called home for this, the summit of his later career. As for Guinness as Fagin, this is a caricature so faultless as to be almost incredible: one doubts the evidence of one's own eyes. But the real villain of the piece is Bill Sikes, who could have no more menacing personification than in the form of Robert Newton, here caught in full ripeness a couple of years before his Hancock period. Cruikshank would have been delighted with them all.

But it was *Great Expectations*, made a couple of years earlier during the first months of recovery from a devastating war, that Richard

OLIVER TWIST. Alec Guinness as Fagin watches Robert Newton attend to Kay Walsh

Winnington called 'the greatest British film yet made'; and there were many who felt bound to agree with him. Again there was a real snapper of an opening, with Pip placing flowers on his mother's grave in the deserted churchyard on a foggy afternoon. Fearfully in the grey light he turns, sensing something in the wind which makes the trees seem to creak and faces to appear on the gnarled trunks. Suddenly he runs almost out of frame into – thud! – the grim figure of a manacled escaped convict. 'Keep still, you young devil, or I'll cut your throat!' A moment later, horror turns to comedy as the convict turns Pip upside down to see if money or food will fall out of his pockets. (So vivid was the impression made by this scene, so cunningly judged, that no one questioned the suitability for the part of Finlay Currie, who was nearly seventy at the time of filming but brought immense strength to his few minutes of screen time.) Pip runs back home across a breathtaking landscape that is part Romney Marsh, part studio (note that the clouds don't reflect in the water), and presently returns with a prize pie for the shivering convict. 'I think you've got the ague, sir.' 'I'm much of your opinion, boy.' But after an exciting chase it's back to the hulks for Magwitch, and we don't really expect to see him again, as we become entangled in Pip's new experiences as he is engaged to play every week with the young niece of eccentric Miss Havisham, who was jilted on her wedding day and ever since has remained in her cobwebbed mansion with the mouldering wedding feast still on the table. Not a very plausible concept, even for Dickens, but so cleverly calculated is Lean's handling that we don't have time to think of plausibility or even of hygiene: the images of these scenes are among the most vividly recollected by filmgoers all over the world, and the face of Martita Hunt became immortal with this one performance.

The classic serial is so well done on television these days that it is hard to recall what a breath of fresh air this production brought with it in 1946. Television is in any case a matter of talking heads, and could never afford or achieve the careful compositions possible in a film studio. The shots of Pip arriving by stagecoach at St Paul's, for instance, took a great deal of careful angling to hide the bombsites which devastated the area. True, the music score is a disappointment, and Pip himself is a bit of a cipher (John Mills was too old for the part, and was straining too hard to look bright-eyed and bushy-tailed); while Valerie Hobson, who appears only in the second half, has a hard time trying to make the contradictory character of Estella even interesting enough for us to care whether there will be a 'happy' ending. (There would probably have been applause from the audience if Pip had caused history to repeat itself by jilting *her*.) As so often with the characters of Dickens, and of Shakespeare come to that, it is the grotesques on the periphery of the narrative who turn the meal into a feast: Francis L. Sullivan as the bullying lawyer Jaggers, Ivor Barnard as Wemmick his clerk, Bernard Miles as Gargery the blacksmith, Freda Jackson as his shrewish wife, Alec Guinness as Herbert Pocket. But even more than the acting, it is those beautifully composed scenes which linger in the memory, and especially the low, chilling aspects of Romney Marsh, its flatness only occasionally interrupted by a building or a gibbet; its water so still and its lanes seldom used. It is a setting worthy of M. R. James, and *aficionados* of that worthy Etonian would certainly wish to see Lean, even at this late stage, tackle *O Whistle and I'll Come to You, My Lad*.

Oliver Twist. GB 1948; monochrome; 116 minutes. Produced by Ronald Neame for Cineguild; released by Rank. Written by David Lean and Stanley Haynes, from the novel by Charles Dickens. Directed by David Lean. Photographed by Guy Green. Music score by Arnold Bax. Production designed by John Bryan. With Alec Guinness as Fagin; John Howard Davies as Oliver; Robert Newton as Bill Sikes; Kay Walsh as Nancy; Francis L. Sullivan as Bumble; Henry Stephenson as Mr Brownlow; Anthony Newley as the Artful Dodger; Mary Clare as Matron; Gibb McLaughlin as Mr Sowerberry; Diana Dors as servant girl.

Great Expectations. GB 1946; monochrome; 118 minutes. Produced by Anthony Havelock-Allan for Cineguild; released by Rank. Written by David Lean, Ronald Neame and Anthony Havelock-Allan, from the novel by Charles Dickens. Directed by David Lean. Photographed by Guy Green. Music score by Walter Goehr. Production designed by John Bryan. With John Mills as Pip; Valerie Hobson as Estella; Martita Hunt as Miss Havisham; Finlay Currie as Magwitch; Bernard Miles as Joe Gargery; Francis L. Sullivan as Jaggers; Alec Guinness as Herbert Pocket; Anthony Wager as Young Pip; Jean Simmons as Young Estella; Ivor Barnard as Wemmick; Hay Petrie as Uncle Pumblechook; Freda Jackson as Mrs Gargery; Torin Thatcher as Bentley Drummle; Eileen Erskine as Biddy.

L'Oiseau Chante Avec Ses Doigts
Orphée

Death as a dark lady falls in love with the poet Orpheus and has his wife Eurydice killed. Orpheus follows her into Hades and Death finally reunites them.

It may be that there is less in *Orphée* than meets the eye. If so, there always was, for superficially it presented to me in 1980 exactly the same mixture of boredom, fascination and stimulation as it did at the Cambridge Arts in 1950, when it was the term's talking point among undergraduates following ecstatic reactions from the London critics:

A film of rare value, often as fantastic as a poem.

James Monahan

It will delight some people and enrage others, but I guarantee it will set them talking, with the eagerness they brought to a discussion of the Roland Petit *Carmen*, the Covent Garden *Salome*, *Ring Round the Moon*, and *The Cocktail Party* . . . I can't pretend to know what it all means, and I have a lurking suspicion that Cocteau doesn't know either, but I do know that it sent me out of the theatre quivering with excitement, and more provocatively engaged than I have been by any film for seasons.

C. A. Lejeune

An unmatched achievement in the telling of a magical adventure ... It reasserts wonder, ritual, the power of illusions and magic, reinterpreting them in a contemporary setting which brings the myth closer, gives it a disturbing edge of reality.

Gavin Lambert

All this, plus a publicity tag-line, 'the immortal thriller', and a poster sketch of Jean Marais from a Cocteau original apparently designed while playing Dotto, was catnip to Cambridge, more than enough to maintain gowned queues around the Arts for a fortnight, with many a midnight discussion over chicken biryani at the Koh-i-Noor.

Even if one did not know that Cocteau was a poet, one would call this film poetic. Its characters are handsome symbols, from whom the normal daily hubbub of life has been removed, for the events above ground all seem to take place on a sunny French Sunday, with roads and city squares devoid of traffic except that directly concerned in the plot. The atmosphere is rarefied, anticipatory, antiseptic. A shower of rain would wash away the drama. Cocteau's previous inspirations had been more medieval, more surrealist; what brought him to the legend of Orpheus is hard to say, though one could guess that he had seen *A Matter of Life and Death*, which very similarly treats love across the void, though from a different angle and in an entirely different mood. One can't even be sure that he intends a modern setting, any more than was necessary to bring in limousines and motor bikes, for his handwritten prologue sets neither time nor place: 'It is the privilege of legends to be ageless. Therefore, as you like it.'

Orphée begins as a mystery story, though addicts of Agatha Christie need not expect a sealed-room solution. Sitting outside the Café des Poètes, Orpheus watches a young fellow scribbler, Cégeste, make a fool of himself under the inscrutable gaze of the dark lady who finances the magazine for which he 'writes'. (It's called *Nudism*, and contains only blank pages.) Suddenly, Cégeste is killed by passing motorcyclists, and the dark lady calls on Orpheus' help to get the body into her limousine. From that moment he is under her spell, but only gradually realizes that he is experiencing something other-worldly. When he mentions the hospital he is told to be quiet. The countryside through which they pass is photographed in negative. Strange messages come over the car radio. 'The bird sings with its fingers.' 'Silence is twice as fast backwards.' 'One glass of water illumines the world.' Arriving at a deserted château, he is disturbed to find that the motorcyclists have preceded them, but after accepting champagne and cigarettes from Chinese waiters he is drawn into some strange dreamlike events. The dead Cégeste is miraculously revived by the dark lady. ('Do you know who I am?' 'My death.') Orpheus watches as, without any farewell, they walk through a mirror which conveniently melts at their touch and reconstitutes itself behind them. Unable to follow, he faints with his face pressed against the mirror (a magnificent double image which was extensively used in the publicity) and wakes to find it changed to a puddle in the sand dunes amid which he now lies. The princess has left her chauffeur Heurtebise, a recent suicide, to take Orpheus home and care for him, and the phlegmatic young man sees that his mistress has fallen in love with the poet: each night she comes through the mirror to watch over him as he sleeps. But Orpheus is irritable, especially when he finds he can receive the curious messages on his own car radio. He doesn't fully recognize their source, but seizes on them as a new form of poetic inspiration. 'The role of the dreamer is to accept his dreams.' 'The mirror would do well to reflect again.' 'Thirty-eight, thirty-nine, forty.' Increasingly churlish to his bewildered wife, Orpheus spends all his time in the garage. 'I am on the trail of the unknown,' he cries, not realizing that the unknown has come to him. 'For a third time,' intones the commentator, 'Orpheus' death came to watch him sleep.' Only after Eurydice has been killed does he learn the true identity of the dark lady. He is astounded, 'You are my death?' he asks the princess. 'If we appeared to mortals in the guise they expect, it would make our task more difficult,' she replies.

The audience realizes suddenly at this point that Death's agents have indeed been going about their duties rather like the spies in *The House on 92nd Street*, obsessed by the mechanics of their work and divided by petty suspicions and jealousies. Now one of them turns double agent: Heurtebise takes pity on the distraught Orpheus and leads him through the mirror into Hades in search of Eurydice's immortal soul. All the equipment he needs is a pair of rubber gloves

ORPHEE. The poet faints at the realization that the princess is from the other world. Jean Marais, Maria Casarès

which, by reverse photography, leap snugly onto his hands and enable him to penetrate the mirror like water. Now of course we are reminded of *Alice Through the Looking Glass*, though in this case the territory on the other side looks more like Berlin after the war, all cold night skies, ruined buildings, draughty alleys and an air of total desolation. Strong winds alternately hold back the travellers and blow them along like wisps of paper. Despite his fears, Orpheus is now a man with a mania. 'Is it Eurydice or Death you seek?' asks Heurtebise. '*Les deux*,' is the reply.

Hades is thinly populated. Only a glazier – why a glazier? – crosses their path. And when they eventually find the dark lady in a bare and windowless room, she is being held by a band of bureaucrats, accused of 'indulging private enterprise' in trying to secure Orpheus for herself. Instructed to reverse her tricks, she complies, and Orpheus finds himself back home with Eurydice restored to health. However, killed himself by her jealous friends the

Bacchantes (no doubt a Lesbian inference here) he is able to make one last trip to the underworld to embrace his princess. 'You burn like ice,' he tells her. She regretfully replies, 'You still have human warmth.'

She knows that their love cannot last, that Orpheus must be restored again to the land of the living to become the man he was before her meddling. In an aside to Cégeste she murmurs: 'If we were in our former world, I'd say let's get drunk.' But here there is no escaping the unpleasant if unspecified fate which is in store for her and for Heurtebise: in a famous shot which is the last in the film the two transgressors are led away by their own motorcyclists, across the rubble-strewn moonlit paths and away from camera through what may be intended as a ruined church. The word '*Fin*', zooming in across this image, seems more than usually appropriate.

The intellectual meaning of this story as a whole is undoubtedly of less importance than the impressions made by fragments of it upon the romantic imagination. What my generation most remembers, for instance, is the tricks with mirrors, though cinematically the devices used are easy to explain: the gloved hands penetrating the glass, for instance, is simply an upended shot of gloved hands pointing down into still water. What impressed us, I think, was the lack of showiness, the total discretion, with which these moments are presented; and the fact that they are handled so simply makes them all the more believable. Buffs were also pleased to note echoes from Cocteau's other works. In *The Blood of a Poet* the action took place during the time it took for an exploded chimney to fall to the ground: here the underworld scenes are sandwiched between the postman inserting a letter into the postbox and the letter falling to the floor of the container. Nicolas Hayer's photography contrasts a terrifying sense of dark areas in the underworld with a neat, grey, utility look for the rooms in Orpheus' house; and Auric's music comes in exactly when required to underline the unease. As for the actors, it would be expected that the dead have better parts than the living, and it is so, with Maria Casarès gratefully seizing the best role of her career as the princess; Marais, Cocteau's favourite leading man, has the looks of a Greek god and does perfectly well, though one somehow misses the full sense of his horrendous dilemma, torn between two loves and two worlds.

For all its arguable failings – and I admit several stretches of dialogue which via sub-titles at least fall limply upon the ear – this is a film which surely deserves revival and revaluation, if only to find out whether the ecstasies which greeted it in 1950 can still be sustained.

Orphée. France 1949; monochrome; 112 minutes (or 95 minutes). Produced by André Paulvé/Films du Palais Royal. Written and directed by Jean Cocteau. Photographed by Nicolas Hayer. Music score by Georges Auric. Art direction by Jean d'Eaubonne. With Jean Marais as Orphée; Maria Déa as Eurydice; Maria Casarès as Death; Eduoard Dermithe as Cégeste; François Périer as Heurtebise.

A Horse in the Bedroom
The Palm Beach Story
The wife of an inventor decides that the best way to help him is to divorce him and latch onto a Florida millionaire who will finance his roof-level airport.

Let us get out of the way first of all the curious echoes of *Midnight*. Claudette Colbert stars in both as a money-hungry, wise-cracking gal stranded in one suit of clothes during a journey (in the one case at the end, in the other at the beginning). In neither film can she raise money for a taxi. In both she accidentally meets a rich man who buys her an unlimited wardrobe, and her true love traces and follows her but is forced to go along with her pretence. Mary Astor is even along on both rides to add her own brand of sophisticated comment, and there are additional echoes in the dialogue: in one film Claudette tells her protector, 'As soon as I saw you look at me, I had an idea you had an idea', and in the other, 'You have no idea what a long-legged gal can do without doing anything.'

In style of course there is little resemblance between the two films: Leisen's direction is ever tactful and controlled, while Sturges is forever dishevelled, bringing in slapstick when he's bored and allowing dialogue scenes to outstay their usefulness and sparkle. It is Sturges however who has the reputation of being a genius, the wild man of Hollywood in the early forties, and it is his unpredictability which makes him so. When you are in his presence, it doesn't matter that he borrows a few ideas from earlier films; even Shakespeare was a partial plagiarist, and Sturges' own 1933 screenplay *The Power and the Glory* was undoubtedly the inspiration for *Citizen Kane*. It is the Sturges style and attitude which are original.

In the technical sense he does everything wrong. He may build up a scene carefully and abandon it abruptly. One point may be made at great 'and repetitive length, the next covered in a montage sequence or obscured by a man falling into a cake. He loves hubbub, but doesn't control it as well as Capra. In his fragments of the American nightmare everybody talks very fast, and the occasional witty line seems to rise almost by accident out of the fog of low repartee. In Sturges' world sentiment alternates with pratfalls, melodrama with sexual innuendo: he is extremely fond of 'Topic A'. If he has a structural formula it is to start very slowly and talkatively, to slip into top gear just past the half-way mark, and to finish in frantic overdrive, though he usually disdains an action finish, having used up his slapstick earlier on to punctuate the dialogue stretches.

Sullivan's Travels, undoubtedly the Sturges masterwork, is treated separately on another page. But the great pleasure given in fits and starts by his other movies can't be ignored, and pride of place is given to *The Palm Beach Story* because at this stage it seems the freshest and sharpest of them, though the least pretentious. Sturges doesn't even bother to explain why his impecunious inventor has to live in a lush Manhattan apartment, but he does, or at least did until the day the film starts, when his wife is being thrown out in favour of a deaf old millionaire who turns out to be her fairy godfather, glad to give her enough money to pay off all the family debts. Her husband when he returns is naturally suspicious:

TOM: So this fellow gave you the look?
GERRY: At his age it was more of a blink.
TOM: Seven hundred dollars and sex didn't even enter into it, I suppose?

Of course sex entered into it, says Gerry, it always does, and that's why she's off to flaunt herself and make some money for Tom. 'And where are all these men who are going to faint at your feet?' he asks. 'They're always there,' she says, 'and in any case they make new ones every year.'

On her journey to the land of luxury Gerry quickly encounters and is aided by a whole group of millionaires in the shape of the Ale

THE PALM BEACH STORY. On the way to a happy ending. Joel McCrea, Mary Astor, Claudette Colbert, Rudy Vallee

and Quail Club, but they prove to be the wrong kind, addicted to getting drunk and shooting up trains. Luckily, while clambering into a top bunk in borrowed pyjamas, she encounters one of the more pliable sort by the simple expedient of stepping on his face and breaking his glasses. John D. Hackensacker III (a marvellous and at the time unexpected performance from Rudy Vallee) travels second class because 'staterooms are unAmerican', and carefully analyzes the different values of a 35 cent and a 55 cent breakfast; he also, because the habit runs in the family, keeps a note of every cent he spends, though he never bothers to total the pages. Mild-mannered he is ('One of the great tragedies of this life is that the men most in need of a beating-up are always enormous'), but also extremely generous. Before long Gerry has not only a proposal but the finance for her 'brother's' airport. She is also adopted as a friend by Hackensacker's predatory sister: 'Stay with us: it will give the servants some exercise. We can look for new husbands together. I'm thinking of an American: it seems more patriotic.'

By now Gerry's conscience is starting to prick, and she needs reassurance: 'Don't you know the best men in the world have told lies and let things be misunderstood if it was useful to them? Didn't you ever hear of a campaign promise?' When Gerry confesses all, the Hackensackers are naturally disappointed, but unabashed. 'You haven't a twin sister, have you?' asks John. But of course she has, if it will enable Sturges to finish the film in a one-minute wrap-up, and Tom has a twin brother too. ('Of course, that's another plot entirely,' he points out.) We see now the point of the frantic action which went on behind the main titles, with one Gerry escaping from another and dashing off to get married. So the twins are recruited for a triple wedding, with only a leery Sturges question mark over the future.

The Lady Eve was Sturges' first big budget comedy with top stars, and in it all his trademarks are fully evident. The first movement on board ship, though too long, has marvellous performances, excellent jokes and some surprisingly sexy dialogue. Henry Fonda is a rather naïve young millionaire, his fortune based on 'Pike's Pale, the ale that won for Yale', and in return for sponsorship he has been allowed to accompany an Amazon explorer for a year, bringing back a rare snake (which Sturges probably saw as a phallic symbol). Aboard the luxury liner which will take him back home he is carefully scrutinized by a couple of cardsharps, Colonel Harrington and his daughter Jean. 'Gee, I hope he's rich,' says Barbara Stanwyck in what may be her finest, most alert and mischievous comedy performance. 'I hope he thinks he's a wizard at cards.' Charles Coburn looks him over and sums up: 'As fine a specimen of the sucker sapiens as I ever saw.' That evening in the dining-room Jean makes derisory comments about the attempts, viewed through her vanity mirror, of every woman in the room to make a play for Pike. After they fail, she ensnares him herself by the simple process of tripping him up. Before long the cards are on the table, and although on the first night Pike makes a gratifying profit, on the second he finds himself 32,000 dollars down. 'This is most embarrassing,' says the colonel; 'just make it out to cash.'

Jean of course foils her father's schemes because by now she has fallen in love with the poor bozo, after seducing him by allowing him to choose her shoes and put them on her feet. 'Would you care to come and see Emma?' he asks. 'That's a new one, isn't it?' she replies. But of course he means the snake. (What with shoes and snakes, this movie is a field day for the fetishists.) They end up in her room. 'See anything you like?' she asks. He looks bewildered.

JEAN: I was just flirting with you.
PIKE: Oh.
JEAN: You're not going to faint, are you?

And later:

JEAN: Don't you think we ought to go right to bed?
PIKE: You're a funny girl for a fellow to meet who's just been up the Amazon for a year.

The fish is hooked, and proposes, but when he discovers Jean's true vocation he opts out in a huff, and she vows revenge, to the consternation of her father. ('Don't be vulgar, dear. Let us be crooked but never common.') Her vengeance takes the form of insinuating herself into Pike's household, with apparently impeccable credentials, as a lately arrived English heiress, and seducing him all over again in this alternative persona. He is so bemused that he keeps falling over things, but within a fortnight there's a wedding, which is just what the lady has been waiting for. In one of Sturges' cleverest sequences, as they honeymoon aboard a speeding train, she pours out to her spouse episodes of a wickedly fictitious past. We don't hear the confessions, Sturges preferring to cut to thunder and lightning, the roar of the train into a tunnel, and the Poet and Peasant overture. Pike gathers up his clothes if not his dignity and leaves her again, falling into the mud as he does so. But Sturges has now had his fun, and there's only another five minutes to the happy ending and the cast roll-up. Along the way he has paused for slapstick feuds between servants, for Eugene Pallette wanting his breakfast, for a horse that wants to get in on a courtship, and for Eric Blore's splendiferous performance as a con man known as Sir Alfred McGlennan Keith, who gets the false Eve into the Pike brand of high society. ('I positively swill in their ale.') Bits and pieces may not make a classic movie, but they do add up to a thoroughly enjoyable extravaganza. You might say of his unpredictable talent what Gerry in *The Palm Beach Story* says about Hackensacker's great wealth, that you can't ignore it any more than you can ignore a horse in a bedroom. (To which Hackensacker's thoughtful reply is: 'I wasn't thinking exactly of that, but it'll serve.')

There may also be a lot of Sturges in Tom's remark: 'I don't mind a little noise, we'll be dead soon enough.'

The Palm Beach Story. US 1942; monochrome; 88 minutes. Produced by Paul Jones for Paramount. Written and directed by Preston Sturges. Photographed by Victor Milner. Music score by Victor Young. Art direction by Hans Dreier and Ernest Fegte. Edited by Stuart Gilmore. With Claudette Colbert as Gerry Jeffers; Joel McCrea as Tom Jeffers; Rudy Vallee as J. D. Hackensacker III; Mary Astor as Princess Centimillia; Sig Arno as Toto; William Demarest, Porter Hall, Robert Warwick, Robert Greig, Torben Meyer, Jack Norton, Chester Conklin, Jimmy Conlin, Roscoe Ates, Alan Bridge as Members of the Ale and Quail Club; Robert Dudley as the Weenie King; Franklin Pangborn as the hotel manager.

The Lady Eve. US 1941; monochrome; 97 minutes. Produced by Paul Jones for Paramount. Written and directed by Preston Sturges from the play by Monckton Hoffe. Photographed by Victor Milner. Music score by Leo Shuken and Charles Bradshaw. Art direction by Hans Dreier and Ernest Fegte. Edited by Stuart Gilmore. With Barbara Stanwyck as Eve; Henry Fonda as Charles Pike; Charles Coburn as Colonel Harrington; William Demarest as Muggsy; Eugene Pallette as Mr Pike; Eric Blore as Sir Alfred McGlennan Keith; Melville Cooper as Gerald; Janet Beecher as Mrs Pike; Robert Greig as the butler.

Mac the Night Watchman Is a Prince Among Men
The Philadelphia Story

An heiress with high moral standards prepares for her second marriage but falls for a journalist covering the occasion and reckons without the wiles of her first husband, who still loves her.

My diary records that when I was twelve I didn't much care for this film. I saw it at the Bolton Capitol, and despite the star cast, which I acknowledged, I found in it only 'a small oasis of merriment in a large desert of talk'. I also remarked that nothing very much happens. Nor does it, if you're expecting earthquakes.

Ten years later I saw it at a matinee at the Cambridge Arts, and hurt myself laughing. By the end of the week it was the talk of the town, and was revived twice that year; when I came to run my own Cambridge cinema it was one of my safest staples. Since then I have seen it whenever I can. Five or six years ago I met the venerable author of the screenplay, Donald Ogden Stewart, who would deserve his fame if for no other reason than his authorship of the last line of the film version of *Dinner at Eight*, where tarty Jean Harlow is leaving the room with Marie Dressler, playing a burlesque of Mrs Patrick Campbell:

HARLOW: You know, I read a book (*Dressler reacts*) and it says machinery is going to take the place of every profession.
DRESSLER (*looking her over*): Oh, my dear, that's something you need *never* worry about!

Stewart was deprecating about his work on *The Philadelphia Story*, and ashamed of winning an Academy Award merely for putting another man's play into film form. However, comparison will show a most valuable tidying-up process in his script, as well as the addition of a score of jewelled lines, including: 'The finest sight in this fine pretty world is the privileged class enjoying its privileges.'

I have no way of knowing whether the Philadelphia élite behave as this film depicts them behaving, or whether they ever did. I hope so: it would be pleasant to know of a group of people so controlled, so urbane, so witty: they would deserve their riches. Of course, the actors who play them should have a major share of the credit, and in this case it would I think be fair to mention first the unassuming and unstarred senior generation. John Halliday, as the mildly philandering Seth Lord, and Mary Nash as his slightly catty but deeply understanding wife, make as attractive a pair of old marrieds as the screen has shown; while Uncle Willie Tracy, as played by Roland Young, is certainly the most pleasing dirty old man on theatrical record. (Being rich naturally helps, as does knowing 'a formula said to pop pennies off the eyelids of dead Irishmen'.)

Centrepiece of the romantic tug of war among the younger set is of course Katharine Hepburn as Tracy Lord, who when told by her ex that she is nothing but a spoilt goddess wishing to remain chaste and virginal, explodes in embarrassment: 'Stop using those foul words!' Despite the elaborate wedding preparations, she clearly isn't going to marry stuffy George Kittredge, 'man of the people', just as boringly well-mannered as the gentry but with none of their accompanying personality spark. The wedding march may be playing, and the parlour full of stuffed shirts and lace, but lo! James Stewart is proposing in the ante-room, James Stewart playing

Macaulay Connor the writer of left-wing novels, who in his journalist capacity (which he assumes whenever he wants to eat) has been sent by *Spy Magazine* to cover the society wedding and has fallen for a few capitalist snares. (He was perhaps overfond of quoting an old Spanish proverb: 'With the rich and mighty, always a little patience.') The heiress knows that for all his good intentions to love her despite her bank balance, the equation won't really come out, so she returns him to the loving arms of his photographer, played with a fine wry detachment by Ruth Hussey. George, having revealed himself as a hypocrite, is already out of the running, so there is no available solution except the one we expected all along, namely for her to remarry her ex, Mr C. K. Dexter Haven. Why else would Cary Grant have been playing him with such guile and hesitant charm, ever ready with the right word at the right time, as when George suspects that there have been goings-on at the pool on the wedding eve:

GEORGE: Tracy, a man expects his wife –
TRACY: To behave herself, naturally.
DEXTER (*agreeing*): To behave herself naturally.

At this point Tracy suspects that under the gaze of almost everybody in the house ('Good Golly, why didn't you sell tickets?') she let herself go too far under the influence of champagne and moonlight, and when Mr Connor, her partner in an innocent late night swim, assures her that she didn't she gets pretty angry:

TRACY: Why, was I so unattractive, so distant, so forbidding?
MACAULAY: You were extremely attractive, and as for distant and forbidding quite the reverse, but you were also a little the worse, or better, for wine, and there are rules about that.

So Dexter pops in at the last minute – he can't have been planning it, he isn't even wearing a tie – and promises that this time, if she will be less intolerant, he will give her less cause. For once we are fairly sure that the happy ending will continue after the credits have rolled up.

I almost forgot to mention the real perpetrator of the plot, the editor of *Spy Magazine*, who blackmails Dexter into easing the journalists into the Lord ménage as guests in return for withholding a malicious story about Seth. 'No mean Machiavelli is smiling,

THE PHILADELPHIA STORY. A young Philadelphia matron knows how to put interlopers in their place. Katherine Hepburn, James Stewart, Ruth Hussey

cynical Sidney Kidd,' Dexter later muses. Henry Daniell, who plays him, has only one short scene and a silent shot at the end, but it is an imperishable performance, like Orson Welles' in *The Third Man*: his thin-lipped, self-confident aura permeates the whole film like hickory smoke. When Dexter comes into his office, his greeting is: 'I understand we understand each other.' 'Quite', is the laconic rejoinder.

Another small but happy talent in this multi-talented film is that of Virginia Weidler as Tracy's mischievous twelve-year-old sister, confusing the guests with her rendering of 'Lydia the Tattooed Lady' and her embarrassing curiosity about the grown-up world. Tracy herself adds to the confusion when she determines to give the journalists more of a story than they bargained for:

TRACY: Yes, Philadelphia is full of ancient relics. And how old are you, Mr Connor?

MACAULAY: Thirty.
TRACY: Two books isn't much for a man of thirty. But I expect you have other interests outside your work. What's the 'Macaulay' for?
MACAULAY: My father taught English history. I'm Mike to my friends.
TRACY: Of whom you have many, I'm sure.

The elements are clearly present for high comedy of the highest order, and none of the cast has ever outpointed his performance in this movie: Hepburn in particular was born to play Tracy, her much imitated but never equalled Bryn Mawr delivery working miracles with even the most ordinary line. George Cukor's direction would win no prizes for originality, but his great virtue is that he allows author and actors to do their thing, contenting himself by staying at a discreet distance and ensuring that they underline every nuance. Franz Waxman's music score, with its echoes of romance, drunkenness and mocking laughter, makes the most of the most memorable few notes in Hollywood history, and in general the presentation is impeccable. Incidentally, anyone who thinks that this kind of filmed play makes itself should see the appalling musical remake *High Society*, in which flat lighting and directions kill more or less the same lines, delivered by quite personable actors, stone dead.

The Philadelphia Story belongs to a sadly dated genre which isn't attempted any more, because modern film-makers will no longer allow the rich to wear their heritage casually. Yet at each viewing it seems to get fresher. It is the world which has aged since 1939, when this film was conceived; if it were rewritten for the 1980s Dexter would have to be a drug addict and Macaulay a communist, and the grand finale would be the destruction of the house by agitators. Best perhaps to leave the Lords in their time capsule, living their elegant lives to the full, with a plenitude of silver fish dishes and old Dutch muffin ears and a guest list filled to overflowing with Cadwaladers and Drexels and *qu'est-ce-que-c'est* Cassats; with kedgeree on the breakfast hotplate and Mac the night watchman ('a prince among men') guarding them while they sleep. Certainly *The Philadelphia Story* is no mere frothy comedy – Philip Barry's plays always had serious meaning – but it is the comedy elements which have survived most triumphantly, and if the talents listed above had found no other showcase, for their felicitous teaming in this magical film they would be rightly cherished.

The Philadelphia Story. US 1940; monochrome; 112 minutes. Produced by Joseph L. Mankiewicz for MGM. Written by Donald Ogden Stewart, from the play by Philip Barry. Directed by George Cukor. Photographed by Joseph Ruttenberg. Music score by Franz Waxman. Art direction by Cedric Gibbons and Wade B. Rubottom. Edited by Frank Sullivan. With Cary Grant as C. K. Dexter Haven; Katharine Hepburn as Tracy Lord; James Stewart as Macaulay Connor; Ruth Hussey as Liz Imbrie; John Halliday as Seth Lord; Mary Nash as Margaret Lord; Virginia Weidler as Dinah Lord; Roland Young as Uncle Willie; John Howard as George Kittredge; Henry Daniell as Sidney Kidd.

All the Cat's Fault
The Picture of Dorian Gray

A Victorian man-about-town finds that while he keeps the appearance of youth, his portrait shows his increasing dissipation.

During my own prolonged youth I had three favourite items of repartee, geared and ready to fit into almost any conversation, and stop it stone dead. If a story were told of someone's outlandish or anti-social behaviour, I would remark: 'How different from the home life of our own dear queen.' (I have of course no knowledge of the private life of the monarch; this remark was allegedly first made by a Victorian matron after witnessing a performance of *Antony and Cleopatra*.) Instead of a boring goodbye or *au revoir*, I have sometimes been known, depending on the company, to say cheerfully: 'See you in the monkey house.' This puzzling but totally irrelevant rejoinder comes from an old sixpenny record, 'Sandy Powell at the Zoo'. Finally, if anyone tells me that I am looking well for my age, my natural reply is: 'I keep a picture in the attic.' This puzzles some people too, but cultists will of course recognize it as a summary of the plot of the film under consideration.

When the London Empire in 1945 first heralded *The Picture of Dorian Gray*, the title rang no bell, as I was dimly acquainted with only the lighter theatrical works of Oscar Wilde, in one of which indeed I had played Canon Chasuble for a local amateur company. What impelled me to see it was the advertising, which claimed: 'They said it couldn't be made.' Being interested like all schoolboys in forbidden things, I dearly wanted to know who *they* were and why they said such a thing, but of course I never did find out. As a film buff I was also intrigued by the evidence that MGM had lavished major production values on a film without a star, for George Sanders at that time would not be expected to sell tickets, and was indeed billed below the title. Clearly the hope for success lay in the story, which I hastened to read, finding it for my taste a little too perfumed and self-conscious in its style. My investigations also brought me into the shadowy world of Albert Lewin, clearly the onlie begetter of the movie: he turned out to have been Irving Thalberg's grey eminence at MGM in the thirties, a university scholar responsible for prodding the young production head into making all those literary classics like *The Barretts of Wimpole Street, David Copperfield, Mutiny on the Bounty* and *Camille*. After Thalberg's demise in 1937 MGM became more blatantly commercial in its choices and the disillusioned Lewin became involved in various independent enterprises with a literary flavour, directing for the first time with *The Moon and Sixpence*, a Maugham adaptation which ironically did much more than cover its small cost. Typically of Lewin's later work, the central figure was an artist, there was much narration from Herbert Marshall as Maugham himself, the dialogue bristled with intellectualism and at the end there were flashes of the artist's paintings (based on Gaugin) in glorious colour. I immensely relished its dry, edgy, literary flavour, and now hoped for more of the same. Alas, Lewin had been lured back to MGM by a big budget which his small talent couldn't properly use, and although *Dorian Gray* certainly has its fascination, Lewin's four subsequent movies are arid curiosities interesting chiefly for his addiction to literary originals, cats and Omar Khayyam, whose moving finger he wears almost to the bone.

In fact, *The Picture of Dorian Gray*, a film best viewed while nibbling Stilton cheese and sipping vintage port, begins and ends with a verse from Omar:

> I sent my soul through the Invisible,
> Some letter of that after-life to spell
> And by and by my soul returned and whispered,
> 'I myself am heaven and hell'.

And whose are the dulcet tones on the sound track, setting the scene and establishing the characters? Uncredited though he mysteriously

THE PICTURE OF DORIAN GRAY. Lord Henry studies the cynic's manual

is, one can't mistake the plummy voice of Cedric Hardwicke, whose longest Hollywood role this may be, so heavy is the film with his narration. Alas, a tale which needs to explain itself so frequently has not been properly translated into cinematic terms. Although Dorian by his very nature must remain handsomely poker-faced, some other way than narration should be found to let us know what he is really thinking: even extracts from a diary would be better than a wholly disembodied voice. The fact is that Lewin was not wholly at ease in the director's chair. The cast is good enough: Hurd Hatfield does as good a job with the callous Dorian as can be expected, and apart from one small girl with an American accent, the minor players seem quite at home in Victorian London. But technically this is an empty and disappointing experience. There are few close ups or reaction shots, almost no camera movement, absolutely no panache. Every scene has the same slow start: we are shown the set and allowed to take in its splendid design and contents; then the actors move cautiously into it from the edges and usually stay too far away for us to feel any involvement with them. Watching it is rather like stepping through the rooms of an elegant private museum: the smell of wax polish is the element most vividly sensed. Virtually the only cinematic moments are the swinging of the lamp to cause violent shadows in the murder scene, and an early glimpse of Lord Henry killing and preserving a struggling butterfly, just as he has mortally wounded the soul of Dorian by his cynicism. As for the famous self-destroying portrait, the work of Ivan Le Lorraine Albright, it is glimpsed too briefly to be studied, and Lewin tantalizes us too long before each glimpse by showing long reactions from those viewing it. Sometimes, rather too subtly, he doesn't even bother to show it at all; but when it is offered, it is offered in flaming colour, a gimmick which tends to distract from the overall black and white mood, especially as it is occasionally seen behind the actors in plain monochrome.

George Sanders, as a reward for his excellent work in the Gaugin role of *The Moon and Sixpence*, had been handed the plum role of Lord Henry Wotton, and with it not only all the epigrams from the novel but, it would seem, every wicked remark with which Wilde was credited through the whole of his life: 'Punctuality is the thief of time.' 'The only way to get rid of a temptation is to yield to it.' 'To regain one's youth one has merely to repeat one's follies.' 'I apologize for the intelligence of my remarks, Sir Thomas, I had forgotten you were a Member of Parliament.' Even his wife gets into the act: 'I love coming to your house, Aunt Agatha, it's one of the few places I'm likely to meet my husband.' These are all very fine, but a crash course in Wilde doesn't really advance the plot, and Sanders surprisingly tends to gabble them, like a vaudeville perfor-mer realizing that his act is too long but at a loss how to get off.

The actual plot could be got through in less than half the time, especially as keen filmgoers will recognize it early on as a slight variation on *Faust* and *Dr Jekyll and Mr Hyde*. Basil Hallward (a nice understated performance by Lowell Gilmore) has painted a striking full-figure portrait of the 22-year-old Dorian. Admiring the work, Dorian wishes that he could always look like that. One of the *objets d'art* in the studio is an elongated feline statuette, and Lord Henry remarks: 'You ought not to express that wish in the presence of that cat: it is one of the seventy-three great gods of Egypt.'

With a hundred minutes to go, there can be no further surprises. In adopting Lord Henry's cynicism, Dorian causes the suicide of the one girl he really loves, and in his despair notices a curl on the lip of his portrait. 'Was the portrait to be an emblem of his conscience? Would it teach him to loathe his own soul?' intones Hardwicke on the soundtrack. Yes, indeed it would, so he moves it up to an attic away from prying eyes, and abandons himself to a life of vice, reading the Yellow Book (tut, tut) and spending night after night in Blue Gate Fields, which seems to offer opium, ladies of the night, and Pedro de Cordoba playing Chopin, all masterminded by an evil dwarf. Hallward asks to see the picture and finds it oozing putrescence; Dorian stabs him in case he blabs, and blackmails another friend, who later commits suicide, into disposing of the body. Twenty years after the portrait was painted, Dorian's waxwork features are still unmarked, but he is hunted by the vengeful sailor brother of his first love. By now the weary Dorian almost welcomes the prospect of his own death, and when the sailor is accidentally killed, resolves to make a start on mending his ways by destroying the portrait. But at the first stroke of his knife into the canvas it is Dorian who staggers and dies, and when his friends find him on the floor, all the marks of his loathsome dissipation are on his face. 'Heaven forgive me,' says Lord Henry. I would have preferred Wilde's original last line: 'It was not until they had examined the rings that they recognized who he was.'

The Picture of Dorian Gray was an extremely odd film to come out of a major Hollywood studio during wartime, for all its horror elements are muted, its suspense is negligible, and what midwestern audiences thought of the epigrammatic dialogue can readily be imagined. But at least it deserves a mark for trying, and MGM deserves a pat on the back for financing it, for I well remember how many young people of my own age were made by it to think about age, youth, life and death. It makes one regret the passing of the old Hollywood all the more when one realizes that such an aberration as this could never happen now. Now we would have gore and filth and explicit sex instead of the epigrams and the art, and modern critics might even approve of that, for Wilde is out of fashion. Perhaps after all it *was* the film that couldn't be made. But Lewin had an interesting try in the circumstances.

The Picture of Dorian Gray. US 1945; monochrome; 110 minutes. Produced by Pandro S. Berman for MGM. Written and directed by Albert Lewin, from the novel by Oscar Wilde. Photographed by Harry Stradling. Music score by Herbert Stothart. Art direction by Cedric Gibbons and Hans Peters. Edited by Ferris Webster. With Hurd

Hatfield as Dorian Gray; George Sanders as Lord Henry Wotton; Donna Reed as Gladys; Lowell Gilmore as Basil Hallward; Angela Lansbury as Sybil Vane; Richard Fraser as James Vane; Miles Mander as Sir Robert Bentley.

Experiment with Time
Portrait of Jennie

An unsuccessful New York artist falls in love with a mysterious girl whom he meets in the park and who seems to grow older with each encounter. Finding eventually that she died years ago in a storm near a lighthouse, he revisits the spot on the anniversary and narrowly escapes being drawn into death with her; but his reputation is made when he paints her portrait.

This is an outlandish example of Hollywood's higher lunacy, stuffed with phoney intellectual pretensions and as batty as a March hare. Similar instances of romance across the void of death were treated in *Berkeley Square, Peter Ibbetson, A Matter of Life and Death, Quest for Love, A Guy Named Joe* and scores of others, but this, when it came out in 1948, received the accolade from cultists as the supreme achievement in its vein. Unfortunately the paying public found it risible, and it was hastily whittled down for double feature exposure; some say that its poor reception was the prime cause of Selznick's premature decline as a producer.

As Mr Magoo almost said on a memorable occasion, 'I don't care if it is a walrus, I like it, I like it.' Its aim, after all, is only to provide a fairy tale for grown-ups, and in our increasingly realistic society we could surely do with a few more of those. For full enjoyment, however, a perfect, lustrous print is required, and here it seems that time has not dealt kindly with the negative, for the only copies now available appear excessively dark and contrasty. Joseph August's magnificent photography, all lamp-posts in the mist and sunsets in leaden skies, now gives the impression of having been added afterwards, like icing on a cake, and his tricky storm sequence, originally printed green and displayed on a giant screen, seems all too obvious a fabrication of reverse printing and random montage. But the effects, though they no longer convince as part of the whole, are stunning when they come singly, and Jennie's first appearances to Eben Adams, on winter days in Central Park, have the kind of eerie quality that can stop the breath and send icicles down the spine, especially as they seem to be photographed through linen. This Alice-in-Wonderland-type child tells the artist among other things that her parents have a trapeze act at Hammerstein's Victoria. The film is set in 1934; Adams knows that the theatre was razed to the ground many years previously. Next time she says through tears that her parents have been killed in an accident, and he later finds that indeed they were, but in nineteen twenty-something. He says she looks much older; she says she is hurrying for him. She says she is being sent to a convent, and when he later meets her there she says she is being sent for the summer to stay with an aunt on the coast of Maine. He never hears from her again, and when he investigates, Sister Mary of Mercy tells him that she died many years before, in a storm off Lands End Light.

Thus the scene is set for the final cataclysm, a sequence devised by Selznick to be a spectacular entertainment in itself. According to one of his many surviving memos, he hopes for 'a D. W. Griffith effect that will have tremendous dramatic power and enormous spectacular value, thereby adding a big showmanship element to the picture'. Earlier in production, however, he was convinced that 'this whole venture is doomed to be one of the most awful experiences any studio ever had'. But when things were at their worst he sailed into action, cutting, reshaping and adding a long pretentious prologue which he discussed in detail with Ben Hecht, wanting it 'to flatter the intelligence of the audience by assuming that they have the same kind of approach to the great questions of life and death as the great philosophers and poets. I can have quotes or not, either actual or Hechtian creations, which we might credit to the Greeks or the Persians if it is necessary to invent a few to say precisely what we want to say.'

In fact the release version of the movie has a spoken prologue over whirling clouds, with Euripides and Keats both quoted during it (whether accurately or not I have failed to check) and Browning following soon after. Selznick saw the theme of the piece as 'a misplacement of two people in time, involving a question of almost Einsteinian relativity', and whether you're in a mood to cry or merely smile at all this, the foreword certainly gets it over with conviction, especially as it follows that daunting Selznick trademark 'in a tradition of quality', with its white colonial house and drive. Portentously the voice intones:

Since time began man has looked into the awesome reaches of infinity and asked the eternal questions: What is time? What is life? What is space? What is death? Through a hundred civilizations, philosophers and scientists have come with answers, but the bewilderment remains . . . Science tells us that nothing ever dies but only changes, that time itself does not pass but curves around us, and that the past and the future are together at our side for ever. Out of the shadows of knowledge, and out of a painting that hung on a museum wall comes our story, the truth of which lies not on our screen but in your hearts.

After that mighty introduction, which many will see as a whopping disclaimer, the little love story which follows may seem like a nut being cracked by a sledgehammer, especially as its only discernible dramatic purpose is to get one not very good painter half drowned in pursuit of a ghost. But on the screen it's magic, for those who believe in magic. Mr Hecht had a similar thought in his introduction to another movie, *The Song of Bernadette*: 'To those who believe, no explanation is necessary. To those who do not believe, no explanation is possible.'

Though in Robert Nathan's novel Jennie becomes real enough to be seen by others, Selznick's dictum during the preparation of the film made her invisible to all but Eben. This means that Joseph Cotten is never off screen, talking either to her or to the choice little gallery of supporting players who, as proper foils should, offer different attitudes to his spiritual malaise. One longs to see less of David Wayne as the whimsical Irish cab driver who sings to his own harp (not while driving); but Ethel Barrymore merits her co-star billing as the warm, fierce, art gallery owner who encourages and understands Eben after first dismissing his work with: 'There isn't a drop of love in any of these.'

Cecil Kellaway, Felix Bressart, Lillian Gish, Henry Hull, Florence Bates, all have effective cameos; but it is on the principals that the main responsibility rests. Cotten understates enough never to become a bore, even though he has such lines to handle as: 'What is it that makes a man and a woman know that of all the men and women in the world they were meant for each other?' And: 'We know so little of the ways of providence; but now I know a little

PORTRAIT OF JENNIE. Ethel Barrymore and Cecil Kellaway approve of Joseph Cotten's work

more.' Even during the climactic storm the lovers are yelling poetic prose at each other:

EBEN: I want you, not dreams of you.
JENNIE: There is no life, my darling, until you love and have been loved. And then there is no death.

This must sound the daftest stuff imaginable, but you have to see it before hooting with laughter, especially when Dmitri Tiomkin's musical custard, after themes by Debussy, is poured over it. As for Jennie herself, Jennie who has to make most of the nonsense work, Jennie who thinks the Kaiser is still on the German throne, Jennifer Jones does much better than one has any right to expect, absolutely maintaining the ethereal quality, constantly leaving striped scarves behind for Cotten to return, disappearing at the drop of a hat and offering no apology or explanation. She even gets away with singing an awful little song:

> Where I come from, nobody knows,
> And where I'm going, everything goes;
> The wind blows,
> The sea flows
> And nobody knows . . .

So why do I enjoy this monumentally dubious concept? Because of the rare intensity and skill with which it is presented, and because part of me is nutty enough to root for a happy ending by wishing Jennie were real. At least I can cheer silently at the end, and release the lump in my throat, when Ethel Barrymore is nursing Cotten back to physical health but can do nothing with his certainty that he has lost Jennie for ever, that nobody even believes she existed, that they think he created her out of his artistic need for self-expression. And perhaps he did. 'You believe in her, that's what matters,' says Barrymore soothingly. But his eyes have lighted on something familiar by his bedside. It is a striped scarf. He looks up wonderingly. She shrugs. 'It was near you when they found you on the beach.' Then light dawns. 'Is it . . . ?' He nods, and there is elation in their eyes as the musical crescendo mounts and the extra-dignified credits begin to roll up. After this, no one can possibly walk out of the theatre feeling that he hasn't had his money's worth.

Portrait of Jennie. US 1948; monochrome; 86 minutes. Produced by David O. Selznick for his own company. Written by Peter Berneis, Paul Osborn and Leonardo Bercovici, from the novel by Robert Nathan. Directed by William Dieterle. Photographed by Joseph August. Music score by Dmitri Tiomkin, after Debussy. With Joseph Cotten as Eben Adams; Jennifer Jones as Jennie; Ethel Barrymore as Miss Spinney; Cecil Kellaway as Matthews; David Wayne as Gus; Felix Bressart as doorman; Albert Sharpe as Mr Moore; Lillian Gish as Mother Mary; Florence Bates as Mrs Jekes; Henry Hull as Eke.

The Thalberg Style
Pride and Prejudice

***An opinionated young lady of the early 19th century attracts a
rich gentleman whom she had at first despised for his pride.***

Two men must share my gratitude for raising the literary tone of
Hollywood during the thirties. They had of course no thought of
turning it into a grove of Academe: that would have been wildly
unsuitable as well as uncommercial. But they set their sights at a
good middlebrow level, and were amply rewarded. They are David
Selznick, who in this volume is duly credited under *The Prisoner Of
Zenda, Portrait of Jennie* and *Rebecca*; and Irving Thalberg, who in his
short but dynamic career as head of MGM production maintained
the flow of high-falutin' Garbo drama despite clear indifference from
the American hinterlands, and propelled into the world's cinemas a
steady flow of expensive literary adaptations, from *A Tale of Two
Cities* to *Dinner at Eight*. These epic entertainments, with their air of
neatly combining enjoyment with instruction, came to the attention
of my infant self via the good offices of the Bolton Capitol, where
they invariably drew packed houses. When *David Copperfield*, for
instance, was heralded, the *Evening News* ad contained, in addition to
pleas to come early, a very unusual line:

WARNING. This film takes *nearly two hours* to screen.

An unthinkable length at that stage of talkie history, even though
the film's second half now seems to need a more leisurely development: too many shredded incidents are compressed into it. Properly
awed, my mother and I joined the long queue sometime after six,
without the ghost of a hope of getting in before the house broke at
eight. The sixpenny queue at the Capitol finally entered through the
starboard door of the front stalls; but this goal was not easily
attained. From the imposing white façade one passed through heavy
glass doors into a side yard, usually stacked high with beer crates
from the pub next door. In the main wall to the right was a little
window at which one purchased tickets. The queue then snaked

PRIDE AND PREJUDICE. The Bingleys entertain. Bruce Lester, Greer Garson, Frieda Inescort, Laurence Olivier

down by the side of the cinema into a maze-like series of crash barriers under a corrugated roof which made the atmosphere very hot and noisy. Very often to relieve the tedium I would nip off down the street to the pasty shop and come back to enjoy in the open air the aromatic tastes of onions, potatoes and minced meat. Once while engaged in this luxurious pursuit I happened to lean against the cinema wall, and was astonished to find that by applying my ear to the bricks I could get a free show in sound only: the tones of W. C. Fields as Mr Micawber were clear as a bell.

Those early reels of *Copperfield*, while the hero is still a much-abused boy, were irresistibly easy to identify with, and for months I imagined myself as Freddie Bartholomew, taking care the following Christmas to be given an illustrated 'book of the film'. The villainies of Basil Rathbone's Murdstone long remained a talking point among family and friends, and 'Barkis is willin'' became a valued catch phrase. The key to the excitement was that while being overwhelmed by a luxurious production and uplifted by our involvement in a great novel, we were richly entertained by a story involving a gallery of grotesque characters: Mr Dick, Mr Micawber, Uriah Heep, Aunt Betsy, the Peggottys. And what made it so perfect was that in the end we knew all could come right for young David, something which in those drab days we couldn't guarantee for ourselves.

Mutiny on the Bounty was another great local event. While relishing the suspense, the excitements, the floggings, the romantic dash of Clark Gable, and the highly imitable rogueries of Charles Laughton (he never in fact says 'cast adrift in an open boat', but 'cast me adrift, would you, thirty five hundred miles from land'), one could reassure oneself not only that these were actors but that this was history, much more direct and assimilable than the stuff in the school books. In the case of *The Good Earth*, we flattered ourselves that we learned a lot about the unfortunate plight of the modern Chinese peasant, though what we really queued to see was the locust plague. Thalberg went a bit far however in expecting the world audience to applaud *Romeo and Juliet*, especially with such mature young lovers as Leslie Howard and Norma Shearer. Dressed to kill as it was, it died a slow death at the box office.

Thalberg's influence went on long after his untimely death in 1937. In 1940, for instance, MGM produced and released what might seem to be the archetypal Thalberg picture in *Pride and Prejudice*: literature streamlined and pre-digested to attract a mass audience. It also happened to be first-class entertainment for almost all heights of brow. The inevitable compromises were not harmful. The plot was taken from the stage version by Helen Jerome rather than from the original novel (which structurally is somewhat diffuse) and tends to move rapidly from one set-piece to another (assembly ball, Netherfields garden party, visit to Rosings). When the fearsome Lady Catherine finally visits Elizabeth in order to persuade her to give up Darcy ('I take no leave of you, Miss Bennet. I send no compliments to your mother. You deserve no such attention. I am most seriously displeased.') the film turns her into an elderly Cupid come to test Elizabeth's love and to tell the waiting Darcy that he has chosen well and Elizabeth will have him. The Empire line fashions appropriate to the original were thought insufficiently flamboyant, so the period was moved on forty years to permit huge hats and crinolines. Aldous Huxley, no less, was brought in to dicker with the dialogue while retaining an aura of breeding and refinement. The cast was packed with familiar faces and topped by two of the brightest stars on the Hollywood horizon. The whole enterprise was suffused with good intentions and only the faintest tinge of commercialism. Without breaking any records in the urban areas, it did respectably enough at the box office for MGM to pat itself on the back for its wise benevolence in making such a cultured entertainment available to an increasingly philistine world.

In fact *Pride and Prejudice* was always the most accessible of classics, its light modern wit and recognizable characters making it seem sometimes impossible that it was written before Waterloo was fought. Essentially it was not so very different in tone from the kind of modern romantic comedy in which Myrna Loy and Melvyn Douglas might have been cast; it simply required a special style in the handling, and it got it. Despite dull direction by Robert Z. Leonard, for whom the best that can be said is that he doesn't get in the way of the performances, it remains richly enjoyable. Perhaps it is one of the few films I might have chosen to see in colour rather than black and white; not the garish hues of forties Hollywood, though, but a hint of water colour. The monochrome photography gleams well enough, but it has a chill grey look which works against the comedy and prevents the full texture of the costumes and furnishings from coming through. Nor are the credits auspicious: a badly etched broken pillar and a couple of windswept trees. Jane Austen would have winced at the funereal impression. But once past the introductory title ('It Happened in Old England . . .') all is joy.

Huxley and his collaborators found no way to incorporate the novel's famous opening line: 'It is a truth universally acknowledged, that a single man in possession of a good fortune must be in want of a wife.' They did however a most skilful job of introducing almost all the characters in one newly devised scene, with the garrulous Mrs Bennet and her five daughters on a visit to the Meriton draper's, watching the new arrivals drive through, and hearing all about them from the local gossips:

MRS BENNET: Is the young woman *Mrs* Bingley?
GOSSIP: No, dear, that's the pleasantest part of it, she's his sister.

MRS BENNET: Five thousand pounds a year and unmarried. That's the best piece of news since Waterloo!

When the family returns home, Mrs Bennet in haste to lay her plans, the script returns fairly faithfully to its source for the scene between the mother hen and her reclusive husband, choicely played by Edmund Gwenn. Indeed it would have been sacrilege to abandon such delightful thrust and parry:

MRS BENNET: Mr Bennet, how can you abuse your own children in such a way! You take delight in vexing me. You have no compassion on my poor nerves.
MR BENNET: You mistake me, my dear. I have a high respect for your nerves. They are my old friends. I have heard you mention them with consideration these twenty years at least.

During the rather underpopulated ball scene we warm to Greer Garson's sharp, witty performance as the impetuous Elizabeth (the best she ever gave) and Laurence Olivier comes decisively into his own as the initially unsympathetic Darcy. It is an entertainment simply to watch him back out of a room, and his way is inimitable with such lines as: 'I am in no humour tonight to give consequence to the middle classes at play.' The resonant love-hate relationship between him and Elizabeth is quickly struck up and conscientiously maintained, despite subsequent moments of doubt:

ELIZABETH: At this moment it is difficult to believe that you are so proud.
DARCY: At this moment it is difficult to believe that you are so prejudiced.

Broader comedy is provided by the fussy, pompous and self-important cleric Mr Collins, a fawning hypocrite who must by entail inherit the Bennet fortune and proposes to make amends by choosing a wife from among the Bennet daughters. Melville Cooper, accompanied by dipping and bowing music whenever he appears, gives the performance of a lifetime in the role, twittering his good intentions, his high moral tone, and his grovelling regard for his patroness to relations who quickly decide that, fortune or no fortune, they would like to see the back of him. Luckily Elizabeth is finally joined to the riches of Pemberley, and we are content that she will dispense them wisely as well as being happy ever after. The film's last word goes to Mrs Bennet, withdrawing from a parlourful of courting couples and exclaiming ecstatically: 'Think of it, Mr

Bennet – three of them married, and the other two tottering on the brink!'

Pride and Prejudice. US 1940; monochrome; 116 minutes. Produced by Hunt Stromberg for MGM. Written by Aldous Huxley and Jane Murfin, from the novel by Jane Austen and the play by Helen Jerome. Directed by Robert Z. Leonard. Photographed by Karl Freund. Music score by Herbert Stothart. Art direction by Paul Groesse. With Laurence Olivier as Darcy; Greer Garson as Elizabeth Bennet; Edmund Gwenn as Mr Bennet; Mary Boland as Mrs Bennet; Melville Cooper as Mr Collins; Edna May Oliver as Lady Catherine de Bourgh; Maureen O'Sullivan as Jane Bennet; Ann Rutherford as Lydia Bennet; Marsha Hunt as Mary Bennet; Heather Angel as Kitty Bennet; Bruce Lester as Bingley; Frieda Inescort as Miss Bingley; Karen Morley as Charlotte Lucas; E. E. Clive as Sir William Lucas; Edward Ashley as Mr Wickham; Marjorie Wood as Lady Lucas; May Beatty as Mrs Philips.

Before the Lights Went Out
The Prisoner of Zenda

An Englishman holidaying in Ruritania is found to resemble the drugged and kidnapped king, for whom he deputizes at his coronation and whom he later rescues from his adversaries.

It predates Bulldog Drummond, Dornford Yates and Mr Chips. It is contemporary with Sherlock Holmes, inhabiting another corner of that cherished Europe which was destroyed for ever when the world went to war in 1914. It belongs to the genre once called Graustarkian, a romantic adventure taking place in the kind of mythical country where Sigmund Romberg and Ivor Novello liked to place their musicals, where the heroes behaved like English gentlemen and the villains like the caricature Nazis of World War II. Its locale is a land as remote as Oz, and even more enchanting. Anthony Hope's novel, first published in 1894, called it Ruritania. Its capital is Strelsau, which according to this version lies between Vienna and Bucharest, and can be reached by stepping off the Orient Express. When Ronald Colman steps off it, we know exactly where we are: in the land of legend.

David O. Selznick, whose 'O' was as imaginary as Ruritania, knew very well what he was making: a means of escape, backwards into time, for the cynical thirties. Silent versions had appeared in 1913 and 1922, but it was quite another matter to entrance audiences with the same story told in dialogue. After the highly successful première he could afford to share a few confessions with university students:

> The great criticism of most of the people in Hollywood who heard that we were going to make it, and of most of the people in our own company, was that we were making a very dated piece of material . . . a story that had no conceivable appeal to present-day audiences. It was an old-fashioned fairy tale and melodrama. I felt that the affectionate memories that most people had of *The Prisoner of Zenda* persisted, that audiences were ready for a great and clean love story which contrasted with the sordid realist pictures of which they had had so many. And I have had, in any case, some success in resurrecting some of the old books and in bringing them to the screen. I felt very candidly that the Windsor case had given new life to an old problem – that of king and commoner, queen and commoner; that it had become a topical problem.

Selznick went on to say that he would not have embarked on the project without Ronald Colman's assurance that he would play the title role. With his wistful blend of nobility and idealism Colman was the only star capable of carrying off the character of Rudolph Rassendyll, the gentleman of London leisure who goes to Ruritania for a fishing holiday and finds that his life is given both a purpose and an aching unattainable love by the adventure on which he promptly if reluctantly embarks. The audience delights in his visibly increasing enthusiasm as the circumstances grow more dangerous, in the wry smile, the nod of the head and the glinting eye. 'Most remarkable wine I had last night,' he quips to the man known to have drugged it; 'slept like a baby.' Fascinated by the villainy around him, impelled by the military code of honour exemplified by Colonel Sapt, he inhales the scent of danger and springs almost gleefully into the kind of action of which a week previously he would not have thought himself capable, bargaining with the smilingly treacherous Rupert of Hentzau (who would cut anybody's throat for a purse of gold) and even bandying resplendent words with him during their final duel:

RASSENDYLL: When did you give up knives for pistols?
HENTZAU: Oh, I left my knife in Michael . . . You may as well face it, Rassendyll, I'm not a gentleman.
(*Rassendyll disarms him with a well-aimed stool.*)
    I cannot get used to fighting with furniture. Where did you learn it?
RASSENDYLL: Oh, that all goes with the old school tie.

Colman was able to personify the idle dreams of every middle-aged clubbable man, though most would have wished to dispense with the noble acts of self-sacrifice which climax both this film and the preceding *Lost Horizon*, the pair for which he is principally remembered and celebrated. The Capra film had stressed the philosophy of modern man; *Zenda* presented the aspect of its star which harked back to yesterday, showcasing him (as Lawrence J. Quirk has written) as 'the courtly, intrepid adventurer, living by a code of unselfish and essential integrity, fielding off all obstacles and adversaries with consummate grace and coursing serenely through all difficulties to a jauntily graceful dénouement'.

So Selznick conceived his film as a star vehicle, but one in which every nuance of production and acting should support the star in the fullest meaning of the word. Memos still exist in which he coaches James Wong Howe in the obtaining of some tiny miracle of lighting, alas quite invisible in the unattractively grainy prints which seem to be all it is possible to get from the dupe negative kept by MGM after they bought up the property for their slavish and spineless 1952 remake. John Cromwell patiently followed all Selznick's directorial demands, but his stately theatrical style was thought insufficiently supple for the duel, so Woody Van Dyke was brought in to add excitement; similarly John Balderston's careful screenplay was augmented by a few one-liners from Donald Ogden Stewart. But if there were several cooks, Selznick was the one who planned the menu and inspected the kitchen daily. *The Prisoner of Zenda* joins *A Tale of Two Cities, Rebecca, David Copperfield* and *The Garden of Allah* in the list of his productions 'in a tradition of excellence', all harking back to the European heritage of light literature. Like the others, it seems these days a shade rusty in its technique and somewhat too humble in its genuflections before the original material. A few more direct cuts instead of Cromwell's interminable fade-outs and fade-ins would have sharpened up the narrative considerably, and he is less nimble than one once thought in moving his camera. Yet there is no gainsaying the care, the cost, or the exact rightness of the approach, the feeling at the end that one has witnessed a hundred minutes of absorbing escapist entertainment which one need not be ashamed to have enjoyed.

The royal mood is captured from the order of the credits.

THE PRISONER OF ZENDA. The false king takes advice. C. Aubrey Smith, Ronald Colman, David Niven

THE PRISONER OF ZENDA

David O. Selznick presents
RONALD COLMAN
in a picturization of
the celebrated novel

An introduction then sets the scene: 'Towards the end of the last century, when history still wore a rose, and politics had not yet outgrown the waltz, a royal scandal was whispered in the anterooms of Europe . . .' The plot is set forth in a few swift narrative strokes. Assorted railway passengers and officials are seen staring open-mouthed at the newly arrived Rassendyll before we see him for ourselves; even then we don't know the reason until on the way out he passes a poster on which the camera lingers. It looks like Rassendyll but is in fact King Rudolph V. Cut to a forest, and Rassendyll happily asleep under a tree, viewed by us between two pairs of army boots. The unmistakable voice of Aubrey Smith says: 'Shave him, and he'd be the king.' It is the old soldier Sapt who for the noblest of motives conceives the great deception: 'As a man grows old he begins to believe in fate. Fate sent you here. Fate sends you now to Strelsau.' So to the coronation, with only a single sign of production economy, when one line of trumpeting heralds becomes two by means of a reverse optical. By the time of the ballroom scene we believe we are really living in June 1897, as the camera tracks incredibly further and further backwards to cover the entrance of Colman and Carroll down an immense marble stairway and between hundreds of enthusiastic courtiers. And when the amateur actor meets the king's villainous half-brother he is confidently in character: 'My dear Michael, I had no idea you were being kept waiting. Why was I not informed? I am most scandalously served.'

But soon the mood grows ruefully heroic, as the king is kidnapped by Hentzau and held at knife point in the impregnable fortress of Zenda, from which rescue is a matter of iron nerve and delicate judgement. The lines grow more curt and epigrammatic: 'One king is enough for any kingdom.' 'If that door is forced, you're not to be alive to tell it.' 'I haven't lived like a king; perhaps I can die like one.' And so the rousing and suspenseful climax, which is all that any schoolboy can desire, especially as the scheming but smiling Hentzau is allowed to escape with his skin after a few more lines of banter:

HENTZAU: You're a man after my own heart, Rassendyll. Frankly, we're the only two worth saving out of this entire affair . . . What did they teach you on the playing fields of England?
RASSENDYLL: Chiefly not to throw knives at other people's backs. Bad-tempered fellow, aren't you, underneath the charm?
HENTZAU: Why don't you let me kill you quietly?
RASSENDYLL: Oh, noise always adds a little cheer.

One regrets the loss of endpapers which were shot and discarded, with the aged Rassendyll in a London club receiving news of Flavia's death. As it is, the final renunciation scene lets down the pace a little, though the heart soars as Colman gallops up the hill, pauses on the crest and disappears into the final fade-out. It's a Prince Charming exit for what has after all been a Cinderella story; and the sense of unreality is underlined not only by the lack of explanation for Rassendyll's being able to speak such fluent Ruritanian, but by the fact that all three heroes, Colman, Smith and Niven, were leading members of the Hollywood cricket team.

The Prisoner of Zenda. US 1937; monochrome; 101 minutes. Produced by David O. Selznick for his own company. Written by John Balderston, Wells Root and Donald Ogden Stewart, from the novel by Anthony Hope. Directed by John Cromwell (and W. S. Van Dyke). Photographed by James Wong Howe. Music score by Alfred Newman. Art direction by Lyle Wheeler. Edited by Hal C. Kern and James E. Newcom. With Ronald Colman as Rudolph Rassendyll/King Rudolph V; Madeleine Carroll as Princess Flavia; Douglas Fairbanks Jnr as Rupert of Hentzau; C. Aubrey Smith as Colonel Sapt; David Niven as Fritz von Tarlenheim; Mary Astor as Antoinette de Mauban; Raymond Massey as Black Michael.

It Begins with a B
Pygmalion

For a wager, a professor of phonetics teaches a cockney flower girl all the social graces, and falls in love with his creation.

When *Pygmalion* played its first local run at the Bolton Odeon in 1938, I had measles. On my regular weekly visits to that palatial hall I had been fascinated for some time by the life-size cut-outs which stood on either side of the paybox, one of Eliza Dolittle before the transformation – a grimy and socially undesirable creature in an atrocious black hat – the other of the same Miss Dolittle afterwards, in white satin with a glittering tiara topping her noble brow. When I asked my mother the meaning of this, she replied that the story was of a guttersnipe transformed into a duchess, and that it must be excellent because it was by George Bernard Shaw, who was known never to write rubbish. I nodded approval and interest, though I imagined at first that the transformation would be accomplished by the waving of a magician's wand; only when I staggered home from the library with the collected works of said Shaw did I understand it to be a matter of speech training. Mother was somewhat less forthcoming when I asked the meaning of the teaser ads which were shortly spattered all over town, reading either *Miss Pygmalion? Not **** Likely!* or less succinctly: *Miss Wendy Hiller as Eliza? Not Pygmalion Likely!* She was pleased enough that I was reading the play and would thus find out for myself: she was simply reluctant personally to take on the task. I barely noticed the swear word: I was more concerned at the discovery that Higgins does not get Eliza in the end. In the play Shaw leaves everything up in the air, adding for readers only a postscript which can't very well satisfy theatregoers. Used to films which purported to represent literary works and in fact kept little more than the title, I felt sure that the forthcoming attraction would handle matters differently. With Shaw's approval, indeed it did, though so strong was the author's contract in this case that a more romantic conclusion was the only concession he made.

As the longest queues of the decade were predicted, I planned to meet my mother after school on the Monday and get the tram straight down to the Odeon; eating was unimportant on such an occasion. And then came the dratted measles, and I was in bed for ten days while visitors came to tell me (from a safe distance) how much they and their friends had enjoyed *Pygmalion*, even though one or two professed to have been mildly shocked. Mother went herself one afternoon, and came back blushing slightly but confident in her view that Miss Hiller was a splendid young woman, that Leslie Howard was the epitome of English gentlemen (she'd have been shocked to know he was Hungarian) and that I was quite old enough to enjoy the picture and wouldn't be harmed by it at all. (She had momentarily forgotten that I had read and savoured it twice.) Alas, runs of more than one week, however successful the picture, were unknown in 1938, so there was nothing to be done but wait impatiently for the second run, which came within a month. The Embassy, a strategically placed bijou with a steep rake parallel to the drop in Bridge Street (the site gave Boot's the Chemist some problems when they took it over) advertised it as occupying a whole week, something unique in the history of this threepenny three-day house which specialized in first run junk and, when such was unobtainable, exploitation revivals, of, say, *Frankenstein* and *Dracula* or *The Vampire Bat* and *The Monster Walks*. At this stage my filmgoing had still to be accompanied, and on this occasion my father volunteered to take me on a Saturday afternoon; he wasn't much of a fan, but as a prominent local Tory he had a healthy respect for the wit of Bernard Shaw, who was of the opposite persuasion. We had to queue for quite a while, but it was reasonably fine and the Embassy was advertising six continuous shows a day, so we got in at about three-thirty. I remember the excitement with which I followed the flickering torch to two excellent seats on the right. *Pygmalion* was nearly over, and I had barely time to relish the shot of Higgins in his trilby hat leaning back in his rocking chair and asking for his slippers before the end title flashed onto the screen and – here came our astonishment – was immediately followed by the censor's certificate heralding the next performance of the film. That was the Embassy's way of covering its no doubt expensive film rental; nothing else was showing at all. No newsreel, no cartoon, and even more oddly, no advertisements or sales interval. Everything was geared to shovelling the queues in and out as fast as possible. There was even a slide: *In view of the queues waiting outside, patrons are requested to leave as soon as they have seen the full programme.* (They projected this over the main titles.) Full programme indeed! I seethed at the thought of Dad's hard-earned sixpence wasted, for he usually enjoyed the newsreel more than the film. I couldn't even understand how they'd worked the trick, for knowing nothing of reels I ignorantly imagined that there must be two full prints and two sets of projection apparatus.

In the circumstances, and considering the suspiciously ratlike smell which even then had begun to infest the Embassy, I enjoyed the film thoroughly. Being an infant English scholar myself, I felt a swell of pride that proper pronunciation, so ignored in everyday life, could become the subject of an absorbing entertainment for all heights of brow. (The swear word was no hindrance: the shocked but delighted reaction to it that Saturday afternoon must have rippled on for well over a minute, drowning the rest of the scene.) Shaw knew that people in those days wanted to better themselves; his neatest trick was merely to sugar the pill. Throughout his play, and especially in the complex character of Dolittle the dustman, he scatters crumbs for the intellectuals, but most of it can be enjoyed as pure comedy of insult on the level of *The Man Who Came to Dinner*. He must also have congratulated himself on the casting of the lovable but professional Leslie Howard, whose relish for the softly spoken word was second to none. Wendy Hiller was not only a revelation but a Lancashire lass, which made us cheer her all the more. Add to them Marie Lohr, as Higgins' imperturbably aristocratic but kindly mother; Scott Sunderland, as Colonel Pickering the most gentlemanly of feeds, and Esmé Percy as the dangerous knowall Aristide

PYGMALION. Professor Higgins reproves his new pupil

Karpathy (invented for the film); and you have a princely cast even without consideration of Wilfrid Lawson's rich rococo warblings as the dustman who, one of the undeserving poor, betters himself despite his own best intentions. His grimy teeth, rolling eyes, wheezing laugh and plainly foul breath are part of a creation as unforgettable as a Walt Disney cartoon, and of course he has some of Shaw's ripest language:

DOLITTLE: The truth is, I've taken a sort of fancy to you, guvnor. And if you want the girl I'm not so set on having her back home again that I might not be open to an arrangement. Regarded in the light of a young woman, she's a fine handsome girl. As a daughter she's not worth her keep; and so I tell you straight. All I asks is my rights as a father; and you're the last man alive to expect me to let her go for nothing; for I see you're one of the straight sort, guvnor. Well, what's a five pound note to you? And what's Eliza to me?

PICKERING: I think you ought to know, Dolittle, that Mr Higgins' intentions are entirely honourable.

DOLITTLE: Course they are, guvnor. If I thought they wasn't I'd ask fifty.

I have said nothing so far about the unobtrusive technical expertise with which this film is assembled. Apart from a couple of fine montages, it contents itself with getting actors and objects to the spots where they can be photographed to the best advantage; it is unfussy but precise and somewhat intellectual, so that one recognizes the presence of fine minds. Honegger's unique music sets it off perfectly. The sheer all-round excellence of the presentation is the more marked by comparison with the musical version which was marketed twenty-five years later under the title *My Fair Lady*, with opulent sets, excellent songs and a bottomless budget. Twice the length of *Pygmalion*, it is in dramatic terms about half as good, its lapses compounded by miscasting, by the inevitable longueurs produced by its anamorphic ratio, by an air of theatrical stateliness and by direction which seems content to hover over the sixth row of the stalls. Eye-popping it may be, but it isn't *Pygmalion*.

That unlikely impresario Gabriel Pascal talked Shaw into three other versions of his plays. Only the first, *Major Barbara*, is of any real interest. As a fantasia on religion and politics, it is harder tack than *Pygmalion*, but its right royal cast ensures that the debates are not unbearably prolonged. I remember *Picture Post* headlining a feature 'British Studios Find a New Kind of Man', and wondering hopefully whether this might be a creature with three legs; but it was only Robert Newton stealing the show as the blustering bully Bill Walker whom audiences loved to hate, either because he was 'the bloke who hit poor Jenny 'ill in the marf' or for repeating his much imitated taunt to the Salvationists for accepting the bribes of Mammon, 'Wot prawce selvytion nah?' (We are indebted to Mr Shaw for this authorized phonetic version.) But also on hand were Rex Harrison banging a drum; and Robert Morley as the armaments king, at twenty-nine as Poohbah-ish as he is now, and at the end providing me with a favourite catch phrase, 'Six o'clock tomorrow morning, Euripides'. When you add Sybil Thorndike and Marie Lohr and Stanley Holloway and Deborah Kerr and Donald Calthrop you have almost a theatrical who's who; but the entertainment remained excessively talkative. The futuristic factory finale gave it some appeal to the groundlings, but by now the war was on and more pressing social matters had to be considered.

Wendy Hiller, of course, was the perfect Barbara, autocratic in her pride and moving in her self-reproach. I loved her more passionately than ever. I met her only once, nearly thirty years later in Hollywood, when she failed to get an Oscar for *A Man for All Seasons* but accepted one for Paul Scofield. She was wearing a high-necked silk gown of vaguely Chinese design, and looked ravishing. We were out there to get interviews for a programme called *Cinema*, and she spoke to us for a minute or two from the runway along which all winners and presenters must proceed after their appearance in order to meet the press. When it was all over, and she stood outside in the night air awaiting her car, I was quite close as fans in the bleachers strained over the ropes to clamour for her autograph. After trying to ignore them she eventually relented, but not before shooting them a sharp reproof: 'Have you really any idea who I am?' And the sad thing was that nine out of ten of them clearly didn't.

Pygmalion. GB 1938; monochrome; 96 minutes. Produced by Gabriel Pascal. Written by Cecil Lewis, Ian Dalrymple, Anthony Asquith and W. P. Lipscomb from the play by Bernard Shaw. Directed by Anthony Asquith and Leslie Howard. Photographed by Harry Stradling. Music score by Arthur Honegger. Art direction by Laurence Irving. Edited by David Lean. With Leslie Howard as Professor Henry Higgins; Wendy Hiller as Eliza Dolittle; Wilfrid Lawson as Dolittle; Scott Sunderland as Colonel Pickering; Marie Lohr as Mrs Higgins; Esmé Percy as Aristide Karpathy; Jean Cadell as Mrs Pearce; David Tree as Freddy; Everley Gregg as Mrs Eynsford-Hill.

The Art of Adaptation
Quartet

Somerset Maugham introduces four of his stories.

In 1948 television had barely touched our lives: Alfred Hitchcock had not thought of presenting anything except one big screen film a year, and Douglas Fairbanks Jnr was regarded as an amiably ageing swashbuckler rather than as a purveyor of tele-playlets by the yard. Those who had a set in their living-rooms were considered either ostentatious or foolhardy, for the entertainment it provided was mainly raucous, the state of the art undeniably primitive. So there was still an eager and appreciative audience for the cinema's latest elegant gimmick: a civilized evening with one of our celebrated literary lions during which he would regale us with four of his neatly turned stories. As television has subsequently been turning out precisely this kind of entertainment for more than thirty years, it is not possible to view *Quartet* in the rarefied atmosphere which attended its première, and certainly not to recapture the immense pleasure it gave me personally, as a contrast to my army life, when I caught up with it at the Cosham Odeon; but at least two of its four anecdotes still present sharp-flavoured screen versions of their amusing originals.

'The Facts of Life', which served as appetizer, actually seemed rather daring at the time, though nobody actually went to bed with anybody. It concerns a well-brought-up young tennis player who goes off to Monte Carlo for a tournament and is warned by his father not to gamble or to have anything to do with women. He does both, and comes up trumps, for when his willing hostess for the night gets up just before dawn to steal his wallet and hide it under a plant pot, he quietly retrieves it before he leaves and finds on the plane that he has picked up her savings as well as his winnings. As his father in perturbation tells his cronies, 'He doesn't see that it was just a fluke. He thinks it was all his own cleverness. It may ruin him. You fellows are men of the world. What am I to do about it?'

The story has been told over bridge at the club, and the anxious father is played by Basil Radford. Ian Fleming is allowed to give him the advice with which Maugham's original story finishes: 'Well, if you want my advice you'll have a drink and forget all about it. My belief is the boy's born lucky, and in the long run that's better than being born clever or rich.' But the film has Naunton Wayne also present to bring back happy memories of his sporting comedy partnership with Radford in *The Lady Vanishes* and a dozen other movies. So he has the last word: 'If you don't mind my saying so I think it's a shame you let him take up tennis. That sort of thing would never have happened to a cricketer.'

The principal virtue of this playlet however is the super-glamorous, almost electrically-charged presence of Mai Zetterling as the high-class casino tart. Oozing sex from every pore, but immensely presentable as the ambassador's wife she claims to be, she even makes a virtue of the censor's blue pencil by standing impudently over young Nicky's uncomfortable sofa bed, which he has volunteered to occupy, and asking with a note of wide-eyed surprise: 'Are you sure you have everything you need?' And of course, this being 1948, he has.

'The Alien Corn' is about a family of Jews who pretend to be frightfully English county. When the rather aimless and stuffy young son discovers his true inheritance he develops an artistic temperament to go with it, and shoots himself when he finds that he will never be more than a moderate pianist. The Jewishness is entirely removed by the film (the Americans might have already produced *Gentleman's Agreement*, but British studios weren't yet up to that sort of thing), and with it went the richness of characterization, half the point of the story, and all the significance of the title, leaving a drab and self-conscious little tale about unbelievable people, enlivened only by Françoise Rosay's appearance as the great pianist who comes to the family seat to give her opinion.

'The Kite' is one of Maugham's more regrettable ventures into the lower-middle-class milieu which he understood not at all. It presents, through the account of a prison visitor, the tall tale of a marriage which breaks up irrevocably when the wife smashes her husband's kite: she has long been jealous of his passion, shared with his parents, for this Saturday sport, and rather than pay her maintenance he goes to prison and stays there. The anecdote chiefly revolves around Hermione Baddeley as his awful mum, a caricatured inverted snob, and it now entertains rather less than it embarrasses.

The prime ingredient in the portmanteau is 'The Colonel's Lady'. It features a clubbable middle-aged man, the possessor of a slightly stately home in Warwickshire and a luscious mistress in Piccadilly, who is both perplexed and embarrassed when his dull-seeming wife writes a best-selling volume of passionate poetry all too clearly based on an extremely physical passion with a man much younger than herself, a man who has caused her much grief by dying. Apart from the percipience of the story and the convincing detail with which it works itself out, much entertainment comes from the playing of a long line of British character actors led by Cecil Parker, here splendidly delineating a man whose contempt for the arts is exceeded only by his ignorance, as shown in his encounter with an egghead critic played by Ernest Thesiger:

DASHWOOD: I was simply bowled over by your wife's book. It's fresh and original, very modern without being obscure.

COLONEL: Yes, I suppose it is.

DASHWOOD: She seems as much at ease in free verse as in classical metre. In fact I'd go so far as to say that some of those short lyrics of hers might have been written by Landor.

COLONEL: Really?

DASHWOOD: But what makes the book so outstanding is the passion that throbs in every line . . . naked, earthy passion. Ah, my dear colonel, how right Heine was when he said that the poet makes little songs out of great sorrows! You know, now and then as I read these heart-rending pages, I thought of Sappho.

COLONEL (*seizing a chance to escape*): Well, it's jolly nice of you to say such nice things about my wife's little book. I'm sure she'll be delighted. (*Sotto voce:*) Idiot!

Maugham's story ends when the colonel takes his lawyer friend's advice to bluff out the situation and pretend he is proud of his wife: 'I suppose you're right. But there's one thing I'll never understand to my dying day. What in the name of heaven did the fellow ever see in her?' In order to satisfy the groundlings the film takes one further step towards a happy ending, by having the colonel blurt out his unhappiness to his wife, only to be told that the mysterious lover was himself as she remembered him, before he grew stodgy. It works well enough, and permits a final clinch and a swell of romantic music, but one is a shade surprised that the urbane and influential Mr Maugham seems so pleased with what has been done to temper his stings for the mass audience, and also that he allowed the lengthy on-camera links which he stammeringly filmed (culling his remarks from his autobiography *The Summing Up*) to be edited down for general release into one short introductory paragraph.

Adaptation is one of the new arts of the twentieth century, and in this case it was in the highly respectable hands of R. C. Sherriff, an observant if unspectacular writer whose immense success with *Journey's End* in 1929 perhaps obscured in the public eye his subsequent deftness as a writer of West End plays perpetuating the British upper-middle-class milieu and of a number of films taking generally the same direction: *Goodbye Mr Chips, The Dam Busters, Odd Man Out, No Highway, The October Man*. In his delightful autobiography *No Leading Lady* (he never married, and took his mother everywhere with him) he describes with quiet relish how in 1933 he was beckoned to Hollywood to adapt H. G. Wells' *The Invisible Man*

QUARTET. Colonel Peregrine at a cocktail party finds himself among revolting highbrows. John Salew, Felix Aylmer, Cecil Parker

into a film. For anyone at all interested in how books become movies, these chapters are essential reading. The story editor at Universal handed Sherriff fourteen different scripts called *The Invisible Man*, but when the writer timidly asked for a copy of the original novel the man barely remembered that there had been one, and assured Sherriff that his fourteen minions must have sucked all the juice out of it. As one of the scripts set the story in the Russian revolution, Sherriff was unconvinced, and began to scour Los Angeles' second-hand bookshops, finally obtaining a copy for fifteen cents from a tray of greasy volumes outside a Chinese greengrocer's. Determined to keep not only Wells' storyline but his marvellous English village humour, he finally produced a script which delighted expatriate English director James Whale; his fear then was that Universal would refuse to pay for something so close to the novel. But Sherriff's faithful pages were hailed by everyone from Carl Laemmle down as a work of original genius.

After *Quartet* two other Maugham compendiums were made, with three stories in each, but which was called *Trio* and which *Encore* is hard to remember. Personally I rated highly the 45-minute adaptation of 'Sanatorium', faithful to Maugham's recollections of the time he had TB and was sent to Scotland, where he watched with wry detachment not only his own medical progress, but the quirks of the assorted types grappling with what was then normally a fatal disease. 'Mr Knowall' gave Nigel Patrick a chance to shine as a shipboard dago bore who proved enough of a gentleman to lose face rather than reveal a lady's deception; 'Winter Cruise' sent on a voyage a twittering English lady who so rattled the crew that they deputed a young engineer to silence her by sleeping with her. 'The Ant and the Grasshopper' was a commendably brief opener, but 'Gigolo and Gigolette' showed Maugham out of his element again, dealing with backstage passions at the circus and not helped by a heavily unconvincing matte shot of a dangerous trapeze dive. Of them all, 'The Verger' was perhaps the most precisely pointed, even if its story was borrowed from Gogol. Here a middle-aged church official is fired when it is discovered that he can neither read nor write. On his despondent way home he finds himself out of tobacco and realizes the lack of supply in this particular area. So he opens a shop, and success is so instant that before long he owns a thriving chain, all in cannily selected sites. Later his lawyer incredulously discovers his deficiency:

LAWYER: Do you mean to say that you've built up this important business and amassed a fortune of thirty thousand pounds without being able to read or write? Good God, man, what would you be now if you had been able to?

MR FOREMAN: I can tell you that, sir. I'd be verger of St Peter's, Nevill Square.

Here at least was a Maugham ending which permitted no improvement.

Quartet. GB 1948; monochrome; 120 minutes. Produced by Sydney Box and Antony Darnborough for Gainsborough and Rank release. Written by R. C. Sherriff from stories by W. Somerset Maugham. Directed by Ralph Smart ('The Facts of Life'); Harold French ('The Alien Corn'); Arthur Crabtree ('The Kite'); Ken Annakin ('The Colonel's Lady'). Photographed by Ray Elton (first three) and Reg Wyer. Music score by John Greenwood.

Skeleton in the Cupboard
Rebecca

An inexperienced girl marries a wealthy Cornish widower and on taking up residence at his mansion is haunted by the memory of his dominating first wife.

In writing these notes I have become more than previously aware that my preference is for films which, though some of them may be based on real places and important truths, are strained through the mesh of Hollywood's magic machinery, with the added lustre of gleaming, impressionist black-and-white photography which distances them still further from reality and sometimes accords to a mere entertainment the status of a myth. Recently the BBC produced a perfectly creditable four-hour televersion of *Rebecca*, made in and near a real stately home and much more faithful than the film version to the letter of the novel. But when the title is mentioned, it is the 1940 film which comes to mind, because it is the film which has remained most vivid in its appeal to the eye and ear. Care was taken in it to eliminate unnecessary details and get all the necessary ones absolutely right; performances were rehearsed and reshot until every nuance of the characters was on the screen. David O. Selznick's ambition in all his films from literary originals was to get as much as possible of the spirit rather than the letter of the book onto the screen, and he was certainly successful here despite the fact that he had to change the central revelation: the Hays Office would not allow Maxim de Winter to be a murderer and go free. So careful was the reworking that most fans of the novel were not even aware of the change; given a choice, they would probably have preferred the Selznick version anyway.

Under the closest technical scrutiny *Rebecca* may now seem lacking in certain respects. Manderley exists only as a model; and for a story hinging on the closeness of the sea we see very little of that element. But that is the trick of great film-making, the trick of making you think you have seen more than you have, of withholding a central element and making the audience's imagination work. For these reasons Daphne du Maurier never gave her heroine a first name; nor does the film. And Rebecca is never seen, because no actress could possibly live up to the audience's expectation of a goddess who must also be a monster. Yet many people who claim to have been enraptured by the film, if asked who played Rebecca, would search their memories and hazard a guess, because in their own imagination she was made to exist.

Every filmgoer of the right age remembers the opening shot of the great gates opening by night and the winding overgrown drive unfolding as the narrator intones: 'Last night I dreamed I went to Manderley again.' Then comes our first view of the great house across the lawn, illuminated by moonlight stealing across it. It can't destroy the spell now to know that the whole scene was shot on a table top; after all, it was the best table top money could buy, and Selznick was spinning a yarn with all the resources at a major studio's command. The BBC only showed us a great house, which we ourselves could see any weekend for 75 pence.

In my selections for this book it seems I can't resist giving first prominence to the works of Alfred Hitchcock. However, I think of *Rebecca* as more Selznick's than Hitchcock's; even though it shows Hitch in full creative flow and at the top of his technical form, it is far from typical of his interests. It was the film for which he first went to Hollywood, and he had to show what he could do. He did first offer a treatment which Selznick discarded more in sorrow than in anger; apparently it started off with the characters being seasick. So Hitch gave in gracefully and played Selznick's game. Like Welles the same year, he was not only paid handsomely but given 'the biggest toy train any boy ever had to play with'; and he used it to the full. The result is one of the most accomplished adult entertainments in film history. Long it is, plot-bound it is, and there are stretches when the gauche behaviour of the inexperienced heroine is irritating to say the least. Yet we view it with pleasure time and time again because the story is told with such masterly professionalism. The rewards are comparable with those of reading a great book in a particularly fine binding.

The opening half hour is in any case marvellously funny, thanks to Florence Bates' snappy portrayal of the dragon-like Mrs Van Hopper, chiding her companion for her shyness in front of their distinguished English fellow guest at the best hotel in Monte Carlo:

REBECCA. Maxim de Winter is furious, and his wife doesn't know why. Joan Fontaine, Laurence Olivier, Gladys Cooper, Reginald Denny

MRS VAN HOPPER: Most girls would give their eyes to see Monte.
MAXIM: Wouldn't that rather defeat the purpose?

Even when he takes her out for a spin, the anonymous heroine thinks he is humouring her:

'I': Oh, I wish I were thirty-five and dressed in black satin.
MAXIM: You would not be with me in this car if you were.

After the wedding and the arrival at Manderley the narrative takes a sombre turn as the heroine learns something of the responsibilities she has taken on and is played with mercilessly, as a cat with a mouse, by the stiff and unyielding housekeeper Mrs Danvers, who loved her former mistress with what seems like more than normal devotion, and still secretly entertains Rebecca's extremely unpleasant cousin Jack Favell. Things seem brighter when Max's hearty cousins Giles and Beatrice persuade the increasingly gloomy and self-torturing Maxim to revive the Manderley ball, though we sense something nasty in the woodshed when Mrs Danvers is unexpectedly helpful in choosing the bride's dress, and of course it turns out to be a replica of the one Rebecca wore at her last ball. The young wife's suicide, urged by the frightful Mrs D, is averted only by rockets signalling the discovery of a wreck in the bay. It is Rebecca's boat, with Rebecca's body still in it, and suddenly the child bride becomes a mature woman, coping with the possibility that her husband will be charged with murder:

'I': How could we be close when I knew you were comparing me with Rebecca? How could I even ask you to love me when I knew you loved Rebecca still?

MAXIM: You thought I loved Rebecca? You thought I killed her, loving her? I hated her! She was incapable of love, or tenderness, or decency.

This is fine Gothic stuff, and no observant reader will have failed to notice the similarities to *Jane Eyre*: gloomy and mature landowner, great house, mysterious first wife. It doesn't matter: before it's over we shall feel as purged as if we have been witnessing Greek tragedy. The pace becomes swifter as we are carried through revelation after revelation, culminating in a record-breaking drive to London, where Rebecca's doctor indicates that she had cancer and may have committed suicide; then back to Manderley to discover that Mrs Danvers, having heard the news, has set the house ablaze. ('That's not the northern lights, that's Manderley!')

Especially notable in this film is Hitch's careful control of his comedy elements. There are many amusing lines, but the story is played absolutely straight, with no winking at the audience and no narrative tricks which draw attention to themselves. Stills exist showing Hitch in his accustomed walk-on part, waiting for George Sanders to emerge from a phone booth; but the shot will not be found in any finished print, for it came too close to the end, and a laugh of recognition would have spoiled the tension.

As for the actors, each is handpicked. Olivier is perhaps a shade too young, but otherwise perfectly lifelike as the mercurial and guilt-ridden hero; he wanted Vivien Leigh as his bride, but one doubts whether she could have convinced as a weakling, and Joan Fontaine, with her ambience of jerseys and pearls and sensible shoes, certainly gave the performance of a lifetime. The obvious casting for Mrs Danvers must have been Gale Sondergaard, but that poor lady was decidedly overexposed in sinister housekeeper roles, of which at that time Hollywood had plenty. Selznick preferred to fetch Judith Anderson from the Broadway stage, and her subtleties are all the more evident when compared with the wide-eyed hysteria of Anna Massey in the BBC version. Similarly the sliminess of Favell could have been left in no better hands than those of George Sanders. The BBC, noting that the character was a car salesman, cast Julian Holloway, who might have been all right for second-hand Volkswagens, but Favell traded in Rolls-Royces. Reginald Denny, Gladys Cooper and Nigel Bruce incomparably filled out the film's ranks of the upper crust, and at a late stage C. Aubrey Smith marched on as the no-nonsense chief constable:

COL. JULYAN: Let me tell you, Favell, blackmail is not much of a profession, and we know how to deal with it in our part of the world – strange as it may seem to you.
FAVELL: I'm sure I don't know what you're talking about, but if you ever need a new car, Colonel, just let me know.

Finally, as a special turn at the end, Hitch's favourite character actor Leo G. Carroll filled the role of the mysterious doctor, with exactly the correct note of professional discretion.

Even at forty years' remove, it is pleasant to contemplate the vivid impression all these characters made on me when I first sat enthralled through *Rebecca* at the Bolton Lido, though I believe I was slightly disappointed that the ghostly presence of Rebecca herself, suggested on the poster, never showed up in the film. Still, Mum and I went at least twice during the unprecedented run of a fortnight; apart from the sheer enjoyment the film provided, it seemed the well-bred thing to do.

Rebecca. US 1940; monochrome; 130 minutes. Produced by David O. Selznick for his own company. Written by Robert E. Sherwood and Joan Harrison, from the novel by Daphne du Maurier. Directed by Alfred Hitchcock. Photographed by George Barnes. Music score by Franz Waxman. Art direction by Lyle Wheeler. Edited by Hal C. Kern. With Joan Fontaine as Mrs de Winter; Laurence Olivier as Maxim de Winter; Judith Anderson as Mrs Danvers; Reginald Denny as Frank Crawley; Nigel Bruce as Giles Lacy; Gladys Cooper as Beatrice Lacy; George Sanders as Jack Favell; Florence Bates as Mrs Van Hopper; C. Aubrey Smith as Colonel Julyan; Melville Cooper as Coroner; Edward Fielding as Frith; Leo G. Carroll as Dr Baker; Leonard Carey as Ben.

Gotta Dance, Gotta Dance
The Red Shoes

A young ballerina, dazzled by success and torn between love and ballet, throws herself under a train.

The years have not diminished this cornerstone of J. Arthur Rank's 'art gallery' of the forties. After the flop of *Caesar and Cleopatra*, dire forebodings were voiced about the commercial chances of a ballet film, but the rare elements in it fused to make a box-office wonder, as much in the States as in Europe. I saw it on a glum autumn day when I was in the army on Salisbury Plain, at a cinema curiously set in the innards of a medieval banqueting house. The glimpse it proffered into an intensely private world was overwhelming: I did not understand the compulsion to dance, and probably still don't, but I emerged full of respect for the fanatical dedication, the triumphing over physical discomfort, and the brilliant talent required to make a ballet star. Luckily prints can still be obtained which duplicate the original glowing colours required to clothe the theme in scintillating raiment.

The least satisfactory part of the entertainment is the plot, conveyed above in one sentence which makes one wince to write it. For well over an hour there is no plot at all, just an account of the success in this strange world of a young dancer played with great delicacy by Moira Shearer and a young composer played in sickly make-up by Marius Goring as an unabashed boor. As soon as they marry, he changes character so radically as to demand that she give up her art to iron his shirts. She decides to leave him instead, but when he reappears in her Monte Carlo dressing-room just before curtain up, sulking like a spoilt schoolboy and not unnaturally evoking a few harsh words from her temperamental impresario, she goes suddenly to pieces and throws herself over a convenient balustrade into the path of a passing train. There is an indication that we are supposed to believe that in doing so she was possessed by her red dancing shoes, as was the heroine of the ballet she was about to perform, based on the Hans Andersen fairy tale; but the film has given no prior warning that we are about to plunge into this kind of fantasy, so it is not effective; nor is the shot of Miss Shearer expiring amid globbets of tomato ketchup. It is as though Powell and Pressburger, having explored every nook and cranny of the ballet world to their satisfaction, had decided that since the end had to come somehow, it might as well be this way as not. But however unsatisfactory it may be from the point of good taste as well as drama, it does provide two memorable brief moments. The first is only fleeting, as Miss Shearer's dresser realizes that her mistress is going to kill herself and runs off arms outstretched in one direction to get help, just as Shearer dances off arms outstretched in the other: there is something impressionist and disturbing in the mirror image. The second is the opportunity it affords for Anton Walbrook's speech before the deep red curtains of the theatre, a speech shouted at the audience through barely-controlled tears: 'Ladies and gentlemen – I'm sorry to tell you – that Miss Page – is unable to dance – tonight. Nor indeed – on any other night. Nevertheless – we have decided to present *The Red Shoes* – it is the ballet that made her name, whose name she made. We present it – because we think – she would have wished it.'

It doesn't sound much on paper, but it has to be experienced through the dark genius of Walbrook's performance, every word apparently torn by its roots from his reluctant larynx and twisted through his Germanic pronunciation which turns gentlemen into shentlemen and the title of the ballet into something that sounds like *Zeredshussssss* . . . His presentation of the word 'nevertheless' is also something special, accompanied by flailing helpless arms and the suggestion of a facial tic. It is a good thing however that we are treated to only a few frames of the ensuing stage performance, in which a moving spotlight replaces the leading lady; it is an impractical idea from which we are mercifully protected by the end title.

Having got the last five minutes out of the way, we can affirm that the rest of the film is all pleasure, except perhaps for the title cards, in which bald non-serif lettering accords badly with the film's artistic pretensions. We open on the dingy upper circle staircase at Covent Garden as half berserk students rush to occupy the uncomfortable seats after queueing for six hours. The film carefully sets up all the characters before the curtain rises. The ballet stars limbering up nervously backstage. Shearer in a box with her aunt, who is

THE RED SHOES. A symbolic grouping. Massine's attention is all for Art but Walbrook and Shearer seem to have divided loyalties

trying to persuade Lermontov to watch her perform. Lermontov hiding behind the curtains of a stage box, wagging a finger to indicate non-acceptance of her invitation. And Goring in the upper circle increasingly livid that the music being played has been stolen from him. As Massine peeps through the curtain at the distinguished audience, and a girl in the front row of the balcony nearly falls over at a glimpse of Lermontov, there is magic in the air.

Eventually Lermontov meets the young heroine at a party:

LERMONTOV: Why do you want to dance?
VICKI: Why do you want to live?
LERMONTOV: I don't know exactly, but I must.
VICKI: That's my answer too.

Later, before giving her her big chance, he expands his theme:

LERMONTOV: I want something more – I want to create. I want to make something big out of something little. But first I must ask you the same question. What do you want of life? To love?
VICKI: To dance!

The role of the lofty, reclusive impresario is a magnificent one for Walbrook, whether lording it in a fading stuccoed villa high above the Mediterranean, flopping around a hotel room in a multi-coloured kaftan and suede shoes, or impeccably attired for rehearsal in dark glasses, black suit and spats.

The main achievement of Powell and Pressburger in this film is to make us look at people through fresh eyes, and to give us a series of vivid impressions of a world which few of us will enter. Massine donning a hair net. Miscellaneous activity in the corners of the Covent Garden labyrinth. The designer (82-year-old Albert Basserman in his last role) in tears because his door has been ruined. The egomania and delusions of grandeur so inseparable from great talent. ('What we have created tonight the whole world will be talking about tomorrow morning.') The transition from overnight triumph to the cold rehearsal room next morning, with the old star taunting the young one. ('*Ça va?* Any swelling? I mean the head.') The chaos of a press conference interrupted by telephone calls and administrative problems. Above all the great and typical Archers moment when a dramatic highlight combines with a piece of technical bravura: Vicki is dancing *Swan Lake* on a wet Saturday afternoon at the tiny Mercury Theatre, and the camera pirouettes with her before fixing on a close-up of Lermontov in the audience, followed by one of Vicki's startled, red-framed eyes.

The central *Ballet of the Red Shoes* is an entertainment I am scarcely qualified to judge. It is pleasing, if rather self-consciously artistic: I have enjoyed other screen ballets better. My favourite sequence in a film overflowing with brilliant touches covers the evening when Vicki receives from Lermontov a curt note: 'I hope you are free this evening: my car will call for you at eight.' The impression of a warm Mediterranean evening is only slightly marred by the fact that when she emerges from her Monte Carlo hotel, dressed to kill, the sun is so clearly casting shadows from overhead that the scene must have been filmed at midday. The limousine takes her as far as it can, to the foot of an apparently endless flight of stone steps overgrown with grass. '*Montes, mademoiselle,*' says the chauffeur, and she does, her voluminous bottle-green gown and twinkling tiara outlined finally against the blue seas to the south. As she steps through a formal garden on a shoulder of the hill, the image which comes to mind is that of Cinderella arriving for the palace ball. But the house proves to be as neglected as the plants, and when she finds Lermontov he is dressed in a powder blue smock, red scarf and old trousers, discussing the future of the ballet company with his intimates. Obviously, his surprised look says, he is too busy a man to take a lady to dinner, and within two minutes she is outside again; but he has promised to make her a star. Within, his friends grudgingly admit that she is charming, but Lermontov has in his eye the gleam of the fanatic: 'I know nothing about her charms, and I care less, but I tell you this, they won't wait till the end, they'll applaud in the middle!'

His colleagues warn him not to be too disappointed if she decides to break her career for marriage. He is scornful:

LERMONTOV: The dancer who relies upon the doubtful comforts of human love will never be a great dancer.
CRASTER: That's all very well, but you can't alter human nature.
LERMONTOV: No? I think you can do even better than that. You can ignore it.

And there starts the plot, to prove him wrong.

The Red Shoes. GB 1948; Technicolor; 136 minutes. Produced, written and directed by Michael Powell and Emeric Pressburger, for Rank. Photographed by Jack Cardiff, Music score by Brian Easdale. Production designed by Hein Heckroth. With Anton Walbrook as Lermontov; Moira Shearer as Vicki; Marius Goring as Julian Craster; Albert Basserman as Ratov; Leonide Massine as Ljubov; Ludmilla Tcherina as Boronskaja; Robert Helpmann as Boleslawsky; Esmond Knight as Livy.

The Devil of an Actor
Rembrandt, Henry VIII and
The Hunchback of Notre Dame

In 1946 C. A Lejeune wrote:

One of the most painful screen phenomena of latter years has been the gradual decline and fall of Charles Laughton from the splendid actor of *The Private Life of Henry VIII, Mutiny on the Bounty* and *Rembrandt* to the mopping and mowing mug of *The Man from Down Under* . . . All that can be said is that Mr Laughton's performances in recent years seem at the best to be made up of lines and touches broken off from his old parts, and combined with the facility of an experienced actor who has long since stopped trying to get down to the core of a character, and is content to amuse himself and the audience with surface decoration.

Well, in still later years Laughton, despite a tendency to allow his already roly-poly figure to run flabbily to seed, retrieved himself somewhat with irresistible serio-comic performances in such entertainments as *Witness for the Prosecution*, *Hobson's Choice* and *Advise and Consent*, and by his sensitive and pictorial direction of *Night of the Hunter*. But in general the accusation could not be denied: his great days were behind him. The man who in the thirties had been a household word for his interpretations of some famous figures of history was now an unattractive ham, still only in his forties but condemned by the Hollywood which had been his haven during the war to vegetate among the supporting casts of inferior epics. A similar fate had befallen such as Aubrey Smith and Cedric Hardwicke, but they took to it with rather more dignity; even when cast in rotten films they refrained from such self-burlesque as Charles displayed in *The Strange Door*, making his acting partner Boris Karloff seem by comparison the very model of reticence.

The truth, we later learned, was that the great performances had come from him with great difficulty, had had to be wrested out of his unlikely physique by the strength and tact of clever directors. Some of these men also deserve medals for patience. If Charles was not in the mood he would simply not appear on the set, or pretend to have difficulty learning his lines. *I, Claudius* had to be abandoned, principally because Charles could not get himself into the part of the shuffling, stammering emperor, though when it was too late he decided he should play it like the abdication speech of Edward VIII. In the case of *Jamaica Inn* Charles insisted that his role as a lecherous mad squire should be separately rewritten by J. B. Priestley, with the result that he seemed to be performing in a different film from anyone else. He stalled however at a scene in which he has to tie up Maureen O'Hara and seem apologetic about it, and disaster was only averted when after many delays he turned up on set beaming at the exasperated Hitchcock and announcing: 'I've got it! I'll play it like a boy of ten who's just wet his pants!'

Readers are now aware, despite Elsa Lanchester's great loyalty to him over a marriage that lasted more than thirty years with many periods of happiness, of Laughton's homosexuality, which certainly contributed to his troublesome self-doubt and made him difficult to work with. Self-consciousness about it may well have caused his early withdrawal from the ranks of the superstars, though the paying public seems never to have been aware of it. A more likely handicap was sheer ignorance of his own best interests. It can't have been good for his career when in order to buy an expensive painting he accepted star billing in the cheaply-made pantomime *Abbott and Costello Meet Captain Kidd*, a clinker which didn't even have laughs to justify it.

Laughton's hangdog looks and chubby figure were initially his fortune, yet he couldn't stand to look at himself in the mirror or even to see his own performances. It was an ironic situation. While still in his twenties he was playing obese and sometimes obscene middle-aged villains and perverts; ironically it was not until he was in his forties and already misshapen of frame that he was called upon, in *The Suspect*, to play a semi-romantic role in which a good-looking girl had to fall for him and he to murder for love. It was a pill not to be swallowed by the audience. His acting was still respected, but he was preferred in heavy disguise: Laughton the actor might still be a star, but not Laughton the man. The unexpectedness of his talent had by now worn off, and Hollywood had only routine supporting roles to offer him, despite the fact that hundreds of impressionists were still getting laughs with his 'delicious debauchery' from *The Sign of the Cross* and 'cast adrift in an open boat' from *Mutiny on the Bounty*. These peaks were now more than ten years behind him, and in Hollywood nothing is more dated than the star of yesterday. He turned to his first love, the theatre, and curiously chose to tour with a rehearsed reading of Shaw's *Don Juan in Hell*. The other members of the self-styled First Drama Quartet, all equipped with evening dress and lectern, were Charles Boyer, Cedric Hardwicke and Agnes Moorehead; I rushed to book my seat when they visited the Manchester Opera House, but I needn't have bothered, for although they did nicely in American university towns, the public was wary of paying advanced prices for what looked like a rehearsal of a very boring play. I couldn't disagree: I found it a curiously stilted enterprise which showed off none of their eminent talents.

There is absolutely no doubt what made Laughton a world star in the first place: it was 1933's *The Private Life of Henry VIII*, which the Hungarian Alexander Korda had had to persuade the British to

REMBRANDT. Though furthest from the camera, the painter is the focus of this dramatic scene. Edward Chapman in black, Charles Laughton, Elsa Lanchester at right

make and which won an Academy Award for Laughton and a nomination for best picture. Unthinkable in those days for a British actor, in a British picture; and the film as a film doesn't stand up. But the performance does. This Henry is an amiable, testy monster: having a few wives beheaded seems part of some cheerful game, and his honeymoon night with Anne of Cleves (played by Elsa), still stuffing herself with food while she awaits his nightgowned approach, is outright farce which might have been written by Ben Travers.

HENRY: Did they not give you enough to eat, madam?
ANNE: Don't shout at me, just because I'm your wife.
HENRY: My wife! Not yet. We have to . . .
ANNE: What?
HENRY: Oh, well, all that stuff about children being found under gooseberry
bushes, that's not true.

ANNE: I know, It was der shtork. Der shtork flies in the air mit der babes und down der chimney drops.

HENRY: Well, no, madam, that isn't true either. Er . . . when a hen lays an egg, it's not entirely her own doing . . .

Above all, perhaps, it was the banquet scene which got Laughton his award, with the court sitting silently in fear of the sharp edge of the king's tongue while he remains morosely at the dinner table, belching loudly and tearing apart the carcass of a chicken whose half-eaten limbs he flings to various parts of the chamber while roaring at the top of his lungs about manners and decorum being things of the past.

By the following year he was entrenched in Hollywood as undoubted star of *The Barretts of Wimpole Street,* sending shivers down female spines as he cast unmistakably lascivious eyes on his invalid daughter. ('They can't censor the gleam in my eye,' he once said.) There followed the malevolent Bligh, a perversion of history but a thoroughly actable role which somehow allowed him to command sympathy while performing unspeakable acts, yet two years after that, following a glowering Javert in *Les Misérables,* he slipped a couple of rungs down the commercial ladder when the much heralded *Rembrandt* failed to set either the Thames or the Hudson on fire. Not that it was despised by the critics: to quote Miss Lejeune again:

Rembrandt is a one-man picture. It is a close-up so intimate that the other figures are thrown inevitably out of focus. Only by laying himself bare to the bone could any actor hope to play it. Only Laughton, I believe, of all screen actors, could hope to play it so movingly and so well . . . He has taken the golden passages like a psalmist. Rembrandt is his great part, his matriculation; full of the intimate moments that test an actor's integrity to the highest . . . probably the finest acting performance ever recorded on celluloid.

Miss Lejeune was also very keen on the picture itself. ('It is produced, set and written with a fastidious feeling for beauty. The pictures shine and glow, the lines ring with music.') As a humble follower I have to agree, for even today it maintains tremendous impact and is a revelation in set design. Yet at the time it made no impact whatever on the world's paying patrons, who found it a boring tour round chilly rooms in the presence of people they didn't understand and didn't want to.

Laughton's opportunity to regain his commercial stature was

rather like the one offered to Bette Davis in *Whatever Happened to Baby Jane?*, except that his was a much better picture. He was cast as *The Hunchback of Notre Dame*, and shot it in the gruelling hot summer of 1939, under many pounds of disfiguring make-up, while Europe prepared for war. There must have been a lot on his mind to unsettle him; yet his Quasimodo is a triumph, a genuine figure of pathos behind the grotesque face supplied for him by the make-up department. It is claimed that no photographs of it were ever taken, to preserve the shock of his first appearance, but the film remains, and it's a corker, a shining demonstration of all that Hollywood under the studio system could do on a big budget. The medieval sets, the vast crowds, the meandering storyline are all handled with immense skill and bravura by Dieterle, a German director of the old school; and Laughton's star performance is perfectly complemented by a number of others from actors all at their best: Hardwicke, Davenport, Mitchell. The impression one takes away, however, is slightly unsettling as one remembers the hunchback caressing a gargoyle and blubbering 'If only I were made of stone, like you'; or admitting to Maureen O'Hara 'I've about as much shape as the man in the moon.' Quasimodo? Or Charles Laughton?

Rembrandt. GB 1936; monochrome; 85 minutes. Produced and directed by Alexander Korda for London Films. Written by Carl Zuckmayer, Arthur Wimperis, Lajos Biro and June Head. Photographed by Georges Perinal and Richard Angst. Music score by Geoffrey Toye. Art direction by Vincent Korda. Edited by William Hornbeck. With Charles Laughton as Rembrandt; Gertrude Lawrence as Geertje; Elsa Lanchester as Henriskje; Edward Chapman as Fabrizius; Walter Hudd as Banning Cocq; Roger Livesy as the beggar; Allan Jeayes as Dr Tulp; John Clements as Gavaert Flink; Raymond Huntley as Ludwick.

The Private Life of Henry VIII. GB 1933; monochrome; 96 minutes. Produced by Alexander Korda for London Films. Written by Arthur Wimperis and Lajos Biro. Directed by Alexander Korda. Photographed by Georges Perinal. Music by Kurt Schroeder. Art direction by Vincent Korda. Edited by Stephen Harrison. With Charles Laughton as Henry; Robert Donat as Culpeper; Merle Oberon as Anne Boleyn; Elsa Lanchester as Anne of Cleves; Binnie Barnes as Katherine Howard; Wendy Barrie as Jane Seymour; Everley Gregg as Katherine Parr; Franklin Dyall as Cromwell; Lady Tree as Nurse.

The Hunchback of Notre Dame. US 1939; monochrome; 117 minutes. Produced by Pandro S. Berman for RKO. Written by Sonya Levien and Bruno Frank from the novel by Victor Hugo. Directed by William Dieterle. Photographed by Joseph H. August. Music score by Alfred Newman. Art direction by Van Nest Polglase. Edited by William Hamilton and Robert Wise. With Charles Laughton as Quasimodo; Maureen O'Hara as Esmeralda; Cedric Hardwicke as Frollo; Harry Davenport as

Louis XI; Thomas Mitchell as Clopin; Edmond O'Brien as Gringoire; Alan Marshal as Phoebus; Walter Hampden as Archbishop; George Zucco as Procurator.

Open Up That Golden Gate
San Francisco

The proprietor of a Barbary Coast night club, cynically running for public office, clashes with a slum landlord over the love of a young singer.

Newsweek, when it first opened, summed it up thus: 'One of the strangest conglomerations ever welded into a film. It has a lusty story of Barbary Coast days, a love triangle, cabaret dancing, opera, comedy, religion, a moral, politics, and the 1906 earthquake.' True, but not necessarily a bad thing. Frank Nugent in *The New York Times* was not merely kinder but sounded as though he was working for the producers: 'Out of the gusty, brawling, catastrophic history of the Barbary Coast in the early century, Metro-Goldwyn-Mayer has fashioned a prodigally generous and completely satisfying screenplay, less a single motion picture than an anthology.' Both writers, in retrospect, are correct. It *is* an odd combination and it *does* work. But according to Anita Loos, who wrote the screenplay, it was she and not MGM who deserved the credit as the studio had to be persuaded into giving its premium talent to the project. It started when, under contract to MGM, she discovered that one of the resident gag writers was Robert Hopkins, who like her had been born in San Francisco. Over a canteen lunch they toyed with the idea of a script which would reflect not only their own childhood experiences but the city's unique style:

We delighted in memories of the city of our youth; its brisk northern climate generates energy, just as the tepid air of Southern California dissipates it. We had a deep love for ancient San Francisco landmarks, of which the entire Los Angeles area had none; we cherished the free-and-easy spirit of forebears who had risked their lives crossing the plains in covered wagons, suffered tremendous hardships, and fallen afoul of attacks by Indians to reach their Eldorado. We shared an equal contempt for those citizens of Southern California who had none of the imagination and braggadocio that motivated our own colourful pioneers.

They decided to base their script on the flamboyant personality of Wilson Mizner, a colourful Barbary Coast gambler of the period who later became a well-known Hollywood resident and international joker. Only Gable, they decided, could play him, but Gable could not be secured until a director considered worthy of him, in this case W. S. Van Dyke, had consented to take the reins. Even then they had trouble when the studio's comparatively highbrow head of production, Irving Thalberg, became ill and was replaced by Bernie Hyman, who proved intent on replacing the loftier portions of the script with action melodrama which would appeal to the lowest common denominator of the potential audience. So much for the oft-voiced public suspicion that epics emerge completed from the studio factory as soon as somebody pushes the right combination of buttons.

Perhaps *San Francisco* is one case where all the compromises worked to the benefit of the movie. Still available in prints as gleaming as those first minted, it can be appreciated as an example of old-time Hollywood at its very best, offering something for everybody in a production which moves so slickly that its minor deficiencies aren't even noticed. Jeanette MacDonald, one might feel, is impossibly pure for such surroundings, and the spirit of the city, the original impetus, is only fleetingly sensed, most notably in the character of the villain's mother, who knew it when:

I'm an old lady and I've been through a lot in me life. I came to Frisco in the winter of '51 in a sailin' vessel round the Horn. When I got here there were a hundred and fifty men to one female. And if I do say it as shouldn't, I wasn't so bad to look at. I started in business in a shack near Portsmouth Square – doin' washin'. Do you know how long me business lasted? About forty-five minutes. Me tub was smashed to smithereens in a free for all fight between five of the town swells – to see which would take me to lunch . . . But I pulled meself together one day and married Burley. Burley was a good solid man. He never got used to wearing a coat till the day he died – but he built me this mansion and every cuspidor in the place was eighteen carat gold!

Two matters sealed the success of *San Francisco*. It is one of Gable's top roles, for here, as in *Gone with the Wind*, he is called on to play a tough smiling rascal whose heart is in the right place, 'as unscrupulous with women as he is ruthless with men.' We may not quite accept his religious conversion at the end – his close friendship with Spencer Tracy's priest would have been enough – but for nearly two hours we have been captivated by his characterization of a lovable rogue, and that is the image we carry home: he is a real live guy who almost bursts out of the screen. Second, and perhaps it should be first, is the magnificent climactic earthquake sequence. It stretches credibility a little when the plot has to come to a head during a talent contest which doesn't reach its peak until after five in the morning, but that historically is when the earthquake struck, and at least it ensures that the principals are all on set, in evening dress, when the timbers begin to shake. And shake they do, most convincingly. Doorways collapse like matchboxes, parallel cracks run up walls so that the bricks between fall forwards, a sudden deep fissure sucks pedestrians from the public street and exposes water and gas mains, gargoyles on high buildings topple into camera, front walls crumple from apartment houses revealing half-clothed inhabitants stumbling out of bed, and, most magnificently, a domed civic building shivers and quakes its slates away one by one until only a romantic ruin is left. The unsung special effects man who masterminded this sequence was Arnold Gillespie, and one hopes that MGM awarded him a nice bonus, for he contributed generously towards one of their biggest box office bonanzas.

A third major factor in the film's success was the title song, which until recent inspection I could have sworn the three leads sang at the end, in a burst of optimistic fervour, as they strode into the sunlight to rebuild their shattered city. So much for memory: what they actually sing is 'The Battle Hymn of the Republic', and not on the rousing topnotes I recalled. 'San Francisco' is not in fact given the full treatment anywhere in the movie. MacDonald has three stabs at it, first in far too slow a tempo, the second adequately but not excitingly, the third in a curious warbling version interrupted by dramatic events. Be that as it may, the ditty swelled in people's minds and is still hummed in bathtubs around the world. In 1979, taking a boat trip round San Francisco harbour, I was ushered ashore by its cadences over a dozen loudspeakers: instantly the sun seemed to shine more powerfully over the fabled city and I half expected to see the ghosts of Gable, MacDonald and Tracy strolling arm in arm towards me along Fisherman's Wharf. The notion of credit where credit is due impels me to mention that the lyric is by Gus Kahn, the music by Bronislau Kaper (himself a recent Euro-

SAN FRANCISCO. The start of the earthquake

pean emigré, so how did he so precisely strike the keynote of a great American city?).

Disaster movies became a regular feature, almost a laughing stock, of the seventies, but to my eye they were never particularly successful in colour. The devastations of *Earthquake*, for instance, despite the added rumblings of Sensurround, do not have a quarter of the conviction of those in *San Francisco*, so meticulously put together in black-and-white. The reason I think may be that in colour we expect absolute realism, whereas black-and-white, being itself an unreal medium, allows us to accept an artist's impression of reality. Or perhaps the old films were just better. The seventies spectacles have without exception reduced their characters to the status of unattractive dramatic dummies about whose fate we could scarcely care less; this could never be said of Gable's Blackie Norton, whom we cheer when we see that he has escaped the falling masonry. Nor would it be true of two excellent black-and-white spectacles which followed the success of *San Francisco*, both from Twentieth Century-Fox's competitive and imitative Darryl F.

Zanuck. *In Old Chicago* climaxes with the great fire started by Mrs O'Leary's cow, but takes care to absorb us first in nearly two hours of dramatic conflict between Tyrone Power and Don Ameche. *The Rains Came*, lovingly photographed by Arthur Miller in 1939, even has the audacity to put its floods in the very middle of the picture, relying on our interest in the problems of the principals to keep us riveted to our seats during the aftermath. This all-Hollywood film gives a better impression of India during the fading days of the British Raj than the nations involved have ever contrived to do, even with the aid of wide screen and colour; the central tragic romance is well acted by Myrna Loy and Tyrone Power, with invaluable assistance from the dignified performances of Maria Ouspenskaya and H. B. Warner as Maharani and Maharaja, but to my mind the best display in the film is given by George Brent, who not only tosses away his cynical lines with quiet wit but wears dinner jackets which are the epitome of sartorial splendour. I hope they came through the flood unscathed.

San Francisco. US 1936; monochrome; 117 minutes. Produced by John Emerson and Bernard H. Hyman for MGM. Written by Anita Loos, from a story by Robert Hopkins. Directed by W. S. Van Dyke II. Photographed by Oliver T. Marsh. Music direction by Herbert Stothart. Art direction by Cedric Gibbons. Special effects by Arnold Gillespie. Montage by John Hoffman. With Clark Gable as Blackie Norton; Jeanette MacDonald as Mary; Spencer Tracy as Father Tim; Jack Holt as Talbot; Jessie Ralph as Mrs Talbot; Ted Healy as Mat.

Shame of a Nation
Scarface and Little Caesar

Two Italian-American hoodlums rise to the top but fall through their own weaknesses.

They are both, of course, modelled on Al Capone, who cut a murderous swathe through Chicago in the twenties, surrendered himself finally on a charge of income tax evasion, and died in Alcatraz of syphilis. The fictitious Rico Bandelli and Tony Camonte perish more picturesquely in a hail of bullets, the one finding time to murmur 'Mother of God, is this the end of Rico?'; the other dropping dead in the gutter below a Cook's Tour sign announcing ironically that 'the world is yours'. They mark two of the high spots of the gangster movie, a form which has never left our screens but was at its most dynamic in the early days of talkies, when the era of the real gangsters was only just over and their snarled gutter language, punctuated by the rattle of tommy guns, was the easiest and simplest form of speech to reproduce from those primitive sound tracks. Even today these sensational melodramas, torn from the headlines of another age, retain their power to thrill, just as more sophisticated audiences squirm pleasurably at the atrocities of Jacobean tragedy. They lack refinement of film style, they are slowly edited, with too many fades to black and practically no music score to underline the narrative; but they were put together by seasoned film journalists who knew how to shock, and they bathed in the talents of art directors and cameramen who knew how to make the most of their drab backgrounds. In *Little Caesar*, Anton Grot begins each new sequence with silent actors distantly viewed in a box set whose jaggedly decorated ceiling sets the tone for what is to follow. In *Scarface*, the 'X' behind the titles reappears traced in light across two scenes featuring a rival gangster who is soon to get his come-uppance, and again in the form of his bowls score just a few seconds before he is mown down. Of such visual touches are memorable movies made.

Little Caesar is not merely of interest to the film archaeologist. On its first release it must have had an electrifying impact, and it set the pattern for hundreds of Warner crime movies which were to come, using the same backlot streets, the same screeching automobiles, and no doubt the same foggy shadows. At a time when other studios were still adjusting their mikes to get the sound of frying eggs off the sound track, here was game little Jack Warner coming up with a cheap picture of superb technical accomplishment, a real movie torn from the pages of the yellow press. It is incredible that only three years had passed since the fumblings of *The Jazz Singer*, here is a riveting delineation of the distortion and evil that can possess men's minds. Not that the film is over-rich in characterization. The supporting characters are mere ciphers, ripe for toppling, like those who stood between Richard Crookback and the Plantagenet throne; and Rico himself is not explained except as a callous hoodlum with an urge to get to the top at whatever cost, a man who fails to understand that he too is not merely vulnerable but mortal. But what an overwhelming incarnation of rancid paranoia attaches to this stocky figure. And what a performance Edward G. Robinson gives in the role, spitting out his lines like daggers and seeming never to blink his basilisk eyes. 'When I get in a tight spot,' he tells his reluctant partner Joe Massara at the beginning as they plot an alibi in a cheap diner, 'I shoot my way out of it. Like tonight. Sure, shoot first, argue afterwards. If you don't, the other guy gets *you*. This game ain't for guys that's soft!'

Rico has only one weak spot, and that is his affection for the rather boring Massara, whom he protects from other gang members and finally wants for his own number two even though Joe has long ago crept away towards a pure romantic attachment and a blameless career as a dancer. Rico's failure to control this situation, in which bullets can't give him the edge, leads directly to his final crumpling and ignominious end; yet his motivation has never in my experience been commented upon, which is odd, as both script and film make it abundantly clear that his feeling for Joe is homosexual. Even when he realizes that Joe has given him away to the police, Rico can't bring himself to squeeze the trigger beneath his finger; though his face is a fearful mask, he backs away and leaves Joe to the woman who is Rico's unconquerable rival. In close parallel, Tony Camonte in *Scarface* brings about his own downfall by his incestuous love for his young sister; his impetuous murder of her paramour is the one crime for which the police are able to bring him to book.

The screenplay of *Little Caesar* is credited to Francis Edward Faragoh, though in his autobiography director Mervyn Le Roy takes credit for 'several scripts'. Certainly Faragoh's published ending was drastically changed, and not for the better. Originally Rico, a symbol of physical purity despite the mental quagmire in which he exists (he neither smokes nor drinks, and takes great pride in his clothes) was to turn himself in after six months on the run and a nervous breakdown, only to be disbelieved by the cops because of the liquor on his breath. Only his glittering diamond ring was to give him away; the police were to follow him and shoot him dead when he reached into his pocket for a comb, which they mistook for a gun. As filmed, Rico is found in a dosshouse, enraged by a newspaper comment on his cowardice in running away. He rings up the police and harangues them so long that his call is traced; when cornered, he shoots it out. The film ends rather lamely on a

SCARFACE. A movie first for incest? Muni, Dvorak

billboard advertising Joe Massara's latest starring film: a remark-able career development in a few months!

Scarface is a more polished film than *Little Caesar*. Both directors exhibit great vigour, but Hawks is more of a cinéaste than Le Roy, whose failings became more apparent as he aged and began to make interminable film versions of stage hits photographed from mid-stalls. *Little Caesar* is the work of a young opportunist with the verve to keep one punchdrunk; *Scarface* exhibits the fancy footwork of a man who understands psychology as well as choreography, who can move right into a scene and keep an audience hypnotized by the cold smell of evil which at any moment, it seems, may slurp down from the screen and contaminate the front rows. Paul Muni is not, like Robinson, a lone figure of menace set among incompetent amateurs; given a family background, he is simply the most dangerous element in a dark fresco of savagery so intense as to seem almost supernatu-ral. The cumulative effect of this remarkable melodrama, good prints of which have been hard to come by for forty years owing to the idiosyncrasies of its owner-producer, Howard Hughes, is to make one shudder for the whole of humanity. The fact that it was set up quite cynically in imitation of a string of commercial hits does not diminish its grandeur. It is no secret that Hughes, fearing he had come upon the scene too late, developed a well-publicized battle with the censors for over a year so that when the film was eventually released the world had its tongue hanging out to see it. Hughes' only concession to governmental concern was to sub-title it *The Shame of a Nation* and to add an entirely hypocritical preface: 'This picture is an indictment of gang rule in America and of the callous indifference of the government to this danger to our safety and our liberty . . . The purpose of the picture is to demand of the government: "What are you doing about it?"' A reasonable answer might have been 'Stop Hollywood from making films which glorify hoodlums', and that in fact is exactly what the government did.

Scarface depicts no bleeding corpses: Sam Peckinpah and *Bonnie and Clyde* were many years in the future. Hawks chills us by suspense. A lone figure is telephoning when we see the shadow of a gunman down the hall, and hear a tune whistled on the sound track; the camera moves slowly away past the debris of a party before we hear the inevitable hail of bullets. Even the St Valentine's Day massacre is staged entirely in silhouette, and our eyes have been averted to the ceiling before the shots ring out and a dog is heard whimpering. And when Boris Karloff, playing a gangster with the most unlikely English accent, is despatched in a bowling alley, what we watch is his last strike, the final skittle spinning crazily on its axis before tumbling into the pit. For a film shot at the beginning of 1931 these are subtleties indeed, with sound and picture perfectly integrated.

Through it all the wide-shouldered star moves like King Kong, with the same passionate but limited range of emotions. His insolent features are first revealed from behind the hot towels in a barber's shop, but the expected shoot-out is denied us; he only strikes a match on the badge of the investigating sheriff, whose tight-lipped retort strikes a prophetic note: 'Someday you're going to fall down in the gutter – right where the horses have been standing – right where you belong!'

Muni as Camonte dynamically displays the child's love of

destruction for its own sake. 'Look at it, Johnny,' he says of his first tommy gun, 'you can carry it around like a baby!' His dynamism makes him attractive to women. He marches in to take possession of the mistress of the partner he has just killed. 'Where's Johnny?' she quivers briefly. 'Where ya think?' he sneers, and we see her lip arch in sheer sexual longing for the murderous beast who will soon possess her. So in the finale, the sister who has come to kill him for murdering her lover is driven instead by his animal power to join him in violent death as the police close in.

After 1932 the gangsters withdrew, or were comicalized, until in 1935 Jack Warner had a brainwave. If he could no longer make heroes of the gangsters, he would have his tough stars play the cops. If Cagney was motivated by a personal vendetta, as in *G Men*, the excitement would be no less than in *Public Enemy*, which had him trussed up like a chicken, riddled with bullets, left to fall into his mother's front doorway when she answered the bell. By the later thirties the hoodlums of the twenties were only a dimly remembered threat, which censors were content to accept as merely symbolic villain figures. The genre has never died. It went through black comedy (*A Slight Case of Murder*), whimsy (*Brother Orchid*), melancholy (*High Sierra*) and docu-drama (*The Enforcer*, 1951 version); and by the time Cagney played the psychopathic Cody Jarrett in *White Heat* at the end of the forties, it seemed but a small step back to *Scarface* and forward to *The Untouchables* and *Bloody Mama*.

Scarface. US 1932; monochrome; 99 minutes. Produced by Howard Hughes. Written by Ben Hecht, Seton I. Miller, John Lee Mahin, W. R. Burnett and Fred Paley, from the novel by Armitage Trail. Directed by Howard Hawks. Photographed by Lee Garmes and L. W. O'Connell. Edited by Edward Curtiss. With Paul Muni as Tony Camonte; Ann Dvorak as Cesca; George Raft as Guido Rinaldo; Osgood Perkins as Johnny Lovo; Boris Karloff as Gaffney; Vince Barnett as Angelo; C. Henry Gordon as Guarino.

Little Caesar. US 1930; monochrome; 80 minutes. Produced by Hal Wallis for Warners. Written by Francis Edward Faragoh from the novel by W. R. Burnett. Directed by Mervyn Le Roy. Photographed by Tony Gaudio. With Edward G. Robinson as Rico; Douglas Fairbanks Jnr as Joe Massara; Glenda Farrell as Olga; William Collier Jnr as Tony Passa; Ralph Ince as Diamond Pete; George E. Stone as Ottero; Sidney Blackmer as The Big Boy; Thomas Jackson as Lt Tom Flaherty; Stanley Fields as Sam Vestri.

Regency Buck
The Scarlet Pimpernel

An apparently foppish Englishman is the secret leader of a band of adventurers who save French aristocrats from the guillotine.

> They seek him here, they seek him there,
> Those Frenchies seek him everywhere.
> Is he in heaven? Is he in hell?
> That damned elusive pimpernel.

In Bolton in 1934, at the elementary school of St Simon and St Jude, all of us six-year-olds were saying it. The Scarlet Pimpernel was the sensation of the moment, a folk hero who brought a distant historical time to vibrant life and made it exciting. The French Revolution was an unpleasant page in our picture books, an era of mob rule and violence. Some of us were already familiar with *A Tale of Two Cities* (I'd had an illustrated children's edition for Christmas), but that had an unhappy ending. Here was a dashing hero who rescued French aristos from a dreadful fate, spirited them away across the Channel under the very noses of those tight-lipped villains Robespierre and Chauvelin, and lived to tell the tale; and he was played not by some athletic pseudo-Fairbanks but by the thoughtful and patrician Leslie Howard, whom one would previously have considered to be more at home in drawing-rooms than leaping in and out of tumbrils in heavy disguise.

There is of course nothing very original about the Scarlet Pimpernel, as his creator Baroness Orczy would probably have been the first to admit. The love of disguise and the apparent omniscience come from Sherlock Holmes, the hidden identity from Robin Hood (who according to legend was the Earl of Locksley when he wasn't romping around Sherwood Forest with his merry men, saving brave Saxons from being crushed under the invading Norman heel). Raffles was an apparent fop who had a double life as a daring crook; Rassendyll in *The Prisoner of Zenda* was an ordinary bloke called upon to play a dangerous impersonation; the hero of *Destry Rides Again* displays a deceptive mildness but roars into action when the crunch comes; Faversham in *The Four Feathers* is an apparent coward who performs heroic deeds in heavy disguise. Our parents had seen Douglas Fairbanks, and we would shortly see Tyrone Power, play another disguised avenger in *The Mark of Zorro*, the scene changed from the French Revolution to Spanish California but the plot proceeding exactly to formula. Later Tony Curtis went back to the original French setting for *The Purple Mask*, and *Omar Khayyam* retold the tale in ancient Persia. (Did you know that the famous poet saved his country with one hand while composing the *Rubaiyat* with the other?) The Incredible Hulk, Superman, Batman and The Green Hornet are but comic strip variations on the same theme, and *The Thief of Baghdad* does it with even more spectacular brands of magic. *Pimpernel Smith*, also with Howard, simply updated the plot by putting in the Nazis instead of Robespierre, and a Cambridge professor instead of a Regency fop. The thrill is the same, that of applauding the exploits of a hero who quietly outwits the villains at every turn while pretending to be a disinterested onlooker so that he can live to fight another day. It is one of the six unsinkable plots of show business.

Still, *The Scarlet Pimpernel* deserves its credit, for it got the mixture right and superimposed a languid style which was sometimes even more nerve-stretching than the action sequences. These are in fact restricted to two, and no longer thrill as they did. The central holding power derives from a triangular suspense situation. Sir Percy has taken on his mission partly because he believes his French wife to be guilty of betraying some friends to the reign of terror. She despises him because he has dwindled from the man she married into a useless fop. Chauvelin, Robespierre's ambassador to London, dare not return without discovering the Pimpernel's identity. Is Lady Blakeney really guilty? Will she, to save her brother, betray her husband? Can Sir Percy afford to take her into his confidence? These questions, and many others, are left unresolved until the nail-biting finish, and along the way there are delicate situations such as the Greville Ball, which the Pimpernel is known to be attending because he has a rendezvous in the library at midnight. Chauvelin knows it too; how will Sir Percy escape discovery? Will the Frenchman see the cold intelligence behind his pretence? ('It was the busiest part of the day: demn it, I was tying my cravat.' Or:

THE SCARLET PIMPERNEL. Sir Percy toys with his arch-rival. Leslie Howard, Raymond Massey

'I've just been to Bath to be cured of the fatigue. And now I'm so fatigued by the cure that I really think I shall have to go back to Bath to be cured of the fatigue.') The Prince of Wales is a help, having taken on Sir Percy as fashion adviser:

PRINCE: Where is that jackanapes?
SIR PERCY: Who, sir?
PRINCE: You, sir.
SIR PERCY: Here, sir.
PRINCE: Odds fish, Percy, you're brainless, spineless and useless, but you do know clothes.

The film displays its period with fascination: these dandies in their uncomfortable clothes really come to life for us, something not to be expected from a cursory inspection of the cast list which includes such character names as Sir Andrew ffoulkes and Armand St Just.

I remember rather ruefully that back in 1934 we loved *The Scarlet Pimpernel* all the more because it was a British film made without Hollywood aid. For some reason that seemed to make it more important than any mere entertainment. Well, its star is of Hungarian descent, its heroine Anglo-Indian, its villain Canadian. The scripting team included two Americans and a Hungarian, which latter nationality was shared not only by the original author but by the producer himself. Photographer, special effects man and nominal director were all American. I say nominal director because it is hard to believe that Harold Young exerted much real influence over this elegant entertainment, as his subsequent career shows no evidence of grace or talent. Korda had had a mid-film disagreement with his first directorial choice, Rowland Brown (another American), and for a while directed the film himself; then finding himself too busy with administration he handed over the routine daytime chores to his editor, having no doubt provided him on the previous evening with a complete storyboard à la Hitchcock. Oddly enough, considering Harold Young's previous experience, the chief lack we now find in watching *The Scarlet Pimpernel* is a lack of dynamic editing. Some shots are clumsily set up and held too long, in others continuity is inexcusably poor. Perhaps because its structure was taken from a play version of the novel, this is never a movie movie, more a sophisticated charade.

What does come through, apart from the personality of the star, is a wild whiff of patriotism. Even though 1934 was a bit early to be arming ourselves against Hitler, the whole thrust of the story is of Englishmen dealing with dastardly foreigners as they deserve. While the Prince of Wales is playing with his smart but impotent troops – 'beer and beef, that's what makes soldiers' – the populace is eager for more tales of the Pimpernel's derring-do. 'Do you know who he is, sir?' the Prince is asked. 'I don't, but I confess I feel a little prouder when I know that he is an Englishman.' We cut to the horror of the guillotine (though the shots of severed heads being removed have been so smartly cut that you have to be expecting them to spot them at all) and to the yet more unspeakable sight of the *tricoteuses*, cackling old harridans doing their knitting as they wait for the next head to fall. We are next shown the aristos in prison, 'waiting to be shaved by the national razor'; in fact the only family we actually meet are due to be saved, and we have already glimpsed a foul old hag with a nose so unlikely that she simply has to be the Pimpernel in disguise. The de Tournays are actually in the tumbril when he snatches them by a diversion; then at the west gate, with a wagon full of fugitives, he gets past the sergeant-at-arms by asserting that his only companion is a boy with the black plague. By an even neater twist, the platoon of French officers who come galloping after him, denouncing the sergeant as a nincompoop, are all the members of the Pimpernel's league, making their own escape in the deftest possible way. The scene with Robespierre, which follows, is admittedly stilted: Ernest Milton plays him in the worst Henry Irving tradition, hands behind back and head slumped between shoulders. But by now it doesn't matter, for the story has taken over, and we can relax and enjoy the sight of Blakeney outwitting his friends and enemies alike. The ball sequence has more than a reminiscence of the similar point in the story of *Pygmalion*, except that this time it is Howard himself and not Eliza Dolittle who may get found out. Needless to say, he doesn't, and the entertainment was popular enough to warrant a sequel, four years later, by which time the allegorical content, the reign of terror being equatable with the Nazis, was more obvious. In 1953 it was dusted down again and turned up as *The Elusive Pimpernel*, but by now either Korda or his associates (Powell and Pressburger) had totally misunderstood the appeal of the story and offered a piece of richly decorated high camp which cost a fortune and satisfied nobody.

Though intermittently trivialized by television, the Pimpernel could come up fresh and sparkling for the eighties; perhaps even a new production of the Orczy play would make a sumptuous attraction for the National Theatre.

The Scarlet Pimpernel. GB 1934; monochrome; 98 minutes. Produced by Alexander Korda for London Films. Written by S. N. Behrman, Robert Sherwood, Lajos Biro and Arthur Wimperis, from the novel by Baroness Orczy and the play by Baroness Orczy and Montague Barstow. Directed by Harold Young. Photographed by Harold Rosson. Music score by Arthur Benjamin. Art direction by Vincent Korda. Edited by William Hornbeck. With Leslie Howard as Sir Percy Blakeney; Merle Oberon as Lady Blakeney; Raymond Massey as Chauvelin; Nigel Bruce as the Prince of Wales; Anthony Bushell as Sir Andrew; Walter Rilla as Armand; Ernest Milton as Robespierre; Bramwell Fletcher as the priest; O. B. Clarence as the Count de Tournay; Joan Gardner as Suzanne de Tournay; Melville Cooper as Romney.

Seaside Postcard
Sing As We Go

When the cotton mills close down during the Depression of the early thirties, a Lancashire girl goes to Blackpool in search of work.

It was my time, and they were my people. My father worked at huge looms in just such a mill, and was unemployed for a fair slice of my infant years. Yet I remember no abject misery: Lancastrians preferred to laugh at hardship, and if Gracie Fields was their inspiration then this film above all was their shield. A raw little comedy with music, it happened to become the best representation on film of the working class north during those unhappy years: even its modest montages were used over and over again in other films which required glimpses of cotton being spun by lean men in overalls, and the only aspect it couldn't capture was the sweet oily smell which pervaded their clothes and was transferred to buses and even to cinema seats. Part of it was filmed in Bolton, and I remember great excitement locally when Gracie herself turned up and stayed with her entourage at the Swan Hotel. It seemed from the *Evening News* reports that she was a bit snappy with the press, and didn't make herself very available for interviews; her PR man said she was very tired. 'Eeh, that doesn't sound like our Gracie,' said my Aunt Edith rather as though she knew her personally; she didn't, but at that time everybody in Lancashire felt he had a proprietary interest in the irrepressible Rochdale lass. After all, it was she who had put us on the map.

A couple of days later I came home from school to find my father, who was temporarily at liberty, looking very pleased with himself as he described some great event to my mother, which was odd in itself as they weren't normally very communicative. It transpired that he had walked to the other side of town to watch Gracie filming mill scenes, and even thought he might have finished up in the crowd shots. I understood him to say that the Mill was Holden's, an imposing new pile in Blackburn Road. When the film opened later that year my mother and I were first in the queue, and as the singing crowd surged into the mill at the end we looked anxiously but in vain for Dad. It was difficult indeed to look at anyone but the magnetic star; the angular figure who marched rather flatfootedly across the cobbles and sang her song of optimism:

> Sing as we go, and let the world go by;
> Sing me a song to chase away the grey skies;
>   Say goodbye to sorrow –
>   There's always tomorrow
> To follow today . . .

Just before the final fade-out she momentarily relaxes her wide camera smile to rebuke a passer-by: 'Hey, who you shoving?' I knew then that I was in the presence of a star.

During the next forty-five years I must have seen and enjoyed *Sing As We Go* a dozen times, as a joy in itself and as a revered relic of my own childhood. In the summer of 1978 my friend Graham Murray, who compiles TV's weekly film programme *Clapperboard*, asked me if I had any ideas for a half-hour film programme on a Lancashire theme. Hazily I suggested a trip from Bolton to Blackpool illustrated by *Sing As We Go*, with a corrective in the form of *Love on the Dole*, in which the young lovers also enjoy a Blackpool holiday but which generally takes a pessimistic and almost tragic view of thirties mill life. The next question was, could I suggest some locations so that Chris Kelly, the presenter, could compare the films with the reality? I thought I could, and was co-opted to travel north for the filming, which was to be accomplished in one day, with clips to be spliced in later. Graham and I took a late afternoon train to Manchester, which preserved its reputation by arranging a cloudburst for our arrival. We commandeered a taxi and toured Pendleton and Moses Gate in a downpour so violent that we could see almost nothing out of the steamy windows. It was dark before we got to Holden's mill, which I quickly realized couldn't be right, after all these years, because its bricks were too red and shiny and it had no gateway of the right width for that final invigorating inrush of singing workers. Dashed, we retired in the direction of a hot toddy and bed, consoling ourselves that early next morning we could investigate the matter at the office of the *Evening News*. Sure enough, the events of 1934 were copiously indexed, and we found that though Gracie had indeed filmed at Holden's, it was for interiors only. The only clue to the exteriors was a mention of 'other local locations including Union Road'. Neither I nor anyone in the office could remember where Union Road was, but the crew was here now and we were wasting time, so I took a chance and led them towards Tonge Moor and a pub named the Starkey: I seemed to remember Union Road being a street on the left as the tram groaned up the hill, a street I had never had occasion to explore. There it was indeed. Left turn; downhill past neat terraces with little gardens; under a railway viaduct; past spare fields, and a mill on the left which couldn't possibly, from its style or aspect, be right. Then at the far end, near a cooling tower, was another group of buildings pretending to be a chemical works. They couldn't fool me. Cotton and Lancashire parted company many years ago, but there were the gates and there were the cobbles. There too was a little doorman, like Albert Tatlock in *Coronation Street*, who as we unpacked the cameras ambled up to see what we wanted. I asked him if he could possibly confirm our suspicions. 'Aye,' he said, 'I can. I were 'ere. Forty-five years, do you say? I suppose it mun be. I were a little piecer then, and now I'm all but retired.'

We got our programme, and for me it evoked not only nostalgia but an awed awareness of time, which can make things so different and yet so much the same. Those gates meant more to me than Shelley's tomb of Ozymandias. Is it my fantasy that we lived more vibrantly and vigorously in the thirties than we do today? *Sing As We Go* seems to suggest that I'm not dreaming. It is still marvellously enjoyable, and you can almost smell the vinegar on the fish and chips. It is a Donald McGill postcard come to life, and we have George Orwell to testify that there is no more vivid form of social history. The excursion trains pulling into Central Station remind me of my own excited journeys at a time when the return fare from Bolton was two-and-ninepence. Gracie in bowler hat and moustache, singing 'Speak, speak, speak to me, Cora' with her Uncle Murgatroyd, remind me of hilarious musical evenings with my Uncle Tom and Auntie Flo, and the house full of clocks is no funnier than my Uncle Albert's tripe shop. Then there's Stanley Holloway in a variety of guises playing what seems to be the only policeman in Blackpool. ('All right, Sam, pick up tha musket,' Gracie tells him in an in-joke that can still be appreciated; and later in the zoo she gets

SING AS WE GO. Streaming out of the famous gate, laughing in the face of unemployment

a startling response from a lion when she demands: 'Hey! Where's young Albert?') There is Gracie nearly being run over by a promenade tram which looks exactly like the models in use today. Gracie demolishing an argumentative friend with: 'Aw, shurrup, you piecan.' Gracie as slavey at Mrs Clotty's boarding house, overwhelmed by change-over day but getting her own back on a randy guest by tipping a bowl of rhubarb over his head. ('Sauce!' says a posh lady. 'It's on the table,' she replies.) Gracie selling Crunchy Wunchy Toffee. Gracie leading choruses in the singing room of Ritz and Fingelstein. Gracie on the Pleasure Beach, playing both the Human Spider and the Vanishing Girl, but choosing the wrong booth in which to make her magical reappearance. Gracie evading pursuers on the Ghost Train, in the Funhouse, and atop Noah's Ark, all unchanged to this very day. Gracie falling among the water ballet at the Tower Circus, of which likewise. Gracie quelling a thousand dancers in the palatial Tower Ballroom with her rendering of 'All Tucked Up in Me Little Bottom Drawer'. Gracie devoting herself to cheering us all up.

I never met her until January 1979, the year she died, and then it was in the unlikeliest of venues, the lift of the elegant Beverly Wilshire Hotel in Los Angeles. I couldn't resist telling her that I was born twelve miles from Rochdale, and had spent all my life regarding her as a distant cousin of whom I could never see enough. Without prompting she sang a line or two of 'Sing As We Go' in the hotel foyer, and said she'd like to see the film again. I promised to fix it for her and gave her my card. Sadly, she never called.

Blackpool has not been well covered on film since *Sing As We Go*. There was another locally popular movie called *Cotton Queen*, starring Will Fyffe and Gibson Gowland (yes, the star of *Greed*), but recent inspection revealed it as a patchy affair. George Formby never filmed in Blackpool, though he sang with splendid *double entendre* of his little stick of Blackpool Rock. And Frank Randle's ramshackle vehicles never strayed far outside the Mancunian Studios where he filmed them with great delay and difficulty through bleary eyes; they don't stand up either. (What does is a *Blackpool Gazette* report of how Mr Randle was arrested one cheerless dawn in the early fifties when he emerged from his Central Pier dressing-room after a night of earnest drinking, climbed into his flash car, shot down the Manchester Road, collided with a tram, and abused the driver unmercifully for being on the wrong side of the street. The police witness reported that Mr Randle then performed an arabesque. 'What is an arabesque?' inquired the magistrate. And, from the well of the court, Mr Randle provided a demonstration. He was fined all the same.)

A world away, and yet in some ways much the same, stands Tati's *Les Vacances de Monsieur Hulot*, an account of a French seaside holiday. The trouble with Tati is and was that he never ends his jokes with a punch line, that he won't take direction, and that for some perverse reason he likes to see his central character on the periphery of the frame. Still, his observation is marvellously accurate, and the first half of this film is a hysterically funny series of little disasters such as might befall a shy and gangling bachelor at a humble summer hotel overlooking a Normandy beach. I resist his later attempts at elaborate sequences involving tennis, and funerals, and fireworks, because he doesn't build them properly; but moments such as his standing on a rope which tautens and propels him into the river, or his mid-ocean collapsing of a collapsible canoe, still make me ache from memories of my first encounter with them. What Hulot needed was Gracie Fields to lick him into shape; and what a meeting that would have been!

Sing As We Go. GB 1934; monochrome; 80 minutes. Produced and directed by Basil Dean for ATP. Written by J. B. Priestley and Basil Dean. Photographed by Robert G. Martin. Songs by Harry Parr Davis and others. With Gracie Fields as Grace Platt; John Loder as Hugh Philips; Dorothy Hyson as Phyllis Logan; Stanley Holloway as the policeman; Frank Pettingell as Uncle Murgatroyd; Norman Walker as Hezekiah; Lawrence Grossmith as Sir William Upton; Maire O'Neill as Madame Osiris; Margaret Yarde as Mrs Clotty.

Fit as a Fiddle and Ready to Dance
Singin' in the Rain

A song-and-dance man in silent Hollywood graduates from stunting to romantic action hero. When talkies come, he exposes the vocal inadequacies of his overbearing leading lady, and marries the girl who is voicing for her.

The entire history of screen musicals could be justified by this one exuberant production, produced by the Arthur Freed unit almost as an afterthought to *An American in Paris*. Presumably they thought less of it because it aims to be funny. The public was not slow to discover its true worth, and it probably now appears in more lists of favourites than any other musical, for its bounce is simply irresistible. Bright and breezy, and witty and gay, and fast moving and satirical, and just plain fun, it wraps up in its amusing tale no fewer than fifteen nostalgic hit songs, most of them written by Freed with Nacio Herb Brown for that forgotten early period of brash and tinny talkies whose manners and mores, in 1952, were still instantly recognizable to most filmgoers. Oddly enough, painstaking research was needed to unearth designs for studio equipment of the time, for Hollywood has always been slow to preserve records of its own fantasies; once used, the evidence is thrown away.

It really doesn't matter to posterity how a movie like this was put

SINGIN' IN THE RAIN. At the première, with a spoof Louella Parsons (Madge Blake) and the beautiful but dumb Lina Lamont (Jean Hagen)

together. Sufficient that it was, that everything clearly went right from the very beginning, and that everyone obviously had a whale of a time making it, even the scriptwriters to whom at first it was a chore to be accepted under duress. Not that their script is particularly funny to read, because a good musical uses a script only to get from one number to another in the fastest possible time; but it does remind one of the visual jokes with which the movie abounds, of the rapid-fire editing which replaces one stunning image with another at profligate speed, and of the fortissimo performances which convince you after the show that you have been in the cheerful company of old friends. Even the strident, scheming Lina Lamont, in the hands of Jean Hagen, becomes a villainess so easy to trip up as to emerge a sympathetic character. Who could fail to warm to an actress so naïve as to tell her assembled fans that 'If we bring a little joy into your humdrum lives, it makes us feel as though our hard work ain't been in vain for nothin'.' Lina has no power of self-criticism: 'What do they think I am – dumb or somethin'? Why, I make more money than Calvin Coolidge – put together!' Nor can she understand how her partner can romance her before the cameras and nowhere else:

LINA: Oh, Donny. You couldn't kiss me like that and not mean it just a teensy-weensy bit.
DON: Meet the greatest actor in the world. I'd rather kiss a tarantula.
LINA: You don't mean that.
DON: Hey, Joe, bring me a tarantula.

There is malicious wit too in the caricature of Louella Parsons, gushing over each new arrival at a Hollywood Boulevard première, including a sexy young starlet arriving with an extremely aged escort:

It's that famous zip girl of the screen, the darling of the flapper set, Zelma Zanders . . . and her new red-hot pash, J. Cumberland Spendrill III, that well-known eligible bachelor. Zelda's had so much unhappiness: I hope this time it's really love. And look who's just arrived, it's that exotic star Olga Mara and her new husband, the Baron de la Bouvet de la Toulon. They've been married two months already, but they're still as happy as newlyweds . . .

Memorable indeed is the restaging of the first demonstration of talkies at a private party, the screen filled by a close-up of an emaciated professor type, speaking with extreme care and deliberation as though to an audience of the deaf:

This is a demonstration of a talking picture. Notice: it is a picture of me, and I am talking. Note how my lips and the sound issuing from them are synchronized together in perfect unison. Since the earliest days of the cinema screen, the concept of simultaneous sound has been the primary object of our pioneer inventors. My voice has been recorded on a record. A talking picture. Thank you. Goodbye.

Obviously, even a smash hit like this isn't put together without a few problems. The major one here is that Freed volunteered a new number, 'Make 'Em Laugh', for Donald O'Connor, and it turned out to be simply a new and unauthorized lyric for 'Be A Clown', a Cole Porter item written for *The Pirate* which Freed had filmed four years earlier. The crew was too embarrassed to comment, Cole Porter maintained a dignified silence, and at least it was a magnificent number for O'Connor. He walks into a wall, is biffed on the head by a passing plank, has a fight with a headless dummy, runs and back-flips up two walls, and hurtles through a third, all in the cause of raising a chuckle; the moments when his facial muscles seem to be out of control are sheer magic. Another curious problem was that when Debbie Reynolds was supposed to be lending a few cultured tones to the Jean Hagen character, her midwestern accent proved intrusive, so the lines were dubbed by Jean Hagen. (Got that?)

Twenty years later, co-director Stanley Donen was deprecatory about *Singin' in the Rain* on British television, labelling it 'old stuff' that he wished people would stop bringing up. He may rest easy in the certainty that there will be no such lingering enthusiasm for his films of the seventies. It sparkles in my memory as the one movie which really lit up the chill anonymity of the Cambridge Regal, and as an attraction which I subsequently queued for at the National Film Theatre, at the Bijou on Hollywood Boulevard and at the Elysée in Paris; while its every appearance on television is a signal for the doors to be locked and the phone taken off the hook. And time and again, it works. Its tunes, incidentally, are almost sufficient recommendation, including 'You Were Meant for Me', 'Good Morning', 'Fit as a Fiddle and Ready for Love', 'Broadway Rhythm' (as the main theme of a knock-out satirical ballet), and of course the title number, performed by Kelly in a studio rainstorm. Comden and Green added a little something of their own in the shape of the song spoofing diction coaches who tried to turn silent stars into talkers by making them work at tongue twisters:

> Moses supposes his toeses are roses,
> But Moses supposes erroneously.
> Moses he knowes his toeses aren't roses
> As Moses supposes his toeses to be.

All the numbers are just great. In fact, here we have all film which comes close to fulfilling that famous claim of the late twenties:

100% singing! 100% dancing! 100% talking!

Gene Kelly is one of the magic names of Hollywood, but although he was working there in 1942 and is still at it, he had only four or five years right at the top, from *On the Town* in 1949 until, say, 1954's *It's Always Fair Weather*, a generally unattractive piece distinguished by his solo dance on roller skates. By then the fashion for musicals was waning, and they had become too costly to produce for a minority audience. *On the Town* was in fact a development of two earlier musicals, the rather dull *Anchors Aweigh*, also about three sailors on leave and memorable for his dance with a cartoon mouse, and *Take Me Out to the Ball Game*, a much zippier affair about three baseball players. Here Kelly did the most Irish number of his career, a George M. Cohan-style romp called 'It Is the Hat My Father Wore Upon St Patrick's Day', and along with Frank Sinatra and Jules Munshin participated in 'O'Brien to Ryan to Goldberg'. The same trio featured in *On The Town*, a simple tale of a crowded day in New York; the first half at least is the equal of *Singin' in the Rain* for sheer brashness and verve, but invention flags in the last couple of reels. This is partly attributable to the character played by Kelly, gloomy Gaby, searching the streets of New York for his lost love and dreaming up a drab classical ballet to drown his sorrows. Nothing however can diminish the zest of 'Prehistoric Man' or 'Come Up to My Place' or the title song:

> New York, New York, it's a wonderful town.
> The Bronx is up and the Battery's down.
> The people ride in a hole in the ground.
> New York, New York, it's a wonderful town.

The critics at the time said there wasn't a tune you could whistle, but they must have lacked the right kind of ear.

Then of course there is the contrasting gossamer splendour of *An American in Paris*. No doubt about the whistleability of these tunes, for they were all by George Gershwin, and because of him, and Paris, and Toulouse-Lautrec, the movie collected a whole gallery of Academy Awards and put Kelly, who co-directed with Vincente Minnelli, at the pinnacle of his fame. In fact by now Mr Kelly's beaming good guy characterization was beginning to wear a little thin, but nobody expected him to act when he could dance like that. (He called it hoofing, but what's in a name?) The big set-piece here is a twenty-minute ballet, much better than the one in *On the Town* but somehow dissociated from the rest of the movie; most instantly likeable is the simple kerbside number with the kids, 'I've Got Rhythm', while I have a distinct preference for comedy numbers like 'By Strauss' and 'Just Listen to My Heart'. What tends to slow down this airy movie is the romance with Leslie Caron, who seems pretty depressed throughout; personally I'm always rooting for the more predatory Nina Foch as the wealthy American patronne who wants more from Kelly than his pictures. Undoubtedly *An American in Paris* is packed with incidental pleasures, but unless you're in absolutely the right mood, sitting through it can be rather like eating one chocolate éclair too many. *Singin' in the Rain* has the sense and skill to end while the appetite is still stimulated.

Singin' in the Rain. US 1952; Technicolor; 103 minutes. Produced by Arthur Freed for MGM. Written by Adolph Green and Betty Comden. Directed by Gene Kelly and Stanley Donen. Photographed by Harold Rosson. Music score by Nacio Herb Brown. Musical direction by Lennie Hayton. Art direction by Cedric Gibbons and Randall Duell. Edited by Adrienne Fazan. With Gene Kelly as Don Lockwood; Donald O'Connor as Cosmo; Debbie Reynolds as Kathy Selden; Jean Hagen as Lina Lamont; Millard Mitchell as R. F. Simpson; Douglas Fowley as Roscoe Dexter; Rita Moreno as Zelda; Cyd Charisse as dancer.

Our Dear Old Friends
Sons of the Desert

Wishing to attend a convention in Chicago, Laurel and Hardy tell their wives that they are going to Honolulu for Olly's health. But the boat on which they were due to return is sunk . . .

In my filmgoing infancy I often found the short supporting subjects more entertaining than the headliner. Every Hollywood studio not only had a cartoon factory but made or distributed comedies, musicals and 'interests' running one or two reels, and since features in those days seldom lasted more than 75 minutes there was room for quite a selection in the average two-hour show. Leon Errol, Unusual Occupations, Edgar Kennedy, Crime Does Not Pay, The Three Stooges, Pete Smith Specialties, Bugs Bunny, Tom and Jerry, Screen Snapshots and John Nesbitt's Passing Parade were all grist to my mill; but two particular stars in this field, in the years up to 1935, rose way above any others in my affections and in the affections of almost all Boltonians, whose 27 cinemas queued up to book reissue after reissue of their two-reelers. Perhaps they were particularly attuned to the Lancashire workers of that time who, like themselves, ambled through life full of good fellowship and blissful ignorance of the world at large.

Once when a new adventure of theirs turned up, the Capitol's publicity man hit upon a particularly apposite turn of phrase. 'In addition', he wrote for the *Evening News* advertisement, 'we have pleasure in presenting our dear old friends, *Mr Laurel and Mr Hardy*.' That was all: not even the title of their new escapade was given, because it wasn't necessary. With Stan and Ollie on the screen, even in something you'd seen before, you could start laughing while you were still in the queue. Just by being themselves, or what we took to be themselves, they were foolish, funny, and entirely sympathetic, like over-indulged members of the family, and I grew up regarding them as just that. Indeed every Sunday morning, when my father and my Uncle Jesse used to put on their best suits and bowlers and saunter down the street for a pre-prandial half of mild at the Greens Arms, I used to whistle Stan and Ollie's cuckoo theme after them; for one was thin and one well-rounded, and by reason of their facial expressions and their basic gentleness they might almost have got themselves jobs at the Hal Roach Studio as stand-ins for the famous pair.

Once you knew and loved their characteristics, there was no great element of surprise about Laurel and Hardy's comedy routines. In fact, what made them funny was that you knew exactly what was going to happen, and it always happened bang on cue. Olly's selfish and childlike pride, for instance in preceding Stan through a doorway, would on all occasions be promptly followed by a savage fall. (Between them they could come through a door in more funny ways than I've had hot dinners.) Stan's infant wonder and curiosity would land the pair of them in one fine mess after another. Whenever, as much-married men, they decided to enjoy an innocent but forbidden night on the tiles, retribution would be swift and cataclysmic, often involving the complete collapse of the vehicle in which they were travelling. If, as occasionally happened, Stan did something mystifyingly clever, such as his celebrated earsy-eyesy-nosey routine, Olly would diligently practise it until he did himself an injury. For Olly knew that he was smarter than Stan; but the fates knew that his smartness was a kind of dumbness. Even when Olly took the reins he was likely to end up in a sooty fireplace with

SONS OF THE DESERT. At the convention, Olly and Stan meet practical jokester Charlie Chase; and Olly is going to get it right in the eye

bricks falling down the chimney onto his head; and when he finally looked up to ensure that the flow had stopped, that would be the cue for one more brick to fall. These basic themes developed but never really varied; they always came up fresh because they were full of human truth.

Once seen, Stan and Olly can never be forgotten, for they are satisfyingly individual and of a piece. Short of stature and intellect, Stan is placid and willing, his long pale face occasionally animated by a parade of larger-than-life expressions and gestures. The beaming self-satisfied smile from ear to ear. The head-scratching with eyebrows raised high. The myopic peer down the tilted nose for closer inspection of something hard to understand. The simple mouth pursed in indignation. The rare determined walk with flailing arms. The infantile tears. The composite of all these was a clown unique in the history of comedy. Olly by contrast had a large and self-satisfied physical presence, which made all the more remarkable

429

his agility on the run. His trademarks were his southern gallantry disguising a basic fear of women, his frequently bruised but never tarnished dignity, and his incurable optimism that their joint fortunes must surely change for the better, despite what he takes to be his friend's weaknesses. Till the better times come he will remain philosophical about the inevitable setbacks, and we shall often be privileged to see his embarrassed tie twiddle and his 'I told you so' camera look, and to hear his long sustained yell as disaster strikes, mercifully offscreen.

Out of a mere hundred essays I could not possibly restrict myself to only one on Laurel and Hardy. I shall therefore postpone discussion of their more fantasticated humour until we get to *Way Out West*, and treat in this space their domestic side as displayed in the very best of their 'realistic' comedies, *Sons of the Desert*. The interesting thing about this piece is that it could easily have been adapted for almost any other comedians one might mention, though of course Stan and Ollie make it so entirely their own that it is in these incarnations that one most often thinks of them. There is certainly more plot than usual, less slapstick, and more characterization. The final resolution depends not on a chase but on whether Stan will tell the truth to his wife. 'Honesty is good for the soul,' she informs him sternly, and almost instantly his tear ducts turn on and to Olly's consternation he is pouring out the whole regrettable story of their secret defection to Chicago and a good time with the Elks and their 'exhausted ruler'. With rich justice the fibbing Olly ends up having the entire contents of the kitchen hurled at him, while Stan, in a silk dressing gown, is wined and fed by his ever-loving spouse. This forms a splendid contrast to the opening reel, when Olly announces that they are going to Chicago because he says so.

OLLY: Every man should be king in his own castle. Do you have to ask your wife everything?
STAN: Well, if I didn't I wouldn't know what she wanted me to do.

On arrival at the Hardy ménage, however, Olly finds himself at the butt end of a torrent of invective, while Stan sits absent-mindedly chewing wax fruit. When it is over he has the last word: 'Well, I may not be king of my castle, but I wouldn't allow my wife to wear any pants.' Stung, Olly evolves a plot. He will assume a nervous breakdown – the kind that is treatable only by Pacific sunshine –

and Stan will bring a doctor willing to testify. Astoundingly, though the doc is a veterinarian who gives Olly horse pills, the scheme works, and Olly is proud of himself. 'To catch a Hardy they've got to get up very early in the morning.' 'What time?' asks Stan.

Meanwhile in two minutes flat Stan has contrived to upset the contents of a footbath over three separate people; but eventually they do go to Chicago, have a hysterical time reverting to second childhood with Charlie Chase, and on the appropriate day turn up on their own doorsteps with leis round their necks, singing 'Honolulu Baby' to small banjos. Just as they discover that they are supposed to be in a shipwreck, the wives turn up in a taxi, and Stan and Ollie are forced to take refuge in their own roof void. Stan is all for confessing, but Olly is adamant: 'If you spill the beans I'll tell Betty I saw you smoking a cigarette.' 'All right,' says Stan, 'you can . . .' (his face falls). 'Would you really tell her that?' In a sense this exchange holds the vital clue to the appeal of Laurel and Hardy. Their pranks and misdemeanours are those of naughty schoolboys in men's clothing. Physically they have grown up, and are married, and in business. But mentally they remain in never-never-land, viewing women and the whole world through glasses of the rosiest hue and with the naïvety of infants.

Meanwhile we approach the final plot complication. Alarming the sleeping wives by a loud noise, they have to escape over the roof, in the pouring rain and in the dark. Descending, Stan finds himself at the bottom of a drainpipe, up to his armpits in a butt of cold water. Looking up, he calls to Olly: 'Spread your legs.' So Olly spreads his legs, and lands bottom first in the tub, arms and legs akimbo. At this point a suspicious cop takes them in charge.

COP: Where do you live?
OLLY (*in his nightshirt*): I'd rather not say.
COP (*to Stan*): Where do you live?
STAN: Next door to him.
COP: And where does he live?
STAN: In there.
OLLY: Here's another fine mess you've gotten me into.

This may or may not sound funny in print, but on the screen it is side-splitting and magnificent. Throughout this film, in fact, the timing is perfect and the acting of both comedians and 'wives' absolutely convincing within its chosen limits: the boys were clearly working with colleagues who appreciated them. They were always fortunate with wives, in other features such as *Blockheads* and *Our Relations* and especially in a few of their best shorts, notably *Come Clean* in which they are sent out to get ice-cream and come back with a lady of the streets whom they have saved from a watery grave and who now demands that they look after her. Wifeless, in *Below Zero* they are dignified but bankrupt street musicians who find a windfall and order a grand restaurant meal: 'And I shall have a demitasse,' declares Olly. 'Yes,' says Stan, 'I'll have one of those, and a cup of coffee too.'

Oddly enough, when they played their own children in *Brats* it hardly worked at all, for childlike behaviour is only funny when performed by professed grown-ups. They were childlike enough in *Towed in a Hole*: as fish salesmen anxious to eliminate the middle man, they buy a boat, paint and wreck it in the same morning. *Their First Mistake* is one with curious overtones: Mrs Hardy, the splendid Mae Busch, wants Stan out of the house and out of Olly's life:

OLLY: She says I think more of you than I do of her.
STAN: Well, you do, don't you?
OLLY: We won't go into that.

What the Hardys need to keep them together, says Stan, is a baby. Olly thinks he's right. 'You bet I'm right,' agrees Stan. 'You know, I'm not so dumb as you look.' So they go out to adopt a baby; but when they return with it, Mrs Hardy has walked out for good and all, and is suing Stan for the alienation of Olly's affections. We had better pass on quickly and finally to their short masterpiece *The Music Box*, which won an Academy Award in 1932. Here it takes them three reels to get a piano to a house atop a flight of steps – and of course to wreck everything in sight. If you haven't seen it, you haven't lived. And if ever you go to Los Angeles, that flight of steps is still very much in evidence, and Sons of the Desert flock to it every weekend in pilgrimage.

Sons of the Desert. US 1933; monochrome; 68 minutes. Produced by Hal Roach. Written by Frank Craven, Nat Hoffberg and Byron Morgan. Directed by William A. Seiter. Photographed by Kenneth Peach. Music score by William Axt, Marvin Hatley and others. With Laurel and Hardy as themselves; Charley Chase as himself; Mae Busch as Mrs Hardy; Dorothy Christie as Mrs Laurel.

Figures in a Landscape
Stagecoach

***Passengers in a stagecoach through Indian country find their
lives changed, even before the Indians attack, by their
influence on each other.***

In 1966 I attended a press conference at Claridge's to hear the views
and intentions of Martin Rackin, who was about to remake this
classic 1939 film by John Ford. For some entirely ill-advised reason
he spent most of the time between drinks in attacking his model. A
has-been leading man, drunken bums for actors, a script that was all
talk, a director who never was box office, and so on. The press
listened in stupefied silence, and made up its communal mind to
dislike Mr Rackin's remake even before they saw it. As it turned out,
it needed no help to fail: it was woodenly written and acted, and the
American critics savaged it. What Mr Rackin had failed to observe
was that it is not the actor himself, but the impression he gives in a
part, that matters, and that *Stagecoach* is not basically an action story
requiring the grand manner, but a series of connected anecdotes
about people. The story on which it was based owes allegiance to de
Maupassant's *Boule de Suif*, and the success of the 1939 version was
largely due to its having a director who knew how to fashion a
sequence, get the most out of the faces in his gallery, and frame a
shot for the utmost dramatic interest.

The negative was never well cared for. Being an independent
production, it passed through various hands, and by the time John
Wayne tried to buy up the rights it was scratched and blemished
almost beyond recall. But it still looks well enough on small-screen
television, which is the way most classics will have to be shown in
the future. It was never a very glossy film anyway: I remember that
when I first saw it at the Bolton Odeon in 1939 it had a B picture
look despite its A picture content. In a sense it isn't much of a
western either. Irrelevant shots of Indians on the warpath appear
under the main title, but that's to obscure the fact that another
eighty minutes are to pass before the next piece of action, which is

433

the famous chase across the salt flats; after that, even the final shoot-up takes place offscreen. The journey with which it concerns itself could equally well have been taken by train or sea: although towards the end interest shifts to the Ringo Kid and his revenge, the character who mainly concerns us is the good-hearted prostitute shunned by her fellow-travellers. So it is Claire Trevor who gets top billing, and it is through her shrewd eyes that we assess the other characters.

They are that miscellaneous crew so beloved of Hollywood: not quite Morino, Halberstadt, Pulaski and O'Brien, but their 1880 equivalents. In God's own country, it seems, there is room for everybody, even the absconding banker played with such splendid huff and puff by Berton Churchill. (One feels that if the Hays Office had allowed him to get away with it in the end, no one would really have minded.) Hatfield, the Southern gentleman gambler, is somehow a less comfortable, less sympathetic creation, although he has the right instincts; perhaps John Carradine was not quite the actor to play him. There are nuances of caste here which are not fully understood by non-Americans: it seems to the average audience that he is far exceeding his moral right in planning to shoot the young mother rather than have her suffer a fate worse than death at the hands of the Apaches. Luckily an Indian arrow gets him just as he squeezes the trigger, but the single shot of Louise Platt clutching her baby and praying, as the muzzle of the gun inches closer and closer to her temple, is one of the most emotive in film history. Miss Platt has little to do but look delicate, and she does that very well. Comedy comes from Donald Meek as the whisky salesman taken by everyone for a parson: it's the best part this little man ever had, and when he gets an arrow in the shoulder it's a genuine shock, though the movie sends us home happy in the knowledge of his recovery. Thomas Mitchell is the boozy doctor, who takes his shingle with him when run out of town, and comes to his senses pretty smartly in such a crisis as an unexpected birth. (*Very* unexpected, to judge from Miss Platt's face and figure.) He completes the official passenger list, with Andy Devine and George Bancroft as driver and riding shotgun to provide a running commentary on the peccadilloes of their passengers. But along the trail John Wayne hitches a ride, and we all know that it can now be only a matter of time before the action starts. Even when he's saying nothing, Wayne exudes such star appeal that it's a matter for wonder how Hollywood let him linger for nine years in bottom-of-the-barrel second features before Ford brought him back into the limelight.

To cram these characters into a tiny stagecoach, three abreast facing each other, often with a seventh lying on the floor between their legs, and to keep the images logical and interesting, is no mean feat: that is one of Ford's two major triumphs in this picture. The other is of course the salt flats sequence, with Apaches on horseback yarooping and yelling as they all but catch up the rattling vehicle, and Yakima Canutt doubling for Wayne and making his famous leap amid the horse team to grab the reins and steer the leading pair to safety. He doesn't quite make it, but the seventh cavalry shows up at just the right moment. We knew they would.

The question has often been asked, why didn't the Indians shoot the horses? The cynical answer is that it would have brought the movie abruptly to an unacceptable end, but Ford himself claims that the horses were what the Indians were really after, so that to shoot them would have defeated their own object. It has also been objected that the final reel, showing Ringo's vengeance on Luke Plummer in Lordsburg, is an anti-climax, but it's a pretty tense affair on its own account and it does work out the romantic side of the plot, leaving Ringo both revenged and free to set up on a farm with Dallas. Besides, the images are menacing and the music memorable, with Tom Tyler as the stone-faced villain seeming to be rehearsing for his role next year as the stalking terror in *The Mummy's Hand*; his return to the bar after the shoot-out, his walk up to the bar and sudden collapse, is a cunningly judged piece of filmcraft.

Although a long film by the standards of its time, *Stagecoach* has no fat on it. Romance, humour and philosophy are made to arise out of the situation; characterization is given on the run. The nearest we get to a moral is that folks gotta do what folks gotta do, as evinced in this dialogue between the doctor and the whore:

DALLAS: Ringo asked me to marry him. Is that wrong? For a girl like me? If a man and woman love each other?

Doc: You're going to be hurt, child, worse than you've ever been hurt. Don't you know that boy's headed for prison? Besides, if you two go into Lordsburg together, he's going to know all about you.

DALLAS: He's not going into Lordsburg. All I want is for you to tell me it's all right.

STAGECOACH. The coming together of director John Ford with Monument Valley, the world's most impressive natural backdrop

Doc: Gosh, child, who am I to tell you what's right or wrong? All right, go ahead, do it if you can. And good luck.

John Ford has told how he had to make *Stagecoach* as an independent because the big studios at that time were chary of westerns, having brought the genre to its knees by robbing it of air. What kind of westerns could survive stars who didn't leave the studio, performing against back projection plates obtained by a second unit? Walter Wanger finally found the money, but wanted Gary Cooper and Marlene Dietrich for the leads: luckily the budget wouldn't run to them. It was Ford who thought of Monument Valley as a splendid setting, and afterwards used it again and again. It was he who devised the final shootout, based on memories of his friend Wyatt Earp and the legendary gunfight at the OK Corral. The total cost of production was just over 200,000 dollars, and even after the previews the giants of the industry were grudging in their praise.

Luckily the public, as so often, knew better, and the film's success had an enormous impact on several careers, as well as on the development of the western.

As to why make westerns at all, Ford had an answer for that too:

I never look at them, but I love to make them. Why? Because they're made mostly on location. You're out there in the open, away from the smog and the freeways. You're with a bunch of stunt men who are your friends, and they keep a pitch game going all the time. You eat well – I always insisted on the best possible food on location. You work from dawn until sunset, and you sleep like a baby at night. It's a great life – who wouldn't like it?

Stagecoach. US 1939; monochrome; 99 minutes. Produced by Walter Wanger for his own company. Written by Dudley Nichols, from the story 'Stage to Lordsburg' by Ernest Haycox. Directed by John Ford. Photographed by Bert Glennon and Ray Binger. Music score by John Leopold and Leo Shuken. Edited by Dorothy Spencer and Walter Reynolds. With John Wayne as the Ringo Kid; Claire Trevor as Dallas; Thomas Mitchell as Doc Boone; George Bancroft as Curley; Berton Churchill as Gatewood; Donald Meek as Peacock; John Carradine as Hatfield; Louise Platt as Lucy Mallory; Andy Devine as Buck; Tom Tyler as Luke Plummer.

Just Plain Folks
Star Spangled Rhythm

When a sailor and his friend dock for one day's leave at San Pedro, his father and girl friend, respectively doorman and telephone operator at Paramount, pretend to be running the studio and persuade all the stars to put on a show for the navy.

With three thousand seats, the Blackpool Odeon was the biggest cinema in England, and I looked forward to inspecting it. It opened just before the war, but my opportunity didn't come until 1943, when the LMS railway put on an excursion with a midnight return back to Bolton, and after an enjoyable day on the sands and in the Tower I finally passed through the delectable portals at about 6.30 P.M., sank blissfully into a perfectly adjusted mid-stalls seat, and watched an impeccably projected print of *Star Spangled Rhythm* unspool itself on the gleaming giant screen. I entered just as Goddard, Lamour and Lake were putting over their self-spoofing number, 'A Sweater, a Sarong and a Peek-a-boo Bang'. I found it rather puzzling, as I didn't know that a bang was a curl of hair, but I was overwhelmed by the sheer pulchritude of that celebrated trio, and delighted when Arthur Treacher, Walter Catlett and Sterling Holloway came on in drag to spoof the spoof. It was just one item in an easy-going movie of which that holiday audience roared its entire approval. Anyone coming fresh to it today would probably find its characterizations faintly embarrassing and its plot contrivances distinctly thin, but what the hell, it was fun, and one can still imagine the effect it must have had on the morale of a world engulfed in total war, with its flagwaving numbers, its generous ragbag of jokes and stunts, and its revelation that the biggest stars were just plain folks at heart who would do anything, even knock off work early, to boost the spirits of the navy.

Perhaps *Star Spangled Rhythm* isn't even the best of the star-studded studio musicals of the forties (for the habit was catching). But it has so many things I like. Its depiction of Paramount Studios is still recognizable; its triumph was that it was able to inveigle Cecil B. de Mille and Preston Sturges into playing themselves and doing so with aplomb. It starts promisingly with a cartoon variation on the regular Paramount mountain-and-stars logo and a fast-moving roller title which goes one better than *The Jolson Story*'s by having all the glamorous names remain visible as they recede into the twinkling sky and grow ever smaller. The plot then has to be set up. Betty Hutton has to do a dozen funny voices and belie her boy friend's assurance to his pals that she's the refined type by leaping over a desk to seize him in an amorous half-Nelson. Cass Daley comes in for no reason, asks 'Shall I do it here?' and does. There are cringe-making lines like: 'It's a pleasure to shake the hand that picked up Dorothy Lamour's option.' Through all this malarkey stalks the harassed figure of Walter Abel, playing the studio head who is convinced by Hutton's devious plans that he has been fired. His character name is G. B. de Soto, and the studio head at the time was B. G. de Sylva: get it?

The style settles down into that of *Hellzapoppin*; soon we shall be surprised by nothing. Hope wanders in to gag about Crosby, Crosby responds. Hope says he has a date with Veronica Lake: 'She's going to show me her other eye.' (The studio obviously had a conscience about foisting the only mildly talented Lake onto the public, for Abel later has a line: 'About that Lake test, I think covering both eyes is too much.') Preston Sturges, believing that de Soto has walked out

STAR SPANGLED RHYTHM. A sweater, a sarong and a peek-a-boo bang: Arthur Treacher, Walter Catlett and Sterling Holloway take off Mesdames Goddard, Lamour and Lake

on his rushes, screams 'I think I'm going to Metro' and falls over a trash can. (Incidentally they might have had Sturges directing something more likely than Dick Powell and Mary Martin singing 'Meet Me on the Road to Dreamland', which is clearly an offcut from another movie.) Nervous Victor Moore as the doorman, hovering indecisively over the executive's chair, asks Hutton what he should do if the phone rings. 'Say it stinks,' she advises him. 'That's the way all the big executives do it.' Not too surprisingly, his first call is from de Mille wanting to know what de Soto thinks of his latest production.

As the big show nears, the movie dissolves into a series of routines and numbers. Betty Hutton and the sailors have a zany jeep ride around town to the song 'I'm Doing It For Defence', with their doubles taking a mighty lot of punishment as the vehicle bounces over a number of solid obstacles. Betty Jane Rhodes, Dona Drake and Marjorie Reynolds share an absurdly shimmering 'factory' number which might now count as camp and includes the immortal lyric:

439

Overtime?
Here's why I'm
Doin' it free –
'Cos baby's with me on the swing shift jamboree!

De Soto returns to his wrecked office and wails: 'Somebody's been sitting in my chair. Somebody's been drinking at my bar. Somebody's been smoking my cigars, and smoked them all up!' Hutton is banned from the studio and tries to get back over the wall, hindered rather than helped by passers-by in the shape of Walter Dare Wahl and Company, proprietors of that irresistible burlesque routine in which three people lock hands and try to get out of it by stepping over each other's arms until they lock themselves in a gruesome anatomical tangle. This in fact is the movie in which Miss Hutton amply demonstrates that she's a girl ready for anything, and for sheer grit probably deserved some sort of Oscar.

The show itself, though wildly applauded by the navy, is a mixed bag. A sketch in which Tone, MacMurray, Milland and Overman show what would happen if men played cards as women do is pretty feeble; the obligatory black number, 'With a Belt in the Back', has production values and not much else; some rationing sketches were funnier at the time. Better is a playlet in which Hope gives the laugh line to Jerry Colonna who, after the wife of the suspicious Hope has protested she is as honest as the day is long, pops out of the wardrobe to enunciate: 'Short day, wasn't it?' And Johnny Johnston's rendering of 'That Old Black Magic', with a dance in the snow by Vera Zorina, is a little classic of its light pop kind, which is rather more than can be said for Bing Crosby's patriotic finale, standing on a hilltop and intoning 'Old Glory' to a crowd of suspiciously typical Americans. All that can be said in defence of this number is that we were trying to win a war at the time.

The Warner all-star extravaganza, *Thank Your Lucky Stars*, emerged a year later. I saw it in Manchester at the old Theatre Royal, the only cinema I ever knew with a lift to take one up to the balcony; when I entered, Ann Sheridan was telling a group of expensively negligéed co-eds that 'Love Isn't Born, It's Made' (and that's why ev'ry window has a window shade). The gimmick here was that all the stars played more or less against type. Errol Flynn, spoofing his own much derided physical prowess, was a boastful cockney in 'That's What You Jolly Well Get'. Olivia de Havilland and Ida Lupino did a jitterbug. And Bette Davis, in an amusing, well-performed but much criticized number, bemoaned the lack of romantic manpower on the home front:

> They're either too young or too old;
> They're either too grey or too grassy green.
> The pickings are poor and the crop is lean.
>   There isn't any gravy;
>   The gravy's in the navy . . .
> Tomorrow I'll go hiking with an eagle scout unless
> I get a call from grandpa for a snappy game of chess . . .
> I'm finding it easy to stay good as gold:
> They're either too young or too old.

Eddie Cantor in a dual role was clearly prepared to spoof the inflated ego of Cantor the entertainer, wanting to produce the show as well as star in it, and singing a song intended as propaganda against the waste of petrol:

> We're staying home tonight, my baby and me,
> Having a patriotic time!

And the black number this time was called 'Ice Cold Katie'. It was all rather like amateur night at Burbank, but it went down effortlessly at the time, and if there were ever a Warner version of *That's Entertainment*, much of it would bear revival.

Oddly enough, the MGM attempt to get all its stars into a patriotic musical, *Thousands Cheer*, lacked humour, while its arty and plotless *Ziegfeld Follies* seemed merely pretentious. Universal didn't try very hard, its roster of musical talent having diminished since 1930 when it commissioned the unique, theatrical and still spellbinding *King of Jazz*, though in 1944 the studio came up with *Follow the Boys*, a feeble account of how Hollywood entertained the troops, with Orson Welles unconvincingly sawing Marlene Dietrich in half. Darryl Zanuck at Fox, however, presented an all-star, all-black movie of some pace and style. *Stormy Weather* had a vaguely morale-building plot purporting to tell the life story, in and out of uniform, of Bill Robinson. The fact that he was there performing, along with Lena Horne, Fats Waller, Katherine Dunham, Cab Calloway and the Nicholas Brothers was what really mattered, but the film was not widely appreciated. Thirty years later, oddly enough, theatrical shows like *Bubbling Brown Sugar* and *Ain't Misbehavin'* used similar elements without the class, and were hugely popular.

Star Spangled Rhythm. US 1942; monochrome; 99 minutes. Produced by Joseph Sistrom for Paramount. Written by Harry Tugend. Directed by George Marshall. Photographed by Leo Tover and Theodor Sparkuhl. Music direction by Robert Emmett Dolan. Songs by Johnny Mercer and Harold Arlen. Edited by Arthur Schmidt. With Betty Hutton as Polly Judson; Eddie Bracken as Jimmy Webster; Victor Moore as Pop Webster; Walter Abel as B. G. de Soto; and the Paramount stars.

Thank Your Lucky Stars. US 1943; monochrome; 127 minutes. Produced by Mark Hellinger for Warners. Written by Norman Panama, Melvin Frank, James V. Kern. Directed by David Butler. Photographed by Arthur Edeson. Music direction by Leo B. Forbstein. Art direction by Anton Grot and Leo E. Kuter. Dance direction by Le Roy Prinz. Songs by Frank Loesser and Arthur Schwartz. With Eddie Cantor as Joe Sampson; Joan Leslie as Pat Dixon; Dennis Morgan as Tommy Randolph; Edward Everett Horton as Farnsworth; S. Z. Sakall as Schlenna; and the Warner stars.

With a Little Bit of Sex
Sullivan's Travels

A film director famous for comedy goes on a safari among the lowest of the land; but his sobering experiences convince him that comedy is what people really need.

Writer, director, inventor, restaurateur, Preston Sturges was a wacky and unpredictable near-genius whose drive, imagination and facility with words and actors took him in the early forties to the highest pinnacle of Hollywood success: his name above the title. Then, for reasons never satisfactorily explained – though drink had a little to do with it – came the downfall. Photographs of him in his heyday show him apparently suffering colossal hangovers; and when his Paramount contract ended in 1944 he had the misfortune to become involved with Howard Hughes, an experience which seems to have driven him abortively to the wrong kind of subject. When he came back to comedy, his talent was almost gone. Perhaps he had simply written himself out, though it is indeed puzzling how this could happen so immediately after *Hail the Conquering Hero*, a prolifically inventive piece. *Unfaithfully Yours*, which came four years later, has its manic moments, but the later films are a sorry lot indeed, and when in 1955 he made *The Diaries of Major Thompson* in France, there was barely a trace left of the talent which fourteen years earlier had gone off over Hollywood like a firework.

At least we have the eight films of his Paramount heyday to be thankful for. They are unique in their combination of satire, sentimentality, near-tragedy and pratfall farce, all presented at twisting, turning speed with a reckless but total command of the film medium. Delightfully, they also use a shifting repertory company of Hollywood's most endearing comedy character actors: genial, shifty Raymond Walburn; pompous, prissy Franklin Pangborn; overbearing gravel-voiced Al Bridge; lugubrious Eric Blore; portly/pompous Eugene Pallette, Robert Greig, Robert Warwick; spidery Jimmy Conlin; explosive Edgar Kennedy; crumple-faced Porter Hall; above all dumb, bossy, lovable William Demarest. Most of them contributed their finest moments to the illumination of Sturges' scripts; and he also did well by some unlikely leads, for example Brian Donlevy, Eddie Bracken, Betty Hutton and Veronica Lake, while almost single-handedly he rescued Joel McCrea from a life on horseback and turned him into a handsome representative of a type of comic uncertainty which seemed appealing at the time, and still does.

If one of these films is singled out above the others it has to be *Sullivan's Travels*, because the confidence which comes of first success was sitting on his shoulders when he made it, because Paramount was clearly willing to give unlimited indulgence in terms of cost and theme to its newly elected boy wonder, and because of the wonderful ease with which he sidesteps from pratfalls into sudden death, from a tear in the eye to a custard pie in the face, with no noticeable grinding of gears, to give a graphic impression of the mixed-up mad parade which, for most people, is life. *Sullivan's Travels* begins with a fight to the death on top of a speeding train, but it quickly turns out to be the last scene of Sullivan's latest dramatic movie, which he is showing to his studio bosses. The ensuing conversation has to be the fastest in screen history:

SULLIVAN: You see the symbolism of it? Capital and labour destroy each other . . . I want this picture to be a commentary on modern ideas . . . stark realism . . . the problems that confront the average man.
Boss A: With a little bit of sex.
SULLIVAN: With a little bit of sex in it, but I don't want to stretch it. I want

this picture to be a document. I want to hold a mirror up to life. I want this to be a picture of dignity . . . a true picture of the sufferings of humanity.

BOSS A: But with a little bit of sex.

SULLIVAN: With a little sex in it.

BOSS B: How about a nice musical?

SULLIVAN: How can you talk about musicals at a time like this, with the world committing suicide, with corpses piling up on the streets, with grim death gargling at you from every corner, with people slaughtered like sheep?

BOSS B: Maybe they'd like to forget that.

SULLIVAN: Then why did they hold this one over for a fifth week at the Music Hall? For the ushers?

BOSS A: It died in Pittsburgh.

BOSS B: Like a dog.

SULLIVAN: What do they know in Pittsburgh?

BOSS A: They know what they like.

SULLIVAN: If they knew what they liked, they wouldn't live in Pittsburgh.

There's no answer to that, but as the sequence ends, with Sullivan getting reluctant approval for his voyage of discovery into America's hinterland, doing personal research for *O Brother Where Art Thou* instead of preparing a sequel to *Ants in Your Pants of 1939*, we sense that before long he's going to be very sorry he started this. And indeed he is, though not till the third movement. The first is outright farce, as he sets out on foot across country, tailed by an enormous trailer filled with studio assistants. When he tries to give them the slip, the massively overloaded vehicle careers after him, to the accompaniment of the *William Tell* overture, in the best slapstick sequence since the Keystone Kops. Lodging at a farm, he finds himself stalked by two frustrated old spinsters, and is glad to make his escape back to Hollywood. Here, breakfasting in a diner, he meets a failed young actress (Veronica Lake in a performance that makes you think she could really act) who doesn't believe a word of his yarn till he takes her back to his Beverley Hills pad (with a swimming pool I've always coveted, one which from the yard continues under a door and comes up right in the living room). Here Sturges makes another of his inimitable stopovers for farce, with pompous people falling into the pool, but the serious point is made by the butler, who counsels Sullivan against making another attempt to study poverty in the raw:

SULLIVAN'S TRAVELS. Joel McCrea suffers from too many well-intentioned nuisances. Byron Foulger, William Demarest, Franklin Pangborn, Margaret Hayes, Veronica Lake, Porter Hall, Robert Warwick

If you'll permit me to say so, the subject is not an interesting one. The poor know all about poverty, and only the morbid rich find the subject glamorous. You see, sir, rich people and theorists, who are usually rich people, think of poverty in the negative, as the lack of riches. But it isn't, sir. Poverty is not the lack of anything, but a positive plague, virulent in itself, contagious as cholera, with filth, criminality, vice and despair as only a few of its symptoms. It is to be stayed away from, even for purposes of study. It is to be shunned.

Any novice must be hooked by a movie in which that speech goes to the *butler*.

Despite the direst warnings, Sullivan sets off again, with the girl this time (disguised as a boy, which evokes some Shakespearian connotations). They hop a ride on a freight train, and this time the studio spies maintain a discreet distance. The controlled experiment is a success; Sullivan gets his script, but he makes the mistake of one more excursion, solo and by night, in order to distribute largesse and thereby assuage his guilt. It is his undoing. He is assaulted and robbed by a hobo, who steals his clothes and is then, in a briefly terrifying sequence, run down by a freight train and mangled beyond recognition. In Hollywood Sullivan is mourned; in reality, temporarily amnesiac from his attack, he suffers a series of undignified misadventures which land him finally in a Georgia chain gang (which seems to have strayed more from twenties fantasy than from forties actuality). Forced one Sunday to attend a religious service in a Negro church, he sees the faces of the downtrodden poor light up when a Mickey Mouse cartoon is projected as part of the simple entertainment; and when a convenient whim of fortune restores him noisily to sanity, fame and the film studio, he refuses to make the socially conscious epic which Bosses A and B now think would result in great publicity. He insists 'There's a lot to be said for making people laugh. It isn't much, but it's all some people have. And it's better than nothing in this cockeyed caravan. Boy!'

A simple moral, but perhaps it contained more truth than even Sturges knew. One also has the feeling at the end of *Sullivan's Travels*, while one is still reeling from the extraordinary mixture of farce and melodrama, that although Sturges clearly had something to get off his mind, he wasn't sure at the end whether or not he had done so successfully. What matters most, forty years on, is that the movie remains just as sporadically brilliant, just as wayward, just as overflowing with wit and character and optimism as it was on that summer evening in 1942 when I encountered it at the Bolton Odeon and promptly fell in love with Veronica Lake.

The critics of the time were in two minds about the Sturges of *Sullivan's Travels*. They had hailed the gentleman as a master of light comedy, and now he was offering them something else, something they couldn't quite put together. *Variety* worried lest the public might think the movie a sequel to *Gulliver's Travels*, and counselled exhibitors to emphasize that it wasn't a cartoon. Its reputation grew with the years, though not always in the right direction; in 1964 to the *Film Society Review* it was 'the most witty and knowing spoof of Hollywood film-making of all time', and in 1969 Eileen Bowser saw it as 'dancing on the grave of thirties social cinema'. I don't think it set out to do these things at all: it is a film unique in itself, to be taken in relation to nothing except Sturges' jaundiced but hopeful view of the world around him. As such I accept and welcome it among my ten favourite films of all.

Sullivans Travels. US 1941; monochrome; 90 minutes. Produced by Paul Jones for Paramount. Written and directed by Preston Sturges. Photographed by John Seitz and Farciot Edouart. Music score by Leo Shuken. Edited by Stuart Gilmore. With Joel McCrea as John Sullivan; Veronica Lake as the girl; Robert Warwick as Mr Lebrand; William Demarest as Mr Jones; Porter Hall as Mr Hadrian; Robert Greig as the butler; Eric Blore as the valet; Franklin Pangborn as Mr Casalsis; Byron Foulger as Mr Valdelle; Torben Meyer as doctor; Jimmy Conlin as trusty; Margaret Hayes as secretary.

Something to Look Down On
Sunset Boulevard and Ace in the Hole

A penniless Hollywood scriptwriter becomes the gigolo of a neurotic star of the silent era, who eventually shoots him. A sensation-seeking reporter keeps a man unnecessarily trapped in a cave for the sake of the headlines.

You have to like a man who describes France as 'a country where the money falls apart in your hands and you can't tear the toilet paper'. Or who, when on his first trip back to stricken Europe after the war, is asked by his wife to bring back a bidet and cables: 'Unable obtain bidet: suggest handstand in shower.' Or who tosses off television as follows: 'It used to be that movies were the lowest form of art. Now we have something to look down on.' Billy Wilder is one of Hollywood's most celebrated European expatriates, a man whose basic good humour has been made bitter by the state of the world, and perhaps too by the fact that half his family died in concentration camps. So his comedies sometimes have a heavy texture and a waspish flavour; and for the purest essence of Wilder I turn to his sardonic melodramas, whose heroes and heroines are never admirable but whose jaundiced view of the world it is easy to applaud. Once you're in the mood.

Sunset Boulevard starts with a shot of a Hollywood gutter, so you know at once that Shirley Temple isn't going to be in it. The narrator, we briskly discover, is already dead, floating head down in a swimming pool; Wilder had to be persuaded to cut long scenes in the morgue. 'Yes', says the dead man (or his shade), 'this is Sunset Boulevard, Los Angeles, California. It's about five o'clock in the morning. And here comes the homicide squad.' So another Wilder-ish day begins. The talkative corpse takes us back six months, to a time when he was *really* down on his luck, with no help forthcoming from his only studio friend, 'a smart producer with a set of ulcers to prove it'. The future is bleak. 'I talked to a couple of yes men at Metro. To me they said no.' In flight from would-be repossessors of his car, he turns into an overgrown drive, and finds himself in what might be the land of Oz, or the house of Miss Havisham in *Great Expectations*. There is even a Miss Havisham on the balcony, behind mosquito blinds and dark glasses: 'You there. Why are you so late? Why have you kept me waiting so long?'

He finds he has been mistaken for a mortician come to provide a white casket for her pet chimpanzee. He is pretty unsympathetic about the whole affair until he suddenly recognizes her:

Joe: You're Norma Desmond. You used to be in silent pictures. You used to be big.
Norma: I am big. It's the pictures that got small.

He tells her about his own wilted career: 'The last one I wrote was about Okies in the dust bowl. You'd never know, when it was released it all played on a torpedo boat.' But he can't compete with her memories of what happened in this faded mausoleum, of the time when Valentino danced the tango on the tiled ballroom floor; or with the memories of Max the mysterious butler: 'There was a maharaja who came all the way from India to beg one of her silk stockings. Later he strangled himself with it.'

In one or other of these voices, the script is filled with the kind of put-downs of Hollywood which on its release persuaded Louis B. Mayer to demand Wilder's permanent exile. In one of his periods of concern for Norma, Joe complains of the system that made her the way she is: 'A dozen press agents working overtime can do terrible things to the human spirit.' She complains about audiences: 'They don't know somebody sits down and writes a picture – they think the actors make it up as they go along.' And one imagines Wilder's tongue must have been well in his cheek when he shows Cecil B de Mille rejecting Norma's *Salome* script as old-fashioned, then turning to roll the cameras on his own stilted epic *Samson and Delilah*. (NB.

SUNSET BOULEVARD. The reluctant gigolo (William Holden) finds that his patroness's demands are excessive . . .

Six years later, Columbia did make *Salome*, and Norma Desmond's script couldn't have been much worse.)

The glittering irony of *Sunset Boulevard* is that Gloria Swanson, who played Norma, was just such a faded star, who in this role managed a spectacular comeback and almost won an Academy Award . . . only once again to fade almost completely from the sight of filmgoers. At the time this seemed incredible, with the memory still fresh of the scene in which, her hands like spider's claws, she finally conquers Joe's resistance and draws him into her bed; and of course the finale is a *tour de force*, with her murdered lover in the morgue and Norma descending the curved staircase to an accompaniment of flash bulbs and vulgar questions, oblivious to them all and murmuring: 'All right, Mr de Mille, I'm ready for my close-up now.'

Although it could benefit from a few cuts, I tend to like best of all Wilder's work *Ace in the Hole*, which gives a view of American life so unpopular as almost to have cost Wilder his career. Again we start by looking down, this time with our noses in gravel. We are in a hot dusty border town in the company of a wandering reporter who has flipped his lid once too often and needs a job. 'I can handle big news and little news, and if there's no news I'll go out and bite a dog,' he tells the sceptical editor, who has never before had an approach from a man who admits that he drinks and can be had for half rate because he once made a play for the boss's wife. Tatum looks the editor up and down and makes one last plea. 'I've lied to men who wear belts and to men who wear suspenders, but I wouldn't be such a fool as to lie to a man who wears both.' He gets the job.

Though the film is based on a genuine case of the twenties, America turned its back as though refusing to believe that for the sake of a scoop a newsman would allow a trapped explorer to die. Yet most of us who have visited New York will recognize the syndrome, for in that welcoming city, if one turns aside to investi-gate a body in the gutter, the amiable townfolk will draw one away, muttering: 'Don't get involved.' Chuck Tatum's sins are many, and they include pride; but he has the stature of a tragic hero, just as Macbeth or Coriolanus. In his case he is torn by the desire to succeed, and go on succeeding: 'Tomorrow this will be yesterday's paper.' As the girl tells him, 'I've met some hard-boiled eggs in my time, but you, you're twenty minutes.' Yet he is a heel not quite without a soul, as the final reels show: the explorer is dead, the carnival of sightseers is breaking up, and Chuck staggers back to die in the newspaper office where we began. 'You can have me for nothing,' he cries, falling headlong into the camera in a masterly final shot.

The whole of Wilder's filmcraft is masterly, but we come to expect no less. We simply wish he would hire a sharper editor; and sometimes more help on the script. *Five Graves to Cairo*, for instance, is enjoyable partly because it is so bad, such a cynical piece of manipulation for the sake of propaganda. Giving the appearance of being torn straight from the headlines – it was on the world's screens in May 1943 when the desert war it depicts was by no means over – with titles printed in type face to increase the sense of actuality and urgency, it was in fact the wildest of fantasies, fabricated hastily by Brackett and Wilder from an obscure play by Lajos Biro. (What would Hollywood have done without Hungarians?) It postulates that in 1937 Field Marshal Rommel, dedicated by the Nazi hierarchy to preparing for the North African war which was to come, visited Tunisia in the guise of an archaeologist, Professor Croenstatter, and supervised the digging of huge pits in which were buried a sufficiency of food, water and ammunition to sustain Rommel's remarkable advances in 1942. The pits, covered by sand, were identifiable by the five letters of the word Egypt on a certain map, and specifically by the decorative dots in the middle of each letter. The action of the film takes place in a bug-ridden seaside hotel, the Empress of Britain, at a hamlet called Sidi Halfaya (Hellfire?). On the day the British evacuate it, a sunstruck British corporal who is the only survivor of a tank left to career away into the endless desert (Wilder starts us off this time by staring at sand), takes refuge there with the reluctant assistance of the proprietor, played by Akim Tamiroff like an agitated S. Z. Sakall. Having taken over the identity of the clubfooted and newly dead waiter, he finds he is posing as a German spy. Rommel's entourage arrives ('The room with the bathroom which doesn't work goes to the Italian general') and after various alarums and excursions our hero, replete with secrets, is sent under Rommel's own safe conduct to prepare the field marshal's triumphant entry into Cairo and specifically to arrange a special performance of *Aida* ('in German, omitting the second act, which is too long and not too good'). This farrago of nonsense is little more than an excuse for a music hall turn by Erich Von Stroheim as Rommel, a fine strutting performance from the back of his glistening neck to the tip of his stylish fly swatter. Franchot Tone as the accidental spy is hilariously unconvincing, especially in the final scene when he has to deliver a mawkish speech over the grave of a French maid who has given her all for the cause. Wilder seems to have had great gleeful fun with this ramshackle vehicle, but he might have remembered, before taking it on, the line he gives to the despised but ebullient Italian general, who has his own view of the Axis: 'When you lie down with dogs, you wake up with fleas.'

Sunset Boulevard. US 1950; monochrome; 110 minutes. Produced by Charles Brackett for Paramount. Written by Charles Brackett, Billy Wilder and D. M. Marshman Jnr. Directed by Billy Wilder. Photographed by John Seitz. Music score by Franz Waxman. Art direction by Hans Dreier and John Meehan. Edited by Doane Harrison and Arthur Schmidt. With Gloria Swanson as Norma Desmond; William Holden as Joe Gillis; Erich Von Stroheim as Max Von Mayerling; Nancy Olson as Betty Schaefer; Fred Clark as Sheldrake; Jack Webb as Artie Green.

Ace in The Hole. US 1951; monochrome; 111 minutes. Produced and directed by Billy Wilder for Paramount. Written by Billy Wilder, Lesser Samuels and Walter Newman. Photographed by Charles Lang Jnr. Music score by Hugo Friedhofer. Art direction by Hal Pereira and Earl Hedrick. Edited by Arthur Schmidt. With Kirk Douglas as Chuck Tatum; Jan Sterling as Lorraine; Porter Hall as Boot; Bob Arthur as Herbie; Richard Benedict as Leo; Ray Teal as Sheriff.

Our Eyes Have Seen Great Wonders
The Thief of Baghdad

With the help of a cheerful young thief, a deposed and blinded king gets back his rightful throne and wins the hand of a beautiful princess.

The story of the making of this remarkable production is a sadly disjointed one. It straddled the outbreak of war, and half-way through shooting the Korda empire evacuated to California. The film therefore involved two sets of supporting actors, three directors, and a range of locations from the backlot at Denham to Bryce Canyon in Utah. For thirty years the movie seemed to have triumphed over these difficulties, until it came to the matter of ordering new prints from the old matrices which are in various stages of dissolution. The best Technicolor now seems able to produce is only a ghost of the original, a faded copy with hues which vary from scene to scene and at best produce rust where once there was gleaming red, with trick work showing itself up against backgrounds which have faded at a different rate, especially in the matte shots where the inserts appear to be curling up at the edges. So an overdose of imagination is required to bring back the vivid but carefully controlled magic which so delighted me on the vast screen of the converted skating rink where I first wallowed in it, in 1940 during one of Bolton's few air raids. To be truthful I had seen the programme round when the sirens sounded, and should have shot off to the shelters with the majority of the audience, but I could not bring myself to forgo another glimpse of the climactic delights of this eye-popping treasure trove of a movie, so I gritted my teeth against fear and sat in almost solitary state through the last three reels. My faith was justified, for the all-clear was heard within ten seconds of the end title appearing on the screen, and I walked home in triumph, enlivening the drabness of Fletcher Street with my inaccurate rendition of Rozsa's haunting theme tune, vocalized by Sabu as 'I want to be a sailor, sailing out to sea . . .' During that walk through the cobbled streets I felt myself capable of anything, even of riding the rainbow on any magic carpet which might happen to make itself available. After a movie like this not only the world but the heavens are one's oyster.

The hero of this book is turning out to be the famous production designer William Cameron Menzies, whom the reader will find lauded also under *Gone with the Wind* and *Things to Come*. On *The Thief of Baghdad*, though credited only as associate producer, he is plainly responsible for the magnificent physical look of the adventure: for the unexpected angle which compels attention, for the breathtaking glass shot of Basra's pink roofs, for the intricacies of the sultan's army of life-size mechanical toys, for the opening shot of the old sailboat with the giant eye painted on its prow, even for the overall style of the costume, and especially (I guess) for the executioner's yellow headgear with its eyeslit the shape of a halibut steak. The vicissitudes described above rob the production of uniformity, but scene for scene it is indeed a cavalcade of riches.

Due homage however must be paid to a stimulating script, which seems to have been written almost singlehandedly by Miles Malleson, with precisely the right *Arabian Nights* balance of humour, awe, cruelty, action and splendour. We are first introduced to the thief as a mongrel dog, the shape into which the evil magician has transformed him. Sitting with his blind master in the market place, he is able to tell good coins from false. Someone in the crowd challenges him: 'O frequenter of tree trunks, which is the true one of these?' He picks it out, and elicits the response: 'This is no dog, but the reincarnation of a tax collector.' With the blind man's story, told to the ladies of the harem whence fate has taken him, we move to romantic vein, for not so long ago he was a king: 'Three hundred and sixty-five wives were mine, but in my heart was no love: with every desire satisfied, I grew empty of desire.' We move on to wit as the king calls Jaffar, his vizier, whom we recognize as the evil genius responsible for Ahmad's plight:

AHMAD: Another execution, Jaffar? Why had he to die?
JAFFAR: He had been thinking, O my master.

THE THIEF OF BAGHDAD. Conrad Veidt is waiting his turn to make more mischief. June Duprez is the damsel in distress

And to the semblance of a wisecrack as a passer-by brushes past a beggar: 'Out of my way, O master of a thousand fleas. May Allah be with you, but I doubt it.'

All these elements are perfectly toned in with the spectacle, and the mixture was promptly imitated by Hollywood, notably by Walter Wanger in his 1941 *Arabian Nights*, but without the original's sharp intelligence Wanger's chocolate box heroics led only to boredom. *The Thief of Baghdad* seems almost inspired by its own magic, as though it were a religion. Even its little asides scintillate, such as Malleson's own comic turn as the sultan, obsessed by the life-size toys which are eventually the death of him: 'I do so prefer these things to my subjects. I have only to turn a key and they do what I want. So often my subjects refuse to do what I want and I have to have their heads cut off.'

Jaffar covets the sultan's daughter, and pleases the old man with the gift of a mechanical flying horse, each section of which comes superbly packed in its own shaped and velvet-lined container. When the girl resists, and the sultan defends her right to do so, Jaffar produces his Silver Maid, a remarkable metallic six-armed lady who gyrates to music and stabs the old man while embracing him, whereupon the princess falls into a deep sleep from which Jaffar is unable to awake her. In true Sleeping Beauty style, she can be roused only by the kiss of her true lover, so Jaffar is obliged for the purpose to turn beggar and dog back into king and thief. Jaffar then smuggles the princess onto a ship bound for distant lands, and tries to bend her to his will; when our heroes follow, their vessel is devastated by a magical storm. Ahmad storms Jaffar's palace and is thrown into a dungeon along with his recalcitrant sweetheart. So the happy ending is up to young Abu, who has been washed up on a beach where he finds a dirty old bottle. When unstoppered, this emits a huge cloud of black smoke, settling down into an extremely large genie with a reverberating voice which tends to cause small earthquakes. Abu wastes two of his regulation three wishes, but with the third manages to steal the All-Seeing Eye from its giant spider guardian which he despatches in a nicely chilling encounter. Unfortunately, all the eye does for him is enable him to see Ahmad's plight more clearly, so he petulantly dashes it against the rocks and is wafted by the explosion into the Land of Legend, 'where everything is possible when seen through the eyes of youth'. The old ruler, self-styled relic of a golden age, allows Abu to steal his private magic carpet, intended for his own imminent journey to the next world; with the additional help of a magic crossbow Abu flies back to Baghdad, kills Jaffar just as he is escaping on the flying horse, and bids the lovers farewell as he flies off to 'some fun and adventure at last'. 'Farewell, little master of the universe,' they cry as the carpet soars into the heavens.

It's all rousing stuff, though you shouldn't expect anyone after a first viewing to recount it in the right order. In the end it's the little trinkets in the wonder box you remember. Rex Ingram's giant genie in his red loin cloth, satisfying Sabu's first desire by producing a pan of sizzling hot sausages in the palm of his hand. Veidt's multi-coloured wardrobe of rich veils, gowns and turbans, backing the irresistible command in his cruel eyes and mouth. Sabu's natural delight in being as nimble and quick-witted as his role demands, crawling up a huge idol's left nostril or conning a beggar into giving him honey for his stolen bread. Veidt taunting the condemned princess: 'Why do you close your eyes? There is little enough time to see him.' Morton Selten as the aged ruler of the land of legend, offering Sabu the crossbow: 'Aim this only at injustice and you cannot fail.' The splendid stage management of the flying carpet, which even contrives to cast shadows. The flying horse falling to pieces in the sky as its rider is killed. The chase through the market, with fruit and vegetables flying everywhere. The gleaming, castellated palace roof on which the action climaxes, a dazzling contrast with the squalor below. There are of course borrowings here from many sources, though not very much perhaps from the stories of Scheherazade. The Fairbanks film of 1924 seems to have provided the balance of pleasure and pain; the final plight of the lovers ('Chain them to opposite walls: in the morning they die the death of a thousand cuts') seems highly reminiscent of Flecker's *Hassan*, where Rafi and Pervaneh did end up as ghosts haunting the golden road to Samarkand.

The Thief of Baghdad took twenty months to make, and apart from the credited directors there were contributions from Korda himself, his brother Zoltan, and William Cameron Menzies. Not surprisingly, it lacks the overall style which would have made it an unchallengeable classic. But it won Academy Awards for colour photography, art direction and special effects; and no one who saw it when it was fresh can fail to have allotted it a comfortable niche in his memory. Its like will not be seen again because it is sustained by flights of fancy rather than by the cruder dictates of commerce: Korda's first consideration was that it should be as good as talent could make it, an attitude seldom encountered these days. Besides, who in the eighties would think it reasonable to spend so prodigiously on a story about a princess of whom it was said that 'her beauty is like the sun and the moon; to look upon her is certain death'?

The Thief of Baghdad. GB 1940; Technicolor; 109 minutes. Produced by Alexander Korda for London Films. Written by Miles Malleson and Lajos Biro. Associate producer and production designer, William Cameron Menzies. Directed by Ludwig Berger, Tim Whelan and Michael Powell. Photographed by Georges Perinal and Osmond Borrodaile. Special effects by Lawrence Butler. Music score by Miklos Rozsa. Edited by William Hornbeck. With Sabu as Abu; Conrad Veidt as Jaffar;

June Duprez as the princess; John Justin as Ahmad; Miles Malleson as the sultan; Rex Ingram as the genie; Morton Selten as Old King; Mary Morris as Halima.

A Cocktail Before Murder
The Thin Man

A detective comes out of retirement to solve the case of an inventor who has disappeared but is suspected of two murders.

To get one thing clear: the thin man is not the detective, Nick Charles, even though Mr Charles' subsequent adventures made up the 'Thin Man' series which ran intermittently for ten years (and should be avoided). The title of the second film, *After the Thin Man*, played fair; but after that the producers got just as muddled as their audiences. No, the real thin man, in the film as in the original novel, is the unfortunate murder victim, the inventor Clyde Wynant, and the point is underlined early on by a pleasing shot in which he casts a long thin shadow along the pavement, as well as by a dénouement which explains that bones found buried in lime must necessarily be his even though a fat man's clothes were buried with them to throw investigators off the scent.

Does all this matter? Only a little more, perhaps, than the Christmas theme which runs through the film and the book (the jacket of which swings into view before the crowded title card). Hard to read now, Dashiell Hammett's novel (which was published in 1931 and had no sequels) conjures up a 41-year-old detective of Greek extraction (real name Charalambides) who for the last four years has retired to the west on the income of his rich 28-year-old wife Nora. A plea by an old acquaintance to help find her missing father is enough to bring him back to the Manhattan murder scene and, before the old man is found, two other bodies turn up in circumstances which clearly demand investigation. It's easy enough to spot the villain, but that doesn't matter. What did matter when the film was premièred in 1934 was that our hero and heroine were not only mature and married, but actually seemed to like the state in which they found themselves and to have a warm wisecracking regard for each other despite the occasional spat. Their other notable characteristic, slightly over-indulged by writers who were no doubt celebrating the end of prohibition, is a tendency to drink to excess; stylishly, but as though grape and grain were about to go out of fashion. Mr Charles, in fact, is first discovered at a bar, dreamy-eyed, giving instructions to the bartender: 'The important thing is the rhythm. The dry martini you always shake to waltz time.'

A reporter later asks Nora whether her husband is working on a case.

'Yes, he is.'

'What case is that?'

'A case of Scotch.'

Then there's the scene in which Nora meets Nick at a bar and he has the man waltz her up a martini. She promptly persuades him to admit that he's on his sixth, so she demands five more lined up before her, just to keep even. In the next shot she is flat on her back on the carpet. No wonder ice packs play a featured role in this movie.

Thanks to a slightly zany script by the Hacketts, the film is much funnier than the rather verbose novel. Detection-wise it's a thoroughly professional job in the fast-moving screen idiom of the early thirties, and in place of pauses for breath we get wisecracks. 'My father's a sexagenarian,' Nora tells a nonplussed reporter, whose bemused reply is 'They'll never put that in the paper.' Nora reads from a paper about Nick's exploits, and calls to him: 'It says you were shot six times in the tabloids.' 'Not true,' he replies. 'He didn't come anywhere near my tabloids.' Sometimes the banter gets quite sharp. 'I think it's a dirty trick,' says Nora, 'to bring me back to New York and make a widow of me.' 'Oh,' murmurs Nick, 'you wouldn't be a widow long. Not with your money.'

Nick and Nora don't appear much in the first half hour, because the murder plot has to be set up, and it's done with the no-nonsense expertise typical of its director, 'One Shot' Woody Van Dyke. He polished off the whole thing in sixteen days instead of the twenty-six MGM would have allowed. His style is splendidly economical. The first shot is of Edward Ellis' shadow on a wall, looking menacing. The camera pulls back to show that he is only an inventor pottering at a bench; then further to reveal the rest of the room and a door through which the next character enters. A murder is set up with equally plain efficiency: a man is about to step up to a house when the door opens slightly and a hand emerges holding a gun, which shoots him dead. Most of the story is played out against interesting high class sets, white in the manner of the period, with depth usually given by heavy shadows. No fancy angles, just everything you need to see. No scene goes on longer than it has to, and at one point there is a veritable plague of wipes, which is the quickest way in film grammar of getting from one point to another, the scene you are watching being replaced by another by means of a straight line which crosses the picture to reveal it. Left to right, right to left, bottom to top, right to left, top to bottom, left to right, right to left. Despite this plethora of opticals we don't get dizzy: a firm hand is in control, the sheer dexterity of the story-telling stimulates us.

The Thin Man is a film which all concerned seem to have enjoyed making, and that enjoyment communicates itself to the audience. I can't have been more than five years old when I first saw it at the Capitol, Bolton, so all the innuendo was over my head, but I did adore the wire-haired terrier, Asta, which shoots under the bureau whenever danger threatens and is given a miniature fire plug for a Christmas present. Today it seems a perfect television film, one to take the phone off the hook for, because from the word go it engrosses the attention and relaxes the mind, and sends you to bed smiling. William Powell and Myrna Loy are of their time rather than ours, but far preferable to the pale imitations of themselves recently presented by Robert Wagner and Stephanie Powers in *Hart to Hart* who are simply not characters one cares about; Nick and Nora, on the other hand, would be welcome in anybody's circle of friends. Nat Pendleton as the not-too-dumb cop gives his best performance, and among the suspects are such splendidly dubious characters as Cesar Romero, Porter Hall and Harold Huber.

It has been theorized that Nick and Nora are so likeable because they have so little dignity. Louis B. Mayer must have been horrified when he found that his most-touted female star makes her first appearance in the film being pulled flat on her face by an over-eager dog. He can't have been too keen either on the party she later arranges in her apartment. The guests include cops, prizefighters, an Irish deadbeat, an ex-con and a little man who keeps crying for his mother and gets permission to ring her in San Francisco. 'Don't bother to announce anyone,' Nora tells the doorman, 'just send them all up.' Her husband too has a rather frivolous attitude to the murder of an old acquaintance. 'I'm going to have a party,' he

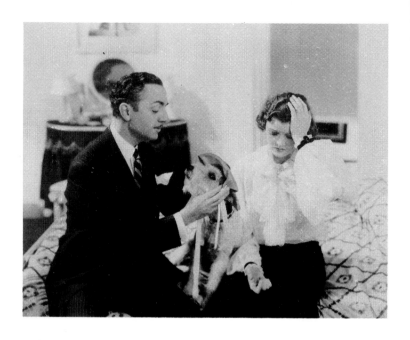

THE THIN MAN. Even Asta has a hangover. William Powell, Myrna Loy

announces airily, 'and invite all the suspects.' And so we proceed to the sealed-room finale so beloved of Charlie Chan, with burly cops masquerading as waiters. Mr Charles rises to make a short speech of welcome. 'The murderer is right in this room. Sitting at this table. Waiter, you may serve the fish.'

You may gather correctly that this is a film best seen after a few drinks, but not so many that you can't appreciate its high polish. You may even suspect that the principals had a few drinks before each day's shooting. I wouldn't put it past them.

Snugly in the *Thin Man* tradition, and made in the same year by William Dieterle for Warners, is *Fog Over Frisco*. It can't boast so personable a sleuth, its plot is confused, and it shamefully kills off Bette Davis in the second reel, but it may well be the fastest film ever made. Hardly a scene spares time to begin or end: we just get the middles: and try to spot an actor given time to enter or exit. Every kind of optical trick – wipe, dissolve, cross-cut – is deployed at top speed, and even the solution seems to be given on the run. From a script by Robert N. Lee and Gene Solow, this complex little mystery was remade during World War II as *Spy Ship*, to little effect.

Another fast-moving mystery from Warners, this time on more traditional lines, was 1933's *The Kennel Murder Case*. It seems that as the thirties wore on puzzles of this kind lost their snap, perhaps because they were padded out to ninety minutes and overblown with romantic interludes. Here, under Michael Curtiz' direction, nothing comes between Philo Vance and his quarry, and the solution of the sealed-room murder is as intricate as devotees of the genre could wish. William Powell's Vance is only different from his Nick Charles in that he stays on the wagon, supported by a cast of Hollywood's most attractive and amusing suspicious characters.

The Mystery of the Wax Museum has a well-deserved section to itself, but deserves mention here because apart from its pioneering horror elements it presents the archetypal image of the wise-cracking girl reporter who solves the mystery despite the interference of the blustering editor (who of course has her in his arms at the fadeout). Glenda Farrell revamped this role in a series of Torchy Blane mysteries, also for Warner, at the end of the thirties, but never had such good lines as this grotesquerie in which she comes face to face with a monster who 'makes Frankenstein look like a lily'.

The Thin Man. US 1934; monochrome; 93 minutes. Produced by Hunt Stromberg for MGM. Written by Frances Goodrich and Albert Hackett, from the novel by Dashiell Hammett. Directed by W. S. Van Dyke. Photographed by James Wong Howe. Music score by William Axt. Edited by Robert J. Kern. Art direction by David Townesend, Edwin B. Willis. With William Powell as Nick Charles; Myrna Loy as Nora Charles; Maureen O'Sullivan as Dorothy; Porter Hall as McCauley; Nat Pendleton as Guild; Minna Gombell as Mimi; Cesar Romero as Chris; Edward Ellis as Wynant.

Prophet with Honour
Things to Come

*A world war, beginning in 1940 and lasting for many years, is
followed by the break-up of European society and by
widespread plague; but airmen build up the nucleus of a new
society in Basra, and by 2036 Everytown, once ruined, is a
gleaming civilization of glass and steel, capable of sending
men to the moon.*

Imagine if you will that the year is 1936, and that a great many
cotton spinners and their families, from the black hinterland of
Lancashire, are enjoying their annual wakes week holiday in the Isle
of Man. Imagine the little they knew for certain about world events
except for the certainty of their own frequent unemployment;
imagine the minute amount of factual information dispensed by the
cinema of that time, with its Charlie Chans and Errol Flynns and
George Formbys doing their cheerful best to obscure the real world
behind a gaudy curtain of girls, fun, adventure, thrills, sentiment
and romance. So imagine the effect on these willing filmgoers, and
especially on the children, when they paid their sixpences to sit one
June night in the vast auditorium of Douglas' Crescent Cinema and
got, instead of some harmless palliative, *Things to Come*.

I for one had seen nothing like it ever before. My parents' friends
had agreed that it should be experienced because it was by Mr H. G.
Wells, who by conviction at any rate was one of them, a wise man
and a socialist, though since he stopped writing novels nobody had
understood much that he said; but nothing had prepared me for the
futuristic pageant at which we all sat gaping. It had no known stars,
it told no conventional story, its music was disturbing, its photographic quality was variable enough at times to be a newsreel. Even
the London Films logo seemed strange, as Big Ben had been caught
on the slant, and the main titles were in a kind of third-dimensional
perspective, those on the right seeming to edge into the auditorium,
while searchlights played over the rock-like letters which made up
the words *Things to Come*, rendering them even more portentous. We

were then shown a town which might have been ours, or anybody's, its architecture seeming to include bits of St Paul's, the Bank of England, Manchester Corn Exchange, Piccadilly Circus and Bolton Town Hall, while in the distance was a hill very like Arthur's Seat in Edinburgh. It was labelled Everytown, and it was Christmas; there was a schoolboy in a cap, just like me, and holly, and newspaper sellers preaching imminent war, but nobody taking any notice as they bought last-minute presents and queued up at the Burleigh Hotel and the Buckingham Theatre and a huge modernistic cinema. Then a date came relentlessly forward: 1940. I remember a cold shiver running down my back at being made to think that far into the future.

We were now taken into the home of one John Cabal, a thinking man and an aircraft engineer who clearly expected war to come: 'These fools are capable of anything.' His more sanguine friend Passworthy had other ideas: 'Another speech by *him*. I tell you there's nothing in it, it's just to buck us up about the air estimates.' In the nursery, Cabal's wife was sad: 'My dear, are you sorry we had these children? Were we selfish?' That night – Christmas Eve – the guns sound and a frantic voice on the radio declares mobilization. Even now Passworthy is optimistic. 'The last war wasn't so bad as people make out. Something great seemed to have got hold of us.'

That proved to be yet another of Mr Wells' uncannily accurate bull's-eyes, but the film doesn't have it so. This is a war pervaded by the smell of death, from the opening montage with Passworthy's small boy marching in the foreground across the bottom of the screen with his tin hat and gas mask, through the devastating air raids and gas attacks, to the final moving away of the war clouds to reveal a devastated Everytown, half of its inhabitants dying of the wandering sickness. Despite the serenity of the final part of the film, it was the opening which stayed in my mind, and on the way back to Mrs Cannell's lodgings I asked my father whether it was going to come true. He puffed at his pipe and said no, no, it was all fancy, 1914 was the war to end wars; but as we sauntered along the promenade he too was scanning the skies of Douglas Bay just in case clouds of bombers over the Irish Sea were being picked out by searchlights.

As one might expect from the directorial hand of William Cameron Menzies, the main power of *Things to Come*, apart from

Arthur Bliss' uniquely stirring music, seeps from its ingenious model sets and its vigorous montages rather than from the acted sequences in between, for Wells has imperfectly translated his ideas into a screenplay. The entertainment remains at pageant level, awesome pageant though it be. The war sequence, for instance, with its panning shots borrowed from *All Quiet on the Western Front*, its fabulous sequence of planes descending on Everytown like locusts, its exploding cinema, its endlessly marching men, is followed by a rather embarassing cameo in which young John Clements as a crashed enemy airman gives away his gas mask and shoots himself rather than submit to his own poison gas; and after this we are treated to a drearily long sequence in which the devastated town in 1966 is ruled by a rough and ready Boss, Rudolph the Victorious, played by Ralph Richardson in a sheepskin, as though he had had a vision of Idi Amin. As he is supported by the most stilted actors that Britain's matinée tradition could produce, we breathe a sigh of relief when Wings Over The World sends a squadron of flying platforms armed with peace gas, and we can move on to the real stuff, the montage of burrowing machines and electronic progress leading to the underground city of the twenty-first century. The Boss' rule had been hampered by petrol shortage, which, when seen from the eighties, must rank as another of Mr Wells' bull's-eyes, and the laugh is inevitable when Derrick de Marney sulks that 'there's not more than three gallons in this accursed town'. But Raymond Massey's 'freemasonry of science' produces new forms of energy leading to a perfected, air-conditioned civilization, in which plate glass turns into a television monitor, nobody walks when they can move by electric scooter or travelator, and the world has had its health, welfare, education and travel restored. One's elation at all this is only slightly tempered by the stiff-skirted costumes, the extremely uncomfortable-looking glass furniture with nowhere to put anything, and the little lecture about the past provoked by a dreadful girl child with a Violet Elizabeth accent.

As a kid I felt on safer ground in this final sequence, 2036 being too far ahead to worry about; in any case I was conditioned to it by *Flash Gordon*. Even here of course there is a villain; not Ming the Merciless but Theotocopulos, a sculptor guilty of a least one huge and ghastly monstrosity but concerned to halt any further progress for mankind and in particular the space gun in which it is proposed

THINGS TO COME. Life in 2040, as seen from 1936

to send to the moon two young people, to wit the progeny of the descendents of our old friends Cabal and Passworthy. Despite the sculptor's mass rally and a dash by helicopter to the launching site, the gun does get fired, and mankind is left to contemplate an unknown, vast and frightening future.

Well, of course, my father was wrong, H. G. Wells was right, and war did come, not in 1940 but a year earlier; it lasted for only six years instead of the thirty-odd predicted: and the pestilence which followed was atomic fallout rather than the wandering sickness. Mr Wells' high scores also include spiralling inflation (newspapers costing four pounds by 1966); space rockets orbiting the moon and being guided back into the Pacific Ocean; and the conflict of science with art, humanity and religion. The result is not a science fiction movie, more a vividly animated pamphlet; or, to adapt an old phrase, like writing the future in flashes of lightning. The characters are walking arguments rather than people, and this is never clearer than in the final confrontation between Cabal the visionary and

465

Passworthy the reactionary after their children have become the first voyagers to the moon. Against a dazzling background of stars seen through the mirror of a giant telescope, the debate concludes:

PASSWORTHY: And if they don't return, my son and daughter? What of that, Cabal?

CABAL: Then, presently, others will go.

PASSWORTHY: My God! Is there never to be an age of happiness? Is there never to be rest?

CABAL: Rest enough for the individual man. Too much of it and too soon, and we call it death. But for Man no rest and no ending. He must go on, conquest beyond conquest. First this little planet with its winds and ways, and all the laws of mind and matter that restrain him. Then the planets about him, and at last across immensity to the stars. And when he has conquered all the deeps of space and all the mysteries of time, still he will be beginning.

PASSWORTHY: But we are such little creatures. Poor humanity. So fragile, so weak. Little animals.

CABAL: If we are no more than animals, we must snatch at our little scraps of happiness and live and suffer and pass, mattering no more than all the other animals do, or have done. (*He points at the stars.*) Is it that, or this? All the universe, or nothingness? Which shall it be, Passworthy? Which shall it be?

And as his voice distorts and echoes for a third time across the universe, to be picked up distantly by a heavenly choir, the lights come up and we go soberly home. Stirring stuff for anybody at any time, these questions which are so rarely asked even now. For a small boy on holiday in 1936, with nigger minstrels and a trip round the island and kippers for tea on his mind, it was a new and awesome concept of a world which had hitherto seemed rather grimy and hard but with many modest compensations – such as a sixpenny seat at the pictures.

Things to Come. GB 1936; monochrome; 100 minutes. Produced by Alexander Korda for London Films. Written by H. G. Wells, from his book *The Shape of Things to Come*. Directed by William Cameron Menzies. Photographed by Georges Perinal. Music score by Arthur Bliss. Production design by William Cameron Menzies, Vincent Korda, John Bryan, Frederick Pusey. Art direction by Vincent Korda. Edited by William Hornbeck. Special effects by Ned Mann, Lawrence Butler, and others. With Raymond Massey as Cabal; Edward Chapman as Passworthy; Ralph Richardson as the Boss; Margaretta Scott as Roxana; Cedric Hardwicke as Theotocopulos; John Clements as airman; Derrick de Marney as Richard Gordon; Sophie Stewart as Mrs Cabal.

No More Waltzes from Vienna
The Third Man

An American in post-war Vienna seeks the old friend who promised him a job, disbelieving the story that he has been killed in an accident.

Though it takes the gloomy view of life which is typical of its author, *The Third Man* is basically no more serious than, say, *The Maltese Falcon*: once the plot is set, it's a matter of suspense situations and a final revelation, not to mention an unromantic ending, and Greene himself labels it one of his 'entertainments'. It was hailed on its release as rather more because of several factors. It was set in war-shocked Vienna, whose real-life settings were photographed with aching vividness and dramatic menace by Robert Krasker. The Anglo-American production team brought in the best of both worlds, and the big names involved made it seem like an international enterprise to compare with Marshall Aid. Culturally, the reteaming of Welles and Cotten brought echoes of *Citizen Kane*. Politically, the 'McGuffin' of black-marketeering in penicillin was topical enough to make audiences think they had been watching a documentary. Trevor Howard as the cynical Intelligence colonel stole all the notices and became an international star. The zither score of Anton Karas, accidentally discovered playing at a Vienna café during production, became a sensational best-seller and provided the film with a unique ambience and a chilling motif.

If it were not for the plangent music, this would be a chill tale indeed, for 1948 Vienna is a humourless background even though the director controls its ruins like studio sets. His villains are not of the old-fashioned kind, activated solely by greed: now they are anti-allied, anti-religious, or anti-human, fugitives from Greeneland who might be familiar to a section of the reading public but presented a new challenge to the average filmgoer. When I first saw the movie there was an additional physical factor to chill my blood, for I unwisely chose to attend a teatime performance on a cold day at the

THE THIRD MAN. Joseph Cotten reluctantly helps Trevor Howard and Bernard Lee in their quest

Cambridge Regal, a charmless hall whose vast empty spaces could be guaranteed to depress the spirit even if the temperature had risen above 58 degrees, which it didn't on that occasion. Forewarned, I snuggled into my overcoat and allowed myself to be transported into the person of the irritable, unlettered and rather foolish Holly Martins, who arrives in Vienna without a nickel and can be made attractive only by the exercise of all Joseph Cotten's charm. Despite this flaw, so great was the combination of talents working on the movie that I was instantly carried along and involved, though I never was able to figure out the exact significance of the title, and nor I suspect can most people who list the movie among their favourites. Lime is supposed to have been killed in a street accident, and witnesses say that afterwards his body was carried across the road to his home by two men. A less prejudiced account however says that there was a third man. The body buried as Lime subsequently turns out to be that of the informer, Joseph Harbin, so presumably the third man was Lime himself, who would surely have been recognized by the onlookers; but the script, having posed the mystery, doesn't bother to explain it, and in any case the point is hardly central to the drama.

A study of the original script reveals that without Karas and the other trimmings it was unlikely to be a huge success. The development is sluggish and repetitive, the hero is a boor, and without the zither there is very little lightness or pace to carry one's interest from one scene to the next. On this showing the movie could have turned out no better than Reed's later *The Man Between*, a solemn variation on the same themes with the locale changed to Berlin. Moreover, space had been allowed for that popular double act of the time, Radford and Wayne, as two stuffy British civil servants. Since *The Lady Vanishes* they had been a welcome addition to any British comedy, but in this particular film they could only have worked against one's involvement in the story. In the event their characters were rolled into one, played by Wilfrid Hyde White: he was acceptable because his persona was then fresh and his scenes extremely brief.

Because the complex post-war division of Vienna needed more explaining for the average audience than had at first been thought necessary, all the filmed pre-credit shots of Cotten flying from Canada were junked. Instead we have simply pleasing credits against a background of zither strings being plucked to the famous music, followed by a brisk first person introduction which I had always assumed to be by Trevor Howard but which on examination proves to come from an anonymous person who has no further connection with the story. The voice, in a last-minute decision, was that of Carol Reed:

I never knew the old Vienna before the war, with its Strauss music, its glamour and easy charm; Constantinople suited me better. I really got to know it in the classic period of the black market – we'd run anything, if people wanted it enough and had the power to pay. Of course, a situation like that does tend to amateurs – (*There follows a shot of a body floating in a river, and an explanation of the four-power zoning.*)

Oh wait, I was going to tell you – I was going to tell you about Holly Martins from America – he came all the way here to visit a friend of his – the name was Lime, Harry Lime. Now Martins was broke, and Lime had offered him – I don't know, some sort of job. Anyway, there he was, poor chap, happy as a lark and without a cent.

A train steams in cheerfully and Martins is having his papers checked by a British officer. 'Lime,' he says, 'Harry Lime. I thought he'd be here to meet me.' And the music cunningly dips and plunges so that we know there is something sinister in Harry's absence.

The entire film is about the search for Harry Lime, but Orson Welles, who plays him, has the shortest role any co-star ever accepted. Officially dead, he has to reappear because Martins is asking too many awkward questions, and is first glimpsed as a pair of well-shined shoes in a shadowy doorway. Martins takes them as belonging to an Intelligence agent shadowing him, and begins to hurl drunken abuse. But a shaft of light hits the face above the shoes, and Martins is shocked to recognize the friend whose murder he is seeking to avenge. There follows a magical chase sequence of bobbing shadows and cobbled alleyways, all to no purpose: Lime has, it turns out, disappeared down the city sewer, which he is using as a private escape route. It is not until Martins sends a secret aggrieved message that the friends meet, in the rotating ferris wheel of a dejected fairground. This is one of the great film conversations, as Holly voices his disappointment in Harry and his horror at the deaths his racketeering has caused. Harry replies with cheerful cynicism.

LIME: Look down there. Would you really feel any pity if one of those dots stopped moving for ever? If I said that you can have twenty thousand pounds for every dot that stops, would you really, old man, tell me to keep my money, or would you calculate how many dots you could afford to spare? Free of income tax, old man, free of income tax.

At one point it seems that Martins may be pitched down from the compartment to join the dots, but the moment passes, and the encounter ends with a famous little speech which it is generally admitted that Welles wrote himself to bolster up his cameo:

Don't be gloomy. After all, it's not that awful. You know what the fellow said . . . in Italy for thirty years under the Borgias they had warfare, terror, murder, bloodshed . . . they produced Michelangelo, Leonardo da Vinci and the Renaissance. In Switzerland they had brotherly love, five hundred years of democracy and peace, and what did that produce? The cuckoo clock.

Such was the impact of his five-minute role that Welles was kept busy for years with radio and television extensions of it. Indeed it caught the public imagination so firmly that 39 episodes were filmed of a series called *The Third Man*, which however had nothing to do with the character or the locale of the film. Michael Rennie played a shrewd and wealthy international manipulator who always had time to help ladies in distress. They used the zither music, though.

If Hitchcock hadn't had more than his share of the limelight elsewhere in this book, I would have found room for a tribute to *Foreign Correspondent*, his 1940 piece which at first sight has a similar theme, i.e. a blundering American getting involved with European tensions which he doesn't fully understand. The mood is of course entirely different: until the final anti-isolationist plea to America, Hitch's purpose is to entertain us with one suspense sequence after another, sugared with a few easy laughs and made memorable by four ingeniously constructed set-pieces: an assassination in the rain, the disappearance of a car into a Dutch windmill, an attempted assassination atop Westminster Cathedral, and a simulated plane crash in the middle of the Atlantic. All this and Robert Benchley too . . .

My headline might have been *Clouds over Europe*, which is also the American title of a most enjoyable spy trifle of 1939, known to the British as *Q Planes*. This is *Boy's Own Paper* stuff, directed by Tim Whelan like a variation on *The 39 Steps*, with no serious points to make about the approaching war. What it does have is Laurence Olivier playing what amounts to a minor Errol Flynn role, and being acted off the screen by Ralph Richardson as an extremely casual British agent whose bowler hat and umbrella keep getting in the way. Patrick MacNee freely admits that it was on Richardson's elegant performance in this very casual romp that he based his performance as Steed in *The Avengers*: it's an ill wind.

The Third Man. GB 1949; monochrome; 104 minutes. Produced by David O. Selznick and Alexander Korda for London Films. Associate producer, Carol Reed. Written by Graham Greene. Directed by Carol Reed. Photographed by Robert Krasker. Music score by Anton Karas. Art direction by Vincent Korda, John Hawkesworth and Joseph Bato. Edited by Oswald Hafenrichter. With Joseph Cotten as Holly Martins; Alida Valli as Ann Schmidt; Trevor Howard as Major Calloway; Orson Welles as Harry Lime; Bernard Lee as Sergeant Paine; Ernst Deutsch as Baron Kurtz; Wilfrid Hyde White as Crabbin.

Innocence Is Running for Your Life
The Thirty-Nine Steps

An amiable colonial in London is suspected of the murder of a pretty woman who begs shelter for the night in his flat. He journeys to Scotland and back in pursuit of the real culprits, a ring of spies.

Many readers may feel that *The Thirty-Nine Steps* should be included under the same heading as *North by Northwest*, for one is merely an extension of the other, presenting a hero in danger, on a journey, following a murder, eluding both the police who want to arrest him and the villains who want to silence him. The difference is that *North by Northwest* is the work of a slightly jaded Hollywood professional telling an old story on a big budget, while *The Thirty-Nine Steps* is the electrically vivid first flowering of a brilliant young British film-maker who hopes we will enjoy his bag of tricks and not reproach him for the backcloths and the *non sequiturs*. He never did grow out of these backcloths, but he did succumb to American elephantiasis: *North by Northwest* is an hour longer than *The Thirty-Nine Steps*, the film which established Hitchcock's international reputation and gave him that kind of instant glory which can never be recaptured or improved upon.

From the standpoint of the eighties *The Thirty-Nine Steps* also has the patina of age which admits it into the antique class; not only its technical qualities but its fashions and a little of its dialogue are deliciously dated. What then are the qualities which make it so much more enjoyable still, so much more certainly a work of art, than the slavish 1959 remake with Kenneth More or the slacker but intermittently vigorous 1978 version with Robert Powell?

I can't be sure where I first saw it. Could it have been the Bolton Atlas, where it was jocularly remarked that they gave you a hammer along with your tuppeny ticket? I know I thoroughly enjoyed it and found some of its moments so haunting that when in 1943 I became secretary of the school film society it was among the first bookings I confirmed. I remember now that splendid winter afternoon in the oak-panelled library, when the heavy curtains were drawn at 4.15 and a sprinkling of masters as well as fifty boys chuckled appreciatively through its twists and turns. Several years later I was amazed, on sitting through it with a packed undergraduate audience at the Cambridge Arts, to discover how sexy some of it was. Had the scene where hero and heroine are handcuffed together, and she is trying to remove her stockings with as little help as possible from him, really been part of the print I projected at school?

The films which draw critical attention to the work of young directors usually have one thing in common: their low budgets ensure that they concentrate on essentials and waste no time. Think of William Dieterle's *The Last Flight*, Michael Curtiz' *The Mystery of the Wax Museum*, Howard Hawks' *Scarface*, John Sturges' *Bad Day at Black Rock*, John Huston's *The Maltese Falcon*, Robert Wise's *The Body Snatcher*, and compare them with the sprawling expensive expanses of the later solemn monuments. Once a film-maker has hit it big, one must regretfully cease to expect from him the peculiar qualities which first took him to the top. So with Hitchcock: though he remained a major director for forty years, as soon as he arrived in Hollywood his proportion of palpable hits became smaller and although almost all the later films have marvellous moments they lack the casual excitement, the sly jokes and the breakneck pace of his British entertainments.

Hitch has never been generous at giving credit to his writers, but here Charles Bennett turned in a marvellous script, albeit with few vestiges of Buchan's novel. Consider the terse conversation with dour John Laurie, the highland crofter from whom Hannay requests accommodation for the night:

CROFTER: Can ye eat the herring?
HANNAY: I could eat half a dozen right now.
CROFTER: Can ye sleep in a box bed?
HANNAY: I can try.
CROFTER: Two and six.

There is the marvellous introduction by the manager of the memory man act at the music hall: 'I ought to add before retiring that Mr Memory has left his brain to the British Museum.' And the inevitable first question from the audience:

PATRON: Where's my old man been since last Saturday night?
MEMORY: You'll have to ask him, madam.
2ND PATRON: How old's Mae West?
MEMORY: I know, sir, but I never reveal a lady's age.

Hitch once called Bennett a ball-tosser, meaning that their scripts evolved from tossing ideas between each other, but the scripting here is so tight as to seem like one man's work. Against this notion must be set the fairly desperate journeyman writing Bennett did a year previously for a hasty monster ripoff called *The Secret of the Loch*, his own ripping-off being done from Conan Doyle's *The Lost World*.

What did come from the book was the opening murder of the spy (now a lady) and the general direction of the chase (north-north-west, come to think of it). The first sequence after the credits, however, was entirely the film-makers' own invention, and by a succession of well-chosen shots they recall a foggy London that never was, a London of opera hats and whelk stalls, of chop houses and steamy trams; the London of Sherlock Holmes only slightly modernized, and recapturable by the cinema only in Hitch's contrasty monochrome. In close up, illuminated letters pass from right to left before us, each lighting up as it reaches centre screen: they spell MUSIC HALL. We see the cash box, admission one shilling (Saturdays and holidays 1/6). We see Hannay's ticket being torn and his feet reaching a seat before we see him; then we take in the tawdry gilt, the shabby orchestra, the plush curtains, and down the side the long bar where the noisier patrons congregate. Soon Mr Memory's act inadvertently starts a riot at the bar, and we see a gun fired, causing further panic. In the crush Hannay's arm is gripped by a veiled *femme fatale*:

MISS SMITH: May I come home with you?
HANNAY: What's the idea?
MISS SMITH: Well, I'd like to.

Safely ensconced in his Portland Place flat, and having furtively established that she can't be seen by the watchers in the street outside, she tells him half a yarn about being a professional spy in the employ of the British government: 'It is only a matter of days, perhaps hours, before the secret is out of the country.' And in the middle of the night we see billowing window curtains and she staggers into his room with a knife in her back (the breadknife he has been waving about while making sandwiches) and shouting: 'Clear out, Hannay, they'll get you next!' (Query: Why didn't they get him then?) All he has to go on is her mentioning going to see an Englishman in Scotland, but luckily her dead hand is clutching a map on which the village of Alt-na-Shellach is ringed. What to do about the sinister watchers who still patrol the street? (Hitch once remarked scornfully that the director of the remake was so foolish as to give us a close-up of them, thus destroying the essential impression of seeing the menace from the hero's viewpoint.)

We all know what Hannay does: impersonates a milkman. And we all remember the subsequent course of events, like a series of Hitchcock cameos. The commercial travellers talking about corsets; the escape on the Forth Bridge; the chase across the moors; the sequence with the crofter and his wife (inspired, Hitch cheerfully admitted, by the bawdy French tale about the guest for the night who preferred cheese to his hostess' bed); the meeting with the gentle laird who after Sunday morning drinks reveals himself as the spymaster and cheerfully shoots Hannay (the bullet luckily lodging in a prayer book). The escape from the situation is not shown, perhaps because Hannay still has to effect so many, notably from the sheriff's office when that worthy doesn't believe him, from the village hall where he is taken for a politician and makes an excellent speech, and from the policemen who arrest him but turn out to be spies. By this time he is handcuffed to Madeleine Carroll (don't ask why, just accept it) and the film dissolves into sexy banter at an inn until he suddenly remembers why he can't get out of his head a catchy little tune. It's Mr Memory's tune, and that must be why Miss Smith went to the music hall. Mr Memory has been paid to memorize the secrets which will be smuggled out of the country in his brain. (There must have been more reliable ways, even in 1935.) So let's rush back to the London Palladium, where Mr Memory is now appearing. Spymaster is up in the stage box: we can see on the rail his right hand with one finger missing. Hannay is in the stalls, but the police are closing in. Why doesn't he do something? He does, as Mr Memory is led on. 'What are the thirty-nine steps?' he cries. And little Mr Memory's pride is his undoing, for he can't resist giving the answer, thus obliging spymaster to shoot him (and be dramatically captured). And what are the thirty-nine steps? Oh, it doesn't really matter, they're just Hitch's McGuffin. All right, then,

THE THIRTY-NINE STEPS. The beginning of the chase: Lucie Mannheim is being followed

they're members of a spy ring. (In the book they were real steps leading down to a landing stage.) Hitch claims that in the excitement of creation he forgot to give the explanation at all and had to add a line after he had already made several takes.

Otis Ferguson called this little melodrama 'a miracle of speed and light'. André Sennwald said it was 'one of the fascinating pictures of the year'. That was enough to start the offers coming. The incredible thing is that so many years later, after so many close or distant copies (including Hitch's own), it is still among the most entertaining ways one can find of spending eighty minutes in a cinema.

The Thirty-Nine Steps. GB 1935; monochrome; 81 minutes. Produced by Michael Balcon and Ivor Montagu for Gaumont British. Written by Charles Bennett and Alma Reville, from the novel by John Buchan. Directed by Alfred Hitchcock. Photographed by Bernard Knowles. Music score by Hubert Bath and Jack Beaver. Music direction by Louis Levy. Art direction by Otto Werndorff and Albert Jullion. Edited by Derek Twist. With Robert Donat as Richard Hannay; Madeleine Carroll as Pamela; Wylie Watson as Mr Memory; Godfrey Tearle as Professor Jordan; Lucie

Mannheim as Miss Smith; John Laurie as the crofter; Peggy Ashcroft as the crofter's wife; Helen Haye as Mrs Jordan; Frank Cellier as the sheriff.

Just the Perfect Blendship
The Three Musketeers (1939) and Abbott and Costello Meet Frankenstein

D'Artagnan and three lackeys posing as musketeers save the queen from embarrassment over a jewel; two porters meet three monsters.

Hope and Crosby sang about teamwork; Laurel and Hardy polished it to perfection; Martin and Lewis thought they'd be better without it. The history of film has generally shown that it's easier to get to the top on one's own, but one only has to think of the above teams, plus Astaire and Rogers, and the Marx Brothers, to realize how deprived we'd all have been without a few examples of multi-headed attractions. I particularly cherish a marvellous number from an otherwise unremarkable British musical of 1938 called *Over She Goes*, in which Stanley Lupino and two colleagues promenade round a stately ballroom, singing 'Side by Side'. If only the act could have been kept together (and of course, this being a British film, it wasn't) it might have been the equivalent of those American fools the Ritz Brothers, whose zany musical lampoons enlivened many a dullish comedy of the thirties. I smile at the memory of them singing 'Hey Pussy Pussy' to Adolphe Menjou in *The Goldwyn Follies*, and cowering in unanimous terror from *The Gorilla*; but perhaps their most sustained outing was the above unassuming but highly satisfying music version of a minor classic, which apart from being very funny is the most exhilarating musketeer movie yet made, with its graceful glass shots standing in for French châteaux and its solid staircases clearly meant for duelling down. The cast alone is worth the price of admission, though only Binnie Barnes has a real moment of glory, when as villainess-in-chief she tucks a vital message down the front of her dress and the Ritzes are instructed to get it back, remembering of course that they are musketeers and gentlemen. They solve the problem ingeniously, by turning her upside-down and shaking her several times. (The first couple of prizes they win are irrelevant *billets doux* concerning assignations behind the shrubbery.) Miss Barnes suffers magnificently, with much the same expectation of indignity to come as is demonstrated by Margaret Dumont when she comes up against the Marxes.

The swashbuckling element in the picture is played straight by Don Ameche as a perfectly acceptable D'Artagnan, who sings that he is off

> To the city that is never melancholy,
> Where the girls are very very very jolly,
>   C'est Paris.

Well, he is so ingratiating that we can even forgive him that. The comedy highlight is a dance performed by the Ritzes with cymbals strapped about their persons, a hilarious example of perfectly drilled movement and sound which lingers fondly in the memory: it even has a medieval air. The other songs are the briefest snatches, though despite the lyrics one remembers with relish 'We're the King's Musketeers on Parade':

> Comrades fond, we're marching along,
> Fighting at
> The drop of a hat . . .
> It's all for one and it's two for five and it's vive la France!

Simultaneously gyrating in a variety of feathered costumes, the Ritzes make you laugh just to look at them, which is fortunate considering some of the dialogue they're handed. When asked, 'My name's D'Artagnan, what's yours?' it is scarcely the height of wit to answer 'A whisky and soda'; but, always led by the rubber-faced Harry, their expressions are a joy to behold when they are expected by D'Artagnan to live up to the legend of their borrowed plumes: 'Think of it, of all the musketeers we are the four selected to die for the queen. This is indeed our lucky day.' They also do an old burlesque routine when called upon to toast the king. Before drinking, they have to wave their brimming tankards from side to side, so the one at the end gets it in the face, no matter where he stands. As there are sixteen kings to be toasted, all called Louis, he gets pretty wet.

The secret of the Ritzes is no more obscure than that they are very funny fellows, three eccentrics going through identical movements, impeccably rehearsed. When they are dressed in costumes that make them look like the card men from *Alice in Wonderland*, so much the better. They even pluck chickens in unison:

> We pluck pluck pluck pluck all day long
> As o'er this pot we stoop.
> We pluck pluck pluck pluck all day long
> As we make chicken soup.

(I did admit that this film's lyrics are not its strongest point.)

I like this little movie because it is funny and exciting at once, because its actors know how to wear costume and inhabit period sets, because it gets through a complicated story more smartly than the serious versions, and because it was made so efficiently and cheaply on studio sets with contract artists. Today you couldn't think of making a period picture with music for less than five million dollars, and the odds are it wouldn't send you home so happy. They might however have done something about the very American heroine, who says Rishyloo when she means Richelieu. Miles Manders bears the affront with fortitude.

Another example of teamwork which really ought to be mentioned in a book like this is the double act of Abbott and Costello, who entertained me pretty solidly throughout my later boyhood and made a mint of money for Universal. Today, alas, all I can stand of them is a few snatches: the 'Slowly I Turned' routine from *Lost in a Harem*, the 'Susquehanna Hat Company, from *In Society*, and 'Who's on First' from *The Naughty Nineties*, whenever they chose to revive it. For various reasons, however I have a soft spot for *Abbott and Costello Meet Frankenstein*, which rescued them from career doldrums in 1948. To begin with, the horror element is played fairly straight, with at least as many chills as were to be found in the previous four Frankenstein pictures, but with the monsters permitting a few jokes at their own expense. Lon Chaney rings up Costello with a warning, all the way from London; but midway through the conversation the full moon shines, and he turns into a growling wolf. Costello concludes the conversation with: 'You're awful silly to call all the way from London just to have your dog talk to me.' Even when they meet, Costello doesn't believe his explanations: 'But you don't

THE THREE MUSKETEERS. The Ritz Brothers are funny fellows, but I wouldn't trust their cooking

understand: every night when the moon is full, I turn into a wolf . . .' 'Yeah,' says Costello, 'you and fifty million other guys!'

It's pleasant too to find Bela Lugosi back as Dracula, trying to find a new brain for the monster and wistfully purring as he strokes Costello's skull: 'What we need is young blood . . . and brains!' The monster is indeed at a low ebb, for on their first encounter it starts back at the sight of Costello, who is paralysed with fright. Lugosi takes the giant hand and soothes it: 'Don't be afraid: he won't hurt you.'

As usual, Abbott is given little to do except stand back and feed the jokes to his partner:

ABBOTT: You stay here, I'm going to explore upstairs.
COSTELLO: I've got two words to say to you.
ABBOTT: What are they?
COSTELLO: Hurry back.

Inevitably Abbott fails to see the ghostly manifestations of which his partner is giving such vivid speechless impersonations, such as the moving candle (it's on Dracula's coffin, and the count is trying to rise) which is always stationary when Abbott turns his head. They even manage to search the cellars without Abbott seeing anything, though Costello sits on the monster's knee without realizing it until he notices that he has three hands, one rather hairy.

In fact this movie is only adequate at what it seeks to do, but adequacy was something Abbott and Costello rarely encountered in their productions except for the old burlesque routines which gagster John Grant lovingly incorporated until the stars got too big for their boots and fired him. They seem to have been an unlovable pair who had no idea how to handle their success, and they were lucky when Universal hit on the idea of salvaging their careers by confronting them with all the monsters under the studio's copyright. *Meet Frankenstein* is undoubtedly the best of these, rising to a splendid crescendo with the electric sparks flying, the monster reactivated at full strength, all three ghouls coming to a sticky but impermanent end, and the voice of the Invisible Man arriving too late for the party. But I have a weakness too, for *Abbott and Costello Meet Dr Jekyll and Mr Hyde*, despite the tacky make-up plastered all over Boris Karloff's face (no doubt in an effort to disguise the athletic double who so frequently stood in for the ageing star). It has an unsurpassed who's-following-whom routine on a rooftop, a zany laboratory sequence in which Costello changes into a guinea pig, and a fittingly foolish finale in which Costello, himself bitten by Hyde, bites half the police force so that they'll all turn into monsters.

To return to *Meet Frankenstein*, my warmth towards it undoubtedly stems from an evening in Cambridge, just before exams, when I had to queue up to see it and it formed an invigorating relief from my study of the works of Edmund Spenser. And a further interesting footnote is that in my experience it chalked up the fourth highest rating ever achieved by a movie on British TV. This was in Granadaland, around 1962. The record is still held, and in view of increased competition always will be, by *The Best Years of Our Lives*, which got 72 per cent of the potential viewing audience. Second came Astaire and Rogers in *Follow the Fleet*, when it played against Granada's prestigious but highly unpopular *The Skin of Our Teeth* with Vivien Leigh; third was *Sherlock Holmes Faces Death*, from the immortal but inexpensive Basil Rathbone series. And then came Abbott and Costello. Sociologists will no doubt explain.

The Three Musketeers (aka: *The Singing Musketeer*). US 1939; monochrome; 72 minutes. Produced by Raymond Griffith for 20th Century-Fox. Written by M. M. Musselman, William A. Drake and Sam Hellman. Directed by Allan Dwan. Photographed by Peverell Marley. Music directed by David Buttolph. Songs by Samuel Pokrass and Walter Bullock. With the Ritz Brothers as the Three Stewards; Don Ameche as D'Artagnan; Miles Mander as Richelieu; Joseph Schildkraut as the King; Gloria Stuart as the Queen; Binnie Barnes as Lady de Winter; Lionel Atwill as de Rochefort; and John Carradine, Douglass Dumbrille, Russell Hicks, Pauline Moore, Gregory Gaye.

Abbott and Costello Meet Frankenstein. US 1948; monochrome; 83 minutes. Produced by Robert Arthur for Universal. Written by Frederick Rinaldo, Robert Lees, John Grant. Directed by Charles Barton. Photographed by Charles Van Enger. Music score by Frank Skinner. Art Direction by Bernard Herzbrun, Hilyard Brown. With Abbott and Costello; Bela Lugosi as Dracula; Lon Chaney Jnr as the Wolf Man; Glenn Strange as the Monster; and Lenore Aubert, Jane Randolph, Frank Ferguson.

Midland and Scottish
The Titfield Thunderbolt and Whisky Galore

Villagers take over a railway which British Rail wants to axe; and Scottish islanders beat the Inland Revenue to a shipwrecked cargo of whisky.

The more metropolitan Ealing comedies have already been dealt with under their champion, *The Lavender Hill Mob*; but Ealing's approach to comedy was so novel and so successful as to deserve two bites at the apple. (Three if you count *The Man in the White Suit*; but that's pure satire.) *The Titfield Thunderbolt* was actually Ealing's last comedy of any consequence, their first in colour, and possibly their most expensive production. I liked it first and foremost for its evocation of the idyllic southern English countryside in its summer mood, a heritage which I wasn't born into but loved all the same. There was one marvellous shot of a cricket match which is abandoned so that the players can run cheering after the village train on its first run. Come to think of it, eight in the morning is a strange time for a cricket match, but never mind: the film works because of these lyrical moments, which today are captured on celluloid only for the benefit of margarine commercials. Alas, the rich but restrained colours of *The Titfield Thunderbolt* can no longer be reproduced, and the BBC's print boasts only muddy green skies and blue trees, which are the best that labs can manage now that the Technicolor process has changed. Best to forget what it looked like at the Leicester Square Odeon in 1953, and watch it in black and white, which at least makes the comedy seem sharper; but then it was never intended to have the edge of *The Lavender Hill Mob* or the pawkiness of *Whisky Galore*. *The Titfield Thunderbolt* is a celebration of the old English country virtues, and if you happen to like trains, that's a bonus. Inventively it marks no advance on T. E. B. Clarke's other scripts, but if you imagine it came first it will not disappoint you as it did the critics of the time. It has a pattern script, even down to the anti-TV joke which was then statutory; it is full of situations which are none the less funny for being telegraphed; it addresses itself to anyone who can appreciate its essential truths, but will appeal most firmly to non-urban upper-class audiences who retain their half-amused esteem for vicars and squires and their disdain without malice for bureaucrats. Early on it also pokes fun at railways in the form of a guard who carefully examines a parcel marked *Fragile* before tossing it onto the platform, and at a trades union official who, when told that management and labour are in accord, can only remark: 'My association will view any such situation as evidence of exploitation.' Bureaucrats get it too, in the shape of the inevitable cups of tea, the insistence on doing things by the book, and the impressive gent who turns up to work at the Ministry of Transport – on a scooter.

As a piece of story-telling it is exemplary. Characters, relationships and situations are all neatly and humorously defined within the first five minutes. The government proposes to close a branch railway line; so, against the interests of a private bus company (the sabotaging villains), manor and church plan to run it themselves.

VICAR: They can't close our line: it's unthinkable.
SQUIRE: What about the old Canterbury–Whitstable line? They closed that.
VICAR: Perhaps there were not men of sufficient faith in Canterbury.

But how to raise the money? The vicar's scheme to put on *The Mikado* again is judged unlikely to be sufficiently profitable. Mr Valentine, the local rich boozer, is a more likely bet. He is found in the pub drinking gin and toasting 'our magnificent generals, General Gordon and General Booth'. Dubious at first, he brings out his chequebook with a flourish on being assured that on his own railway he can drink at nine in the morning if he likes. And on the day of the first service he is out of the house early, a rose in his buttonhole. 'Do you know what time it is?' his wife calls after him. 'Yes, my love: summer double time.' Once settled at his private bar, even opposition from a steamroller fails to disturb him: 'Oh, a duel; how very delightful.'

After the exposition, the plot has but one point of suspense: can the amateurs outwit the would-be saboteurs and satisfy the inspector of railways? No prizes are offered for guessing that they do, despite bullet holes in the water tower and a derailment of their engine. One group steals a locomotive from the main line turntable and drives it back by night through the village streets, a marvellous image with the local bobby careering after it on his bicycle. More successfully, others borrow a nineteenth-century Rocket-type loco from the museum, attaching to it as rolling stock the converted carriage in which their poaching footplateman makes his home. Unfortunately he is under arrest, but a bishop happens along and, being a railway fanatic, is recruited. ('Oh, Sam! One's first sermon all over again!')

This is a delightful, stimulating film about people with the drive and energy to sustain their own enthusiasms, set to music which perfectly reflects the English love of playing with trains. It is also packed with memorable characterizations: George Relph as the vicar, Stanley Holloway as the toper, Godfrey Tearle as the bishop, little old Edie Martin as all things to all men. And there is no shortage of pleasantries. 'Running at a profit? This is dreadful. The next thing you know, we shall be nationalized.'

To many people the best Ealing of all has always been *Whisky Galore*, known in America as *Tight Little Island*. Certainly it is this film more than any other which gives the world its image of the dry and dour Scots, and especially of the self-sufficient Outer Hebrideans. 'A happy people, with few and simple pleasures,' intones the commentator at the beginning, as a dozen children of graded size scamper out of a crofter's cottage. The islands are, we're told, a hundred miles from the mainland. 'To the west, there is nothing. Except

America.' It is 1943, and the war has barely touched the island of Todday except for the shortage of whisky. That is quite bad enough: the islanders are in mourning 'for a departed spirit'. The joke takes some time to develop. Twenty-five pleasant minutes pass before a ship full of whisky is wrecked on a nearby reef; but it is then only a matter of deciding how the locals will contrive to snatch a good deal of it from under the watchful eye of the Sassenach home guard commander. (Basil Radford in this role is clearly the prototype of Arthur Lowe's Captain Mainwaring in *Dad's Army*.) Meanwhile we have enjoyed scores of small jokes, and slid comfortably between them are idyllic scenes on deserted sunlit beaches and in sand dunes, graphic compositions of firelit faces showing their canniness by a flicker of the eye. Sash windows, stone walls, corrugated iron porches, broken flagstones and smoky peat-fired chimneys sum up for us the Calvinistic puritanism of this neglected village straggling out on its hillshore, surmounted by the tall black steeple of its church. By the time the film ends you know it so well as to feel like a resident, which is no small tribute to the production team's unerring eye for angle and detail.

It is the church which gives a false start to the criminal adventure of the islanders, for no sooner have all those in authority over the wreck been cunningly despatched to the mainland than the locals dash to the moonlit harbour, only to discover that the Sabbath has struck. For twenty-four hours, apart from restless sessions in church and at private prayer, the cliffs are strewn with black-suited, bowler-hatted men gazing wistfully at the wreck like sober wingless birds. But the midnight clock no sooner chimes than the streets are filled with scurrying figures on their way to an entirely understandable spot of smuggling; after all, the wreck is about to submerge, and it is surely better for the whisky to be put to good use than to disappear beneath the waves. So a large stock is hidden in a handy cave, and after a good deal of private rejoicing it remains only to outwit the customs and excise men, who arrive silently and by night on a surprise visit. But five minutes' warning is all the islanders need. A party is rapidly abandoned, and bottles of Scotch are secreted in milk churns, in pies, in hot water bottles, in violin cases, in badger holes, in gutters, under babies. When the searchers have departed, fuming, the master of the house absent-mindedly pours himself a dram from the kitchen tap; while whisky in the tank of a

WHISKY GALORE. John Gregson, Morland Graham and Wylie Watson find that true Scottish spirit has unsuspected uses

stalled truck allows the last lot of smugglers to escape. One would be hard put to find anywhere in cinema such a prodigally inventive ten minutes as this comedy climax with its succession of fast funny shots, all perfectly framed and timed: it reaches heights which even Ealing was never to achieve again.

The Titfield Thunderbolt. GB 1953; Technicolor; 84 minutes. Produced by Michael Truman for Ealing Studios. Written by T. E. B. Clarke. Directed by Charles Crichton. Photographed by Douglas Slocombe. Music score by Georges Auric. Edited by Seth Holt. Art direction by C. P. Norman. With Stanley Holloway as Valentine; George Relph as the vicar; John Gregson as the squire; Naunton Wayne as Blakeworth; Godfrey Tearle as the bishop; Edie Martin as Emily; Gabrielle Brune as Joan; Hugh Griffith as Dan; Sidney James as Hawkins; Jack McGowran as Crump; Ewan Roberts as Pearce; Reginald Beckwith as union representative.

Whisky Galore. GB 1949; monochrome; 82 minutes. Produced by Monja Danischewsky for Ealing Studios. Written by Compton Mackenzie and Angus Macphail from the novel by Compton Mackenzie. Directed by Alexander Mackendrick. Photographed by Gerald Gibbs. Music score by Ernest Irving. Art direction by Jim Morahan. Edited by Joseph Sterling. With Basil Radford as Captain Waggett; Joan Greenwood as Peggy Macroon; Catherine Lacey as Mrs Waggett; James Robertson Justice as Dr Maclaren; Wylie Watson as Joseph Macroon; John Gregson as Sammy; Jean Cadell as Mrs Campbell; Gordon Jackson as George Campbell; Morland Graham as the Biffer; Bruce Seton as Sergeant Odd; Henry Mollinson as Farquharson.

It'll Get a Terrific Laugh
To Be or Not to Be

When the Nazis invade Warsaw, temporarily unemployed actors find themselves acting as spies for the Allied cause.

In these tasteless days of *The Devils*, *The Exorcist* and *The Life of Brian*, it is a little difficult to understand the howls of dismay which greeted this brilliant film when it first appeared in 1942. Part of the trouble, undoubtedly, was that its iridescent star, Carole Lombard, had just been killed in an air crash during a war bond sales tour: it was just too poignant to watch her being so decorative up there on the silver screen. 'You can't think of her except in the present tense,' wrote James Shelley Hamilton for the National Board of Review. 'Her death dampened one's ardour for the film,' said Herman G. Weinberg years later. 'One has the strange feeling,' wrote Bosley Crowther in the *New York Times*, 'that Mr Lubitsch is a Nero, fiddling while Rome burns.' Theodore Duff has recalled that '*To Be or Not to Be* was called callous, a picture of confusing moods, lacking in taste, its subject not suitable for fun-making.'

Today it can be seen, and certainly is by me, as one of Hollywood's most polished and perfectly controlled masterworks. Technically it is one of the finest comedy screenplays ever constructed, a bravura piece of ensemble acting, of running gags which all pay off. The lines, dryly delivered, still evoke an appreciative smile. 'So they call me Concentration Camp Ehrhardt.' 'Just like our Führer.' 'It'll get a terrific laugh.' 'They named a brandy after Napoleon, a herring after Bismarck, and Hitler is going to finish up as a piece of cheese.' And more. True, it takes a little time to warm up, and the heavy commentator sounds as though he has strayed from *The March of Time*. The opening shows peacetime Poland, with shops owned by such as Rosnanski, Posnanski, Maslowski and Kubinski, all astonished to see Adolf Hitler, unaccompanied, strutting around their pavements. But he proves to be an actor, trying to test his make-up, and Josef Tura's company is putting on a play about the Gestapo. (The uniforms will come in useful later on.) War comes, and the shops are in ruins. The theatre is closed. But a young Polish flyer has escaped to England, the same ardent young man who each night during Hamlet's most famous soliloquy put Josef Tura off his stroke by taking the cue to exit from the second row for an assignation with Tura's wife in her dressing room. ('What a husband doesn't know won't hurt his wife,' she assures him.) One winter's night in 1940, after ten minutes of straight spy melodrama, the airman parachutes into Poland with the urgent need to foil a Nazi plot, and enlists Mrs Tura in the cause. A Professor Siletsky has obtained the names of the leaders of the Polish underground, and proposes to hand the list to the local Nazi commandant, Colonel Ehrhardt. He must be stopped; and the structure for the ensuing comedy is complex. She goes to Siletsky's heavily guarded hotel room. The jokes start to creep back, hesitantly at first. 'Wait a minute,' says Tura when he hears of the plan; 'I'll decide with whom my wife is going to have dinner and who she's going to kill.' The actors don their uniforms and Siletsky is called to see a bogus Ehrhardt, Tura in disguise. He becomes suspicious and is shot in a splendidly melodramatic scene in an empty theatre. Tura now becomes Siletsky and goes to rescue his wife, but is called to see the real Ehrhardt. By his second visit next morning the Nazis have found the real Siletsky's body, but Tura, a ham with all the succulent flavour of Donald Wolfit or Lionel Barrymore, bluffs his way out, only to be 'rescued' by his own colleagues in Nazi disguise. The finale has the actors impersonating Hitler and his entourage and taking over the Führer's own plane to make their escape to London; after which Tura achieves his ambition to play Hamlet in the land of Shakespeare; but during the soliloquy an English officer excuses himself from the third row . . .

So initial realism has made way for an alternation of high comedy and low farce, but how superbly its intricacies are presented. Perhaps it offended because it was so well done, its textured photography and its superb art direction of Warsaw in winter making one feel that one is experiencing these unlikely events. Yet it now looks like a first-class piece of propaganda, its final polonaise sending one home intent on winning that long-ago war. After all, during those years every low comedian tried his hand at spoofing the Nazis, and nobody complained; was Lubitsch's sin that he did it too well?

In what she has to do, Lombard is beautiful and efficient, whether flirting with the flyer who can 'drop three tons of dynamite in two minutes' or with the susceptible Siletsky. ('Shall we drink to a blitzkrieg?' 'I prefer a slow encirclement.') Robert Stack as the flyer is a handsome cipher; but the rest of the cast provides richness indeed. Felix Bressart has one of his best roles as the spear carrier who wants to play Shylock, though oddly enough Hollywood of that day does not allow the script to label him Jewish, except obliquely. ('What you are,' he says to an over-emphatic fellow-actor. 'I wouldn't eat'; and even Shakespeare is amended to read 'have I not eyes' instead of 'Has a Jew not eyes'.) Lionel Atwill is a joy as the ham in question, overplaying his hand when backing Tura's impersonation, with stentorian laughs and such little jokes as 'The British lion will drink his tea/From saucers made in Germany.' ('How did that man get to be a general?' asks Siletsky. – 'He's Goering's brother-in-law.') The villainous professor evokes a deliciously smooth performance from the underrated Stanley Ridges, clearly chosen for his physical resemblance to the star who has to impersonate him. And the star is Jack Benny.

Jack Benny? Lubitsch's choice at the time brought ripples of surprise and concealed mirth, but Benny was more than a brilliant stand-up comic. Given proper direction, as here, he was an accomplished comedy actor, never forcing the pace and well capable of handling the melodrama as well as the gags. Disguised as a Nazi, he is unable to resist frequent mentions of his real self. 'That great, great Polish actor Josef Tura: you must have heard of him.' Twice he gets a mystified shake of the head, but on the third occasion he is well served by Ehrhardt. 'Oh yes, I saw him once. What he did to Shakespeare, we are now doing to Poland.' This line, hilarious in context, was the one most attacked at the time, and caused Lubitsch to defend himself in an open letter to the press:

When in *To Be or Not to Be* I have referred to the destruction of Warsaw I have shown it in all seriousness; the commentation under the shots of the devastated Warsaw speaks for itself and cannot leave any doubt in the spectator's mind what my view and attitude is towards these acts of horror. What I have satirized in this picture are the Nazis and their ridiculous

TO BE OR NOT TO BE. The heroes escape. Charles Halton, Tom Dugan, Lionel Atwill, Jack Benny, Carole Lombard, Robert Stack

ideology. I have also satirized actors who remain actors however dangerous the situation might be, which I believe is a true observation.

Well, Lubitsch was born in Berlin, so he was no doubt as touchy on the subject as any of his detractors; he was also Jewish, so his real attitude to the Nazis can hardly have been in doubt. To understand the fuss one should perhaps consider the impossibility today of a comedy about the IRA; but then one should forget the whole argument and simply enjoy the picture.

Lubitsch as director and Edwin Justus Mayer as scriptwriter are matched in their ingenuity and precision, and to my mind everyone behind the camera deserves enthusiastic recognition; but a special award should go to Sig Rumann, a magnificent comedy actor who, playing the dreaded Ehrhardt, does not appear until the picture has been running for an hour, and then walks away with it. A refugee, in Hollywood from 1934, he never had star billing but proved himself the equal of the best comedians in the business. He was the chief butt of Marxian barbs at the opera, at the races and in Casablanca. In *Ninotchka* he was the biggest and best of the Russian commissars who so easily adjusted to life in the royal suite. ('Do you want to be alone, comrade?' he asked Garbo.) For thirty years he served Hollywood well, but in *To Be or Not to Be* he found his finest half hour as the supposed bane of the Poles. 'So they call me Concentration Camp Ehrhardt?' he asks delightedly of Tura, who has been using the line in his Ehrhardt disguise and now answers: 'I thought you'd react in just that way.' (The follow-up line also caused offence: 'We do the concentrating and the Poles do the camping.') Ehrhardt's other idiosyncrasy is his reluctance to admit responsibility for his own mistakes; he prefers to yell for his assistant. Even when he is finally made to think that he has surprised the Führer in a clandestine liaison, and commits suicide behind a locked door, the sound of his body falling to the floor is followed by the despairing cry: 'Schultz!'

To Be or Not to Be. US 1942; monochrome; 99 minutes. Produced by Ernst Lubitsch for Alexander Korda. Written by Edwin Justus Mayer. Directed by Ernst Lubitsch. Photographed by Rudolph Maté. Music score by Werner Heymann. Art direction by Vincent Korda. Edited by Dorothy Spencer. With Jack Benny as Josef Tura; Carole Lombard as Maria Tura; Felix Bressart as Greenberg; Sig Rumann as Ehrhardt; Tom Dugan as Bronski; Lionel Atwill as Kawitch; Robert Stack as Stanislav Sobinski; Stanley Ridges as Siletsky; Charles Halton as Dobosh; Henry Victor as Schultz.

Cosmo Topper, Alfalfa Switzer and David Wark Griffith
Topper Returns

While staying at an eerie mansion, a wisecracking showgirl is murdered in mistake for her heiress friend. Her ghost persuades a casual acquaintance, banker Cosmo Topper, to help her solve the mystery.

This third and final entry in the *Topper* series was despised on its release because it forsakes the casual sophisticated banter of the earlier films, and with it the elegant persona of Cary Grant and Constance Bennett, for a spoof thunderstorm mystery serving as a prop for the then current popularity of light supernatural themes and for a nap hand of producer Hal Roach's favourite farce gags, most of them dating back to Our Gang and the silent period. Revolving furniture, performing animals, a sinister house with hidden passages, a dumb bully of a cop and a frightened black servant who repeatedly falls down a chute into the inky waters of a secret lagoon; these are just a few of the elements tossed into the brew. No holds are barred, absolutely none at all; and if I had a criticism when I first saw the movie at the Queen's, Bolton, it was that with so many comedians featured, by the time they have all been given something to do there is no way that characterization can develop within the confines of an average feature, and the principals are left stranded and helpless, lucky to get a look in as this rickety vaudeville show lurches to its hilarious conclusion.

In the end, favouritism is shown to Eddie 'Rochester' Anderson, registering twenty different kinds of terror as his wide eyes watch an invisible ghost making footsteps in the snow ('Enough is enough, and that's what I've had a sufficiency of'); but there are good moments too for Billie Burke as twittering Mrs Topper, who is given to such fragments of philosophy as 'My my, it's strange how it's always cold in the winter and warm in the summer, isn't it?' Patsy Kelly as her maid manages to register little except incredulity at the general goings-on; crooked-faced Donald MacBride however doesn't need lines to impress as the bullying, bellowing cop called in to investigate a murder only to find (of course) that the body has disappeared. His half-raised upper lip reveals a vicious set of molars as he reacts violently to each astounding revelation; he and James Finlayson must have competed for the coveted title, Supreme Master of the Double Take. There are also a couple of gloomy butlers with lines like 'Goodnight, I hope you rest in peace'; and Rafaela Ottiano (in the regrettable absence of Gale Sondergaard) is the black-garbed housekeeper, who even adapts a line from *The Cat and the Canary* to explain that the house is full of spirits, but deserves her reward, which is a line Bob Hope must have thought about but wisely discarded:

HOUSEKEEPER: For twenty years they've been calling, calling, calling to someone who never answers.
GUEST: Just like the Pot O'Gold programme.

After dialogue like that we have no regrets when the housekeeper sits on the Sweeney-Todd-style armchair so invitingly placed on the library carpet, and rapidly disappears from view.

More figures emerge from the old oak woodwork. Suavely spoken George Zucco is on hand to play yet another sinister lawyer. Or is it doctor? No matter, he doesn't actually do anything except rove his eyes, fold his lips and give an ambivalent edge to such lines as 'Are the young ladies comfortable?' which in his hands emerges as a definite threat. Dear old H. B. Warner is the invalid owner of the house (but never trust invalids or cripples in this kind of movie). Then we have the alleged principals, romantic and otherwise. Carole Landis as the heiress in danger is for decoration only, and Dennis O'Keefe as the cab driver who waits for his fare and ends up winning the girl might have more claim on our sympathy if he could resist falling off a log after saying something is as easy as falling off a log. (It should be remembered that the director is an old Mack Sennett gag man, and clearly had no resistance to bits of schtick like this, or the shot in which one of the girls lifts her skirt to get a lift and we hear a grinding of gears and brakes followed by a grainy old stock shot of a car half-way up a tree with its dazed and dishevelled driver.) Joan Blondell is the lively ghost who can well take care of herself, but her role declines into a series of elegant invisibility tricks. We are not allowed to feel sorry for her sudden death because she doesn't seem sorry for herself; and besides her wisecracks get even worse after she's dead than they were before. Finally, holding it all together in his diffident way, often indeed required to make bricks with inferior straw, is dear self-effacing Roland Young, who may be third-billed but is certainly first in presence.

All these people and a story line in 87 minutes? Well, this zany movie is so peppily paced that the answer is yes, most decidedly. Within its own slender terms, the plot even makes sense.

It begins with a splendid credit sequence in which the sinister shadow of a caped and goggled figure moves stealthily around darkened rooms to the accompaniment of a shivery little theme tune which manages to be both ominous and cheerful at the same time: pom pom poppo poppo pom pom *pom*, poppo pom pom *pom*, poppo pom pom *pom*. And as a door closes on the last credit, a dagger is hurled into it, quivering. Within seconds the same black-caped figure is seen for real, shooting from behind a rock at a cab carrying

493

TOPPER RETURNS. A bemused Roland Young with invisible ghostly assistance finds himself threatening a whole crowd of familiar players including Donald MacBride and Billie Burke

the two girls. The tyre explodes, and for a nasty moment the vehicle teeters over the edge of a cliff, but then along comes Cosmo Topper to give them a lift, and later to wish that he'd gone home the other way. The girls finally make it to the hall, and the heiress is welcomed by genial, wheelchair-ridden long-lost dad; by Mr Zucco (yes, he must be a doctor because he takes Mr Carrington's temperature); and by the formidable Miss Ottiano. The murder sequence which follows is genuinely rather spooky, but soon an indignant Blondell, in her shroud-like negligée, is walking across the clouds to Topper's house and blackmailing him into finding the murderer. (Come to think of it, shouldn't a ghost know everything?) Easily persuaded, in view of the proximity of his very jealous wife who is unlikely to exempt transparent ladies from her wrath, he rouses his black chauffeur, who for reasons unexplained has gone to bed in his racoon coat. (Can't the Toppers afford central heating? And how did the studios keep actors cool for scenes like this, in raging California summers before air conditioning?) The dialogue is none the less hilarious for being predictable:

CHAUFFEUR: What we going to the Carrington place for, boss?
TOPPER: To look for a body.
CHAUFFEUR (*blenching*): Better look for one for me too, 'cos the one I'm using is *numb*.

Before long Rochester is packing:

CHAUFFEUR: I'm going back!
TOPPER: Where?
CHAUFFEUR: To Massa Benny. Ain't nothing like this ever happened there!
MRS TOPPER: Come, come, darkness never hurt anybody.
CHAUFFEUR: 'Tain't the darkness, it's what's in it.

But nobody finally backs away from the nocturnal adventure, and before long our timid banker is being accused of house-breaking as well as murder. Mr MacBride is summoned, and addresses the housekeeper as 'Rebecca'; urged to think before acting, his response is: 'I'm not supposed to think, I'm from City Hall.' A little later, the entire cast, more or less, finds itself imprisoned in a room-size refrigerator, which gives Mrs Topper just cause to reprove her errant spouse: 'Getting out of a nice warm bed to sit in someone's icebox: I can't understand it!'

The seal has by now made several appearances, and the ghost has got drunk, so Mrs Topper gets a little addlepated ('I'm going to scream. There. That's fun, isn't it! Come on, let's all do it together'), and we are approaching the sealed-room finale which to the surprise of nobody in the audience reveals honey-voiced H. B. Warner to be the masked man. (How dare Chang of *Lost Horizon* be guilty of such heinous crimes?) Escaping by car, he runs smack into a tree, and it is left for his ghost to recapitulate the plot to the ghost of the girl he killed, who is reproving but friendly. ('I'd hate to be in your shoes. First murder, then reckless driving.') Meanwhile the police detective has expressed his general warning for what's left of the cast: 'Don't any of you ever park near a fire plug!'

Topper Returns clearly has affiliations with other forties comedies about ghosts and devils: *Here Comes Mr Jordan*, *Angel on My Shoulder*, *Blithe Spirit*. However, it borrows its basic apparatus – a bulging gag book – from Bob Hope, Abbott and Costello and Mack Sennett. To me it stands not only as a well-seasoned ragout of many and various ingredients but a convenient portmanteau of the penchants of producer Hal Roach, the great impresario of such gag comedians as Laurel and Hardy and Charlie Chase and Our Gang. Around the same time as *Topper Returns* he made three others in the same 'anything goes' vein, slightly less successful but nevertheless worthy of attention. *Turnabout*, also derived from the works of Thorne Smith, postulates a magical switch of bodies between bored husband and wife, even getting past the Hays Office with a finale in which hubby has a baby. *The Housekeeper's Daughter* is a black comedy mix of the newspaper and gangster genres, with a little bit of sex; it concludes with a riotous battle of fireworks on the roof of a New York apartment building. *Road Show*, weakest of the trio but with compensations, transgresses the borders of taste with a yarn about lunatics joining a travelling circus. Each is slightly weakened by the casting as romantic lead of John Hubbard, who was to Roach what Robert Cummings was to the Major studios; each benefits immensely from the presence in a major character role of Adolphe Menjou, a much underrated actor who can now be seen as the Walter Matthau of his time and place. They all, along with the first two *Toppers*, add to my conviction that Hal Roach contributed more to Hollywood comedy style than he has been given credit for, even if one ignores the serious achievement of *Of Mice and Men* and the splendid absurdity, with or without the oft-alleged assistance of D. W. Griffith, of *One Million Years BC*.

Topper Returns. US 1941; monochrome; 87 minutes. Produced by Hal Roach. Written by Jonathan Latimer and Gordon Douglas from the characters created by Thorne Smith. Directed by Gordon Douglas. Photographed by Norbert Brodine. Music score by Werner Heymann. Art direction by Nicolai Remisoff. Edited by James Newcom. With Roland Young as Cosmo Topper; Joan Blondell as Gail Richards; Carole Landis as Ann Carrington; H. B. Warner as Mr Carrington; Dennis O'Keefe as Bob; Billie Burke as Mrs Topper; Eddie 'Rochester' Anderson as chauffeur; Patsy Kelly as maid; George Zucco as Dr Jeris; Donald MacBride as Sgt. Roberts; Rafaela Ottiano as Lilian.

Night, Youth, Paris and the Moon
Trouble in Paradise

Gaston and Lily are international jewel thieves who double cross each other from Venice to Paris but finally get together despite his infatuation with one of his victims.

I believe I share with Alistair Cooke my rapturous delight in this old-fashioned comedy of bad manners: he once told me that he begged off an important dinner in order to catch it once more on television. Personally I hadn't seen it for ten years when I made a special effort for the purpose of this revaluation, as every time it appears on television or at the National Film Theatre fates conspire to send me out of the country. But it has been in my mind and my heart since the Sunday morning in 1949 when Cambridge's Film Society, a thousand strong, rose to it as one man and gave it a deafening ovation; later I booked it at the Rex as a double bill with *French Without Tears*, and although it started quietly, by Saturday we had to turn hundreds away, after which it became as firm a favourite as *Genevieve*, *The Lavender Hill Mob*, or anything starring the Marx Brothers.

Lubitsch, as everyone knows, or used to know, was a man with a touch – 'the Lubitsch touch, that means so much'. This indicated merely that he tried to tell his society comedies by picture as well as dialogue; in his hands a doorknob turning or a clock ticking could mean as much as a page of script. He also liked to use repeated gags and images as a comedy framework, getting a bigger laugh with them each time; instances here are the constant references to room two fifty three, five, seven and nine; the frequent exchanging of booty between the thieves; and the shot of Herbert Marshall running up the spiral stair (an in-joke in itself, since Marshall had a wooden leg, couldn't run anywhere, and had to use a double). The famous touch deserted him as often as not, and many of his films now seem flat and dry, but *Trouble in Paradise* is vintage champagne from beginning to end.

The fun starts with the main title. To the strains of romantic violin music, the words fade in one by one, and just as we are expecting *Paradise* the music becomes sickly sweet and we are shown a double bed. Within seconds the film has begun with a shot of a gondolier plying his way along a Venetian canal, singing a barcarolle; the image is almost unbearably romantic. But in the next shot the gondolier alights on a jetty and proves to be the garbage collector, depositing bins full of refuse into his craft before gliding gently away into the nocturnal mist, still singing. Any film which begins at this level simply has to take the audience along with it. Lubitsch's favourite writer Samson Raphaelson, who worked on *Trouble in Paradise* (and also, curiously, on such clinkers as *That Lady in Ermine*) can't remember who first thought of the dustbin gag but thinks that, like so many others, it was the outcome of happy collaboration between Lubitsch and himself.

Another of the film's running gags is Edward Everett Horton's constant feeling that he has seen Marshall somewhere before, not realizing that he is the thief who knocked him cold in room two fifty three, five, seven and nine. (There we go again.) Yet another is the excessively polite rivalry between himself and Charlie Ruggles for the hand of perfume queen Kay Francis. ('It isn't how you look, it isn't how you talk, it's how you smell that counts,' runs her advertising.) And we mustn't overlook the tongue-in-cheek romantic banter which runs high between the jewel thieves at each meeting:

LILY: When I came here tonight it was for a little adventure, a game you play tonight and forget tomorrow. But now I have a confession to make to you. Baron, you are a crook. *You* robbed the gentleman in room two fifty three, five, seven and nine.

GASTON: Countess, believe me, before you left this room I would have told you everything. And let me say this with love in my heart: Countess, you are a thief. The wallet of the gentleman in room two fifty three, five, seven and nine is in your possession. I knew it very well when you took it out of my pocket. But your embrace was so sweet . . . (*He hands her something.*) By the way, your pin.

LILY (*suddenly missing it*): Thank you, Baron.

GASTON: It has one very good stone in it.

LILY: What time is it? (*He misses his watch and looks startled. She hands it to him from her bag.*) I regulated it for you: it was five minutes slow.

GASTON (*pocketing the watch with a smile, and holding up another item*): I hope you don't mind if I keep your garter.

TROUBLE IN PARADISE. How happy would he be with either. Francis, Marshall, Hopkins

The perfume queen comes into the picture when Gaston steals her handbag and, returning it, finds ahead of him a grimy Bolshevik, behaving as Bolsheviks in the early thirties were supposed to do:

BOLSHEVIK: So you have lost your handbag, madame?
MARIANNE: Yes.
BOLSHEVIK: And it had diamonds in the back.
MARIANNE: Yes.
BOLSHEVIK: And diamonds in the front.
MARIANNE: Yes.
BOLSHEVIK: Diamonds all over?
MARIANNE: Yes, have you found it?
BOLSHEVIK (*shouting*): No! But let me tell you – any woman who spends a fortune in times like these for a handbag – phooey! phooey!! phooey!!!

When the fake baron promptly ushers out this nuisance, madame is in his debt at once, and in his arms soon after. The precise progress of the plot hardly matters, but it is deftly charted: the characters go to the opera at least once; and in a neat reversal of one's expectations

499

C. Aubrey Smith turns out to be a swindler. It is all as sweetly toothsome as ever it was, and should be sought out and savoured. When it came out it was of course caviare to the general, though the critics positively showered it with praise. Georges Sadoul compared it aptly to watching a championship tennis match; the *New York Times* found it 'a shimmering piece of work'. Dwight MacDonald was ecstatic: 'It comes as close to perfection as anything I have ever seen in the movies ... the list of virtues is endless ... it almost makes one believe in Hollywood again.'

Trouble in Paradise has echoes in other Lubitsch films, but most of all in *Ninotchka*, which also concerns itself with stolen jewels (which the communists have stolen from a noble Russian household and propose to sell). The suave jewel thief has become an equally suave lawyer played by Melvyn Douglas, though he is fairly moral and confines his wit to sardonic remarks about the USSR. ('Comrade, I have been fascinated by your five-year plan for the last fifteen years.') The Bolshevik has become three comic commissars sent to Paris to sell the jewels, and the perfume queen who falls for a thief is reversed into a Russian envoy extraordinary who falls for Paris. The script by Billy Wilder, Charles Brackett and Walter Reisch has at least a first half as funny as Raphaelson's, notably when a reluctant Commissar Buljanoff is being persuaded to join his less principled colleagues in the Royal suite at the Hotel Clarence instead of a room without bath at the Hotel Terminus where Moscow has booked them:

KOPALSKI: Are you the Buljanoff who fought on the barricades? And now you are afraid to take a room with a bath?
BULJANOFF: I don't want to go to Siberia.
IRANOFF: I don't want to go to the Hotel Terminus.
KOPALSKI: If Lenin were alive he would say, 'Buljanoff, you can't afford to live in a cheap hotel. Doesn't the prestige of the Bolsheviks mean anything to you? Do you want to live in a hotel where you press for the hot water and cold water comes, and when you press for the cold water nothing comes at all? Phooey, Buljanoff!
BULJANOFF (*shrugging*): I still say our place is with the common people, but who am I to contradict Lenin? Let's go in.

The picture of course is conceived as a vehicle for Garbo, who insofar as the script allows gives a funny and flexible performance:

KOPALSKI: If we had known, we would have greeted you with flowers.
NINOTCHKA: Don't make an issue of my womanhood.
BULJANOFF: How are things in Moscow?
NINOTCHKA: Very good. The last mass trials were a great success. There are going to be fewer but better Russians.

When she meets debonair Melvyn Douglas she is predictably unimpressed:

NINOTCHKA: Must you flirt?
LEON: Well, I don't have to but I find it natural.
NINOTCHKA: Suppress it. What do you do for mankind?
LEON: For mankind, nothing. For womankind, the outlook is not quite so bleak.
NINOTCHKA: You are something we do not have in Russia.
LEON: Thank you.
NINOTCHKA: That is why I believe in the future of my country.

Unfortunately the humanizing and westernizing of Ninotchka, which is the story's main concern, drives most of the sardonic humour from the script and ushers in the warm wind of sentiment. The three commissars all but disappear from the fray, and after the unconvincing scene in which, as the publicists of the time assured us, 'Garbo laughs', there is precious little to laugh at before the long-delayed happy ending. *Ninotchka* as a whole is unbalanced by its message; *Trouble in Paradise* is perfection in itself, and content to have no message at all.

Trouble in Paradise. US 1932; monochrome; 83 minutes. Produced and directed by Ernst Lubitsch for Paramount. Written by Samson Raphaelson, from the play, *The Honest Finder* by Laszlo Aladar. Photographed by Victor Milner. Songs by W. Franke Harling and Leon Robin. With Herbert Marshall as Gaston Monescu; Miriam Hopkins as Lily; Kay Francis as Mariette; Charles Ruggles as The Major; Edward Everett Horton as Filiba; C. Aubrey Smith as Adolphe Giron; Robert Greig as Jacques; Leonid Kinskey as the radical.

Ninotchka. US 1939; monochrome; 110 minutes. Produced and directed by Ernst Lubitsch for MGM. Written by Charles Brackett, Billy Wilder and Walter Reisch, from a story by Melchior Lengyel. Photographed by William Daniels. Music by Werner Heymann. Art direction by Cedric Gibbons, Randall Duell and Edwin B. Willis. With Greta Garbo as Ninotchka; Melvyn Douglas as Leon; Ina Claire as Swana; Sig Rumann as Iranoff; Felix Bressart as Buljanoff; Alexander Granach as Kopalski; Bela Lugosi as Razinin.

Let Right Be Done
Twelve Angry Men

The jury on a murder case gradually reverses its first impressions.

One would not expect it to be cinematic at all. A celebrated piece of live television, which means that it was primarily a matter of talking heads, it was filmed almost exactly as originally devised, except that there was now more time to get the detail and the composition right. Apart from the briefest of scenes at beginning and end, there is only one set, and that is a bare and unlovely room big enough for a large oblong table and twelve chairs. At the far end, behind a glass partition, is a toilet and washroom. Outside the grimy windows we are made to feel the sweltering air of New York on a muggy day when thunderstorms constantly threaten and eventually make good that threat, darkening the room and making it even more oppressive.

Here twelve strangers meet, after sitting side by side in court for a week. Their mission is to discuss a case we have not seen tried and to come to a decision as to the defendant's guilt or innocence. Everything we learn about him and his supposed crime comes from their conversation, and to follow the nuances of character and the exactitude of evidence requires careful attention. The trouble is amply repaid, for this is a film which lodges itself uncomfortably in the memory, both as a feast of ensemble acting and as a warning against prejudice and careless assumption. Valuable points are being made all the way, not only about the jury system but about human nature; while the student dramatist will be dazzled by the way Reginald Rose ensures that we gradually come to know each of the twelve characters so precisely that we would recognize them instantly in the street. Dramatically the only flaw, if it counts as one, is that from the moment one man stands out against an instant vote of guilty, we know that there must be a total reversal: it's the only way to go. One might also admit that the final conversion of the most recalcitrant character is accompanied by a shade too much

TWELVE ANGRY MEN. Henry Fonda is not impressed; nor is Joseph Sweeney

melodrama. Well, the Greeks overemphasized too; and without this excess we could scarcely feel the catharsis, the immense relief of the final scene, when we emerge from the claustrophobic room into the open air, almost smelling its sweetness after the storm, elated that justice has been done and that the system for once has triumphed over those who would demean it by their petty greeds and jealousies:

One by one they walk into the rain, each reacting with his own maneuvers. One turns up his collar. One pulls down his hat. One holds a newspaper over his head. They begin to move down the steps, in groups and singly now. Juror number eight is alone. He walks into close-up, rain beating his face. He raises his collar, looks around, and then walks off. The others begin to spread out now. Some turning left, some right, some going straight ahead. Camera moves back up, ending with a long shot, through the pelting rain, of the steps and the jurors spreading out silently in all directions, never to see each other again. And finally they are gone, and the rain beats down on the empty steps.

There was a stage version too, which failed to work because we in the audience could not get close enough to the actors' faces and because half of them had to sit with their backs to the audience unless excuses were made to have them stand up and face us. This is a subject for film, and this film is no cheap rip-off shot from the sixth row of the stalls, but a cunningly composed piece of screencraft in which every single shot is calculated to have the fullest possible dramatic impact. Would that Sidney Lumet had approached all his subsequent films with such confidence and care! His direction here is both painstaking and subtle, telling us much about character simply from the way he sets up his shots. There are a few long takes: much sharp and exciting work has taken place in the editing rooms. Even in these restricting circumstances the eye is never once allowed to get bored. Helped immeasurably by Boris Kaufman's superior cinematography, the actors make their characters live even when they are only peripherally in shot.

A more able cast could scarcely have been assembled. Henry Fonda, who plays the first doubting juror, number eight, was apparently the driving force behind the production and is still saddened and puzzled by its failure to make money. It is an archetypal Fonda performance, subtle and caring, yet despite being the catalyst of the drama he seems the least interesting of the group: virtue has the drawback of being sometimes a little dull.

Even without the peg of a name on which to hang their characterizations, the other eleven members of the cast are at least his equal in their claims on our attention:

Number one, the foreman, is Martin Balsam, a small nervous fellow trying not to show how pleased he is at his election. 'Now you gentlemen can handle this any way you want to. I mean, I'm not going to make any rules.'

Number two, John Fiedler, has least to say: a Milquetoast without the courage of his own convictions, until almost by accident he comes out with a clinching piece of observation; before that he has domestic worries on his mind. 'I wonder if they'll let us go home in case we don't finish tonight. I got a boy with mumps.'

Lee J. Cobb has one of the most dominating roles as number three, the loud-mouthed bully who has family reasons for distrusting modern youth and is determined to take out his prejudices on the defendant. 'It's the kids, the way they are nowadays. Listen, when I was his age I used to call my father sir. That's right. Sir! You ever hear a boy call his father that any more?'

The intellectual view is presented by E. G. Marshall as number four. He prides himself on his clear understanding of the facts, and is tough to convince, but not above admitting his mistake. 'I have a reasonable doubt now.'

Jack Klugman as number five is a well-meaning nonentity who constantly tries to pour oil on troubled waters but is roused to anger when it's suggested that slums breed nothing but crime. 'I lived in a slum all my life. I used to play in a back yard that was filled with garbage. Maybe it still smells on me.'

Number six, Edward Binns, is a dull fellow who listens earnestly but always sides with the majority. 'I'm not used to supposing. I'm just a working man. My boss does the supposing.'

Jack Warden makes number seven a harmless slob whose main objective is to get away in time for the football game. 'All this yakkin's getting us nowhere. I'm changing my vote to not guilty.'

Fonda as number eight presents the case that defence counsel so obviously failed to prepare. 'Look, this boy's been kicked around all his life. He's had a pretty terrible nineteen years. I think maybe we owe him a few words, that's all.'

Number nine is a frail elderly man, Joseph Sweeney, with a kind of native wisdom and a capacity for anger when ignored. 'If you keep shouting at the top of your lungs . . . I'd like to be a little younger.'

Ed Begley makes number ten an unattractive bigot with a touch of fascist and some irritating mannerisms. 'You can talk till your tongue is draggin' on the floor. The boy is guilty. Period. Know what I mean, my friend?'

Number eleven, George Voskovec, is a European refugee watch-maker, quick to champion the underdog. 'I have always thought that a man was entitled to have unpopular opinions in this country. That is why I came here.'

And number twelve, Robert Webber, is a brainless young adver-tising executive who prefers doodling to giving the case his full attention. 'It had a lot of interest for me. No dead spots. I tell you, we were lucky to get a murder case. I figured us for a burglary or an assault or something. Those can be the dullest. Say, isn't that the Woolworth building?'

Twelve rounded characterizations, plus the unravelling of a mystery in ninety-odd minutes, is value for money in anybody's language; but as Fonda discovered, the public felt cheated when word of mouth described *Twelve Angry Men* as a film shot in one cheap set. I first encountered it as manager of the Ambassador, Slough. I played it from Monday to Wednesday, one cold week in February. We did moderately with it, and a few patrons commented that it was a film they'd remember; but we trebled the daily income at the end of the week with a double bill of Audie Murphy and Abbott and Costello.

Twelve Angry Men. US 1957; monochrome; 95 minutes. Produced by Henry Fonda and Reginald Rose for United Artists. Written by Reginald Rose. Directed by Sidney Lumet. Photographed by Boris Kaufman. Music score by Kenyon Hopkins. Cast as above.

On the Trail of the Lonesome Pine
Way Out West

In Brushwood Gulch, Laurel and Hardy deliver a goldmine deed to the wrong person.

It's a Stan Laurel production, so for once there is no one to blame but him: he controls and devises all the gags. And of course there is no blame, for they all work perfectly. The pacing is impeccably sustained from first shot to last, and even allows for an introductory first reel in which the stars do not appear, a reel which, with its rowdy saloon atmosphere, can be fairly compared with *Destry Rides Again*. Generously, Stan even allows a few gags to pop-eyed James Finlayson as Mickey Finn the proprietor, who notes that when he presses the one dollar key on the cash register, only ten cents rings up. 'This thing ain't working properly,' he tells the bartender. 'It's working all right for me,' is the reply. This is a cue for Finlayson's famous 'double take and fade away', which has to be seen and not explained.

Way Out West is acclaimed by many as the best film Laurel and Hardy ever made. One wouldn't be inclined to argue: it's marvellous. But perhaps one should qualify the accolade slightly by calling it the best of their non-domestic films, the ones which set the comics in various times and places, from Toyland to Hollywood's idea of the Swiss Alps, thus severing them from any need to restrain the fantasies of their imagination. Of course, even in Brushwood Gulch they still wear bowler hats, but on their first appearance Stan is leading a mule which pulls the sleeping Olly along on a kind of primitive land raft. Olly doesn't even notice at once when the procession stops in the middle of a deep ford; but as soon as the dampness percolates, and he steps forward to wreak vengeance on Stan, he falls off an underwater ledge and disappears completely. (The film manages two more variations on this gag and gets bigger laughs each time.) As is the way with comedies, he soon dries off, and as soon as Stan has stopped a stagecoach by showing his leg (for the regular audience, a reminiscence of Claudette Colbert in *It Happened One Night*), Olly is travelling in style and at his courtliest, chatting up an uneasy matron with such saucy remarks as 'A lot of weather we've been having lately' and 'It's only four months to Christmas'.

Arriving in town, the boys pause before business for one of their most cherished sequences, an eccentric dance with the Avalon Boys as accompaniment. Why are we surprised that they can dance so gracefully? Perhaps only because it seems so incongruous. For the same reason, probably, we relish their next act, a vocal rendering of 'The Trail of the Lonesome Pine'; such are the mysteries of pop music that it climbed into the charts forty years after they recorded it. But while they are performing, the crafty Finn, apprised of their mission, is arranging for his hard-bitten wife to impersonate the real owner of the deed and receive it from them:

LOLA: Tell me about my daddy. Is he really dead?
STAN: Well, we hope he is: they buried him.
LOLA: What did he die of?
STAN: He died of a Tuesday. Or was it a Wednesday? Anyway, now that you've got the mine, I'll bet you'll be a swell gold digger.

Experimenting as always, Stan builds into this picture curious aphorisms for himself, such as 'Every bird can build a nest, but it isn't everybody that can lay an egg.' There are also grotesque physical jokes. His big toe, sticking out through a hole in his shoe, is seized by Olly and pulled out like a rubber balloon before it snaps back into place. Later he reciprocates, when Olly is trapped by the neck between floorboards, by seizing the head and pulling until

Olly's neck is five feet long. Then it transpires that he can turn his hand into a lighter, flicking his thumb until it sets ablaze so that he can nonchalantly light his pipe with it. Several times Olly tries in vain to imitate him: when it finally happens, he yells out in pain and fright. All the jokes are incidental to the pair's efforts to retrieve the deed, and after one abject failure Olly insists that Stan carry out his promise: 'We'll get the deed or I'll eat your hat.' Stan is tearful at first, but quickly finds that he rather enjoys the flavour, especially with the addition of salt and pepper. Creditably to the continuity, Olly goes through the rest of the film in a hat with teethmarks round the brim. And despite Stan's being the boss, or perhaps because of it, Olly is here at his sunniest and most relaxed.

It will be clear by now that *Way Out West* does not depend on plot but is simply an hour of connected highspots on a related theme. Among them:

1. The boys get the deed back and Stan thrusts it into his bosom. Wicked Lola however locks the bedroom door behind her and gets it back by tickling him, in a scene that almost amounts to comedy rape with the usual roles reversed.

2. They want to break into the saloon by night, and Stan suggests using the mule to hoist Olly up over a block and tackle. Olly submits to having the rope tied round his waist, but looks at the camera and crosses his fingers. Sure enough, he ends up in a nice deep hole in the ground, with the mule on the balcony.

3. Olly is stuck in the flooring with only his head showing and Finn is on the prowl. Hysterically Stan hides Olly's head under a bucket, sits on it, and puts another bucket over his head.

It's all magic, and magic shouldn't be analyzed too closely. Better simply to remind ourselves, as frequently as possible, of the great riches in the Laurel and Hardy canon, which despite poor care of the negatives has survived very nearly intact, and can be seen to contain much greater genius than that of Chaplin, who was so lauded during his lifetime.

A typical Laurel and Hardy invention was the tit-for-tat routine. Sometimes they devoted a whole film to it, as in *Them Thar Hills* and *Tit For Tat* itself; on other occasions it merely formed the climax to such films as *You're Darn Tootin'*, which finishes with a score of shin-kicking, trouser-ripping fanatics making war on the sidewalk. The basic ingredient is an exchange of physical violence, usually with a third party, starting with a light unintentional blow but growing in inventiveness and fury until the scene takes on the appearance of a national disaster area. Necessary features are the slow burns which punctuate the mayhem: each injured party, instead of seeking immediate retribution on his attacker, quietly fumes while thinking up his next onslaught, and when he has decided on his course it is the turn of his opponent to wait, in silent apprehension, while the gluepot or the flour bin is being prepared, and to wince only as the blow is being struck. This is directly opposite in technique to Mack Sennett's way with custard pies: he wrote that 'non-anticipation on the part of the recipient of the pastry is the chief ingredient of the recipe'. With Laurel and Hardy the joke is all the funnier because it is seen to be inevitable.

A prime example of a tit-for-tat routine is the 1930 two-reeler *Big Business*, and it is doubly pleasant to linger over because it gives equal screen time to their old sparring partner James Finlayson. He has a house, and they have a truck, from which they are selling Christmas trees. In California. Richly attired in overcoat and gloves, Olly signals Stan to stop at this likely prospect. He alights, selects a firm tree, and rings the bell. Finlayson's grim visage when he answers makes it clear that the interview will be short. He doesn't want to buy a tree. Stan manages to get first the tree, then Olly's coat, caught in the door as Finlayson slams it. Undeterred, they ring again to ask whether they may take his order for *next* year. Breathing heavily by now, Fin brings out a pair of garden shears and turns their tree into a shrub. Olly cuts off from Fin's head a few hairs he can't afford to lose. Fin smashes Olly's watch. Olly pulls Fin's doorbell from its socket. Fin starts to call the police. Stan cuts the cord. Fin cuts off the tail of Olly's shirt, and as an afterthought snips his tie. Stan and Olly train the garden hose on its owner. Teetering on the edge of DTs, Fin pulls the headlamp off their truck and throws it through the windscreen. Having carefully inspected the damage, Stan and Olly remove their coats and return to the fray at the front door. The doorlamp goes through the window. Fin returns to the car, falling over a tree in his eagerness, and rips off a door. Stan and Olly take the house door off its hinges and toss it away. A policeman drives up and watches silently, hypnotized by the balletic timing with which the three of them dash from the house to the car

WAY OUT WEST. At the ball, that's all: Laurel and Hardy succumb to the charms of Terpsichore

and back again. Fin tosses all the trees into the road. Olly axes Fin's garden tree. Stan throws a lamp through the house window. Olly axes a bigger tree. Fin wrenches off a mudguard, and demolishes the bonnet and radiator; the car goes up in flames and Fin does a war dance. Olly begins to dig up the lawn. Stan, inside, throws all the furniture through the biggest window, and Olly uses his spade as a baseball bat. Olly attacks the chimneystack; Stan smashes the piano. Then suddenly, they notice the policeman and begin to look ashamed of themselves. Stan cries. Olly cries. The policeman cries. Fin cries. The assembled crowd, pretty numerous by now, cries. The three contestants are induced to shake hands, and Stan hands Fin a cigar. He lights it and it explodes. Stan and Olly roar with laughter and are chased up the road by the policeman.

They made over a hundred films together and only a handful of duds. At least a score are positive masterpieces. Even the titles make me smile. *Hog Wild. Double Whoopee. Our Wife. Dirty Work. Midnight Patrol. Laughing Gravy. Two Tars. The Finishing Touch. The Perfect Day.*

Night Owls. Below Zero. Beau Hunks. Fra Diavolo. Towed in a Hole. Scram. A Chump at Oxford. Blockheads. Liberty. Helpmates. And one must include the first reel of *County Hospital*, in which Stan takes the invalid Olly some hardboiled eggs and nuts, and within minutes, by his childlike curiosity about things mechanical, has the patient hanging from the ceiling by his plaster-covered leg. I fall about laughing just thinking of that scene.

When Olly died, there were thousands of devoted fans who felt an intense personal loss. At least Stan lived to see their films coming back into critical esteem, and even got an Academy Award for his services to the cinema. As for me, just let me hear that silly little signature tune of theirs and I'm happy. I whistle it every morning when I round the corner, as a signal to my wife to put the kettle on.

Way Out West. US 1937; monochrome; 66 minutes. Produced by Stan Laurel for Hal Roach. Written by Charles Rogers, Felix Adler, Jack Jevne and James Parrott. Directed by James W. Horne. Photographed by Art Lloyd and Walter Lundin. Music score by Marvin Hatley. Art direction by Arthur I. Royce. Edited by Bert Jordan. With Stan and Ollie as themselves; James Finlayson as Mickey Finn; Sharon Lynne as Lola Marcel; Rosina Lawrence as Mary Roberts.

Pie in the Sky
The Wizard of Oz and The Blue Bird

A discontented little girl flees from her farm home in Kansas, is caught up in a whirlwind, and dreams that she has been transported to the magical land of Oz. Another girl seeks happiness in the past, the present and the future.

It was all Miss Gulch's fault, really, for trying to have Dorothy's little dog Toto impounded. And dear Aunt Em simply wouldn't stand up to her. As for Professor Marvel, whose caravan home she visited while on the run, he simply told her that happiness was in her own back yard and she should return and fight for her rights. But then she saw the towering whirlwind approaching black and frightening from the horizon, and something hit her head, and before she knew where she was the house was flying high in the sky, with Miss Gulch still cycling past and changing as she did so into some kind of witch. The house had to land somewhere, and when it did, with a gentle bump, it happened to kill the Wicked Witch of the East, who had been terrorizing the little Munchkins on whose multi-coloured territory Dorothy now found herself. They even sang about it:

> Heigh-ho, the witch is dead!
> Rub your eyes, get out of bed.
> Heigh-ho, the wicked witch is dead . . .
> She's gone where the goblins go,
> Below, below, below, yo ho,
> And ring the bell out . . .

And after a little musical comedy work they were fixing Dorothy up with the wicked witch's red shoes and sending her off to seek advice on the best way home from the all-powerful Oz who ruled the Emerald City . . .

> Follow the yellow brick road.
> Follow the yellow brick road.
> Follow, follow, follow, follow, follow the yellow brick road.
> We're off to see the wizard the wonderful wizard of Oz.
> We hear he is a whiz of a wiz, if ever a wiz there was.
> If ever a wever a wiz there was,
> The Wizard of Oz is one because,
> Because, because, because, because, because . . .
> Because of the wonderful things he does . . .

Come to think of it, these lyrics weren't noted for their wit, but they struck the right simple note of freshness and charm. Anyway, Dorothy was sufficiently impressed to set out on her travels, taking with her on the way a scarecrow who needed a brain, a tin man badly in want of a heart, and a lion who thought the wizard might give him some courage. After sundry exciting adventures they vanquished the Wicked Witch of the West, only to find that the all-powerful Oz was a modest conjuror from the United States, who one day had drifted over the rainbow in his home-made balloon and had been welcomed as a god by the people of Oz. Being a fast thinker, he was able to satisfy Dorothy's friends by awarding them, respectively, a diploma, a medal, and a testimonial, but as for Dorothy herself he could only suggest dusting off his balloon and making the journey with her. Unluckily, just before take-off she had to jump out after Toto, and the wizard was carried away without her; but three taps on her red shoes woke her up at last, and her family and friends were gathered about her (looking just like characters in her dream), and she just knew that she'd never run away again.

The oddest thing about this much-cherished film fairy tale, now a television staple for which large sums of money change hands annually, is that its original reviews were grudging to say the least, and in Britain its commercial prospects were so little thought of that it went the rounds as second feature to Anna Neagle as *Irene*. In order to see it from the start I had to be at the Bolton Capitol no later than 6.40 P.M., and found the house not exactly a hive of activity. I remember that I liked the 'bookends' being in sepia, but as for the rest of it there were fewer trick effects than I'd expected, the colour was garish, and the ending a let-down. It all seemed pleasing enough but rather empty, like a well-rehearsed pantomime to which somebody had forgotten to add any jokes. However, I came away humming the songs and remembering the three jolly creatures who had helped the heroine to sing them, and deciding that in order to be scrupulously fair I would see it again with a full house, which I managed to accomplish one Saturday night four months later when it came to the Majestic, a converted skating rink in which, if you wanted to see the picture, you had to make sure of one of the few seats not on the flat. Its advantage was a softer screen which removed some of the flash from the colour, and the suburban audience that night rose to the movie with enthusiasm I could still sense afterwards as I strolled down the road with them towards the nearest fish and chip shop.

It must have been the increasingly emotional aura which developed around Judy Garland that in later years broadened and intensified the adult appeal of *The Wizard of Oz*; or perhaps the enthusiasts were simply wallowing in nostalgia for their own childhood. At any rate it took off again in the mid-fifties, with long revival runs at the London Ritz and a popular holiday re-release, coupled with *The Glass Slipper* or *Queen Christina* according to the sophistication of one's district. The seventies brought MGM's auction of its old props, including Judy's red shoes; the success on Broadway of a black version called *The Wiz*; and the first of many Christmastime showings on the BBC. The thing had become a monument, and none of the survivors from it could dissociate themselves from their long-ago roles. When Jack Haley appeared on the Academy Awards Show shortly before his death in 1979, his

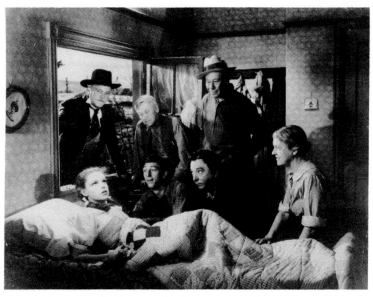

THE WIZARD OF OZ. Back home, there's a happy ending

patter was entirely about the Tin Man, and in the same year Ray Bolger was doing a margarine commercial dressed in his Scarecrow costume. Bert Lahr's son wrote a biography of the comedian called *Notes on a Cowardly Lion*, bringing back instantly the sound of Mr Lahr's Bronx accent issuing from that comical heap of fur:

> Oh, it's sad to be admittin',
> I'm as vicious as a kitten,
>   Without de vim and voive;
> I could show off my prowess,
> Be a lion, not a mowess,
>   If I only had the noive.

Margaret Hamilton had a long career in coffee commercials, trading on her one star role as the Wicked Witch of the West, alias Miss Gulch. And Judy, of course, for the rest of her troubled life, had only to sit on the stage in a spotlight, her feet flopping over the orchestra pit, and sing 'Over the Rainbow' to bring the house down. (As is well known, this song was almost deleted from the movie after the first preview because it held up the action.) Frank Baum's original book, the American equivalent of *Alice in Wonderland*, now comes out in heavily annotated editions, and a fat volume about the making of the film has emerged. On the intellectual front, a sixties magazine of some notoriety was called *Oz*, and a seventies fantasy movie of excruciating impenetrability called its villain *Zardoz* (wiZARD of OZ, get it?). Oz has become an industry, and the original film – well, not quite the original, for there was one in 1924 with Oliver Hardy as the tin man – is more than forty years old and getting younger and more attractive each time one sees it.

Ironically it is a work of much less imagination than one which at the time set up as its rival, failed, and is now almost completely forgotten. The story goes that Louis B. Mayer wanted Shirley Temple for *Oz*, thinking Garland a shade too mature and too thick about the waist (which, to an uncharitable eye, she certainly is). Darryl Zanuck refused to lend Shirley, and set up a rival project with virtually the same plot. Maurice Maeterlinck's *The Blue Bird* features children discontented with their existence in a woodcutter's cottage; losing their bluebird, the symbol of happiness, they seek it in the past, the present and the future, finally discovering that it was after all right in their own back yard. Money was lavished unsparingly on the production, and some of the sequences have a magnificence unmatched in their field; yet the movie flopped badly both as a road show attraction and as a regular release. Years later its black and white bookends were crudely lopped off for television release, and it is hard to find a complete print.

The reasons for its neglect are not too difficult to divine. It has no songs, to begin with, and precious few jokes; this is a fairy tale for serious-minded children. Its star, Shirley Temple, was approaching the awkward age, and her popularity was waning. A strong all-family film might have revived it, but here she was cast as a spoilt and petulant girl who does not become sympathetic until the story is virtually told. It was surely also a mistake to kill off the cat in a forest fire, especially as she had turned into Gale Sondergaard; for audience satisfaction she should have been back on her hearthrug at the end, in her original form, spitting at the dog. Most of all, the tenor of the tale was too creepy for all but the staunchest-hearted children, being filled with those elements usually omitted from junior editions of Grimm's Fairy Tales. The land of children waiting to be born has a decidedly shivery climate, and at the other extreme Mytyl goes to see her long-dead grandparents, having found that the way to the past lies through the cemetery, and that the dead wake up only when the living think about them.

For all these commercial failings, *The Blue Bird* is a splendid testimonial to the superlative Hollywood techniques of its day, and a hundred times more successful than the Russian co-produced remake of the seventies. For Richard Day's art direction alone I hope a pristine negative is safe in the care of the American Film Institute.

The Wizard of Oz. US 1939; Technicolor and monochrome; 102 minutes. Produced by Mervyn Le Roy for MGM. Directed by Victor Fleming. Written by Noel Langley, Florence Ryerson and Edgar Allan Wolfe, from the story by L. Frank Baum. Photographed by Harold Rosson. Music score by Herbert Stothart. Songs by E. Y. Harburg and Harold Arlen. Art direction by Cedric Gibbons and William A. Horning. Special effects by Arnold Gillespie. Make-up by Jack Dawn. Edited by Blanche Sewell. With Judy Garland as Dorothy; Frank Morgan as the Wizard; Ray Bolger as the Scarecrow; Jack Haley as the Tin Man; Bert Lahr as the Lion; Billie Burke as Glinda; Margaret Hamilton as the Wicked Witch; Charley Grapewin as Uncle Henry; Clara Blandick as Aunt Em.

The Blue Bird. US 1940; Technicolor and monochrome; 98 minutes. Produced by Gene Markey for Twentieth Century-Fox. Written by Ernest Pascal, from the play by Maurice Maeterlinck. Directed by Walter Lang. Photographed by Arthur Miller and Ray Rennahan. Music score by Alfred Newman. Art direction by Richard Day. Edited by Robert Bischoff. With Shirley Temple as Mytyl; Johnny Russell as Tyltyl; Eddie Collins as Tylo; Gale Sondergaard as Tylette; Spring Byington as Mummy Tyl; Russell Hicks as Daddy Tyl; Jessie Ralph as Fairy Berylune; Nigel Bruce as Mr Luxury; Helen Ericson as Light; Cecilia Loftus as Granny Tyl; Al Shean as Grandpa Tyl.

Index

NB: Principal references are in bold type.

Paladin Reference Books

A Dictionary of Mythologies £2.50 ☐
Max Shapiro and Rhoda Hendricks
The first concise yet comprehensive dictionary of world mythologies. It is fully cross-referenced, so that the universal themes in common to all myths are easily recognized, and the cultural differences easily compared.

Test Your Own Wordpower 95p ☐
Hunter Diack
Test your own vocabulary by attempting these carefully devised tests. Shakespeare's was over 35,000 and the national average around 12,000.

The Encyclopaedia of Reality £2.25 ☐
Katinka Matson
An indispensable reference book of alternative thought and of the ideas of the key revolutionary thinkers of the past and modern times.

To order direct from the publisher just tick the titles you want and fill in the order form.

PAL14282

Paladin Reference Books

A Dictionary of Operations   £2.50 ☐
Dr Andrew Stanway
A lucid commonsense guide to hospitals and how they affect the patient plus an A-Z of operations and an alphabetical list of procedures and investigations.

A Dictionary of Symbols   £2.95 ☐
Tom Chetwynd
Tom Chetwynd has drawn from the collective wisdom of the great psychologists, particularly Jung, to create a comprehensive and thought-provoking guide to the language of symbols.

Trees and Bushes of Britain and Europe   £2.95 ☐
Oleg Polunin
A superb and definitive guide. Fully illustrated in colour and carefully organized for use in the field.

Halliwell's Film Guide (Second Edition)   £5.95 ☐
Leslie Halliwell
A mammoth new Guide covering fifty years of English-language talkies and 10,000 films.

Halliwell's Filmgoer's Companion (Seventh Edition)   £4.95 ☐
A gargantuan compilation of film facts. 'Totally indispensable' — *Film Review Annual.*

To order direct from the publisher just tick the titles you want and fill in the order form.   **PAL14182**

All these books are available at your local bookshop or newsagent, or can be ordered direct from the publisher.

To order direct from the publisher just tick the titles you want and fill in the form below.

Name _____

Address _____

Send to:
Paladin Cash Sales
PO Box 11, Falmouth, Cornwall TR10 9EN.

Please enclose remittance to the value of the cover price plus:

UK 45p for the first book, 20p for the second book plus 14p per copy for each additional book ordered to a maximum charge of £1.63.

BFPO and Eire 45p for the first book, 20p for the second book plus 14p per copy for the next 7 books, thereafter 8p per book.

Overseas 75p for the first book and 21p for each additional book.

Paladin Books reserve the right to show new retail prices on covers, which may differ from those previously advertised in the text or elsewhere.